E-LEARNING - INSTRUCTIONAL DESIGN, ORGANIZATIONAL STRATEGY AND MANAGEMENT

Edited by **Boyka Gradinarova**

E-Learning - Instructional Design, Organizational Strategy and Management
http://dx.doi.org/10.5772/59896
Edited by Boyka Gradinarova

Contributors

John Wall, Mildred Atieno Ayere, Mouenis Anouar Tadlaoui, Souhaib Aammou, Khaldi Mohamed, Todorka Atanasova Glushkova, Martin Lesage, Gilles Raîche, Martin Riopel, Dalila Sebkhi, Frédérick Fortin, Charles Potter, Andrej Jerman-Blazic, Borka Jerman Blazic, Maureen Snow Andrade, Salvador Oton, Hector Amado, Jose Ramon Hilera, Eva Garcia, Antonio Garcia, Robert Repnik, Dominik Robic, Igor Pesek, Nicoleta Gudanescu Nicolau, Susan Renes, Ileana Hamburg, Michela Ponticorvo, Orazio Miglino, Luigia Simona Sica, Viliam Fedak, Pavel Záskalický, Andrée Roy, Ahmad Rafi, Khairulanuar Samsudin, Hafizul Fahri Hanafi, Kueichih Chuang, Hye-Jung Lee, Ana Alice Vilas Boas, Gustavo Henrique Nogueira De Andrade

Published by InTech

Janeza Trdine 9, 51000 Rijeka, Croatia

Publishing Process Manager Iva Lipovic

Technical Editor InTech DTP team

Cover InTech Design team

First published October, 2015

Printed in Croatia

Additional hard copies can be obtained from orders@intechopen.com

E-Learning - Instructional Design, Organizational Strategy and Management , Edited by Boyka Gradinarova

p. cm.

ISBN 978-953-51-2188-6

For EU product safety concerns:
IN TECH d.o.o., Prolaz Marije Krucifikse Kozulić 3, 51000 Rijeka, Croatia,
info@intechopen.com or visit our website at intechopen.com.

Meet the editor

Boyka Gradinarova is the Head of the Distance Learning Centre and lecturer in Information Technologies in the Department of Computer Science and Technology at the Technical University of Varna. She holds a Ph.D. in Educational Methodology and Instructional Technology from the Sofia University of Bulgaria. Her research and teaching focus is in the area of e-learning (web-based learning, tele-learning, online learning, flexible learning and instruction, semantic web technologies, etc.), computer networks and communications, web design and software agents. Her last published book is titled *Methodological Requirements for the Design and Implementation of E-learning* (Technical University of Varna, 2014). She is a member of the Association of Scientists in Bulgaria and the National Committee of IFIP, IFIP WG 3.5 (Informatics in Secondary Education).

Contents

Preface

One quite certain fact for the future is the rise of e-learning. E-learning offers substantial advantages to people and companies looking to develop a new content program or curricula. Nowadays, we frequently see new online learning options that can incorporate new technologies into educational processes. The authors of this book come from all over the world; their ideas, studies, findings and experiences are a beneficial contribution to enhance our knowledge in the field of e-learning. The book is divided into three sections, and their respective chapters refer to three main macro areas. The first section of the book covers Instructional Design of E-learning, considering methodology and tools for designing e-learning environments and courseware including examples for effective ways of gaming and educating. The second section is about Organizational Strategy and Management. The last section deals with the new Developments in E-learning Technology, emphasizing subjects like knowledge building by mobile e-learning systems, cloud computing and new proposals for virtual learning environments/platforms.

Boyka Gradinarova
Technical University Varna,
Bulgaria

Section 1

Instructional Design of E-learning

Chapter 1

Support for Learning of Dynamic Performance of Electrical Rotating Machines by Virtual Models

Viliam Fedák and Pavel Záskalický

Additional information is available at the end of the chapter

http://dx.doi.org/10.5772/60723

Abstract

The undergraduate electrical machines course belongs to basic courses in electrical engineering. It is especially crucial for the students studying continuing subjects like electrical drives and control of electrical drives. Thus, a good knowledge of the behavior of electrical machines in various control modes and various supply and the changeable parameters of machines is needed to understand the behavior of machines. This chapter deals with the development of virtual models of two electrical machines in MATLAB GUIDE: an one-phase motor and a stepper motor. It serves as a guide for similar applications; only the necessary explanation of the machines operation and their mathematical models is presented, which creates a core of developed virtual models. The graphical user interfaces contribute in modernizing the electrical machines course and in enriching their attractiveness by a fast and comfortable visualization of the machine performance at their changeable control modes and parameters. They also serve as an introduction to the measurement of real machines in the laboratory. Of course, the teacher is expected to clarify the obtained graphical results and phenomena running in real machines corresponding to the machine behavior.

Keywords: Virtual model, one-phase induction motor, stepper motor, MATLAB GUI, simulation

1. Introduction

An electrical machine is a complex device being multidomain by nature, involving electromagnetic, mechanical, and thermal phenomena. Thus, the subject of electrical machines is highly multidisciplinary and holds a significant position in engineering education. The knowledge obtained in the electrical machines subject presents a starting point in the whole series of subjects like electrical drives, controlled drives, motion control, control of robots, control of mechatronic systems (industrial lines), etc.

This is why the subject Electrical Machines requires a solid understanding of energy conversion and a good knowledge of physics and physical thinking, supported by mathematical background. Here a student learns the principles of motion and the operation of various types of electrical machines in order to evaluate the influence of various changeable parameters on the performance of the machine. The contribution describes one of possibilities how to improve training methods from the subject of electrical machines.

The main objective of practical training from the subject Electrical Machines is to verify theoretical knowledge from the lectures. It is required that the students should have a good knowledge about the machine construction and its behavior before they enter the laboratory to measure to investigate the machine. There they learn how to understand deeper the substance of the measured machines, to avoid any damage of equipment, and to maintain safety of the work. Classical lectures and printed materials cannot offer students enough possibility to prepare themselves satisfactory for the labs. They give theoretical explanation, but the deep understanding of the machine behavior can be grasped through hands-on experimentation. Also, the time and the space available within courses on electrical machines are not elastic for the verification of various modes and for checking the influence of changeable parameters of a machine on its performance and characteristics.

Various animation models used for the explanation of the phenomena usually do not offer the required variety of a virtual experimentation to get information about the real data of the machine. By contrast, various simulation models offer a possibility to verify the machine performance, but a problem arises here-the learner should master a simulation program. Moreover, a possibility of obtaining false results is very high, not speaking about any user-friendly changing parameters of the machine and other optional parameters to change machine dynamics.

Like pointed out by Dongmei et al in [1], the verification of static and dynamic properties of electrical machines by the application of virtual models, where the mathematical and simulation models are hidden and working in the background, is becoming a key element of modern electrical engineering school. The readiness of the application of virtual dynamical models of electrical machines and drive systems for their analyzing is not disputable (not speaking about cost and time saving). Nice application of using simulation techniques applied to the learning of Electrical Machines is shown in Djeghloud et al in [2]. An example of simulation of a synchronous generator based on it a remote access to the electrical machines remote lab has been published by Martis et al in [3].

MATLAB GUI (graphical user interface) in connection with the Simulink program (and also with some special toolboxes like SimPowerSystems, SymbolicMath toolbox and Control toolbox) presents an extremely suitable tool for the development of purpose-oriented virtual model of any dynamical system. Easy and comfortable change of parameters by control elements, such as push and radio buttons, text boxes, and visualization of results, enables the operation of virtual models either without any deep knowledge of their substance or without any complex programming and debugging of the models.

The proposed chapter presents an extension of the knowledge presented in a series publications by Fedak et al. [5-7] and a continuation of the development of the teaching aids by the application of the virtual models to more specialized topics not described there – a single-phase machine and a stepper machine, including their supply and modes of the operation. This chapter is more-or-less technically oriented and presents a practical guide for the development of a whole series of virtual models of electrical machines to be utilized in the teaching process.

This chapter is organized as follows: for each motor, it starts with its brief description and some peculiarities of motor starting, followed by mathematical and simulation models, and continued by a series of graphs from the simulation to document the behavior and correctness of the model. The simulation model creates a core of the virtual model. The screen of the virtual model was carefully designed from a pedagogical point of view, having in mind easy operation and well arrangement of input (sliders, buttons, and text boxes) and output elements (graphs). Finally, the experience of using the virtual models in teaching several subjects is described, and an evaluation of questionnaires is presented.

2. Methodology of virtual models design of electrical machines

In designing successful virtual models, it is necessary to preserve some basic rules, especially in designing the screen, which are as follows:

- The model should be easy to operate, without any special guide.
- The screen should contain the basic information and cannot be overcrowded by supplementary information taking the learner's attention and concentration. For example, the parameters of the machine that input into the solution in the beginning of any simulation should be hidden, usually on the second screen.
- A proper ergonomic arrangement of the elements upon the screen should be kept. It covers the placement of:
    - controlling elements like buttons, sliders, etc.
    - edit/text boxes (input data, system parameters, and various scales), and
    - output information to display-graphs, number, texts, and figures.

Basic rules to place the control, input, and output elements as well as the procedures were published in previous publications [5-7].

3. Virtual model development of a single-phase induction machine

Single-phase induction motors are widely used in applications, and they excel in its simplicity, undemandingness, and reliability. They are also affordably priced. Usually, they are of smaller powers, approximate in the range of tens of watts to kilowatts units, and typically they are used in household appliances (because usually the single-phase supply system is available in the home distribution of electrical energy).

3.1. Principle of operation

The mechanical construction of the single-phase induction motor does not differ much from the three-phase one. Different is the way of arrangement of the stator winding and supply: one winding in the stator of the single-phase induction motor cannot create rotating magnetic field necessary for running the machine, but it produces only a vibrant field. The rotor will not start without any auxiliary winding. This is why the motor has two stator windings – the main and the auxiliary ones. The motor power is transmitted through the main winding, which is stored in two-thirds of the stator slots and is supplied directly from the single-phase network. The auxiliary winding is rated for lower current than the main winding. In interactivity having the main winding, its aim is to develop rotating magnetic field with the form approaching as the most to the circular shape.

The single-phase induction motors are distinguished by the structure of the rotor motor with wound rotor and squirrel cage rotor. The cage motor is used only for small performances.

3.2. Modes of starting

To get the rotating magnetic field, the current in the auxiliary winding shall be displaced by 90° from the current in the main winding. This is achieved by connecting an inductor or a capacitor in series with the auxiliary winding and parallel connection of the circuit to the main winding connected to the supply. For this reason, a suitable reactance is connected into the auxiliary winding (Figure 1). Here we recognize the following:

a. Starting with inductor (Figure 1a). This is seldom used (it results in a lower efficiency)

b. Starting with capacitor (Figure 1b): connected full time or by a double capacitor.

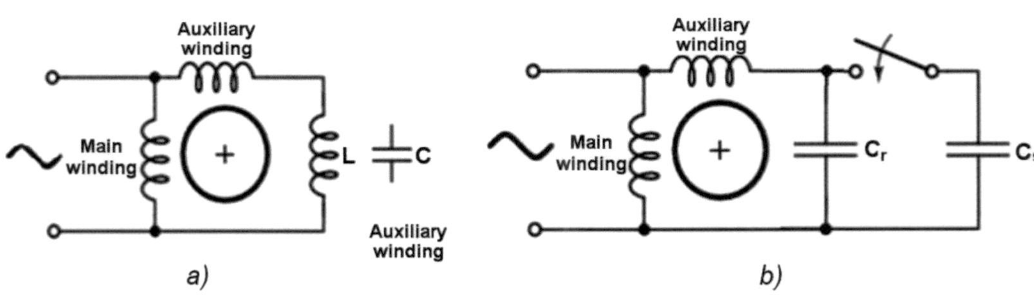

Figure 1. Starting modes of one-phase induction machine.

The capacitor C_r connected into the auxiliary phase is optimally calculated according to the following equation:

http://dx.doi.org/10.5772/60723

$$C_{\mathrm{r}} = 2200 \frac{P_{\mathrm{N}}}{U_{\mathrm{N}}^2} \left[\mu\mathrm{F};\ \mathrm{W},\ \mathrm{V} \right] \tag{1}$$

The one-phase induction motor is supplied by an alternating sinusoidal harmonic voltage that is generated by a simple harmonic oscillator in the model, having on its output the signal of harmonic voltage with the amplitude U_{1n} and frequency f_1 corresponding to the supply net. To achieve the starting torque, which is equal to the nominal, two to three times larger capacitor C_{s} is required, i.e.,

$$C_{\mathrm{s}} = (2 \div 3) C_{\mathrm{r}} \tag{2}$$

3.3. The one-phase induction motor model

The motor mathematical model consists of models of electrical and mechanical parts. The electrical part is represented by the scheme in Figure 2.

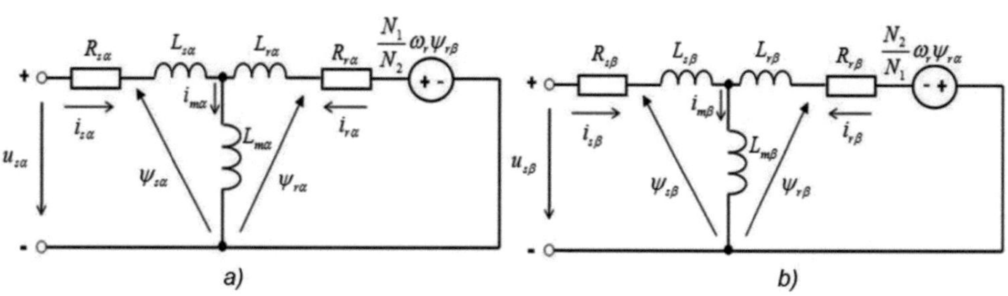

Figure 2. Equivalent circuits: (a) the main winding and (b) the auxiliary winding.

Based on the equivalent circuits and dynamic equation of the motor, the mathematical equations with their representations are shown in Table 1.

Equation for	Mathematical model (equations)	Simulation model in Simulink
stator magnetic flux	$\psi_{s\alpha} = L_{s\alpha} i_{s\alpha} + L_{m\alpha} i_{r\alpha}$	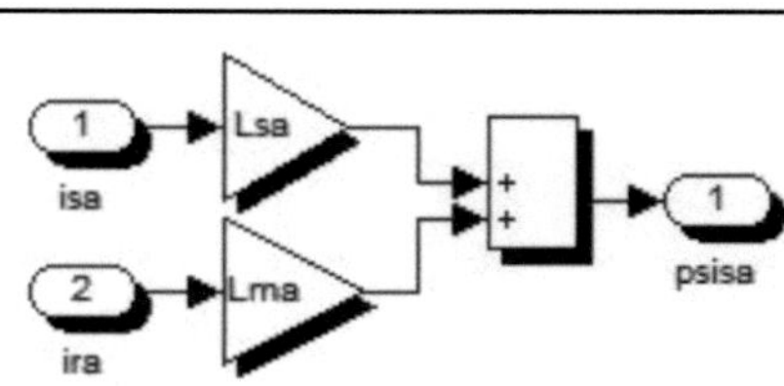
	$\psi_{s\beta} = L_{s\beta} i_{s\beta} + L_{m\beta} i_{r\beta}$	A similar simulation scheme to the previos one with corresponding parameters and variables

Equation for	Mathematical model (equations)	Simulation model in Simulink
rotor agnetic flux	$\psi_{r\alpha}=L_{m\alpha}i_{s\alpha}+L_{r\alpha}i_{r\alpha}$	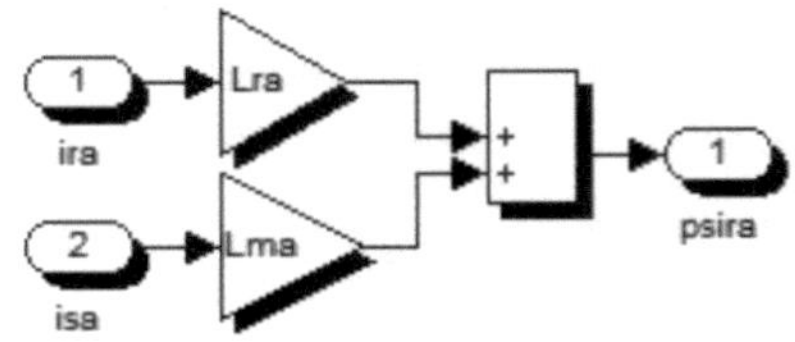
	$\psi_{r\beta}=L_{m\beta}i_{s\beta}+L_{r\beta}i_{r\beta}$	A similar simulation scheme with corresponding parameters and variables
stator currents	$i_{s\alpha}=\frac{1}{L_{s\alpha}}(\psi_{s\alpha}-L_{m\alpha}i_{r\alpha})$	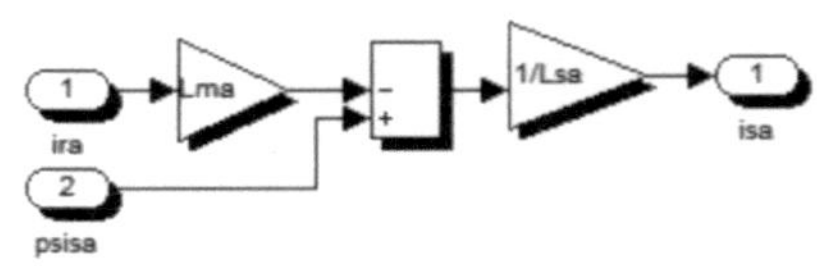
	$i_{s\beta}=\frac{1}{L_{s\beta}}(\psi_{s\beta}-L_{m\beta}i_{r\beta})$	A similar simulation scheme with corresponding parameters and variables
rotor currents	$i_{s\alpha}=\frac{1}{L_{s\alpha}}(\psi_{s\alpha}-L_{m\alpha}i_{r\alpha})$	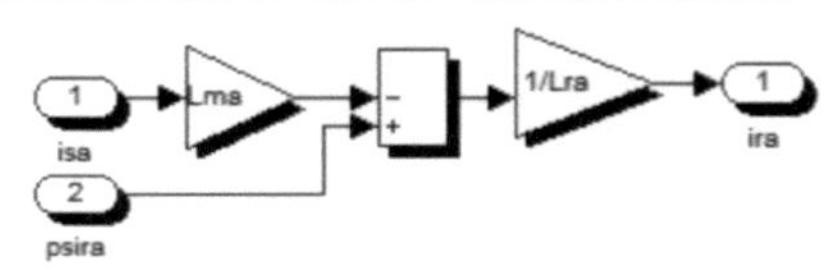
	$i_{r\beta}=\frac{1}{L_{r\beta}}(\psi_{r\beta}-L_{m\beta}i_{s\beta})$	A similar simulation scheme with corresponding parameters and variables
motor torque	$M_m=p\left(\frac{N_1}{N_2}\psi_{r\beta}i_{r\alpha}-\frac{N_2}{N_1}\psi_{r\alpha}i_{r\beta}\right)$	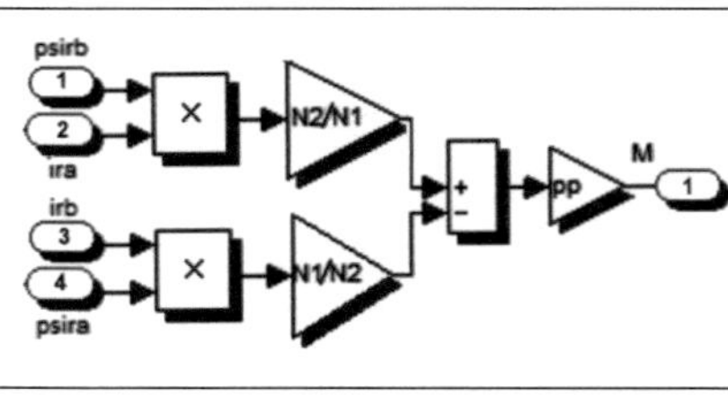
dynamic equation	$\frac{d\omega}{dt}=\frac{1}{J}\cdot(M_m-M_{load})$	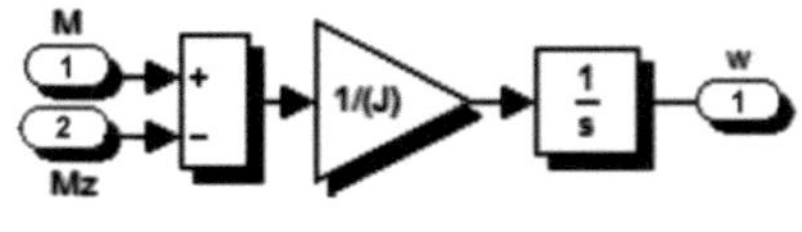

Table 1. Mathematical and simulation models of subsystems of the one-phase induction machine

Combining all schemes together, we get the block diagram of the motor (Figure 3), which presents a core of the virtual model enabling deeper understanding of the phenomena in the motor at various modes of operation and supply.

http://dx.doi.org/10.5772/60723

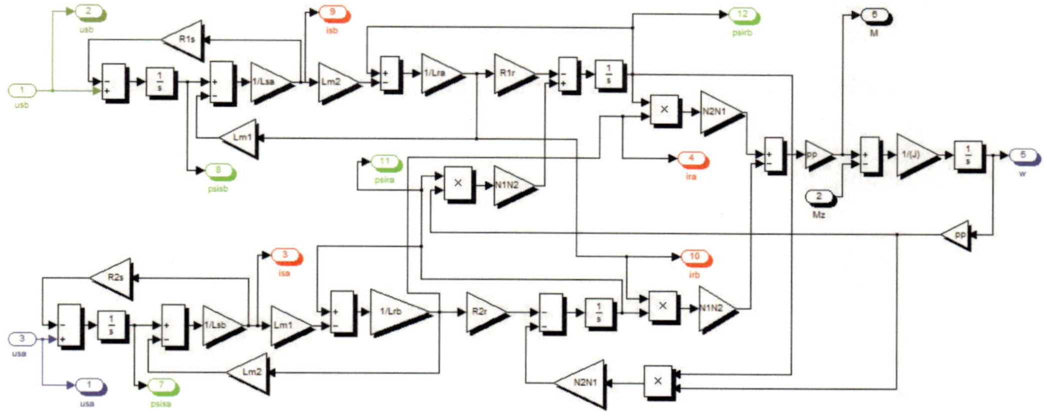

Figure 3. Simulink block diagram of one-phase induction motor.

In investigating various modes of starting and operation, it is suitable to complete the model by supplementary blocks, like harmonic oscillator generating sinus and cosinus voltages, by the switches switching the capacitors according to the chose mode of operation, and by block generating the load torque in the optional time instant of loading the machine. The final scheme, used for the virtual model, is shown in Figure 4.

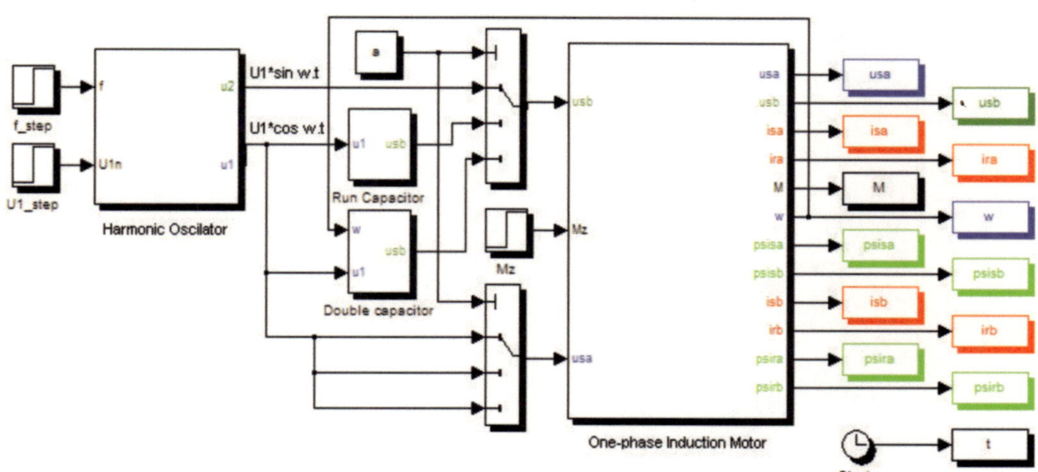

Figure 4. The model of the motor with connected inputs and outputs enabling to simulate capacitor run and double capacitor starting the motor.

3.4. Verification of the motor model with permanently connected capacitor

The speed can be changed by the frequency, by changing the number of poles, and-in a small scale-by change of the voltage or value of the capacitor. The change of the direction of rotation is simply done by the pole change of the auxiliary winding.

Time courses of the motor basic variables, motor torque, speed, and currents in both windings, are shown in Figure 5.

Simulation parameters:

$$U_1 = 230\text{ V}, f_1 = 50\text{ Hz}, M_{load} = 5\text{ Nm}, C_r = 32\ \mu\text{F}, T_{sim} = 0.8\text{ s}, T_{load} = 0.5\text{ s}.$$

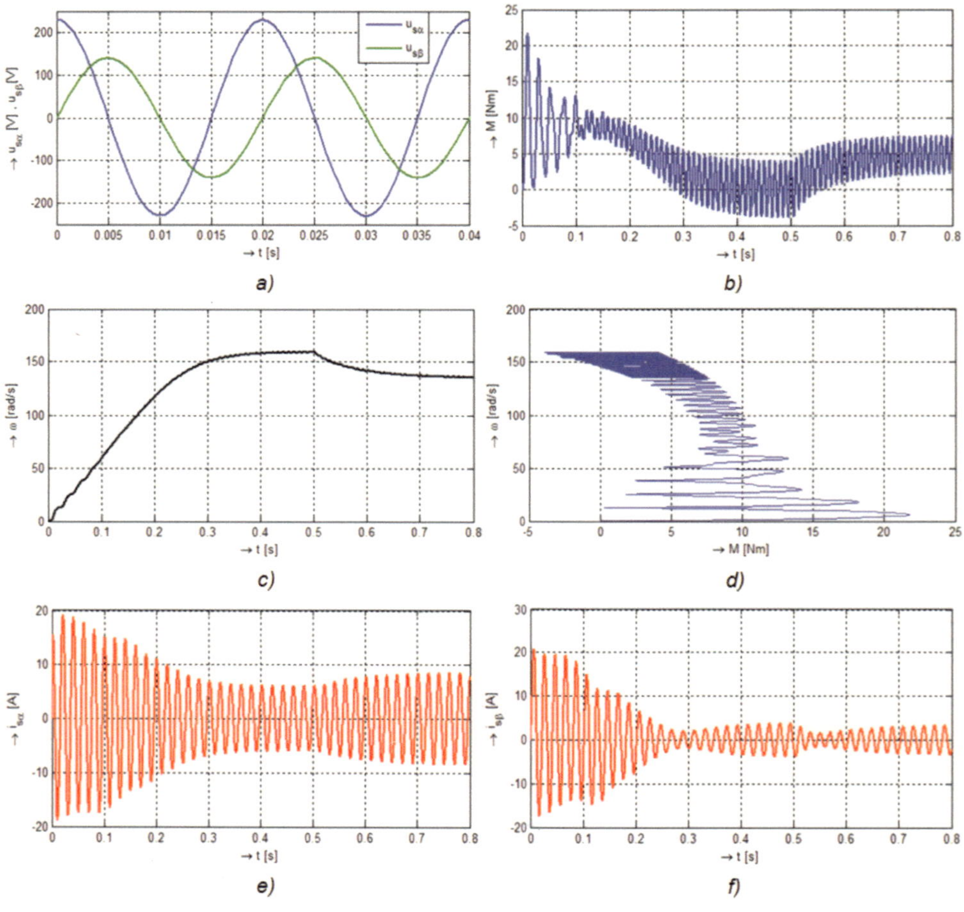

Figure 5. Time responses of the one-phase induction motor with the permanently connected capacitor in the stator reference frame $\{\alpha,\beta\}$ at starting and loading the motor in the time 0.5 s: (a) supply voltages $u_{s\alpha}$, $u_{s\beta}$ of the motor mode; (b) motor torque M ; (c) angular speed ω; (d) static characteristic of the motor ω/M; and (d) stator currents: torque producing component $i_{s\alpha}$ and magnetic flow component $i_{s\beta}$.

3.5. One-phase motor with a double capacitor

To improve the motor performance during start period, a higher capacity is required in the auxiliary phase circuit. This is done by a capacitor C_s connected in parallel to the existing one (Figure 1b) up to the time instant the motor runs by speed about 70% $\omega_{N,}$ which is followed by a centrifugal switch. After disconnecting, only the capacitor C_r of a lower value remains connected permanently. The next figure (Figure 6) shows performance graphs of the motor with double capacitor.

Simulation parameters: $U_1 = 230$ V, $f_1 = 50$ Hz, $M_{load} = 5$ Nm, $C_s = 53$ μF, $C_r = 32$ μF, $\omega_n = 110$ rad/s, $T_{sim} = 0.8$ s, and $T_{load} = 0.5$ s.

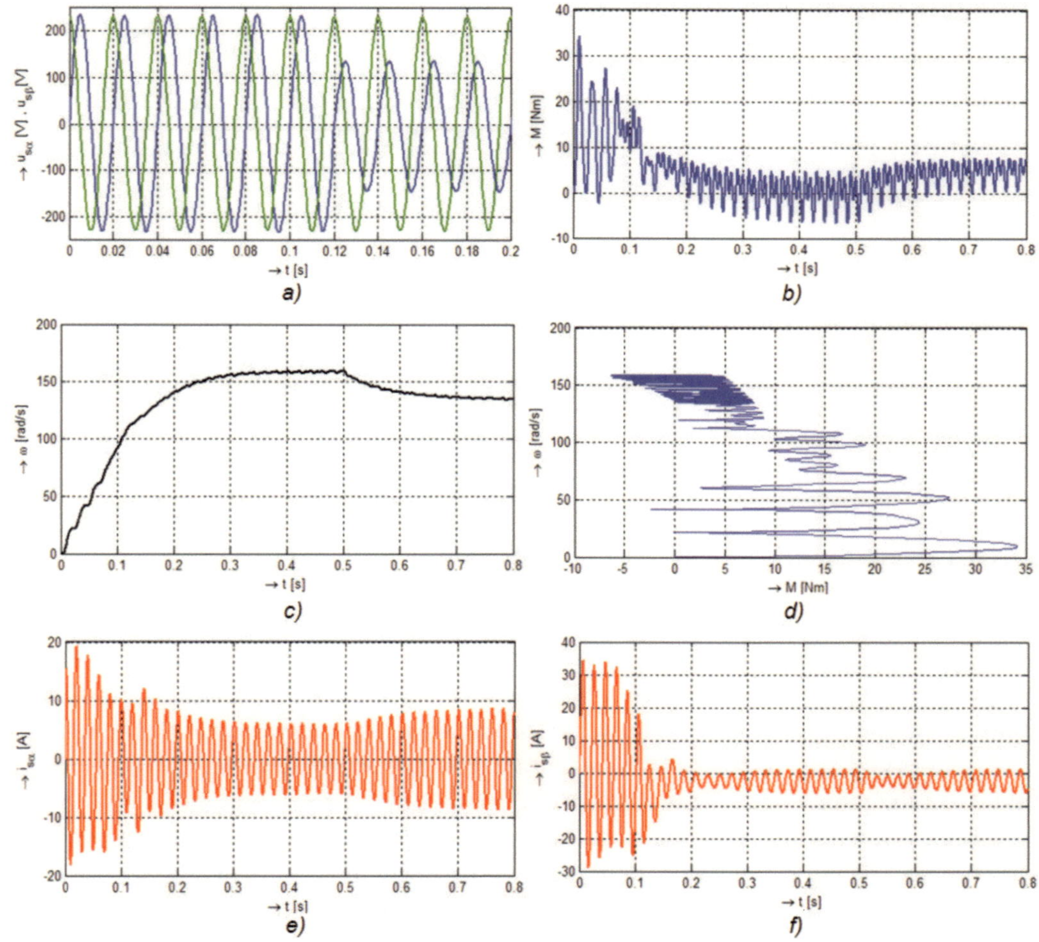

Figure 6. Time responses of the one-phase induction motor with the double-starting capacitor in the stator reference frame $\{\alpha,\beta\}$ while starting and loading the motor at time 0.5 s: (a) supply voltages $u_{s\alpha}$, $u_{s\beta}$ of the motor mode; (b) motor torque M ; (c) angular speed ω; (d) static characteristic of the motor $\omega = f(M)$; (e, f) stator currents: torque producing component $i_{s\alpha}$ and magnetic flow component $i_{s\beta}$

3.6. Comparison of the motor performance supplied by the voltages of different frequencies

To get the best motor performance, the constant stator flux must be preserved at various supply frequencies. From this condition, it follows up that U/f = const. (Figure 7).

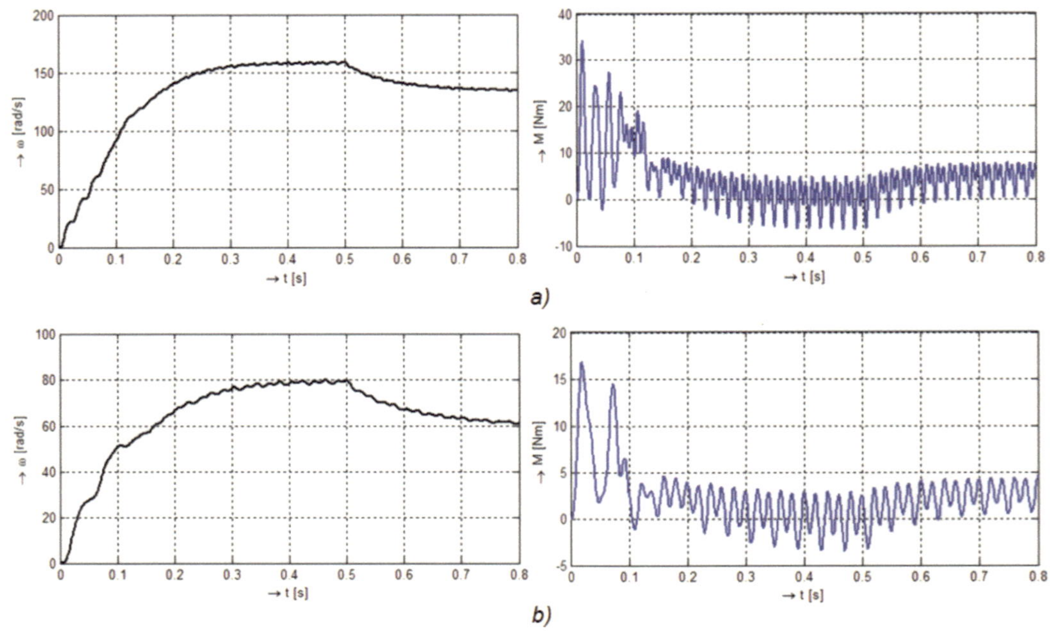

Figure 7. Time courses of the angular speed ω and motor torque at various frequencies of the supply voltage: (a) U = 230 V, f = 50 Hz, C_s= 53 μF C_r = 32 μF; (b) U = 115 V, f = 25 Hz, C_{sb} = 28 μF, C_r = 14 μF.

3.7. GUI application for the one-phase induction motor

After the verification of the mathematical model of the single-phase motor by simulation, we can design and develop the motor virtual model-graphical user interface in the MATLAB program. The application is designed so that the user is granted simple handling in adjusting motor parameters, and waveforms show typical values of the motor. Graphical user interface (GUI) allows you to visualize four different graphs: the input supply voltage, torque, angular velocity of the rotor, components of stator and rotor currents, and components of magnetic fluxes motor when starting the motor, during steady-state operation, and after loading it the chosen time. The ergonomics of handling and pedagogical respects should be strictly taken into consideration, as widely analyzed in the previous publications [1-3]. Moreover, these aspects of using the model should be also considered-they should be suitable.

1. for explanation at lectures the phenomena and motor behavior during various operating modes and

2. for preparation of the students for the experimentation in the labs.

http://dx.doi.org/10.5772/60723

3.8. GUI screen description

The developed GUI for the one-phase induction motor consists of two screens:

1. The first (auxiliary) screen (Figure 8) serves:

    a. for explanation – it displays equivalent diagram of the motor on the left side and its mathematical model on the right side. The basic differential equations describing the motor that are in boxes, the color of which corresponds to the color of the graphs

    b. for inputting the motor basic parameters.

2. The second (main) screen (Figure 9) shows the graphs of the motor variables and contains control elements for simulation models and displaying the graphs.

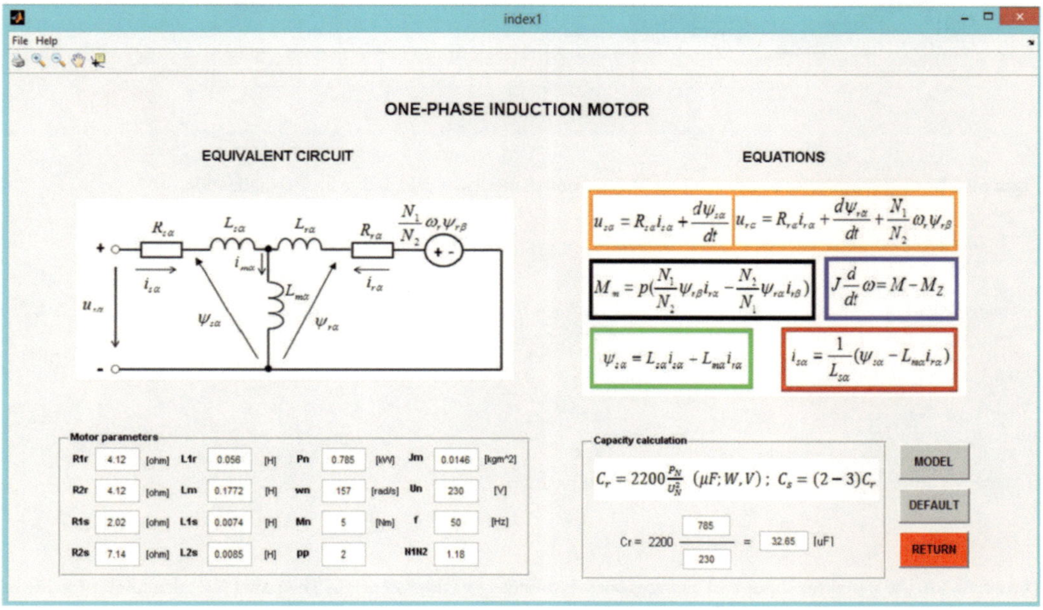

Figure 8. The screen for inputting parameters for the model of single-phase motor displaying motor equivalent diagram, equations of the model, and input motor parameters.

The panel *Motor Parameters* (Figure 10a) enable to input motor parameters and thus to verify and compare behavior of various motors. After pushing the return button, the main program starts model simulation with the actual parameters.

In the bottom-right corner, there are three buttons: the *model* button displays the motor model in the Simulink program, as shown in Figure 4 (and inside the block of the motor, the full scheme appears according to the Figure 3). The *default* button sets the preset values of the parameters, and the *return* button causes return to the second screen with the graphs, and immediately, the simulation starts with the set parameters.

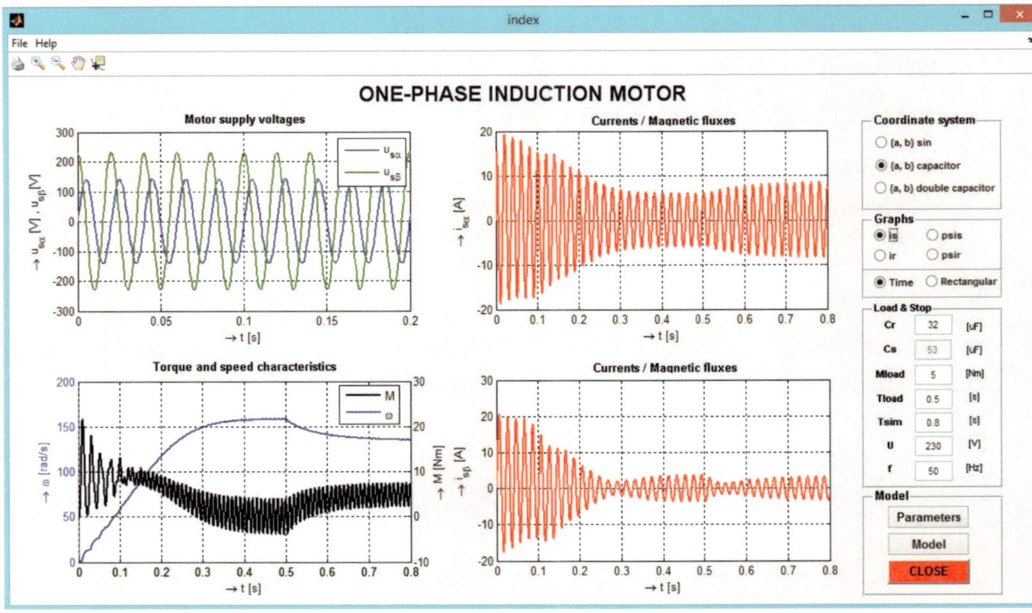

Figure 9. The GUI main screen with the graphs and control modes of calculation and visualization.

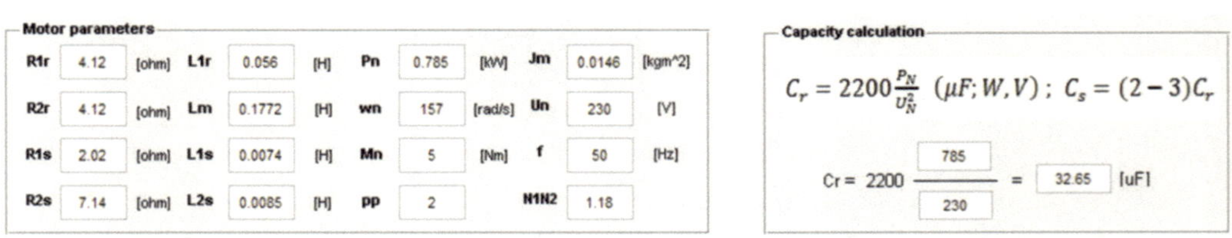

a) b)

Figure 10. (a) The panel for input and changes basic parameters of the motor. (b) The panel for calculation of value of the capacitor connected into the auxiliary phase.

3.9. Description of the control panels

The panel *Coordinate system* (Figure 11a) contains three switches to choose the supply mode: (1) supply by the harmonic voltage in the $\{\alpha, \beta\}$ coordinate system connected with the stator, (2) supply with the permanently connected capacitor, and (3) supply with the double capacitor.

The panel *Graphs* (Figure 11b) consists of two parts: the upper one contains four buttons serving to choose the graphs to display stator/rotor currents or stator/rotor magnetic fluxes. By the buttons in the lower part, the time graphs ($i = f_1(t)$, $\psi = f_2(t)$) or mutual dependence of the variables is chosen ($i_\alpha = g_1(i_\beta)$, $\psi_\alpha = g_1(\psi_\beta)$). The variables of the motor we are intend to display (stator or rotor) are selected by the above-mentioned buttons.

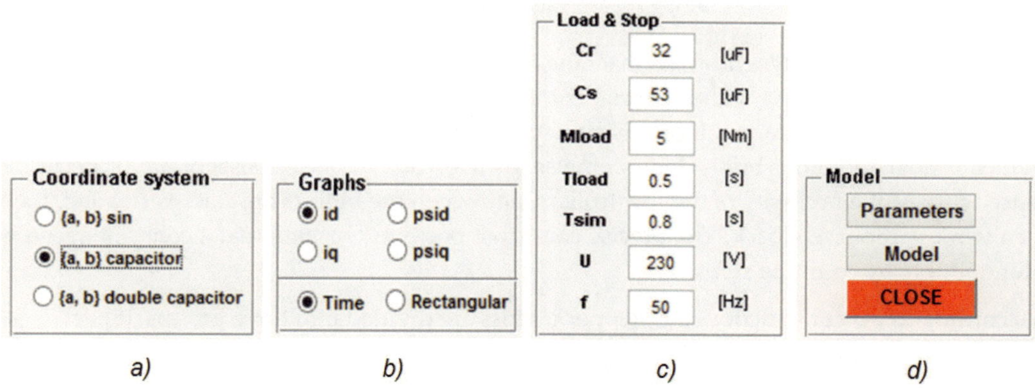

Figure 11. The GUI panels: (a) Coordinate system; (b) Graphs; (c) Load and Stop; (d) Model.

The panel *Load and Stop* (Figure 11c) shows the edit boxes for setting the values of the capacitors: permanently connected C_r, starting capacitor C_s, load torque M_{load}, time of loading T_{load}, time of simulation T_{sim}, and supply voltage U and its frequency f.

The panel *Model* (Figure 11d) contains the possibility to finish simulation and exit from the program (*Close*), displaying motor model in Simulink (*Model*), and after pushing the button *Parameters,* we switch to the screen with parameters (Figures 8 and 10a).

The panel of tools (Table 2) makes the work with the GUI comfortable. The *Tools* panel consists of five icons. The *Context* menu enables to set up line widths for the simulation courses (Line Width), to make a copy of the screen (screenshot) by saving it (Save), to run help (Help), and to close the graphical interface (Close).

	**Print** - printing graphs	The context menu:
	**Pan** - shifting the graph	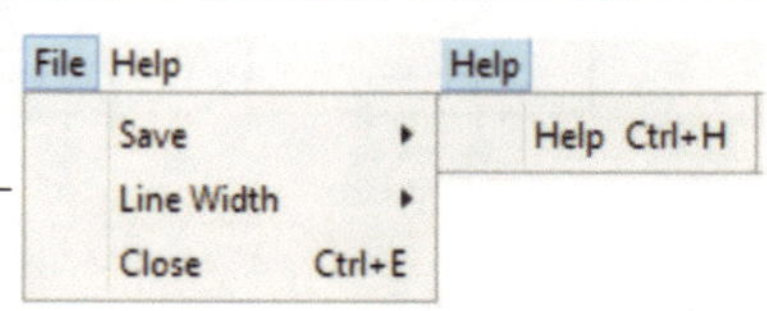
	**Zoom out** - decreasing the graph	
	**Zoom in** - zooming the graph	
	**Data cursor** - showing coordinates of the points (by clicking on graph)	

Table 2. Panel of tools and menu of the graphical user Interface

4. Virtual model development of a stepper motor

Stepper motor is an asynchronous machine, the stator of which contains a control winding. The rotor is either fitted with a permanent magnet or made up of a toothed ferromagnetic magnetic circuit. The stepper motor is an impulse-excited electric machine, the movement of which is not continuous but is done stepwise. Its main advantage consists of motor performance without the necessity of any controllers, and when the motors are not overloaded, they can work without feedback. The precise control of position or rotation at a constant speed is done simply by counting steps.

According to the construction, the stepper motors are divided into three groups, [8]:

a. Stepper motors with variable reluctance

b. Stepper motors with permanent magnets

c. Hybrid stepper motors

4.1. Hybrid stepper motor

The hybrid stepper motor accumulates benefits both of stepper motors with variable reluctance and permanent magnets. It has a very small step and high power per unit of weight. The arrangement of the stator winding is similar to this stepper motor with variable reluctance. It differentiates by the rotor that is made from a cylinder permanent magnet with mounted rotor poles along the circumference having teeth. The number of teeth determinates an angle step. Typically, the motors with 50 teeth are produced, in which one step is equal to the angle of 1.8°. In the stator of the hybrid stepper motor, there are usually two windings having terminals arranged as shown in Figure 12.

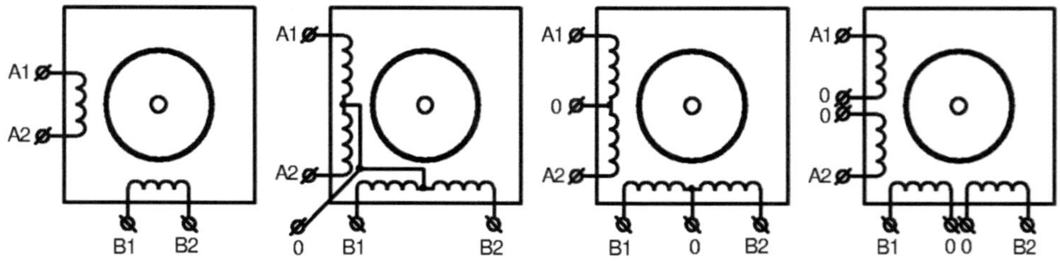

Figure 12. Twelve ways of arranging the stator windings of a two-phase hybrid stepper motor: (a) 4 wires-only start and end points are led to terminals; (b) 5 wires-also the common middle point is led out to terminals; (c) 6 wires-the middle point of each phase is led out to terminals; and (d) 8 wires-the phases are divided into the halves and the start and end points are led to the terminals.

4.2. Control of stepper motors

According to the types of the windings, the stepper motors are divided into the unipolar stepper motor and the bipolar one. Similarly, the control of the stepper motors is divided into the following:

http://dx.doi.org/10.5772/60723

- Unipolar control, which is mostly used for a four-phase stepper motor with variable reluctance or for hybrid stepper motors.
- Bipolar control, which is used for stepper motors with permanent magnets of for hybrid stepper motors. In this type of control, the current flows through the windings are placed opposed.

4.2.1. Four-tact control magnetizing one phase

In a simple drawing (Figure 13), the rotor is replaced by a rotating permanent magnet having the north pole (red) and the south pole (blue). By switching the stator winding phases in the in the opposite coils, the north and the south poles are also excited.

The principle of the control consists of exciting (and magnetizing) one phase only. According to the cyclogram in Figure 13a, the sequence of excitation A1-B1-A2-B2 ensures the rotation of the magnetic field in the positive direction. The change of the direction is done through reverse switching of the motor phases. Here the current flows through one winding only.

In case of bipolar control (Figure 13b), the current flows simultaneously through two opposite coils. This means the current is twice higher in comparison with the unipolar type. The bipolar control differs by the necessity of change the current direction.

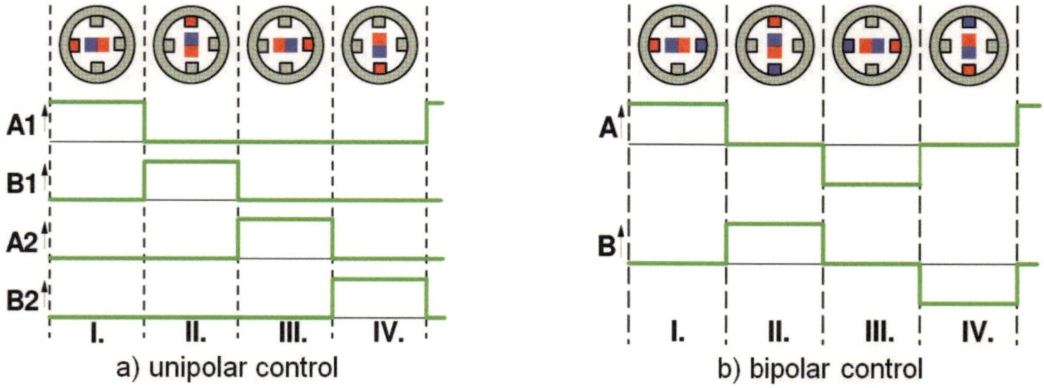

Figure 13. Cyclogram of four-tact control magnetizing one phase of a hybrid stepper motor.

4.2.2. Four-tact control magnetizing two phases

When two neighboring coils are excited simultaneously, according to the cyclogram in Figure 14, the motor torque is $\sqrt{2}$ times higher. The position of the rotor will follow the vector sum of magnetic fluxes of both phases. At this type of control, the current flows through all four windings. This type of control is used the most often.

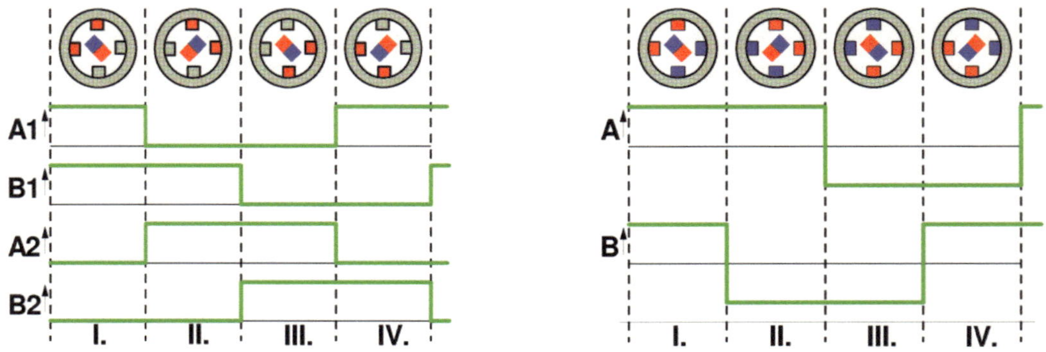

Figure 14. Cyclogram of four-tact control of a hybrid stepper motor.

4.2.3. *Eight-tact control*

Combining the previous two control algorithms leads to doubling the number of stable states (cyclogram in Figure 15). Consequently, an increase of positioning accuracy is achieved (called "soften up"), without changing the structural adjustment. The previous commutation (four-tact control) was the symmetrical one, and the asymmetrical eight-tact commutation causes doubling of the number of rotor steps.

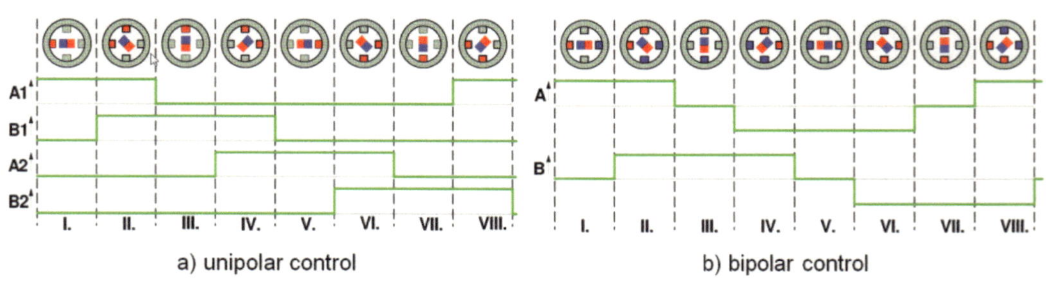

Figure 15. Eight-tact control of a hybrid stepper motor: (a) unipolar control; (b) bipolar control.

4.2.4. *Further modes of the control*

Other ways of controlling hybrid stepper motors exist, but due to simplification, we do not deal with them in detail here (although the modes are also included into the virtual model):

- Vector control. The commutation consists in simultaneous supplying both phases by different voltages. This enables to rotate the stator magnetic field vector by a softer step.
- Microstepper. This is done by commutation at supplying the coils by harmonic voltages that are mutually shifted by $\pi/2$. This causes a smooth, continuous movement of the rotor.

http://dx.doi.org/10.5772/60723

4.3. Simulation model of the hybrid stepper motor

The model of the motor consists of the electrical part (Figure 16) and mechanical part, described by the dynamic equation.

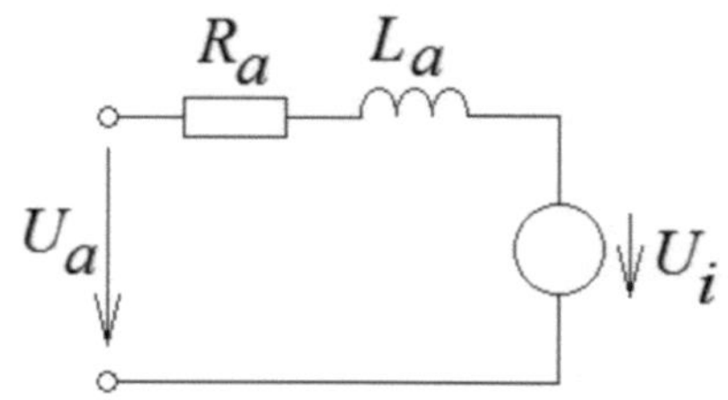

Figure 16. Equivalent circuit diagram of hybrid bipolar stepper motor for phase A; L_a presents the inductance, R_a is the resistance of phase A winding, and U_i is the electromotive force depending on the angle of the rotor.

The mathematical models of all motor subsystems together with corresponding simulation schemes are displayed in Table 3.

Equation for	Mathematical model (equations)	Simulation model in Simulink
phase currents	$\frac{di_a}{dt}=\frac{U_a}{L_a}-\frac{R_a}{L_a}\cdot i_a+\frac{K_m}{L_a}\cdot\omega\cdot\sin(N_r\cdot\theta)$	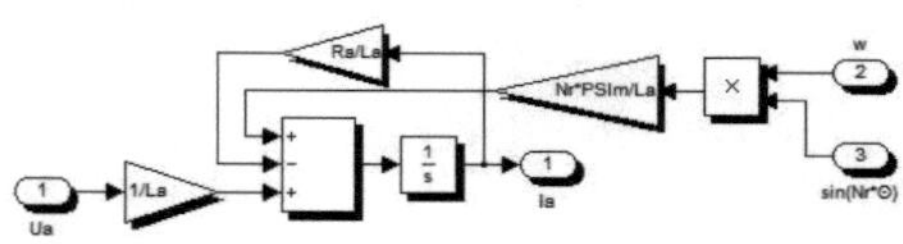
	$\frac{di_b}{dt}=\frac{U_b}{L_b}-\frac{R_b}{L_b}\cdot i_b-\frac{K_m}{L_b}\cdot\omega\cdot\sin(N_r\cdot\theta-\pi/2)$	A similar simulation scheme with corresponding parameters and variables
phase torques	$M_a=-K_m\cdot i_a\cdot\sin(N_r\cdot\theta)$	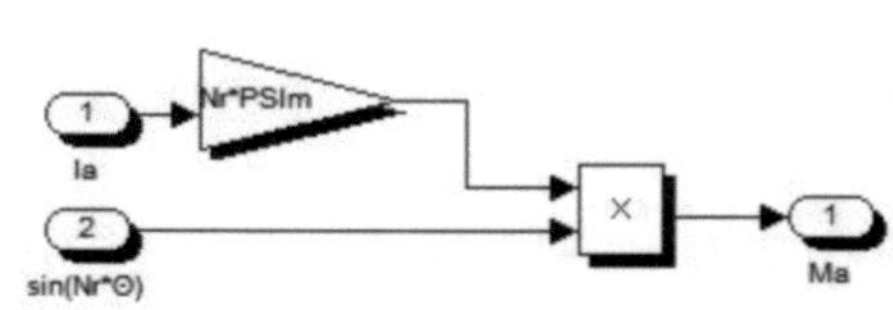
	$M_b=-K_m\cdot i_b\cdot\sin(N_r\cdot\theta-\pi/2)$	A similar simulation scheme with corresponding parameters and variables
aretating torque	$M_d=-T_{dm}\cdot\sin(N_r\cdot\theta)$	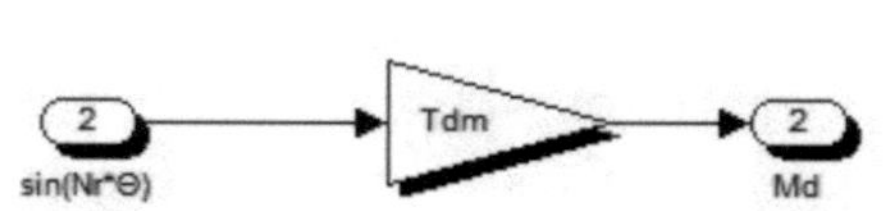

Equation for	Mathematical model (equations)	Simulation model in Simulink
Total motor torque	$M_c = M_a + M_b + M_d$	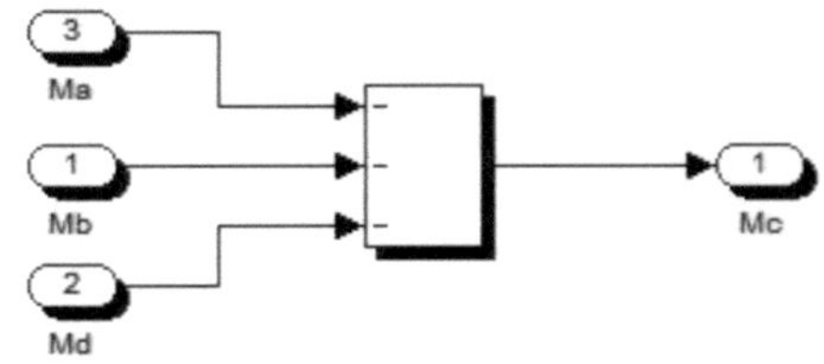
motion equation	$\frac{d\omega}{dt} = \frac{1}{J} \cdot (M_c - b_m \cdot \omega - M_{load})$	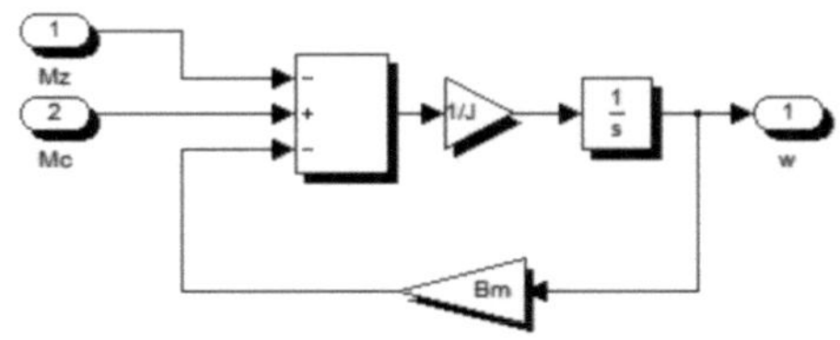
relation angle -speed	$\frac{d\theta}{dt} = \omega$	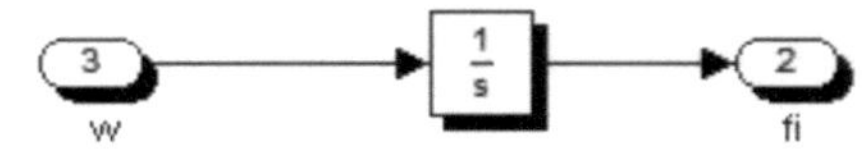

Table 3. Mathematical and simulation models of subsystems of the hybrid bipolar stepper motor

Figure 17 shows the complete simulation scheme consisting of the schemes of subsystems.

4.4. Simulation results of hybrid bipolar stepper motor at various control modes

A series of experiments before developing the GUI was done in order to verify correctness of the developed motor simulation model.

The hybrid bipolar stepper motor parameters used for simulation are as follows: $L_a = L_b = 0.058$ H, $R_a = R_b = 30\ \Omega$, $S_a = 1.8°$, $N_r = 50$, $K_m = 0.8$ Nm/A, $T_d = 0$ Nm, $b_m = 8.10^{-4}$ Nms/rad (damping coefficient), $M_{load} = 0.1$ Nm, $U = 12$ V, and $J = 6.10^{-6}$ kg m^2.

The motor simulation schemes were completed by schemes of simplified voltage sources, enabling control of the chosen stepper motor by whether the full step, half step, reduced (or shortened) step, or microstep.

Just note that the time courses in Figures 18-22 were obtained from the graphical user interface of the hybrid bipolar stepper motor (explained in detail later, in the subchapter 4.5). The graphs display the motor torque M, the angular speed ω, and the angle of displacement θ, and there are courses of the current and supply voltage at the bottom.

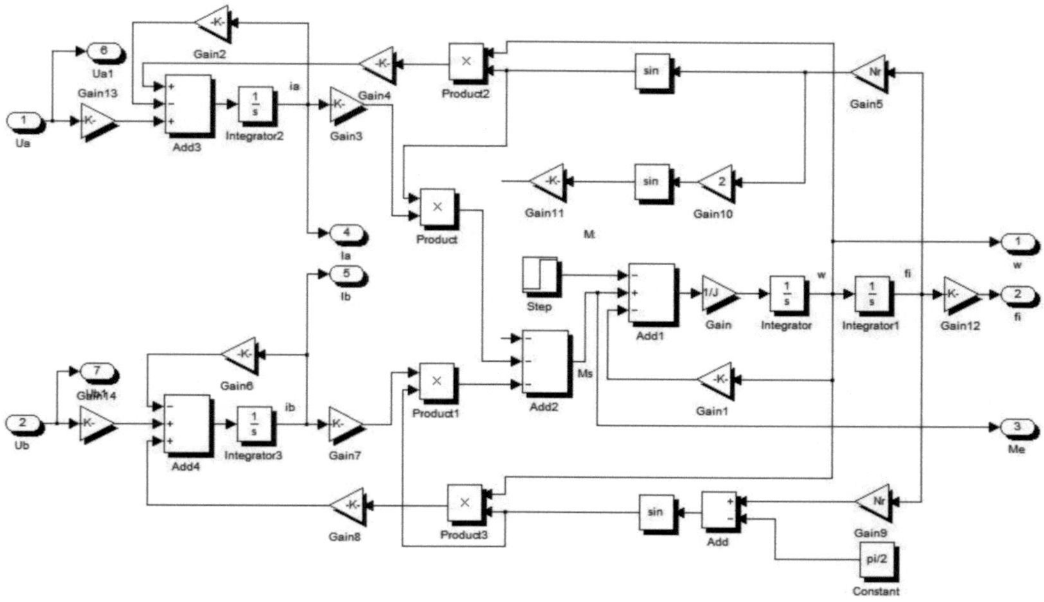

Figure 17. Simulation model of a hybrid bipolar stepper motor in Simulink

4.4.1. Motor control at full step and magnetizing one phase only

The angular displacement starts after the voltage is connected to phase B (Figure 18). The angular step displacement is 1.8° (i.e., 90/50). The load torque influence on the angular displacement is very small.

4.4.2. Motor control at full step and magnetizing two phases

The step displacement in this control mode control comes to a half in comparison with the previous case 0.9° (Figure 19). Also, the load torque has lesser influence on the angular displacement like in the previous case.

4.4.3. Motor control at the half step

Interchange of active coils results in a varying torque and angular velocity, as shown in the simulation results of half-step (Figure 20). The angle displacement step is 0.9°.

4.4.4. Vector control of the motor

In the vector control, two phases are supplied by different voltages (Figure 21). This allows the rotation of the vector of the stator magnetic field. In our case, the nominal value of the voltages U_1 and the second one has the value that ensures the constant step. In this case, this is $U_2 = 0.4U_1$.

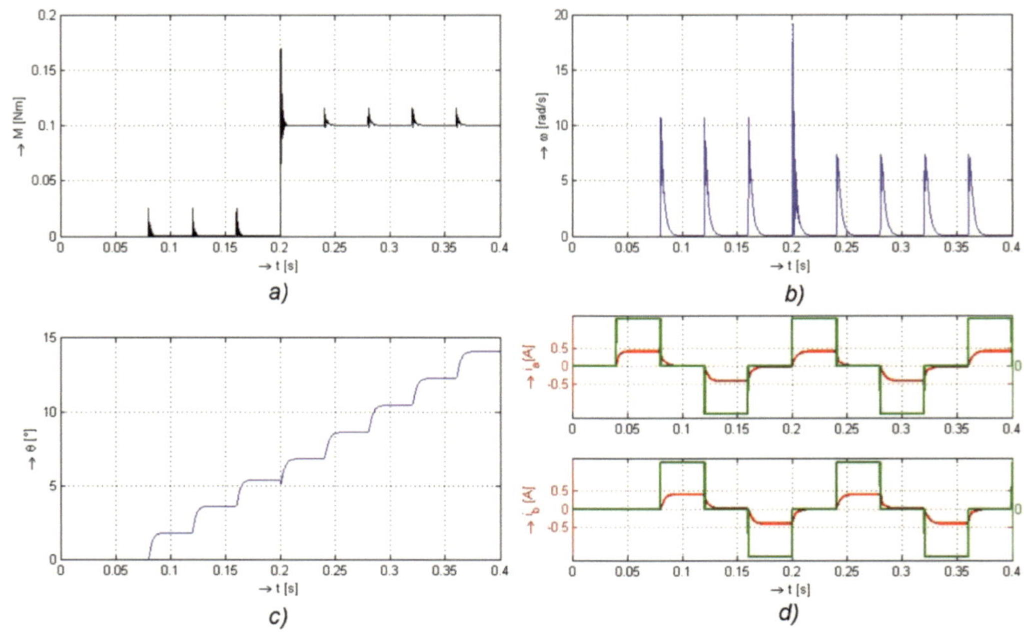

Figure 18. Time courses of the hybrid bipolar stepper motor at full step and magnetizing one phase.

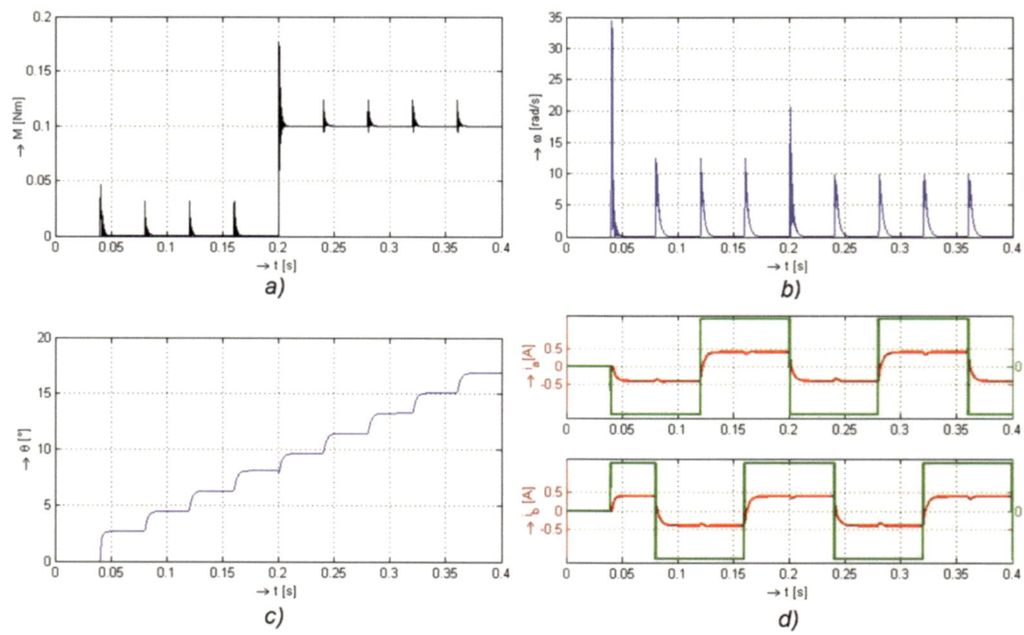

Figure 19. Time courses at the full step and magnetizing both phases.

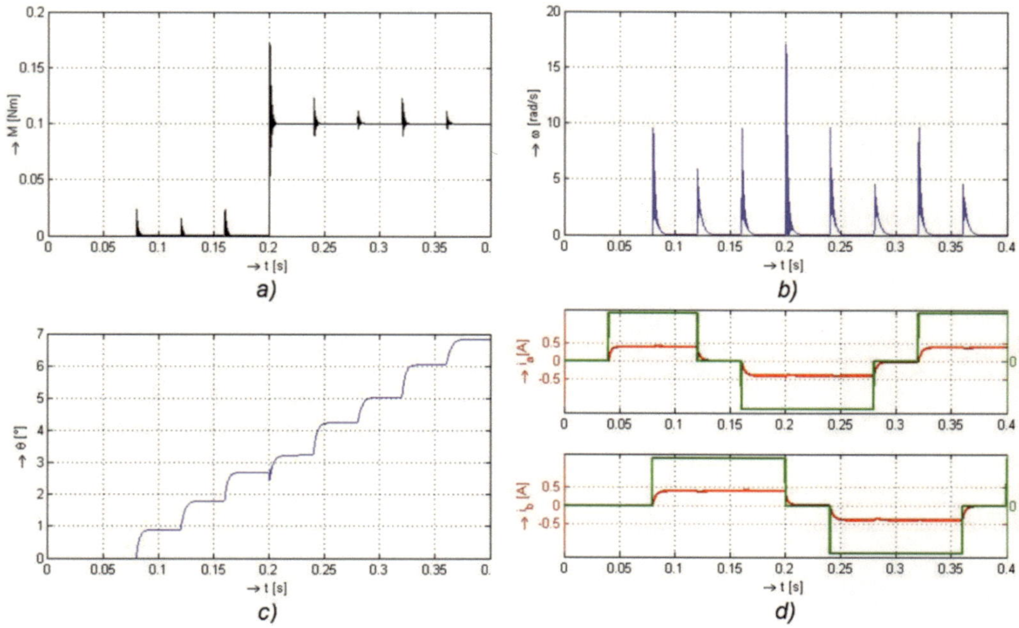

Figure 20. Time courses for the chosen half step.

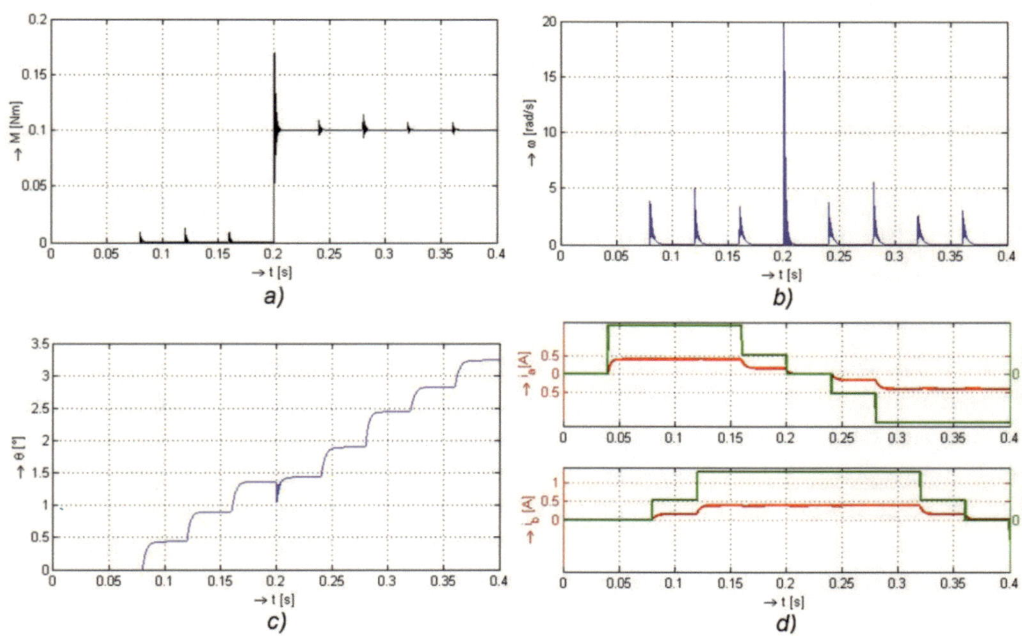

Figure 21. Time courses for vector control and step equal to 0.45°

4.4.5. Microstepper of the motor

At microstepper, one phase is supplied by the sine voltage and the second phase by the cosine voltage (Figure 22). It is possible to replace the harmonic voltage by a discrete course with a low frequency of 1.5 Hz. The achieved final step is 0.21°.

4.5. GUI for the hybrid stepper motors

Similarly, like in the previous case, GUI application was developed for analyzing both the bipolar and unipolar hybrid stepper motors. The chosen supply mode is selected by a button. The application allows to implement a simple change of parameters to choose the mode of the motor run to load the motor and to visualize results in four basic charts: for the motor torque, angular speed, the angle of the rotation of the rotor and the line voltage, and the currents in the respective phases.

4.5.1. Description of the screen with graphs

The GUI screen (Figure 23) displays the motor torque M, the angular speed ω, the angle of displacement θ, and there are courses of the current and supply voltage at the bottom.

The panel *Type of Motor* (upper right) contains two buttons: Bipolar SM and Unipolar SM, where the user selects the mode of basic control of the stepper motor. After selecting the chosen mode, the button turns green.

The panel *Control Mode* (Figure 24a) contains three further subpanels. In the subpanel *Direction*, a direction of rotation is chosen; in the subpanel *Step Modes*, a value of the step is chosen from the choice: full step, half step, reduced or shortened step for the vector control, and, the last choice, microstep. In the last subpanel *Power Supply Phase*, it is possible to choose either the active one or both phases of the motor (this possibility is available only when the full step is chosen).

In the panel *Other Simulation Parameters* (Figure 24b), the user inputs further information required by some modes of control. Here the first panel box is accessible only if a reduced step is chosen in the control mode panel. This gives a possibility to choose a reduced step divided into four parts or into eight. The next panel box is available when the microstep is chosen. The choice gives a possibility to change the frequency of the input sinus-cosinus signals. By the Slider Step Size, it is possible to soften the step size. In the last panel box, it is possible to change the time of simulation T_s, and the parameter T_v is related to the microstepper (the text box is available only when the microstepper mode is chosen).

The tools panel and the context menu have similar meaning like in the previous case (see Table 2). At the mentioned step choice, the user can change the direction of rotation of the motor to select other cyclogram of motor supply, to choose the length of each cyclogram (by the parameter T_v), to change the frequency of a voltage supply at the microstepper, and to choose the step size when the movement of the rotor is continuous.

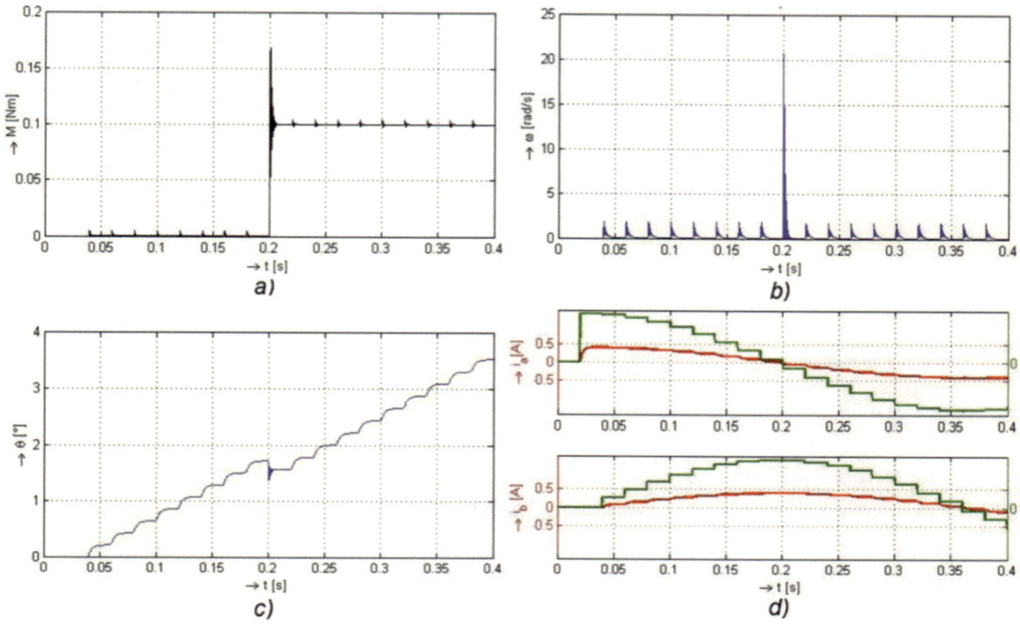

Figure 22. Time courses at the microstepper with the step 0.21°.

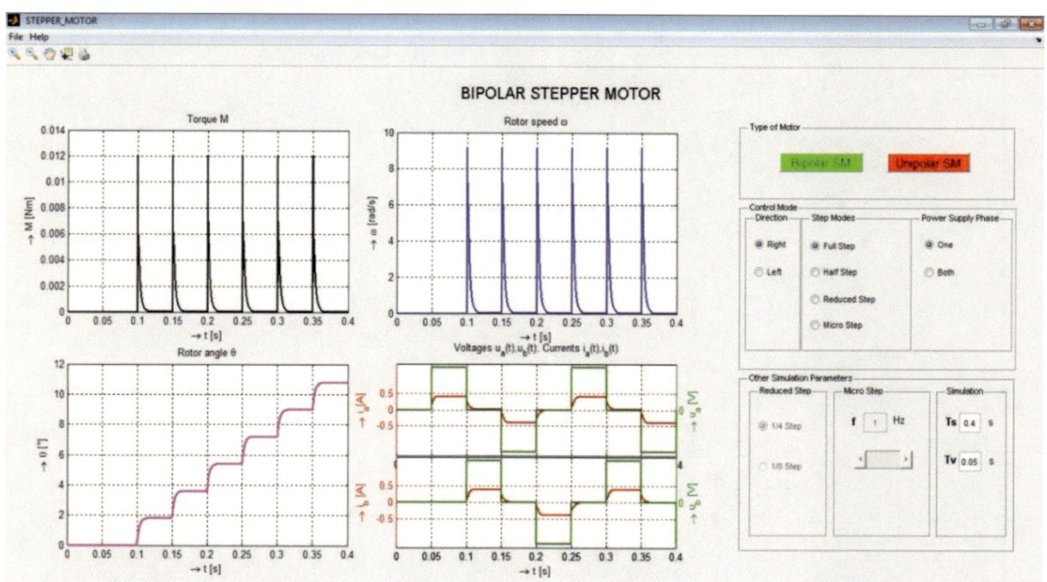

Figure 23. GUI screen for the stepper motor.

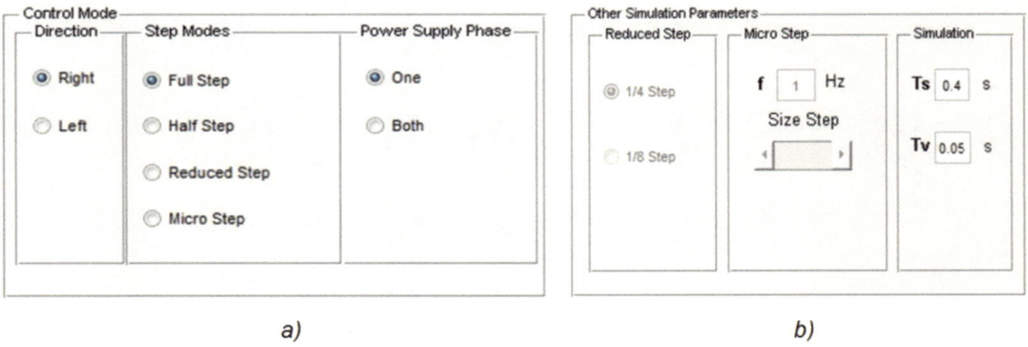

Figure 24. The panels (a) for selection of the stepper motor control mode and (b) for inputting control and simulation parameters.

4.5.2. The screen for inputting parameters of the bipolar stepper motor

The GUI screen enables easy change of parameters of a chosen stepper motor. This GUI screen (Figure 25) appears after choice of bipolar motor-the button *Bipolar SM* in the panel *Type of Motor* (see the GUI main screen in Figure 23). The screen also displays differential equations of the mathematical model of the bipolar stepper motor and equivalent diagram of the motor one phase.

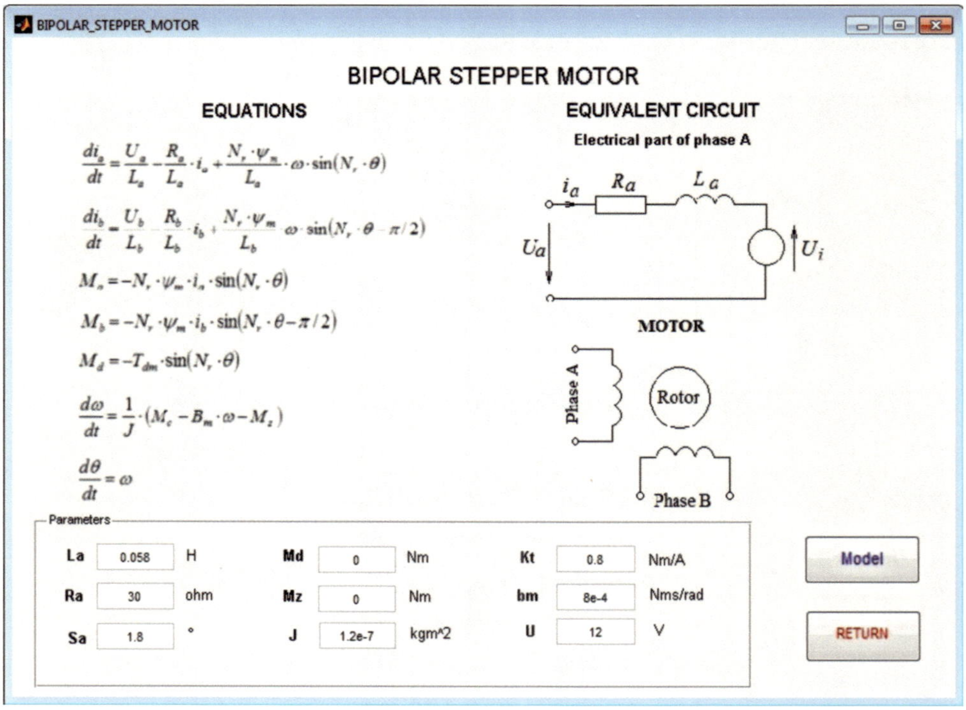

Figure 25. The GUI screen for inputting parameters for the model of bipolar hybrid stepper motor.

The parameters for any arbitrary bipolar motor are set in the bottom panel *Parameters*. After clicking the model, the Simulink model of the motor is displayed. Pushing the return button causes switch over the main screen.

4.5.3. The screen for inputting parameters of the unipolar stepper motor

After choosing the unipolar stepper motor (the button **Unipolar SM** in the main screen, Figure 22), a screen for inputting unipolar stepper motor parameters is displayed (Figure 26).

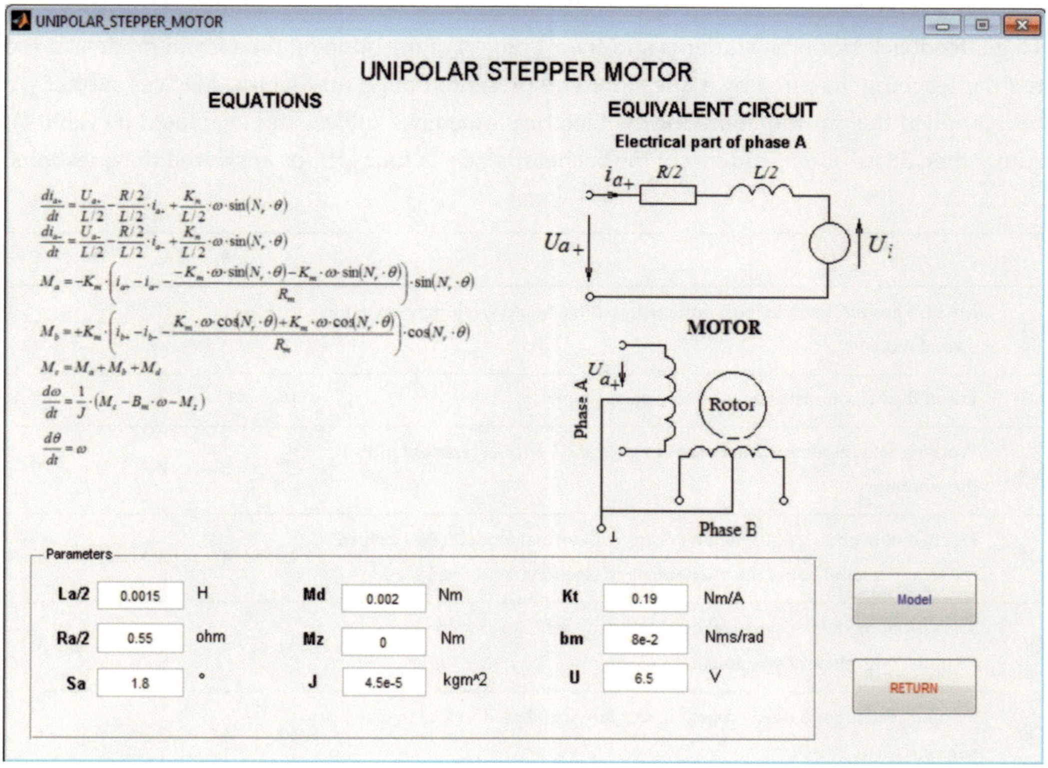

Figure 26. The GUI screen for inputting parameters for the model unipolar hybrid stepper motor.

4.6. Integration of the realized virtual models into virtual laboratory of electrical machines

The subject electrical machines taught in the second year of the undergraduate course is devoted to the explanation of the phenomena in the machine, which is supported by various animation models. During lectures, when explaining static and dynamic characteristics of each machine by presentation of demo pictures, animations, videos, and of course using the blackboard for derivation of the dependencies, the virtual models are briefly introduced. The students have a free access to the models through the institutional LAN (the access is also available in the student hostels).

In the laboratory, they measure the characteristics of the motors and compare them with those from virtual models. They also discuss and explain in detail the motor behavior and the influence of motor parameters on the characteristics.

The work with the virtual models saves time at virtual experimentation, but it requires a careful and detailed explanation and analysis of the obtained characteristics by the teacher-how and why is the behavior of the motor corresponding to the form of the characteristics. Otherwise, the students do not fully understand the graphs.

To get feedback from the students and their opinion of introducing the virtual models in the regular teaching, inspired by a questionnaire presented in [9] for Electrical Drives subject we have applied the questionnaire for the Electrical Machines subject and evaluated it (Table 4). Altogether, 36 full-time students of the bachelor study in four groups answered the questions.

#		A	B	C	D	E
Q1	My background knowledge is sufficient to understand working with of the virtual models	11	18	5	2	0
Q2	I need the help of instructor to understand graphs	16	13	3	2	2
Q3	Working with models helped me to understand better experimentation in the laboratory	27	5	2	2	0
Q4	I gained new knowledge when working with virtual models (they helped me to understand better the phenomena in electrical machines)	29	4	2	1	0
Q5	The virtual models of electrical machines are useful and I recommend to continue with their development	30	5	1	0	0
Q6	I would recommend development of similar virtual models also in other subjects	30	4	2	0	0

Evaluation criteria: A - strongly agree, B - agree, C - neutral, D - disagree, E - strongly disagree

Table 4. Questionnaire statements and their evaluation

The student ratings on the evaluation of incorporating the virtual models into teaching – both into lectures and prior laboratory work – are generally positive. It was observed that majority of students found it useful, interesting, and contributing to increasing knowledge about the subject.

The students works with the virtual models also in the following years in the subjects like:

http://dx.doi.org/10.5772/60723

- The subject Electrical Drives where the dynamic characteristics and the influence of parameters on the motor behavior are analyzed in connection with the power electronic converter.
- The subject Controlled Drives, for which specialized virtual modules for the subject were developed, which facilitate the calculation and verification of controllers and enable to analyze the influence of the controller parameters on the dynamic behavior of the controlled electrical drives. Of course, a connection with the practical realization is pointed out at each utilization of the virtual model.

5. Conclusion

The aim of this study was to present the methodology and results in the development of virtual models of two types of electrical machines in the MATLAB graphical development environment: the one-phase induction motor used in home applications and the stepper motor used widely in automation.

The MATLAB GUIDE, on the one hand, presents a comfortable tool enabling the development of GUI in a very easy and understandable way. On the other hand, it limits the utilization of virtual models by the necessity of the MATLAB program purchase. We do consider it as a limitation because MATLAB is widely distributed and presents a standard tool at the universities. Another solution is to use MATLAB server features through the Internet, which enables registered users (students) to utilize the developed interfaces for free. In the boundary case, a stand-alone .exe program can also be developed, but here, some special features of the MATLAB program are lost (Simulink, SymbolicMath toolbox, Animation toolbox, and some other specialties), and they are replaced by bothersome programming.

The two developed GUIs of the one-phase induction motor and of the stepper motor complete the series of virtual modules developed earlier [5] for the subject of electrical machines, like the virtual models of the DC motor, the three-phase AC motors, and the BLDC motor. The virtual models show system performance in various working points and analyze the influence of variable system parameters, modes of supply, and control parameters on system behavior.

The virtual dynamical models, on one hand, contribute to the e-learning support of teaching and, on the other hand, serve for preparation of students before entering the laboratory experimentation. Their utilization also supports and makes more attractive lectures and considerably enhances the explanation of properties of machines.

Acknowledgements

The financial support of the Slovak Grant Agency VEGA under the contract VEGA 1/0121/15 is acknowledged. The research was also supported by the project VEGA No 1/0464/15 "Research of New Principles and Methods for Design of Electrotechnical Systems".

Author details

Viliam Fedák* and Pavel Záskalický

*Address all correspondence to: Viliam.Fedak@tuke.sk

Department of Electrical Engineering and Mechatronics, Faculty of Electrical Engineering and Informatics, Technical University of Košice, Slovakia

References

[1] Dongmei Wang, Lingshun Liu, Yan Li. Discussion on teaching reform of electric machinery and drive course. In: 30-31 July 2011; Singapore. p. 1-3. DOI: ISBN 978-1-4577-0859-6

[2] Djeghloud H, Larakeb M., Bentounsi A.. Virtual labs of conventional electric machines. In: 2012 IEEE International Conference on Interactive Mobile and Computer Aided Learning (IMCL); 6-8 Nov. 2012; Amman. IEEE; 2012. p. 52-57. DOI: ISBN 978-1-4673-4924-6

[3] Martis C.S., Hedesiu H.C., Szabo L., Tataranu B., Jurca F., Oprea C.. Electrical machines virtual laboratory: grid connection of a synchronous generator. In: 12th Power Electronics and Motion Control Conference, EPE-PEMC 2006; Portoroz, Slovenia. p. 1709-1714.

[4] Mehmet Dal. Teaching electric drives control course: incorporation of active learning into the classroom. IEEE Transactions on Education. Nov. 2013;56(4):459-469.

[5] Fedak V., Balogh T., Zaskalicky P.. Dynamic simulation of electrical machines and drive systems using MATLAB GUI. In: Dr. Sergio Kofuji, editor. E-Learning. Book 4 ed. Rijeka, Croatia: INTECH-Open Access publisher of Scientific Books and Journals; 2012. p. 317-342. DOI: ISBN 979-953-307-774-0

[6] Fedak V., Durovsky F., Keusch P.. E-learning in mechatronic systems supported by virtual experimentation. In: Dr. Sergio Kofuji, editor. E-Learning. Book 4 ed. Rijeka, Croatia: INTECH-Open Access publisher of Scientific Books and Journals; 2012. p. 84-106. DOI: ISBN 979-953-307-774-0

[7] Fedak V., Balogh T., Ismeal G.A.. Virtual models of dynamic systems: design, methodology, applications, and experiences in learning of mechatronics. In: Jakab F., editor. 10th IEEE International Conference on Emerging eLearning Technologies and Applications; 8-9 Nov. 2012; StaráLesná, High Tatras, Slovakia. 2012: IEEE, Budapest; 2012. p. 111-116. DOI: ISBN 978-1-4673-5123-2

[8] Zaskalicky P.,. Krokový motor/Stepper motor. Košice: C-PRESS Košice; 2007. 97 ISBN 978-80-8073-778-8

[9] Mehmet Dal. Teaching Electric Drives Control Course: Incorporation of Active Learning Into the Classroom. IEEE Transactions on Education. Nov. 2013;56(4): 459-469.

Chapter 2

Effective eLearning and eTeaching — A Theoretical Model

Maureen Snow Andrade

Additional information is available at the end of the chapter

http://dx.doi.org/10.5772/60578

Abstract

Distance learning is increasingly becoming an option for learners that were previously denied higher education opportunities due to elitist systems, cost, academic preparation, or personal circumstances. It is also a means to help nations meet goals to increase the percentage of individuals with post-secondary education in order to address workforce needs. However, learners and instructors often have concerns with their ability to be successful in a distance learning environment. This chapter presents a theoretical model for eLearning and eTeaching aimed at helping learners and instructors successfully navigate distance learning courses. Examples of course activities corresponding to the model components are shared. A qualitative analysis of learner self-reflections demonstrates the efficacy of the model in terms of increased autonomy, self-regulation, and targeted skills.

Keywords: distance language learning, self-regulation, eTeaching and eLearning, online instructor training, distance education

1. Introduction

Knowledge, an end in itself as well as the surest route to higher wages and longer lives, is measured by degree attainment and school enrollment [1]. eLearning provides access to higher education for a wide range of learners. These include traditional students in university classrooms, individuals in the workplace seeking to formalize their work experience through the pursuit of a degree or to transition into a different career path, and those who need flexible scheduling options or prefer to not participate in traditional learning environments. These learners can select courses and degree programs from institutions of higher education in their local areas or from providers across the globe. eLearning increases access, which has historically been denied to many due to elite education systems, and offers choice—choice in providers, programs, scheduling, cost, and content.

Elitist views of tertiary education are receding [2-6], with recognition of the benefits of a well-educated workforce in terms of economic development, economic stability, health and well-being, and decreased crime [7], factors that are encouraging governments to lower the barriers to higher education and set goals for degree attainment [7,8]. The appeal of eLearning is readily recognized as instrumental in these endeavors [8-11], evidenced by increased enrollments in online courses. In the United States, for example, the number of university students taking an online course increased from 1.6 million to 7.1 million in a 10-year time span (2002-2012) [12]. Many of these learners are nontraditional in terms of age, marital condition, and employment status [13].

In spite of demand, involving university instructors in developing, implementing, and teaching online courses can be challenging due to concerns with quality, nontraditional methods of interaction with students, low student performance, pedagogical skill, technological knowledge, workload, time intensiveness, large class sizes, and course ownership [14-16]. Learners may struggle with the discipline needed in eLearning contexts, which are generally less structured than face-to-face settings, feel intimidated by the technological expertise required to navigate courses and submit assignments, lack motivation, or simply be convinced that learning in a more traditional format in which they can engage in class with other learners and an instructor is preferable.

This chapter introduces common challenges with eLearning in terms of learner success and instructor expertise, and suggests solutions to these challenges through the framework of self-regulated learning [17-21] and the supporting theories of transactional distance [22-24] and collaborative control [25]. The chapter provides a guiding model for course design and pedagogy, illustrated with specific course content and activities. The theoretical model of eLearning and eTeaching helps learners overcome barriers to success while parallel training based on the same principles prepares instructors to facilitate effective online learning experiences. Learner and teacher self-reflections were examined to identify the presence of the model's components, and are shared to demonstrate the model's efficacy. Additional recommendations for evaluating the model are provided. The approach is illustrated with online English language courses and a related instructor training course; however, the model and its elements can be applied to courses in any discipline and be examined quantitatively or qualitatively to determine its effectiveness in facilitating learner success.

2. Problem statement

While global growth in technology-based learning, and online learning in particular, presents significant opportunities for learners to access higher levels of education that were previously out of reach, and for institutions wanting to address challenges associated with the resources needed to expand their physical infrastructure to accommodate enrollment increases, or desiring to take advantage of outreach beyond their state or national borders, the fact remains that many stakeholders are concerned with the efficacy of this delivery method. Anecdotes of negative distance teaching and learning experiences abound on many university campuses in spite of growing evidence to the contrary and increasing interest and participation. Views toward distance education tend to be polarizing, as expressed in the following statement:

> At one end of this continuum, we detect what some might argue is an overly sanguine view of what distance education has already achieved and how much it has influenced pedagogy and the academy. At the other extreme is the pessimistic perspective that this phenomenon is a scourge threatening the quality and integrity of academe [26].

Related to the latter extreme, concerns involve accreditation, institutional support, scalability, technological literacy, instructional strategies, rigor, expertise, and fear of taking missteps into this new territory due to possible negative repercussions. Each of these issues has and can be addressed. The focus of this chapter is on online teaching and learning, and specifically, approaches that situate both learners and instructors to have a positive experience.

3. Theoretical foundations: Literature review

In all educational contexts, every effort must be made to ensure that learners succeed. This involves pedagogical considerations, understanding learner backgrounds and approaches to learning, instructor skill, and course design and management. Distance learning presents its own set of factors related to success such as a less structured experience for learners in that they do not meet regularly in a classroom; a possible learning curve related to course delivery technologies, which is a potential concern for both learners and instructors; different strategies for sharing and discussing information than would be present in a face-to-face context; and specific to teachers, the need to adapt and expand on traditional face-to-face instructional tools. In effect, novice online learners and instructors must be prepared and supported in this new learning endeavor. While success for students in any learning context, and particularly in distance learning, is dependent on a number of factors, not all of which are within the control of an instructor, much can be done to anticipate and alleviate challenges inherent in an online course. Similarly, instructors who have a solid understanding of online teaching approaches and the ability to apply them will be able to provide a more positive learning environment for their students and fully enjoy their teaching experience.

Self-regulated learning [17-21] is an educational theory which can be maximized in an online class to provide learners with the needed scaffolding to manage their learning. The theory of transactional distance [22-24], from the field of distance education, provides insights into the relationship among the course, learners, and instructor, and how the psychological distance created by the physical gap between the learner and teacher can be mitigated. The concept of collaborative control [25], most frequently applied to distance language learning, addresses the myth that online learning is synonymous with independent learning (although this is a possibility), and suggests strategies for collaboration. These three concepts can be applied to course design and instructor training to maximize the opportunities associated with distance learning and assist learners and instructors in developing the requisite skills and abilities for success.

4. Self-regulated learning

The concept of self-regulated learning has been applied to the teaching and learning process to increase student achievement across age, educational levels, and delivery modes [17,18, 27-33]. It is most commonly defined as the ability to control the elements and circumstances that affect learning [17,18]. A useful framework is the six-dimension model, which consists of motive, method, time, social environment, physical environment, and performance [17,18, 19-21]. These dimensions address the questions why, how, when, with whom, where, and what. Figure 1 provides additional details about the dimensions.

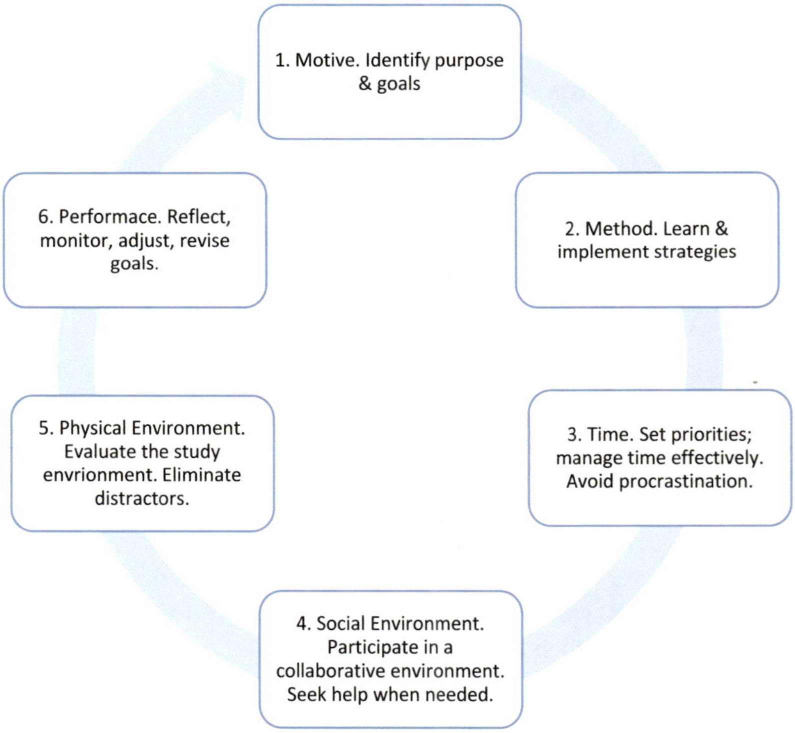

Figure 1. The cycle of self-regulated learning.

Another commonly applied self-regulated learning framework consists of three phases—"the *forethought* phase refers to processes and beliefs that occur *before* efforts to learn, the *perform-*

ance phase refers to processes that occur *during* behavioral implementation, and *self-reflection* refers to processes that occur *after* each learning effort" [21, p. 67]. Forethought is similar to *motive* in that it encompasses goal setting, motivation, and examining beliefs about learning. Performance is most closely related to *methods* as depicted Figure 1; it involves strategy identification, implementation, and monitoring of the strategies applied to determine their effectiveness. Methods might also include consideration of areas such as time management and social and physical environments in that learners must determine strategies to improve their performance by using time effectively, getting help from others, and eliminating physical distractors where and when they study. Finally, self-reflection consists of reviewing learning outcomes and comparing them to a standard. It is similar to the performance dimension in Figure 1, which involves examining the achievement of goals and learning outcomes and determining the next steps.

While both frameworks are valuable, the former is particularly helpful in guiding learners. The specificity of the various areas needing consideration assists learners in analyzing their current practices in relation to their study approaches and making needed changes by following the cyclical process of goal-setting, strategy implementation, control of time and environmental factors, and review of performance. Goals can be set related to any of the dimensions (e.g., methods, time, social environment, physical environment) depending on individual strengths and weaknesses. Methods involve strategies for processing and acquiring knowledge and improving skill. In the case of language learning, strategies might focus on vocabulary learning with note cards, using the context to guess the meaning of words, recognizing error patterns in written grammatical usage, or using headings to find the main ideas in reading passages. Outside of language study, more general learning methods can be applied such as various strategies for reading (e.g., previewing, mapping main ideas and supporting details, asking questions, paraphrasing, and summarizing), studying and recalling information (e.g., listening, identifying transitional phrases, note-taking), writing (organization, idea development, revision, and editing), improving performance on assignments and tests (e.g., following instructions, understanding distractors in multiple choice tests, organizing a response to a short answer or essay exam question), and interaction and discussion (teamwork, collaboration, class participation). Many methods or learning or strategies are applicable across content areas.

The six-dimension framework can serve as the foundation to online course design to assist learners in controlling the factors that affect their learning concurrent with gaining content knowledge for a given discipline or increasing skills to perform specific tasks. Course assignments involving goal setting, examining motive for learning, gaining awareness of various learning strategies, recognizing the role of the social and physical environments in learning, and monitoring and reflecting on performance can be integrated into the course. This design approach can increase the achievement of learning outcomes [27,29], particularly if the self-regulated learning components are required rather than optional; students rarely complete optional assignments. For many students, considering various approaches to learning is completely new, as illustrated in the following quotation from an English language learner who discusses his use of methods of learning, specifically, taking reading notes and composing study questions.

> Taking this course helps me to know how important it is to use my study materials. Throughout my junior and high school, I always thought that using my study materials was a waste of time because I thought that I wouldn't really understand if I used my study materials compared to asking my teachers to explain how to do the activity. Every time I read an assignment my mind was not really focused. I didn't pay attention so I ended up not knowing what the assignment was all about. I didn't make notes of what I read or write down questions as I read the assignment or paragraph. But today I can say that using my study materials is really important.

This quote provides evidence that the learner has become more autonomous through the use of methods of learning. Instead of relying on the teacher to explain assignments, he has recognized that he can read, take notes, and write down questions to help him understand the material. This indicates self-regulation.

5. Transactional distance and collaborative control

Two other theories have relevance to online course design and instructor support and can be integrated with the self-regulated learning framework. The first is the theory of transactional distance [22-24]. This theory has three components: structure, dialogue, and autonomy. Structure is provided by course materials, content, assignments, and deadlines, which are fixed prior to a course being made available to students. Structure is a helpful pedagogical tool as it provides learners with predictability in determining how the course is organized, sequencing of instructional modules and assignments, and deadlines for assignment submission. Generally, courses are designed so that each lesson has the same sections and various pages in the course have the same formatting, similar to a textbook. This helps learners know what to expect as they progress through the course. A course syllabus is also part of the structure as it guides students through the course and its requirements and provides needed information about policies, procedures, requirements, and grading. Structure can also be provided through communication for the purpose of guiding and supporting learners. This communication is referred to as dialogue, and includes any type of exchange or interaction in a course. It can be among the learners or between learners and the instructor. It includes course features such as discussion boards, peer review of assignments, instructor announcements, instructor feedback on assignments, student questions, e-mail, and live conferencing. Dialogue provides socialization, particularly through peer interaction. Instructor dialogue can motivate learners, help them identify their strengths and weaknesses, and assist them in making needed improvements.

The amount of structure and dialogue in a course affects autonomy, which is defined as choice characterized by elements of self-direction. Lower levels of structure and dialogue support greater levels of autonomy. Some learners are able to function well with low levels of structure and dialogue while others need greater support. Autonomous learners are able to determine learning goals and steps for reaching those goals. They have both instrumental independence and emotional independence [22-24]. In other words, they can progress through the course with little help and need little encouragement. One could expect that learners might become more autonomous over the weeks they are enrolled in an online course as they understand expectations and gain confidence in their ability to be successful. Instructors can facilitate this confidence building. The goal of structure, dialogue, and autonomy is to support the achievement of learning outcomes and prevent student attrition. The theory of transactional distance has similarities to that of self-regulated learning. The self-regulated learning framework in Figure 1 provides a type of structure for learners to help them set goals, practice strategy application, make use of dialogue (i.e., the social environment) to get help when needed, and self-evaluate in order to have greater capacity for autonomous learning.

Finally, the concept of collaborative control [25] provides greater understanding of the social environment aspect of self-regulated learning and the dialogue component of the theory of transactional distance. Rather than conceiving of distance learning as an independent activity, collaborative control acknowledges that learners can learn from and help each other and also that the instructor can facilitate learner interaction and success. Help-seeking is a positive practice as long as learners are not overly dependent on others. They need to recognize when they need help, identify the best sources of help, and evaluate the effectiveness of the help received [34]. As the name of the concept implies, collaborative control occurs when learners and the instructor collaborate to complete tasks, thereby improving learning outcomes. Instructors must be aware that the goal of collaboration is to encourage greater levels of self-regulation or autonomy so that learners can make sound choices and have the confidence to succeed. However, as a common criticism of distance learning is the purported lack of social interaction and exchange among learners; thus, course designers and instructors should always be aware of opportunities to provide for this aspect of learning.

6. Theoretical integration

Figure 2 demonstrates the integration of various aspects of the three theories. Online courses that require learners to engage in forethought (goal-setting), performance (strategy application and monitoring), and self-reflection (review of progress); that are designed with a specific structure (organized content), opportunities for dialogue (peer and instructor communications), use of the social environment (help-seeking), and collaborative control (learner and teacher collaboration on tasks), all of which are facilitated by the instructor; and that use these features to help learners gradually develop greater autonomy (capacity for self-direction and making choices), self-regulation (ability to control factors affecting learning), and targeted skills and knowledge (course content and related outcomes) as they set goals, apply what they are learning, and reflect on their learning demonstrate how the three theories work synergistically to improve the online learning experience.

The model demonstrates how the theories of self-regulation and transactional distance and the practice of collaborative control can guide distance learning and teaching approaches.

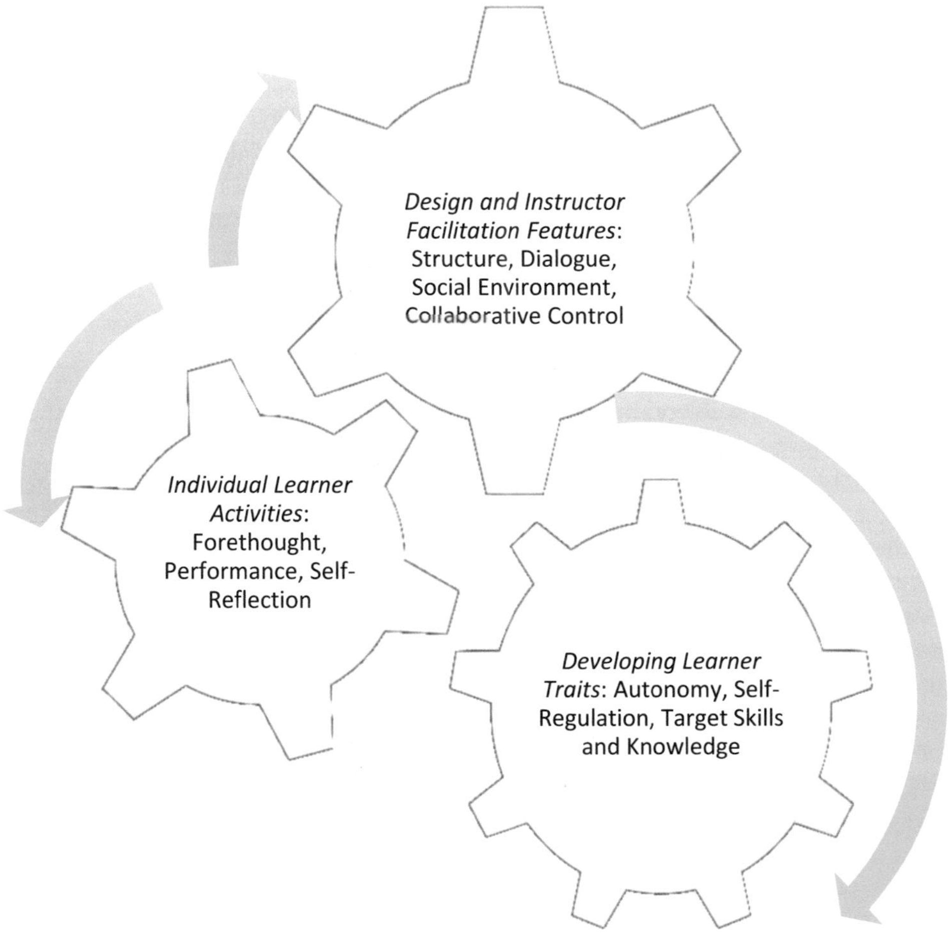

Figure 2. Model of eLearning and eTeaching.

Although the design and instructor facilitation features in the model overlap, each concept has distinct characteristics that help to inform design choices and instructional approaches. The model can be applied to both online student courses and related training for online instructors. In the latter case, the learner is the instructor.

7. Applying the model: Principles and practice

To address the challenges inherent in eLearning, course designers and instructors must consider ways to facilitate effective student learning and course completion. In the process, students enrolled in the course can acquire lifelong learning strategies with broad applicability. Additionally, administrators, or those responsible for assigning instructors to courses, must ensure that these instructors are prepared for and skilled in online teaching. This can be accomplished through required instructor training that models the student online learning experience.

This section of the chapter identifies principles based on the theoretical model presented in Figure 2. The principles are designed to help learners be successful eLearners and to prepare instructors to make the transition from traditional pedagogies to those that facilitate eLearning [27,30]. A primary consideration for instructors is communication with learners through dialogue and response strategies [22-24]. The discussion is organized around the three areas of the model of eLearning and eTeaching (see Figure 2). For each area, key principles are identified with examples of applications for a student course and an associated teacher training course.

8. Individual learner activities

While every online course contains a variety of learner activities, the focus in this section is on those related to the three phases of self-regulated learning: forethought, performance, and self-reflection. For purposes of delineating this portion of the model, both students and instructors are considered learners; both are applying the principles of self-regulated learning in their respective courses—students are learning about a specific content area or discipline or acquiring a related skill while instructors are honing their online pedagogical skills. The courses provide the opportunity for individuals in each group to set goals, apply strategies, and reflect on their performance. An additional benefit of these self-regulated learning activities for instructors is that they are experiencing what their students will be doing in the student course. It is strongly recommended that these activities be required so that all learners will benefit from them.

The forethought stage of self-regulated learning can be integrated into online courses and online teacher training through activities that help individuals examine their beliefs about learning, diagnose their strengths and weaknesses in the subject area or in relation to needed teaching and learning strategies, and to set goals [28, 29, 31]. The six-component framework in Figure 1 can help learners generate areas of focus for goals as can some type of diagnostic evaluation. The forethought stage should be initiated at the beginning of the course, possibly in the introductory module of a course. It helps set expectations for learner responsibility and raise awareness of course content.

Next, the performance stage involves the use and monitoring of strategies. Strategies should be introduced and linked to the assignments in the course. For example, if students are required to compose a writing assignment, part of the instruction for the assignment might include strategies for revision and editing or learning how to evaluate the appropriateness of sources [34]. It could also involve discussion of the particular genre expected, e.g., a critique of an art exhibit for an art class or the summary of an academic journal article for a psychology course. In keeping with the six dimensions of self-regulated learning [17-21], strategies could also be introduced related to effective time management or evaluating the physical environment to determine its conduciveness to learning. In the teacher training course, strategies would include those related to online pedagogies such as using whole-class feedback rather than responding to students individually, providing supplementary materials to address identified learner weaknesses, facilitating a discussion board, or incorporating the use of a new form of technology [27, 29, 30].

The third and last area, self-reflection, is designed to help learners evaluate the benefits of the various strategies they have applied. They can then examine reasons for their outcomes and modify their methods accordingly. "Overall, the available research evidence suggests that promoting self-reflection, self-regulation and self-monitoring leads to more positive online learning outcomes. Features such as prompts for reflection, self-explanation and self-monitoring strategies have shown promise for improving online learning outcomes" [35, p. 45]. As such, this is critical for students and also important for teachers as it involves taking the time to carefully consider teaching approaches and also to experience directly what they are asking their students to do. Possible activities for each of the three areas are summarized in Table 1.

Principle	**Student Course**	**Instructor Training Course**
Learning can be improved through identifying the purpose for learning, goal-setting, and examining beliefs about learning (forethought); learning, practicing, and monitoring strategies (performance); measuring performance against a self-imposed or external benchmark, and modifying goals and strategies as needed (self-reflection).		
Forethought	· Introduction activity in which learners post information about themselves, their background in the subject area, and their purpose for learning; posts can be written or oral (video recordings); learners are required to respond to a specific number of peer posts. · Appoint students to take turns to facilitate the discussion board throughout the semester to increase comprehension of the subject matter and help them gain confidence. · Introductory writing assignment stating previous experience with the subject area and reasons for wanting to learn more. Peer or teacher response to assignment.	· Introduction activity in which teachers post information on a discussion board about themselves, their teaching or professional backgrounds, and their purpose for teaching online; posts can be written or oral (video recordings); teachers are required to respond to a specific number of peer posts. · Appoint teachers to take turns to facilitate the discussion board throughout the semester to practice the skills they will use in the course they are teaching. · Introductory writing assignment stating previous experience with online learning and reasons for wanting to learn more. Peer or trainer response to assignment.

Principle **Learning can be improved through identifying the purpose for learning, goal-setting, and examining beliefs about learning (forethought); learning, practicing, and monitoring strategies (performance); measuring performance against a self-imposed or external benchmark, and modifying goals and strategies as needed (self-reflection).**	Student Course	Instructor Training Course
	· Completion of an instrument identifying learners' self-beliefs about learning (e.g., intelligence is fixed vs. intelligence can be developed) [36]. · Diagnostic survey to help learners identify strengths and weaknesses related to the subject area or to the use of academic learning strategies. · Identification of goals related to strengths and weaknesses in the subject area or learning in general; goals should be specific, measurable, achievable, result-oriented, and time-bound (SMART).	· Writing assignment may include asking teachers to provide their philosophy of teaching, perspectives of online teaching and learning, previous successes with distance education as a student or a teacher, or any other prompt that helps teachers dialogue with each other and create community. · Online survey listing various online teaching practices, particularly those relevant to the course, from which teachers determine their strengths and weaknesses. · Identification of goals related to what teachers hope to learn in the course and what they anticipate their needs to be in terms of online teaching based on the survey.
Performance	· Strategy instruction integrated with course content; learners apply strategies as they complete course assignments. · Activity choices focused on the six dimensions of self-regulated learning (motive, methods, time, physical environment, social environment, performance). · Opportunities to select appropriate strategies to accomplish course assignments.	· Learn about and practice methods for online instruction and responding to students. This instruction includes becoming familiar with the theoretical foundation for the course. · Opportunities to adapt familiar face-to-face teaching strategies to an online environment. · Introduction to technology-based instruction and application activities, including tools available through the course management system.

Principle **Learning can be improved through identifying the purpose for learning, goal-setting, and examining beliefs about learning (forethought); learning, practicing, and monitoring strategies (performance); measuring performance against a self-imposed or external benchmark, and modifying goals and strategies as needed (self-reflection).**	Student Course	Instructor Training Course
Self-reflection	· Discussion boards, learning journals, or survey instruments that provide prompts for reflection on goals at regular intervals in the course (e.g., weekly, monthly, midterm, end of course). · Opportunities to share reflections with peers or the instructor for feedback. · Inclusion of goal modification and next steps as part of reflection.	· Discussion boards, learning journals, or survey instruments that provide prompts for reflection on goals at regular intervals in the course (e.g., weekly, monthly, midterm, end of course). · Opportunities to share reflections with colleagues or the trainer for feedback. · Inclusion of goal modification and next steps as part of reflection.

Table 1. Activities for the Three Phases of Self-regulated Learning

9. Design and instructor facilitation features

Although learners engage in the three phases of self-regulated learning independently, and set goals and practice the specific dimensions of self-regulated learning (motive, method, time, physical environment, social environment, performance) largely on their own, the process is facilitated through course design and instructor dialogue. The four components of this part of the model—structure, dialogue, social environment, and collaborative control—have a theoretical basis, described in the previous section, and are built into the course design. They also have implications for instructor behavior.

As indicated earlier, the structure of the course helps guide learners and provides predictability while dialogue entails communication among course participants and the teacher for purposes of socialization and learning support. These two elements affect autonomy. Figure 3 indicates the relationship among structure, dialogue, and autonomy.

When structure and dialogue are low, the learner is able to make choices about learning independently. However, structure and dialogue may be needed when necessary information is not included in the course or if the information is incomplete, or when learners need greater levels of support. When structure and dialogue are high, autonomy decreases. As instructors work with students, they can tailor the instruction and support to the level of the learner

http://dx.doi.org/10.5772/60578

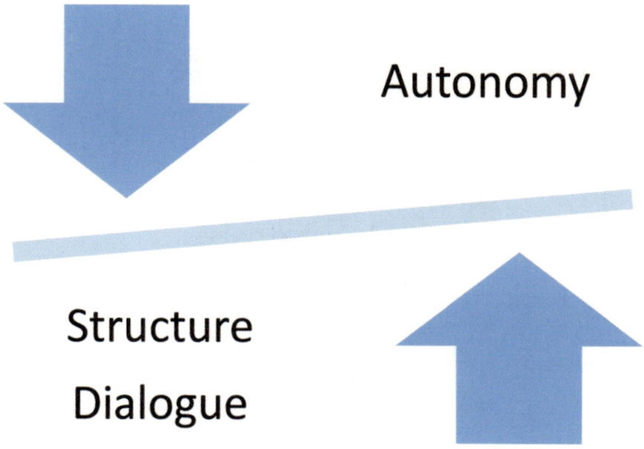

Figure 3. The interaction among structure, dialogue, and autonomy.

through the use of dialogue. As the learners' skills improve, the amount of dialogue will likely decrease. The following example demonstrates structure in the form of assignment instructions that are set in the course, and instructor dialogue that provides additional information to help learners successfully compete the assignment. Instructor dialogue can be provided as an announcement (oral or written), a supplemental page in the course, in a brief video, or in an e-mail to the class.

9.1. Assignment

Read the article about the spread of English as an international language and then write a one-paragraph summary of the main ideas. Organize your ideas clearly and upload the paragraph for your teacher's review.

9.2. Instructor dialogue

In order to complete this assignment, you need to know how to write a summary. See the steps below to help you complete the article summary assignment.

1. Understanding the reading

The first step in writing a summary is to read through the article carefully and make sure you understand it.

- Check any vocabulary you don't know
- Find the author's thesis statement or main point
- Find the main idea (topic sentence) of each paragraph or section of the article
- Underline main ideas as you read
- Reread the article and take notes—use your own words; put exact words in quotation marks
- Explain what you read to someone else

2. Writing the first sentence

The first sentence of a summary follows a specific format. See the instructions and examples that follow.

- The first sentence of a summary includes the following:
    - The author's name—usually the family name only
    - The title of the article, book, magazine, or chapter
    - A restatement of the author's thesis
    - Examples:
- According to their article, "A Model for Self-regulated Distance Language Learning," Andrade and Bunker claim that learning a language through distance education is a challenge due to the learner's limited opportunity for real-life interaction.
- In "A Model for Self-regulated Distance Language Learning," Andrade and Bunker observe that distance language learning is particularly difficult due to the lack of opportunity for learners to hear and use the language.

3. Completing the summary

When you are certain you understand the content of the reading and have practiced expressing it orally, and you have written your first sentence for the summary using one of the patterns, use your notes to draft the remainder of the summary paragraph. Be sure to review the paragraph carefully and edit as needed so that your language is as accurate as possible.

- Write a sentence or two summarizing each main idea of section of thought
- Put the sentences in the same order of the ideas in the original article
- Use transitions to connect the ideas
- Check your use of punctuation
- Check sentence structure, verb tense, and other grammar
- Add your reference list (see the writing tip on how to format references)
- Remember that a summary
    - explains the main ideas of the original article in your own words
    - does not contain your own opinion
    - is usually 1/4 to 1/3 the length of the original

The assignment instructions assume that learners know how to write a summary. The dialogue, in the form of supplemental materials, provided by the instructor gives them specific steps to follow. The teacher also needs to include an example summary paragraph and instruction about reference list formatting. Even though the materials in an online course are

http://dx.doi.org/10.5772/60578

already established; in other words, the structure is present, skilled online teachers know their learners and recognize when additional information is needed. This situation is similar to using a textbook in a course; the teacher determines what to use from the textbook and what to add based on a needs analysis of the learner. As instructors teach a course regularly, they have a better sense of where learners will struggle and how to assist them. This is a principle that needs to be included in online teacher training and addresses the viewpoint that is sometimes present among instructors that online teachers are glorified graders. The opposite is true—effective pedagogy and interaction is critical in an online course.

The next example demonstrates how instructors can facilitate learning through dialogue in the form of response to assignments. The instructions for the assignment are an example of structure, complete with specifics for how to formulate the post, word count, and deadlines, while the instructor feedback guides learners toward better utilization of this structure so as to meet expectations for the assignment.

Assignment

Post a response to ONE of the following questions about the article you summarized. Clearly state your point of view and use information from the reading and your own experience to support your answer. Respond to at least two of your classmates' posts. Your initial post should be at least 100-150 words in length. Responses to your classmates must be 50-75 words. Your initial post is due Monday at 11:59 pm. Your two responses to classmates are due Thursday at 11:59 pm. Be sure to check the discussion each day.

Questions

1. Is English an instrument for global economic expansion or does it simply increase inequalities between those who are proficient and those who aren't? Explain.

2. Does the spread of English decrease cultural uniqueness across the world or does it serve to connect people across cultures and increase intercultural understanding? Explain.

3. Will English maintain its status as a global language or will another language supplant it at some point in the future? Explain.

Student post

English provides people with opportunities for education and better jobs. This is why I am studying English. I want to go to school in the UK. Then, when I come back home, I can get work and look after my future wife and children better.

Instructor dialogue

You have important reasons for wanting to improve your English skills. Please make sure you focus on the topic in the question. You have mostly talked about your personal reasons for wanting to learn English. You need to bring in ideas from the article, take a position on the topic, and support your viewpoint. These are skills that you will need in academic writing. The discussion board assignment is designed to help you practice and develop these writing skills. You also need to make sure your response is 100-150 words. Always make sure you read the instructions and follow them carefully. If there is something you don't understand, I am here to help. Please also review the example responses that I posted in the announcements this week. I look forward to your next post.

The instructor response example follows the sandwich approach, which entails starting and ending with positive comments (the two slices of bread) while the middle portion (the filling) provides specific recommendations for improvement. The purpose is to encourage learners while helping them improve. Instructor dialogue in the form of feedback on assignments can be individualized, as in the example above, or it can be provided to the entire class, which is the purpose of the announcement the instructor refers to. The whole-class approach allows the instructor to provide a more extensive response with examples and models. To do this, the instructor notes commonalities in strengths and weaknesses in the students' interactions and provides feedback, examples, and direction to the entire class similar to what would occur in a face-to-face course. Some of this information, depending on the length, could also be posted in the discussion board itself—during the time period that students are doing the assignment. Students do need to know where to find the information, so it is best to have a common practice for this.

Providing a rubric for assignments and including it with the instructions also provides structure and helps learners know how they will be graded. However, often learners need to be reminded to examine the rubric carefully and compare their work to it. An option related to this is to use the practice of collaborative control to help learners develop their own evaluation abilities. Learners could be paired or assigned to small groups and asked to review and discuss each other's posts and then evaluate them with the rubric, providing rationale for the scores assigned. Although students may tend to give each other high scores, the activity at least increases their awareness of the rubric and helps them explore common or differing understandings of it. This is also an example of how the social environment can be integrated into a course. Another way to use the social environment is to simply have an open discussion board in which students post their own questions about anything related to the course to other students. In this way, students can get help on their own that is not instructor-focused. This supports the development of autonomy and self-regulated learning in that they are selecting topics of need and taking responsibility for factors affecting their learning.

This discussion has included guidelines for instructors related to the components of structure, dialogue, social environment, and collaborative control. In the instructor course, structure is provided in the set course modules on various topics—introduction to the university mission and English language program, logistics about the course they will be teaching and the learning management system, understanding their role as online instructors, planning and preparing, and exploring techniques for response. Dialogue and the social environment are incorporated into the course design with opportunities for instructors to share perspectives on the information in the various modules such as how to apply the teaching strategies presented. Examples such as those shared regarding student posts and corresponding instructor feedback can be included in the course to help teachers see models of response. Additionally, strategies for individual and whole-class response, use of technology, and other pedagogical information relating to the principles of structure, dialogue, social environment, and collaborative control should be included and practiced in the training course. The instruction needs to introduce these features, the philosophical foundation for the student course and related research, and also give the teachers the opportunity to discuss these areas much in the same way the learners are discussing the global nature of English in their discussion board in the example shared previously.

10. Developing learner traits

The goal of online instruction based on the model of eLearning and eTeaching is characterized in following quote: "The capacity to learn autonomously is seen to develop from a state of self-awareness and willingness to take an active part. In order for learners to achieve this state, teachers must also play their part" [37, p. 220]. The first component of the model accounts for the need to develop learners' awareness and engagement by having them examine their purpose for learning, beliefs about learning, and by setting goals. They take an active part as they learn and apply strategies, monitor their outcomes, and modify their approaches. Taking an active part also involves the social environment and dialogue with others in the course. The model provides guidance for how instructors can "play their part" to help learners become more self-aware, fully participate in the learning process, and take control of their learning. Teachers facilitate this through practices related to structure, dialogue, the social environment, and collaborative control. They model these behaviors in the teacher training course.

The aim of the model of eLearning and eTeaching, reflected in the third component—developing learner traits—is to help learners develop greater capacity for autonomy and self-regulation, and to meet learning objectives related to the targeted skills and knowledge of the course. For teachers in a training course, the model assists in giving them direct experience with self-regulation and related theoretical components in order to understand the course design philosophy and how they can facilitate the goals of the model as they interact with learners.

In this section, I review possible methods for determining evidence of the model validity. The first possibility involves using the self-reflection instruments that are built into the course as a means to determine learners' experiences and their views of their own learning. In both the student and the teacher training courses, participants are involved in self-reflection through some type of journal, discussion board post, formal paper, or video recording. These may be required at various points in the course such as weekly or at the middle and end of the term. Prompts for reflection can be specific to the course content, focused on learning in general, and be formative or summative as the examples in Table 2 illustrate. All of the examples are focused on the self-reflection aspect of self-regulated learning.

Purpose	Reflection Prompt: Students	Formative Summative	Reflection Prompt: Teachers	Formative Summative	Model/Theory Elements
Specific to course content and activities	What did you learn about organizing a paragraph in this week's lesson? How did it make a difference in the way you write?	Summative	How can you help students become more self-regulated? What types of feedback can you provide that will help students increase their self-regulated behaviors and strategies?	Formative	Methods Dialogue Social environment
	What was the most helpful thing you learned about vocabulary study this week? How will you apply this in the future?	Formative	What did you learn this week about types of technology you can use to communicate with students? How will this make a difference in your teaching this semester?	Formative	Methods Dialogue Social environment
	How did the course help you improve your academic writing skills?	Summative	How did the training course help you change your perspective of online learning and teaching?	Summative	Methods Performance
	Review the diagnostic survey you took at the beginning of the semester and the goals you set based on the areas in which you wanted to improve. Evaluate your progress on your goals and explain what you will do in the next half of the course to continue to make improvement. This may include modifying your goals.	Formative	What strategies did you learn in the module for creating a community of learners online? Which of these will you use in your course? Why?	Formative	Forethought Performance Dialogue Social Environment
General learning/ teaching strategies	Think about the readings you discussed with your	Formative	What do you think of the whole-class	Formative	Forethought Performance

http://dx.doi.org/10.5772/60578

Purpose	Reflection Prompt: Students	Formative Summative	Reflection Prompt: Teachers	Formative Summative	Model/Theory Elements
	classmates this week. Share one idea or insight you learned from a classmate. How will that insight help you be a better learner?		feedback approach? How is it similar to what you would do in a face-to-face class? How do you think you might utilize it?		Dialogue Social environment Collaborative control
	How have you used feedback from your tutor appointment to improve your language skills or solve a problem?	Summative	What can you do to provide feedback to students to help them synthesize their learning for the week, identify needed areas of improvement, and set related goals? How can you help students recognize the progress they are making?	Formative	Performance Methods Forethought Dialogue Social environment Collaborative control
	How will you apply the learning strategies you practiced in this course to future learning? Give an example.	Formative	How do you view your role as an online teacher? How can you apply your skill as a face-to-face teacher to an online environment? What advantages and disadvantages are there to having the content of the course set? How can you respond to student needs when the content is already established in the course?	Formative	Methods Performance Dialogue
	Discuss the two most effective strategies or skills you learned in the course.	Summative	Think about your experience this semester as an online teacher. Consider the materials in the course and the goals you set for each unit. Reflect on how your perspectives have changed.	Summative	Performance Methods Forethought

Purpose	Reflection Prompt: Students	Formative Summative	Reflection Prompt: Teachers	Formative Summative	Model/Theory Elements
			Comment on your goals and to what degree you achieved them.		

Table 2. Self-reflection Prompts and Theoretical Connections

11. Research on model validity

One method of providing evidence of the efficacy of the model is to examine learner self-reflections. The examples below, from students and teachers, illustrate learner perceptions of various aspects of the model, and particularly the six dimensions of self-regulated learning (motive, methods, time, physical environment, social environment, performance). The examples are taken from weekly, midterm, and final reflections in the student class, and end-of-module and end-of-course reflections for teachers. The model elements are indicated in parentheses following each quotation.

Students

- I learned a lot of things through this wonderful activity about identifying values and setting goals. First of all, I need to understand my motivation before I set goals Sometimes, it was difficult for me to set a meaningful goal for I did not understand my desire and vision. I was like a visitor without a compass and map, and I got lost. Therefore, I need to evaluate my motivation and needs before I set my goals. (Motive)
- I reviewed the goals I set for the course to see if I am making progress. I need to see if I have made any changes. I need to make some changes from what I have done before to now in order to get better grades. These are new goals for the second half: first, try to distinguish between important things and unimportant things. Second, try to improve reading speed, and the last one is improve on finding main ideas in readings (Performance, Methods, Target Skills)
- The course activities are good activities because these activities can help me to become a better learner. Reviewing the activities, I found that I learned a lot. For example, I found out my learning styles, my strengths and weaknesses as an English language learner, and my reading strategies. These three activities help me to study better. Besides, I found out how to schedule my study time and have a study plan and to study in short segments. These two activities help me to have a better time management. (Methods, Time, Performance)
- Online distance learning program are quite strenuous compared to traditional classroom learning, notwithstanding this fact I felt it was fun and balanced. The structures set up to help the student know, do and become is just awesome, most significant of all is sharing ideas and learning from each other, furthermore our speaking partners made it more interesting. (Structure, Dialogue, Social Environment, Collaborative Control)

Instructors

- My goal is to create an assignment where students write an explanation of the directions BEFORE they do it. Then they need to write a self-evaluation on how well they followed the directions. My hope is to get a better idea of how much they understand from the directions, as well as for them to better understand and evaluate what is expected of them and how well they are meeting these expectations. (Forethought, Methods, Target Skills)
- The whole-class feedback approach is helpful. There are sometimes patterns of mistakes and collective misunderstandings that we should recognize and respond to. I will use this approach and I believe students can really benefit from it. It is my responsibility to give them extra tips, advice, or even reviews so they can make progress. (Forethought, Methods, Target Skills)
- I have been taking notes on students' individual weaknesses and strengths all semester. I can see how those who have followed my advice and have actively worked on their mistakes are actually improving faster than those who are going through the motions only. (Methods, Performance, Target Skills)
- I have tried individual and whole-class feedback. They both work well. The discussions have been one of the most effective ways for students to interact with each other. I would like to try video feedback and online office hours in the future. (Methods, Performance, Target Skills).

Compiling these comments and using qualitative analysis methods to determine categories and themes [38] can provide insights into the effectiveness of the course activities and learners' evaluations of their success in achieving course outcomes. The examples above indicate clear evidence that students and teachers benefitted from the structure and dialogue in the course, the opportunity to examine their motivation, goal setting activities, engagement in the social environment, and the instruction and practice activities related to methods and strategies. Outcomes indicate that they acquired new strategies, increased their self-regulation behaviors, and achieved the target skills and knowledge for the courses.

Another way to measure the effectiveness of the model is to have students complete a formal survey with specific questions about course activities and then analyze the data. Questions might be both forced choice (e.g., multiple choice or ranking) and open-ended. Forced choice questions could consist of asking learners to rank the activities in the course grouped by model component (e.g., for dialogue/social environment/collaborative control, these could include the discussion board, video postings, peer review of writing drafts, group writing project), evaluate the instructor on a Likert scale (e.g., value of instructor feedback, response time, knowledge, quality of interactions), or the effectiveness of the course design and content (ease of navigation, technology use, organization of the home page, clarity of instructions). Examples of open-ended questions might include the following: What aspects of the course did you feel were the most valuable? What specific learning (or teaching strategies) were new to you and which did you have the most success with? What were the greatest strengths of your instructor? What suggestions for improvement do you have for your instructor? This approach is a little more structured than the course self-reflections, particularly if quantitative responses are included. These can be collected over several semesters and the results compared to help inform administrators and designers of needed changes in the content and structure of the course.

Additionally, instructors should be given the opportunity to provide feedback about the course materials. As they are teaching, they will notice inconsistencies in the course, unclear instructions, portions of the course that students have difficulty with, and poorly worded or incorrect content and test items. They will also have suggestions for content changes and different pedagogical and presentation approaches. While course designers and administrators responsible for the course would not want to implement all of these recommendations or respond immediately except in cases where simple corrections or typos are needed, this feedback should be compiled and analyzed to determine needed revisions to the course. Also, if the course is part of a sequence of courses, feedback should be obtained from instructors teaching the next level course in the series to determine if the course and instructional techniques are preparing learners adequately.

Other ways to evaluate the model would be through course completion and test scores. The latter would be dependent on ensuring that instructors are rating student work and applying rubrics consistently in the case of assignments such as essays or projects. Comparisons could be made between courses in which teachers have been trained and those in which instructors have not been trained in the model or between courses with embedded learning strategy activities and those without.

12. Implications and conclusions

A limitation of the information presented in this chapter is that the model of eLearning and eTeaching has been applied to only English language learning courses and related teacher training courses, although the theoretical components of the model are well-established as being effective in improving learning in both online and face-to-face contexts [17-21]. Further application of the model should be extended to other disciplines and those using it should assess its value in helping learners and teachers become successful in an online context.

The model does much to address concerns with online learning and teaching from students and faculty members. It provides students with structure and the potential to improve their strategies and approaches to learning so as to be effective in a technology-based distance course. It addresses instructor concerns and myths about teaching online, particularly that online instructors are limited to a grading rather than a teaching role. It expands awareness on the part of both the learner and the teacher of the value of taking responsibility for learning and the role of autonomy, and addresses the misperception that distance courses involve largely independent study with no social interaction or learning from others. It also helps define the role of the instructor in an online course and indicates how instructors can facilitate autonomy through collaborative control, a concept expressed in the following quotation: "What matters most in language advising for autonomy, however, is the [teacher's] ability to help learners make informed decisions about their learning without making those decisions for them" [39, p. 17]. This is the goal of instruction—to help learners develop the capacity to make sound decisions about what and how to learn.

Evidence of the efficacy of the model has been established through a qualitative examination of learner and teacher self-reflections that are embedded into both the student and teacher training courses. This examination demonstrated that the elements of self-regulated learning, transactional distance, and collaborative control, when applied in English language learning and teacher training contexts, assists participants in goal setting, the application of new learning and teaching methods, reflection on these methods, and improved performance. Practices and activities involving dialogue, the social environment, and collaborative control support this process and provide critical elements for the development of autonomy, the acquisition of targeted skills, and overall, successful eLearning and eTeaching.

With increasing demand for higher education, and movements in the United States, the United Kingdom, Europe, and elsewhere to expand the numbers of individuals with post-secondary education [2-4, 8,9], eLearning will continue to grow to fill this need. Indeed, the use of technology, and specifically, online learning, is a strategy to reduce the time spent in class and provide alternate pathways that support degree completion by allowing students greater access to the coursework they need. This can help students avoid excess credits, address the common problem that courses are not offered when needed, not offered at convenient times, or not offered frequently enough [40]. Online learning is convenient to the schedules and lifestyles of today's diverse learners in higher education [13]. However, those involved in its development and delivery must take action to ensure its success for all stakeholders. The model of eLearning and eTeaching is an important step in this direction.

Author details

Maureen Snow Andrade

Address all correspondence to: maureen.andrade@uvu.edu

Academic Programs, Office of Academic Affairs Utah Valley University, Orem, UT, USA

References

[1] Lewis K, Burd-Sharps S. American Human Development Report. The Measure of America. Brooklyn, NY: American Human Development Project and the United Way; 2014. http://www.measureofamerica.org/wp-content/uploads/2013/06/MOA-III.pdf (accessed 29 November 2014).

[2] Corver M. Trends in Young Participation in Higher Education: Core Results for England. Bristol, UK: Higher Education Funding Council for England; 2010. http://www.hefce.ac.uk/pubs/hefce/2010/10_03/ (accessed 29 November 2014).

[3] Higher Education Funding Council for England. Strategic Plan 2006-11; 2009. http://www.hefce.ac.uk/pubs/hefce/2009/09_21/ (accessed 29 November 2014).

[4] Higher Education Funding Council for England. National Strategy for Access and Student Success in Higher Education; 2014. https://www.gov.uk/government/uploads/system/uploads/attachment_data/file/299689/bis-14-516-national-strategy-for-access-and-student-success.pdf (accessed 29 November 2014).

[5] Trow MA. Reflections on the Transition from Elite to Mass to Universal Access: Forms and Phases of Higher Education in Modern Societies since WWII. Berkeley, CA: UC Berkeley Institute of Governmental Studies; 2005. http://escholarship.org/uc/item/96p3s213 (accessed 29 November 2014).

[6] Kamenetz A. DIY U: Edupunks, Edupreneurs, and the Coming Transformation of Higher Education. White River Junction, VT: Chelsea Green Publishing Company; 2010.

[7] Baum S, Ma J, Payea K. Education Pays 2013: The Benefits of Higher Education for Individuals and Society. Washington, DC: College Board; 2013. http://trends.collegeboard.org/sites/default/files/education-pays-2013-full-report.pdf (accessed 29 November 2014).

[8] Lee JM, Rawls A. The College Completion Agenda, 2010 Progress Report. New York, NY: National College Board Advocacy and Policy Center; 2010. http://completionagenda.collegeboard.org/sites/default/files/reports_pdf/Progress_Report_2010.pdf (accessed 29 November 2014).

[9] Lumina Foundation for Education. A Stronger Nation through Higher Education. Indianapolis, IN; 2010. http://www.luminafoundation.org/states_landing/a_stronger_nation_through_education/ (accessed 29 November 2014).

[10] International Council for Open and Distance Education, European Association of Distance Teaching Universities. Maastricht Message 2009. Oslo, Norway, Heerlen, Netherlands; 2009. http://www.ou.nl/Docs/Campagnes/ICDE2009/M-2009_Maastricht_Message.pdf (accessed 29 November 2014).

[11] Altbach PG, Reisberg L, Rumbley LE. Trends in Global Higher Education: Tracking an Academic Revolution. Paris: UNESCO; 2010. http://www.uis.unesco.org/Library/Documents/trends-global-higher-education-2009-world-conference-en.pdf (accessed 29 November 2014).

[12] Allen IE, Seaman J. Grade Change: Tracking Online Education in the United States. Oakland, CA: Babson Survey Research Group, San Francisco, CA: Quahog Research

Group, LLC; 2014. http://www.onlinelearningsurvey.com/reports/gradechange.pdf (accessed 29 November 2014).

[13] Radford AW. Learning at a Distance. Undergraduate Enrollment in Distance Education Courses and Degree Programs. Washington, DC: U.S. Department of Education; 2011. http://nces.ed.gov/pubsearch/pubsinfo.asp?pubid=2012154 (accessed 29 November 2014).

[14] Pundak D, Dvir Y. Engineering college lecturers reluctance to adopt online courses. European Journal of Open, Distance, and e-Learning 2014. DOI: 10.1080/01587919.2014.926803. http://www.eurodl.org/?p=current&article=637 (accessed 29 November 2014).

[15] Shulte M. University instructors' perceptions of factors in distance education transactions. Online Journal of Distance Learning Administration: 2010;13(11). http://www.westga.edu/~distance/ojdla/summer132/schulte132.html (accessed 29 November 2014).

[16] Worthen H. How the Working Conditions of Online Teaching Affect the Work Lives of Online Faculty: Report from the Coalition of Contingent Academic Labor (COCAL) United Association for Labor Education (UALE) Working Group on Online Learning Survey, October-December 2012; 2013. http://uale.org/papers-and-presentations-from-2013-conference (accessed 29 November 2014).

[17] Dembo MH, Eaton MJ. Self-regulation of academic learning in middle-level schools. Elementary School Journal 2000; 100(5) 473-490.

[18] Dembo MH, Junge LG, Lynch R. Becoming a Self-regulated Learner: Implications for Web-Based Education. In: O'Neil HF, Perez, RS. (eds) Web-Based Learning: Theory, Research, and Practice. Mahwah, NJ: Erlbaum; 2006. p. 473-490.

[19] Zimmerman BJ. Self-regulated learning and academic achievement: an overview. Educational Psychologist 1990;25(1) 3-17.

[20] Zimmerman BJ, Risemberg R. Self-regulatory dimensions of academic learning and motivation. In: Phye, GD (ed) Handbook of Academic Learning: Construction of Knowledge. San Diego, CA: Academic Press; 1997. p. 105-125.

[21] Zimmerman BJ. Becoming a self-regulated learner. Theory Into Practice 2002:41(2) 64-70.

[22] Moore, MG. Learner autonomy: The second dimension of independent learning. Convergence 1972;5(2): 76-88. http://www.ajde.com/Documents/theory.pdf (accessed 15 January 2015).

[23] Moore, MG. The theory of transactional distance. In: Moore MG. (ed.), Handbook of Distance Education (2nd ed.), Mahwah, NJ: Lawrence Erlbaum; 2007. p. 89-105.

[24] Moore MG. The theory of transactional distance. In: Moore, MG (ed.), Handbook of Distance Education (3rd ed.). Mahwah, NJ: Lawrence Erlbaum; 2013. p. 66-85.

[25] White C. Language Learning in Distance Education. Cambridge: Cambridge University Press; 2003.

[26] Beaudoin, M. Issues in distance education: A primer for higher education decision-makers. In: Andrade MS (ed.) New Directions in Higher Education. Special Issue on Distance Education. Hoboken, NJ: John Wiley & Sons (in press).

[27] Andrade MS. Building community and learner autonomy: An instructor training model for online learning. Middle East and North Africa (MENA) Higher Education Leadership Forum: Proceedings of the 2nd Middle East and North Africa (MENA) Higher Education Leadership Forum, 10-11 November 2015, Dubai, United Arab Emirates.

[28] Andrade MS. Course embedded support for online English language learners. Open Praxis 2014;6(1): 65-73. http://openpraxis.org/index.php/OpenPraxis/issue/view/7/showToc (accessed 29 November 2014).

[29] Andrade MS. Dialogue and structure: Enabling learner self-regulation in technology enhanced learning environments. European Journal of Educational Research 2014;13(5): 563-574. www.wwwords.eu/eerj/content/pdfs/13/issue13_5.asp (accessed 29 November 2014).

[30] Andrade MS (2014, August). Effective whole class feedback for second language writers. Annual Conference on Distance Teaching and Learning: Proceedings of the 30th Annual Conference on Distance Teaching and Learning, 12-14 August 2014, Madison, Wisconsin.

[31] Andrade MS. Self-regulated learning activities: supporting success in online courses. In: Moore, JS (ed.) Distance Learning. Rijeka: InTech; 2012. p. 111-132. Available from http://www.intechopen.com/articles/show/title/self-regulated-learning-activities-supporting-success-in-online-courses (accessed 29 November 2014).

[32] Andrade MS, Bunker EL. Developing self-regulated distance language learners: A promising practice. Targeted Cooperative Network of European Institutions (STELLAR-TACONET): Proceedings of the Fourth Annual Self-regulated Learning in Technology Enhanced Learning Environments Conference, 10-12 May 2011, Barcelona, Spain.

[33] Andrade MS, Bunker EL. Language learning from a distance: a new model for success. Distance Education 2009;30(1): 47-61.

[34] Andrade, MS, Evans, NW. Principles and Practices for Teacher Response in Second Language Writing: Developing Self-regulated Learners. New York: Routledge; 2013.

[35] Means, B, Toyama, Y, Murphy, R, Bakia, M, Jones, K. Evaluation of Evidence-Based Practices in Online Learning: A Meta-Analysis and Review of Online Learning Stud-

ies. Washington, DC: U.S. Department of Education; 2010. http://www2.ed.gov/rschstat/eval/tech/evidence-based-practices/finalreport.pdf (accessed 15 January 2015).

[36] Means, B., Toyama, Y., Murphy, R., Bakia, M., & Jones, K. Evaluation of Evidence-Based Practices in Online Learning: A Meta-Analysis and Review of Online Learning Studies. Washington, DC: U.S. Department of Education; 2010. http://www2.ed.gov/rschstat/eval/tech/evidence-based-practices/finalreport.pdf (accessed 15 January 2015).

[37] Hurd, S. Autonomy at any price? Issues and concerns from a British HE perspective. Foreign Language Annals 1998; 31(2), 219-230.

[38] Strauss, A. & Corbin, J. Basics of Qualitative Research: Grounded Theory Procedures and Techniques, Newbury Park, CA: Sage Publications; 1990.

[39] Benson, P. What's new in autonomy? The Language Teacher 2012; 35(4) 15-18.

[40] Complete College America. Time is the Enemy. http://completecollege.org/docs/Time_Is_the_Enemy.pdf (accessed 29 November 2014).

Chapter 3

Theoretical Perspectives of Hands-On Educational Practices — From a Review of Psychological Theories to Block Magic and INF@NZIA DIGI.Tales 3.6 Projects

Orazio Miglino, Michela Ponticorvo and Luigia Simona Sica

Additional information is available at the end of the chapter

http://dx.doi.org/10.5772/60922

Abstract

In this chapter, the main theories related to cognitive development are discussed, starting from psychological discussion up to theories application to training, pedagogical and formation sciences issues.

We start from the classical contribution by Vygotsky and Piaget to arrive to the recent embodied cognition approach.

This theoretical excursus leads us to describe two projects we are involved in: the Block Magic project and INF@NZIA DIGI.tales 3.6. The goal of Block Magic is to introduce a new teaching methodology and technology targeting young children between the ages of 2.5 and 7 who are attending pre-school or the early years of primary school. The project aims at helping young learners to learn autonomously. This, the authors believe, is a basic life skill, of critical importance for their future development.

We then describe INF@NZIA DIGI.tales 3.6 project, an Italian project aimed to promote the use of ICT technologies and the latest paradigms of human–computer interaction (augmented reality, RFID/NFC sensors, handwriting and speech recognition, motion detection, etc.) in order to define psycho-educational practices, which are able to enhance curricular activities and facilitate acquisition processes for skills and knowledge for pupils.

Keywords: Hands-on practices, Embodied cognition, ICT tools for learning, Logic blocks, Learning processes

1. Introduction

Digital learning games have become a reference point in the educational field, in terms of positive effect of their use on learning and motivation [1,2]. However, why they are used in education is an interesting issue to be investigated from a broad perspective including, on one hand, the psychological processes underlying learning and, on the other, the potential new technologies offer. In this chapter, we will try to describe both mentioned perspectives and to illustrate how they may concretely interact through two project descriptions.

Since their birth and maybe even before, children start learning about the world around them. Day by day they can count on wider sensorimotor functions that open their cognitive development in new ways.

In the period of their life that goes from few months to 3–4 years, the hands are fundamental in conveying knowledge. A child points something and he/she handles, touches, tastes and manipulates while understanding an object's features and functions.

These everyday observations eminently reflect in psychologists' perspectives; consider, for example, Piaget [3], Papert [4] and Bruner [5] who recognise a fundamental role to manipulative activities for psychological development and cognitive representations at birth. Also Vygotsky [6], the other giant father of cognitive development theory, believed that interaction with the environment was an important way a child could learn, not the only one indeed. In his opinion, cognitive development relies on input from other people as well, thus underlying the importance of the historical and cultural context children live in.

Of course, learning in adults is not limited to pointing, reaching, touching and manipulating as, along human cognitive development and thanks to learning processes, the 'concrete' manipulative acts are gradually interiorised and become part of our neurocognitive structures. They are not actually performed as they are but they become 'simulated' actions (symbolic acts) in a virtual (mind) space [7].

In spite of this interiorisation, the use of hands (or more in general, the body) together with the related cognitive representation of physical space is a latent and essential psychological resource for learning and developmental processes. They can emerge when the context and the environmental conditions allow humans to use hands and their representation. It is a sort of bias that is, probably, the main reason why we think about Internet as a geometrical (virtual) space or why the (computer) 'mouse' and the 'touch screens' are immediately intuitive. Adopting this view, the mouse extends 'pointing' and 'reaching' actions in a computer screen graphic space, and the current 'touch-screen' technology allows us to manipulate digital virtual objects. Recently, new technologies are candidates to enhance our attitude to learn by manipulating. If we equip common objects with sensors and connect them in wireless mode with a remote computer, we build something similar to what is called Internet of Things [8] that permits an easy interaction with (smart) objects through new interfaces (glasses, gloves, visors, etc.) or by traditional manipulation coupled with (sophisticated) computer programs (see, e.g. handwriting recognition systems).

We think that the new chances offered by the smart object technology could produce innovative learning/teaching environments to enhance neurocognitive development especially in training context. Moreover, with these tools, we could recover traditional and well-known psycho-pedagogical practices that are not widely and massively applied because of their expensiveness. For example, these technologies can be applied to traditional educational materials like logic blocks or teaching tiles. These are manipulative materials specifically designed to teach a wide range of subjects (mathematics, geometry, languages, geography, etc.) and abilities or soft skills (problem solving, creative thinking, cooperative behaviour, etc.) for children aged from 3 to 10. These materials have a strong drawback: they can be used individually or in small groups of students (3–4 children maximum) and require a constant supervision by teachers, parents, educators, etc. This represents a strong constraint, also economic, for their wide employment. But we think that smart technologies (software and hardware) can be exploited to overcome this constraint and express the huge educational potential lying in these materials/practices.

The aim of this chapter is to explore the principal approaches to the learning process from the cognitive one to the embodied cognition through the constructivism. This theoretical excursus will lead us to describe two projects we are involved in: the Block Magic project and the INF@NZIA DIGI.tales 3.6 project. These projects have produced interesting educational applications that can help in enhancing traditional educational materials to make them meet the technological challenge.

2. Theoretical perspectives: General principles

Learning can be defined as an enduring and stable change in the individual potential behaviour, as a result of practice or experience (Fig. 1). Learning occurs throughout life for animals, and learned behaviour represents a large proportion of all behaviours in higher animals, especially humans. In humans, learning is strictly connected to development in cognitive, emotional and social sphere, and it implies the human skill of giving sense, coherence and meaning to experience too. The complexity of this process is evident for the reader when he/she thinks that everyone is constantly subject to a huge amount of information coming from the context the individual is immersed in. This information can potentially become learning materials, but actually most of them disappear in an individual's mental life, whereas some others are recorded in memory.

From a psychological perspective, there are three key-points of learning process (consider the definition at the beginning of this paragraph): 1) observed change in the individual's behaviour, 2) change resulting from experience and 3) 'potential' behavioural change that does not have to be actual.

Furthermore, Gagné [9] emphasises that learning is a change, observable in behaviour, that can affect attitudes or human ability, which can be stored and which cannot be simply attributed to growth.

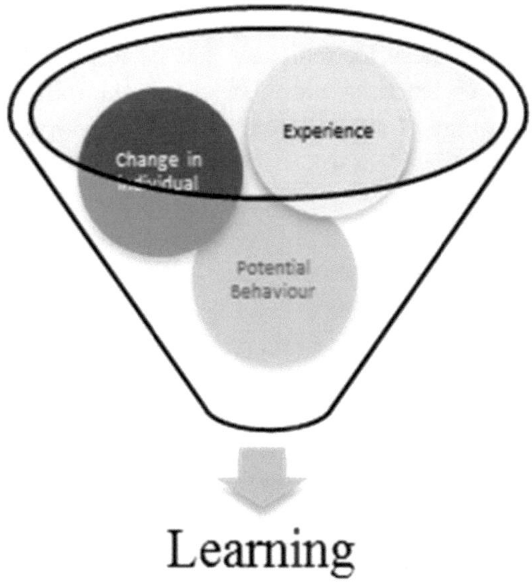

Figure 1. What is learning?

In a more practical view, learning 'programming is not seen simply as a technological development incorporating previously established learning principles, but rather as one particular form of the ordering of stimulus and response events designed to bring about productive learning.... (If) one wants to investigate the effects of an experimental treatment on the behaviour of individuals or groups who start from the same point, he would be well advised to measure and map out for each individual the learning sets relevant to the experimental task' [10].

Even if the practical aspect of the teaching/learning process depends on the specific didactic topics, it is possible to underline various common steps that Gagné and Briggs [11] have focused on in order to describe the learning process events. The author has broken down the process into an elementary task sequence or behavioural objectives that were presented to the learner who was given immediate feedback on his/her responses (Fig. 2).

How to accomplish these steps and how to promote and stimulate learning are relevant issues that have been variously interpreted in psychological literature. Here we report three approaches that provide interpretative frameworks and operational guidelines that are significant in educational psychology and pedagogy too: behaviourist, cognitive and embodied cognition approaches. These three approaches can be seen as points along a continuum, with continuity and discontinuity elements, leading to embodied cognition notions that represent the starting point of Block Magic project rationale referred to in this chapter.

http://dx.doi.org/10.5772/60922

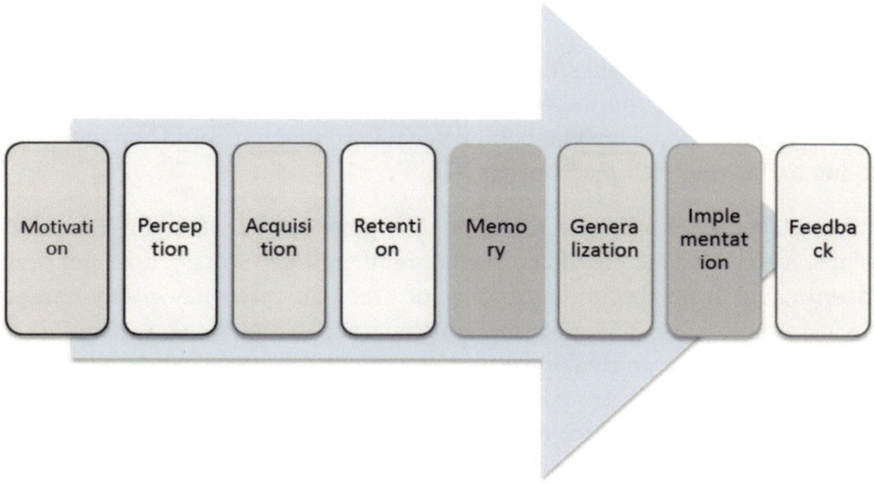

Figure 2. Basic principles of learning process

3. A Behaviorist perspective: Associative learning

According to the behaviorist approach [12], learning is seen in terms of connections (associations) between stimulus (or stimulus–situation) and response and between response and reinforcement. Learning means that behaviour (objectively observable) can be modified by reinforcements that in turn can produce conditioning [13] or operant conditioning (Fig. 3). In this context, environment is fundamental, because it can produce learning only if it is properly structured.

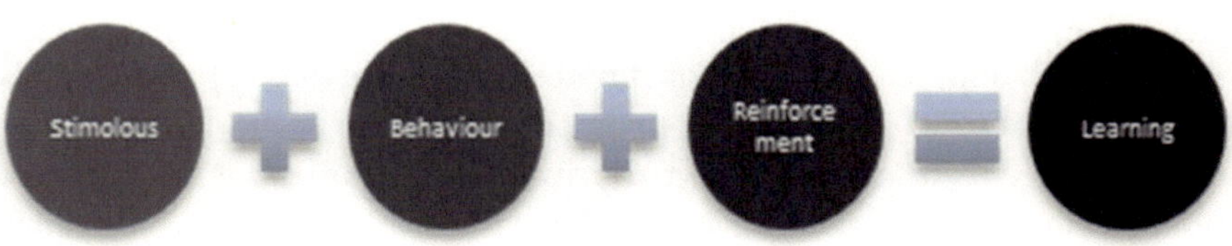

Figure 3. Operant conditioning

Pedagogy practice based on associative principles involves identifying the components of learning competences, sequencing these in complexity terms and providing clear tasks with immediate feedback. The sequence is then adjusted according to learner performance. The underlying assumption is that learning consists of building on simpler behaviours, a quantitative increase where existing knowledge and procedures are merely added to the previous ones.

3.1. A cognitive perspective: Piaget, Vygotsky and Bruner and the constructivist approach

Since the 1950s and 1960s, thanks to Gestalt psychology, Tolman and Piaget contribution, psychologists have focused on the cognitive process underlying learning. In opposition to behaviorism, they explored what was behind behaviour: thought, mind and mental representation, trying to describe their mechanisms (Fig. 4).

In cognitive perspective, learning is not a sum of fragmented activities, but the knowledge of relationships, meanings and situations. Furthermore, problem solving does not derive from trial and error, but from the understanding of a certain problematic situation structure. Cognitive learning involves higher mental functions such as attention, perception, memory, intelligence and general cognitive processes belonging to humans: the change is not only in the behaviour but in internal structures and processes too, which in turn acts on individual behaviour. This change can arise from active thoughtful participation, whereas learning arises from the interaction between new experiences and existing internal pattern.

In this context, the central issue is how we represent knowledge and develop our concepts and understandings. According to McKendry [14], we learn as a result of the interaction between new experiences and existing understanding structures, previously created.

It is worth underlining that cognitivist authors have formulated some of the most relevant theories in educational and developmental psychology. We will now briefly describe the ones which have direct implications for our discussion on learning.

According to cognitive perspective, Piaget [3] – who is, as reminded above, one of the most influential developmental psychologist – has explored the process by which children develop their knowledge of the world in cognitive terms. Using a clinical–critical approach and by observing his children for a long time, Piaget came to the conclusion that two cognitive processes are responsible for human cognitive development: assimilation and accommodation. These processes are the basis of learning process and define children development in cognitive terms.

The first one (assimilation) refers to the acquisition of an object/event in pre-existing cognitive or behavioural schema; the second one (accommodation) refers to the change of the schema subsequent to new events/objects. These two processes alternate in order to achieve a dynamic equilibrium. In other words, learning is based on the balance between assimilation and accommodation, and it is based on the new information integration in pre-existing cognitive structures. The development of these structures is innate and fixed, and it is organised in universal subsequent steps/stages. Learning, in this perspective, develops with doing. The educational context can only tune itself with the developmental stage the child is in, so as to offer the proper chance of doing to learn.

According to traditional interpretation, the Piaget approach can be seen in opposition to the Vygotsky conception of learning. The key-point of this opposition is the context role. From the Piagetian point of view, social and cultural context does not play an important role in cognitive development, whereas for the Vygotskian framework, context promotes learning and development in cognitive sphere.

Vygotsky [6] holds that child cognitive development derives from the interaction between person and social context. More specifically, an individual interiorises cognitive functions through language that shapes social interaction. The social context (or other significant people in the learner's life) can help, support and facilitate the learning process and, in particular, it may have an impact on the zone of proximal development (ZPD). The ZPD is a cognitive area where the child can go beyond his/her current knowledge level and development through the support of a competent adult, representing a social stimulus. The higher mental processes are created through socially meaningful mediated activity.

Translated in pedagogical language, teachers have to encourage learners to build their own mental structures through interaction with the environment. Moreover, Vygotsky has introduced the 'scaffolding' notion to suggest that an important role is played by learners who, with the assistance by someone more experienced, can achieve cognitive results they would be otherwise unable to. The teacher's role as scaffolder involves guiding students towards activities that they are likely to find engaging and from which they will probably learn. However, rather than playing a didactic role, the teacher must encourage students to think by themselves, to raise issues and questions related to didactic activity and to identify problems they can face and solve. In brief, pedagogy based on constructivist approach bases on the following principles: creating an environment where learners can become actively involved, setting up activities that encourage experimentation and discovery and interactive and student-centred activities, locating learning within the ZPD and scaffolding through encouragement and support for raising questions and reflecting on principles.

Building on Piaget and Vygotsky theories, Bruner [5, 15], in his theory, has stressed both the learner active involvement (Piaget) and social context (Vygotsky) roles, and he has proposed a cultural approach to learning process and cognitive development. According to Bruner [16, 17], learning is a complex activity in which three processes interact: 1) information acquisition, 2) information transformation/manipulation in a new form that is suitable for problem solving and 3) checking of this transformation efficacy. Information modification (2) is linked to three representational methods that depend on individual culture and maturation: action system, iconic system and symbolic system [18].

From an ontological point of view, child learning can be divided in four stages: 1) ability of acquisition, 2) reflexivity, 3) sharing and 4) culture. Extending the social context and language importance underlined by Vygotsky, Bruner emphasises the role of culture in human development. Culture is a collective and shared interpretation of reality, and the individual mind has an interpersonal nature. Learning is an interpersonal and relational activity strictly linked to the 'where and how' of the knowledge; in other words, learning is a 'situated cognitive action' [19].

In Bruner's words: "the active participation in the learning process by the child might result in the following hypothesized benefits: an increase in intellectual potency so as to make the acquired information more readily viable in problem solving, the action of the learning activities in terms of the intrinsic reward of discovery itself (as contrasted with the drive-reduction model of learning), learning the heuristics of discovery, and making material more readily accessible in memory" [20].

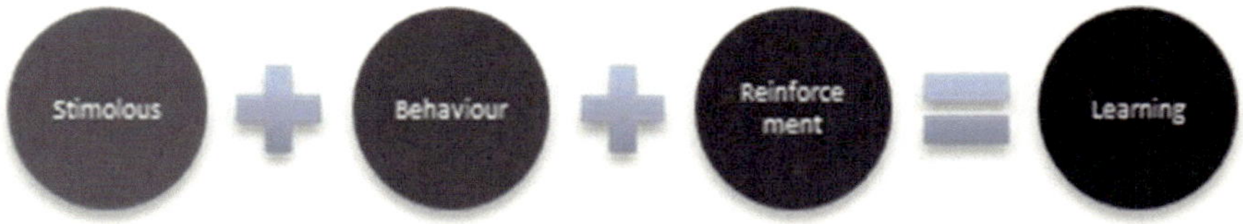

Figure 4. The learning process from a cognitive perspective

Bruner intuitions have given important hints to successive cognitive authors; consider, for example, Papert and Jonassen who have emphasised the person's active role in experience comprehension using cultural and contextual resources. Other important concepts of constructivist approach such as 'discovery learning' [21] and 'meaningful learning' [22] are based on Bruner's conceptualisation of culture and manipulation.

3.2. Situated learning: The role of embodiment

As it is evident from the previous paragraphs, activity has a central role in learning process: it is a core process in Piaget theory, it is fundamental in Bruner approach and it has a transformative power if supported by external stimuli for Vygotsky. In particular, the concept of action becomes central for the situated learning theories [23, 24]. These theories belong to a theoretical framework in which authors emphasise sociocultural aspects of learning and cognition. The idea is that the knower cannot be separated from the known; knowledge and learning are the results of social activity in context [25, 26]. Therefore, situated learning includes participation as a key concept; participation can be seen as 'being a part' with a critical importance of contextualisation in learning. Teaching strategies based upon participation can encourage collaboration amongst learners [27]. This way, learners can become part of the community. Learning can be described in terms of action and participation in a community of practice. In this framework (as well as in the previous cognitive theories), the concept of activity defines a cognitive process somehow detached from the body. In the traditional vision of learning, the attention on the person complexity was simplified, focusing on mind in terms of cognitive processes.

However, it should not be neglected that the body plays a fundamental role in the interaction between the person and context. In a wider perspective, having a body is essential for agents of different kinds, and it becomes a powerful vehicle to acquire knowledge.

Let us consider, for example, artificial agents provided with bodies with sensors and actuators, such as robots [28] that have to orient in space, a quite complex cognitive task. Being embodied allows these agents to find effective solutions to spatial tasks [29, 30]: embodiment conveys knowledge. In authors' words: embodied cognition view 'emphasizes the role of coupled interactions between organisms and the environment in the development of cognitive processes, capturing the way mind, body and world interact and influence one another to promote the adaptive success of an organism' [31].

Also authors in cognitive psychology framework regarding humans exalt the body role as well.

Piaget describes it as one of the first instruments used to know the world (e.g. see sensorimotor stage in the Piagetian theory). In more recent years, Galperin [32] retrieves the body importance too. According to this author, the mental object-oriented activity is the result of initially materialised object-oriented activity. Or, in other words, the physical manipulation of objects represents the basis of human thought. Rambush and Ziemke [33] identify in Galperin approach a bridge between situated learning and embodied cognition research that affirms that cognition is a continuous process with changing boundaries and much more than what takes place within the individual mind. This idea has been considered by an increasing number of scientists in various areas of research (e.g. see [34] for neurosciences and [35] for philosophy).

As Rambush and Ziemke argued, 'the embodied cognition is in many aspect a very social process, and that embodied social process such as mimicry and imitation are significant for social relations as they help people connect, making it possible for them to communicate and to understand each other' [33]. In this trace, Roth [36] demonstrated that gestures not only reflect learning but also contribute to it, serving not only to communicate content to a public but also to help the speaker in making things clearer and more understandable.

3.3. CAI, LOGO and smart objects: Making connections between technology and learning

Learning theories have their counterpart in pedagogical practices and in learning technology. Technology is a mirror of the times, and the development of educational practices is reciprocally linked to technology advancement.

In this respect, although teaching machines may be historical artefacts, theoretical perspectives have stimulated technological applications. Behaviorist principles underlie methods such as computer-assisted instruction (CAI) where rapid feedback is given on the correctness of learner response (e.g. mathematical routines presented as a game with extrinsic rewards).

Cognitive principles underlie methods such as LOGO [37, 38], a programming language created as the first children toys with built-in computation, described as follows: 'children might come to want to learn it because they would use it in building these models. And if they did want to learn it they would, even if teaching were poor or possibly nonexistent. Moreover, since one of the reasons for poor teaching is that teachers do not enjoy teaching reluctant children, it is not implausible that teaching would become better as well as becoming less necessary. So changes in the opportunities for construction could in principle lead to deeper changes in the learning of mathematics than changes in knowledge about instruction or any amount of "teacher-proof" computer-aided instruction' [39]. LOGO and Lego/LOGO constitute outstanding examples of how technology can provide new ways to learn.

In recent years, the technology progress produced smart objects, everyday objects augmented with computational services [40] that can have a central role in educational psychology based on both situated learning and embodied cognition principles. In addition, mobile devices that are mainly used for communication, entertainment and as electronic assistants may be used as intermediaries between us and the smart objects in our surroundings for their increasing computational, storage, communicational and multimedia capabilities [41].

Starting from the innovation in the individual–environment interaction offered by the smart objects technology, our idea is that we can produce innovative learning/teaching environments (according to constructivist learning theories and extant pedagogical practices) to enhance neurocognitive development especially in training context. This proposal will be discussed in detail in the next paragraphs.

4. From TEL to STELT: Technology-enhanced learning becomes smart technologies to enhanced learning and teaching

The review proposed in the previous section highlights the fundamental role played by learning theories for building effective educational tools. Technology can be a powerful weapon in this battle, provided that we conceive it as an empty bin whose sense is given by the reference theory. In Dror's words [42], 'learning means that the cognitive system acquires information and stores it for further use...regardless whether the objective is learning new information, acquiring new skills, or knowledge sharing and transfer within or across organisations — the processes of acquiring, storing and applying the information are critical. The question is how to achieve these cornerstones of learning and whether technology can enhance them. The answer is clear: learning must fit human cognition...the difficult and tricky challenge is how to translate this theoretical and academic research into practical ways to utilise technology so as to enhance learning'. An entire area of research, known with the acronym TEL, developed in recent decades.

Technology can obviously enhance learning if it mirrors how cognition works. This can be achieved through the appropriate design. Design is indeed fundamental to the successful development of any technology-enhanced learning scenario and requires input from many diverse areas of expertise and multiple perspectives [43].

Some technologies are precisely fit to stimulate learning by doing, as they are based on the theoretical framework already described. These technologies are not purely instructional: in the past years, many tools have been conceived as teacher substitutes in a vertical unidirectional lesson transmitting their specific knowledge domain. More recently, technology offered new chances, thus allowing to build TEL environments that can offer direct experience to the learners. In particular, we would like to introduce the STELT platform precisely devoted to build active environments for learning [44, 45], represented in Fig. 5.

STELT is a software platform that combines the management of hardware components (sensors and actuators) and software components (libraries for the storyboard and provision of feedback, authoring systems to be used by nonprogrammers) which are required to construct educational, teaching and play materials that exploit the potential of new technologies into a single development environment. STELT is able to support environments based on the handling of physical object that have a central role in learning by doing framework.

STELT, created by AIDVANCED SRL, implements augmented reality systems based on RFID (radio-frequency identification) and NFC (near field communication) technology. The labels

http://dx.doi.org/10.5772/60922

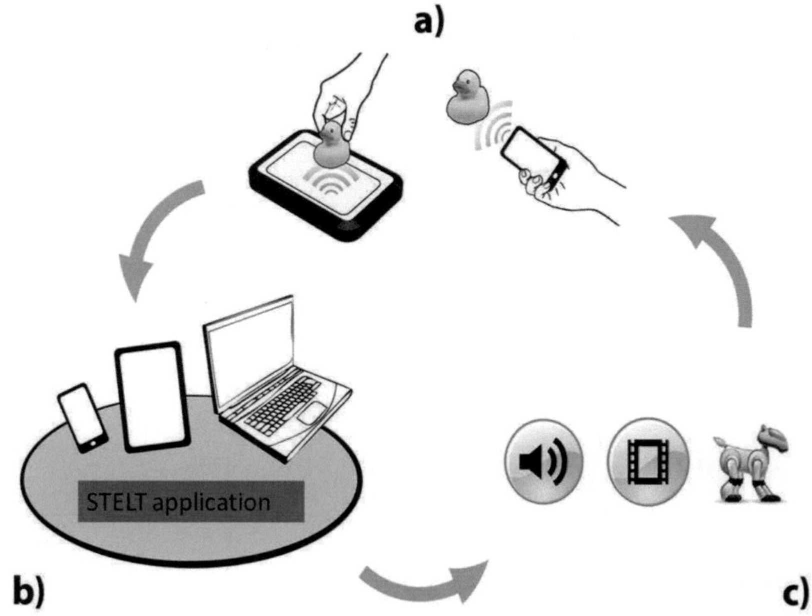

Figure 5. STELT platform functional representation

RFID/NFC (tag) are very thin transponders that can be applied to any type of object and are detected by small readers. The reader can be connected to a computer with either a wired or wireless connection or integrated into standard equipment on smartphones and tablets (NFC sensor). STELT combines communication protocols with the various hardware devices (readers and output devices), a storyboarding environment for creating various interaction scenarios, a database for tracking the user's behaviour and an adapting tutoring system that can build a user profile providing customised feedback.

This platform is functionally represented in Fig. 5: a) the learner places a «tagged» object onto a tablet reader or moves a reader or smartphone close to the «tagged» object; b) the signal containing the object's code is sent to a computer (desktop, notebook, tablet or smartphone) containing the STELT platform; and c) once it has entered the STELT system, the signal generates a number of actions from the output devices (audio system, monitors) depending on the current scenario created with the storyboarding module. Furthermore, the same signal is memorised and analysed by the adapting tutoring module, so that a customised profile is created for the user that guides the subsequent system responses. Human–machine interaction takes places solely by the handling/identification of physical objects and by the activation of audio or visual feedback. The originality of STELT resides in the combination of communication protocols with various hardware devices (readers and output devices), a storyboarding environment that allows to design many different scenarios, a database for tracking the user's behaviour that collects huge information amount and an adapting tutoring system that can analyse and interpret such behaviour and provide relevant feedback. All these components are provided into a single development environment. This combination allows the creation of different and easily customisable application environments and the direct tracking of all the activities during the session. From a technical point of view, STELT is a SDK (software development kit) containing software libraries for sensor, storyboarding, monitoring and adapting tutoring management and for the creation of applications in Windows (Vista, 7 and 8), Android and iOS environment. The SDK also contains authoring systems that allows nontechnical people with no specific technical background to directly design educational scenarios.

STELT platform has been used to implement different products. In the next section, we will describe Block Magic, a hybrid physical/software tool that enhances traditional blocks and methods for teaching in kindergarten and primary schools.

5. Block Magic project

Block Magic is a prototype for educational materials developed in a successful European research project under the framework of LLP-Comenius programme. It aimed at creating a bridge between physical manipulation and digital technology in education. Block Magic developed a functional prototypal system that enhanced the logic blocks box. The prototype is made up of an active desk/board able to recognise concrete blocks equipped with the RFID passive tag and to communicate with a PC, an augmented reality system.

In Figs. 6 and 7, BM kit and BM functional representation are reported.

Figure 6. Block Magic kit

The BM platform consists of a set of magic blocks (48 traditional logic blocks), a magic board/ tablet device and a specific software. It is based on STELT platform introduced above and links together smart technologies and physical material to support children learning processes. It unites the manipulative approach and touch-screen technologies.

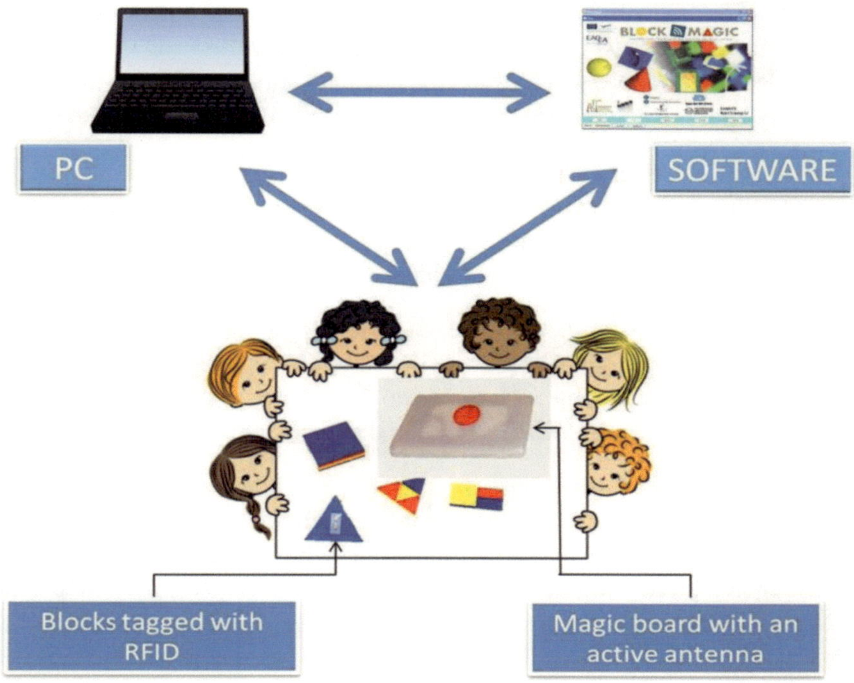

Figure 7. Block Magic functional representation

BM materials derive from structured materials, classically used in education. Structured materials have fixed numbers of 'n' elements, 'm' categories and rules to connect single parts that represent the structure. Logic blocks, cards, teaching tiles, etc., are structured materials typical examples. These materials promote analytical thought, as they segregate single qualities (e.g. dimension, shape, colour, etc.) and allow first to focalise attention on an object single part and then to develop clustering and serialisation ability in order to understand the objects' features.

The technology used in the BM project is the RFID/NFC, radio-frequency identification/near field communication. The RFID system consists of an antenna and a transceiver, which is able to read the radio frequency and transfer the information to a device, and a small and low-cost tag, which is an integrated circuit containing the RF circuitry and information to be transmitted.

These technologies are simple to use, so they are interesting for applications rather than on technical level.

The BM teaching kit consisted of a set of magic blocks (48 traditional logic blocks) and a magic board/tablet device. Magic blocks are derived from logic blocks which are didactic materials used worldwide in kindergartens and primary schools [46]. They are made up of a set of blocks (usually 48 pieces) divided in four groups according to different attributes: geometric shape (triangular, squared, rectangular and circular), thickness (thick and thin), colour (red, yellow and blue) and dimension (big and small).

The BM project proposes a hybrid version that allows an enhancement of traditional logic blocks, equipping them with RFID tags. This configuration permits to a PC or a table, with BM software installed on, to connect with BM Magic Table, another relevant BM material. The Magic Table has a hidden antenna that recognises each block, sends a signal to the PC/tablets and produces a feedback coherently with pupils' learning path.

Each augmented magic block had an integrated/attached passive RFID sensor for wireless identification of each single block. A specially designed wireless RFID reader device, an active board, is used which could read the RFID of a block and transmit the result to the BM software.

The BM system aimed to stimulate and teach different skills such as logic, mathematics, languages, etc.; therefore, the described BM-enriched blocks together with the Magic Table are complemented with a software that includes a series of exercises that researchers involved in BM project built on the teachers' feedback and on their previous experience in pedagogy.

The BM software is mainly formed by two parts: the first one is devoted to receiving input from the active board and generating an 'action' (aural and visual). These actions implement the direct feedbacks the user can receive interacting with the system. These feedbacks are regulated by an adaptive tutor system embedded that ensures autonomous interaction between the user and the system, receiving active support, corrective indications, feedback and positive reinforcement from the digital assistant on the outcome of the actions performed.

The second software component is devoted to customisation too, but it is dedicated to teachers, educators, etc., allowing them to choose the exercises to be proposed to the child, focusing the attention on the skills the child needs to train more. The BM software moreover can collect data about the exercises.

Preliminary trials with Block Magic prototype were run in various schools in Germany, Greece, Italy and Spain, involving children aged 3 to 7. Observations were run on children and the teachers were involved in after-session focus groups Results confirmed Block Magic educational platform effectiveness in educational context. In particular BM attractiveness emerged strongly: the tool is very attractive for children for many reasons. They especially like to use the tablet and the computer and are attracted by visual and aural stimulation as well as the mascot 'Blocki'. It is motivating for the students to use a computer-based system that the manipulation of real objects makes it even more fun. Teachers think that children found both visual and aural presentation of the tool attractive, and the use of text, graphics, sound and pictures is perceived as balanced so the children did not get bored. They stayed happily until the end of each session and even wanted to continue playing.

Teachers also notice that children like to hear their names from the computer and feel like participating in a real game. Also receiving an appropriate feedback is crucial to keep a high motivation level. Children with special needs find the tool attractive too.

The researchers investigated BM use in relation with specific skills: in teachers' opinion, it contributes to develop specific cognitive skills; in particular it is fit to improve mathematical and logical skills. All teachers accepted that the tool offers a variety of activities that encourage children to develop mathematical skills. Also imagination is stimulated by BM. In detail, the

'Creative Drawing', 'Logic Train' and 'Slice the Shape' were identified as the exercises that motivate children to use their imagination.

Then the questionnaire and the focus group compared the use of BM with traditional blocks: teachers agreed that the most relevant aspect was the feedback provided by BM system that allowed many children, especially the older ones, to interact autonomously with exercises. Block Magic meets the new IT generation and is an interactive tool, but there are constraints in terms of creativity and imagination that, on the contrary, are better stimulated by traditional blocks. Moreover, teachers underlined that Block Magic creates more possibilities for the teachers than the traditional logical blocks: there is a wider variety of exercises, some of which are more difficult to play in traditional settings. With Block Magic, children can work (almost) unattended and they can spend more time with it.

It is useful to underline that these aspects emerged in all trials, thus meaning that children interact with BM platform in a similar way across different countries and cultures.

6. INF@NZIA DIGI.tales 3.6 project

The second project we are going to describe in this chapter is INF@NZIA DIGI.tales 3.6. It is an Italian project aimed to promote the use of ICT technologies and the latest paradigms of human–computer interaction (augmented reality, RFID/NFC sensors, handwriting and speech recognition, motion detection, etc.) in order to define psycho-educational practices, which are able to enhance curricular activities and facilitate acquisition processes for skills and knowledge for pupils.

According to the literature described in the first part of this chapter and basing on evidences from Block Magic, the INF@NZIA DIGI.tales 3.6 project addresses a specific topic related to the link between cognitive development in childhood and technology use in both formal and informal teaching/learning contexts. Developmental psychology highlighted that multiple levels of organisation contribute to child growth: biological, psychological and environmental conditions influence each other in a dynamical way. This interaction is easily observable during school time (kindergarten and primary school), a period in which the complexity of systems and environments that begin to interact with each other is amplified. It is precisely the interaction between different factors (cognitive and socio-relational) and different settings to highlight gaps. One of these gaps, particularly relevant in our opinion, is that many children today are living with a serious technological gap between the various educational contexts in their lives: on one hand, they attend schools that are still technologically stagnant; on the other hand, they can use much technology at home, made up by platforms for game consoles, smartphones, Internet, etc. This technological imbalance has increased recently, due to the introduction of touch-screen tablets and their numerous 'educational' applications, which are particularly suitable for very small children (2–6 age group). Indeed, the domestic environment is experiencing an ever-increasing use of technology: it is foreseen that tablet use in Italy, for example, will increase from 15 % to 28 % by 2016 (source: eMarketer), while greater increases have been projected for other European nations, such as the UK, Germany, France and Spain.

Projections issued by the International Data Corporation (IDC), updated in March 2013, predict that the global tablet market reaches 190.9 million units this year, an increase of 11 % between 2013 and 2016 that will reach 350 million by the end of 2017.

Tablet technology for children aged 2 or more precisely has a strong educational potential as confirmed by large-scale distribution and commercial success of educational Apps both for iOS and for Android (to mention the most popular operating systems) implemented by compatible software house. These new technologies and their content cognitively stimulate children, but the downside is that they often engage children alone and without the intervention and supervision of a responsible adult.

Specifically in Italian context, the Digital School curriculum of the Ministry for Education has ensured that Italian schools are gradually making use of the well-known interactive digital whiteboards, but distribution is still marginal and the technology, in the meantime, has been rendered obsolete by more modern touch-screen technologies. Most of the instruments used in preprimary and primary schools are not based on ICT technology: preprimary institutions mainly use materials which involve handling, as is the case for the first years of the primary cycle where initial fundamental learning is based on the acquisition of cognitive skills by way of developing natural motor and sensory abilities.

In order to achieve this gap overcoming, the INF@NZIA DIGI.tales 3.6 project is defining psycho-educational practices able to foster curricular activities and facilitate the acquisition processes of skills and knowledge in pupils and to implement an innovative model for the digital educational publishing for the primary school. Thus, this model will support the curricular school activities through the digital and technological empowering of the materials (e.g. schoolbooks) of the institutional and regulatory educational framework (see European Digital Agenda 2012). The sphere of action chosen for the project is constituted by preprimary and primary school system, which has been charged by the Italian Ministry for Education to promote the development, identity and abilities of our youngest citizens and introducing them to their civic duties, in accordance with the right to education and care, in coherence with principles of cultural pluralism as stated in our constitution, the International Convention on the Rights of the Child and in various other reference documents of the European Union. More specifically, the INF@NZIA DIGI.tales 3.6 project is aimed at children aged 3 to 6, thus including the first year of primary school, with the goal of renewing teaching and learning models in an educational context in this teaching segment. The INF@NZIA DIGI.tales 3.6 project also involves the 'significant others', actors of teaching/learning process in both formal and informal contexts: teachers, parents and families.

In brief, the model consists of interactions between different components and steps. The first of these steps consists of transforming curricular activities in digital micro-games that could be selected by teachers or tutoring systems. The child answers (in other words, the successful/not successful conclusion of micro-games) impact on the proposal of subsequent micro-games in a manner akin to the personalisation of school curriculum. A broader tutoring system could retrieve and analyse the data/answers to micro-games and socialise the results to the other actors of the teaching/learning process.

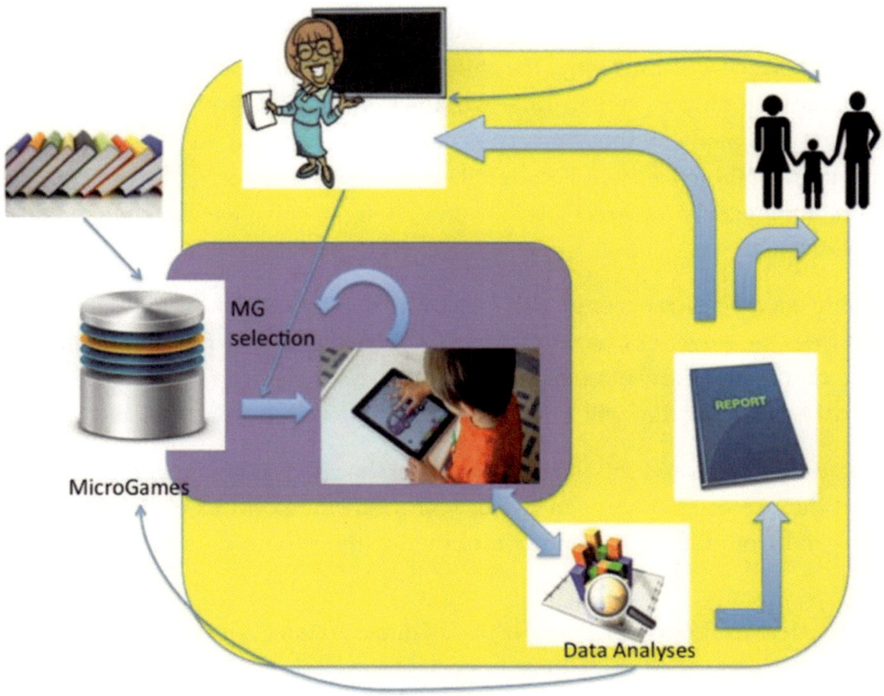

Figure 8. The INF@NZIA DIGI.tales 3.6 functional model

More in detail, on the basis of the state of art in the field of developmental psychology, school activities and new technologies, the INF@NZIA DIGI.tales 3.6 project individuates the following key elements as central for the empowering of the current curricular learning materials:

- Multimedia = the ability to develop a digital and empowered learning material available on different tools and OS. This approach allows different learning processes and different stimuli that each teacher could tailor on his/her own needs.

- Multimodal = the opportunity of the platform to exploit more interactive solutions. The user will interact with the platform developed in the project with different modes, i.e. voice, gesture, materials, handwriting and touch.

- Computing = the technologies that allow the customisation of the contents and the advanced adaptive assessment and assistance for the users.

In our opinion, these key elements could be essential for modernised learning, teaching and assessment practices through digital technologies, namely, through the following actions:

- Tracking the learner data during the execution of the training activities: the system could record each activity during the game session, and then the teacher will be able to access the personal control panel to check the raw tracking data collected from the platform.
- Using an immediate feedback for the learning activity: the child has immediate confirmation of response correctness. Currently, the child has to perform exercises, but the feedback is given collectively only in certain time windows, which can potentially be far from the intellectual effort made by the child. This discrepancy can lead, in the worst cases, to the ineffectiveness of the correction. The digital technologies could easily prevent this problem, correcting immediately incorrect answers and giving positive feedback when the exercise is well performed.
- Developing advanced reporting: the system will provide data analysis about results obtained from the exercises execution, which will be visible only to certain users (teachers, enabled parents, etc.). Teachers and parents will be able to see the pupil's learning evolution, with a final assessment that will contain tips, suggestions and observations.
- Allowing the surprise and interactivity increase: the child will have a higher satisfaction degree in the use of interactive material, both from the point of view of internal game dynamics and from the recognition point of view (the system calls by name every single child).

A secondary effect of the use of INF@NZIA DIGI.tales model addresses the social identity formation process that is one of the most important developmental tasks for the child, and it is strictly linked to learning. According to this view, the building of knowledge emerges concurrently and is facilitated by the formation of a social identity, which is shared with the community, by means of carrying out common activities. INF@NZIA DIGI.tales allows to achieve both learning and social identity through 1) conceiving designing and creating Smart Learning & Teaching Environments, which can be integrated into the school curriculum cycle; 2) creating favourable conditions for learning, maturity and teaching, in accordance with the principles of continuity and the wholesome and harmonious youngest members of society growth; and 3) building areas for free expression and multisensory experience which permit symbolic play, the greater and more incisive participation of different people involved in education process. With regard to the child, the INF@NZIA DIGI.tales model addresses socialisation and cooperation with classmates during school hours: interaction with peers, friends and parents outside school hours, communication dynamics, using cultural stimuli, which may be rooted in the local area.

7. Conclusions

The aim of this chapter was to illustrate the close connection between psychological/cognitive processes and using and building new technologies especially in the education field.

In doing so, we have examined the classical approaches to human learning, highlighting continuity and discontinuity in psychological theories. Overall, the nature of teaching/learning process is mainly interactive, based on context and culture, actually relational. Various approaches (cognitive approach, behaviourist theory, cultural psychology, constructivism and embodiment cognition) have tried to explain the process of interaction between person and context in different ways, but all these have taken in consideration its transactional nature. The person and context, during the learning process, are mutually interrelated, and a change in one element implies a change in the other element. This 'intimacy' is well evidenced by the embodiment cognition theory and by the successive and continuous development of new technologies in the educational field. Indeed, this latter pays most attention on the teaching/learning context and tools analyses. Context and tools constitute key elements in children, adolescent and adult learning process. They are sensitive to individual development (in cognitive, emotional and psychological terms) and cultural stimuli.

Following this circular approach (in which individual context and tools affect each other), in this chapter we have described two projects (Block Magic and INF@NZIA DIGI.tales 3.6), which offer two examples of new technologies used in supporting teaching/learning processes.

The Block Magic project was aimed at creating a bridge between physical manipulation and digital technology in education; to do this, Block Magic developed a functional prototypal system that enhanced the traditional logic blocks box. The INF@NZIA DIGI.tales 3.6 project aimed to promote the use of ICT technologies and the latest paradigms of human–computer interaction in order to define psycho-educational practices in order to enhance curricular activities and facilitate acquisition processes for skills and knowledge for pupils. Both projects were built on STELT platform that links together smart technologies and physical material to support children learning processes. The two projects, basing on STELT technology, show a possible methodology to unify the manipulative approach to the learning processes and touch-screen technologies.

According to encouraging preliminary findings of the projects, our conclusion is that they could offer examples of new technologies used in educational contexts and that they both are in line with previous research providing effectiveness of use for new technologies in the learning process. In conclusion, this chapter has set out to provide additional insights and new research models for using new technologies in formal and informal learning contexts for children.

Acknowledgements

The Block Magic project has been funded with support from the European Commission under Life Long Learning Programme Comenius.

The INF@NZIA DIGI.tales has been funded by the Italian Ministry for Education, University and Research under PON-Smart Cities for Social Inclusion Programme.

Author details

Orazio Miglino, Michela Ponticorvo* and Luigia Simona Sica

*Address all correspondence to: michela.ponticorvo@unina.it

Department of Humanistic Studies, University of Naples "Federico II"- Naples, Italy

References

[1] Connolly TM, Boyle EA, MacArthur E, Hainey, T, Boyle, JM. A systematic literature review of empirical evidence on computer games and serious games. Computers & Education. 2012;59:661–686. DOI: http://dx.doi.org/10.1016/j.compedu.2012.03.004.

[2] Erhel S, Jamet E. Digital game-based learning: Impact of instructions and feedback on motivation and learning effectiveness. Computers & Education. 2013; 67, 156–167.

[3] Piaget J. Origins of intelligence in the child. London: Routledge & Kegan Paul, 1936.

[4] Papert S. Teaching children thinking (AI Memo No. 247 and Logo Memo No. 2). Cambridge, MA: MIT Artificial Intelligence Laboratory, 1970.

[5] Bruner J. Acts of meaning. Cambridge, MA: Harvard University Press, 1990.

[6] Vygotsky L. Interaction between learning and development. In: Gauvain M, Cole M (eds) Readings on the development of children. New York: Scientific, 1978, 34–41.

[7] Newcombe NS, Shipley TF. Thinking about spatial thinking: New typology, new assessments. Studying visual and spatial reasoning for design creativity. New York: Springer, 2012.

[8] Atzori L, Iera A, Morabito G. The internet of things: A survey. Computer Networks. 2010; 54(15), 2787–2805.

[9] Gagnè RM. Le condizioni dell'apprendimento. Roma: Armando editore, 1973.

[10] Gagné RM. The acquisition of knowledge. Psychological Review. 1962; 69(4), 355–365. DOI: 10.1037/h0042650.

[11] Gagne RM, Briggs LJ. Principles of instructional design. New York: Holt, Rinehart & Winston, 1974.

[12] Skinner BF. Science and human behavior. New York: Simon and Schuster, 1953.

[13] Pavlov IP. The work of the digestive glands. London: Charles Griffin, 1902.

[14] McKendry E. Theory and practice in language teaching and learning. An overview of second language. Teaching Methods and Approaches. 2006.

[15] Bruner J. The act of discovery. Harvard Educational Review. 1962, 31, 21–32.

[16] Bruner J. The process of education. Cambridge, MA: Harvard University Press, 1960.

[17] Bruner JS, Anglin J. Beyond the information given: Studies in the psychology of knowing. New York: Norton.

[18] Bruner J, Goodnow A, Austin A. Study of thinking. New York: Wiley, 1956.

[19] Brown JS, Collins A, Duguid P. Situated cognition and the culture of learning. Educational Researcher. 1989, 18(1), 32–42.

[20] Bruner J. Going beyond the information given. New York: Norton, 1973.

[21] Papert S, Harel I. Situating constructionism. Norwood: Ablex Publishing Corporation, 1991, 193–206.

[22] Jonassen DH, Reeves TC. Learning with technology: Using computers as cognitive tools. In: Jonassen DH (ed) Handbook of research for educational. Columbus, OH: Merrill/Prentice-Hall, 1996.

[23] Levine JM, Resnick LB, Higgins ET. Social foundations of cognition. Annual Review of Psychology. 1993; 44(1), 585–612.

[24] Clancey WJ. Situated cognition: On human knowledge and computer representations. New York: Cambridge University Press, 1997.

[25] Barab SA, Plucker JA. Smart people or smart contexts? Cognition, ability, and talent development in an age of situated approaches to knowing and learning. Educational Psychologist. 2002; 37(3), 165–182.

[26] Greeno JG. The situativity of knowing, learning, and research. American Psychologist. 1998, 53(1), 5.

[27] McMahon M. Social constructivism and the world wide web – A paradigm for learning. In: ASCILITE conference, Perth, 1997.

[28] Miglino O, Lund HH, Nolfi S. Evolving mobile robots in simulated and real environments. Artificial Life. 1995; 2(4), 41.

[29] Miglino O, Lund HH. Do rats need cognitive maps of environmental shapes? Cognitive Processing. 2001; 4, 1–9.

[30] Ponticorvo M, Miglino O. Encoding geometric and non-geometric information: A study with evolved agents. Animal Cognition. 2010; 13(1), 157–174.

[31] Ponticorvo M, Walker R, Miglino O. Evolutionary Robotics as a tool to investigate spatial cognition in artificial and natural systems. In: Loula AC, Gudwin R, Queirz J (eds) Artificial cognition systems. Hershey, PA: Idea Group, 2006, 210–237.

[32] Galperin P I. The problem of activity in soviet psychology. Journal of Russian and East European Psychology. 1992; 30(4), 37–59.

[33] Rambusch J, Ziemke T. The role of embodiment in situated learning. In: Proceedings of the 27th annual conference of the cognitive science society, Mahwah, NJ: Lawrence Erlbaum, 2005, 1803–1808.

[34] Rizzolatti G, Craighero L. The mirror-neuron system. Annual Review of Neuroscience. 2004; 27, 169–192.

[35] Clark A, Boden MA. Being there: putting brain, body, and world together again. Cambridge, MA: MIT Press, 1997.

[36] Roth WM. From action to discourse: The bridging function of gestures. Cognitive Systems Research, 2002; 3(3), 535–554.

[37] Papert S. Mindstorms. New York: Basic Books, 1980.

[38] Papert S. The children's machine: Rethinking school in the age of the computer. New York: Basic Books, 1993.

[39] Harel IE, Papert, S. Constructionism. Norwood: Ablex Publishing, 1991.

[40] Kallman M, Thalmann D. Modeling objects for interaction tasks. In: Proceedings of the Eurographics workshop on animation and simulation, Springer, 1998, 73–86.

[41] de Ipiña DL, Vázquez I, García D, Fernández J, García I. A reflective middleware for controlling smart objects from mobile devices. In: Proceedings of the 2005 joint conference on smart objects and ambient intelligence: innovative context-aware services: usages and technologies, Grenolbe, 2005; 213–218.

[42] Dror IE. Technology enhanced learning: The good, the bad, and the ugly. Pragmatics & Cognition. 2008; 16(2), 215–223.

[43] Mor Y, Winters N. Design approaches in technology-enhanced learning. Interactive Learning Environments. 2007; 15(1), 61–75.

[44] Miglino O, Di Ferdinando A, Schembri M, Caretti M, Rega A, Ricci C. STELT (Smart Technologies to Enhance Learning and Teaching): una piattaforma per realizzare ambienti di realt aumentata per apprendere, insegnare e giocare. Sistemi intelligenti. 2013, 25(2), 397–404.

[45] Miglino O, Di Ferdinando A, Di Fuccio R, Rega A. Ricci C. Bridging digital and physical educational games using RFID/NFC technologies. JE-LKS: Journal of E-Learning and Knowledge Society; 2014, 10(3).

[46] Dienes ZP. Large plastic set, and learning logic, logical games. New York: Herder and Herder, 1972.

Chapter 4

The Internet Implementation of the Hierarchical Aggregate Assessment Process with the "Cluster" Wi-Fi E-Learning and E-Assessment Application — A Particular Case of Teamwork Assessment

Martin Lesage, Gilles Raîche, Martin Riopel,
Frédérick Fortin and Dalila Sebkhi

Additional information is available at the end of the chapter

http://dx.doi.org/10.5772/60850

Abstract

A Wi-Fi e-learning and e-assessment Internet application named "Cluster" was developed in the context of a research project concerning the implementation of a teamwork assessment mobile application able to assess teams with several levels of hierarchy. Usually, teamwork assessment software and Internet applications for several hierarchy level teams are included in the field of Management Information Systems (MIS). However, some assessment tasks in teams with several levels of hierarchy and assessment may be performed in an educational context, and the existing applications for the assessment and evaluation of teams with several levels of hierarchy are not applications dedicated to the assessment of students in an educational context. The "Cluster" application is able to present the course material, to train the students in teams as well as to present individual and team assessment tasks. The application's special functionalities enable it to assess the teams at several levels of hierarchy, which constitute the hierarchical aggregate assessment process. In effect, the members of the teams may have appointments of team member, team leader and team administrator that supervises team leaders. This application can therefore evaluate simultaneously different knowledge and skills in the same assessment task based on the hierarchical position of the team member. The summative evaluation of the application consists of work to submit as well as objective examinations in HTML format, while the formative evaluation is composed of assessment grid computer forms of self-assessment and peer assessment. The application contains two mutually exclusive modes, the assessor mode and the student mode. The assessor mode allows the teacher to create courses, manage students, form the teams and also assess the students and the teams in a summative manner. The student mode allows the students to follow courses, write exams, submit homework, perform in teams and submit self- and peers formative assessment. The theoretical consideration of the project establishes the link between hierarchical aggregate assessment applications and management information systems (MIS). The application is an electronic portfolio (e-portfolio) management system in the competency-based learning and an Internet test administration system in the mastery learning approach. The aim of the chapter is to introduce the reader to the field of hierarchical aggregate assessment and to show how to implement complex assessment tasks with several levels of hierarchy into an Internet software application.

Keywords: E-learning, E-assessment, Teamwork assessment, Hierarchical aggregate assessment

1. Introduction

1.1. General

The current research project is in the assessment field of education. The members of the project has developed an Internet Wi-Fi application that can assess teams with several levels of hierarchy. This application could be considered as an assessment management system (AMS). The application is a complex assessment task in collaborative mode display engine. In fact, during the assessment task, team members can be appointed as team members, team leaders and team administrators that supervise team leaders. These appointments define the hierarchical levels used in the software application. This application is able to process and manage courses, course material, students, teams, hierarchical appointments, assessment tasks, student's curriculums, student's progression in courses and also summative and formative assessments. The application stores all the assessment data to accelerate the organization's assessment process at all hierarchy levels. Hierarchical aggregate assessment of learning in the education domain is a subfield of teamwork assessment where teams have several levels of hierarchy and supervision. Team members are either students or members of any organization that participates in teams in a collaborative mode complex assessment task. In the mastery learning paradigm, this application is a system that presents exams [1] or a system that presents tests to be solved in teams [2] that is a test management system in comparison with the competency-based approach paradigm that defines the application as a collaborative mode complex assessment task display engine [3] and an electronic portfolio (e-portfolio) management system[4] because the application stores all the summative and the formative assessments of presented tests and tasks in its database.

Hierarchical aggregate assessment is a teamwork assessment project that groups students in teams with several levels of hierarchy and assign them a hierarchical position as team member, team leader and team administrator to present them complex assessment tasks in a collaborative mode in an authentic context. When the assessment task is completed, the actual teams are dissolved and the team members are grouped in new teams with new hierarchical positions to perform another assessment task. One of the goals of this chapter is that the term "hierarchical aggregate assessment" to be accepted by the scientific community. This process is shown in Figure 1.

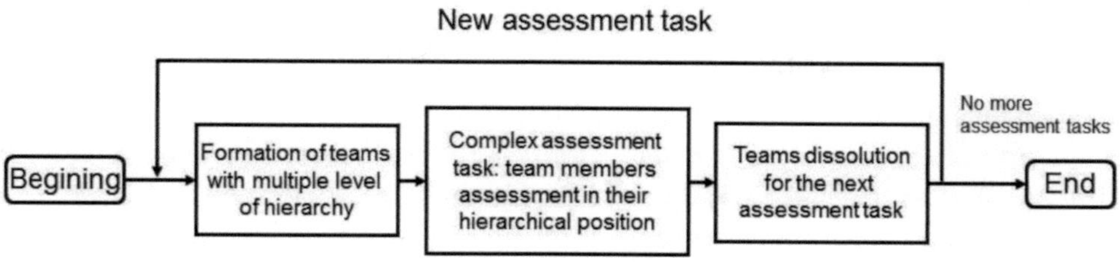

Figure 1. Hierarchical aggregate assessment process

Hierarchical assessment process is applied everywhere teams have several levels of hierarchy. This process could execute itself either manually or automatically with computerized algorithms executed on computer or Internet servers driving Wi-Fi applications. This process finds its origins in the management field where it is applied since human race worked in teams in large organizations. This process surely has been executed by Julius Caesars's generals to assess combat effectiveness of soldiers and their officer's leadership to lead troops in combat.

Hierarchical aggregate assessment includes the standard or the conventional assessment field that provides the same type of assessment for all the students in the class. Hence standard or conventional assessment process is the assessment of the same abilities, performances, knowledge and skills in the same assessment task. So standard or conventional assessment is a particular case of the hierarchical aggregate assessment field. Hierarchical aggregate assessment includes the standard or the conventional assessment and is the assessment of different abilities, performances, knowledge and skills in the same assessment tasks according to the hierarchical position assigned to the team member as shown in figure 2.

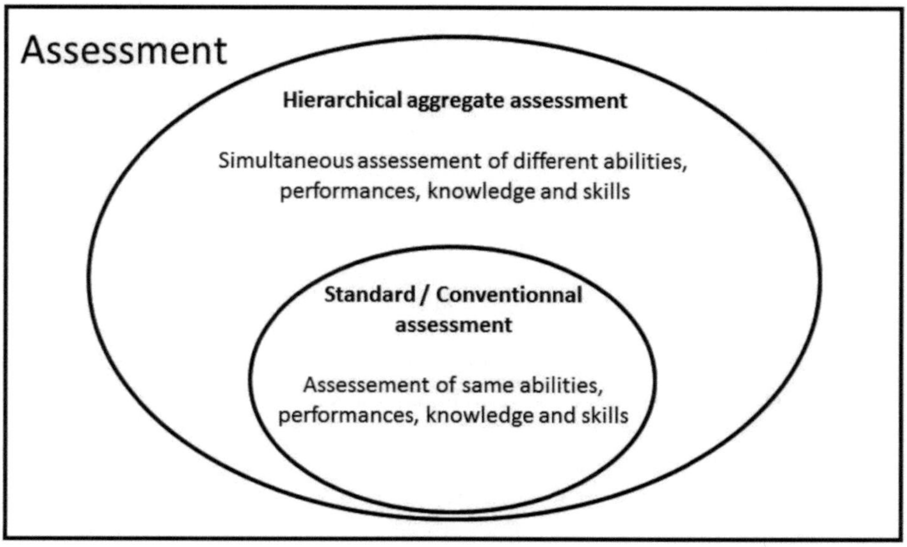

Figure 2. Situation of hierarchical aggregate assessment in the assessment field

1.2. Objectives of the actual research

The objectives of the actual research that is also the subject of a doctoral dissertation is the automation and the computerization of the hierarchical aggregate assessment process with Internet applications and mobile technologies (Wi-Fi). With computer algorithms, Internet applications and mobile technologies, teamwork could be done over the Internet with collaborative work applications used by team members. An Internet application named "Cluster" was developed by researchers of the CDAME [5] laboratory for a PhD project to automate and computerize the hierarchical assessment process with the research and development (R & D) methodology for the development of educative products stated by Harvey and Loiselle [6]. This application currently resides at the following address: http://eval.uqam.ca/cluster/.

1.3. Fields and application domains

The process of hierarchical aggregate assessment has been performed everywhere by mankind throughout the ages. Although the process of hierarchical aggregate assessment was performed through ages, no scientist has considered to define a particular case of teamwork assessment where team members have several levels of hierarchy. The domain of hierarchical aggregate assessment first situates itself in the field of management and its computerization is in the field of computer science. However, the actual research also wants to situate this process in the field of education through complex assessment tasks in collaborative mode with an authentic context, as shown in Figure 3.

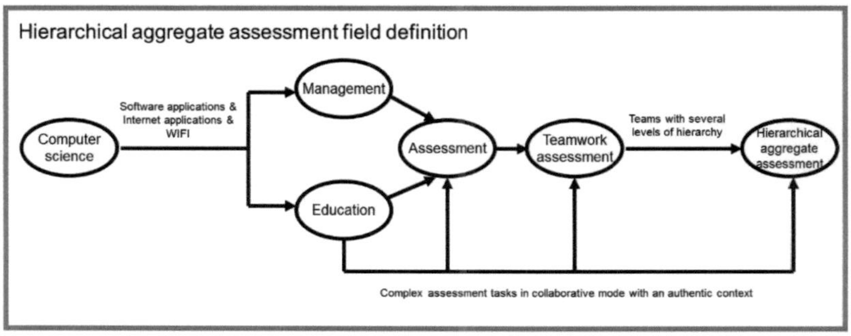

Figure 3. The field of hierarchical aggregate assessment

In effect, in the field of education, it can happen that courses or complex assessment tasks that could be performed in teams can have several hierarchical levels. The authentic context under the hierarchical aggregate assessment occurs when students perform the task in a similar environment to the workplace. This context also applies to the use of mobile technologies (Wi-Fi) in the workplace through which students can perform a complex assessment task in collaborative mode through their cell phone, iPad, iPod or laptop. The use of information technologies in the process of hierarchical aggregate assessment ensures that this process can take place in the field of mobile learning and especially in the mobile assessment field.

The "Cluster" Internet application is a complex assessment task presentation engine in collaborative mode with an authentic context that implements the hierarchical aggregate assessment process. One of the goals of this chapter is to formally define the domain of hierarchical aggregate assessment to be accepted and recognized by the scientific community.

1.4. Chapter structure and organization

This chapter will first define the problematics and the theoretical framework of the hierarchical aggregate assessment field. This chapter will then describe the computerized implementation of the hierarchical aggregate assessment process in the field of education. This process is actually implemented with the research and development (R & D) methodology of educational products defined by Harvey and Loiselle [6] using the "Cluster" Internet application. This chapter will finally present and discuss the results of testing of the "Cluster" application by high school students of the school board of Montreal in the study of geology and by army cadets for the learning of cartography by performing navigation patrols in teams.

2. Problematics

2.1. General

None of the teamwork assessment authors in the education domain as Sugrue, Seger, Kerridge, Sloane and Deane [7], Volkov and Volkov [8] and Baker and Salas [9] have specifically studied the field of teamwork assessment where teams have several levels of hierarchy. Usually, the assessment of organizations with several levels of hierarchy and supervision is part of the Management Information Systems (MIS) field. However, some teamwork assessment tasks in the field of education can have several levels of hierarchy. So, it is important to explore this domain to add new research and theories into the education and assessment field. This new field of research could develop interesting Internet software application as assessment management systems in competency-based learning (AMS) and test assessment systems (TAS) in mastery learning.

Until now, no scientist and no domain expert in the fields of management, information technology, education and assessment has studied and defined hierarchical aggregate assessment. No scientist has yet found a name to define an assessment process with several levels of hierarchy that has always been applied everywhere and has always existed. This process executes itself when individuals are grouped in teams with several hierarchy levels in order to accomplish a task. The research described in this chapter will cause changes and provide a name of this complex process that will be "hierarchical aggregate assessment". This definition will eventually be recognized by the scientific community.

2.2. Teamwork assessment

The problematics that is at the base of the process automation foundations of the assessment process of teams with several hierarchy levels resides in the development of a procedure or a computer application. According to Loiselle [10], the research and development methodology (R & D) of educational products is at the origin of the creation of educational products and the induction of theories produced by researchers throughout the development cycles of educational product development. In the case of the actual research, an Internet application implementing the hierarchical aggregate assessment process has been developed by researchers of the CDAME laboratory according to the research and development methodology (R & D) of educational products. The process of hierarchical aggregate assessment is the theory induced by the process of research and development for the implementation of an Internet application able to process the assessment of teams with several levels of hierarchy, as shown in Figure 4.

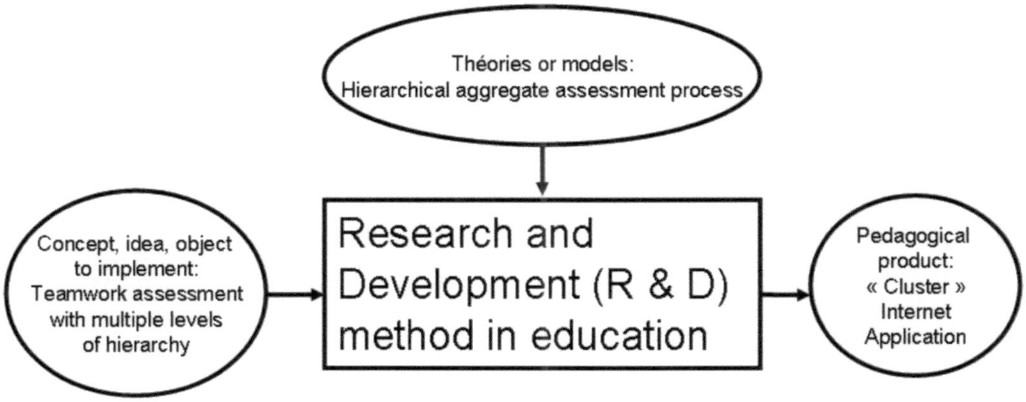

Figure 4. Hierarchical aggregate assessment in the field of education

The hierarchical aggregate field defines itself as a subfield of teamwork assessment. Teamwork assessment is part of both management and education domain. So the hierarchical aggregate assessment field is a common field of education and business administration domains. This states the problematics origin of the hierarchical aggregate assessment where the assessment of teams with several levels of hierarchy has been mostly studied by management and information systems researchers while very few work has been done on several levels of hierarchy teamwork assessment in the education field even if complex assessment tasks with several levels of hierarchy could be performed in a classroom of professional training, as shown in Figure 5.

A large amount of work and research have been done in the assessment field regarding teamwork assessment. Throughout the research and the produced literature, authors such as Sugrue, Seger, Kerridge, Sloane and Deane [7]; Volkov and Volkov [8]; Baker and Salas [9]; Zaccaro, Mumford, Connelly, Marks and Gilbert [11]; MacMillan, Paley, Entin and Entin [12]; Furnham, Pendelton and Steele [13]; Freeman and McKenzie [14, 15]; Ritchie and Cameron [16]; and Lurie, Schultz and Lamanna [17] performed researches and developed theories and assessment grids regarding the dynamics of teamwork with a single level of hierarchy that includes a single leader who runs one or more team members. So far, very few authors, scientists and researchers in the field of assessment teams produced research or theories

http://dx.doi.org/10.5772/60850

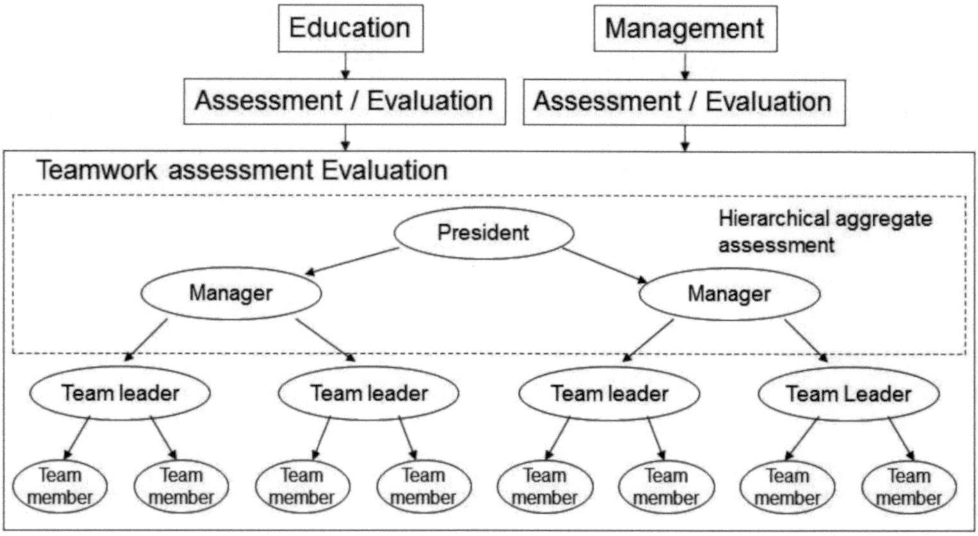

Figure 5. Problematics origin of hierarchical aggregate assessment

regarding the assessment of teams with several hierarchy levels (Lesage, Raîche, Riopel & Sebkhi [18]; Lesage, Raîche, Riopel, Fortin & Sebkhi [19, 20]; Sebkhi, Raîche Riopel & Lesage, [21]). This problematic funnel is described in Figure 6.

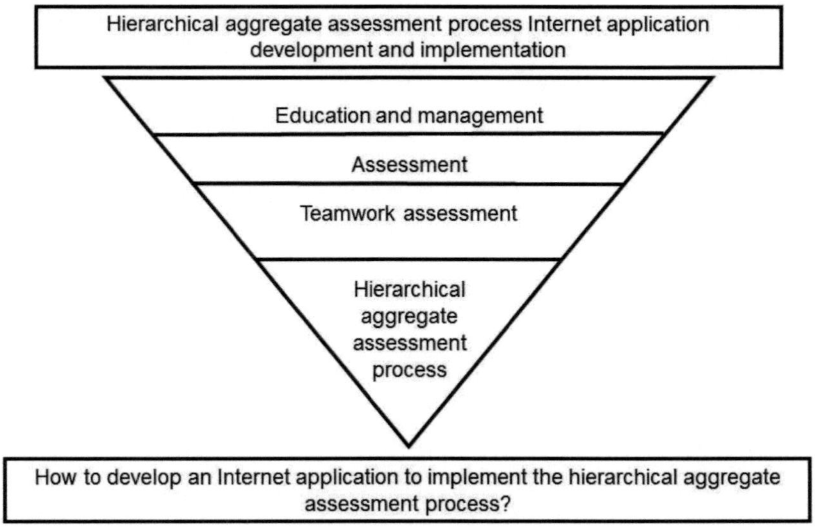

Figure 6. Problematics funnel of hierarchical aggregate assessment

The process of hierarchical aggregate assessment brings together team members into teams that include multiple levels of hierarchy where these people can occupy the hierarchical positions of president, team manager, team leader as well as team member, as shown in Figure 7. The structure of the team is in the form of a pyramid or an inverted tree representing an organizational chart in which each branch is a team which is a team member aggregate. The process of hierarchical aggregate assessment is the action of grouping team members together in a hierarchical organizational structure on several levels and then make an assessment process for each member of the team that is a leaf of the tree or a node of the organizational structure. The Internet application "Cluster" has implemented this data structure located in its MySQL [22] database, and its complex assessment task presentation engine in collaborative mode can perform assessment procedures for each team member or each node of the tree. So in one assessment task, the application can assess different objectives, skills, abilities and knowledge. This feature has not been implemented completely in other distance learning applications such as Moodle [23], Blackboard [24] and WebCT [24], and this statement defines the fundamentals of the problematics of this research.

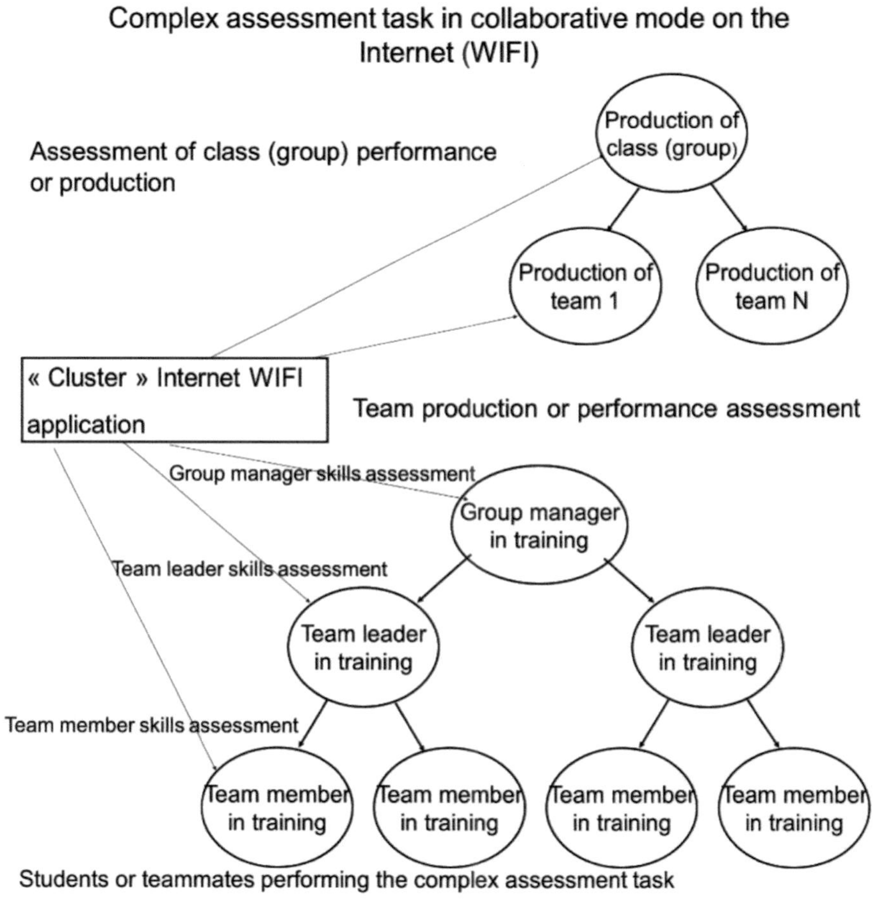

Figure 7. Hierarchical aggregate assessment process capabilities for simultaneous assessment of multiple skills

2.3. Available internet teamwork assessment applications

Online learning software (e-learning) and online assessment software (e-assessment) commercially available are Moodle [23], Blackboard [24] and WebCT [24]. These applications can implement collaborative learning via the Internet by the formation of virtual classrooms where a student may be a member of one or more working groups and may attend one or more classes. They have basic assessment features such as homework submission in electronic format by uploading files to be given to the teacher as well as possessing database repositories of many multiple-choice questions that are part of HTML autocorrecting tests. However, none of these applications have the data structure and software architecture to group or aggregate groups of individuals or teams of students to several hierarchical levels in order to achieve complex assessment tasks in collaborative mode as the "Cluster" application does.

Few of the applications mentioned in the literature is capable of simultaneous assessment of different skills and knowledge according to the hierarchical status of the learner in the same assessment task. The following authors studied peer assessment, but only for the assessment of the same skills and knowledge of team members having the same hierarchical status: Sugrue, Seger, Kerridge, Sloane and Deane [7]; Volkov and Volkov [8]; Baker and Salas [9]; Zaccaro, Mumford, Connelly, Marks and Gilbert [11]; MacMillan, Paley, Entin and Entin [12]; Furnham, Pendelton and Steele [13]; Freeman and McKenzie [14, 15]; Ritchie and Cameron [16]; and Lurie, Schultz and Lamanna [17]. The "Cluster" application data structure is designed to record the group organizational tree structure that contains the hierarchical levels, linking the team members together, while the Moodle [23], Blackboard [24] and WebCT [24] Internet application only allows them to record virtual classes without several levels of hierarchy.

3. Theoretical framework

3.1. General

The theories and research produced by the actual project are an extension of previous work made by Nance [25] that is using a similar aggregation process as the "Cluster" application to form teams with several levels of hierarchy for educational purposes to manage project teams in software engineering courses and also the work of Freeman and McKenzie [14, 15] on the development of the "SPARK" software application that is an Internet distance assessment system managing self-assessment and peer assessment made with assessment grids. Peer assessment is in level 5 of Krathwohl's affective domain taxonomy (Legendre [1]; Lavallée [26]; Krathwohl, Bloom and Masia [27]). Competency assessment in the field of hierarchical aggregate assessment can be made with observation grids or competencies assessment grids (Hubert & Denis [28]; Jeunesse [29]) and also with portfolio (Allal [4]) that usually contains self-assessments (Endrizzi and Ray [30]).

The actual research is based on the development of the "Cluster" Internet application which implements the process of hierarchical aggregate assessment. This application is a presentation engine of collaborative mode complex assessment tasks in an authentic context. The development of the "Cluster" Internet application finds its theoretical foundations in (1) the complex assessment tasks (Louis & Bernard [31]; Tardif [32]), (2) authentic context assessment (Palm

[33], p. 6; Louis & Bernard [31]; Wiggins [34, 35]; Hart [36]; Allal [4]; Rennert-Ariev [37]), (3) teamwork assessment (Baker & Salas [9]; Marin-Garcia & Lloret [38]), (4) collaborative work assessment (Swan, Shen & Hiltz [39]; Volkov & Volkov [8]; Boud, Cohen & Sampson [40]; MacDonald [41]; Swan, Shen & Hiltz [39]; Worcester Polytechnic Institute[42]), and (5) assessment grids (Durham, Knight & Locke [43]; Marin-Gracia & Lloret [38]) as well as self-assessment and peer assessment (Lingard [44]; Goldfinch [45]; Goldfinch & Raeside [46]; Northrup & Northrup [47]).

3.2. Definition of hierarchical aggregate assessment process in general terms

The hierarchical aggregate assessment is defined in general terms as a process that groups teams as well as a subfield of teamwork assessment in which teams have several levels of hierarchy and supervision (Lesage, Raîche Riopel & Sebkhi [18]; Lesage, Raîche Riopel, Fortin & Sebkhi [19, 20]; Sebkhi, Raîche Riopel & Lesage [21]). This assessment process with several levels of hierarchy and supervision in the field of education, that is one of the main theoretical contributions of this research project, has been named "hierarchical aggregate assessment". This process includes the formation of teams with several levels of hierarchy, the display of exams or complex assessment tasks to the teams and also the dismantling of the teams for the next assessment task in teams, as shown in Figure 1.

3.3. Definition of hierarchical aggregate assessment process in education

In the education field, the process of hierarchical aggregate assessment is defined as a team grouping process and a teamwork assessment subfield. In this subfield, teams have several levels of hierarchy and supervision where team leaders that could be students are assessed by one or many group managers that could be other students, teachers or professors (Lesage, Raîche, Riopel & Sebkhi [18]; Lesage, Raîche, Riopel, Fortin & Sebkhi [19, 20]; Sebkhi, Raîche, Riopel & Lesage [21]).

3.4. Situation of the field of hierarchical aggregate assessment process in the mastery learning paradigm

The assessment process in the mastery learning paradigm wants to determine the level at which the educational objectives are mastered or attained (Legendre [1]). Bloom's [48] cognitive level taxonomy of educational objectives allows to determine educational objectives by a statement describing knowledge, skill or performance and a description concerning the application of this knowledge, skill or performance. Bloom's cognitive level taxonomy of comprehension, application, analysis and synthesis is considered to represent the most important goals of the education field. This constatation has provided a foundation to raise the complexity level of tests and teaching programs towards educational objectives that could be in the higher levels of Bloom's taxonomy (Krathwohl [49]). According to some authors as Wiggins [34], traditional tests based on educational objectives are using out-of-context rote learning or open questions needing a few words for answers as an exam on multiplication tables. Those type of tests or exams are verifying if the students meet the criteria mentioned in the course curriculum.

The hierarchical assessment process is based on teamwork assessment. According to the mastery learning paradigm, the assessment process is realized by tests or exams that could contain items [49], questions and tests (De Ketele & Gérard [2]) and also work to accomplish [48]. As stated by the mastery learning paradigm, an exam or a test done in teams needs an accurate work or performance accomplished by a team at the end of a course or a study program [1]. Exam questions and learning objectives, concerning work or team performances, are included in the levels of Bloom's cognitive level taxonomy. In the hierarchical assessment process, the tests and exams are done in teams, so the persons taking part in the team exam can assess quantitatively and qualitatively the work done in teams to determine if the production or the performance meets the determined criteria; this type of assessment being part of level 6 of Bloom's [48] cognitive level taxonomy is named "evaluation". In some exams taken in teams, the persons taking part in the exam could do self-assessment and peer assessment. The peers' assessment process is part of level 5 of Krathwohl's [27] affective level taxonomy which interprets value or belief system classification [01, 26, 27].

3.5. Situation of the field of hierarchical aggregate assessment process in the competency-based approach paradigm

In the competency-based paradigm, the execution of a competency is based on resource mobilization to solve a complex situation (Van Kempen [3]). Competencies include the grouping of skills, attitudes and knowledge allowing a person to perform tasks (Bastiaens [50]). The competency-based approach paradigm replaces classical tests based on objectives by assessment tasks or situations that include social interaction (Allal [4]). Assessment tasks are evaluation tools that use or mobilize resources to solve a problematic situation or to perform a complex task. These tools are used to develop competencies with complex tasks allowing knowledge synthesis (Saskatchewan Professional Development Unit [51]; Olivier [52]; Louis and Bernard [31]; Tardif [32]; Van Kempen [3]; De Ketele & Gérard [2]).

The objectives of learning and assessment situations are to develop disciplinary and transversal competencies and to assess all students that must prove that they can resolve a problematic situation with their knowledge and skills (Bibeau [53]). The aim of competency assessment is to verify if the student has well used all available resources to accomplish a task successfully. During this process, students should be involved in their own assessment and perform their self-assessment (Jeunesse [29]). The competency formative assessment process is based on interactive regulation that comes with student-teacher interaction, interactions with peers and learning tools. The learner can imply himself in the assessment process with self-assessment, peer assessment and co-evaluation (Allal [4]). The hierarchical assessment process in the competency-based approach paradigm is the implementation of complex assessment tasks in teams. These tasks could include summative assessment that are performance or tasks to accomplish either individually or in teams and also includes formative assessment that is produced by self-assessment and peer assessment of team members. The competency-based approach in the hierarchical aggregate assessment field could be performed with observation grids or competency assessment grids as shown in Figures 21, 22 and 23 (Hubert & Denis [28];

Jeunesse [29]) and also with portfolio assessment (Allal [4]) that usually contains self-assessment (Endrizzi & Ray [30]).

3.6. Previous work and similar available existing internet applications

The current research project finds its origins and its theoretical framework in other previous research and through other distance assessment Internet applications that have been developed with a research and development methodology (R & D). These applications are SPARK developed by Freeman and McKenzie [14, 15] and Willey and Freeman [54, 55]; MLE developed by Marshall-Mies, Fleischman, Martin, Zaccaro, Baughman and McGee [56]; Mega Code developed by Kaye and Mancini [57]; and the application that is most similar to the current research project is a collaborative work management Internet application developed by Nance [25].

SPARK [14, 15, 54, 55] is a remote rating system that calculates the results of self-assessment and peer assessment grids to determine the final grade of engineering students on projects during practical work in engineering. This primarily detects the team members who have not done their fair share of work by giving poor performance in their team by letting others do their work for them.

MLE [56] is an application that predicts and assesses the leadership potential of high-level military managers such as colonels and generals with complex assessment tasks that are case studies and resolution of war scenarios.

Mega Code [57] is a software application used in the field of medicine and that is a cardiac arrest simulator. This application is used to assess the performance of resident doctors and nurses when they hold the role of leader of a resuscitation team who treated the case of patients who suffered a cardiac arrest according to the five main roles that are (1) the doctor who is in charge of the team, (2) the controller of respiration, (3) the head of the defibrillator, (4) the head of chest compressions and (5) the head of injections and intravenous infusions. The assessment of the team leader is made using an assessment grid that checks the two main aspects of cardiac resuscitation that are the team effort and the process and directions given to the members of the team by the team leader to resuscitate the patient.

The collaborative work management Web application developed by Nance [25] is used by students of engineering and computer science faculties. This application uses a multiple-level aggregation process for the grouping of teams that is similar to the aggregation process implemented in this research and in the "Cluster" Internet application. Nance's research [25] consists of the implementation of an Internet-based collaborative work application that is used to manage and assess the projects and the productions of engineering and computer science students. This application has the features needed to group students in teams that have multiple levels of hierarchy and supervision including team leaders and project managers (bosses) and project administrators (bosses of bosses (BOB)) supervising several project managers in the field of engineering and computer science. Nance's application collaborative work implementation is based on electronic mail (E-mail) and a discussion forum website.

3.7. Link between hierarchical aggregate assessment applications and Management Information Systems (MIS)

A management information system (MIS) software application "uses computer equipment and software, databases, manual procedures, models for analysis, planning, control and decision-making" (Davis, Olson, Ajenstat & Peaucelle [58]). These systems may contain information about the function, department and the hierarchical position of the members of the organization that are stored in hierarchical databases (Burch & Grudnitski [59]; Davis & Olson [60]; Davis, Olson, Ajenstat & Peaucelle [58]; Laudon & Laudon [61]; Laudon, Laudon & Brabston [62]). Some authors such as Kanter [63] indicate that the employee file can be sorted by order of position or assignment to identify employees who have the same hierarchical position. A database diagram illustrating an employee's position is shown in Figure 8. A hierarchical aggregate assessment software application is therefore a management information system where the employees to manage are students who have a hierarchical position.

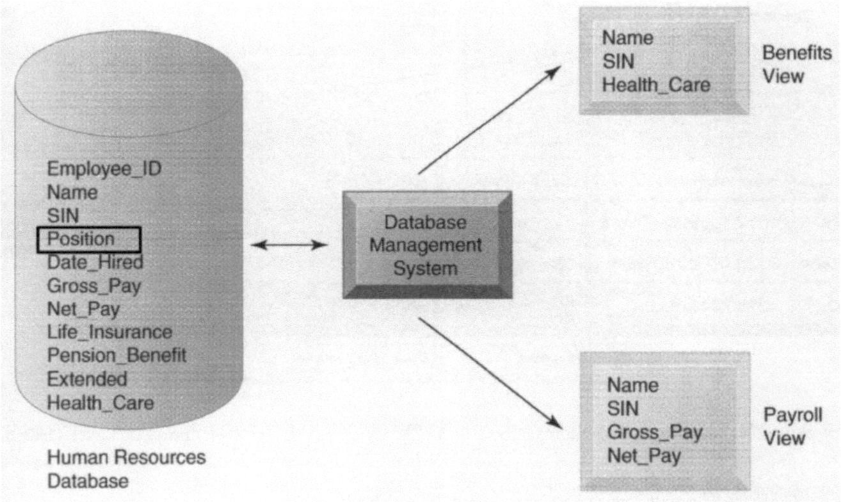

Figure 8. The record of an employee in a management information system database [62]

In the actual paradigm, there is a major difference between distance assessment systems and management information system software applications. A distance assessment system software application is a question bank repository stored in a database that usually presents the same questions or the same assessment tasks to all the students to assess the same skills and knowledge and there is no hierarchical relationship or hierarchy levels between the students. A management information system (MIS) is a software application that stores and processes management data and information on employees to produce information used for decision-making. The assessment data that a management information system produces and computes for the employees are usually sales data and production performance. Management information systems are able to record the hierarchical relations and positions of the employees, while distance assessment applications cannot.

In the hierarchical aggregate assessment paradigm, there is only a slight difference between hierarchical aggregate assessment applications and management information systems because both records the hierarchical relations and positions of the employees. The only difference is that the management information system processes management data, while the hierarchical aggregate assessment software application processes assessment data, course material, question banks and complex assessment tasks with several levels of hierarchy. Hence, any management information system could be modified to record course material and question banks to present complex assessment tasks with several levels of hierarchy. So the modified management information system has now been added hierarchical aggregate assessment capability and is equally now a hierarchical aggregate assessment software application, as shown in Figure 9.

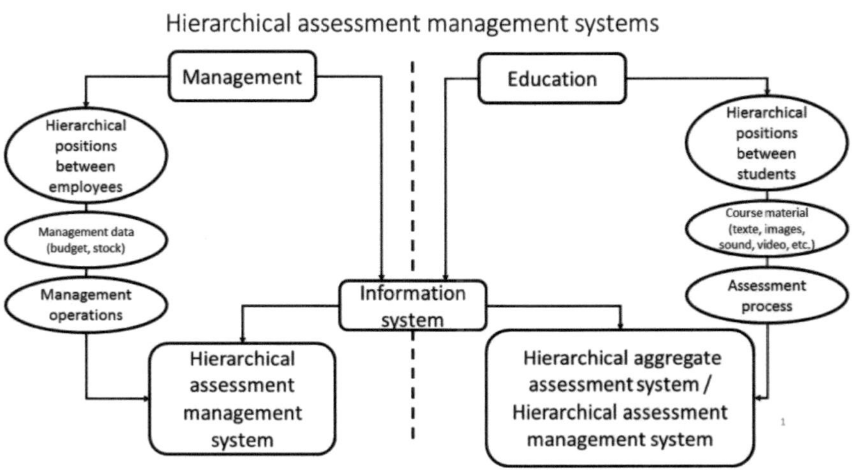

Figure 9. Link between hierarchical aggregate assessment applications and management information systems (MIS)

4. Methodology

4.1. Choice of methodology and software application design process

The implementation of teamwork complex assessment tasks with several levels of hierarchy is the implementation concept that was at the beginning of the research and development process (R & D) used to develop an Internet software application named "Cluster" that will be an educational product. The educational research and development model used is the one implemented by the authors Harvey and Loiselle [6]. The research project's objectives are to develop an Internet multilevel teamwork assessment application in accordance with the Harvey and Loiselle [6] model and to test the application with high school students and Canadian army cadets that will assess his usability with the Questionnaire for User Interaction Satisfaction ("QUIS") [64]. The Harvey and Loiselle [6] research and development process used in the present research project will give two results, the first result will be the "Cluster" Internet application and the second result will be the theoretical statement of the hierarchical aggregate assessment process for his acceptance by the scientific community.

The actual research project is the development of an educational tool that implements the hierarchical aggregate assessment process. Richey and Nelson [65] states that the development of a software application that will be used as an educational tool is part of the research and development (R & D) methodology for educational products. The development of the "Cluster" Internet application and its use by students and teachers will place this research in the paradigm of the research and development (R & D) methodology with mixed data analysis using qualitative and quantitative methods. The qualitative aspect is in the field of the interpretivist epistemology paradigm [66, 67] and used primarily to determine if users like to use the software, resistance-to-change factors as well as the assessment of the proper functioning of the software. The quantitative aspect of the research project, for its consideration, is in the field of the positivist epistemology paradigm [66, 67] and used to assess the increase in knowledge and the course success and dropout rate of students.

Regarding the choice of a research and development model, several authors have proposed models or developed research approaches such as Borg and Gall [68], Nonnon [69], Cervera [70], Van der Maren [71] and Harvey and Loiselle [6]. In all cases, these models include the phases of (1) problem analysis, (2) project planning, (3) production or development, (4) testing, (5) evaluation and (6) review [10]. The model chosen is the one developed by Harvey and Loiselle [6] because it is newer than Nonnon's model [69, 72], and it summarizes all stages of the research and development models of the previously cited authors. The research and development model used in the current research project is the model of Harvey and Loiselle [6] which includes five phases: (1) determination of the cause of the research, (2) determination of the theoretical background, (3) determination of methodology, (4) implementation or development of the educational product and (5) production of the results, as shown in Figure 10.

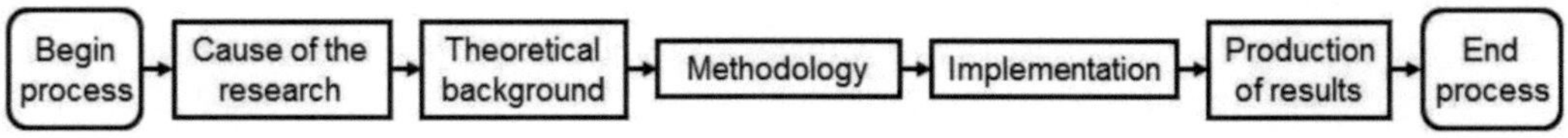

Figure 10. The research and development model of Harvey and Loiselle [6]

The research and development methodology is similar to the technical development of durable and consumable products used in engineering. Loiselle [10] defined the research and development methodology as an iterative process that involves seven steps that are (1) the preliminary analysis; (2) the prototype design and evaluation; (3) testing phase; (4) evaluation, revision and correction phase; (5) publication of results phase; (6) distribution phase; and (7) marketing phase. If the developed product has some lacks, failures or defects in the final stages of the development process such as evaluation, revision and correction, publication of results, distribution and marketing phases, the process returns to the analysis phase to find a solution to correct the defects of the product, as shown in Figure 11. The first functional tests or alpha tests were conducted by the authors of this chapter to ensure that the "Cluster" Internet application was ready to use by teachers and students. Once the functional tests were completed, the second series of tests or beta tests were performed by Mrs. Dalila Sebkhi's high school students [18, 19, 20, 21] during her third education bachelor internship where she taught geology for high school students of the Montreal School Board (CSDM). Then after, other beta tests were made by the authors through the distance learning implementation of map using for Canadian army cadets with navigation patrols in teams [18, 19, 21]

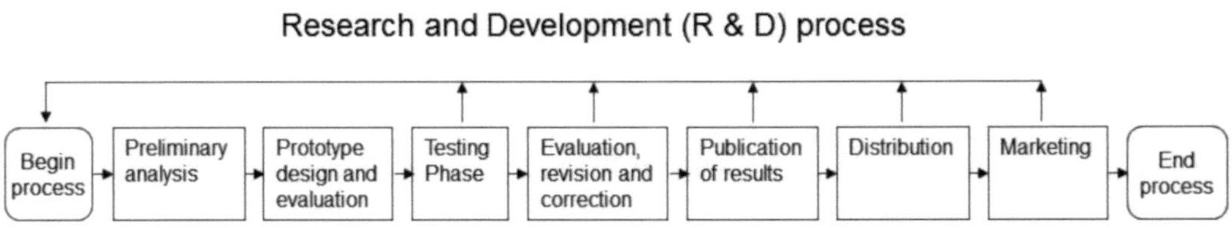

Figure 11. General research and development process (R & D) [10]

4.2. The testing of the "Cluster" internet application with high school students

The "Cluster" Internet application has first been tested with high school students during teaching assignments III and IV of Mrs. Dalila Sebkhi [18, 19, 20, 21]. These teaching assignments are part of the Université du Québec à Montréal's bachelor in education curriculum. This application has been used during Mrs. Dalila Sebkhi's teaching assignment III as an educational tool used as a teaching aid to support the learning of high school students for science and technology classes in the "La Voie" high school of the "Commission Scolaire de Montréal (CSDM)".

The experimental subjects were 113 (N = 113) 9th grade high school students divided into four classes. The course studied was a geology course that included sections on the solar system, the relief and also the rocks and minerals. The course content has been converted to electronic format and placed in the database of the "Cluster" Internet application so that students could access the course material at home outside school hours. This experiment only used qualitative methods and was based on the analysis of the testimonies of students and school officials who used the application. Mrs. Sebkhi would also have wanted to use the "Cluster" Internet application during her teaching assignment IV that included 118 11th grade high school students of the « St-Luc » high school divided into four classes which also belong to the "Commission Scolaire de Montréal (CSDM)". The course studied was thermodynamics. However, this experiment did not take place due to resistance to change because Mrs. Sebkhi's teaching assignment IV directors felt that too much time would be needed for students to learn to use the "Cluster" Internet application effectively.

4.3. The testing of the "Cluster" internet application with canadian army cadets

The "Cluster" Internet application was also experimented by the Royal Canadian Army Cadets with an experimental group of 27 young army cadets (N = 27) and with a control group of 12 cadets (N = 12) [18, 19, 20, 21]. All experimentation subjects came from two cadet corps of the Quebec province in Canada and had an average of 14 years of age. The current study was a military map-using course entitled "PO 122 – Identify a location using a map". The theoretical content of the course is found in the book "*A-CR-CCP-701/PF-001, Green Star, Instructional guides*" published by the staff of the Royal Canadian Army Cadets [73].

Both groups used in the experimentation had to study topography and map using to perform navigation patrols in teams. The experimentation group had to use the "Cluster" Internet application to study map using, while the control group has also to study map using but in a classroom with traditional teaching methods that are Canadian force instructional techniques. Subjects in the experimentation group were from the cadet corps "2567 Dunkerque" from the city of Laval, while subjects in the control group were part of the cadet corps "2595 St-Jean" from the city of Saint-Jean-sur-Richelieu. The cadet corps "2595 St-Jean" resides in the buildings of the Royal Military College Saint-Jean.

The classes given were part of a topography and map-using course that included five theoretical lessons that were (1) the different types of maps, (2) marginal information found on a map, (3) map symbols and conventional signs, (4) map contour lines and (5) four-, six- and eight-digit coordinates. The course material has been converted to electronic format and placed in the "Cluster" Internet application database. The topography and map-using course was divided into two parts: a first theoretical part where the experimentation subjects were studying the course material and a second practical part where the subjects were patrolling in the training area between two eight-digit coordinates given by the experimenter. Subjects or students in the control group had to study with traditional teaching manners the theoretical part in a classroom with a teacher, who in the military is called an instructor. Subjects in the experimental group, for their part, had to study the theoretical part of the group at home using the "Cluster" Internet application. However, both groups had to do the practical part of the course that consisted in navigation patrols in teams in training areas to prove the validity of the learning in presence and the distance learning on the Internet.

The validity of the experimentation was conducted using mixed methodology grouping tools of quantitative and qualitative methods. The experiment used qualitative research methods such as observation, interview and post-exercise report analysis. This is to determine whether the application was easy to use, the accuracy of training and if the test subjects had enjoyed using the "Cluster" Internet application. Usability and user interface conviviality factors are crucial to mitigate the effect of resistance to change during the implementation of software that will be used to make a transition from traditional education in class to e-learning.

Quantitative research methods used in the experiment were used to determine the levels of user interface conviviality and the influence of the "Cluster" Internet application on student learning rates. Quantitative instruments used in the experiment were (1) initial knowledge exam, (2) HTML auto-correcting objective exams, (3) work to submit by upload in electronic format, (4) final knowledge exam, (5) electronic self-assessment forms, (6) electronic peer assessment forms, (7) course module confirmation examinations and (8) QUIS questionnaire (Questionnaire for User Interaction Satisfaction) [64, 74]. Formative assessment is given by the students of the course using electronic forms of self-assessment and peer assessment, while summative assessment is provided by HTML questionnaires, homework to submit and course module confirmation examinations and also by the mark given by the teacher or evaluator for the practical part of the course consisting of navigation patrols in teams. These complex assessment tasks in collaborative mode consist of navigation patrols in teams using a topographic map. The results of the initial and final knowledge tests are not included in the course final result. The results of the initial and final knowledge tests are only used for the purpose of establishing research findings and conclusions regarding the increase of knowledge for both experimental and control groups. The QUIS questionnaire is used to quantitatively assess the levels of user interface conviviality of the computer application and the satisfaction level of the users, as shown in Figure 12.

The curriculum or course progression for a student is (1) to take the initial knowledge exam, (2) to achieve the five course modules performed in class for the control group and at distance with the "Cluster" Internet application for the experimental group that include a test based on a HTML objective exam at the end of each module that accounts for 50 % of the final mark, (3) to participate in at least three navigation patrols that will count for the other 50 % of the final grade in which the student successively held the team member, team leader and group administrator assignments and (4) to complete the self-assessment and peers evaluation forms after each patrol and (5) the teacher or the assessor is responsible for assessing the patrol team and will assign each student a mark for all the work he did during patrols and that will count for the other 50 % of the final grade and (6) the student will write the final or end-of-course knowledge exam.

5. Results

5.1. General

The "Cluster" application is now fully functional and resides at the address http://eval.uqam.ca/cluster/. The application is relatively easy to use and constitutes a software-programmable shell to implement courses. To create courses in assessor mode, the teacher needs the course material, the course schedule, the assessment tasks definition, the student's names and the team's organogram. The teacher has to enter all these data in the application's database to implement a course. Once the course is started, the teacher can form the students in teams and assess individual and teamwork tasks. To follow a course, the student has to login into the application. After the login, the student has to select the course he wants to follow. Once entered in the course, the student can study the course material, write exams, submit homework, participate in assessment tasks and submit self-assessment and peer assessment. The "Cluster" Internet application experimentation results with high school students and army cadets stated resistance to change by the users and the need to implement some software modifications to the application that were the addition of (1) a field identifying the name of the student group or class to the database, (2) return buttons to avoid the students to get stuck in the interface and course modules and (3) a course progression matrix for each student group or class.

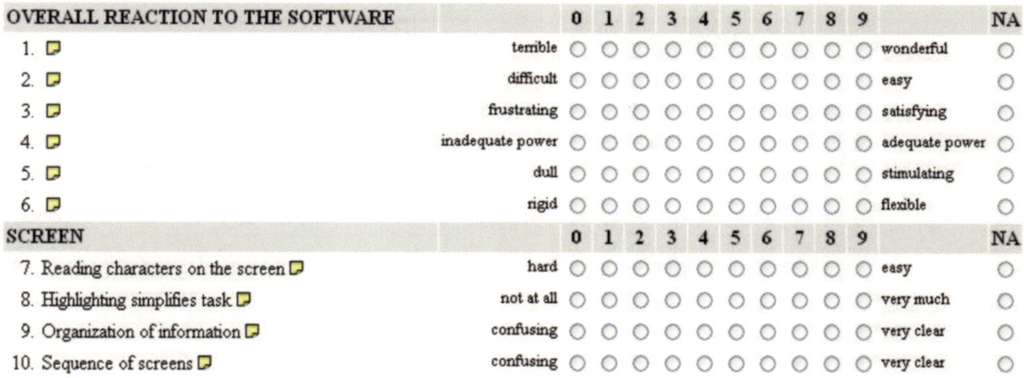

OVERALL REACTION TO THE SOFTWARE		0	1	2	3	4	5	6	7	8	9		NA
1.	terrible	○	○	○	○	○	○	○	○	○	○	wonderful	○
2.	difficult	○	○	○	○	○	○	○	○	○	○	easy	○
3.	frustrating	○	○	○	○	○	○	○	○	○	○	satisfying	○
4.	inadequate power	○	○	○	○	○	○	○	○	○	○	adequate power	○
5.	dull	○	○	○	○	○	○	○	○	○	○	stimulating	○
6.	rigid	○	○	○	○	○	○	○	○	○	○	flexible	○
SCREEN		0	1	2	3	4	5	6	7	8	9		NA
7. Reading characters on the screen	hard	○	○	○	○	○	○	○	○	○	○	easy	○
8. Highlighting simplifies task	not at all	○	○	○	○	○	○	○	○	○	○	very much	○
9. Organization of information	confusing	○	○	○	○	○	○	○	○	○	○	very clear	○
10. Sequence of screens	confusing	○	○	○	○	○	○	○	○	○	○	very clear	○

Figure 12. A section of the QUIS questionnaire [64, 74]

The actual doctoral project aims to computerize the assessment of teams on several hierarchical levels using a research and development methodology of educational products. Since the process of research and development in education not only gives educational products, but also theories, this research will produce the following results: (1) the definition of the hierarchical aggregate assessment process, (2) the "Cluster" Internet application, (3) considerations and changes caused by an experiment on high school students and (4) considerations caused by experimentation on army cadets.

5.2. Hierarchical aggregate assessment process

The process of grouping students into teams with several hierarchical levels that is implemented in the "Cluster" Internet application was the object of theoretical considerations of the research and development process that led to the statement of its definition. The actual doctoral project researchers would like that the term hierarchical aggregate assessment be accepted and recognized by the scientific community as a whole because this process has always existed and occurred in large organizations.

5.3. The "Cluster" internet distance assessment application

The "Cluster" distance assessment Internet application (e-assessment) is a collaborative mode presentation engine in authentic context. This computer application is developed in PHP and supported by a MySQL database. Phases of preliminary analysis and functional analysis of the software development process of the "Cluster" Internet application were done by the CDAME software analysts. The application development with the PHP programming language and also the software application database management system (DBMS) modelling and design in MySQL [22] were done by Frédérick Fortin [19, 20], information systems analyst and a programmer for the "LabMECAS (Laboratoire mobile pour l'étude des cheminements d'apprentissage en sciences (FCI))" [75]. The software architecture of the "Cluster" Internet application is shown in Figure 13.

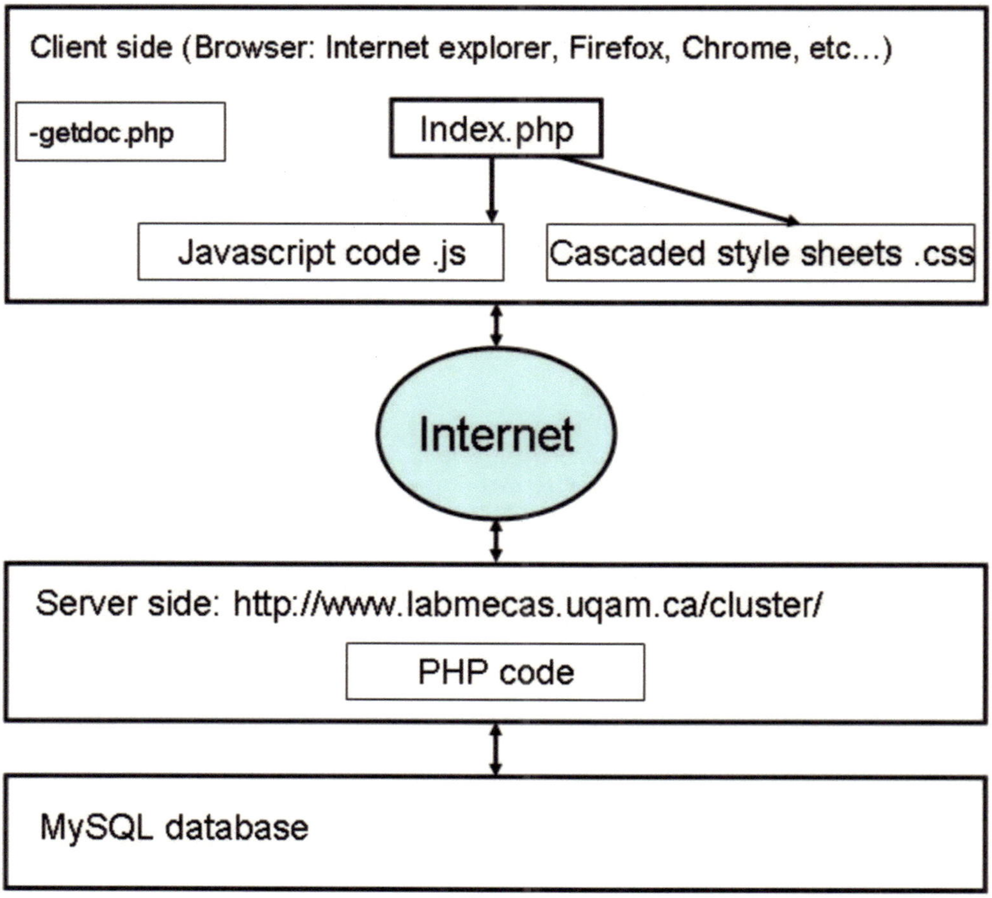

Figure 13. "Cluster" Internet application software architecture

The database management system of the "Cluster" Internet application is able to manage (1) student data, (2) course material, (3) team formation, (4) courses, (5) formative and summative assessments and (6) hierarchical relationships between team members who may have several levels. In the data structure, a course is broken down into modules, and modules include tasks that may have assessment or not. This assessment can be individual or in teams. Individual assessment consists of either HTML objective questionnaire examinations or homework to submit in electronic format with the system's upload functionality. Assessment tasks in teams include formative assessments that are self-assessment and peer assessment and also summative assessment that is the mark given to the team by the assessor for a production, task or performance. The database architecture of the "Cluster" Internet application is shown in Figure 14.

The application has two mutually exclusive operating modes: student mode and the administrator or assessor mode. In fact, the system does not allow an individual with an administrator

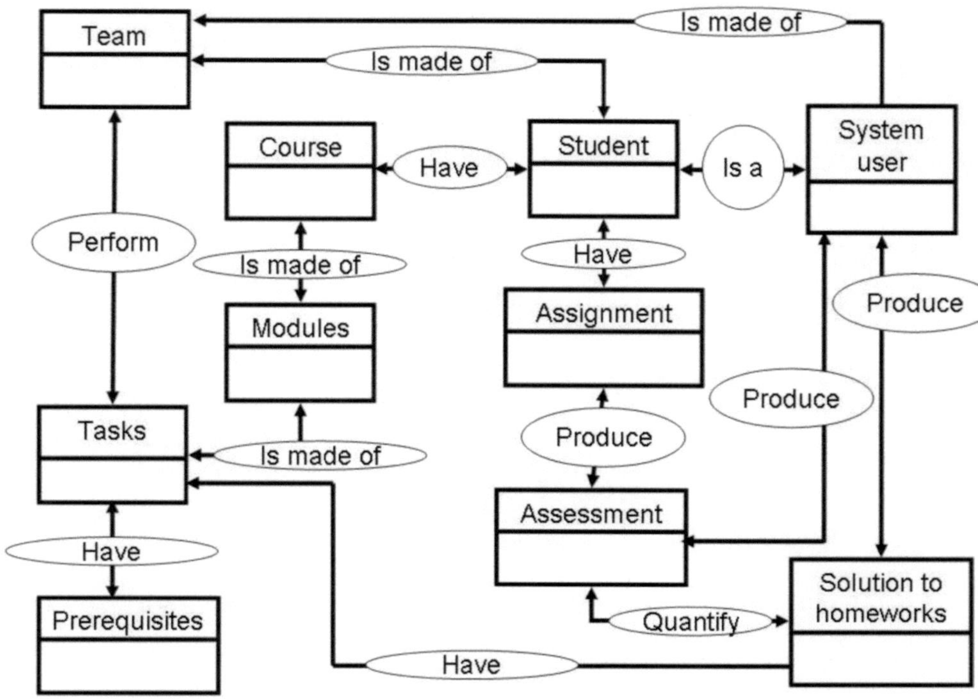

Figure 14. "Cluster" Internet application database architecture

or assessor status to study the course material as well as to participate in an assessment task as a team member. Furthermore, the system does not allow an individual with student status to change over the databases and students or to execute some system administrator commands. In the student mode, a user cannot give summative assessments and assess homework as well as team tasks. The mode of application is determined when connecting to the system with the login page when the system recognizes if the username belongs to a student, an assessor or an administrator. The home page contains the login parameters entry fields for username and password and is shown in Figure 15.

The student mode is only used by students or candidates on distance courses given with the "Cluster" Internet application. Student mode allows candidates on courses to (1) study the course material; (2) check out the curriculum record sheet to know what course modules are done and their progression through course modules; (3) perform HTML examinations; (4) submit homework; (5) be part of a team to perform a complex evaluation task in teams; (6) occupy a hierarchical position in the team as a team member, team leader and group administrator; and (7) fill in forms of self-assessment and peer assessment. Once the students have begun a session in the application, they can choose the course they want to study if they are registered in several courses with the form shown in Figure 16.

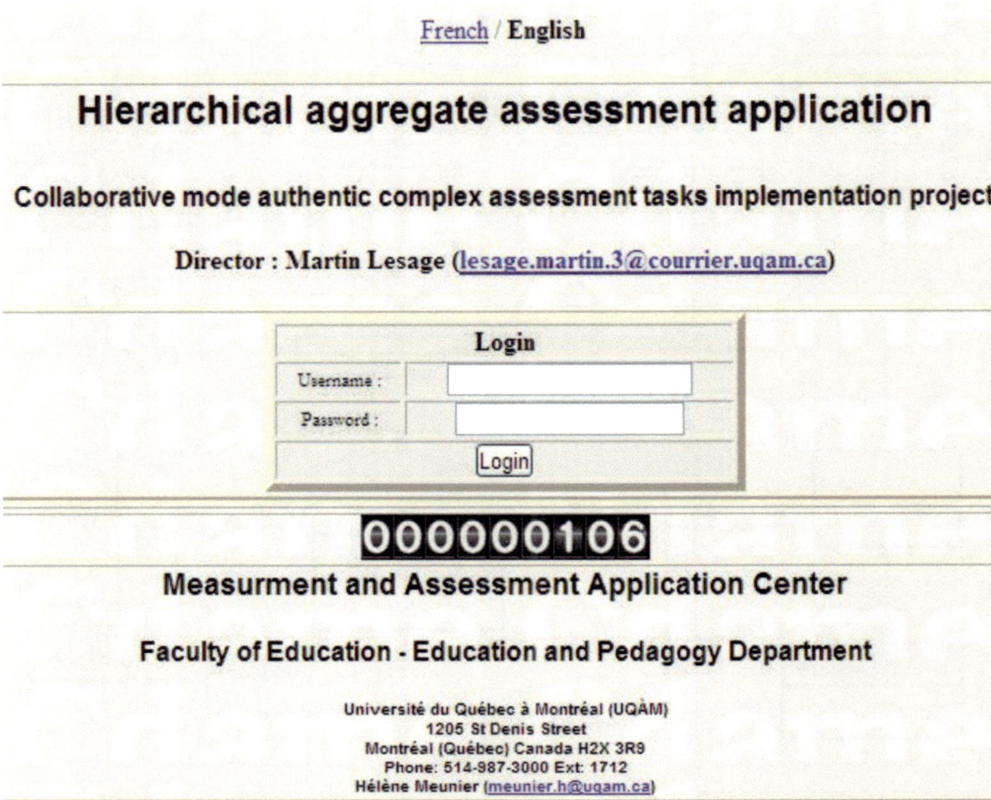

Figure 15. « Cluster » Internet application login page

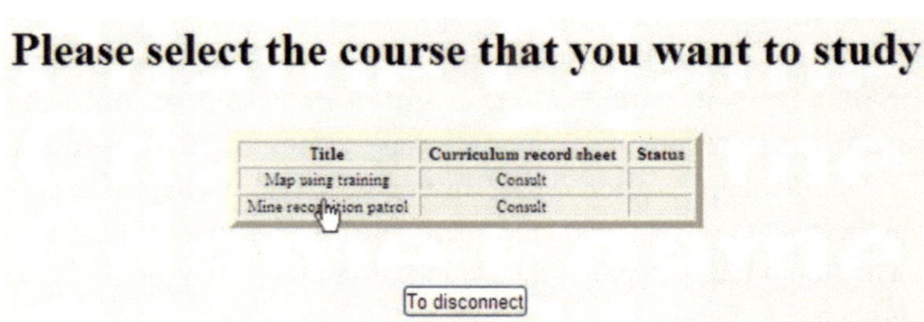

Figure 16. Course selection screen

Once the student has chosen the course he wants to study, the user interface drop-down menu allows access to the modules of the course. The course module selection menu is shown in Figure 17.

The menu allows the student to study the course material sequentially from the first module to the last. An application functionality prevents the student from browsing or to navigate randomly in the course modules. The student is only allowed to study the course material in

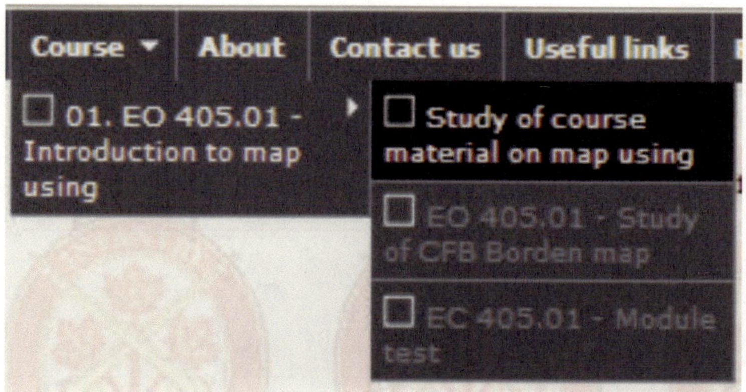

Figure 17. Course module selection menu

course modules from the first to the last, the last module being the end of the course. The application displays the course material for the student to be able to read it on the screen. When displaying the course material, a pop-up menu allows the student to save or print the displayed course material for future revisions. The course material is displayed using the computer screen shown in Figure 18.

The student can consult at any time the curriculum record sheet that shows the progress of students in the course modules and tasks. The computer screen representing the curriculum record sheet is shown in Figure 19.

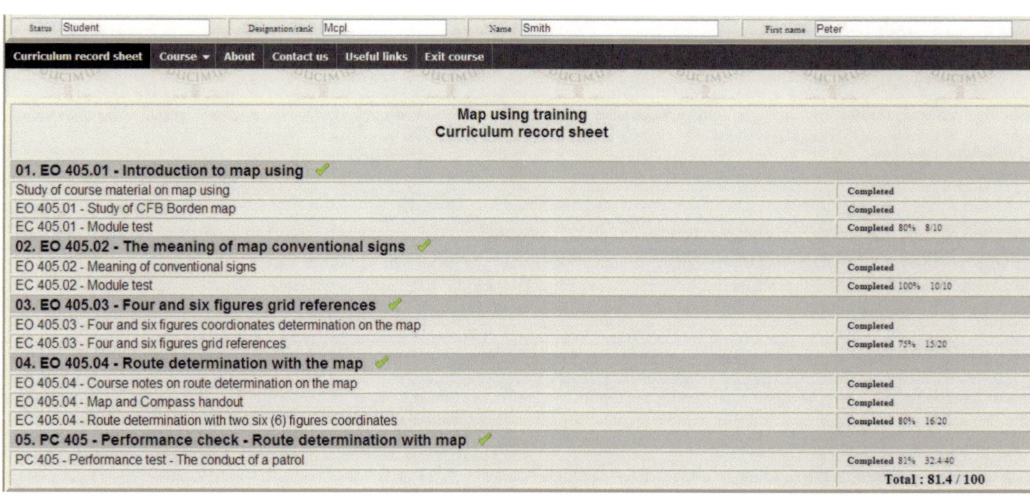

Figure 19. Curriculum record sheet display screen

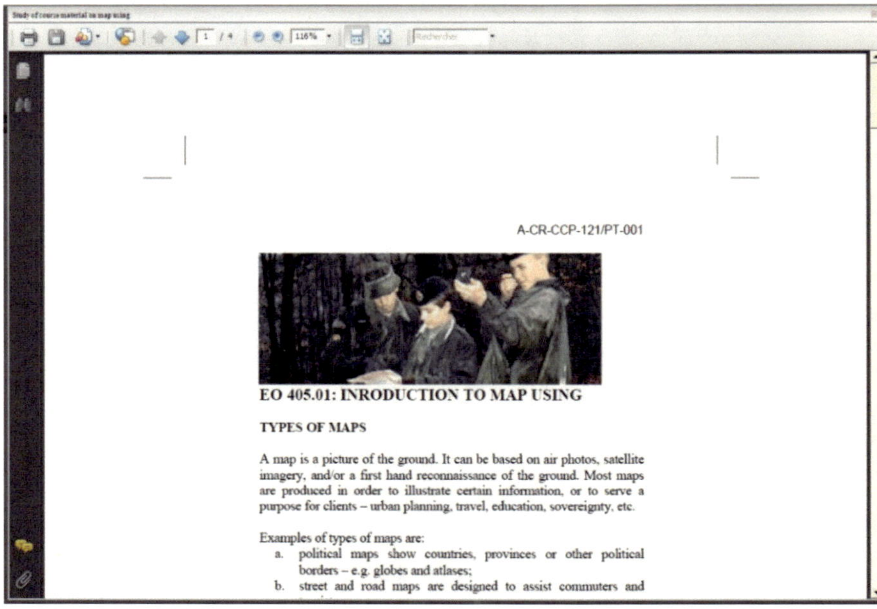

Figure 18. Course material display screen

PO 122.01 Test

Identify the type of maps
Weignt: 5% of final score

Question 1 - What is a topographic map? *(Choose only one answer)*	A contour lines representation A document that shows roads emplacement A reprsentation of the ground A document that locates political boundairies of countries, states and cities An electronic document that could by downloaded in a GPS
Question 2 - What detail or information is not shown on a topographic map? *(Choose only one answer)*	Rivers Forests Elevations Roads Production data for mines and petroleum troughout the country
Question 3 - What is to avoid when a map is used? *(Choose only one answer)*	Write on it with a pen Plastify or laminate the map Put the map in a plastic bag Spread or expand the map when it is wet to dry it Fold the map
Question 4 - Which type of map is similar to orientation maps? *(Choose only one answer)*	Road maps Statistical maps Political maps Topographic maps Nautical maps
Question 5 - What data, document or information is used to produce topographic maps? *(Choose only one answer)*	Street emplacements Tourist guides Mundial atlas Landscape sketches Aerial photos

Submit your answers

Figure 20. HTML objective questionnaire

The "Cluster" Internet application has two assessment modes: the individual assessment and the assessment in teams or teamwork assessment. The individual assessment will be processed with HTML objective exams and homework submission in electronic format by an upload function, while the teamwork assessment is done by the teacher and the assessor that can observe the team or assess a performance or a production with a mark. The HTML objective questionnaire is shown in Figure 20.

Performances, work and productions of the students will be submitted using a standard upload computer screen shown in Figure 21.

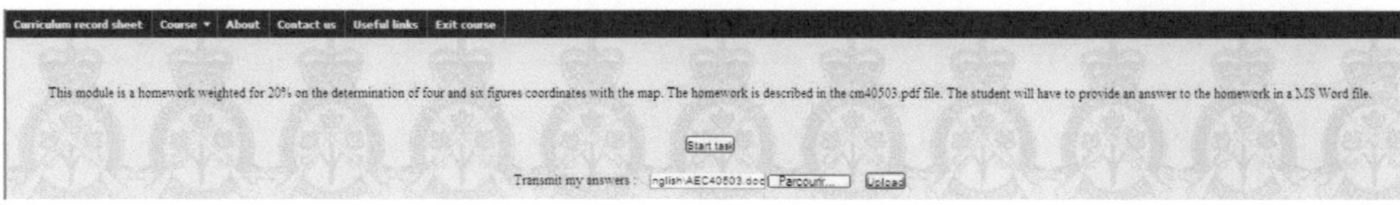

Figure 21. Standard upload computer screen

The "Cluster" Internet application is able to assess different knowledge, skills, productions and performances simultaneously in the same assessment task in teams. Hence, a student participating in an assessment task in teams can occupy team member, team leader and group administrator hierarchical positions. When the student completes an assessment task, he must complete the self-assessment and the peer assessment forms. It is therefore necessary that the self-assessment and peer assessment forms have different assessment criteria based on the hierarchical position of the assessed student that could be a team member, team leader or group administrator. The team member assessment form is shown in Figure 22.

The team leader assessment form is shown in Figure 23.

The group manager assessment form is shown in Figure 24.

The administrator or assessor mode is the operating mode used by system administrators, teachers, assessors as well as distance learning courses developers on the Internet (e-learning) to (1) manage and modify the student database, (2) manage and modify the course material database, (3) mark the students' homework submitted in electronic format, (4) assess the performance of the students in teams, (5) group students into teams and (6) assign team members hierarchical positions as team member, team leader and group manager in order to implement the tree structure made by the hierarchical aggregation of team members. The student management computer screen is shown in Figure 25 and allows the teacher or the assessor to create a new student as well as to modify or delete the record of an existing student.

The course task management form is shown in Figure 26 and allows the teacher or the evaluator to create a new course task as well as modify or destroy an existing task from the course material database.

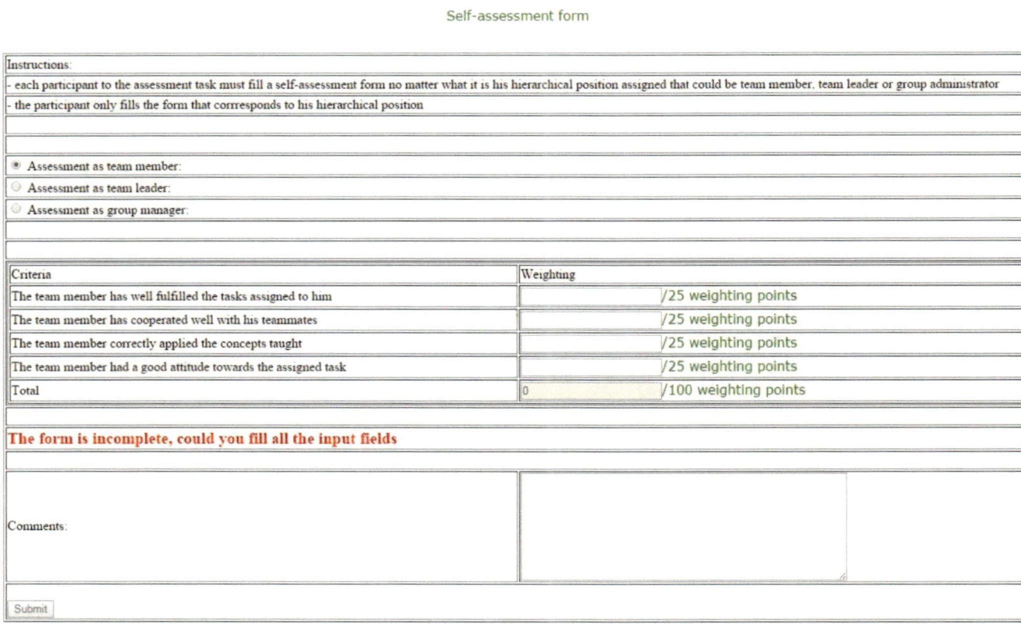

Self-assessment form

Instructions:
- each participant to the assessment task must fill a self-assessment form no matter what it is his hierarchical position assigned that could be team member, team leader or group administrator
- the participant only fills the form that corresponds to his hierarchical position

◉ Assessment as team member:
○ Assessment as team leader:
○ Assessment as group manager:

Criteria	Weighting
The team member has well fulfilled the tasks assigned to him	/25 weighting points
The team member has cooperated well with his teammates	/25 weighting points
The team member correctly applied the concepts taught	/25 weighting points
The team member had a good attitude towards the assigned task	/25 weighting points
Total	0 /100 weighting points

The form is incomplete, could you fill all the input fields

Comments:

Submit

Figure 22. Team member assessment form

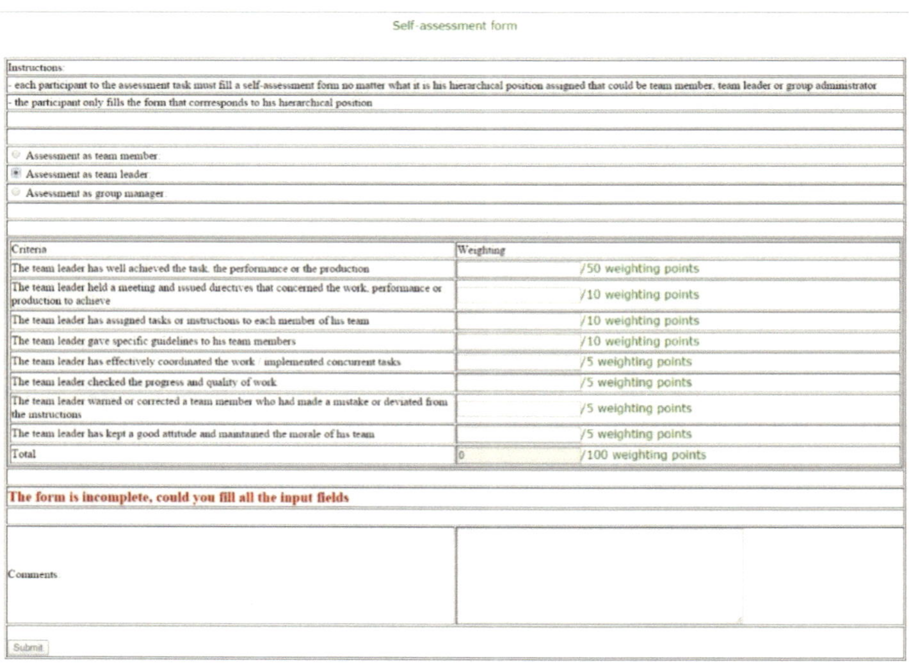

Self-assessment form

Instructions:
- each participant to the assessment task must fill a self-assessment form no matter what it is his hierarchical position assigned that could be team member, team leader or group administrator
- the participant only fills the form that corresponds to his hierarchical position

○ Assessment as team member:
◉ Assessment as team leader:
○ Assessment as group manager:

Criteria	Weighting
The team leader has well achieved the task, the performance or the production	/50 weighting points
The team leader held a meeting and issued directives that concerned the work, performance or production to achieve	/10 weighting points
The team leader has assigned tasks or instructions to each member of his team	/10 weighting points
The team leader gave specific guidelines to his team members	/10 weighting points
The team leader has effectively coordinated the work / implemented concurrent tasks	/5 weighting points
The team leader checked the progress and quality of work	/5 weighting points
The team leader warned or corrected a team member who had made a mistake or deviated from the instructions	/5 weighting points
The team leader has kept a good attitude and maintained the morale of his team	/5 weighting points
Total	0 /100 weighting points

The form is incomplete, could you fill all the input fields

Comments:

Submit

Figure 23. Team leader assessment form

http://dx.doi.org/10.5772/60850

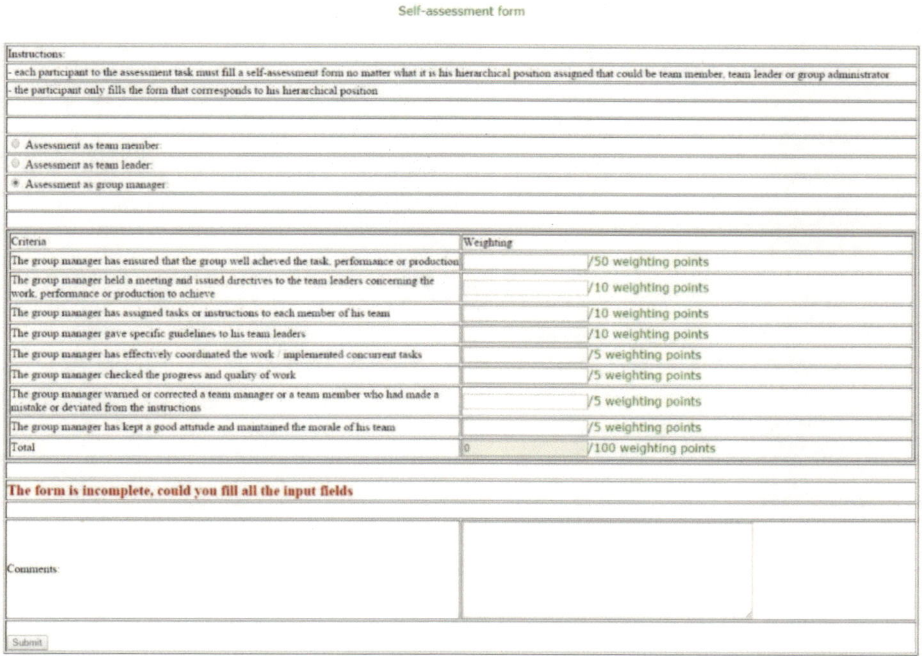

Figure 24. Group manager assessment form

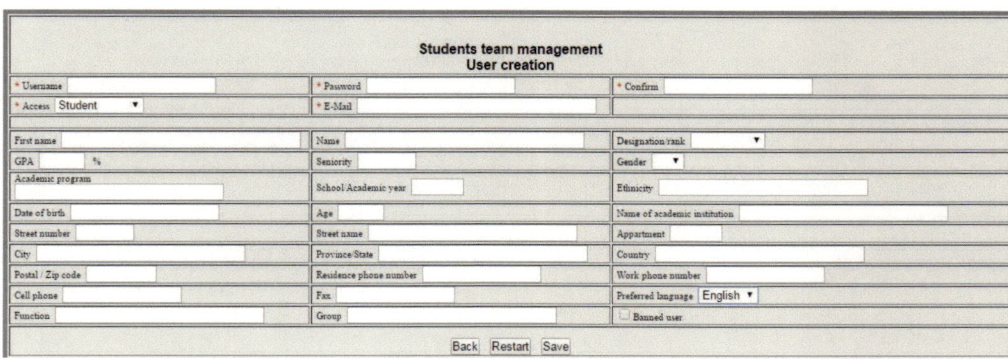

Figure 25. Student management form

The teacher or assessor may mark individual homework or assignments submitted in electronic format and write comments about a student's performance with the work or performance assessment form shown in Figure 27. This form is only used by the teacher or assessor for summative assessment purposes to give marks to work uploaded by students.

Figure 28 is a computer form that allows the teacher or the assessor to perform teamwork assessment. In fact, during a teamwork assessment task, each student is assessed twice: the student first receives marks or assessment data that is a formative assessment concerning his individual performance as team member, team leader and team or group manager. The student

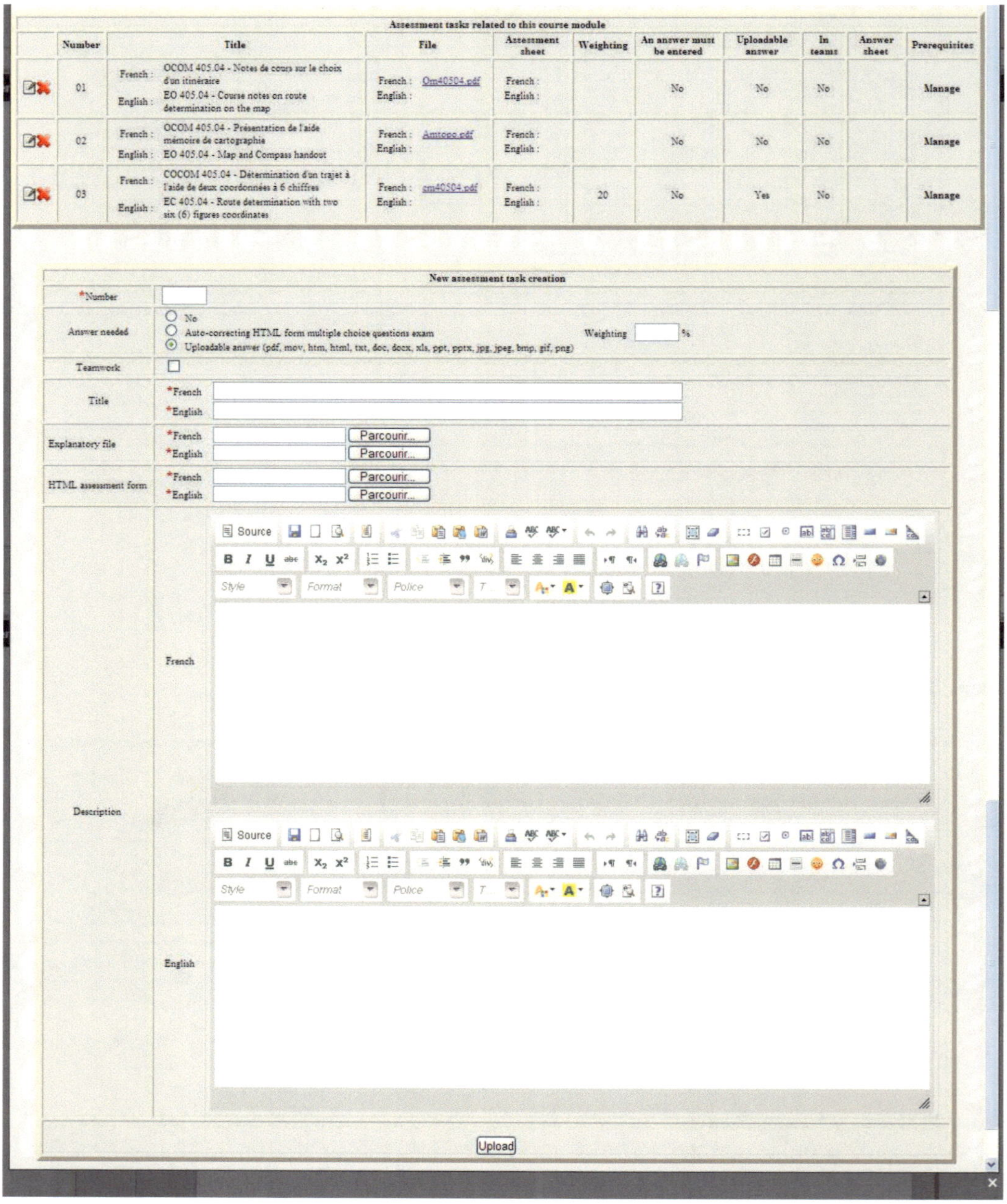

Figure 26. Course task management form

also receives a score that is a summative assessment for the performance he gives during the teamwork assessment tasks and for his individual performances that are homework submitted in electronic format and HTML exams. The teacher or assessor can assess each student performance during a teamwork task with the team member assessment form shown in Figure

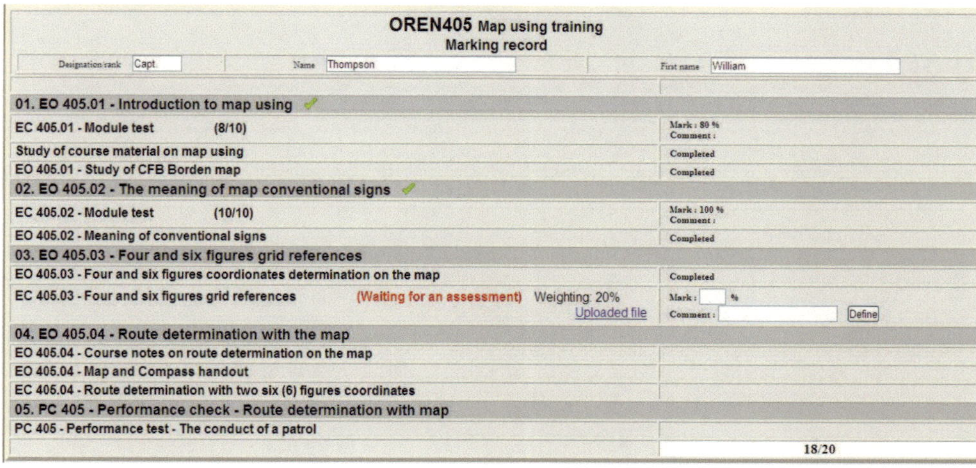

OREN405 Map using training
Marking record

Designation/rank: Capt. | Name: Thompson | First name: William

01. EO 405.01 - Introduction to map using	
EC 405.01 - Module test (8/10)	Mark : 80 % Comment :
Study of course material on map using	Completed
EO 405.01 - Study of CFB Borden map	Completed
02. EO 405.02 - The meaning of map conventional signs	
EC 405.02 - Module test (10/10)	Mark : 100 % Comment :
EO 405.02 - Meaning of conventional signs	Completed
03. EO 405.03 - Four and six figures grid references	
EO 405.03 - Four and six figures coordionates determination on the map	Completed
EC 405.03 - Four and six figures grid references (Waiting for an assessment) Weighting: 20% Uploaded file	Mark : % Comment : Define
04. EO 405.04 - Route determination with the map	
EO 405.04 - Course notes on route determination on the map	
EO 405.04 - Map and Compass handout	
EC 405.04 - Route determination with two six (6) figures coordinates	
05. PC 405 - Performance check - Route determination with map	
PC 405 - Performance test - The conduct of a patrol	
	18/20

Figure 27. Student's individual work or performance assessment form

28, which is the same form used by students to give self-assessment and peer assessment previously shown in Figure 22. This assessment form then has two functions: first, it is used for formative assessment by students who use them for self-assessment and peer assessment. Secondly, it is used to make summative assessment by teachers or assessors to mark the individual performance of the student in his team.

The software application team member individual assessment screen is shown in Figure 29.

Once all individual formative assessment is done by team members with the completion of self-assessment and peer assessment forms, a data entry form shown in Figure 30 is presented to the assessor to enter the mark or the score for the assessment of the task done in a team.

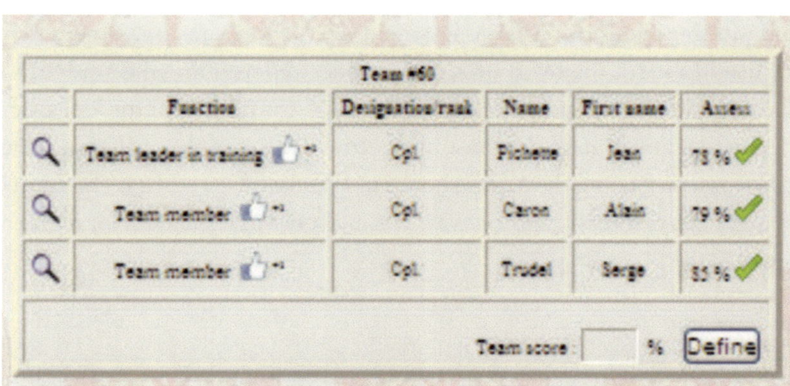

Team #60

	Function	Designation/rank	Name	First name	Assess
	Team leader in training	Cpl.	Pichette	Jean	78 %
	Team member	Cpl.	Caron	Alain	79 %
	Team member	Cpl.	Trudel	Serge	55 %

Team score: % Define

Figure 30. Screen for the assessment of a task in a team

The teacher or the assessor gives summative assessment to the student by observing his team performance based on his hierarchical position, which can be either as team member, team

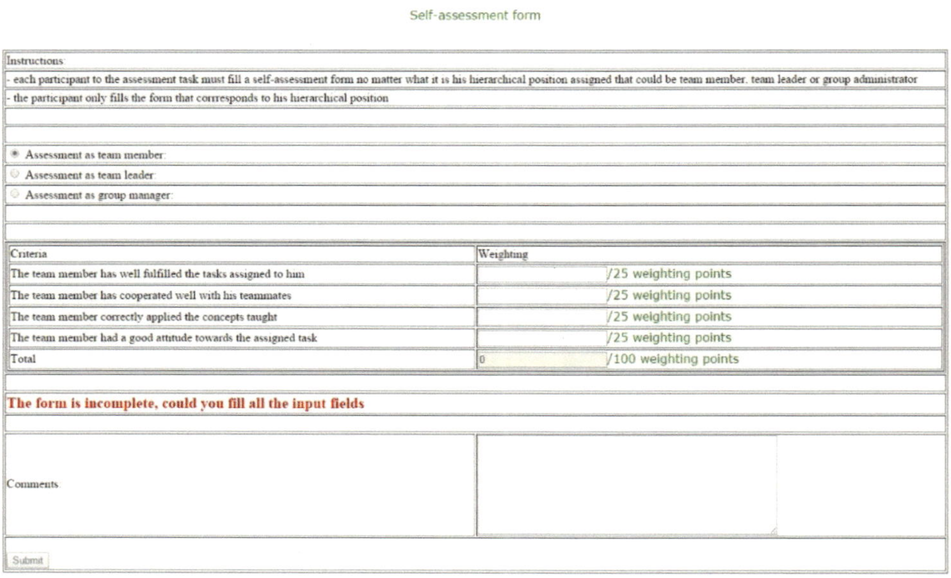

Self-assessment form

Instructions
- each participant to the assessment task must fill a self-assessment form no matter what it is his hierarchical position assigned that could be team member, team leader or group administrator
- the participant only fills the form that corresponds to his hierarchical position

Assessment as team member
Assessment as team leader
Assessment as group manager

Criteria	Weighting
The team member has well fulfilled the tasks assigned to him	/25 weighting points
The team member has cooperated well with his teammates	/25 weighting points
The team member correctly applied the concepts taught	/25 weighting points
The team member had a good attitude towards the assigned task	/25 weighting points
Total	0 /100 weighting points

The form is incomplete, could you fill all the input fields

Comments

Submit

Figure 28. Team member assessment form

leader or group manager. The assessment criteria on the assessment forms are different depending on the hierarchical position occupied by the student, as shown by Figures 22, 23 and 24. This feature is a direct implementation of the problematics of teamwork assessment with several hierarchical levels. This functionality is currently only implemented in the "Cluster" Internet application and is not found in any other e-learning and e-assessment Internet applications such as Moodle, WebCT and Blackboard.

During the teamwork assessment process, the teacher or the assessor has to produce both formative and summative individual assessment and teamwork assessment. These assessments will be used to mark the team productions and to determine the student's final grade for a given course. To assess a student and assign grades, the teacher or the assessor can consult the "Cluster" Internet application database and retrieve the student's self-assessments as well as all the peer assessment using the forms shown in Figures 22, 23 and 24. The computer screen that displays all of the results of self-assessments and peer assessments for a given student is shown in Figure 31.

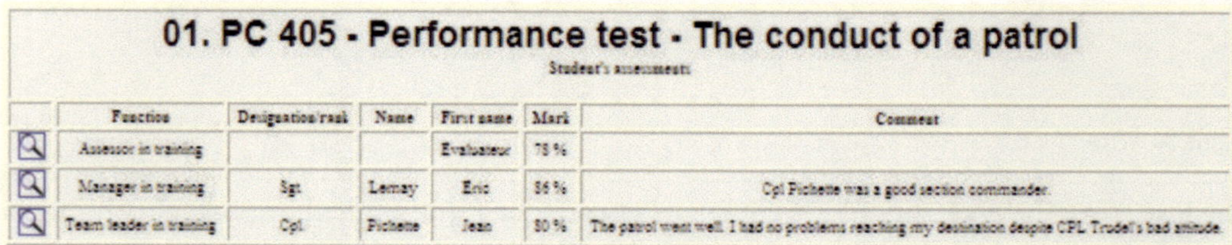

01. PC 405 - Performance test - The conduct of a patrol

Student's assessments

	Function	Designation/rank	Name	First name	Mark	Comment
	Assessor in training			Evaluateur	78 %	
	Manager in training	Sgt	Lemay	Eric	86 %	Cpl Pichette was a good section commander.
	Team leader in training	Cpl	Pichette	Jean	80 %	The patrol went well. I had no problems reaching my destination despite CPL Trudel's bad attitude.

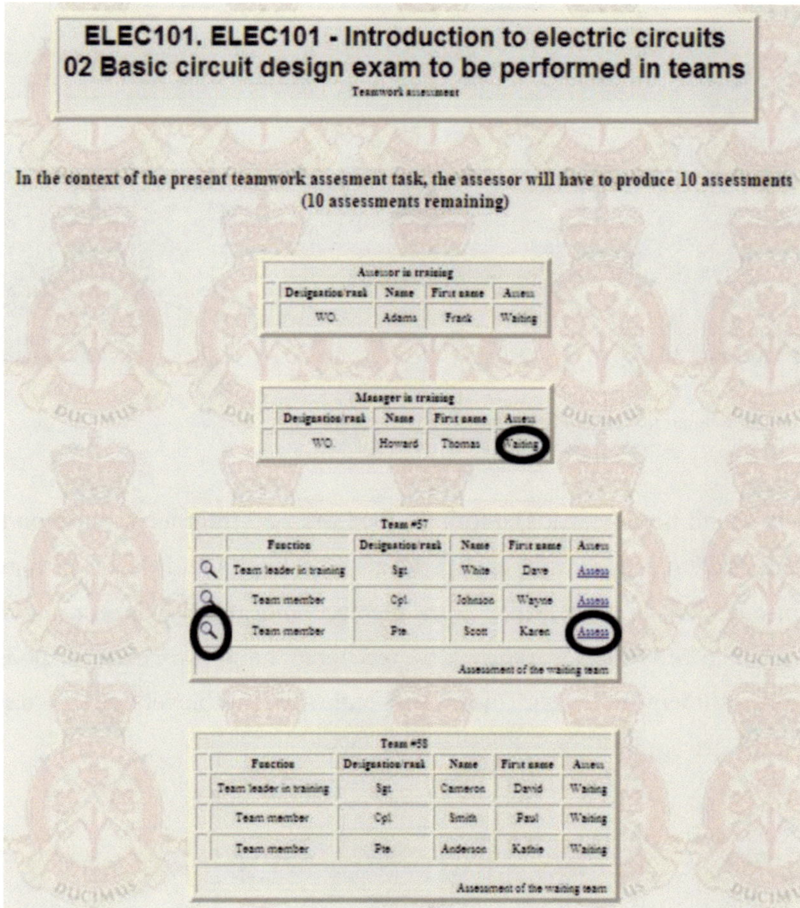

Figure 29. Team member individual assessment screen

Figure 31. Self-assessment and peer assessment display screen

The course final grade is computed by (1) the sum of all the individual scores that includes HTML exams and homework to submit in the course modules and (2) the sum of all scores assigned by the teacher or the assessor to the student for the tasks he performed as a team member. Finally, the main innovation of the "Cluster" Internet application at the origin of current doctoral project is the aggregation function whose tree data structure is implemented into the application's database and thereby allows the grouping of students into teams with multiple hierarchical levels. This feature allows the system to assign the student hierarchical functions such as team member, team leader and group manager. The aggregation function is accessible from the main menu of the application that is shown in Figure 32.

The aggregation functionality implemented in the "Cluster" Internet application provides a solution to the problem of the current research project concerning the implementation of an assessment process for the teams with several hierarchical levels that is less implemented in

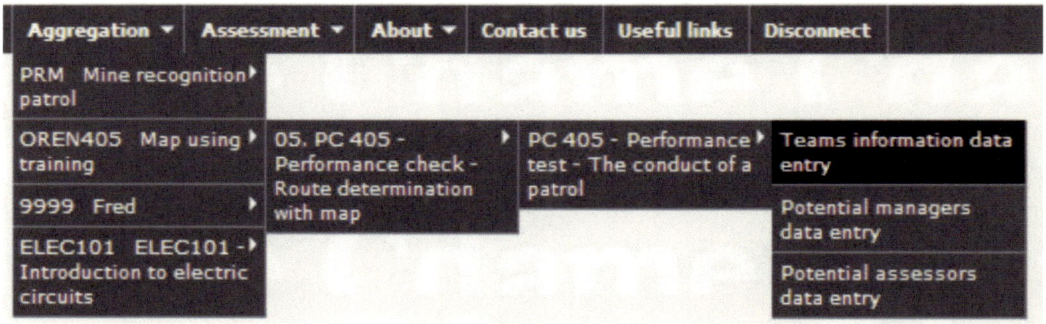

Figure 32. Aggregation menu for team formation

Moodle, WebCT and Blackboard. The form of the "Cluster" Internet application that implements the aggregation process that groups teams of students with levels of hierarchy and assigns team members as team leader, team member and group manager is the computer screen shown in Figure 33. The form enables the teacher or the assessor to begin the aggregation process to group students in teams. This process builds the multilevel tree structure stored in the MySQL database application.

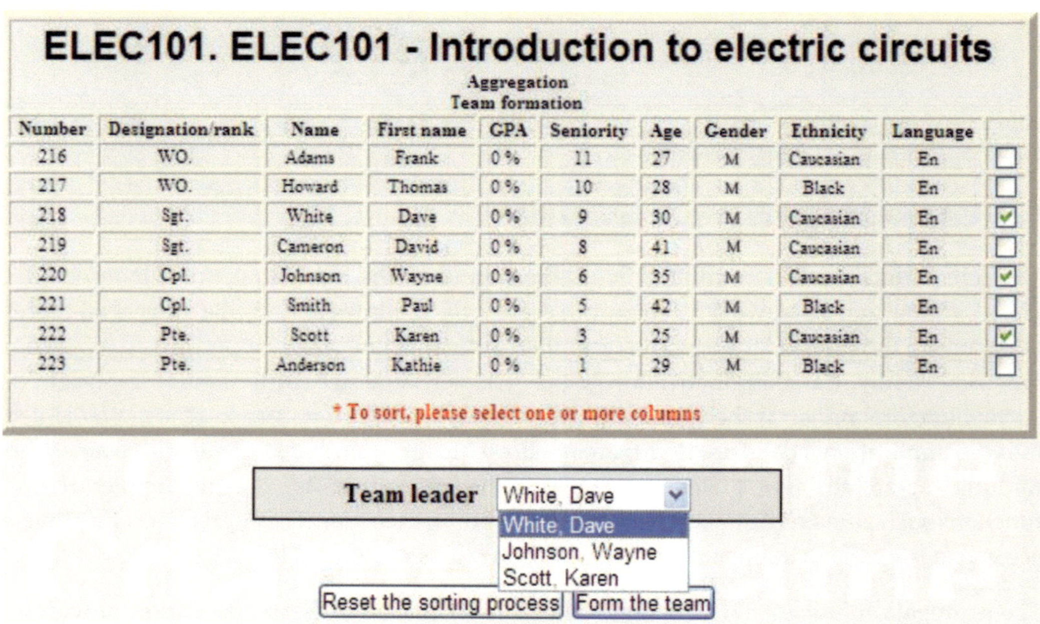

Figure 33. Aggregation process and team formation screen

5.4. Experimentation with high school students

The testing of the "Cluster" Internet application performed on high school students by Mrs. Dalila Sebkhi [18, 19, 20, 21] were the first beta tests used to experiment the application on a large population of over 100 students (N > 100). Alpha tests were done before Mrs. Dalila Sebkhi's experimentation by the CDAME researchers [18, 19, 20, 21]. In this experiment, the "Cluster" Internet application was used by high school students of the province of Quebec as an alternative method to teach geology courses. The results of the experiment were purely qualitative and were based on Mrs. Sebkhi's observations during the experiment where students used the application in their geology classes. Several students who used the application "Cluster" and some directors of the Montreal School Board argued that the application user interface was too rigid and not friendly enough for students who were teenagers from 12 to 16 years of age.

The high school students wanted the applications' user interface to make more use of multimedia elements such as videos and animated graphics so that the course would be more like a video game with avatars as in the "Mecanika" application implemented by François Boucher-Genesse [76] rather than the actual "Cluster" Internet application's basic drop-down menus user interface. However, for some students, learning to use the "Cluster" Internet application was simple and easy. These students did not had any problem to study the course material, review all the course modules and take the geology course exams placed at the end of course modules while the less talented students had experienced various problems when using the "Cluster" Internet application such as (1) resistance to change, (2) losses of usernames and passwords, (3) errors while filling the HTML exams, (4) being lost in navigation when studying the course material, (5) impossibility to go back in the user interface navigation if the course material is not understood or saved and that the student wants to regain access to the course materials or to the previous sections and (6) difficulty for teachers or course assessors to keep track of progress while performing modules and examinations for groups or classes having a large number of students.

Mrs. Sebkhi's high school students faced the described problems; she therefore requested that four modifications could be made to the "Cluster" Internet application user interface [18, 19, 20, 21]. These changes were implemented a few months after the end of his teaching assignment III so that Mrs. Sebkhi could use the new functionalities of the application to the start of her teaching assignment IV. The first modification shown in Figure 34 was the addition of a field in the database to identify the group or the student's class so that all students in the database are divided into classes or groups.

The second modification is the implementation of a back button allowing the student to be able to return to the previous module or chapter, as shown in Figure 35.

The third modification shown in Figure 36 is the implementation of a form to access the curriculum record sheet of all the students registered in the "Cluster" Internet application database. This form will allow the teacher or the assessor to access the curriculum record sheet of a given student to know his progression into the course modules without having to open a session (login) into the account of the student.

The fourth modification shown in Figure 37 is the implementation of a form that displays a matrix that shows the progress in the course modules for all students in a class or a group.

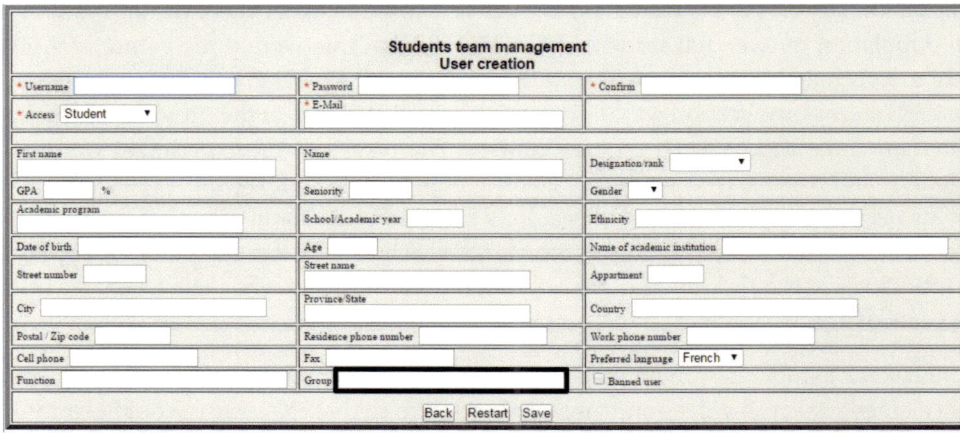

Figure 34. Addition of a field for the group or the class of the student

Figure 35. Implementation of a button to return to the previous module

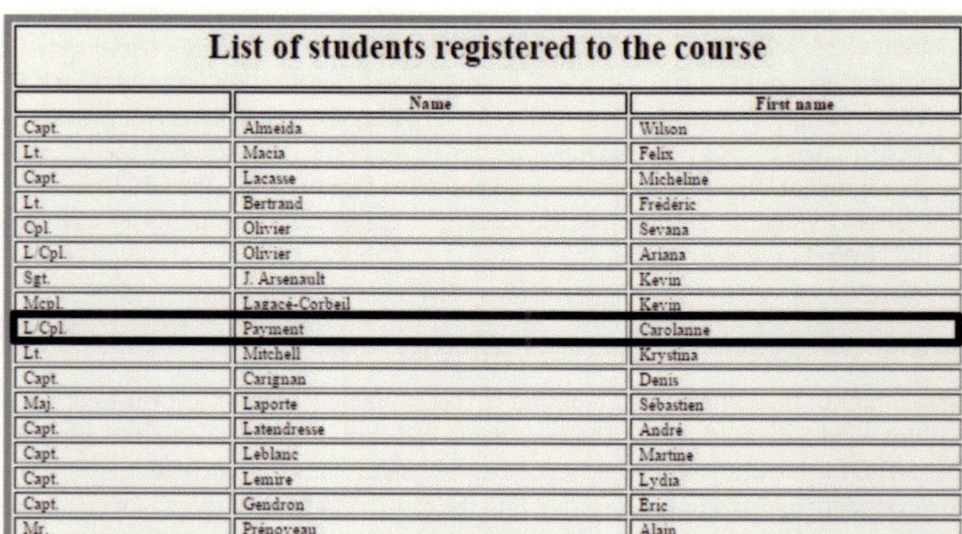

List of students registered to the course

	Name	First name
Capt.	Almeida	Wilson
Lt.	Macia	Felix
Capt.	Lacasse	Micheline
Lt.	Bertrand	Frédéric
Cpl.	Olivier	Sevana
L/Cpl.	Olivier	Ariana
Sgt.	J. Arsenault	Kevin
Mcpl.	Lagacé-Corbeil	Kevin
L/Cpl.	Payment	Carolanne
Lt.	Mitchell	Krystina
Capt.	Carignan	Denis
Maj.	Laporte	Sébastien
Capt.	Latendresse	André
Capt.	Leblanc	Martine
Capt.	Lemire	Lydia
Capt.	Gendron	Eric
Mr.	Prénoveau	Alain

Figure 36. Curriculum record sheet access screen

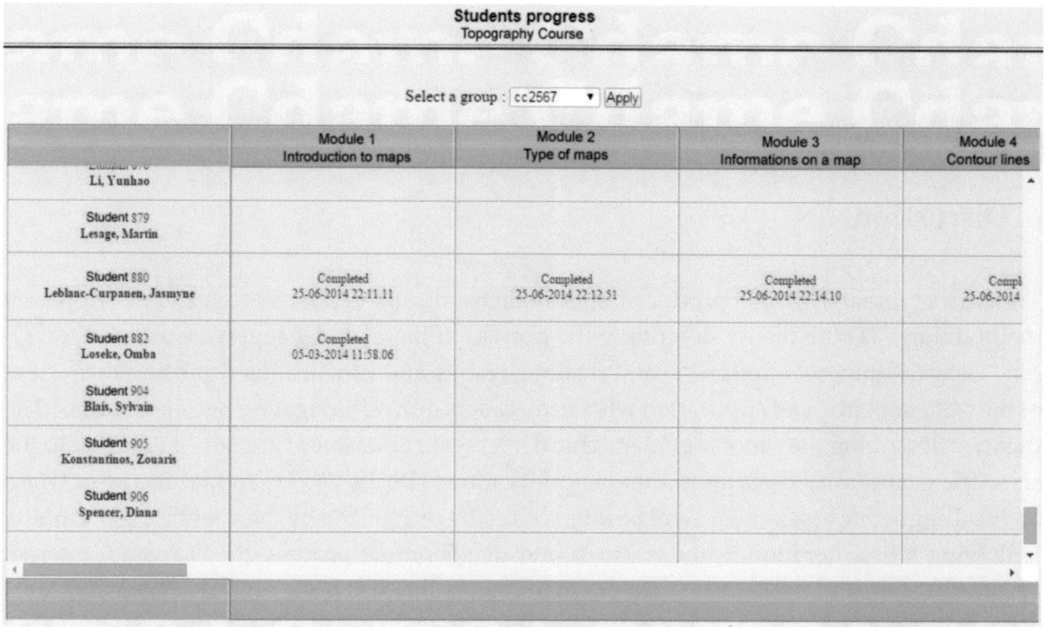

Figure 37. Student progress matrix screen

5.5. Experimentation with Canadian army cadets

The results of the experiment of the "Cluster" Internet application with Canadian army cadets are shown in Table 1 [18, 19, 20, 21].

	Experimentation group	Control group
Population (N)	27	12
Topography course pretest	12.81 %	7 %
Topography course post-test	63.40 %	55 %
Topography course overall score	83.45 %	66.15 %
Knowledge increase rate	50.59 %	48 %
Number of candidates that has succeeded the course	6	10
Course abandon (dropout)	21	2
Success rate	22 %	83 %
User interface satisfaction rate (QUIS)	- Liked : user friendliness - Disliked :	Not applicable

	Experimentation group	Control group
	Feedback, terminology and resistance to change	

Table 1. Experimentation of the "Cluster" on Canadian army cadets for navigation courses in teams using the map

6. Discussion

The current research project produced three main results under the research and development methodology: (1) the theory describing the process of hierarchical aggregate assessment, (2) the "Cluster" Internet application and (3) data, results and conclusions regarding the testing of the "Cluster" Internet application with army cadets during navigation patrols in teams. The theories describing the process of hierarchical aggregate assessment are now submitted to the scientific community through numerous publications [18, 19, 20, 21] so that the term "hierarchical aggregate assessment" will be internationally recognized by the scientific community. Following a first iteration in the research and development process, the "Cluster" Internet application has undergone a first set of amendments that has been proposed by Mrs. Dalila Sebkhi during her teaching assignment III at the Université du Québec à Montréal (UQAM). These results were presented and discussed in the « Results » section of this chapter, and the « Cluster » Internet application is now fully operational. Although the experiment is over, the organization of the army cadet has found useful "Cluster" Internet application in the cadet movement to provide distance learning and help for cadets with learning disabilities and to help late entry cadets of 15 to 18 years of age to progress faster in their career. This application is now used by the cadets to provide distance courses on topography, navigation patrols, instructional techniques and general military knowledge. The results for the testing of the application "Cluster" by the army cadets demonstrate that the increase of knowledge produced with the "Cluster" Internet application is 50.59 %, an increase which is almost identical to that produced by the traditional classroom teaching methods that is of 48 %. This similarity of percentages for the increase of knowledge in both cases could be explained by the "Clark [77]-Kozma [78] debate" where Clark (Clark, 1983, p 44.) states that "the media are only a vehicle transporting knowledge and do not influence knowledge".

However, the success rate for the learning of topography using the "Cluster" Internet application is only 22 % compared to the control group which is 83 %. The success rate of 22 % produced by distance learning can be explained by the fact that many of the cadets in the experimental group were having learning disabilities. Some of the major drawbacks of distance learning are to leave the student alone in his learning process without being in the classroom and lacking the presence of a teacher or colleagues to help him. Very often, students with learning disabilities registered in distance courses became confused by the lack of classroom dynamics that destroys motivation and desire to learn.

http://dx.doi.org/10.5772/60850

7. Conclusion

The actual research project wants that the term "hierarchical aggregate assessment" will be accepted and recognized by the entire scientific community. The process of hierarchical aggregate assessment has been used everywhere and throughout the ages without any researcher or scientist having the idea to define this process by a name or a term. One of the goals of the present research project is to resolve this issue by proposing the term "hierarchical aggregate assessment". The work done in this research was to implement this process in the areas of education, assessment and information technologies (IT). Further work and future research performed by the CDAME researchers will focus on (1) improving the user interface in the fields mentioned by the "QUIS" questionnaire that are feedback, terminology and resistance to change, (2) the implementation of the process of hierarchical aggregate assessment in the field of management and (3) the determination of the "Cluster" Internet application influence on knowledge increase, user satisfaction and student success rates.

Author details

Martin Lesage*, Gilles Raîche, Martin Riopel, Frédérick Fortin and Dalila Sebkhi

*Address all correspondence to: lesagelm@hotmail.com

Faculty of Education, Education and Pedagogy Department, Université du Québec à Montréal (UQÀM), C.P., Montréal, Canada

References

[1] Legendre, R. (2005). *Dictionnaire actuel de l'éducation* (3rd Edition). Montréal: Guérin.

[2] De Ketele, J. M., & Gérard, F.-M. (2005). La validation des épreuves d'évaluation selon l'approche par les compétences. *Mesures et Évaluation en Éducation, 28* (3), 1-26.

[3] Van Kempen, J. L. (2008). *Pourquoi a-t-on développé les compétences à l'école?* [On Line]. Union des Fédérations d'Associations de Parents de l'Enseignement Catholique (UFAPEC). Access: http://www.ufapec.be/nos-analyses/pourquoi-a-t-on-developpe-les-compétences-a-l-ecole/.

[4] Allal, L. (2002). Acquisition et évaluation des compétences en milieu scolaire. In J., Dolz, & E., Ollagnier (Eds.), *L'énigme de la compétence en éducation* (p. 77-94). Bruxelles: de Boeck.

[5] CDAME. (2013). *Site Internet du Centre CDAME (Collectif pour le Développement et les Applications en Mesure et Évaluation)* [On Line]. Access: http://www.cdame.uqam.ca.

[6] Harvey, S. & Loiselle, J. (2009). Proposition d'un modèle de recherche développement. *Recherches qualitatives, 28* (2), 95-117.

[7] Sugrue, M., Seger, M., Kerridge, R., Sloane, D. & Deane, S. (1995). A prospective study of the performance of the trauma team leader. *The Journal of Trauma: Injury, Infection and Critical Care, 38* (1), 79-82.

[8] Volkov, A. & Volkov, M. (2007). Teamwork and assessment: A critique. *e-Journal of Business Education & Scholarship of Teaching, 1*, 59-64.

[9] Baker, D. P. & Salas, E. (1992). Principles for measuring teamwork skills. *Human Factors, 34*, 469-475.

[10] Loiselle, J. (2001). La recherche développement en éducation: sa nature et ses caractéristiques. In D. M. Anadón, & M. L'Hostie (Eds), *Nouvelles dynamiques de recherche en éducation* (p. 77-97). Québec: Les Presses de l'Université Laval.

[11] Zaccaro, S. J., Mumford, M. D., Conelly, M. S., Marks, M. A. & Gilbert, J. A. (2000). Assessment of leader problem-solving capabilities. *Leadership Quarterly, 11* (1), 37-64.

[12] MacMillan, J., Paley, M. J., Entin, E. B. & Entin, E. E. (2004). Questionnaires for distributed assessment of team mutual awareness. In N. A. Stanton, A. Hedge, K. Brookhuis, E. Salas, & H. W. Hendrick (Eds.), *Handbook of human factors and ergonomic methods*. Boca Raton: Taylor and Francis.

[13] Furnham, A., Steele, H. & Pendelton, D. (1993). A psychometric assessment of the Belbin Team-Role Self-Perception Inventory. *Journal of Occupational and Organizational Psychology, 66*, 245-257.

[14] Freeman, M. & McKenzie, J. (2000). Self and peer assessment of student teamwork: Designing, implementing and evaluating SPARK, a confidential, web based system [On Line]. In *Flexible learning for a flexible society*. Proceedings of ASET-HERDSA 2000 Conference. Toowoomba, Qld, 2-5 July. ASET and HERDSA. Access: http://www.aset.org.au/confs/aset-herdsa2000/procs/freeman.html.

[15] Freeman, M. & McKenzie, J. (2002). SPARK, a confidential web-based template for self and peer assessment of student teamwork: Benefits of evaluating across different subjects. *British Journal of Educational Technology, 33* (5), 551-569.

[16] Ritchie, P. D. & Cameron, P. A. (1999). An evaluation of trauma team leader performance by video recording. *Australian and New Zealand Journal of Surgery, 69*, 183-186.

[17] Lurie, S. J., Schultz, S. H. & Lamanna, G. (2011). Assessing teamwork: A reliable five-question survey. *Family Medicine, 43* (10), 731-734.

[18] Lesage, M., Raîche, G., Riopel, M. & Sebkhi, D. (2013). *Le développement d'une application Internet d'évaluation hiérarchique des apprentissages (évaluation agrégée) selon une méthodologie de recherche développement (R & D)*. Association Francophone Internationale de Recherche Scientifique en éducation (AFIRSE).

[19] Lesage, M., Raîche, G., Riopel, M., Fortin, F. & Sebkhi, D. (2014). An E-Assessment Website To Implement Hierarchical Aggregate Assessment. *ICCSSE 2014: International Conference on Computer Science and Software Engineering*, Rio de Janeiro, Brazil.

[20] Lesage, M., Raîche, G., Riopel, M., Fortin, F. & Sebkhi, D. (2014). An E-Assessment Website to Implement Hierarchical Aggregate Assessment. *World Academy of Science, Engineering and Technology, International Science Index 86, 8* (2), 925-933.

[21] Sebkhi, D., Raîche, G., Riopel, M. & M. Lesage. (2013). *Une première mise à l'essai d'une application Internet d'évaluation hiérarchique des apprentissages (évaluation agrégée) avec des élèves du secondaire dans le cadre des stages III et IV de l'UQAM en accord avec l'approche par compétence du Ministère de l'Éducation des Loisirs et des Sports du Québec (MELS).* Association Francophone Internationale de Recherche Scientifique en éducation (AFIRSE).

[22] MySQL. (2013). *MySQL Website* [On Line]. Access: http://www.mysql.com.

[23] Moodle. (2013). *Moodle Website* [On Line]. Access: http://www.moodle.org.

[24] Blackboard. (2013). *Blackboard* [On Line]. Access: http://www.blackboard.com.

[25] Nance, W. D. (2000). Improving information systems students' teamwork and project management capabilities: Experiences from an innovative classroom. *Information Technology and Management, 1* (4), 293-306.

[26] Lavallée, M. (1969). *Taxonomie des objectifs pédagogiques. Tome 1: Domaine cognitif.* Québec: Presses de l'Université du Québec (Éducation nouvelle).

[27] Krathwohl, D. R., Bloom, B. S. & Masia, B. B. (Eds.). (1964). *Taxonomy of educational objectives: Handbook II: The affective domain.* New York: McKay.

[28] Hubert, S. & Denis, B. (2000). Des outils pour évaluer les compétences transversales, *Actes du 1er Congrès des chercheurs en Éducation*, 24-25 mai 2000, Bruxelles.

[29] Jeunesse, C. (2007). Évaluer un apprentissage en ligne : éléments théoriques & pistes de réflexion. In J. C. Manderscheid, & C. Jeunesse (Eds.), *L'enseignement en ligne à l'université et dans les formations professionnelles. Pourquoi? Comment?* Louvain-la-Neuve: De Boeck.

[30] Endrizzi, L. & Rey, O. (2008). *L'évaluation au cœur des apprentissages* [On Line]. Dossier d'actualité n°39, Service de veille scientifique et technologique INRP. Access: http://www.scribd.com/doc/8574511/levaluation-au-coeur-des-apprentissages.

[31] Louis, R. & Bernard, H. (2004). *L'évaluation des apprentissages en classe: théorie et pratique.* Montréal: Groupe Beauchemin, éditeur ltée.

[32] Tardif, J. (2006). *L'évaluation des compétences. Documenter le parcours de développement.* Montréal: Chenelière Éducation.

[33] Palm, T. (2008). Performance assessment and authentic assessment: A conceptual analysis of the literature [On Line]. *Practical Assessment, Research & Evaluation, 13* (4). Access: http://pareonline.net/pdf/v13n4.pdf.

[34] Wiggins, G. (1990). The case for authentic assessment [On Line]. *Practical Assessment, Research & Evaluation, 2* (2). Access: http://PAREonline.net/getvn.asp?v=2&n=2.

[35] Wiggins, G. (1993). Assessment: Authenticity, context and validity. *The Phi Delta Kappan, 75* (3), 200-214.

[36] Hart, D. (1994). *Authentic assessment: A handbook for educators*. New York: Addison Wesley.

[37] Rennert-Ariev, P. (2005). A theoretical model for the authentic assessment of teaching [On Line]. *Practical Assessment, Research & Evaluation, 10* (2). Access: http://pareonline.net/pdf/v10n2.pdf.

[38] Marin-Garcia, J. A. & Lloret, J. (2008). Improving teamwork with university engineering students. The effect of an assessment method to prevent shirking. *WSEAS Transactions on Advances in Engineering Education, 1* (5), 1-11.

[39] Swan, K., Shen, J. & Hiltz, R. (2006). Assessment and collaboration in online learning. *Journal of Asynchronous Learning Networks, 10* (1), 45-62.

[40] Boud, D., Cohen, R. & Sampson, J. (1999). Peer learning and assessment. *Assessment & Evaluation in Higher Education, 24* (4), 413-426.

[41] MacDonald, J. (2003). Assessing online collaborative learning: Process and product. *Computer & Education, 40*, 377-391.

[42] Worcester Polytechnic Institute (WPI) (2011). *Teamwork and teamwork assessment* [On Line]. Access: http://www.wpi.edu/Images/CMS/IQP/teamworkandteamworkassessment.doc.

[43] Durham, C. C., Knight, D. & Locke, E. A. (1997). Effects of leader role, team-set goal difficulty, efficacy, and tactics on team effectiveness. *Organizational Behavior and Human Decision Process, 72* (2), 203-231.

[44] Lingard, R. W. (2010). Teaching and assessing teamwork skills in engineering and computer science. *Journal of Systemics, Cybernetics and Informatics, 18* (1), 34-37.

[45] Goldfinch, J. (1994). Further developments in peer assessment of group projects. *Assessment & Evaluation in Higher Education, 19* (1), 29-35.

[46] Goldfinch, J. & Raeside, R. (1990). Development of a peer assessment technique for obtaining individual marks on a group project. *Assessment & Evaluation in Higher Education, 15* (3), 210-231.

[47] Northrup, S. G. & Northrup, D. A. (2006) *Multidisciplinary teamwork assessment: Individual contributions and interdisciplinary interaction*. Communication présentée à la 36ième conférence ASEE/IEEE Frontiers in Education,Octobre 28-31, San Diego.

[48] Bloom, B. S., Engelhart, M. D., Furst, E. J., Hill, W. H. & Krathwohl, D. R. (Eds.). (1956). *Taxonomy of educational objectives: The classification of educational goals. Handbook I: Cognitive domain*. New York: Davis McKay.

[49] Krathwohl, D. R. (2002). A revision of Bloom's taxonomy: An overview. *Theory into Practice, 41* (4), 212-218.

[50] Bastiaens, T. (2007). *Instructional design of authentic E-learning environments*. Oral presentation at E-Learn 2007, Québec, Canada.

[51] Saskatchewan Professional Development Unit (2003). *Performance Assessments: A wealth of possibilities* [On Line]. Access: http://www.sasked.gov.sk.ca/branches/aar/afl/docs/assessment_support/perfassess.pdf.

[52] Olivier, L. (2002). *L'évaluation des apprentissages* [On Line]. Commission Scolaire de Montréal. Access: http://www.csdm.qc.ca/Csdm/Administration/pdf/reforme_vol1_no2.pdf.

[53] Bibeau, R. (2007). Des situations d'apprentissage et d'évaluation (SAE) sur Internet. *Revue de l'association EPI* [On Line], 91. Access: http://www.epi.asso.fr/revue/articles/a0701a.htm.

[54] Willey, K. & Freeman M. (2006). *Completing the learning cycle: The role of formative feedback when using self and peer assessment to improve teamwork and engagement*. Proceedings of the 17th Annual Conference of the Australasian Association for Engineering Education, 10-13 décembre 2006, Auckland, New Zealand.

[55] Willey, K. & Freeman, M. (2006). Improving teamwork and engagement: The case for self and peer assessment [On Line]. *Australasian Journal of Engineering Education, 02*. Access: http://www.aaee.com.au/journal/2006/willey0106.pdf.

[56] Marshall-Mies, J. C., Fleishman, E. A., Martin, J. A., Zaccaro, S. J., Baughman, W. A. & McGee, M. L. (2000). Development and evaluation of cognitive and metacognitive measures for predicting leadership potential. *Leadership Quarterly, 11* (1), 135-153.

[57] Kaye, W. & Mancini, M. E. (1986). Use of the Mega Code to evaluate team leader performance during advanced cardiac life support. *Critical Care Medicine, 14* (2), 99-104.

[58] Davis, G. B., Olson, M. H., Ajenstat, J. & Peaucelle, J. L. (1986). *Systèmes d'information pour le management. Volume I: Les bases*. Boucherville: Éditions G. vermette Inc.

[59] Burch, J. G. & Grudnitski, G. (1989). *Information systems: Theory and practice* (5th Edition). New York: John Wiley.

[60] Davis, G. B. & Olson, M. H. (1985). *Management information systems: Conceptual foundations, structure, and development*. New York: McGraw-Hill.

[61] Laudon, K. C. & Laudon, J. P. (2000). *Management information systems: Organization and technology in the networked enterprise* (6th Edition). Upper saddle River: Prentice Hall.

[62] Laudon, K. C., Laudon, J. P. & Brabston, M. E. (2011). *Management information systems: Managing the digital firm* (5th édition canadienne). Toronto: Pearson Education Canada Inc.

[63] Kanter, J. (1984). *Management information systems* (3th Edition). New Jersey: Prentice Hall.

[64] Chin, J. P., Diehl, V. A. & Norman, K. L. (1988). *Development of an instrument measuring user satisfaction of the human-computer interface*. Proceedings of SIGCHI '88, p. 213-218, New York. ACM/SIGCHI.

[65] Richey, R. C. & Nelson, W. A. (1996). Developmental research. In D. H. Jonassen (Ed.), *Handbook of research for educational communications and technology* (p. 1213-1245). New-York: Mac Millan.

[66] Savoie-Zajc, L. (2004). La recherche qualitative/interprétative en éducation. In T. Karsenti & L. Savoie-Zajc (Eds.), *La recherche en éducation: étapes et approches* (p. 123-150). Sherbrooke: Éditions du CRP.

[67] Savoie-Zajc, L. & Karsenti, T. (2004). La méthodologie. In T. Karsenti & L. Savoie-Zajc (Eds.), *La recherche en éducation: étapes et approches* (p. 109-121). Sherbrooke: Éditions du CRP.

[68] Borg, W. R. & Gall, M. D. (1983). *Educational research: An introduction* (4th Edition). New York: Longman.

[69] Nonnon, P. (1993). *Proposition d'un modèle de recherche Développement (R&D) technologique en éducation*. Regards sur la robotique pédagogique. Technologies nouvelles et éducation. Publications du service de technologie de l'éducation de l'Université de Liège et de l'Institut nation de recherche pédagogique, Paris, pp. 147-154.

[70] Cervera, D. (1997). *Élaboration d'un environnement d'expérimentation en simulation incluant un cadre théorique pour l'apprentissage de l'énergie des fluides*. Thèse de doctorat inédite, Université de Montréal.

[71] Van der Maren, J. M. (2003). *La recherche appliquée en pédagogie: Des modèles pour l'enseignement* (2ième Édition). Bruxelles: De Boeck.

[72] Nonnon, P. (2002). *La R&D en éducation*. Contribution aux actes du symposium international francophone sur les technologies en éducation de l'INRP sous la direction de Georges Louis Baron & Éric Bruillard, Paris, France (p. 53-59).

[73] Ministère de la défense nationale, Gouvernement du Canada. (2007). *A-CR-CCP-701/ PF-002 – Guides pédagogiques de l'étoile verte*. Ottawa, Ministère de la défense nationale, Cadets royaux de l'armée canadienne.

http://dx.doi.org/10.5772/60850

[74] Sittig, D. F., Kuperman, G. J. & Fiskio J. (1999). Evaluating physician satisfaction regarding user interactions with an electronic medical record system. *Proceedings of the American Medical Informatics Association (AMIA) Annual Symposium*, 400-404.

[75] LabMÉCAS. (2013). *Laboratoire mobile pour l'étude des cheminements d'apprentissage en science (LabMÉCAS)* [En ligne]: Access: www.labmecas.uqam.ca/.

[76] Boucher-Genesse, F., Riopel, M. & Potvin, P. (2011). Research results for Mecanika, a game to learn Newtonian concepts. In *Games, learning and society*. Conference proceedings, Madison, Wisconsin.

[77] Clark, R. E. (1983). Reconsidering research on learning from media. *Review of Educational Research, 17* (2), 445-459.

[78] Kozma, R. B. (1994). Will media influence learning: Reframing the debate. *Educational Technology Research and Development (ETR&D), 42* (2), 7-19.

Chapter 5

Personalization and User Modeling in Adaptive E-Learning Systems for Schools

Todorka Glushkova

Additional information is available at the end of the chapter

http://dx.doi.org/10.5772/61084

Abstract

The manuscript presents a model for the personalization of e-Learning systems in secondary schools. Approaches are discussed about the implementation of this model by the application of the SCORM-standard, ITL (ITL-Interval and temporal logic), policies, etc. Comments on the possibilities for increasing the relevance of e-Learning systems in the real classroom environment schools are also included.

Keywords: E-Learning, User Modelling, Personalization, Adaptation, Interaction, SCORM, ITL

1. Introduction

Dynamically changing realities in modern society require more dynamic and adequate changes in education, which is inherently conservative. Every innovation and change in the traditional school system requires a long time for synchronizing the legal basis, approbation, and implementation in school practice. This generates a continuous delay in the fast increasing requirements to the educational system, which makes it difficult to meet public expectations. The world community sees a way to solve this problem through the application of ICT and e-Learning in the educational process. Environments that offer a variety of teaching materials and services to different user groups, such as students, parents, learners, employees, etc., are created. As a rule, all these systems are developed faster and cost much cheaper than their traditional equivalents. They enable the implementation of new and different approaches from the traditional and provide solutions as well as access to educational materials within the process of learning. The standardization of individual modules and processes bring order to the variety of systems for computer training and make it possible to use them independently because of the software and hardware platform features. All this seemed to solve the problems of didactic theory and practice, but the reality is different. There is a delay in the process of implementation and actual use of these systems despite the rapid development of information and communication technologies. Research groups from different universities and educational communities define the main reason as learning by means of ICT is an innovative process that requires in-depth research by pedagogical science and practice [1]. Psychological attitudes, motivation, and cognitive characteristics of students of different age groups are different in terms of learning processes. The didactic theory and practice for many years examine these processes and provide solutions for the improvement of the traditional forms of training, however, the mechanisms in e-Learning environments of educational portals are still not well investigated and explained. There is a gap between the expectations of developers and real results in the educational practice. The rapid development of computer science and technology for the creation of learning environments requires a high level of qualification and experience of the developers of such systems. These developers are highly qualified and highly specialized IT professionals who create systems in accordance to their abstract vision of the learning process. However, they rarely or never are pedagogical specialists and therefore, do not know the actual in-depth psychological processes of learning. This leads to the fact that institutions have learning environments that have a good software perspective quality but poor quality as a pedagogical tool. To these reasons, we can add the difference in terminology, the desire to maximize profits of software vendors, unclear criteria for evaluation of the learning process, etc. As a result, we see many factors that negatively affect the whole process and can significantly hinder it.

Despite these problems, there are many areas in which the results are very good. Summarizing the results of higher education in the analysis of the Sloan Consortium in [2], successfully use of e-Learning environments in the USA and Canada grew by 20% over the last few years. The indicators are particularly good for students who are trained in a distance form of teaching, as well as with electronic training courses that are similar in nature to the traditional teaching process. Secondary schools also have sectors that experience very good results. Examples are as follows: the using of educational environments in blended learning (classroom training and independent work) and the creation of a portfolio of students who successfully combined with project training [3].

The problem analysis allows us to conclude that the creation of training systems must comply with specifics of the particular educational institution and be developed in direct communication with educational experts as were probed directly in the real learning environment. This publication will present a model for personalizing learning systems for electronic and distance learning in secondary schools by application of didactic methodology, setting of educational goals and objectives, the motivation of the student, and his or her personal goals, plans, and ambitions.

The structure of the manuscript corresponds to the described methodology. In section 2, "Interaction and Adaptation" discusses various aspects of interactivity and adaptability

http://dx.doi.org/10.5772/61084

connected with the personalization of the learning process and provides access to educational resources. Here, the adaptive levels of the system in horizontal and vertical plans are reviewed.

Section 3, "Adaptive levels and interaction Student-Learning system", describes the three adaptive levels and some mechanisms for their implementation of the SCORM-based e-learning system.

Section 4, “Personalization and User modelling”, are connected with the opportunities for development of the personalization and UM on different adaptive levels according to the described methodology. An algorithm is proposed for the implementation of the model in the e-Learning environment.

The results of the partial implementation of the proposed model of e-Learning in secondary schools are encouraging. Work on the realization of the full adaptive model continues.

2. Interaction and adaptation

According to the definitions in [4], [5], and [6] e-Learning is a computer and an internet-based learning, in which the delivery of electronic learning resources is carried out on the principles of dynamic interaction with the educational system and the other participants in the learning process, according to didactic set goals and objectives and according to the characteristics of the course and the personal characteristics of the student. Based on this definition, the team of University of Plovdiv, together with partners from the Institute of Information Technologies (BG), University of Limerick (Ireland), De Montfort University in Leicester (UK), Humboldt University (Germany), Secondary school in Brezovo (BG), etc., developed a system for electronic and distance training (DeLC[1]). As part of this project, an environment is developed for e-Learning and distance training for secondary schools. In order to minimize the problems mentioned above, we chose a methodology by which, together with pedagogical specialists, creates step by step the different prototypes of the system and tested them directly in the real learning environment (Figure 1).

To create an interactive and adaptive system that meets these requirements, it is necessary to model the different interactive levels and adaptive aspects. We accept the definition in [7] and define it as a dialog between users and the learning system and will view it at the following three levels:

- Standard Experience – the physical structure and hierarchy of the learning content remains unchanged;
- Personal Experience – the hierarchy of content changes and adapts to the user’s behaviour and selections;
- Open Experience – an open and live system with continuous engagement between the producer, user, and message.

1 DeLC- Distributed eLearning Centre

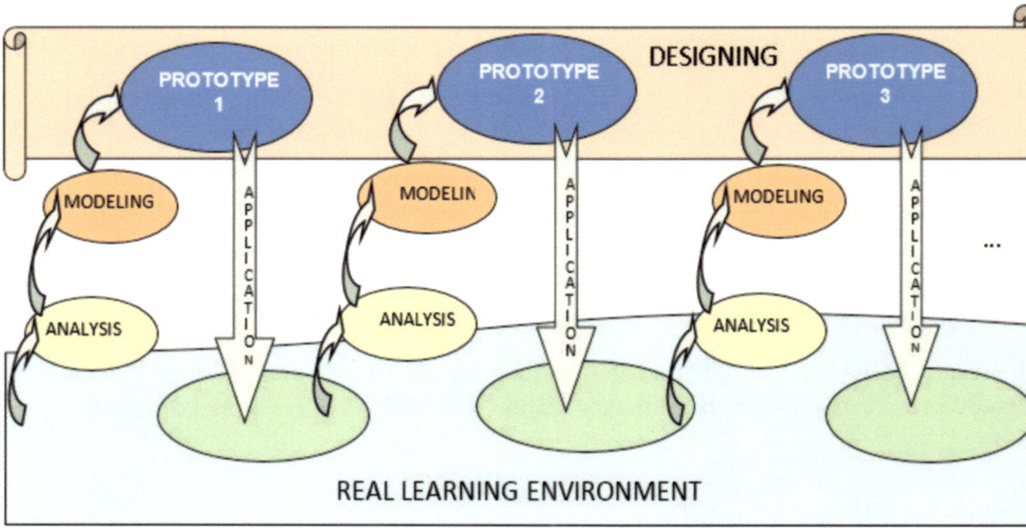

Figure 1. Iterative model of research methodology

Within these levels, there are six categories of interactivity: Feedback; Control; Productivity; Creativity; Communication and Adaptation. Ensuring interactivity for each level and related categories requires the development of a comprehensive adaptive model to provide personalization of the training through: the basic knowledge of the student; his plans and purposes; his cognitive characteristics; his preferences and habits; emotional profile, and so on (see [8]).

According to various aspects of the application and the use of e-Learning systems, the adaptability can be defined differently. We will define adaptability as a feature of the training system to be adapting itself and changed according to the requirements and the characteristics of the users before and during use of it. The main elements of the adaptive model are "condition-action" rules that change the parameters of the environment and realize the adaptation to a user's knowledge, goals, abilities, preferences, etc. The different methods and frameworks for creation of adaptive models are as follows:

- Rule-based – we look at these systems from some aspects: as a declarative interpretation of rules; as a hybrid representation based on logical deduction; as a users' stereotypes; as an overlay model of connecting and co-interacting with the model of the relevant applied area. Presenting the cognitions is connected with the accommodation of the system conventions, the attitude and the convictions of the users, and the stereotypes and the user groups that can be activated dynamically with the particular conditions, etc.

- Frame and Network-based – these models are associated with figuring the sciences as interrelations between separate facts of semantic net and frame structures. It can be used successfully on a small applied domain that can be easily identified and structured.

- Supposition-based – Such systems work with a multitude assumptions of the consumer that forms on the student's knowledge base and domain independent rules. The suppositions are facts on the user that the system takes with a certain level in security and cogency. The degree of cogency in the system is being raised if the user gives a good feedback and falls if he gives a bad one. The suppositions, established on the base of the direct communication with the user, are better defined that the system is adopted on the base of logical deductions. Formally, we can differentiate the system assumptions on three categories: what the student knows; what he doesn't know; and the student's aims, tasks, and plans. The first two can be realized by stereotype and overlay models as the knowledge of students are being adapted to relevant domain ontology. The third group is part of the Goal and Task Model of the e-Learning system. The most simple is the method of linearly parameterization. It is more complex but more reliable as the model uses formulas, predicates, ITL, policies, and grid models.

- Based on statistical rules and theoretical conclusions – This model permits the adapting of rules according to the state of the entrance data. The opportunities for setting-up the adaptation are based on the information from past learning sessions.

For the development of the adaptive model, we use separate elements from each of these methods we: use the stereotypes and the overlay model at the initial determination of common behaviours rules; define the concrete dependencies from the described school subject domain, by using of domain ontologies; make a system from assumptions for the learner, based on his stereotype, cognitions, and goals; store the information from the last learning sessions and processed it statistically; and deduced abstract conclusions for the user groups and the separate learners. The implementation of the model requires the consideration of the various adaptability aspects of horizontal and vertical principles. The first one is connected with the adaptation to some personal characteristics of the student. This model of realization in this aspect is discussed in [9]. There are two types of adaptation – adaptivity and adaptability. The first allows users to use different facilities for presentation and navigation in predetermined learning content. The second level includes mechanisms for adaptation to knowledge and preferences of students dynamically in the learning process. On this basis, we will distinguish the following three adaptive levels: Elementary Adaptive Level, Static Adaptive Level, and Dynamic Adaptive Level. The first two are connected with adaptivity, and the last one – with adaptability.

In the next section, we will look at these adaptive levels. We will focus our attention on the Static Adaptive Level and will comment on some ideas for the realization of the Dynamic Adaptive Level.

3. Adaptive levels and student-learning system interaction

Elementary adaptive level (EAL) – the adaptation in this level is connected by the use of static user information such as type of training, grade, class, name, access to learning material (by mobile or fixed device), etc. Here, we can use a stereotype approach. The authors of educational resources develop packages of lessons, tests, etc., in accordance with government educational requirements and standards for the typical student, school subject, the class and form of training. The created educational resources are common for all students in the described groups.

We can realize an adaptation on this level by the preparation of training materials, common for all students in the phase before the start of the learning process. These characteristics prove the relationship with the first interactive level – Standard Experience, because the physical structure and hierarchy of the learning content remains unchanged. However physical and cognitive interaction occurs for the users. The student receives the entire information independently if he knows it. At this level, users are an abstract group of people with common characteristics – background knowledge, preferences, cognitive performance, and more. This personalization is the lowest formal level. Although users have their accounts in the school e-Learning environment, they can work in it only on the predetermined way for all other users in the same stereotyped group.

Static adaptive level (SAL) – this level is based on the elementary level and is directly related with mechanisms to provide adequate learning materials for individual students according to their knowledge base, personal goals, and plans.

Before we present the adaptive mechanisms of this level, we will comment on the concept of persona as an aggregated user type. The persona is a description of a fictitious learner. This description is based on different methods, including the personal experience of the teachers, hypotheses, statistical methods, and heuristic analysis [10].

Adaptability of this level is realized through the collection preparation of educational materials and services, foreseeing the actions and behaviour of the persona. The realization is based on the log-information about past interactions between the student and LMS according to the set of rules defined by the teachers. It is necessary to define the background knowledge of this student. We can determine the knowledge in different ways – by initial testing, by results from completed to this moment training sessions, etc. Based on these values, the system joins this student to the persona, who is closest to these characteristics. The system compares the individual characteristics, plans, and objectives of the student with the typical didactic aims, defined in BES. As a result, this lesson that most closely matches with the basic knowledge, goals, plans, and personal characteristics of the student that is associated with this persona starts from the Lesson repository.

Moreover, special attention will be paid to the creation of courses by pedagogical specialists in the article. In accordance with pedagogical theory, this process is cyclical and begins by placing the main didactic aims, passes through specifying learning tasks, develops the profiles of aggregated user types (personas), the establishes learning scenarios with different personas, develops prototypes of the training process, shares this prototype among specialized pedagogical community of educators, experts and heuristic evaluation of this prototype testing in real learning environment, and corrects existing errors and inaccuracies. Each stage of this process requires a qualitative evaluation and heuristic analysis of the pedagogical community and the implementation of appropriate tools in a common environment – ex. Integrated Learning Design Environment (ILDE) [11] (Figure 2).

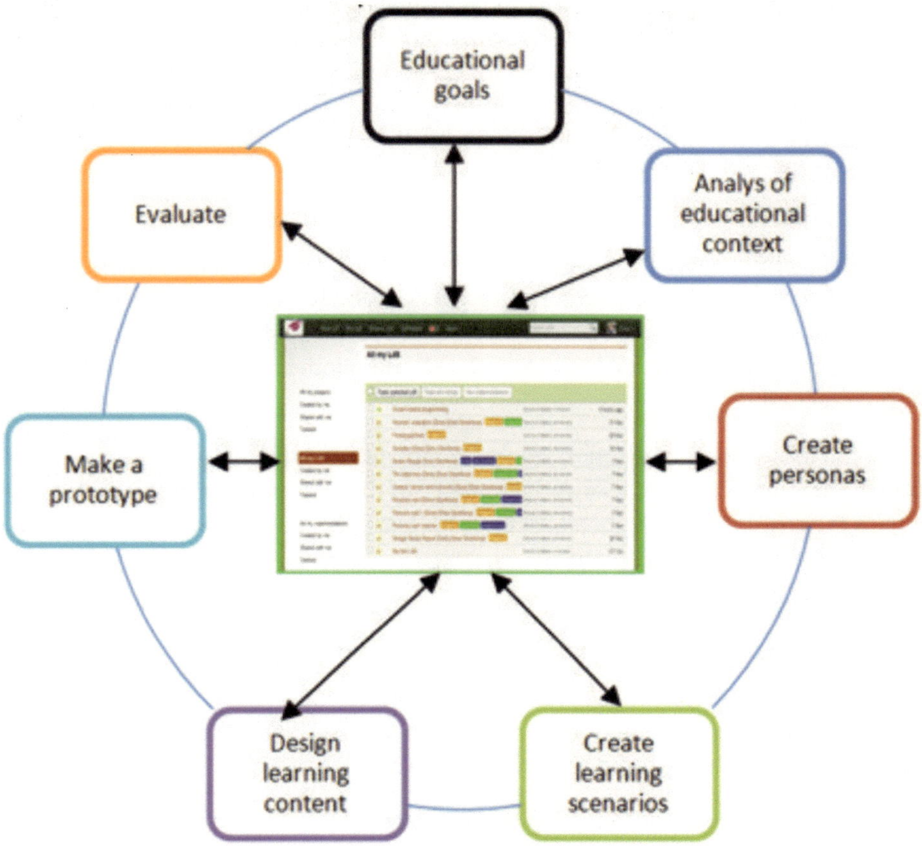

Figure 2. Creation of learning course in ILDE

Creation of the training course, according to the developed scenario is realized based on the selected standard for e-Learning. In developing the DeLC-system, we use the standard SCORM[2] [12]. The team developed a special SCORM-editor for the teachers and authors of the educational content – SELBO [13].

We will concentrate our attention on the two basic characteristics of the lesson – the content and the structure. The content of lessons is related with specific topics that are connected with some school subject domains. The e-lesson presents a semantic structure of the knowledge that is connected with some school subjects. The formalization can be realized through the creation of ontologies in which each concept from the respective area are associated with real information resources that represent them in the lesson. According to the main characteristics of the school subject domain, the authors of e-content in accordance with didactic aims define the structure of the lesson. The didactic aims are related with type of the lesson (for new knowledge, for exercises, summary, and testing). We use Bloom's taxonomy to formalize these

2 SCORM- Sharable Content Object Reference Model

aims with the cognitive levels – knowledge, comprehension, application, analysis, synthesis, and evaluation [14]. The teacher could structure the lesson in different ways depending on the predefined didactic aims. We came to the conclusion that there is a correspondence between the different types of e-lessons and the cognitive levels of Bloom's taxonomy. Therefore, we can formalize the different types of e-lessons according to didactic aims by creating standard scenarios for training and templates that describe them. The template is a combination of structure and learning scenarios.

To create electronic lessons by using algorithm requires a thorough knowledge of the standard SCORM, which creates objective problems for teachers who are not IT specialists. To partly solve this problem, we can use the SCORM Best Practices Guide for Content Developers (BPG) [15], which offers a number of basic templates and models that correspond to different educational scenarios.

In order to increase the formalization level of templates and models, we created a system for its parameterization. Thus, we received a number of different groups of templates that more fully meets the requirements and objectives of the learning process. We can use the following for the parameterization of templates:

- Number_of_SCOs – type Integer, to describe the number of SCOs[3] in the template. If the parameter value Has_test is "yes", the number of questions Num_Quest =Number_of_SCOs – 1;
- Has_test – type Boolean to determine whether there is a final test or not in the template. Defaults to "yes" and is realized with the last SCO;
- Num_Quest – number of questions in the final test
- The ordered pair (objective_n, min_value_n) connects each target variable (objective) and the minimum value for which LMS will mark it as successfully passed (n<Number_of_SCOs);
- The ordered pair (SCOn, template_num), for each n <Number_of_SCOs and template_num <= 10, which connects each SCO with instance of the main BPG-template;

Let's define two operatios:

- Set (SCO_Number_of_SCOs (Asset k); Objective_k) – for setting values of k-th target variable for the k-th issue of the last SCO, where k <Number_of_SCOs, and
- Read (SCO_k, Objective_k) – start-up of the information SCO_k if Objective_k has a value less than the predetermined.

In dialogue with the SCORM-based authoring tool for generating of electronic lessons, the teacher will determine the values of these parameters and the system will generate the structure of the desired template. If specific values of the parameters are not mentioned, the system will get the default values. After the parameterization, the teacher will receive the

3 SCO- Sharable Content Object

parameterized template with the SCORM rules that served as a guide to the sequence of educational activities in the educational scenario depending on the behaviour of the individual student.

For example, if we get parameter values: number_of_SCOs = 10; has_test = "yes"; (objective_n; 0.75) for each n <10; (SCO_n, template_2), for each n <10; Set (SCO10 (asset_n), objective_n) for each n <10; Read (SCO_n, objective_n) for each n <10, we get the following chart describing the scenario of the lesson (Figure 3):

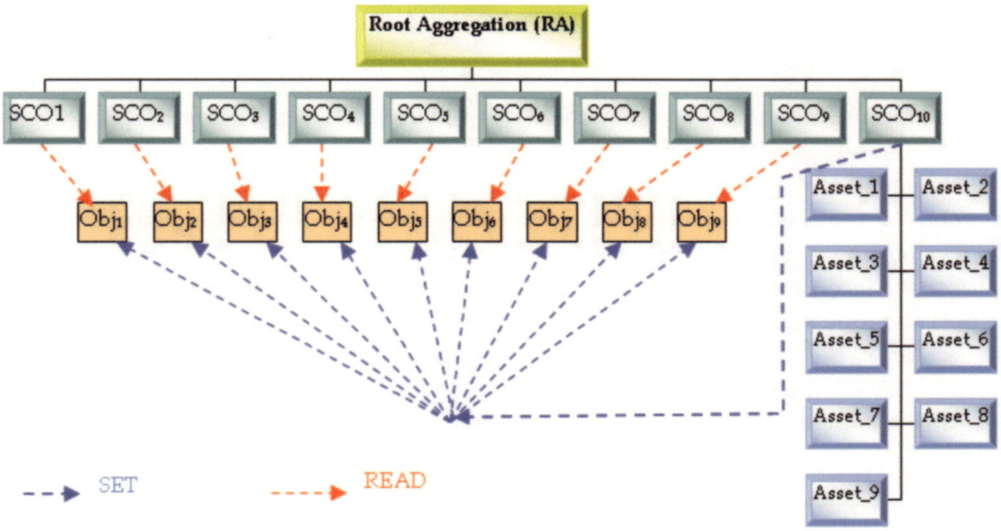

Figure 3. Parametrized Content Structure Diagram

Therefore, based on the Bloom taxonomy of didactic purposes, lesson types formalization of their structure and navigation rules can be created by the step by step algorithm for creating of e-lessons.

The teacher in some school subjects create e-lessons in a specialized development environment, which is in dynamic interaction with the respective ontology. This author's tool has to maintain information about the compulsory concepts in the relevant discipline according to Bulgarian Educational Standards. Concepts that are mandatory taught according to BES and those that are determined from the teacher for this lesson are marked with AND and those that contain additional information are marked with OR. The algorithm includes the following steps:

1. Through a dialogue with the system (e.g. personal assistant), the teacher defines the class, form of training, and didactic aims of establishing a lesson. The system filters relevant domain ontology and retrieves concepts – mandatory and complementary.

2. Depending on the subject area and selected didactic aims, the system offers the most appropriate templates that can be selected from.

3. In a step by step process, the teacher determines the values of parameters such as the number of data objects (SCOs), presence of preliminary and final test, minimum values of the target variables for their passing, number of attempts to solve the tests, etc. As a result, the system generates a parameterized template, which includes the structure of the lesson (SCORM CAM[4]) and the rules that will manage the learning process (SCORM Sequence & Navigation Model[5]).

4. The author connects the SCOs with nodes of the structural graph in the template of the lesson.

5. The author ccreated lesson (the system generates zip-package and imsmanifest.xml)

6. He upload created lesson in SCORM-environment of the education portal.

E-Learning resources (SCOs) are associated with concepts of relevant ontology. They are stored in some online SCOs Repository. In ontologies and related items, SCOs are presented into the development environment for creating electronic lessons [16]. The authors determine the structure of the e-lesson by using the parameterization of some basic templates. In this way, they create an instance of the template in which there are no free parameters. LMS manages educational processes and determines the training scenario in accordance with the structure of the lesson and learning scenario, which are related to the didactic aims, behaviour, and basic knowledge of the students. The e-lesson will be presented in the system as a specific instance of some basic template, which, by setting the values of parameters, is associated with specific learning resources.

One example is the Lesson "Summary on complex verb tenses» for 7th grade students for independent distance training". The didactic aim is to reach higher levels of Bloom's taxonomy – application, analysis, synthesis, and evaluation. The system offers BPG-templates №7, 8, and 10, and the teacher chooses Template 7. In this template, SCOs containing learning information are grouped in a separate Aggregation B. The student must answer questions from the preliminary test and if wrong (i.e. target variables that monitor test results are less than the minimum values), he has to become familiar with the educational content of the information SCOs. Then, he will make the final test in the last SCO. The template can be used in the creation of educational resources, which is necessary to verify and ensure a certain volume of background knowledge. It is essential to fill the gaps and to allow the student to successfully pass the final test. LMS manages the values of the variables (objectives) and only if they are larger than the specified minimum, the training is considered to be successfully completed. The teacher gives the following values of the parameters through a dialogue in a step-by-step process: Number_of_SCOs=9; Has_pre_test="yes"; Num_Quest=9; Has_post_test="yes"; (Obj_n,1) – i.e., answered correctly for all questions from 1 to 9; (Obj_n; 0,75) – gave a very good answer to the questions for $\forall n \in [10, 18]$; (SCOn, pattern_2) for $\forall$ °$n \in [3, 11]$; Set(SCO1 (Asset_k); Obj_k) for $\forall k \in [1, 9]$; Set (SCO2 (Asset_k); Obj_k) for $\forall k \in [10, 18]$; Read (SCO (k +2), Obj_k) for $\forall k \in [1, 9]$. The system generates a CAM- model and S & N rules. The teacher

4 CAM-SCORM Content Aggregation Model

5 S&N Model- SCORM Sequence and Navigation Model

writes the test questions and puts the SCOs in Aggregation B. These data objects (SCOs) include both basic information on various complex verb tenses as well as tasks and exercises for students who will have to pass successively through the levels «application» – «analysis» – «synthesis» – «evaluation». The teacher makes a SCORM-package of the lesson and uploads it in the SCORM-based school education portal (http://sou-brezovo.org). These characteristics prove the relationship with the second interactive level – Personal Experience – because the hierarchy of content changes and adapts to the user's behaviours and selections.

Dynamic adaptive level (DAL) – This level is related to the dynamic interaction between students and the system during the training process (in run-time). After selecting the most appropriate e-lesson from the Lesson DB, the LMS starts the learning process according to the training scenario. The learning scenario is realized by a sequence of actions that is previously defined by the author of the lesson. The system observes the intermediate results during the training and information from the already completed training sessions. Based on this information, the LMS adapts itself dynamically to the changing characteristics of the learning environment as it generates new "condition-action" rules and either continues the training process or stops it. If the parameters are not appropriate, the system has to choose and to start a new and more appropriate e-lesson.

We are convinced that in the process of dynamic interaction between the learners and the training system, it is essential to use intelligent agents who interact with the system and with each other to provide a flexible change of training scenarios depending on the behaviours and actions of the individual student. For the managing of the dynamic adaptation of LMS, we can use Interval temporal logic (ITL) and policies.

Morris Sloman in [17] defines the policies as a set of rules for activating different states and actions, depending on the behaviour of the consumers or the current state of the system. There are different techniques to formalize the policies – graphical modelling, using the object-oriented methods for defining of policies, etc. We will use the opportunities provided from ITL [18] as it builds on a classical logic tier and allows to describe dynamic processes in the course of their implementation. It is a flexible notation for handling events that varied in time intervals, allows series, and parallel compositing using a well-defined mathematical proof system. ITL includes four components – logic tier, temporal structures, conditions, and intervals. Classical logic manages variables, constants, functions, and predicates. If we want to describe the dynamic processes, it is necessary to add temporal structures as skip, chop, and chopstar. The states are specific transmission of values to the observed variables and the intervals are sequences of states.

We will describe the next three sets: S-set of students, O-set of available objects or resources, and A-actions that can be performed with these resources. Then, we can introduce the user authentication as one of the Boolean variables:

- $Autho^+(S, O, A)$ – Positive identification of the user S, who has right to use the resource O by performing action A. For example $Autho^+$(Ivan, Lesson1, Read) or $Autho^+$(Ivan, Test1, Write);

- $Autho^{-}(S, O, A)$ – Negative identification – the user S refusal to use the resource O by performing action A. For example $Autho^{-}$ (Ivan, Lesson1, Write).

Upon the initial start-up of the system, these variables have a default value of "false". The mathematical model of **Autho** is a matrix with 3 columns – users, objects, actions, and n-number of lines for all users in the system. The access to resources will be allowed if they satisfied certain "condition-action" rules of the type: $F \rightarrow W$ i.e., F always followed by W in the final state of the observed subinterval. According to this definition, the Access Rules take the following form: $F \rightarrow autho^{+}(S, O, A)$– rule for positive identification and $F \rightarrow Autho^{-}(S, O, A)$ – rule for negative identification. For example: If in the initial step the access was denied, but in the next moment, it is authorized in the duration of 10 time units then: $((Autho^{-}(S, O, A) \wedge skip) \vee (Autho^{+}(S, O, A) \wedge len <= 10) \rightarrow Autho^{+}(S, O, A))$. If two users M and N are grouped and one of them has access, then the second one also receives access: $In(M, N) \wedge Autho^{+}(M, O, A) \rightarrow Autho^{+}(N, O, A)$.

The Access Rules determine whether the particular user is entitled to access this learning resource or service. To realize the access itself, the management passes the Implementation Rules, which has the following more general form: $F \rightarrow Autho(S, O, A)$. There are two alternatives in access: Open Access and Restricted Access. Open Access has low security – i.e., if access is not prohibited, it is allowed: $\neg Autho^{-}(S, O, A) \rightarrow Autho(S, O, A)$. Restricted Access means the system checks whether access is allowed and it has meanwhile been prohibited i.e., $(Autho^{+}(S, O, A) \wedge \neg Autho^{-}(S, O, A)) \rightarrow Autho(S, O, A)$.

Another way to access learning resources is the delegation of rights to the unauthorized user. For example, the teacher gives access rights to other teachers for reading a lesson: $Teacher(S, Lesson) \rightarrow Candeleg^{+}(S, \_, Lesson, Read)$. The rules for delegating access, which author A1 gives teacher T2 to make corrections in Lesson1 is: $(Autho(A1, Lesson1, Write) \wedge Candeleg(A1, T1, Lesson1, Write)) \rightarrow Autho(T1, Lesson1, Write)$.

The policy P is a collection of rules: $P \cong (w \wedge (\Lambda\, ri) \wedge fin)$, where w is the initial state, w' is the final state, and Λr_i is a conjunction of intermediate states. For example, the policy for Author of Lesson1 (Author), teacher, who use this Lesson1 (Teacher), and student (Student) is:

$$
\begin{gathered}
P1 \cong ((Author(S, Lesson1) \rightarrow Autho^{+}(S, Lesson1, Read)) \\
(Author(S, Lesson1) \rightarrow Autho^{+}(S, Lesson1, Write)) \\
(Teacher(S, Lesson1) \rightarrow Autho^{+}(S, Lesson1, Read)) \\
(Teacher(S, Lesson1) \rightarrow Autho^{-}(S, Lesson1, Write)) \\
(Student(S, Lesson1) \rightarrow Autho^{+}(S, Lesson1, Read)) \\
(Autho^{+}(S, Lesson1, A) Autho^{-}(S, Lesson1, A)) \rightarrow Autho(S, Lesson1, A))
\end{gathered}
$$

The first step towards the creation of our school e-Learning system is the standardization of key processes associated with the personalization of access to e-lessons.

The teachers create e-lessons in specialized SCORM-compliant and ontology-based development environment, then publish them in the education portal in a special Lesson-DB. Further to SCORM-metadata, we will use some additional specifications such as:

- **Info** – title of the lesson, school subject, author, etc. features that are supported by the SCORM-metadata;
- **Subdomain** – matrix with concepts that will be included in the lesson and the extent of their studying Subdomain(concept, m), where m=1,2,3 as: 1 – low level of studying (mandatory minimum, according to BES); 2 – good level и 3 – high level;
- **Num_Grade** (the grade, for which is intended the lesson) – an integer from 1 to 12;
- **Form_of_training** (form of training): 1 – regular training; 2 – self training;
- **Lesson_Status** (status of the lesson) – an integer between 1 and 4: 4-free for use by all users in this and other portals in DeLC-education network; 3-free for use only by students and teachers in the portal; 2-authorized use only for certain users; 1-unavailable for other users, except for the author; **Didactic_aims** (didactic aims, according to Bloom's taxonomy) – an integer between 1 and 5: 1 acquisition of new knowledge (level "knowledge" and "comprehension" in the Bloom's taxonomy); 2 actualization of old knowledge (level "comprehension", "application", and "analysis"); 3 exercise and improvement of knowledge (level "application", "analysis", and "synthesis"); 4-generalization (levels "analysis", "synthesis", and "evaluation"); and 5-exam (level "evaluation").

Therefore, any electronic lesson in the education portal is a vector with the above dimensions:

$$\mathbf{Lesson}\big(\text{Info}\big(\text{ID, title, domain, author,...}\big), \text{ Subdomain}\big(\text{concept}, \text{m}\big), \\ \text{Num\_Grade, Form\_of\_training, Lesson\_status, Didactic\_aims}\big)$$

For example, the lesson "Past imperfect tense of the verb", school subject "Bulgarian language", for 5th grade; author Sarafov, with concepts from matrix Subdomain, designed for regular students, free for use for all users in the education system, and is a lesson for new knowledge we get:

$$\text{Lesson1 }\big(\text{Info}\big(\text{ID, Past imperfect tense of the verb,Bulgarian language, Sarafov,...}\big), \\ \text{Subdomain * 5, 2, 4, 1}\big),$$

where Subdomain* is present with Table 1.

Conceptions	Level of Studying
Verb	3
Person of the verb	2
Tense of the verb	2
Communication moment	3
Moment of action	3
Main orientation moment	2
Additional orientation moment	2

Table 1. Subdomain

When the student requires launching of a lesson around a chosen theme, the system checks the availability of the appropriate e-lesson from the Lesson DB. Lessons that meet the initial user requirements are usually more than one, so the system should provide an appropriate mechanism for selecting the most appropriate among them. After a dialogue with the student, the personal agent defines his personal aims, preferences, etc., and transmits this vector to the system for choices. After the comparison with the vectors of the uploaded e-lessons in the Lesson DB, the e-Lessons with the highest level of similarity are extracted. The result will be a number of e-lessons andthe system should choose the most appropriate. This selection can be realized by the use of some intelligent algorithm (ex. CBR-approach).

The preferences and personal goals of each student can also formalize the policy which defines the sequence of actions in this training scenario. After the identification of the student in the training environment, based on the profile and persona-stereotypical information and a dialogue with his personal agent, the system receives the necessary initial values of the observed variables. After determining the initial state, the policy management can be transferred to a special Policy-Engine, which is part of the infrastructure of the run-time environment of the educational e-Learning portal. Initially, based on the dialogue with the student, the Policy of Preferences registers in the Policy-Engine and then starts the Mechanism for Selecting of Lesson that makes a request to the Lesson DB. After the selection a particular lesson, this e-lesson is filed to SCORM-Learning Management System for implementation. The scenario, which will run activities in the learning process, are described and formalized in the SCORM Sequence & Navigation-model and the corresponding parameterized template by which is created this lesson. Policy-Engine can continually modify policies according to the information coming from the behaviour of the learner.

The learning scenario may include mandatory implementation actions (e.g. solving tests). If a student fails to successfully complete these actions, the learning process falls in a critical condition and the Policy-Engine has to choose more appropriate lessons. In this case, the learning process is temporarily interrupted and the LMS restarts the training process with the new lesson.

http://dx.doi.org/10.5772/61084

The Policy of Preferences is expressed by the rules of condition-action types. Conditions present a number of behaviors that trigger certain actions. The formal semantics of the model is based on ITL as the rules are the following:

when B [increase | decrease] preference in Lesson [low | medium | high], where B is behaviour and Lesson is the e-lesson.

The degree of preference can be expressed as an integer. The larger number represents a higher degree of preference. It is initially assumed that the student doesn't have any preferences and all values are 0. We define the meaning of low, medium, and high level of preferences as 1, 2, and 3. We will look at an example of training with two lessons on the same learning material. The first lesson is more difficult and presents the studying concepts in a higher level than the second one. The student initially has not decided what his preferences are. In the Policy-Engine, there are defined policies, which specify that the lessons that guarantee more than 70% results in the final test are preferable than those that only guarantee between 50% to 70% and the lessons that ensure less than 50% are not preferred. We can express the policy with the following rules:

Score (Lesson1, Lesson2):

When (1: test_result >= 70%) increase preference in Lesson to high

When (2: 50%<=test_result <70%) decrease preference in Lesson to medium

When (3:test_result<50) decrease preference in Lesson to low

The Policy-Engine determines the information needed for the implementation according to these rules. LMS through the SCORM RTE[6] and the mechanism of the target variables (objectives) determines the outcome of the student in solving the test. After each experience, the Policy-Engine checks the assumption as defined by the rules and determines whether they are appropriate. Let's assume that the student has an aim to study the learning material at a high level (3). The system starts Lesson1 and the results of the three consecutive attempts to resolve the final test are 55, 49%, and 60%. After the first attempt to solve the final test, the Policy-Engine activates the second rule because the result is between 50% and 70%. This determines the preference in 2. The next value is <50%. According to rule three, the Policy-Engine reduces the preference from 2 to 1. The last attempt to solve the test starts again with rule two and increases the preference from 1 to 2. This result is unsatisfactory for the personal aims of the student and as a result, the Policy-Engine defines the lesson as inappropriate. The learning process suspends the former lesson and continues with Lesson 2. The student's results from solving the final test for this lesson are 64%, 68%, and 72%. At the first attempt, the preferences rise to 2, the second is retained the same level, while the third attempt increases it to 3, which is quite satisfactory for the student's personal aims that the student has set.

The dynamic adaptive levels most directly correspond to the third type of interaction – Open Experience – because the communication is dynamic with continuous engagement between the system and student.

6 RTE- Run-Time Environment

4. Personalization and user modeling

User modelling is an important feature of any e-learning system, to personalize and tailor the e-Learning to individual characteristics, knowledge, didactic aims, and the preferences of the students [19], [20], [21]. On the basis of the previous section, we can describe the adaptability of the system for e-Learning to knowledge and the preferences of students in elementary, static, and dynamic levels [22].

The Elementary Adaptive Level is guaranteed by the profile information about the student before starting his training process in the system. Based only on this adaptive level, the e-learning system offers only learning resources that are common to all students of the same grade and form of training.

The Static Adaptive Level is based on the model for selecting the most appropriate lesson from the Lessons DB as the student is joined to a particular persona in the stereotypical hierarchy. By personas, students with similar characteristics are presented in the e-learning system together. The lessons are prebuilt by the parameterization of the basic BPG-templates and models from the authors of e-learning content in a special authoring environment. These lessons are placed in a special repository – Lesson DB – and are described in metadata as described above.

The Dynamic Adaptive Level is implemented through the Policies of Preferences and Policy-Engine, which dynamically monitors the behaviours of student and his preferences with the relevant lesson in the actual learning process and can replace the current lesson with another that is more appropriate for the individual student.

In the adaptation process in terms of the user modelling, we will look at: the information athering about the learner, processing the information and its update, and finding and presenting the appropriate training resources for the considered student. The model describes the notion of the e-learning system for user knowledge, for his preferences, and aims. This model must be continuously updated according to the dynamic changes in the process of accumulation of knowledge about the particular student (Figure 4). The algorithm includes the following steps:

- Step 1. Filling the static profile information. According to the grade and form of training, the student is associated to any persona in a stereotypical hierarchy. The initial parameters are filled in interactive mode or the system gets the default values from the general stereotype model. Stereotyping and personas are used to transfer more general information about the group in the assumption of the individual user.

- Step 2. According to the persona, which is associated with the student, the system determines the common characteristics of the group and includes default values. Then, in the dialogue mode,the school subject, topic, and personal didactic aims of the student are determined. The rules are updated on the basis of collected information. The Policy-Engine launches the Searching Mechanism for the more appropriate lesson from the Lesson DB and submits it to the LMS for implementation.

- Step 3. The system manages individualized learning process. If there are any discrepancy found between personal aims,the knowledge of the student, and the rules, the Policy-Engine interrupts the current training scenario and restarts the Searching Mechanism for a new choice.
- Step 4. The system stores the new values of the parameters and change the rules by which Policy-Engine manages personal learning process of the individual student.

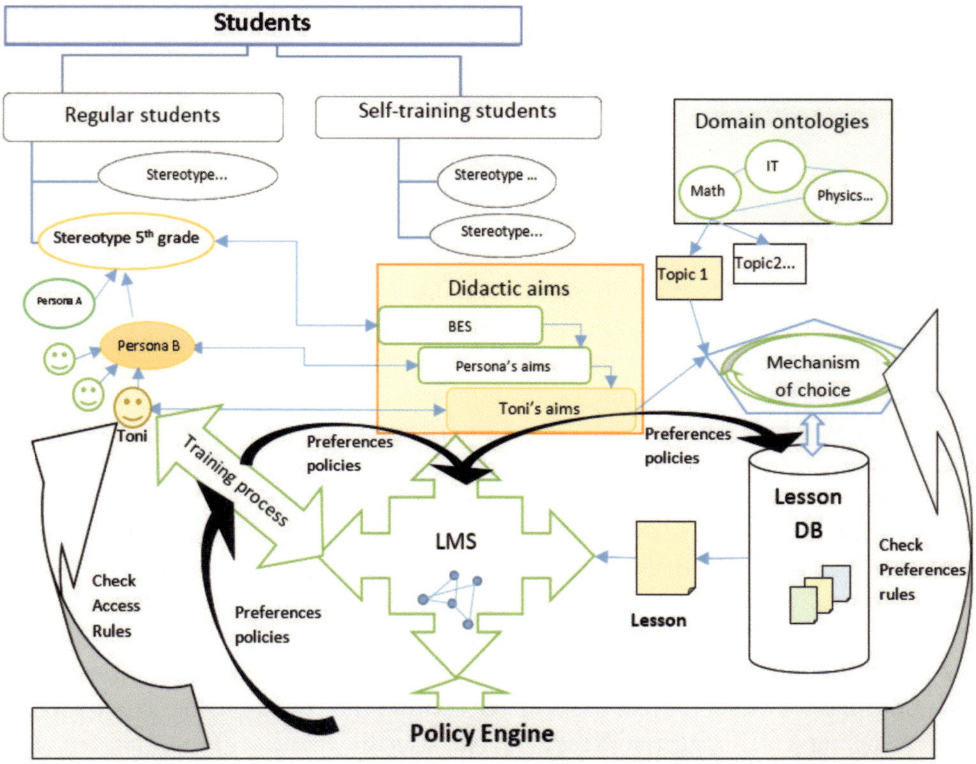

Figure 4. User modelling and personalization

The information in this user model can be considered as information specific to the school subject domain and information that is independent of it. The first type includes the data connected with the Dynamic Adaptive Level as an evaluation of the student; his background knowledge and records of his behavior (number of passed lessons, number of errors during solving test, number of inappropriate lessons, etc.). The information that is not dependent on the some subject domain is related to the personal goals of the learner, with his motivation, experience, preferences, interests, and personal data such as name, years, type of training, etc.

The presented algorithm provides a continuous actualization of information. Such one is independent from the specific school subject domain and one that is domain-dependent. The model is continuously updated to correctly present the student in the e-Learning environment.

We created several versions of SCORM-based e-Learning portal of the secondary school "Hristo Smirnenski"-Brezovo, which is based on the conceptual framework of the system DeLC and supports SCORM RTE [23]. The latest version of the environment ensures the personalization in the elementary and static levels. We developed the mechanism of parameterization of the basic BPG-templates and models, and created an authoring tool for the designing and packaging of SCORM-based e-lessons. Ontologies provide developers with predefined resources covering a specific school subject domain that can be used directly in the content. The establishment of educational environment is based on the adaptation of the corporate portal of the Delphi group. For the realization of the educational portal, we used the portal framework Liferay (http://liferay.com), which has implemented LMS of SCORM RTE [24]. There are many services implemented into the portal that supports the training process in different subjects and raises the level of interactivity in learning.

5. Conclusions and future work

The proposed user model allows to increase the level of personalization in the e-Learning system. This is essential for learners from all forms of training, but is particularly important for students using the distance form of training, pupils with special educational needs, and disabled children. The implementation at the elementary level of the model is provided by the Autho - rules, which depend on stereotyped groups and personas with their access rights to portal resources. Users could be students, teachers, parents, authors of learning content, and so on. If they are students, access must be allowed to educational materials for the appropriate grade, form of training, and so on. If they are teachers, according to their stereotypical information, the mechanism provides them an access to learning resources and services related to their school subjects. If they are authors of educational content, they are allowed access to the Lesson DB for editing and adding of e-Lessons. If they are parents, they are allowed an access to information about their children. Different scenarios for access formalize a sequence of different rules for each group of users managed from the Policy-Engine. The second level of user-modelling is realized through the model for selecting the most appropriate lesson from the repository of lessons – lesson DB and their meta-description by the lesson-vector. The Dynamic Adaptive Level is implemented through the set of Policies of Preferences. The Policy-Engine monitors the behaviour of students and their preference at the relevant lesson and can dynamically replace the current lesson with a more appropriate one.

Based on the MOOC Integrated Learning Environment (http://ilde.upf.edu/handson3), the authors of e-Learning resources successively pass through several steps – the definition of didactic aims, analysis of educational content, creation of personas, designing of learning scenario, creation of e-Lesson in specialized SCORM authoring environment, share a draft version of the created e-lesson for evaluation, and heuristic analysis from other pedagogical specialists. At each step, the authors directly share with their counterparts in the integrated environment. After the completion of the first cycle and depending on the evaluation, authors can then correct their lessons and again pass through the step-by-step cycle or publish the e-lesson in the Lesson DB of education portal. This process is cyclical and leads to the continuous improvement and refinement of the developed learning resources. It meets specified in figure 1 workflow. The published lessons are created in dialogue with educational specialists and tested directly in the real learning environment. This largely ensures the sustainability of the model and overcomes some of the problems in the development of e-Learning.The report is part of the work on the project IT 15- FMIIT-004 "Research in the field of innovative ICT business orientation and training" to fund "Scientific Researches" of Plovdiv University "Paisii Hilendarski".

Author details

Todorka Glushkova*

Address all correspondence to: todorka.glushkova@gmail.com

Plovdiv University "Paisii Hilendarski", Bulgaria

References

[1] Carliner, S., Patti Shank, editors, The e-Learning handbook: past promises, present challenges. 1st ed. USA: Pfeiffer; 2008. 560 p., ISBN: 978-0-7879-7831-0

[2] Allen, I. Elaine; Seaman, Jeff. Entering the Mainstream: The Quality and Extent of Online Education in the United States, 2003 and 2004. 1st ed. USA: Sloan Consortium (Sloan-C); 2004. 27 p., ISBN:0-9677741-8-7

[3] Abrami, R., Barrett, H., Directions for research and development on electronic portfolios. Canadian Journal of Learning and Technology. 2005; 31(3):1-15, ISSN 1499-6685

[4] Drucker, P., Need to Know: Integrating e-Learning with High Velocity Value Chains. 1st ed. USA: Delphi Group; 2000. 12 p., Delphi Group White Paper

[5] Stoyanov, S., I. Ganchev, I. Popchev, M. O'Droma, From CBT to e-Learning. Information Technologies and Control. 2005;3(4):2-10, ISSN 1312-2622.

[6] Stoyanovich, L.,Staab S., Studer R.,. e- Learning, based on the Semantic Web. In: WebNet2001-World Conference on the WWW and Internet; 23-27.10.2001; Orlando, Florida. USA:2001. p. 23-27, ISBN 1-880094-46-0.

[7] Shedroff, N., A unified field theory of Design. In: Jacobsen R., editor. Information Interaction Design. Cambridge: MIT Press; 1999. p. 267-292.

[8] Glushkova, T., Adaptive Model for E-Learning in Secondary School. In: Elvis Pontes, editor. E-Learning – Long-Distance and Lifelong Perspectives. 1st ed. Croatia: InTech; 2012. p. 3-22, ISBN 978-953-51-0250-2. DOI: 10.5772/29342

[9] Glushkova, T., Adaptive environment for e-Learning in secondary schools [PhD thesis]. Plovdiv University: Plovdiv University; 2011. 220 p. Available from: http://procedures.uni-plovdiv.bg/docs/procedure/163/1820394915693780406.pdf

[10] Lene, N., Personas. In: Rikke Friis, editor. The Encyclopedia of Human-Computer Interaction. 2nd ed. Denmark: The Interaction Design Foundation; 2014. https://www.interaction-design.org/encyclopedia/personas.html.

[11] Mor, Y., Mogilevsky, O., Learning Design Studio: Educational Practice as Design Inquiry of Learning. In: EC-TEL 20013; 17-21 September 2013; Paphos. Berlin: Springer; 2013. p. 233-245.

[12] Glushkova, T., Trendafilova, M.,Uzunova, N., Application of SCORM standard for e-Learning in secondary school. In: Informatics in the Scientific Knowlege- ISK'2006; 18-22 June 2006; Varna. Varna: VFU; 2006. p. 205-216, ISSN 1313-4345, ISBN – 10:954-715-303-X, ISBN-13:978-954-715-303-5.

[13] Stoyanov, S., D. Mitev, I. Minov, T. Glushkova. E-Learning Development Environment for Software Engineering Selbo 2. In: 19th Database and Expert Systems Application (DEXA 2008); 1-5 September 2008; Turin. Springer: 2008. p. 100-104, ISBN: 978-3-540-85653-5. DOI: 10.1109/DEXA.2008.89

[14] Bloom, B., Taxonomy of Educational Objectives Book 1: Cognitive Domain. 2nd ed. Addison Wesley Publishing Company; 1984 (first published June 1956). 204 p., ISBN13: 9780582280106

[15] Learning System Architecture Lab. SCORM Best Practices Guide for Content Developers. 1st ed. Pittsburgh, USA: Carnegie Mellon University; 2003. 80 p.

[16] Mitev, D., Popchev I. Intelligent agents and sevices in eLearning development environment Selbo 2. In: ISK'2008; 26-28 June 2008; Varna. Bulgaria: ISK; 2008. p. 275-284. DOI: ISBN-13:978-954-715-303-5

[17] Sloman, M.. Policy driven management for distributed systems. Journal of network and Systems Management. 1994; 2(3):333-360, ISSN 1064-75-70 (Print), 1573-7705(online).

[18] Moskowski, B. Reasoning about Digital Circuits [Dissertation]. Department of computer science: Stanford University Stanford, CA, USA; 1983. 148 p. Available from: http://dl.acm.org/citation.cfm?id=911281 DOI: AAI8329756

[19] Kobsa, A. User modelling and user-Adapted Interaction. Springer Netherlands. 2004; 14(5):469-475, ISSN: 0924-1868(paper) 1573-1391(online). DOI: 10.1007/s11257-005-2618-3

[20] Glushkova,T., User modelling of distributed e-Learning system for secondary school. In: DIDMATHTECH; 2006; Komarno. Slovakia: DIDMATHTECH; 2006. p. 117-123. ISBN: 978-80-89234-23-3

[21] Brusilovsky, P. Adaptive hypermedia. User Modelling and User Adapted Interaction, Ten Year Anniversary Issue. 2001; 11(1-2):87-110, ISSN: 0924-1868.

[22] Glushkova, T., Stoyanova, A., Interaction and adaptation to the specificity of the subject domains in the system for e-Learning and Distance training DeLC. In: Informatics in the Scientific Knowlege; 17-20 June 2008; Varna. Bulgaria: ISK; 2008. p. 295-307. ISSN: 1313-4345, ISBN: 13:978-954-715-303-526-28

[23] Glushkova, T, Stoyanov, S., Trendafilova, M, Cholakov, G., Adaptation of DeLC system for e_learning in Secondary school. In: CompSysTech'2005; 16-18 June 2005; Varna. Bulgaria: CompSysTech; 2005. p. IV.15.1-15.6. ISBN: 954-9641-38-4

[24] Glushkova, T., E-Learning environment for supporting of secodary school education. Cybernetics and Information Technologies. 2007; 7(3):89-106, ISSN: 1311-9702.

Chapter 6

A Knowledge-building Process in Interaction-based E-Learning

Hye-Jung Lee

Additional information is available at the end of the chapter

http://dx.doi.org/10.5772/61518

Abstract

This research articulates a knowledge-building process in interaction-based e-learning. For exploration of a knowledge-building process, an interaction-based e-learning program was developed and implemented at a college level course. Throughout the course, quantitative and qualitative data including students' perceived knowledge-building process from questionnaires, online messages, interview data, and participatory observation journal were collected and analyzed. As results, an observable action model and a conceptual model of the knowledge-building process were derived, which students and experts verified. Cognitive achievement factors and satisfaction factors were also considered in the knowledge building process model. Meaning and implication of each stage in the model were discussed.

Keywords: Learning process mechanism, CSCL, knowledge building, distance learning, interactive e-learning

1. Introduction

Education at a distance is becoming increasingly *interactive* with the ever sophisticated advances in web technology and therefore, interactive learning supported by the technology becomes a more significant field than ever, raising lots of critical issues in research and practice. Interaction-based e-learning may host many modes of communication, such as threaded discussion forums, chat, email, wiki-based boards, etc. Most of the research persists positive effects of interaction and present various strategies to improve the interaction for better learning [1, 2].

Although much of the research emphasizes the effectiveness of interaction and strategies to make the interaction more active and effective in an e-learning environment, why and how the interaction or strategies are effective has not yet been studied enough. There are some conceptual and theoretical articles on knowledge-building [3, 4]. However, there is a lack of theoretical research on a knowledge-building process based on empirical implementation. To find out more effective instructional strategies in interactive distance learning, we need to first understand how the knowledge-building process works in interaction-based e-learning[1].

Knowledge-building is said to be differentiated from *learning* [3, 5]. In [3], "Learning is an internal, unobservable process that results in changes of belief, attitude, or skill. Knowledge-building, by contrast, results in the creation or modification of public knowledge"(p. 1371). [3] also described that "knowledge-building environments enable ideas to get out into the world and onto a path of continual improvement in a form that allows them to be discussed, interconnected, revised, and superseded"(p. 1372). It focuses more on building knowledge-in-the-world as opposed to knowledge-in-the-head. To understand how the process mechanism is going and to find out better instructional strategy in interaction-based e-learning, the observable knowledge-building process rather than the internal learning process would be more useful. Also, the knowledge-building process should be more clearly disclosed in an interaction-based learning environment with active social communication, rather than resource-based instruction for basically individual learning.

The purpose of this chapter, therefore, is to articulate a knowledge-building process in interaction-based e-learning. This research is concerned with how individuals and groups build their knowledge and construct meaning in interaction-based e-learning. This research also considers learning outputs, such as cognitive achievement or satisfaction levels, for better comprehensive understanding of the knowledge-building process.

This research will focus on a process-oriented approach; such an approach is focused on '*where* it makes a difference' rather than '*whether* it makes a difference'. Many other studies that utilize a learning *product-oriented* approach—such as comparative studies of learning results with the application of certain strategies—showed various differences on their effectiveness. However, it is said to be no significant difference by meta-analysis of each research result [6]. This 'no significant difference phenomena' indicates that research needs to shift from finding differences to reasoning the cause of differences. This research focuses more on *process* than product, and presents a more meaningful contribution in the theory and practice of interactive e-learning.

2. Theoretical background

The learning process has been studied by learning psychologists in behaviorism, cognitivism, or constructivism; however, learning mainly occurs in our brain which is basically non-

1 Since there is a kind of e-learning that is for self-learning based on e-contents with little to no interpersonal interaction, this research specifies interaction-based e-learning to focus more on highly interactive e-learning. Computer and network technology have contributed into two ways in teaching and learning; one is for developing effective contents, and the other is for enhancing interpersonal interaction. Contents-based self-learning, pretty popular in Korea, is based on one-way e-contents mostly in the form of VOD (video-on-demand) or WBI (web-based instruction). To eliminate the contents factor, the course developed in this research was interaction-based, with the minimum pre-developed contents.

observable. Only the consequences of learning can be observed. So many studies have dealt with the learning consequences rather than the learning process. However, in many cases, those studies generally turn out to be statistically insignificant when one tries to be rigorous about the learning outcome [6]. Therefore, [5] suggests that we should use the term, knowledge-building rather than learning, especially in regard to collaborative and interactive learning. According to Stahl [4, 5], knowledge-building is more tangible, concrete, and descriptive than learning. This term, knowledge-building, seems to include the whole process of external activity influencing on learning as well as internal learning itself within the brain. With care and practice, the knowledge-building process can be observed directly and empirically, because it accounts for externally observable activities and artifacts as experiential evidence. Therefore, we will use the term knowledge-building instead of learning to specify the observable and empirical approach to this research.

One who tried to disclose the knowledge-building process in interactive e-learning, such as Computer-supported Collaborative Learning (CSCL), was Stahl [4]. Stahl presented a diagram of a knowledge-building process in CSCL from theoretical discussion. His diagram consisted of two circles: one of personal understanding and the other of social knowledge-building (see Figure 1). Stahl [4] described the diagram as "*The convention in the diagram is that arrows represent transformative processes and that rectangles represent the products of these processes: forms of knowledge. To take this limited representation too seriously would be to reify a complex and fluid development—to put it into boxes and to assume that it always follows the same path. In particular, the diagram gives the impression of a sequential process whereas the relations among the elements can take infinitely varied and complex forms. Indeed the identification of the particular set of elements is arbitrary and incomplete. Perhaps despite such limitations and potential distortions the diagram can provide a starting point for discussing a cognitive theory of computer support for knowledge-building. It remains to be seen if such a phase model provides the most useful representation (In [4], pp.71).*"

He explicitly considered the relationship of processes associated with individual minds to those processes considered to be socio-cultural. The significance of Stahl's model is that he indicates the importance of social learning, which is considered to be essentially different from individual self-learning. He suggests that knowledge would be shared and constructed by social interaction in a CSCL environment. He is taking a social constructivist's perspective in which his work impresses upon a sequential process to knowledge-building and provides a starting point for discussing cognitive theory of CSCL as indicated in his research [4]. However, his model was derived from theoretical discussion and it wasn't verified by empirical evidence. As he mentioned in several papers [4, 5, 7], the research community should elaborate upon the knowledge-building process model by utilizing empirical research.

Besides, many studies on modeling the learning process have been reported [8]. Most of them, however, use a face-to-face learning environment or do not utilize empirical evidence. Moreover, they present linear learning procedures and do not consider other factors such as influential relationship between process and product. Therefore, a study on a comprehensive knowledge-building process that considers the learning output variables, such as cognitive achievement and satisfaction levels, as a form of empirical evidence is needed.

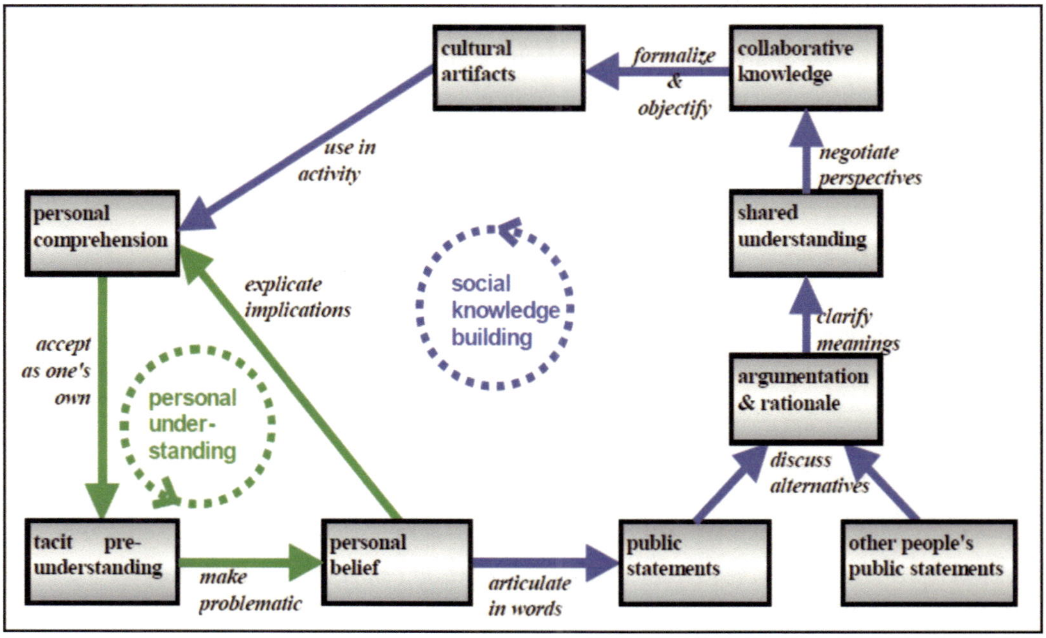

Figure 1. A diagram of the knowledge-building processes [4].

3. Method

In order to articulate a knowledge-building process, an interaction-based e-learning course at college level was developed. Four experts in instructional design practice verified the course program throughout the development process. The subject of the program was 'General Understanding of Distance Education'. Fifty-six juniors at K Cyber University in Korea, from ages 20 to 50, were required to partake in team interactions assigned in the class for a period of eight weeks. Throughout the course, the students' perceived knowledge-building process was collected and analyzed from questionnaires. Cognitive achievement tests, satisfaction queries, online messages, interviews, and participatory observation data were also collected and analyzed. Various methods of statistical analysis including correlation analyses, contents analyses, t-tests, frequency analyses, etc. were applied to the data as well. For students' perceived knowledge-building process, each student was required to describe his/her own knowledge-building process four times during the course. Four times investigations helped how students' perception changed throughout the course progress. Average return rate of the each questionnaire was 84% out of all 56 students. Question items were as follows:

- How many hours per week do you spend for this course?

- Which learning step do you spend the most time on? Write your answers in order.
- What influences your examination the most?
- While working on an assignment, what do you rely on the most?
- What is the most critical satisfactory factor in this course?
- What was dissatisfactory in the course?
- How often do you access to the web class?
- Describe your knowledge-building process in order. Write every single visit and activity on the web class site during your stay as detailed as possible.

For evaluation reliability, three evaluators graded 10% of the students' answer sheets and their responses were correlated (Pearson $r=0.84$, $p<0.01$). In terms of satisfaction level, a satisfaction measurement tool that was developed and validated by [9] was used after modification (reliability alpha=0.93).

After the course, 10 students were interviewed by telephone for 1–2 hours to verify all the quantitative data and to provide more detailed information regarding the factors of the knowledge-building process. The interview first started with the questions similar to the questionnaires in a flexible and unstructured manner and proceeded naturally to verify the knowledge-building models (an observable action model and a conceptual model reflecting the action model and other previous literature). All interview data were recorded and analyzed afterwards.

In the end, the conceptual model was verified by five experts (Ph.Ds. in Education) and ten students in the class. Respondents used a 5-point Likert scale (5 = fully verified, 1 = not verified), which was developed based on previous literature [1, 10] to rate validity, explicability, usability, generality, and comprehensibility of the conceptual model. Average rate of experts was 4.30 and average rate of students was 4.11 out of 5.00.

This study followed Rubinstein's [11] proposed procedure for modeling the knowledge-building process. According to Rubinstein, the modeling procedure is to achieve a simple high level of abstraction. So the procedure needs to be iterative until we get an abstractive pattern. In considerations of Rubinstein's perspective, the procedure in this research was as follows; Development of a treatment instructional program → Implementation of the program and collecting data → Coding questionnaire data → Deriving a rough pattern of the knowledge-building process → Analysis of learning output variables → Correlation of learning output variables and each stage of the knowledge-building process → Verification of the knowledge-building process action model by interview with learners → Conceptualization of knowledge-building process and its actual visualization → Verification of the conceptualized knowledge-building process model by experts and learners → Production of the verified conceptual diagram of the knowledge-building process in interaction-based e-learning. The more detailed procedure is shown in Table 1.

The modeling procedure of the Learning Process in this study	Product
Develop a treatment instructional program	Interaction-based e-learning program
↓	↓
Implement the program and collect data	4 questionnaires and online message analysis
↓	↓
Make first coding of four questionnaires	17 steps of the knowledge-building procedure
↓	↓
Make second coding of four questionnaires	10 main stages and some sub-steps of the knowledge-building procedure
↓	↓
Derive a rough pattern of the knowledge-building procedure	Visualization of the knowledge-building procedure
↓	↓
Analyze learning output variables	Student achievement, satisfaction
↓	↓
Correlate learning output variables and each stage of the knowledge-building process	First visualization of an action model of the knowledge-building process in consideration of learning output variables
↓	↓
Implement interview with learners	Interview recording data with 10 learners
↓	↓
Analyze interview results to verify the model	Decoding the recording, → contents analysis, → first categorization, → coding and second categorization
↓	↓
Derive a verified action model of the knowledge-building process	Visualization the action model of the knowledge-building process
↓	↓
Conceptualize the knowledge-building action process	Visualization of the conceptualized knowledge-building process
↓	↓
Validate the conceptual model of a knowledge-building process	Validation the conceptual model of a knowledge-building process by 5 experts and 10 students
↓	↓
Produce the verified conceptual model of the knowledge-building process	The verified conceptual model of a knowledge-building process in interaction-based e-learning

Table 1. Research procedure of this study.

4. Results and discussion

4.1. An observable action model

To explore a knowledge-building process in interaction-based e-learning, we coded 56 students' perceived learning procedures in questionnaires and derived an average pattern of the students' knowledge-building process. The students' perceived learning procedure after first coding was composed of 17 stages as follows:

1. reading notices & information of the department
2. reading notice of the course
3. reading the Q/A board
4. posting messages on the free board or the Q/A board
5. reading messages on the discussion board
6. studying web-based material
7. editing and printing web-text
8. doing assignments
9. searching other materials for reference
10. reviewing peers' posting and teacher's feedback on it
11. posting questions or replies on the discussion board
12. offline interaction (telephone or offline meetings)
13. assignment submissions
14. checking the teacher's feedback
15. reflection
16. resubmitting assignments after revision
17. checking my individual learning pace in the LMS (learning management system)

Among these items, activities receiving less than 10% frequency of use were removed after first coding, and the learning procedure was re-coded iteratively until an average main pattern of the process was found. Thus, #1, #12, and #17 items were removed, and other items were relocated to the basic default procedure of #6, #8, #13 cycle; studying web-based material, doing assignments, assignment submission. Finally, ten main stages and some sub-steps were induced. For main stages: #6, #8, #13 basic cycle (studying web-based material, doing assignments, assignment submission); #14, #15, #16 activity (checking the teacher's feedback, reflection, resubmission after revision); #4, #5, #10, #11 activity (posting messages on the free board, Q/A board, discussion board, reviewing peers' posting and teacher's feedback on it, posing questions and replies on the discussion board). Sub-steps that students do sometimes but are not that critical according to the frequency are #2, #3, #7, and #9 (reading notice, Q/A board, editing and printing web-text, searching other materials for reference). All stages were analyzed and correlated with learning output variables such as cognitive achievement testing or satisfaction queries. In addition, all messages on each web board were analyzed and categorized by characteristics of message content, SDU (Social Discussion Unit), PDU (Procedural Discussion Unit), and CDU (Contents Discussion Unit), following the classification of [12]. An observable action model of knowledge-building process, in which all stages were rearranged with a logical sequence, was finally derived as shown in Figure 2.

In Figure 2, subscript 1) represents a cognitive achievement factor and subscript 2) indicates a satisfaction factor. Subscript 3) shows features of messages, such as SDU (Social Discussion Unit), PDU (Procedural Discussion Unit), and CDU (Contents Discussion Unit), categorized by [12]. Subscript 4) represents the form of interaction, such as S-C (Student-Contents), S-T (Student-Teacher), S-S (Student-Student), categorized by [13].

In the student-contents interaction (S-C) circle, students come in contact with the web material and are then involved in the process of doing the assignments. While students process their assignments, they interact with other students. This kind of action leads to the student-student interaction (S-S) circle. Meanwhile, when students get feedback from their instructor after submitting their assignments, they check and reflect the teacher's feedback. These steps are for production of assignments. This kind of action is categorized as student-teacher interaction (S-T). Throughout this entire process, students read notices and information on the bulletin board concurrently.

In the student-student interaction (S-S) circle, students referred to peers' finished assignments, read messages on the discussion board, and post messages that are social, procedural, and academic in characteristic. Students were able to see other classmates' finished assignments because all students were supposed to post their assignments on an open discussion board for this research.

In the student-teacher interaction (S-T) circle, after submitting their assignments, students receive and review the teacher's feedback on their work. After reflection, some students revised their assignments and resubmitted them.

Regarding posting messages, the numbers of postings of each student were analyzed with achievement score by correlation analysis. Only CDU was significantly correlated to achievement score by $r=0.455(p<0.05, N=52)$, and to satisfaction score by $r=0.407(p<0.01, N=52)$. As expected, posting SDUs or PDUs did not show significant correlation with cognitive achievement.

Satisfaction level result measured by a modified satisfaction scale of [9] 's was correlated to each stage of the action model in Figure 2, and found significant correlations only with "check the teacher's feedback", "read the messages on the discussion board", and "post CDU"($p<0.05$). With respect to the cognitive achievement factor, the students who checked the teacher's feedback showed significantly higher scores than the students who didn't check the teacher's feedback (Table 2). Table 3 shows that students reading messages on the board had higher scores in the final examination than students who did not read the messages.

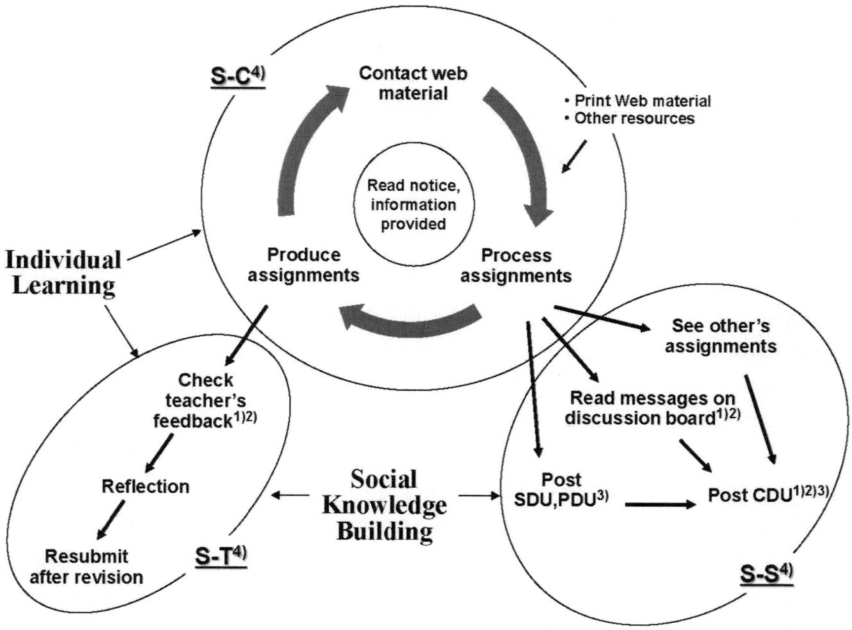

Figure 2. An observable action model of a knowledge-building process in interaction-based e-learning: 1) Cognitive achievement factor; 2) Satisfaction factor; 3) SDU(Social Discussion Unit), PDU(Procedural Discussion Unit), CDU(Contents Discussion Unit); 4) Interaction types (Students-Contents(S-C), Students-Students(S-S), Students-Teacher(S-T).

Group	N	Mean	St. Dev.	df	T
Students who checked the teacher's feedback	19	66.63	21.10	24.07	2.43
Students who did not check the teacher's feedback	33	79.33	11.31		

$p< 0.05$

Table 2. t-test result: Whether checking the teacher's feedback is a critical achievement factor.

Group	N	Mean	St. Dev.	df	T
Students who read the messages on the board	11	65.82	23.09	50	2.06
Students who did not read the messages on the board	41	79.07	13.80		

$^{*}p< 0.05$

Table 3. t-test result: Whether checking the teacher's feedback is a critical achievement factor.

Reading messages on the discussion board, posting CDUs, and reviewing the teacher's feedback are figured as satisfaction factors by frequency analysis and correlation analysis ($p<0.05$). Unexpectedly, the student achievement factors are the same as satisfaction factors in this case, but this could not always happen in other cases. It needs further investigation to differentiate the influence of achievement and satisfaction.

4.2. A conceptual model

The observable action model is abstracted into a conceptual diagram (Figure 3) in consideration of previous research [4, 14]. In Figure 3, the bold solid arrows show a major knowledge-building process and the fine solid arrows show a back process or a minor process that did not occur all the time. The conceptual model of the knowledge-building process in interaction-based e-learning constitutes two phases: a minor individual learning phase and a major social knowledge-building phase. Even though social learning is a major part of the knowledge-building process in interaction-based e-learning, individual learning occurs almost concurrently or alternately with social learning. Although the instructional program in this research was designed mainly for interactive learning, students experienced self-learning with brief material provided in the class to learn basic information for discussion preparation. So an individual learning cycle must be shown with the social knowledge-building cycle concurrently. Explanations of each stage are described below.

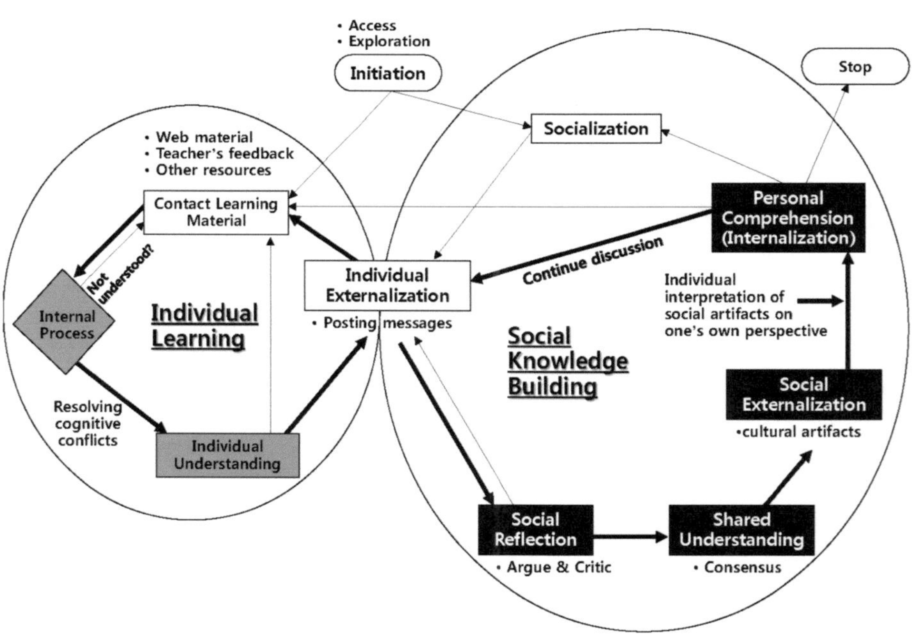

Figure 3. A conceptual model of a knowledge-building process in interaction-based e-learning (▭: from empirical evidence, ▭: from previous literature, ■: from previous literature and empirical evidence; : major knowledge-building process, : minor knowledge-building process).

4.2.1. Initiation

In the individual learning phase, the process begins with initiation. Initiation includes access and exploration of the program sites such as reading notices or announcements, clicking menu options, etc. But this activity is not a main learning process; rather it is a pre-activity before the learning process. Once students get used to navigating their way around the site, they usually skip this stage and go to the main learning process directly. So the initiation phase is located outside of the learning cycle.

4.2.2. Contact with the learning material

After initiation, learners come in contact with the learning material that includes the web-based instruction program, ongoing teacher's feedback, or other online/offline resources. The reason why we differentiated the stage of contact with the learning material from other stages such as internal process and understanding is because even though students come in contact with the web lecture, it doesn't mean that they are really engaged in learning. If students enter the web lecture and click each page of the web material, it is possible that they are just clicking through the program, which is far from genuine learning. So this stage of coming in contact with the learning material should be differentiated for articulation.

4.2.3. Internal process

When learners digest the learning material, an internal process must take effect in their brain, which is not observable but explained by many learning theories. This is for intra-personal communication represented by thought. What's going on in this internal process will not be discussed here because it is beyond this study's scope, but it is obviously appropriate to put this step as one of the stages in the learning process model here. If students understand the contents well enough after the internal process, they arrive at an individual understanding. Otherwise, they return to the learning material and repeat this cycle until they understand the material.

4.2.4. Individual understanding

If a learner's cognitive conflicts are resolved through this internal process, students arrive at an individual understanding. Similar to Stahl's model [4], this is distinguished from personal comprehension by internalization. Although we guess that we understand something, we often find that we are unable to explain what we have learned immediately. That is because the knowledge is not fully internalized yet, though it may be slightly understood. Individual understanding, therefore, could be considered a lower level of comprehension. That is, knowledge is not internalized to a learner yet in the stage of individual understanding.

4.2.5. Individual externalization

In the e-learning course in this study, students post what they learned from the material after individual-understanding; this action is conceptualized as individual externalization in this research. Students also post messages following socialization or internalization on the knowledge-building cycle. That is, students express what they learned from social learning or individual learning. So this stage shows two facets: one is a summary of the individual learning phase and the other is the first step to the knowledge-building phase, which also follows the socialization or internalization process. The stage of individual externalization seems to be similar to making personal belief elicit to public statements in Stahl's model [4].

4.2.6. Socialization

Students participate in discussions by posting messages of what they learned through individual learning or just by socialization. In the knowledge-building phase, students begin to take part in the discussions by posting social messages (SDUs) or asking about procedure (PDUs); this non-academic activity is for their social affinity and rapport. This is conceptualized as socialization in this study. This does not always happen. Once students are socialized enough (SDU), they usually skip this stage and go straight to posting CDUs (individual externalization) after final personal comprehension of one thing. In this study, only 16% of the messages were SDUs. They are shown as fine solid arrows rather than bold arrows in order to represent a minor process. After socialization, students post content-related academic messages (CDUs) on the discussion board, which is expressed as individual externalization, as mentioned above.

4.2.7. Social reflection

When several individuals' messages are posted on the web board, students argue and criticize others' opinions. That is called social reflection in this study. Stahl [4] presents this stage as critic and argument of other people's public statements and discussion of alternatives. Social reflection is a corresponding concept to individual reflection; while one is from inter-personal interaction and the other is from intra-personal interaction, both are basically similar activities in regard to learning in a precise and concrete manner.

4.2.8. Shared understanding

Through social reflection, students obtain consensus on a topic to arrive at shared understanding. Shared understanding is distinguished from individual understanding. This stage implicates that meaning is constructed by social practice as [4]. Social constructivists assert that meaning is constructed by social interaction until people share a common understanding. Shared understanding is from interpersonal interaction, whereas individual understanding is from intra-personal interaction.

4.2.9. Social externalization

When one of the team members summarizes his/her cultural artifacts—product of discussion, summary of consensus like Stahl [4] mentioned—this activity is conceptualized as social externalization that is differentiated from individual externalization. While individual externalization consists of activities such as note-taking or summarizing of what students understand individually, social externalization consists of external expression of socially constructed and shared understanding. Usually one of the team members posts his/her summary or conclusion after discussion, while other team members watch and apply corrections if there is something incorrect or missing.

4.2.10. Internalization

Finally, students internalize knowledge into their personal comprehension schema. How knowledge is internalized into a personal comprehension schema after social externalization is one of the critical issues. In [7] on Meaning and Interpretation, he indicates that meanings in computer-supported collaborative learning are necessarily shared and must be interpreted by individuals. That is, learners interpret social artifacts, which are constructed by social interaction, on each individual's own perspective to reach personal comprehension. This is the only stage of intra-personal and non-observable stage in social knowledge-building, whereas other stages are mostly inter-personal and observable.

Another piece of empirical evidence of this process is that students who only read messages were found not to be inferior to students who write and post messages in terms of cognitive achievement ($p<0.05$). In this research, reading messages as well as writing and posting messages were found to be a critical achievement factor and a satisfaction factor. This finding implicates that one can get meaningful learning though he/she doesn't partake in social externalization after obtaining shared understanding; if one is not a team representative who is summarizing their discussion, he/she is hardly able to get an opportunity to externalize what they share from social reflection and just to watch and read other's externalized messages. In spite of not partaking in social discussion, these students showed high cognitive achievement just like those who posted social externalization messages. This means that there is some process for those who don't undertake observable externalization. It may be explained that people internalize their shared understanding by interpreting of social artifacts with each individual's own perspective to reach personal comprehension.

Regarding satisfaction, there was no significant difference between students who actively participated in social discussion by writing and posting messages and students who only read messages on the board ($p<0.05$). This implicates that students who only read messages also get meaningful learning and satisfaction through the dynamic interaction in the web class and there must be a certain stage to go to internalization. One study [15] gives a significant implication in this context. In [15], perception of overall interaction was a critical predictor of satisfaction. They suggested that overall dynamics in interaction might have a stronger impact on learners' satisfaction than strict personal participation. That is, vicarious interaction within the class as a whole than overt engagement of each participant may result in greater learner satisfaction. Therefore, reading only in a certain period of knowledge-building process could be considered as a meaningful learning activity.

5. Conclusion

This research was conducted to explore and articulate the knowledge-building process in interaction-based e-learning. For exploration of a knowledge-building process, an interaction-based e-learning program was developed and implemented at a college level course. Throughout the course, quantitative and qualitative data including the students' perceived knowledge-building process from questionnaires, online messages, interview data, and participatory observation journal were collected and analyzed. As results, an observable action model and a conceptual model of the knowledge-building process were derived, which students and experts verified. Cognitive achievement factors and satisfaction factors were also considered in the knowledge-building process model. Meaning and implication of each stage in the model were discussed.

The significance of this research is as follows: first of all, this study provides a conceptual framework for understanding a knowledge-building process in interaction-based e-learning such as online discussion learning. The model presented here was better articulated and elaborated based on empirical evidences, indicating social knowledge-building cycle is critically important in interaction-based learning. Historically learning has believed to occur within one's brain from an ultimately individual process. The results in this research provided a conceptual framework saying that there are two cycles and the social learning process as well as individual learning process is critical in interaction-based e-learning. Personal cognition and social activity might not be able to be separated artificially like the model in this research. Stahl [4] indicates by citing Hegel that it is the nature of a relationship of mutually constituting subjects: neither can exist without the other. But this kind of sequential visualization provides a more useful and clearer understanding of the knowledge-building process in interaction-based e-learning.

Second, this article provides a beginning to explain a mechanism of certain effectiveness of observable phenomena. For example, the report in [15] that vicarious interaction was a significant predictor of learning output could be correlated with the result that reading—as well as writing—messages on the discussion board was an achievement factor and a satisfaction factor. It is possible to explain that people learn sometimes by only reading even in interactive learning because people interpret social artifacts from socially shared understanding with an individual's own perspective to get to personal comprehension.

Third, several instructional design strategies such as externalization or group dynamics can be recommended. An interesting implication of this research is that if a student does not externalize either individually or socially, he/she cannot internalize the knowledge properly. This implies that instructors need to design *externalization* of a student's understanding as a requirement such as a 'Reflection paper' or 'Today's learning note', etc. Students who did not post messages actively during the class discussion could be required to wrap up the fierce discussions in order to experience group dynamics as well as externalization.

Besides, the knowledge-building process research in a resource-based self-learning environment or their comparative study can be proposed for further study. Research of more cases in various learning contexts or considering more various learners' characteristics will also contribute to elaborate and generalize the model presented in this research and will enrich understanding of the theory and practice of interactive e-learning.

http://dx.doi.org/10.5772/61518

Author details

Hye-Jung Lee*

Address all correspondence to: hyejung@snu.ac.kr

Institute for Education and Innovation, South Korea

Note. This research was conducted while the author was at Seoul National University in Korea. An early version of this chapter was presented at 2008 ICCE (Lee, 2008). Lee, Hye-Jung (2008). A Learning Process Mechanism in CSCL. Proceedings of ICCE 2008, Taipei, Taiwan, pp. 261-268.

References

[1] Lee H.-J., Rha I. Influence of 'Structure' and 'Interaction' on Student Achievement and Satisfaction in Web-Based Distance Learning. Educational Technology and Society. 2009;12(4):372-382.

[2] Kanuka H., Rourke L., Laflamme E. The influence of instructional methods on the quality of online discussion. British Journal of Educational Technology. 2007;38(2): 260-271.

[3] Bereite, C., Scardamalia M. Technology and literacies: From print literacy to dialogic literacy. In N. Bascia, A. Cumming, A. Datnow, K. Leithwood, & D. Livingstone (Eds.), International Handbook of Educational Policy. Dordrecht, Netherlands: Springer. 2005; p.749-761).

[4] Stahl G. A Model of collaborative knowledge-building. In B. Fishman & S. O'Connor-Divelbiss (Eds.), Fourth International Conference of the Learning Sciences Malwah, NJ; Erlbaum. 2000; p. 70-77.

[5] Stahl G. Contributions to a theoretical framework for CSCL. In: Proceedings of the Conference on Computer Support for Collaborative Learning: Foundations for a CSCL Community. International Society of the Learning Sciences. 2002. Available from http://gerrystahl.net/publications/conferences/2002/cscl2002/cscl2002.pdf [Accessed: 2015-07-11].

[6] Russell T. The no significant difference phenomenon: A comparative research annotated bibliography on technology for distance education: As reported in 355 research reports, summaries and papers. North Carolina State University, 1999. Available from http://www.nosignificantdifference.org/ [Accessed: 2015-07-11].

[7] Stahl G. Meaning and interpretation in collaboration. In: Proceedings of the International Conference on Computer Supported Collaborative Learning. 2003. Bergen, Norway.

[8] Brown R.E. The process of community-building in distance learning classes. Journal of Asynchronous learning networks. 2001;5(2):18-35.

[9] Kim J., & Ryu, H. Evaluation of teaching and learning system. Korea National Open University Press: Seoul; 2000.

[10] Rha I., Hong S. A study on exploring at the process model of online learning community development. Journal of Educational Technology. 2004;19(3):101-122.

[11] Rubinstein M. Patterns of Problem Solving. Englewood Cliffs. NJ: Prentice-hall, Inc. 1975.

[12] Oren A., Mioduser D., Nachmias R. The development of social climate in virtual learning discussion groups. International Review of Research in Open and Distance Learning. 2002;3(1). Available from http://www.irrodl.org/index.php/irrodl/article/view/80/154 [Accessed: 2015-07-11].

[13] Moore M.G. Three types of interaction. American Journal of Distance Education, 1989;3(2):1-6.

[14] Lee H.-J. New perspectives of theoretical research in web-based distance education: Beyond Moore's Concepts. Korean Journal of Educational Research. 2004;42(1): 137-168.

[15] Fulford C.P., Zhang, S. Perceptions of interaction: The critical predictor in distance education. The American Journal of Distance Education. 1993; 7(3):8-21.

Chapter 7

Learner Modeling Based on Bayesian Networks

Anouar Tadlaoui Mouenis, Aammou Souhaib and
Khaldi Mohamed

Additional information is available at the end of the chapter

http://dx.doi.org/10.5772/61021

Abstract

The work presented in this chapter lies within Learner modeling in an adaptive educational system construed as a computational modeling of the learner. All actions of the learner in a learning situation on an adaptive hypermedia systems are not limited to valid or invalid actions (true and false), but they are a set of actions that characterize the learning path of his formation. Thus, we cannot represent the information from the system of each learner using relative data. It requires putting our work in a probabilistic context due to the changes in the learner model information during formation. We propose in this work to use Bayesian networks as a probabilistic framework to resolve the issue of dynamic management and update of the learner model. The experiments and results presented in this work are arguments in favor of our hypothesis, and can also promote reusing the modeling obtained through different systems and similar modeling situations.

Keywords: Learner model, adaptive Hypermedia educational systems, Bayesian networks, Cognitive diagnosis, Uncertainty

1. Introduction

First of all, to clarify our purpose, it seems important to note that the work presented in this chapter lies within learner modeling in an adaptive educational system, construed as a computational modeling of the learner; that is to say, the representation and specification of the learner's knowledge. Different approaches have been taken to manage modeling of the learner with multiple objectives, from the evaluation of the learner's knowledge to the recognition of the plan followed in problem solving.

Despite these various attempts at modeling learning characterized by a dynamic aspect, we always find that there are difficulties in achieving this goal. The proposed approaches provide us with only a static view of the learner model, yet this model is always in development (the learner's knowledge is evolving within the same module). Therefore, a dynamic view is essential. In order to monitor the behavior of the learner in real time and during formation, we must adopt a dynamic modeling approach when managing learner modeling.

The actions of the learner in a learning situation are not limited to valid or invalid actions (true and false), yet it is the actions that characterize the formation of the learning path. From this observation, we cannot represent information from the system of each learner using relative data. Rather, we must place our work in a probabilistic context due to changes in the learner model during formation.

The problems presented in this chapter can be summarized as follows: How should we represent the different functions of a learner model? And what approaches can be used to perform updates on the different characteristics of such a model?

In this work, we propose the use of Bayesian networks as a probabilistic formalism to resolve the issue of management and dynamic update of the learner model. To resolve this issue, we must first ask: Why and how can we represent a learner model with Bayesian networks? How can we go from a dynamic representation of the Unified modeling language diagram of the model to a probabilistic representation with Bayesian networks? Is this consideration experimentally justified?

2. Theoretical approaches

The purpose of this section is to provide the readers with knowledge required in the field of learner modeling. In this section, we address the definitions and terminologies of the chapter's key words.

2.1. Model of the learner

2.1.1. Definition

Learner modeling is the modeling of all the important features that affect the learner (knowledge, preferences, goals, etc.). It identifies relevant information, and structures, initializes, updates and exploits it. By replacing the word "learning" with the term "user", this definition is also applicable to the model of the user. An application other than the learner's educational model is called the user model.

The main goal of a learner model is to store learner information, such as the learner's level of knowledge or skill pertaining to a given topic, and his or her personal information, such as psychological characteristics and preferences.

http://dx.doi.org/10.5772/61021

Zaitseva [1] defines the learner model as a set of structured information about the learning process, in which the characteristics of the learner are considered to be the values of this structure. According to Beck [2], the learner model acts as the key to system adaptation by providing the necessary data to other modules.

The uncertainty of the information contained within the learner model and the intention behind its creation have been the focus of many studies. Thus, a learner model represents system beliefs about learners' beliefs, accumulated during the diagnostic process.

The learner model can be an integral part of adaptive hypermedia systems, as it can be shared with multiple systems. In this last case, we discuss user modeling servers [3]. This type of server is used in environments where more distributed adaptive systems access the server to query or update user information. CUMULATE is one of the most known and used systems for user modeling servers.

2.1.2. Foundations of the learner model

Self [4] defined a formalization of the learner model that is based on the beliefs and knowledge of the system and the learner. Beliefs are represented by formulas in propositional calculus. Objects of belief are called propositions. Beliefs are related to the behavior of an agent (A), a user (U) or a system (S). BA = {p/BAP} is the set of beliefs of agent A. BAP are the proposals themselves.

BSU = {p / BSBUp} is the set of proposals that system S believes are believed by user U (see Fig. 1).

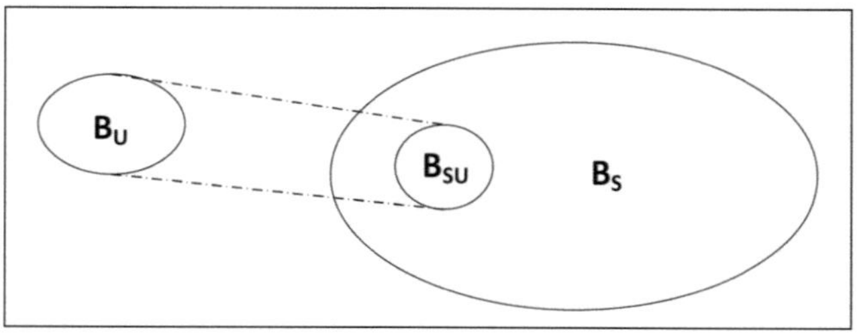

Figure 1. The representation of the system and user beliefs

The learner model can be defined by a set of proposals that the system S thinks about learner U: UM = BS (U) = {p / BSp (U)}

Belief can be replaced by knowledge; therefore, KAP = BAp.

To distinguish between the different aspects of the learner model, Self distinguishes the following proposals:

- Proposals that are dependent on a field that a learner acquires in a system.
- Independent clauses of the system domain. These clauses are also called the background.

This proposal describes the cognitive and personal characteristics of the learner, also known as behavioral skills, which include preferences, tasks, goals and experience.

2.2. Bayesian networks

Before describing our investigation of the use of Bayesian networks in learner modeling, we'll define such networks and address the meaning of inference in this context.

In the rest of this section, we'll take a typology of nodes inspired by Conati [5], and found in different terms in the literature. The field layer is the set of nodes modeling epistemic knowledge of the learner, and the task layer is the set of nodes modeling the actions of the learner.

2.2.1. *Definition*

Numerous models have been created through the representation of knowledge. Probabilistic graphical models, and especially Bayesian networks initiated by Pearl [6] in the 1980s, have proven to be useful tools for representing uncertain knowledge and reasoning from incomplete information.

A Bayesian network is a directed acyclic graph in which the nodes correspond to the variables (user properties), and the links represent probabilistic relationships of influence. These variables can belong to the field of knowledge, the base knowledge and / or the cognitive model. Each node represents the system's belief about possible values (levels, states) of the variable. Thus, the conditional probability distribution must be specified for each node. If the variables are discrete, they can be presented as a table.

The graph is also called the "structure" of the model, and the probability tables are its "parameters". They can be provided by experts, or calculated from data; generally speaking, the structure is defined by experts and the calculated parameters are from experimental data.

Consider a Bayesian network $B=(G, N)$ defined by
$G=(X, E)$, an acyclic directed graph with various vertices associated with a set of random variables $X=(X, ..., Xn)$;N= {P(Xi | Pa(Xi))} All the probabilities of each node Xi are conditional to the state of its parents Pa(Xi) in G.

According to Mayo [7], a Bayesian network allows compact representation of the joint probability distribution over a set of variables:

$$P(X1,X2,\cdots,Xn)=\prod_{i=1}^{n}P(Xi \mid Pa(Xi))$$

These methods obviously use the concept of conditional probability, i.e., what is the probability of Xi knowing that I have observed Xj ; but they also use the Bayes theorem, which calculates, conversely, the probability of Xj knowing Xi, when P(Xi | Xj) is known.

2.2.2. *Bayesian network construction*

To specify a Bayesian network in a comprehensive way, it is necessary, as we have seen in the definition, to specify the network structure (the acyclic graph) and the network parameters (the probability tables). To reach this specification, there are two approaches: 1) the collection of expertise, and 2) the machine learning, which is one of the attractions of Bayesian networks. A combination of these two approaches is also possible.

In the first approach, the collection of expertise, we must begin by defining the network structure, starting with identifying the possible nodes, and then we distinguish between hypothetical (unobservable) variables and informational (observable) variables. The next step concerns the analysis of the existing arc in terms of the influence of one variable upon another. Traditionally, if an arc is directed from A to B, A is a cause of B; however, in the case of learner modeling, we will see that the interpretation is not so simple. The parameters are in turn attached to approximations using qualitative or frequentists' information.

A Bayesian network is considered as a probability distribution. By using maximum likelihood as a statistical learning parameter criterion, the result is a Bayesian network with a fixed structure and with E as a comprehensive basis of example. If the parameters of the Bayesian network are equal to the frequencies of the same features observed in E, the maximum likelihood will be achieved. A test is necessary to determine the conditional independence of random variables in the statistical learning structure.

3. Learner modeling

In this section, we present the steps to follow when modeling the learner in an adaptive educational system, beginning with the user meta-model and then moving to use of the case diagram, and regrouping all actions of the learner in an adaptive system.

3.1. The metamodel

Here we discuss a specific user meta-model for e-learning, as presented by Aammou [8]. This model features a combination of models for e-learning and adaptive hypermedia. It takes into account elements, such as the history of actions that are missing in formal models. The construction of this model allows us to understand the user's creative process model for adaptive hypermedia, helping us to build our hypernym model.

In our user model for e-learning, we want to be able to:

- Define the characteristics attributes, essential and common to all users (name, username, password and age).
- Define attribute categories to separate the user's preferences, school / career and other attributes. This distinction will facilitate importing data, system maintenance, as well as communication with external systems; the attributes are differentiated according to their nature.
- Retain documents that have been covered by the user in either of these two ways: 1) by inclusion of the documents in a whole, greater course. Or by having documents specifically related to the concept that the user has investigated. The aim of this historical duplication

is such that when the user wishes to come back to a concept already brought to his attention, he is presented with documents that are the same as those from his first learning of the concept.

The UML class diagram representation of our user model is given in Fig. 2.

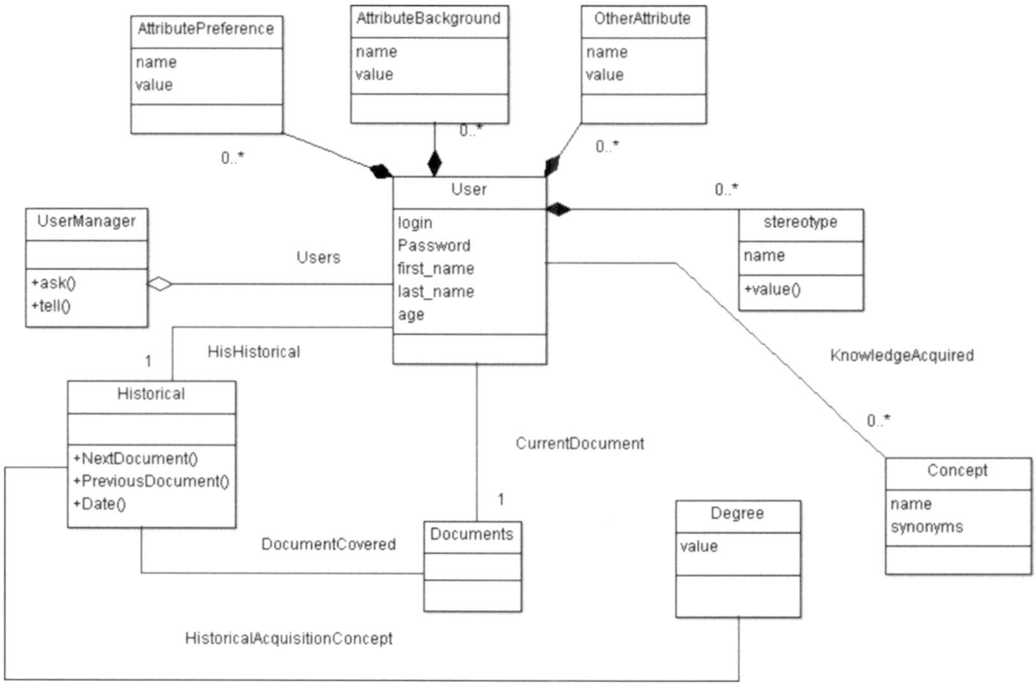

Figure 2. UML class diagram representing the user metamodel

- The **User Manager** class is responsible for interfacing with the other components of adaptive hypermedia systems. For this purpose, the Ask and Tell methods are used to ask questions and provide answers to the external components (domain model, adaptation model). The User Manager class is connected to all users, and is responsible for managing by an aggregation relationship.
- The **User** class is responsible for representing information pertaining to a particular user. It is composed of predefined attributes: name, username, password and age.
- The **Attribute Preference** class is responsible for representing the preferences of the user. These are view preferences: font size, color problems, contrasts, etc., as well as presentation preferences. The user may prefer textual or graphic elements, and may not want an audio element, for example.
- The **Attribute Background** class is responsible for representing the user attributes related to academic / professional background.

- The **Stereotype** class is responsible for representing the various categories of stereotypes to which the user belongs. By definition, a stereotype is an image or fixed design and schematic of an aspect of reality. In our model, a stereotype consists of a name and a value. The name sets the stereotype (e.g., "learning rate"), and the value is used to characterize the user (e.g., "quick" for the stereotype "learning rate"). The number of possible values is often reduced to a given stereotype. Values are often based on other attributes. Stereotypes differ from other attributes in their schematic characterization of the user, as they can represent much more granular elements.

- The **Other Attribute** class is responsible for representing user attributes that are not related to the user's career and are not preferences, e.g., a data encryption key. The purpose of this class is to ensure compatibility of the model with standard models like IMS or PAPI Learner, because some attributes do not fit into the other categories of attributes defined above.

- **Degree** is an association class that is responsible for giving a value to the knowledge of a concept by the user. The possible values are: very low, low, average, good, and excellent. This scale is a range of values that allows good precision with respect to a binary classification, and avoids a degree of accuracy that is too high, and therefore it is very useful for adaptation.

- The **Historical** class is in charge of representing a historical document covered in the learner path, allowing one to give the date of the course of a document, and the browsing history in the order of a historical path [it contains two methods, NextDocument() and PreviousDocument()]. The historical class can be used to represent all the documents covered by a user's history, or to represent the historical documents covered to reach a certain degree of knowledge for a given concept.

The classes of Document and Concept are detailed in the model domain.

3.2. The use case diagram

Based on the meta-model, we were able to map out the functionality of the learner using the use case diagram (Fig. 3) to reflect a portion of the student's actions in an adaptive system. In this section, we will explain each of these actions, and consider the relationships of these actions with each other and within the system operation process.

Based upon the meta-model presented in the previous section, we have illustrated a learner's actions in a learning situation in an adaptive educational system (Table 1).

Learner's actions
- Follow courses
- Take pretest
- Take evaluation

Table 1. The mains actions of a learner in a learning situation in an adaptive system

In Fig. 3, a main actor is identified, named "the learner". The figure shows the generalization relationships between use cases and the learner, and the generalization relationships of inclusion and extension between use cases.

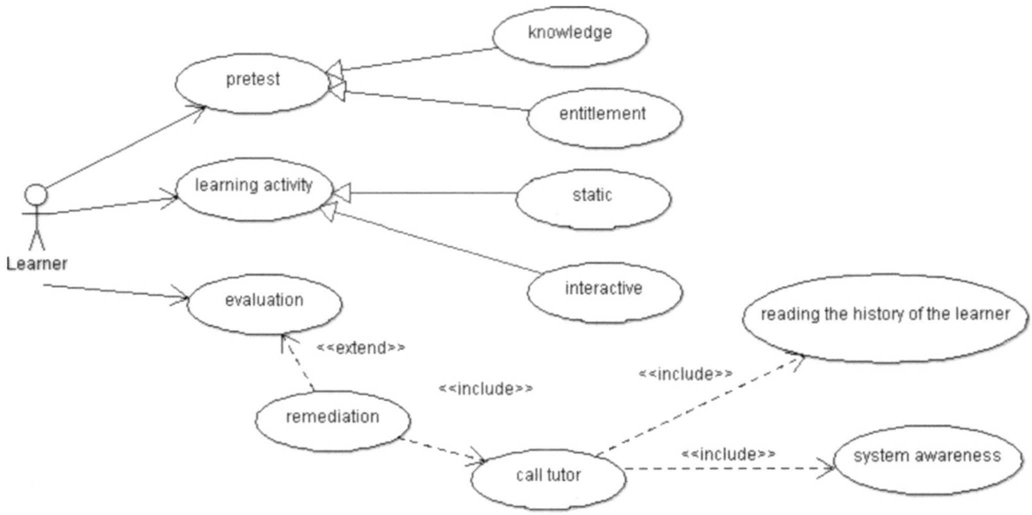

Figure 3. Use case diagram UML representing the learner actions

In particular, the functional requirement of "Learner" represents all information about the learner in the hypermedia system (the learner's knowledge, skills, personal information, etc.). This functional requirement is shown with a generalization relationship with three functional requirements:

- "**Pretest**" – this represents information about the pretest the learner has to take before entering the learning situation. The pretest is composed of two types of evaluation components: 1) tests of knowledge depicted with the functional requirement "*knowledge*", and 2) the functional requirement "*skills*", which represents the test through which we will evaluate the learner's skills.

- "**Learning Activity**" – this functional requirement represents information about the learning activities. Each learning activity in an adaptive educational hypermedia system is of two types: 1) static activities represented by the functional requirement "*Static*", and 2) interactive activities represented by the functional requirement "*Interactive*".

- "**Evaluation**" – this represents the information about the evaluation tests the learner has to take after completion of each learning activity. If the learner fails in the evaluation, the learner must pass to remediation; which is represented by the functional requirement "*Remediation*", which is connected to the functional requirement "*Evaluation*" through an extension of relationship.

In the case of remediation, the functional requirement "Remediation" involves activation of the functional requirement "Call Tutor" through an inclusion relation. This requirement represents activation of the tutor to help the student to return to shortcomings in the learning activity.

Another inclusion relation is represented in Fig. 3. The actions of the learner in an adaptive system are represented, appearing in the relationship between the functional requirement "Call Tutor" and the requirement of "Reading the History of the Learner", which activates the return of the system to the profile and the learner's course information. The requirement "System Awareness" enables the system to follow the course of the learner after remediation.

4. Bayesian network development

In this section, we present the transformation of our use case diagram representing the learner model, as presented in [9], into a Bayesian network.

4.1. The development rules of a Bayesian network

4.1.1. The generalization relationship transformation

A generalized type of use case represents a functionality that allows all instances of specialized use cases. The transformation of this type of relationship to nodes of a Bayesian network is considered simple.

In Fig. 4, use case A is a generalization of use cases A1 and A2, and we represent the functional requirements of A1 and A2 as being descendant of the functional requirement A.

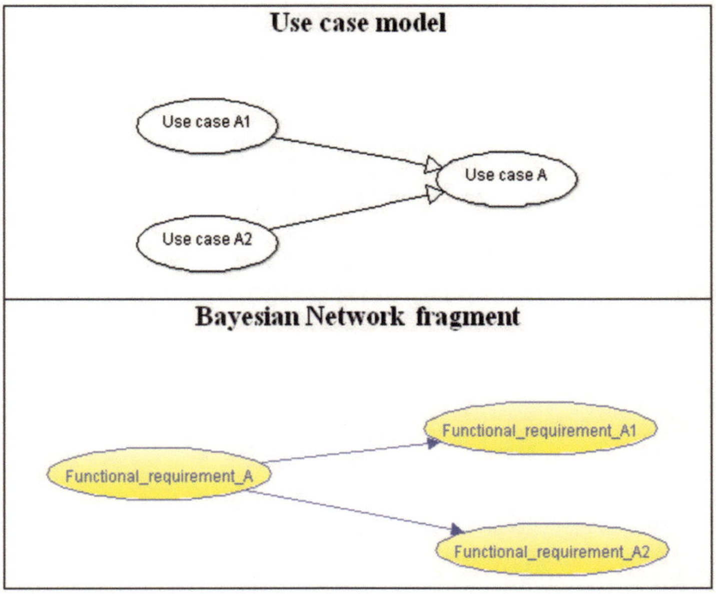

Figure 4. The generalization relationship transformed into a Bayesian network fragment

This results in a Bayesian network with a similar structure. The direction of the arc flows from A to A1 and A2 reflects top-down decomposition. This indicates that one is more likely to encounter a general case with specific functional requirements, including those in the Bayesian network, having developed the information that is represented by the arrows of the use case. Therefore,

$$P(A) = prior$$
$$P(A1 \mid A) = P(A \mid A1)P(A1) / P(A)$$
$$P(A2 \mid A) = P(A \mid A21)P(A2) / P(A)$$

4.1.2. The inclusion relationship transformation

The inclusion relation in a use case diagram represents the situation in which a use case is composed of a number of various use cases. For inclusion, a high level of use cases cannot be executed without the implementation of sub use cases.

Figure 5 represents this relationship, with case A including cases A1 and A2 if the behavior described by case A includes descendant behavior; that is, if A depends on A1. When A is pressed, the east must, as part of A.

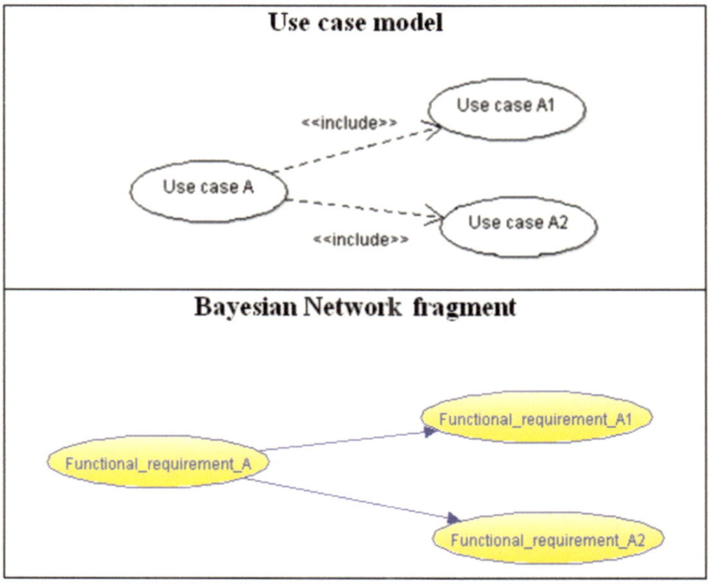

Figure 5. The inclusion relationship transformed into a Bayesian network fragment

This results in a Bayesian network with a similar structure. The direction of the arc flowing from A to A1 and A2 represents a bottom-up composition. This indicates that one is more likely to encounter a general case with specific functional requirements, and the functional require-

http://dx.doi.org/10.5772/61021

ments, including those in the Bayesian network, have developed the information that is represented by the arrows of the use case. Therefore,

$$P(A) = prior$$
$$P(A1 \mid A) = P(A \mid A1)P(A1) \;/\; P(A)$$
$$P(A2 \mid A) = P(A \mid A21)P(A2) \;/\; P(A)$$

4.1.3. The extension relationship transformation

The extension relationship is probably the most useful because it has semantic meaning; it represents a particular use case branched additional behavior, given the satisfaction of certain conditions.

Figure 6 represents use case A, which extends to use case A1, when use case A can be called during execution in the case of A1 use. Run A1 can possibly lead to the execution of A; unlike the inclusion, the extension is optional.

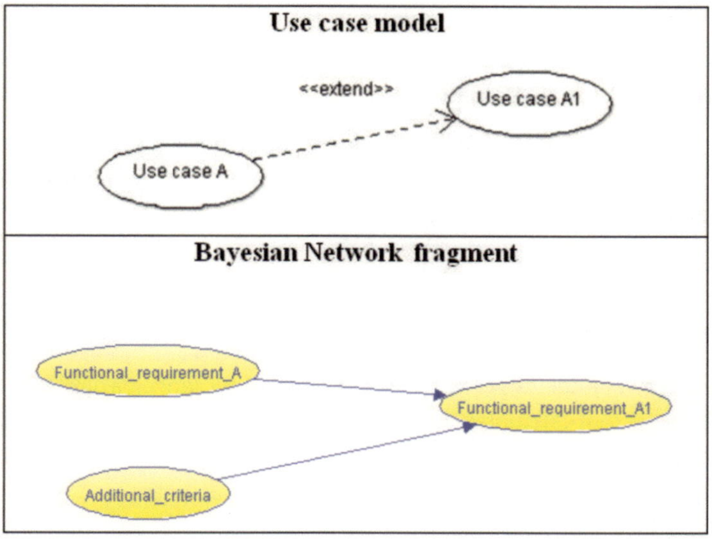

Figure 6. The extension relationship transformed into a Bayesian network fragment

The additional criterion is described in the flow of events in textual description as another functional requirement node. The direction of the implication is an additional criterion (AC) to the functional requirement A1, and functional requirements are included in the Bayesian network, with information represented in cases of use arrows. Therefore:

$$P(A1 \mid A, AC) = \frac{P(A \mid A1, AC)P(A1 \mid AC)}{P(A \mid AC)}$$

4.2. The Bayesian network developed

The development of a Bayesian network based on the use case diagram for modeling the learner in an adaptive educational system passes through two essential steps:

4.2.1. Specification of the model structure

Taking the case of the node "Learner" to illustrate the stages of development of our Bayesian network representing the learner model, note that this node has three parent nodes (Pretest, Learning Activity and Evaluation), and that each of these nodes is composed of child nodes. Links to these nodes are prerequisite relationships:

- **Learning Activity –** In this node, all students following the course must go through activities of two types, static and interactive, in the adaptive system.
- **Pretest –** All learners must take a pre-test before engaging in the learning activities of each course, The pre-test consists of two types of evaluations:
    - Knowledge: the student must answer more than ten questions to measure his or her wealth of knowledge. This type of evaluation reflects the evaluated portion of knowledge of the learner.
    - Skills: This is written proof of whether the student can apply the knowledge gained in the module. This type of evaluation reflects the skills portion of the learner.
- **Evaluation** –After the student follows the learning activity, an evaluation is conducted to determine the student's level of knowledge and skill within the module. The evaluation is essential to guide the course of the learner.

The value measuring the relative importance of each condition varies from 0 to 1, and the values of each evaluation element are defined by the teacher, who in this case is the teacher of the module "Database".

The relationship between the target variable (T) and the evidence variable (E) move from T to E, because the process that calculates the posterior probability of the target variable is the proof of knowledge of the diagnosis. Therefore, if the evidence variable has no children, the parents must be the target variables. There are two types of relationships:

- Prerequisite relations between target variables.
- Diagnostic relations of target variables to evidence variables. The control of concepts (targets) affects confidence of evidence. However, if the learner has failed a test, it is unclear if this is due to his lack of knowledge or ability, because there can be an unexpected error.

4.2.2. The specification of variable values

Once the use case diagrams have been created, it is easy to create the structure of the Bayesian network using the rules described in previous sections. Figure 7 represents the Bayesian network constructed from the use case diagram shown in the previous section. Notice how conditional independence was directly modeled by applying the rules as shown.

http://dx.doi.org/10.5772/61021

In the Bayesian network developed, we observe that the node learner (L) has three parents: Learning Activity (A), Evaluation (E) and Pretest (T), which in turn correspond to three weights of prerequisite relationship: w1 = 0.1, w2 = 0.5, w3 = 0.4. Conditional probability of (L) is computed as follows:

$$P(L|A,E,T) = w1^{*}h1 + w2^{*}h2 + w3^{*}h3$$

Where

$$h1 = \begin{cases} \frac{1 \; if \; A = L}{0 \; otherwise} \end{cases}$$

$$h2 = \begin{cases} \frac{1 \; if \; E = L}{0 \; otherwise} \end{cases}$$

$$h3 = \begin{cases} \frac{1 \; if \; T = L}{0 \; otherwise} \end{cases}$$

We should state that {L, A, E, T} is a complete set of mutually exclusive variables, each of which is also a random and binary variable.

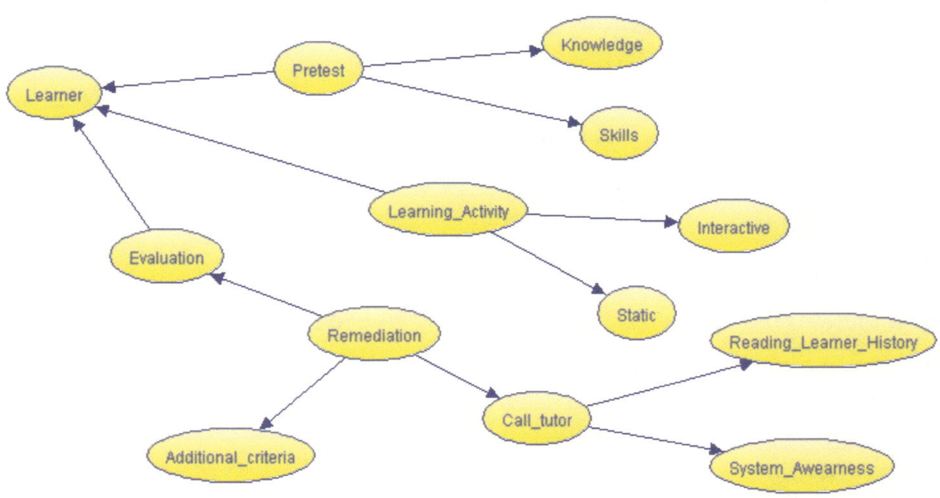

Figure 7. The Bayesian network developed of the learner model

Generalizing the formula below, we state that:

$$P(X = 1| Y1, Y2 \ldots Yn) = \sum_{i=1}^{n} wi^{*}hi$$

where $h1=\begin{cases}1 \text{ if } Yi=X \\ 0 \text{ otherwise}\end{cases}$ with given random binary variables X and Yi. Obviously, $P(not\ X \mid Y1, Y2, ..., Yn)=1-P(X \mid Y1, Y2, ..., Yn)$.

a. The Conditional Probability Table of the Node "Learner"

Table 2 represents the CPT of each child node of the parent node Learner.

A	T	E	P(J=1)	1-P(J=1) P(J=0)
1	1	1	1.0 (0.1*1 + 0.4*1+ 0.5*1)	0.0
1	0	1	0.6 (0.1*1 + 0.4*0+ 0.5*1)	0.4
1	1	0	0.5 (0.1*1 + 0.4*1+ 0.5*0)	0.5
1	0	0	0.1 (0.1*1 + 0.4*0+ 0.5*0)	0.9
0	1	1	0.9 (0.1*0 + 0.4*1+ 0.5*1)	0.1
0	0	1	0.5 (0.1*0 + 0.4*0+ 0.5*1)	0.5
0	1	0	0.4 (0.1*0 + 0.4*1+ 0.5*0)	0.4
0	0	0	0.0 (0.1*0 + 0.4*0+ 0.5*0)	1.0

Table 2. The conditional probability table of "Learner" node

Because concepts A, E, and T have no prerequisite knowledge for understanding, their CPTs are specified as prior probabilities obeying uniform distribution, as stated in Table 3 (assigned medium value of 0.5 in most cases).

P(A=1)	P(A=0)	P(T=1)	P(T=1)	P(E=1)	P(E=1)
0.5	0.5	0.5	0.5	0.5	0.5

Table 3. The conditional probability table of "Learner" parents

b. The Conditional Probability Table of the Node "Pretest"

Table 4 represents the CPT of each child node of the parent node Pretest.

K	P(J=1)	P(J=0) 1-p(J=1)
1	0.8(0.8*1)	0.2
0	0.0(0.8*0)	1.0
Sk	P(J=1)	P(J=0) 1-p(J=1)
1	0.2(0.2*1)	0.8
0	0.0(0.8*0)	1.0

Table 4. The conditional probability table of "Pretest" node

c. The Conditional Probability Table of the Node "Learning Activity"

Table 5 represents the CPT of each child node of the parent node Learning Activity.

S	P(J=1)	P(J=0) 1-p(J=1)
1	0.6(0.6*1)	0.4
0	0.0(0.6*0)	1.0
D	P(J=1)	P(J=0) 1-p(J=1)
1	0.4(0.4*1)	0.6
0	0.0(0.6*0)	1.0

Table 5. The conditional probability table of "Learning Activity" node

5. Experiment and validation

In this section, we present the validation tests of the Bayesian network derived from our model of the learner.

The learners involved in the experiment presented herein are students of the module "Database", in the first year of DUT (Technical university diploma) at the Ecole Normale Superieure of Tétouan at Abdelmalek Essaâdi University.

5.1. UnBBayes software

UnBBayes [10] is a probabilistic network framework written in Java. It has both a GUI and an API with inference, sampling, learning and evaluation. It supports BN, ID, MSBN, OOBN, HBN, MEBN/PR-OWL, PRM, structure, parameter and incremental learning.

JAVA UnBBayes uses a technique to reason by odds in intelligent systems. Through a probabilistic network–graph where the nodes are likely variables representing domain knowledge and the arcs represent relationships between them, we can estimate probabilities conditioned to evidence that assists us in decision making. This calculation is called probabilistic inference. With the addition of tree techniques, inferences in probabilistic networks can be made with high efficiency.

To make this technique easy to use, we create the JAVA UnBBayes, which is a visual system that is interactive and platform independent, making it possible to edit, build networks, and show evidence of entry and probabilistic reasoning.

5.2. Metrics

In this section, before presenting the results of our tests, we introduce the metric through which we measure the performance of a learner module modeled using Bayesian networks. The UnBBayes software allows us to evaluate the performance of each node in our network dynamically and in real time. Here are the metrics we used to evaluate our Bayesian network:

- **The global confusion matrix (GCM),** computed for the selected target node and all the chosen evidence nodes.
- **Probability of Correct Classification (PCC):** The probability of correct classification calculated from the global confusion matrix considering all evidence nodes in the Bayesian network.
- **Marginal PCC (MPCC):** The probability of correct classification calculated from the global confusion matrix considering all evidence nodes in the Bayesian network other than the one presented in the row.
- **Marginal Improvement (MI):** The probability of correct classification calculated from the global confusion matrix considering all evidence nodes in the Bayesian network and gained by adding the node presented in the row to the rest of other nodes.
- **Individual PCC (IPCC):** The probability of correct classification computed from the LCM considering only the evidence presented in the row.
- **Cost Rate:** The individual probability of correct classification over the cost ratio.

5.3. The combined Bayesian network

Before presenting the evaluation results of each node of our Bayesian network modeling the learner model in an adaptive system, we begin by presenting the combined Bayesian network through the UnBBayes software.

Figure 8 provides a map of the combined network, in which marginal variables of each node of our network are developed. We can observe the change in the marginal variables of each node in our network, simply by changing one or more marginal variable of one or more parent nodes of the selected node.

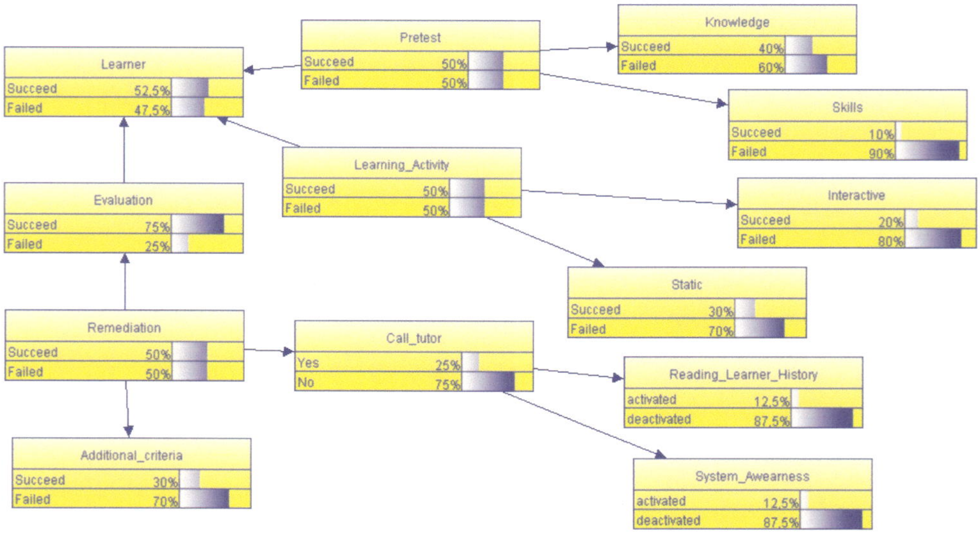

Figure 8. The combined Bayesian network of the learner model

http://dx.doi.org/10.5772/61021

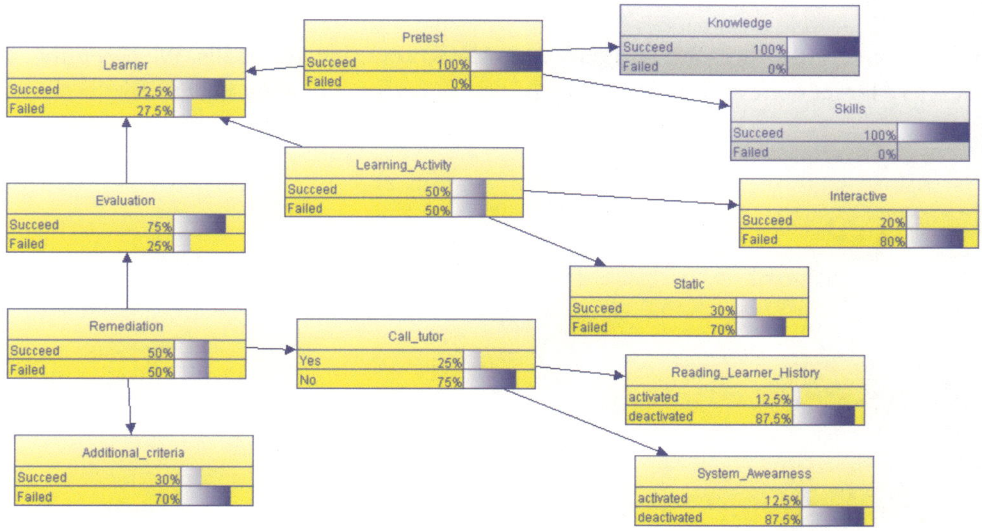

Figure 9. The combined Bayesian network of the learner model

If we change the marginal variable "Succeed" of the node "Knowledge" from 40 % to 100 %, and the marginal variable "Succeed" of the node "Skills" from 10 % to 100 %, we notice that in Fig. 9, the marginal variable "Succeed" of the parent node "Pretest" will change from the initial state of 50 % into a total of 100 % completion. We also notice that a marginal variable of the parent's node of the node "Pretest"—the node "Learner"—will also change from 50 % to 72.5 %.

By changing the information of each node, and after compiling our network, all marginal variables will change automatically, giving us the ability to track in a dynamic way the flow of the learner's path, and to detect the causes of change during all stages of the learning situation.

6. Results

In this section, we present all the results of our experiments on our Bayesian network.

6.1. Node evaluation

To evaluate the performance of each node of our network and its contribution value within a single node or within the entire network, we first began by choosing the node we wanted to evaluate as an evidence node, and chose the parents of these nodes as target nodes. We then defined a sample size that represented how often the software would repeat the simulations.

Using the metrics presented in the previous section, we evaluated the influence of each node within its parent node and within our entire Bayesian network built.

6.1.1. Evaluation of the node "Pretest"

For the pretest node, there are two parent nodes: Knowledge and Skills. We chose the node Pretest as a target node and its parents as evidences nodes, and obtained the results shown in Fig. 10.

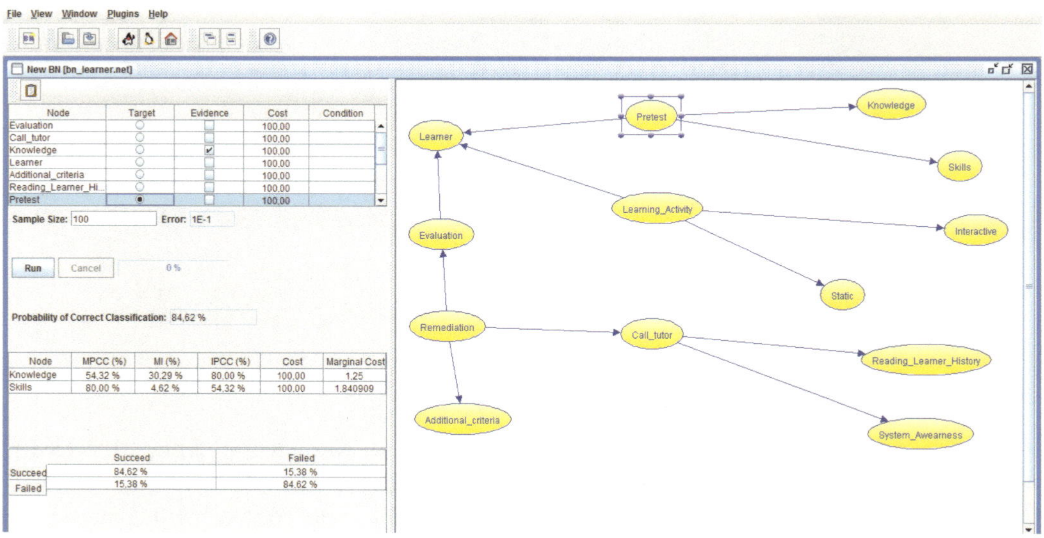

Figure 10. The evaluation results of the node Pretest

According to the results presented in the table, we find the following. By adding evidence nodes into our evaluation of the target node, the percentage of the probability of correct classifications increases. Furthermore, by measuring the probability of correct classification of each node, we see how each node contributes independently to classification. In this evaluation, we find that the node "Skills" is the node that contributes the most.

We also find how each node contributes with respect to the set of nodes in front of it. In this evaluation, the marginal improvement of the node "Skills" mean that the influence of this node is larger compared to that of the target node. We also notice that even if the marginal cost of the two different sensors is the same, the sensor that is the most evolved reflects the marginal cost of the variables of the node "Skills".

All of this reflects that to pass the pretest, the learner in this learning situation must rely more on skills than on knowledge.

6.1.2. Evaluation of the node "Learning activity"

For the "Learning Activity" node, there are two parent nodes: Static and Interactive. We chose Learning Activity as a target node and its parents as evidence nodes, and obtained the results shown in Fig. 11.

http://dx.doi.org/10.5772/61021

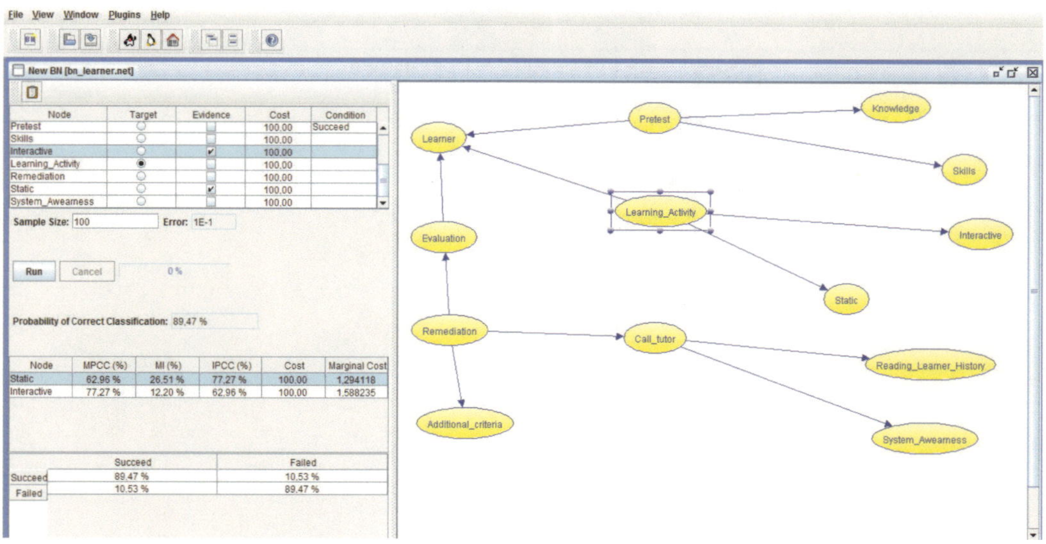

Figure 11. The evaluation results of the node learning activity

According to the results in the table, we find the following. By adding evidence nodes into our evaluation of the target node, the percentage of the probability of correct classifications increases. Furthermore, by measuring the probability of correct classification of each node, we see how each node contributes independently to classification. In this evaluation, we find that the node "Static" is the node that contributes the most.

We also find how each node contributes with respect to the set of nodes in front of it. In this evaluation, the marginal improvement of the node "Static" means that the influence of this node is larger compared to that of the target node. We also notice that even if the marginal cost of the two different sensors is the same, the sensor that is the most evolved reflects the marginal cost of the variables of the node "Static".

All this reflects that the learner in the learning situation has followed a learning activity; the learner must focus on static activity grains more than the grains of interactive activities to increase the chances of succeeding in this learning activity.

6.1.3. Evaluation of the node "Learner"

For the Learner node, there are three parent nodes: Pretest, Learning Activity and Evaluation. By choosing Learner node as a target node and its parents as evidence nodes, we obtain the results shown in Fig. 12.

According to the results in the table, we find the following. By adding evidence nodes into our evaluation of the target node, the percentage of the probability of correct classifications increases. Furthermore, by measuring the probability of correct classification of each node, we see how each node contributes independently to classification. In this evaluation, we find that the node "Learning Activity" is the node that contributes the most.

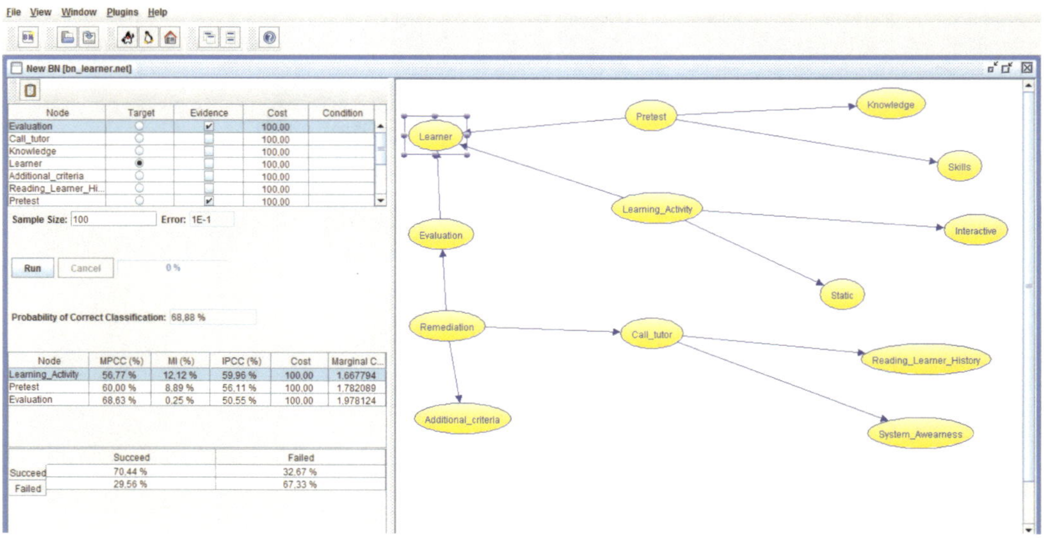

Figure 12. The evaluation results of the node Learner

We also find how each node contributes with respect to the set of nodes in front of it. In this evaluation, the marginal improvement of the node "Learning Activity" mean that the influence of this node is larger compared to the target node. We also notice that even if the marginal cost of the two different sensors is the same, the sensor that is the most evolved reflects the marginal cost of the variables of the node "Learning Activity".

All this reflects that the success of a learner in the learning situation pertains his success in the learning activity more than in the assessment or pretest.

6.2. Bayesian network evaluation

We validated each node of our learner model Bayesian network, and present in this section the validation results of the entire Bayesian network.

Figure 13 presents the entire Bayesian network validation results. In this evaluation of our network, we consider that the learner has successfully passed the pretest and the learning situation. The marginal variable of the node evaluation is 79.71 % in this case. A change in one of these two nodes will affect the marginal variables of our network in a probabilistic manner.

Based on the results and validation of each node of the Bayesian network, we were able to manage the operation of the network in a comprehensive manner.

When a learner begins to take a course in an adaptive hypermedia system, he must first successfully pass the functional requirement "Pretest", which is composed of two functional requirements that measure the learner's knowledge and skills in the chosen field. After validation of the pretest, the learner is automatically assigned to the functional requirement "Learning Activity", which is composed of two types, static and dynamic. At the end of the

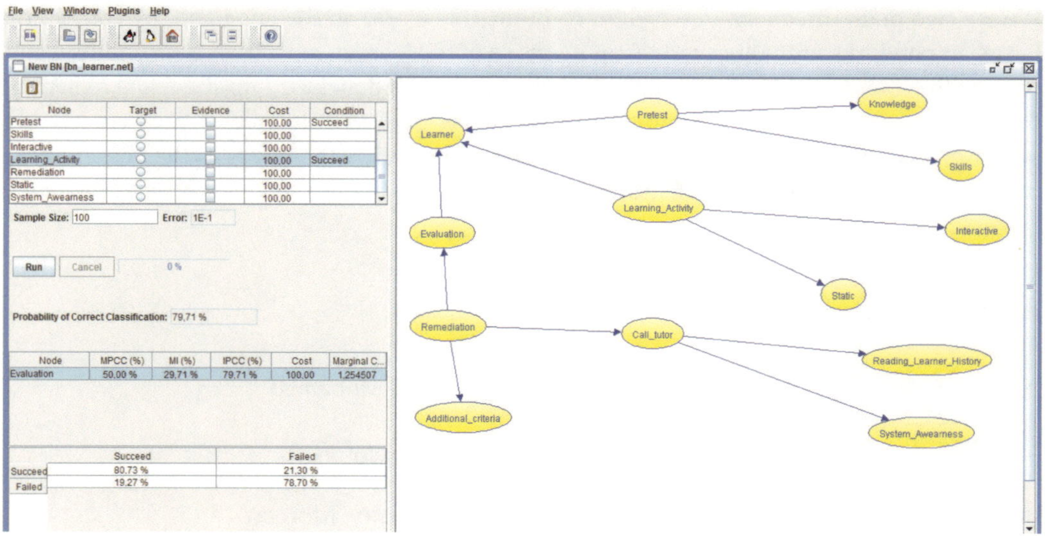

Figure 13. The evaluation of the entire learner model's Bayesian network

course, the learner takes an evaluation expressed in the functional requirement "Evaluation", and the result of this test takes the learner in the case of failure to the functional requirement "Remediation", to retake the learning activities in which the student could not succeed.

Failure in a learning situation requires calling a tutor by activating the functional requirement "Call Tutor", which then activate two functional requirements, "System Awareness" and "Reading History Learner". These two requirements are related to features of the hypermedia system.

7. Conclusion and perspective

We have shown how from a theoretical point of view and considering the analysis of the literature, it seems justified to select Bayesian networks as an effective tool to manage the learner model. The use of Bayesian networks to formally manage the problem of uncertainty in the learner model in an adaptive educational system gives us satisfactory results to address the problem of probabilistic and real-time management of all of a learner's actions in a learning situation.

The experiments presented in this article are arguments in favor of our hypothesis on the modeling of the learner model in a probabilistic way, using all the nodes as sensors to measure and evaluate the entire model.

The proposed rules for processing use case diagrams that schematize the actions of a learner in an adaptive system can be applied to many use cases in different systems.

We see two main directions in which to continue this work; on the one hand, by combining Bayesian networks with other modeling methods of the learner, such as overlay models; and on the other hand, by transforming the Bayesian networks developed for the management of the learner model into a machine-readable language, such as ontologies. Or, as we already proposed [11], by using probabilistic ontologies as a formalism that gives us the possibility to combine Bayesian networks with ontologies.

Author details

Anouar Tadlaoui Mouenis*, Aammou Souhaib and Khaldi Mohamed

*Address all correspondence to: tadlaouimouenis@gmail.com

LIROSA / Faculty of Sciences, Abdelmalek Essaâdi University, Morocco

References

[1] Zaitseva L., Boule C. (2005). Learning systems in professional training. Proceedings of Workshop "Industry meets research" within the conference Interactive Computer Aided Learning, ICL Villach, Austria.

[2] Beck J., Stern M., Haugsjaa E. (1996). Applications of AI in education. Crossroads, 3(1), 11–15.

[3] Brusilovsky P., Millan E. (1991). User models for adaptive hypermedia and adaptive educational systems. The Adaptive Web Book. Springer, Berlin/Heidelberg, 2007.

[4] Self J. Formal Approaches to Student Modeling. Technical Report AI-59, Lancaster University, England.

[5] Conati C., Gertner A., Vanlehn K. (2002). Using Bayesian networks to manage uncertainty in student modeling. Journal of User Modeling and User-Adapted Interaction, 12(4), 371–417.

[6] Pearl J. (1988). Probabilistic reasoning in intelligent systems. Morgan Kaufmann, San Mateo.

[7] Mayo M., Mitrovic A. (2001). Optimising ITS behaviour with Bayesian networks and decision theory. International Journal of Artificial Intelligence in Education, 12, 124–153.

[8] Souhaib A. (2013). Conception de l'intéropérabilité sémantique des systèmes hypermédia adaptatifs éducatifs, basée sur les ontologies. Ph.D thesis, Abdelmalek Essaidi University.

[9] Mouenis A.T., Souhaib A., Mohamed K. (2015). Development of Bayesian networks from unified modeling language for learner modelling. International Journal of Advanced Computer Science and Applications, 6(2).

[10] Costa P.C.G., Ladeira M., Carvalho R.N., Laskey K.B., Santos L.L., Matsumoto S. (2008). A first-order Bayesian tool for probabilistic ontologies. Proceedings of the 21st Florida FLAIRS UNBBayes-MEBN, Coconut Grove, FL, USA.

[11] Mouenis A.T., Mohamed K., Souhaib A. (2014). Towards probabilistic ontology based on Bayesian Networks. International Journal of Software and Web Sciences, 1(10), 102–106.

Chapter 8

Study of the Assessment Criteria on e-Learning Websites

Kuei-Chih K.C. Chuang and Mei Chuan Tsai

Additional information is available at the end of the chapter

http://dx.doi.org/10.5772/61062

Abstract

This study aimed at exploring and discussing cognizance of teachers and students toward construction of e-learning websites. It was evaluated and it developed five assessment indexes required as "Assessment Guidelines on e-Learning Websites." These five assessment indexes were "teaching material and the structure," "layout design," "interface design," "interaction design," and "establishment of system configuration." The development of survey questionnaires was based on the above five assessment indexes as well. In this study, several goals are achieved, for example, teaching resources could be augmented, quality of Web-based instruction could be improved, learners' time and efforts in Web-based learning could be saved, and effects of Web-based teaching and learning could be highlighted. In the end, a digital Taiwan can become possible when the Web-based instructions follow the assessment guidelines and prevail over the aggressive competition.

Keywords: Assessment guidelines of an instructional website, Internet, Instructional websites, Internet server end, Assessment guidelines

1. Introduction

The twenty-first century has been now called the Internet Age which is greatly affected by the various computerized multimedia technologies, such as the Internet. With the wide range of interactive computer and Web technologies, it tends to produce more effective methods of transferring skills and knowledge than the traditional lecture-style approaches. For example, the professors can integrate notes, graphics, diagrams, full-motion video segments, audio segments, and hyper link texts and materials into a comprehensive website as a cognitive and motivational tool to facilitate teaching and learning. In addition, the students can acquire and construct knowledge and skills by accessing their learning performance and take part in discussing with instant feedbacks [1].

In the way of online learning theory and application, teachers and students can get advantages from flexible teaching and learning, and make much progress step by step. Teachers easily get the feedback by students' on-line questions and reply the answers to students as soon as possible. Besides, setting up the instructional websites from teachers by professional knowledge and skills makes effective responses for the demands by students. Eventually, teachers and students get the win-win advantages for each other from such a valid and cognitive system. However, educational curriculum designers and faculty face great challenges and potentials by new teaching experiences. More and more researches have focused on teaching and learning characteristics, learning styles, and interactions between teachers and students about Web-based instructional setting. Nowadays, it has become the greatest concern for all the teachers on what the criteria should be and how to design and evaluate an effective and interactive Web-based instructional setting. We have seen in the cases presented that clearly articulated assessment strategies are vital to the effective design of online courses and programs. The peer assessment case demonstrates a program-level solution to the need to provide a tool that assesses professional skills in group-level and individual-level performance within an online context. McCracken, Cho, Sharif, Wilson, and Miller [2] made a conclusion that "it presented that clearly articulated assessment strategies are vital to the effective design of online courses and programs. The peer assessment case demonstrates a program-level solution to the need to provide a tool that assesses professional skills in group-level and individual-level performance within an online context." Therefore, the more requirement for e-learning environments grows in higher education, the more needs for website application of learning and educational assessment strategy theory to design, develop, and deliver in e-learning environments.

Graff [3] pointed out that "evaluation feedback from participants indicated that each online task was rated positively." And Smith [4] made a comment that "it is suggested that as instructors make the transition from traditional to blended/online instruction, they consider jettisoning the traditional essay requirement and replace it with some form of 'assignment essay/peer review' system such as the one described. Contemporary Learning Management Systems facilitate peer review and peer assessment approaches in ways that were not available in traditional offline education." Somehow, doing the assessment study should consider that there are numerous limitations on how to learn performance that is evaluated by assessment theories and skills. The patterns as online testing show are usually in the form of multiple choice questions without any essay type of learning assessment. Most of the reasons for offering multiple choice tasks in e-learning are for the sake of ease of implementation and ease of managing learners' replies.

The study purposes were to establish a set of criteria for assessing instructional websites by using instructors' and students' perception of current experiences in instructional websites specifically for undergraduate- and graduate- level courses in order to meet the following objectives: collecting and understanding the settings and operating rules of the present instructional websites, analyzing and developing the updated policies of the instructional websites, exploring the users' and designers' perceptions, and providing tips for building an effective instructional website. Web evaluation criteria include ideas for incorporating Web evaluation into the curricula that promote information literacy. In particular, we intended to explore five-section criteria related to the website evaluation. The five criteria were (1) website material development, (2) website graphic design, (3) website interface, (4) website communication interaction, and (5) website system.

The study measures included collecting and reviewing reference papers related to instructional websites, analyzing and inducting the websites' advantages and disadvantages, interviewing experts, and analyzing evaluation of e-learning website. During the study period, the research targets covered 33 instructors who established their own instructional websites at the first semester of the academic year 2013 at National Yunlin University of Science and Technology, 35 teachers who participated in the teacher workshop of research methods for teachers of science and technology in south Taiwan, and 240 college students of the National Yunlin University of Science and Technology. From the participants' responses of the survey questionnaires, the most essential features and characteristics required for a quality instructional website were concluded as the assessment guidelines of an instructional website.

The expert group had revised the assessment guidelines of instructional websites twice, and the effectiveness of the guidelines was high. From the analysis of data collected, it was found that the items of indexes for the assessment guidelines of instructional websites were recognized by the research targets including navigation group, teacher group, and student group. Furthermore, these items were consistent with the hypothesis of the study and results of the analysis of pilot test data conducted by the navigation group. As a result, the guidelines which resulted from the five assessment indexes displayed much high value. The research results were also regarded as database where teachers of all disciplines could refer to whenever they would develop their own instructional websites.

2. Methods

2.1. Participants

The samples of this study consisted of three groups. In the first group called control group for pilot test as well, there were 20 pre-teaching teachers who still were students enrolled in the Teacher Education Program at the National Yunlin University of Science and Technology (NYUST). In the second group, there were 33 professors who had built instructional websites for their courses at NYUST since academic year 2012, and for the other group, there were 45 teachers who attended "The Research Methods Conference of Southern Institute and College" held by NYUST in 2012. In the third group, there were 240 current NYUST students enrolled in the College of Engineering, College of Management, College of Design, and College of Humanities and Science.

2.2. Instrument and return rate

A descriptive survey method was used to collect data. After a close review of studies [5, 6, 7, 8] and particular website guidelines [9, 10, 11], a closed-ended questionnaire, called Criteria of Instructional Website, was designed to gather data related to participants' perceptions of experiences on instructional websites. The questions related to each of the five criteria are listed in Table 1 including six variables, gender, professional field, years of hands-on experience of Internet surfing, educational background, years of teaching (for faculty only), and purposes of using the Internet, also set up for analyzing vocational education faculty's and students' perceptions of instructional websites. The overall response rate for this study was 77.6 %.

Item of criteria	Sample question
1. Website material development	The material should be genuinely related to the Web name that tells
2. Website graphic design	The instructional website design should contain multimedia effects, such as sounds, 3-D pictures
3. Website interface	The web should offer an exact time for downloading each file
4. Website communication interaction (interactivity)	The instructional website should offer some kinds of sections for motivating students to participate in discussion
5. Website system	The instructional website should offer a diversity of learning assessment

Table 1. Sample questionnaire

3. Results

3.1. Control group (n = 20)

The number of pre-teaching teachers of the control group was 20 (n = 20). Among the participants, 75 % were females, 55 % with master degree, 30 % were studying in College of Management, and 70 % with experiences of Internet surfing for less than four years. And they were all sharing similar purposes of Internet surfing, such as e-mails, chatting on-line, gathering information, on-line games, and on-line learning. In addition, the results indicated that the participants rated the hypothesized five criteria as important elements with an average of more than 3.4 of the five-point Likert scale on the same variables mentioned above.

Among pre-teaching teachers who attended the seminar hosted by the National Yunlin University of Science and Technology Teachers' Center in 2012, the distribution percentages were as follows: male teachers with 25 % and female teachers with 75 %.

Among pre-teaching teachers who attended the seminar hosted by the National Yunlin University of Science and Technology Teachers' Center in 2012, the distribution percentages were as follows: College of Management with 30 %, College of Design with 25 %, College of Engineering with 20 %, and College of Humanities and Applied Sciences with 25 %.

http://dx.doi.org/10.5772/61062

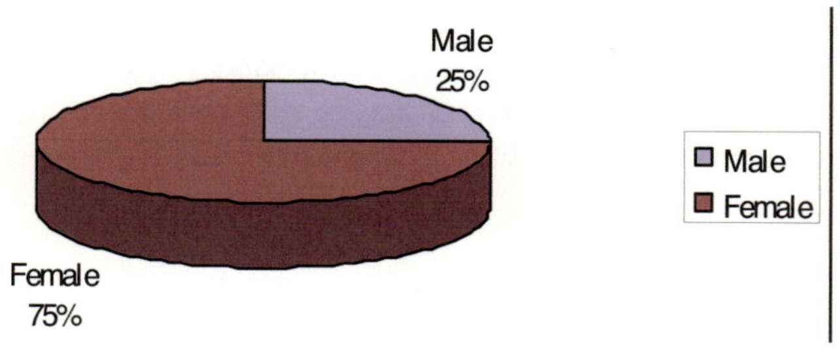

Figure 1. distribution of gender of pre-teaching teachers

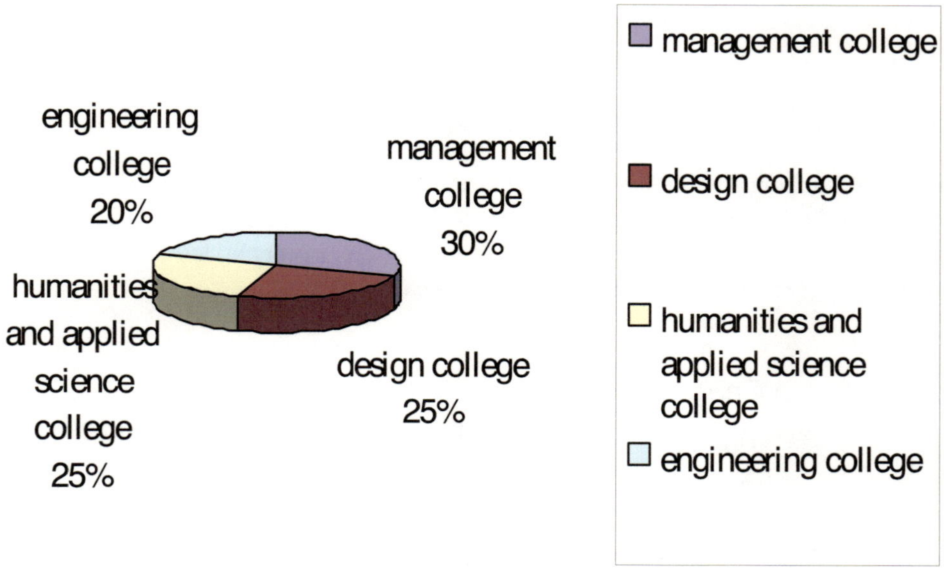

Figure 2. distribution of pre-teaching teachers who studied in college

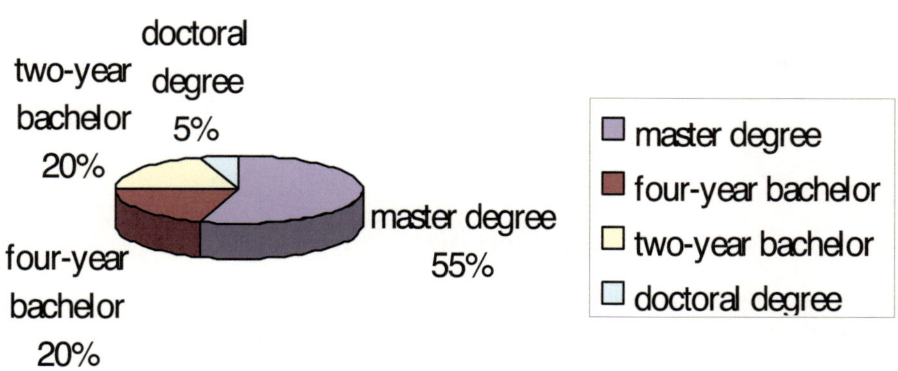

Figure 3. distribution of pre-teaching teachers

Among pre-teaching teachers who attended the seminar hosted by the Center of Teacher Education in the National Yunlin University of Science and Technology Teachers' Center in 2012, the percentages were as follows: master degree with 55 %, four-year bachelor's degree with 20 %, two-year bachelor's degree with 20 %, and doctoral degree with 5 %.

Figure 4. distribution of time in using Internet for pre-teaching teachers

Among pre-teaching teachers who attended the seminar hosted by the Center of Teacher Education in the National Yunlin University of Science and Technology Teachers' Center in 2012, the percentages were as follows: never used with 0 %, 1 year and less with 30 %, 2-4 years with 40 %, 5-7 years with 30 %, and more than 7 years with 0 %.

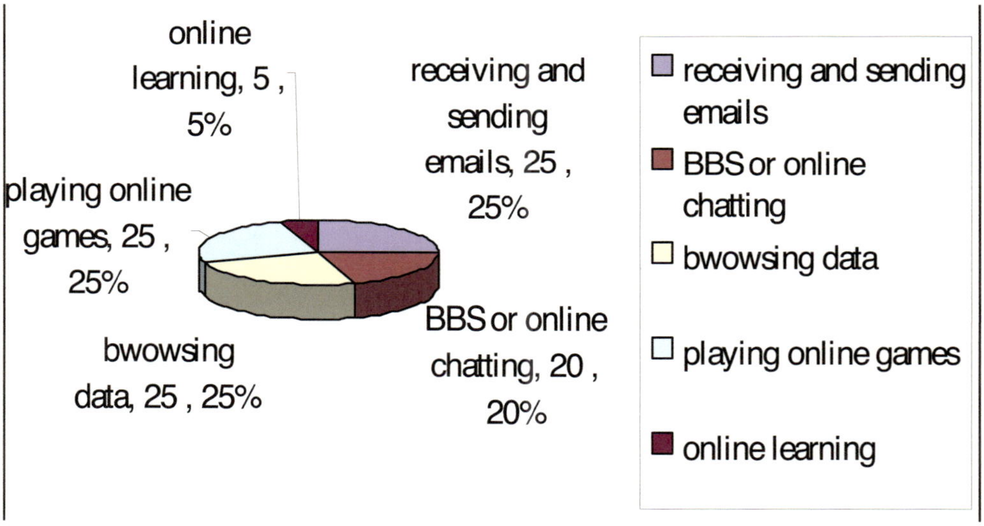

Figure 5. Distribution of the purposes of using Internet for pre-teaching teachers

Among pre-teaching teachers who attended the seminar hosted by the Center of Teacher Education in the National Yunlin University of Science and Technology Teachers' Center in 2012, the percentages were as follows: receiving and sending e-mails with 25 %, BBS or online chatting with 20 %, browsing data with 25 %, playing online games with 25 %, and online learning with 5 %

3.2. Teachers group: (n = 78)

Two thirds of the participants were males teaching in the College of Management with 20.8 %, College of Art and Design with 20.8 %, College of Humanities with 20.8 %, and College of Engineering with 37.5 %. One fourth of them had less than 15 years of teaching experiences. Interestingly, a teacher who had more than 10 years of teaching experiences indicated that the main purpose of Internet surfing was only for e-mail sending/receiving rather than instructional purposes. Compared with others, most of the teachers indicated that they used Internet for class activities with 83.3 %, and information collection with 77.5 %. More importantly, there was not significant difference between the control group and the teacher group for the perception of the instructional website based on the hypothesized five criteria at the probability of 0.05. Nevertheless, different college faculties shared slightly different opinions about the importance of item 1 of the criteria of website material development (e.g. the material should be compatible with the title which it belonged to) as shown in Table 2. Also, different college faculties shared slightly different perceptions on the items of the appropriate location of frame design in the criteria of "website interface" based on the Schaffer test.

College N	**N**	**Alpha =0.05**	
		1	**2**
Management	29	3.52	
Engineering	3	4.00	4.00
Art and Design	21	4.24	4.24
Humanities	6		4.83
		0.465	0.335

Table 2. Website material development, item #1 Schaffer test

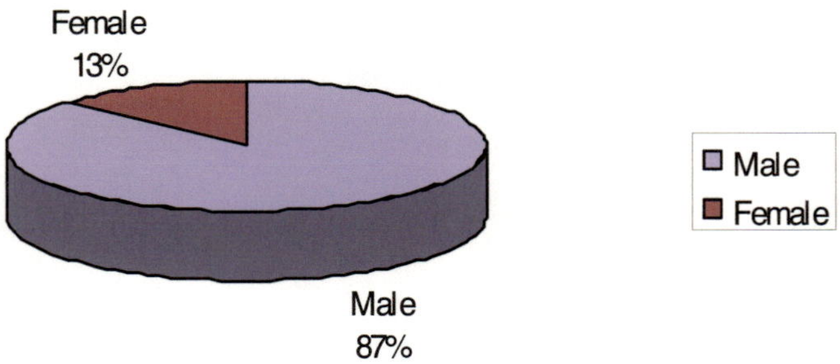

Figure 6. Distribution of gender of YUNST teachers who have built web pages as teaching aids

Among YUNST teachers who have built Web pages as teaching aids, the percentages were as follows: male with 87 % and female with 13 %.

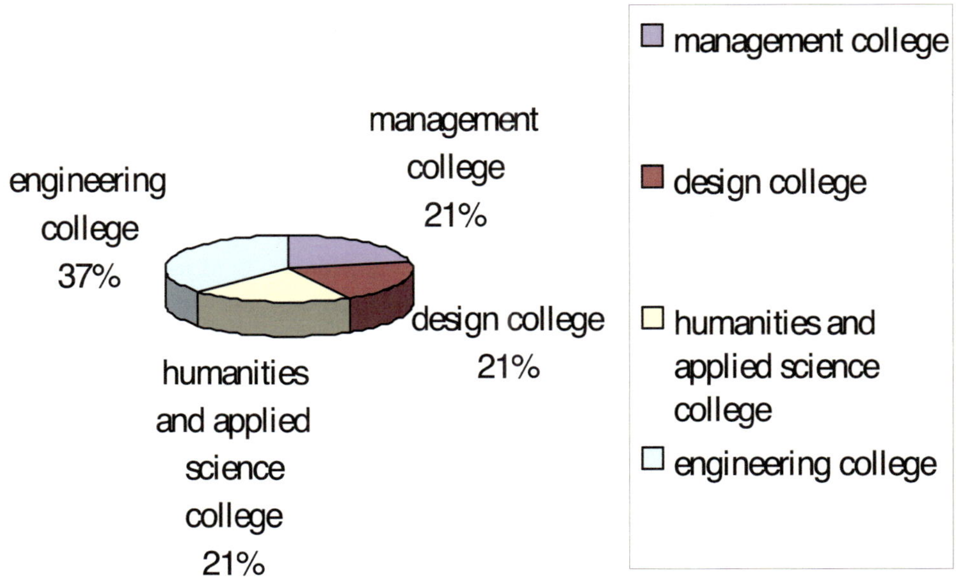

Figure 7. Distribution of YUNST teachers who have built Web pages as teaching aids

Among the college of YUNST teachers who had built Web pages as teaching aids, the percentages were as follows: College of Management with 21 %, College of Design with 21 %, College of Humanities and Applied Sciences 21 % and College of Engineering with 37 %.

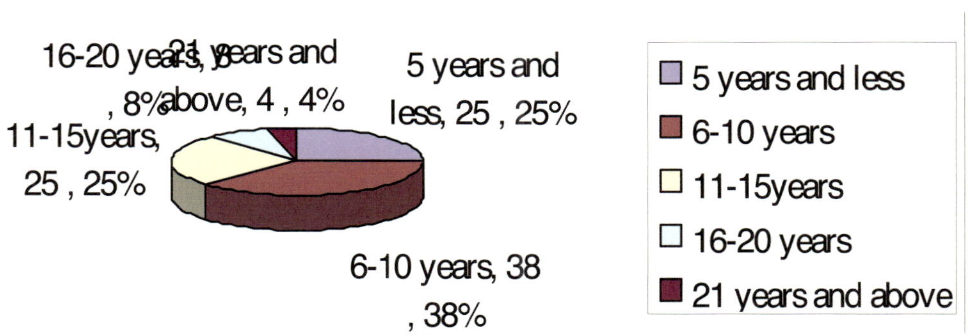

Figure 8. Distribution of seniority of YUNST teachers who have built Web pages as teaching aids

Among seniority of YUNST teachers who have built Web pages as teaching aids, the percentages were as follows: 5 years and less with 25 %, 6-10 years with 38 %, 11-15 years with 25 %, 16-20 years with 8 %, and 21 years and above with 4 %.

Among the time YUNST teachers who have built Web pages as teaching aids used the Internet, never used was 0 %, one year and less 46 %, 2-4 years 50 %, 5-7 years 0 %, 7-10 years 0 %, and more than 10 years 4 %.

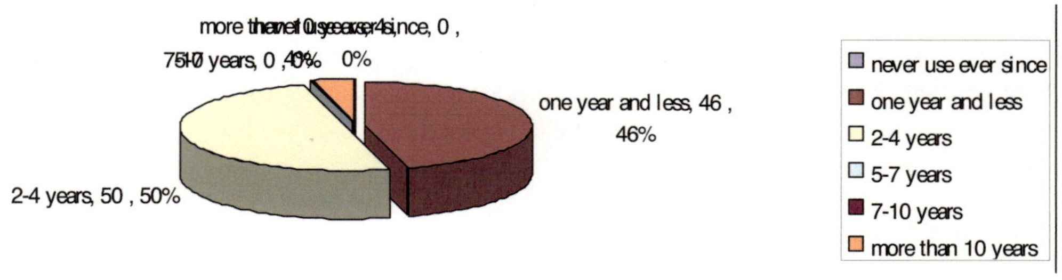

Figure 9. Distribution diagram of time YUNST teachers who have built Web pages as teaching aids used the Internet

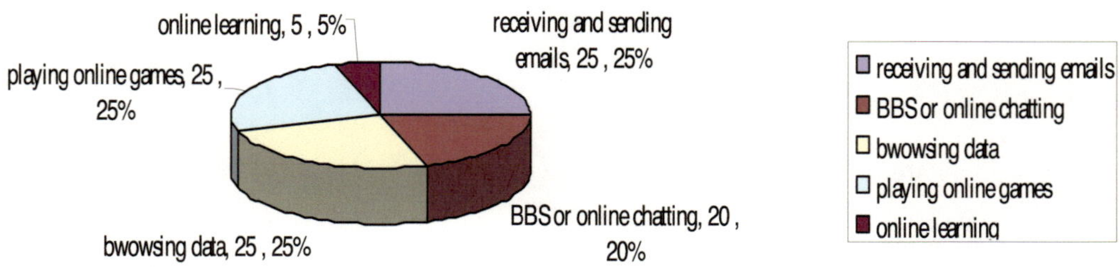

Figure 10. Distribution program of the purpose of YUNST teachers who have built Web pages as teaching aids to use the Internet

Among the purpose of YUNST teachers who have built Web pages as teaching aids to use the Internet, the percentages were as follows: receiving and sending e-mails with 25 %, browsing data with 25 %, BBS or online chatting with 20 %, playing online games with 25 %, and online learning with 5 %.

3.3. NYUST students group (n = 240)

About half of the respondents were male or female. Most of them studied in the College of Management (31.8 %) and College of Engineering (31.3 %) with a college degree (47.0 %), and two- to four-year Internet application experience (55.6 %). The results also revealed that the major purposes of surfing the Internet were for e-mail (69.7 %) and information collection (76.1 %). Based on the results of t-test analysis, there was no significant difference between the control group and the student group for the perceptions of the instructional website based on the hypothesized five criteria at the probability of 0.05. However, different college students have slightly different perceptions on the items of the appropriate updated relevant information given on the side of the site in the criteria of "website material development" based on the Schaffer test.

Third, NYUST students (n = 240), about half of the respondents were male/female. Most of them studied in the College of Management (31.8 %) and Engineering (31.3 %) with a college degree (47.0 %) and two- to four-year Internet application experience (55.6 %). The results also revealed that the major purposes of surfing the Internet were for email (69.7 %) and information collection (76.1 %). Based on the results of t-test analysis, there was no significant difference between the control group and the student group for the perceptions of the instructional website based on the hypothesized five criteria at the probability of 0.05. However, different college students have slightly different perceptions on the items of the appropriate updated relevant information given on the side of the site in the criteria of "website material development" based on the Schaffer test.

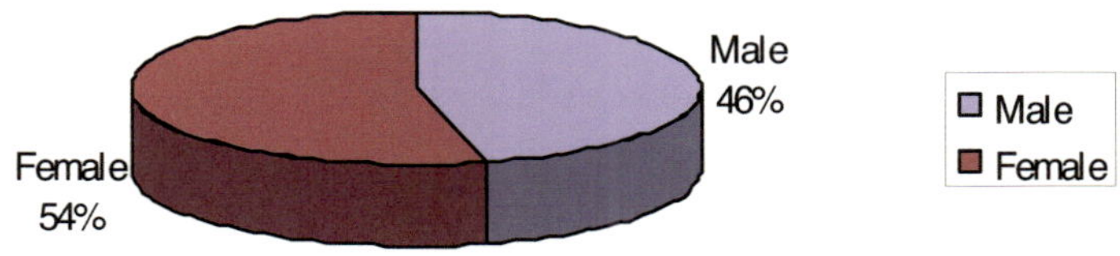

Figure 11. Distribution of gender of YUNST students

Among YUNST students, the percentages were as follows: male with 46 %, and female with 54 %.

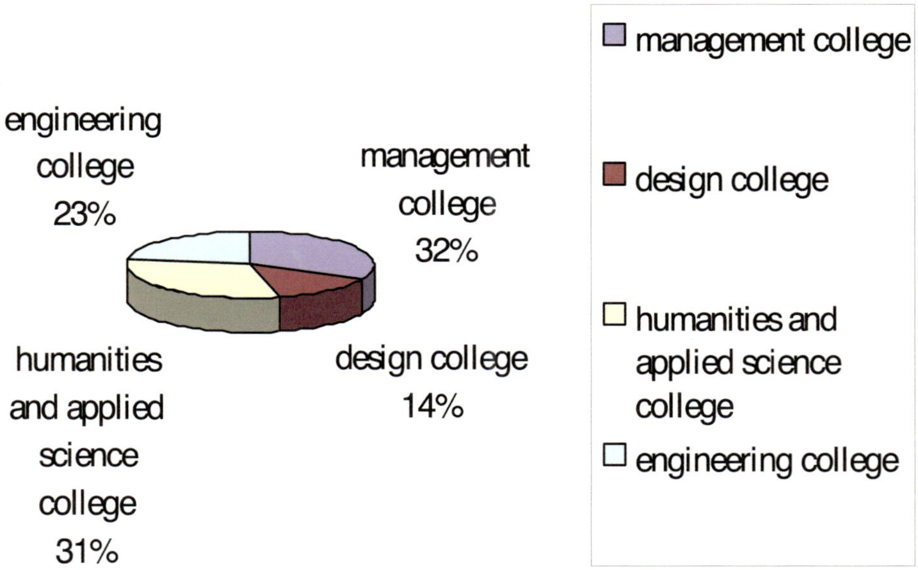

Figure 12. Distribution of college students at YUNST

Among students at YUNST, the percentages were as follows: College of Management with 32 %, College of Design with 14 %, College of Engineering with 23 %, and College of Humanities and Applied Sciences with 31 %.

Among the degrees of YUNST students, the percentages were as follows: master's with 25 %, four-year bachelor's with 47 %, two-year bachelor's with 21 %, and doctoral with 7 %.

http://dx.doi.org/10.5772/61062

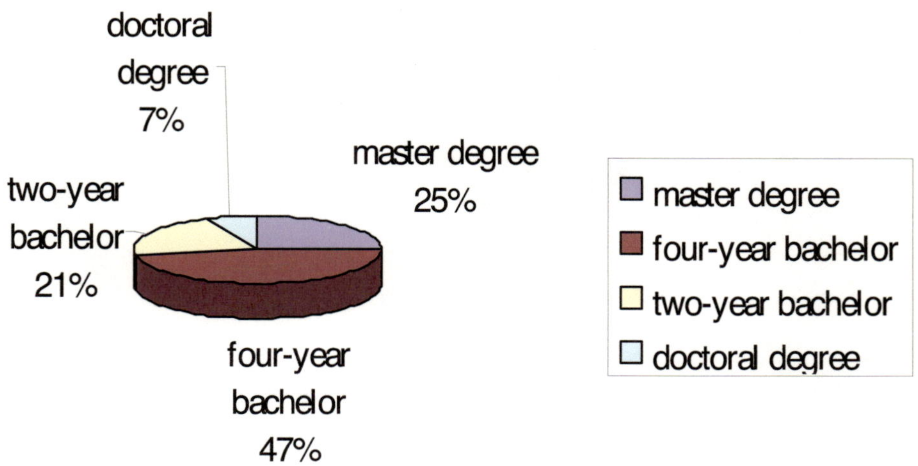

Figure 13. Distribution of students' degree at YUNST

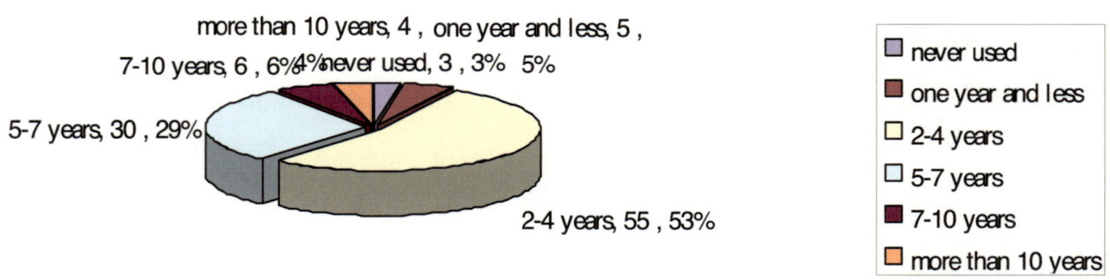

Figure 14. Distribution of years in using the Internet of YUNST students

Among the years YUNST students have used the Internet, the percentages were as follows: never used with 3 %, less than 1 year with 5 %, 2-4 years with 53 %, 5-7 years with 30 %, and 7-10 years with 6 % and more than 10 year with 4 %.

Among the purpose of YUNST students in using the Internet, the percentages were as follows: receiving and sending e-mails with 43 %, BBS or online chatting with 7 %, browsing data with 45 %, playing online games with 2 %, and online learning with 3 %.

4. Conclusion

The central concern of this study was to develop efficient ideas of instructional websites criteria for teachers and instructional Web designers to use and build excellent instructional Web environment. The results revealed that hypothesized criteria were perceived as a highly significant contribution. Indeed, the results could help Web designers construct highly effective and interactive instructional Web environment and bring up education in Taiwan

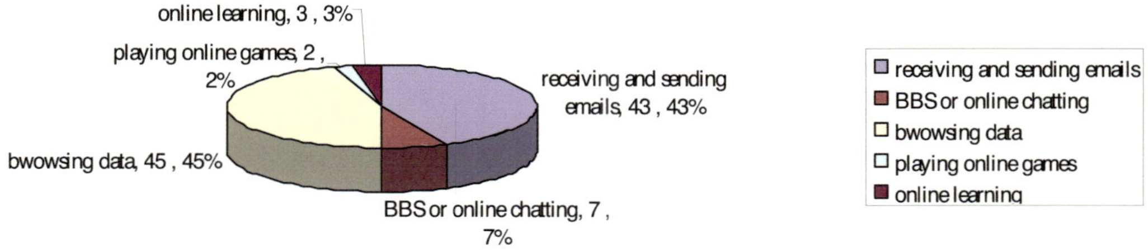

Figure 15. Distribution of purpose of YUNST students in using the Internet

into a higher-level digital learning situation. Based on the results, the study provided some recommendations for further instructional Web establishment and further studies as follows:

1. Instructors should be flexible in constructing their instructional websites specifically to the target students' educational backgrounds.
2. A comparative study for perception of long-term teaching experienced teacher versus new or short-term teaching experienced teacher on criteria of instructional website was suggested for further study.
3. Researches must go on to expand to other schools, faculty and students to deepen scopes and verify the findings.

Acknowledgements

The authors would like to thank the National Science Council and National Yunlin University of Science and Technology for the grant support.

The study has much appreciated the enthusiastic participants including three instructors who established their own instructional websites in the first semester of the academic year 2013 at the National Yunlin University of Science and Technology, 35 teachers who participated in the teacher workshop on research methods for teachers of science and technology in south Taiwan, and 240 college students of the National Yunlin University of Science and Technology.

Author details

Kuei-Chih K.C. Chuang* and Mei Chuan Tsai

*Address all correspondence to: chuangkc@yuntech.edu.tw

Graduate Institute of Technological and Vocational Education, National Yunlin University of Science and Technology, , Sec.3, University Rd., Douliu, Yunlin, Taiwan, R.O.C

http://dx.doi.org/10.5772/61062

References

[1] Kuo, C.H. & Chang, T.S. English On-line: Designing a Web-based EST Course. Proceedings of 2003 International Conference on English Teaching and Learning in the Republic of China. Providence University Taichung (2003).

[2] McCracken, J., Cho, S., Sharif, A., Wilson, B., & Miller, J. "Principled Assessment Strategy Design for Online Courses and Programs." Electronic Journal of E-learning, 10.1, (2012):107-119.

[3] Graff, Martin. "Cognitive style and attitudes towards using online learning and assessment methods." Electronic Journal of e-learning 1.1, (2003): 21-28.

[4] Smith, Martin. "Can Online Peer Review Assignments Replace Essays in Third Year University Courses? And If So, What Are the Challenges?." Electronic Journal of e-Learning 10.1, (2012): 147-158.

[5] Martinez, M. Successful Web Learning Environments: New Design Guidelines. ERIC Document ED 446745 (2000).

[6] Ministry of Education. Education in the Republic of China. Bureau of Statistics, MOE: Taipei. (1996)

[7] Ministry of Education. (2001). Education in the Republic of China. Taipei: MOE.

[8] Pan, A. C. (1998). Optimize the Web for Better Instruction. ERIC Document 421098.

[9] Technology for all Americans Projects. Technology for All Americans: A Rationale and Structure for the study of technology. Blacksburg: VA(1997)

[10] Summary, R. & Summary, L. (1998). The Effectiveness of the World Wide Web as an Instructional Tool. ERIC Document 431393.

[11] Wang, J. & Chuang, K.C. (2003). A Study of Instructional Website Guidelines. World Conference on E-Learn in Corp., Govt., Health, & Higher Ed., Vol. 2002, Issue 1, pp. 999-1005.

Chapter 9

Physics Learning in Primary and Secondary Schools with Computer Games—An Example — Angry Birds

Robert Repnik, Dominik Robič and Igor Pesek

Additional information is available at the end of the chapter

http://dx.doi.org/10.5772/60604

Abstract

In this paper, we discuss how we can make physics lessons more interesting with the use of information and communications technology (ICT). We explain why physics teachers need to be ICT competent and which ICT tools teachers can use to improve their lessons. Nowadays, many learners spend their free time playing computer games that use basic physics laws for game mechanics. One of our goals was to find out which computer games would be appropriate for learning physics and how to include those games in the learning process. We also show an example how to teach physics using the computer game *Angry Birds*, where we take into account primary and secondary school curriculum. Finally, we analyze how teaching physics with computer games affect students and what are the benefits and weaknesses using this method. In addition, we conduct a survey to gain insight on the opinion of physics teachers about the appropriateness of the computer game *Angry Birds* for teaching physics in elementary and high school. Surprisingly, the teachers find the game more appropriate for the teaching of physics in elementary school, despite of the fact that there are physics themes mostly from high school physics included in the game.

Keywords: ICT, Angry Birds, computer games, physics, teaching, e-learning, curriculum

1. Introduction

The fast penetration of information and communication technology (ICT) into our lives and society is causing how, when, and where we work and study. School-aged children nowadays spend their free time immersed in a media-rich, ubiquitous, always-connected world where most of the time they usually play computer games. For two decades, scientists were trying to figure out why are computer games so motivating and why children spend so much time playing them [1]. The results of research were three features: challenge, fantasy, and curiosity. The same three features are also very important aspects in learning. Challenge helps us to stay motivated to achieve our goal, fantasy helps us to better imagine how things should work, and curiosity drives us to figure out things that we did not know.

Educators around the world in the last 50 years try to incorporate ICT and computers into the education system. Four threads have been identified [2]. The first thread, computer-assisted instruction (CAI) and lately intelligent tutoring systems (ITS), has promised a new way of how learners would learn but never gained much attention. Second thread, computer science and computer programming, is gaining momentum lately as few countries are bringing them as obligatory subjects in school curriculum. The third thread is cognitive development and problem solving skills, which are getting much of attention as problem solving is one of the key competencies for 21st century citizen. The fourth thread is Internet use for gathering information and as a tool for improving problem solving skills. Perhaps the greatest potential for ICT in education is the improvement of traditional teaching with the inclusion of different tools in the classrooms.

The next generation of jobs will be characterized by increased technology use, extensive problem solving, and complex communication [3]. These are the skills that go beyond typical reading, writing, and arithmetic of years past. It is not only what students need to learn that is shifting but also how and when they learn. Students of today are growing up with laptops, tablets, cell phones, and video call, and they expect to use this technology in their daily interactions [4].

One area of significant promise in this regard is a movement toward the use of educational computer games as learning tools in schools [5]. We will tackle this area in subsequent sections.

This chapter is structured as follows, we first categorize computer and educational games, and then we introduce the computer game *Angry Birds* and describe how *Angry Birds* can be used in physics curriculum. Next we explain which computer programs and how to use them with *Angry Birds* in the classroom. We conclude this chapter with the survey on how teachers would use *Angry Birds* in classrooms.

2. Computer and educational games

For the purposes of this paper, we will define a game as a system in which players engage in artificial conflict, defined by rules, that results in quantifiable outcome [6]. A definition of digital game requires a game system to incorporate technology. Simulations, augmented reality, and traditional computer games meet the requirement. However, purely virtual worlds, such as Second Life, would not be games because there is no quantifiable outcome [5].

The different types of computer games are as follows [7]:

- **Card games**—Its computerized version of typical card games and games where game mechanics involves playing with cards where graphics can make card more alive in the virtual world. Examples *Poker, Solitaire,* and *Black Jack.*

- **Board Games**—These are virtual presentation of classic board games like *Chess, Monopoly, and Backgammon.*

- **Puzzles**—These are games that are mostly evolved around problems. In these games, the player must figure out a solution for the given problem using different in-game tools to solve an enigma. Good examples are *Tetris, Mastermind, Brain Age, Ilomilo.*

- **Maze**—The basic mechanics of this is evolved by problem of navigation, where a player's main objective is to get out of the maze. Examples are *Pack Man, Doom, Wolfenstien 3D.*

- **Fighting**—Fighting games involve characters who usually fight hand-to-hand in one-on-one combat situation. Examples are *Street Fighter* and *Avengers* [7].

- **Action**—These types of games involve control of a character who proceeds through story and shoots to objects and enemies. Nowadays, we can also refer to this type of games as first-person shooter (FPS) games. These are very popular and can be played online against other players. Examples are *Counter-Strike, Call of Duty, Unreal Tournament,* and *America's Army.*

- **Adventure**—Adventure games are similar to action games, but they evolve more around the story and mystery behind it. Players are often placed in historical environment where they try to solve a mystery. Examples are *Zork: Grand Inquisitor, Quest for Glory IV, Grim Fandango,* and *Gone Home.*

- **Role playing**—In role-playing games, players can choose between different types of character. Play style depends from what type of character you have chosen. Characters may differ from gender, abilities, races, specializations, profession, and other specifics that games have to offer. When a character is chosen, you can adventure in the virtual world where you can go on a quest where you deal with different problems and adversaries. During quests, you upgrade your character in agility, strength or magic. This type of game is very popular nowadays, and it is mostly played online. This type of game is called massively multiplayer online role-playing game (MMORPG). Examples are *Diablo, Titan Quest, World of Warcraft,* and *Skyrim.*

- **Strategy**—strategy games emphasize on involving a strategy to defeat your opponent. In this game, players need to resolve a problem of resources, economy, defense, and attack. Most known strategy games are *Age of Empires, Warcraft, Civilization, Europa Universalis, Total War,* and *Stronghold.*

- **Sports**—These games are mostly a virtual presentation of real-life sports, where the player picks a team or individual and compete in sport discipline. Most known are *FIFA, NHL,* and *NBA,* among others.

- **Simulation**—There are two types of simulation games, training and management. At training simulation game, designers try to simulate a real-world environment, where you can practice. Good examples of training simulation games are games *Wheels of Steels, Flight Simulator*, and *Ship Simulator*. Management simulation games are about managing community and economy. Good examples of these games are *Tycoon* series, *The Sims, and SimCity*.

These games are mostly a product of big entertainment companies, which can provide enough funding for game designers and programmers to develop new games and to sustain old ones up to date. If we can compare these games with didactic games, we can surely get to the conclusion that designers of nondidactical games put more effort to make games fun and graphically appealable and, in this case, also more playable. Another factor is freedom of game designers at nondidactical computer games. They do not need to evolve game around lessons that should be learned in certain stage of game, but they have more freedom at designing environment details and effects. Also, they put more focus on playability of the game rather than learning a certain lesson. That gives nondidactical computer games advantage in popularity.

Research in the United States has shown that majority of children and adolescents nowadays are playing computer games for at least 1 hour per day [6]. This indicates that computer games take a great part not only in children's but also in adolescents' everyday life. Many parents are worried that playing games to much could lead to addiction, violence, and depression of their children, but they mostly overreact because they fail to see the positive effects of playing computer games and are mostly mislead by media. Computer games changed dramatically, and they became much more complex, diverse, and social in nature, which means that they offer much more to players than they did in a previous decade. Let us check what we can gain and what the benefits at playing computer games are. Research has shown that computer games can improve cognitive brain functions. Numerous studies has shown that computer games can help at faster and more accurate attention allocation, higher spatial resolution in visual processing, and enhanced mental rotation abilities. It is also interesting that spatial skills can be trained relatively quickly and skills like this can be easily transferred in real-life usage. Preliminary research has also demonstrated that these cognitive advantages manifest in measurable changes in neural processing and efficiency, which means that players of computer games can filter irrelevant information much faster than nonplayers. However, we must say that these benefits do not apply to all genres of games but mostly to games where 3D environment is included.

Great benefit can be also gained with problem solving skills, which is dependent on game complexity. It seems that nowadays children have evolved around the aspect of problem solving. We rarely see someone reading a manual, but they mostly learn by trial and error, which can also be related to computer games where game designers often offer very little instructions how to solve a problem. A final cognitive benefit from playing computer games is enhanced creativity. Another benefit from playing video games also shows up in the motivation of players. It seems that many computer games are stimulating just enough frustration that players stay highly motivated to solve the problem and take great pleasure succeeding. It seems that challenge in games provides enough motivation and fun for players to play the game, and that makes a positive effect on them in a way to attain better motivation and persistence, which can also lead to better marks at school if the same can be applied to learning. Another benefit from playing computer games is on the emotional state of a player. Gaming may be among the most efficient and effective means by which children and youth generate positive feelings. Puzzle games like for instance *Angry Birds*, which has minimal interfaces, short-term commitments, and high-degree of accessibility can improve player moods, promote relaxation, and ward off anxiety, which can also result in higher self-esteem and better grades in school. If playing a game can make a person happier, then this is a great factor that we can gain from playing games and may result in various positive effects such better inspiration and connectivity. Computer games stimulate not only positive emotions but also negative ones, which may not be as grim as it sounds. By stimulating just enough negative emotions such anger, anxiety, frustration, and sadness, we are able to take control of those feelings and learn how to react on them, which can also lead to better adaptive behavior. Playing computer games also improves our social skills. We already said that games changed a lot from last decade, and they also changed in social prospective. Majority of players nowadays play computer games with their friends and rarely alone, which also indicates that they must obtain certain social skills to be able to communicate with friends. Nowadays, some online games provide players with lots of social possibilities where they chat and even send emoticons to each other. Game designers also enforce collaboration between them, so players have to work together to defeat greater adversaries, and that mostly requires good communication skills and coordination [8]. Due to all of benefits that we can gain from computer games, why not use them as a teaching material.

Computer games that were designed for learning are called educational games [2]. What makes games "educational" are specific characteristics [1]. Educational games should also have appropriate methods for learning contents, which depends on nature of contents. For example, we must distinguish between learning of knowledge, processes, procedures, and casual principles. Each of those requires different learning methods that depend on content's complexity. Methods that are used for learning also affect game structure and game mechanics. Finally, what every educational game should have is a feedback system that provides players with information of learning success. We described key characteristics of educational games, where we found out that game structure and game mechanics depend on game content and methods of learning [5]. On the other hand, we need to ask ourselves why children prefer playing classic computer games than educational computer games. The key element is that educational games are not primarily designed for fun only, and major software companies do not develop educational games. Those companies have expert knowledge in computer graphics and game designs, but they have discovered that educational games are not commercially successful and revenue is too small for them. So to get good learning results in computer games, we should either design and develop better educational games or find those computer games that are popular and could be used for educational purposes.

At this point, we must also mention game-based learning, which is defined as "an innovative learning approach derived from the use of computer games that possess educational value or different kinds of software applications that use games for learning and education purposes such as learning support, teaching enhancement, assessment and evaluation of learners" [9].

Some computer games are using actual physics as their game mechanics, and children are very eager to spend hours playing them. So why don't we use those as a teaching tools for physics? One of those games that are using actual physics as their game mechanics is the very popular computer game *Angry Birds* but is not specifically made for teaching.

3. Computer games and physics

Nowadays, a lot of pupils at the end of their secondary school are discouraged to go to study physics. If we would ask them, why is that so, we would get a common answer that physics is boring, hard to understand, and not interesting. This response from pupils mainly results from physics teacher's old-fashioned methods of teaching. Most of teachers are using main-frame (or traditional) method, teaching by telling, which seems to be less effective and boring for students than inquiry-oriented teaching [1]. A great help for this method is the use of information and communications technology (ICT). To use all these, the physics teacher needs to be e-competent [10]. It means that the physics teacher should be able to successfully use ICT as tool for teaching. The use of ICT gives us access to a lot of information, and it is also essential for the support and development of functional skills required in life. It is also a great motivational factor because many of the pupils have highly developed skills of using ICT, and it allows pupils to maintain their concentration longer [10,11]. With the use of ICT, we can effectively collect, display, and introduce data to pupils, and it is also a great tool to deepen knowledge. Teacher priority should not be only to teach physics and deliver information to pupils but also to teach them how to find this information (collecting information) and define which information are correct and useful for them (selecting information).

Learners are not always aware that the game that they are playing is using basic physics laws for game mechanics. Consequently, we could use these games as a didactical tool to teach them physics and make physics lessons more interesting for them. All we need is a computer and a software that measures and shows analyzed data from computer game. There is a variety of games that can be used for experiment. A well-known game and still very popular is the game *Super Mario Bros*. It can be used with problem-based approach for calculating basic kinematics and studying different problems within Mario world [12]. A very interesting game for learning physics is also *Scorched 3D*. In this game, a player must set the power, angle, direction of a projectile to hit another tank while considering the wind affecting the projectile course. In this game, we can learn the physics of projectile motion and introduce it clearly to the students [13]. Sometimes you have to fail in game to figure out how to complete the mission. A game that is made on this concept is called *Angry Birds* [14], where you use different birds as projectiles to destroy green pigs. We can use this game to teach various concepts in physics. Next, we present an example of how to provide physics teaching with *Angry Birds*.

4. Angry Birds

Angry Birds games are a product of a Finnish company called Rovio entertainment. The first game was released in year 2009 for Apple's iOS Android, Symbian, and Windows Phone operating systems. Since then, Rovio entertainment upgraded the game that can also be used on PCs and game consoles. Its addictive gameplay, comical design style, and low price has made the game very popular in almost any age-group. Its popularity also encouraged the company to make new sequels with different themes. From the first game *Angry Birds* to latest sequel *Angry Birds Transformers*, eight more sequels are listed, with different themes and game mechanics [14].

4.1. Game insight

The basic story of *Angry Birds* is about evil green pigs called "bad piggies," which are constantly stealing unwatched eggs from birds, desiring to cook and eat them. The pigs are under the command of King Pig, who commands his army of pigs to construct as many structures as possible to keep the birds from reaching him. The main protagonists of the game are the birds, which are trying to get their eggs back before the evil pigs can eat them. Red (Bird) is the main character of the *Angry Birds* series and also the leader of the flock. He does not have any special abilities and has appeared in every version except *Angry Birds Stella*. There are also Chuck the yellow bird, who has the ability to drastically accelerate; Jay, Jack, and Jim called "The Blues" with the ability to separate in three same-sized birds; Bomb the black bird, who has the ability to explode; and Matilda the white bird, whose ability is to drop one egg on the pigs. There is also Hal the boomerang, who can be seen as the green bird in many sequels and has the ability is to fly back like a boomerang. Bubbles the orange bird is also one of the flock crew members. He has the ability is to drastically expand and push all obstacles away. The newest member of the flock is Stella. She has different abilities like trapping objects into bubbles, speeding up when screen is tapped, and rebounding of walls [15].

4.2. Game mechanics and materials

In the game, a slingshot is used to shoot birds in a way to eliminate all green pigs that may be protected with different materials, which can be destroyed easier with a specific bird's ability. The game is also designed wherein you gain difficulty in every level, and sometimes it requires you to do the same level many times before you finish it. With difficulty scaling with every level, it also motivates and drags you to play the game. When you successfully complete a level, you can also keep track of the score that you achieved, which is measured by the stars that you gain. The final mark of how you preformed in a specific level is dependent on how many objects you destroyed and how many birds you used to eliminate green pigs [14]. We already mentioned that we have different materials (Figure 1) in the game, and we know that different materials have different properties, and it is also the same in *Angry Birds*. The basic materials in the game are stone, wood, and glass [15].

Figure 1. *Angry Birds* gameplay showing an example how to shoot a bird to destroy pigs hiding inside the walls. Stone, wood, and glass are the basics materials. How hard are they to destroy is not always dependent on the material but also on the shape of the material. Small square-shaped blocks are mostly harder to destroy than long square-shaped blocks.

5. Why is physics not popular?

Physics is not very popular among students, and consequently, the educators all over the world are facing the same problem in stimulating students to study physics (Figure 2). Most of the countries have shortage of physics teachers and scientists. The question is why is physics so unpopular among the students? The common beliefs that we encounter about physics are that physics is not an easy subject, it requires a high degree of dedication, and it is mostly meant for intelligent people who are sometimes socially discriminated, and because of that, they are discouraged to study physics. The most common replies that we get about physics when we ask people who finished high school or are still studying are as follows: "physics is boring," "physics is difficult," "physics is for boys," and "physics is strange and only crazy people are doing it" [16]. Why are most responses so negative? What is the problem? It seems that pupils in elementary school show big interest in physics when you ask them about topics that can be found in physics curricula like, for example, electricity, magnetism, force, universe, and others. However, it seems that interests are greatly lowered in high school when they are actually faced with a higher degree of knowledge about them, which includes the use of mathematic at higher degree and this causes students difficulties at understanding physics and also discourage them [17].

It seems that teaching methods and math involvement at a higher degree of education are the origin why students get lack of interest in physics. The question is What can we change to motivate students and to show them that physics is one of the essential science disciplines that not only brings great results at developing technologies but also gives us understanding how nature is working? Also, physics teachers often do not enjoy teaching physics. The main reason may be hidden behind physics curricula, which give really small flexibility at lesson distribution during the year, and the teacher really does not have time to improve their lessons because they have to deal with the lesson schedule for the year. There seems to be two crucial problems.

http://dx.doi.org/10.5772/60604

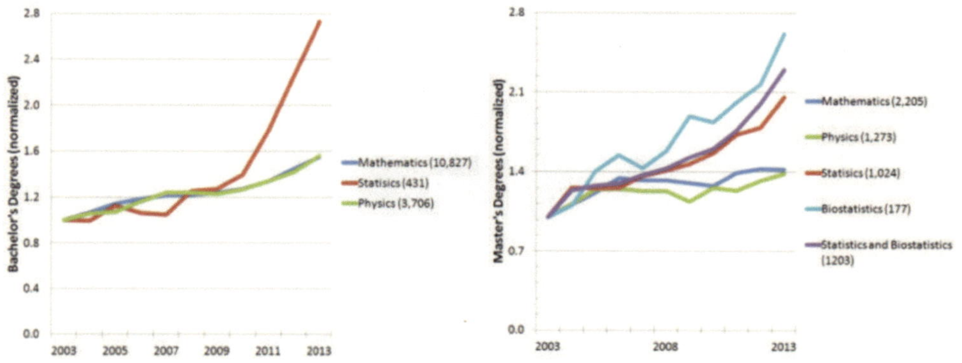

Figure 2. We can see from the ASA Community research that physics is far behind other science disciplines in master's degree. On the left chart, we can see that physics and mathematics bachelors who finished the degree are rising very slow compared to statistics. On the right chart, the number of students who finished master's degree is far behind other disciplines like biostatics and statistics [18].

One of them is a problem on how to introduce knowledge to students in that they will find it interesting, which is basically the problem of teaching methods. The other problem is physics curricula. It seems that physics curricula in many countries is not flexible enough for teachers and, as a result, is unfriendly to students. The solution to this problem would be to redesign physics curricula in a way to give the teacher more flexibility and hereby also relieve teachers from pressure so they could actually enjoy teaching physics and give full dedication to more attractive lessons. A great solution for teaching methods could be to include physics in other subjects such as computer science, where students could solve physics problem with the use of ICT. Games are also a great solution, where students could learn parts of physics simply by playing games and gain necessary knowledge. One of appropriate computer games from which students could learn physics is *Angry Birds*. We present which themes from physics curricula could be appropriate to teach concepts of physics.

6. Physics curricula and *Angry Birds*

All over the world in every school, teachers must follow a teaching plan called curriculum. In every curriculum, there are mandatory themes that consist of subthemes that are building the whole teaching process in certain order. How this process consists may differ from country to country. We may also say that the system of learning physics is concentric (Figure 3). Each physics curriculum is constructed from basic themes. The most important difference between curricula in different countries is in subthemes and their order. In physics, cores of concentric circles are the main themes, which are mechanics, matter, waves and optics, thermal physics, electricity and magnetism, modern physics, and astronomy [19].

The basic themes of physics curriculum are defined, so we studied which of those we may find in the computer game *Angry Birds* and which of them we can analyze.

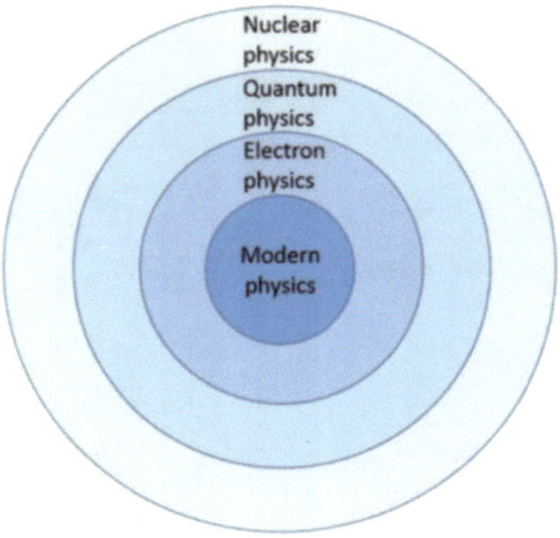

Figure 3. Example of concentric circle in physics. Outer layers may differ in number of subthemes and variety of subthemes titles, but the core stays the same.

7. Mechanics

7.1. Forces and Newton's law, collision, and explosion

We know that when we launch a bird from the slingshot, the only force that is affecting the bird is the force of gravity $\vec{F_g}$. The air resistance force is in the game excluded. We also know that when the bird will collide with a wooden wall, it will be affected with the force of wall $\vec{F_w}$ that is resisting bird's movement in the opposite direction of its movement (Figure 4). Children can monitor and watch examples of collisions and explain how forces are working on the observed object. We already mentioned that black bird has an ability to explode from which we could observe effects of explosion to teach children the basic physics behind it.

Figure 4. We can see that the force of gravity $\vec{F_g}$. is the only force that affects the bird in the flight. Also, we can predict that when the bird hits the wall, it will slow down because the force of the wall is resisting the bird's motion.

http://dx.doi.org/10.5772/60604

7.2. Friction and motion

With the help of *Angry Birds*, we can also explain friction. After finishing the flight, the bird is touching and then rolling on the ground with some speed in the direction of the vector of velocity $\vec{v}$. The bird is slowing down because of friction $\vec{F_f}$, which is working on the bird in opposite direction and causing the bird eventually to stop (Figure 5). With this example, we could explain how friction is working on a (rolling) bird.

Figure 5. We can see that force friction is working in the opposite direction of the bird, causing the bird to slow down.

7.3. Circular motion and gravity

We mentioned before that Rovio entertainment released many sequels. One of much known sequel is called *Angry Birds Space* (Figure 6), where the game environment is in space and the gravity of objects affects the bird's flight. In designing this sequel, Rovio Entertainment worked with NASA, which helped at programming gravity effects and also tested them in actual space. In the game, we could learn the effects of gravity. Also, we can learn the basics of circular motion if we launch the bird in the angle where the bird would circle around the small planet, which is affecting the bird with its microgravity.

Figure 6. We can see that the force of gravity is pointing in the center of the small planet's mass, therefore also affecting the path of the bird's movement, which would circle for longer time if the force of gravity would be smaller or the velocity of the bird would be higher.

7.4. Work, energy, and power

We know that birds are moving with certain velocity $\vec{v}$ when we launch them. We also know that they change height when they are launched (Figure 7). From that aspect, we can also explain the change of kinetic and potential energy, where potential energy is changing according to change of height:

$$E_p = mgh, \tag{1}$$

Figure 7. If we know height and velocity, we can determine potential and kinetic energy; therefore, we can also know how much work and power the birds need when we shoot them.

where E_p is the potential energy, m is the mass of bird, g is the gravitational acceleration, and h is the height where the bird is located in correspondence to the ground. We could also explain the change of kinetic energy as follows:

$$E_k = \frac{1}{2}mv^2, \tag{2}$$

where E_k is the kinetic energy of bird and v is its velocity. We can also determine work as a result of energy change as follows:

$$W = \Delta E, \tag{3}$$

where W is work and ΔE is change of energy. From that, we can also determine average power as follows:

http://dx.doi.org/10.5772/60604

$$P_{avg} = \frac{\Delta W}{\Delta t}, \tag{4}$$

where P_{avg} is the average power, and ΔW is the change of work in time interval Δt [20].

We can see that with the computer game *Angry Birds*, we can cover and explain most of the mechanics. Other themes are not so well covered, but we can still can find something. For example, we can explain buoyancy.

7.5. Buoyancy

We can explain that buoyancy is upward force $\vec{F_b}$ exerted by a fluid that opposes the weight of an immersed object, which is shown by gravity force $\vec{F_g}$. We can also see that one piggy is floating, which is the result of comparison of the average density of piggy to density of liquid in which piggy is located. For floating of the piggy, its density has to be smaller (Figure 8).

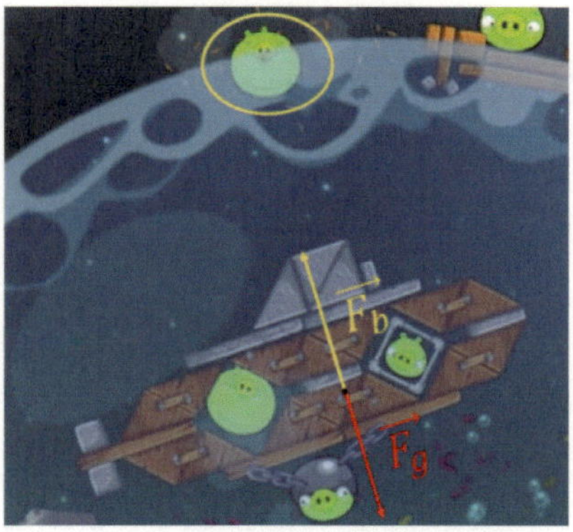

Figure 8. Here we can see an example where force buoyancy is working in the opposite direction as gravity force, causing the material and the pigs to float to the surface [21].

We showed some examples where we could use the computer game *Angry Birds* as a didactical tool for main topics in physics curriculum. However, we did not talk about experimental work and measurement, which is the main topic in following chapter.

8. Teaching with *Angry Birds*

We described some topics where the computer game *Angry Birds* could be appropriate for teaching physics. It contains many mandatory topics of physics curriculum, and it can either be used as a motivational tool, where children could get more comfortable with physics while using ICT or it can be used as an experiment to show children simulation of actual physics. From the experiment, we could define exercises where children could get basic knowledge about physics and calculus behind it. In this chapter, we show an example of how we can teach the physics of projectile motion using the computer game *Angry Birds*. Before we can explain the physics of *Angry Birds*, we have to make footage of *Angry Birds* gameplay, and after that, we can analyze data in that footage. For that, we need some additional programs appropriate for classroom usage, for which we present some examples.

8.1. LioLo Game Recorder

The recommended software for making gameplay footage is a program called LoiLo Game Recorder. You can download it for free from their website [22] and install the program on your computer. LoiLo Game Recorder is a program that enables us to record game sessions. It also supports Motion-JPEG file format that provides with the best balance between file size and image quality. For our purpose, we recorded full-HD videos, and file size is still manageable. When you downloaded and installed the program, simply start the program and the game in which you want to make a recording. Before you start to play, press F6 on keyboard and program will start recording (Figure 9). After you finish playing, press key F6 again and the program will stop recording and save the footage in your PC's video directory. Now you can use the footage for analysis. To minimize the measurement errors at analysis of gameplay, the footage must be smooth and without delays [22]. We will do our analysis in program called Tracker.

Figure 9. This is the LoiLo Game Recorder's user interface where we can see options available in program. We can also see an example of the footage that we made in *Angry Birds*.

8.2. Tracker

Tracker is a free video analysis and modeling tool built on the open source physics (OSP) Java framework. It is designed to be used in physics education and can be easily run from USB drive. Requirements for using Tracker are small, and it only requires that you have installed Java 1.6 or higher. It has a variety of tools to help user to analyze the data from recording where we can read what happened with physical quantity on the graphs (Figure 10). To analyze data from recording, we simply start the program Tracker in which we can open video that we have made with the program Loilo and start the measurements with different tools [23]. Before we can acquire the measurements for discussing physics problem, we need to set starting point to place our bird in space. We do that with calibration tool where we set the coordinate system in the foot of slingshot, which will be our starting point. We also need our measuring unit, which in our case will be the slingshot size. When we determined starting point and basic measuring unit, we use tracking tool to track bird's movement in the footage. When tracking is finished, we see all measurements in the graphs, which we can analyze with measurement analyzing tool. The program Tracker also has a video-analyzing tool where we can depart video frame by frame. For final results, we use measurement-analyzing tools where the data are displayed in different graphs.

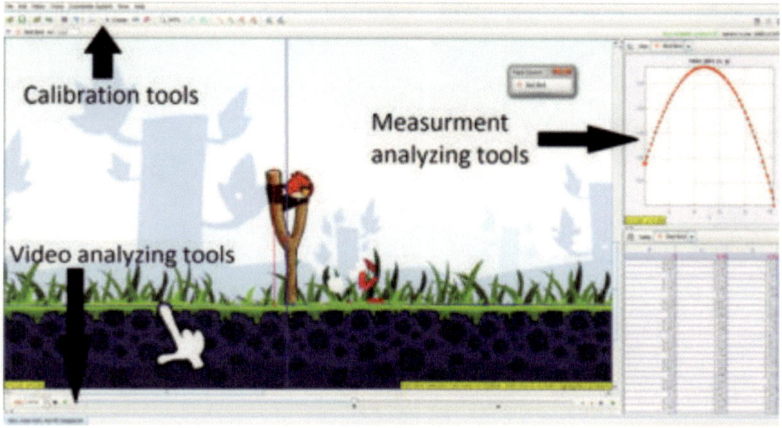

Figure 10. The program has many tools to offer; the most essential of them are the calibration tool, which we can find at the top; the measurement analyzing tools at the right; and the video analyzing tool at the bottom of program interface.

8.3. Physics of *Angry Birds*

When we have analyzed the data with the program Tracker, we can start talking about physics in games. Projectile motion is a case of motion which we can describe it as motion in two dimensions: vertical and horizontal. In this particular case, we can neglect air resistance because the game was not designed to include air resistance in projectile motion. We know that when we shot a bird slingshot, its initial speed ($\vec{v}_0$) is

$$\vec{v}_0 = (v_{0x}, v_{0y}), \quad (5)$$

where v_{0x} is the size of the horizontal component of initial velocity and v_{0y} is the size of the vertical component of initial velocity [20]. The only force that is affecting the bird during the flight is gravitational force. That is why acceleration of bird is equal to the gravitational acceleration.

We also know that the horizontal component of velocity is not changing in size because acceleration only got vertical component. That is why we can define the movement of bird in time t:

$$x_{finished} = \left(v_{0x} \cos\theta\right)t + x_{starting}, \tag{6}$$

where $x_{finished}$ is the location where bird has finished movement in time t in his horizontal path and $x_{starting}$ is the initial location from where bird has started moving in horizontal path. θ is the angle by which we shot the bird from slingshot [19]. As a result, we get Figure 11, which shows us that the body was moving in horizontal direction with constant velocity v_{0x} equal to 3.31 U/s [24].

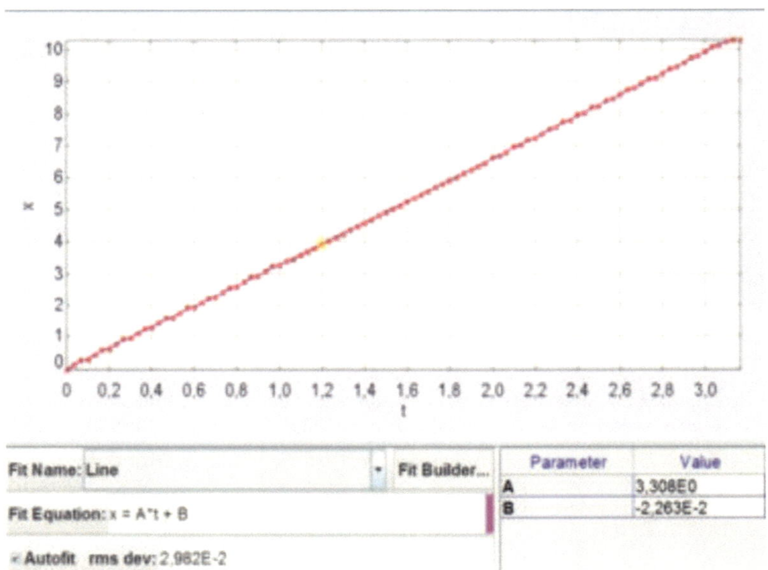

Figure 11. From the measurement, we can read that the horizontal component of velocity (A) is 3.31 U/s, and we can see that dependency position from time is linear.

For motion in vertical direction, we know that acceleration is constant. That is why we can define motion in vertical direction as

$$y_{highest} = (v_{0y} \sin\theta)t - \frac{1}{2}gt^2 + y_{starting}, \tag{7}$$

where $y_{starting}$ is the starting height from which the birds was shot in vertical direction from angle θ and $y_{highest}$ is the maximum height that the birds will reach in at time t. We also see that acceleration is equal to gravitational acceleration g if our game is happening on Earth. From the measurement, we see that vertical motion fits to quadric equation (Figure 12), which also shows us that acceleration in vertical direction is constant and is equal to –1.9 U/ s^2 [25].

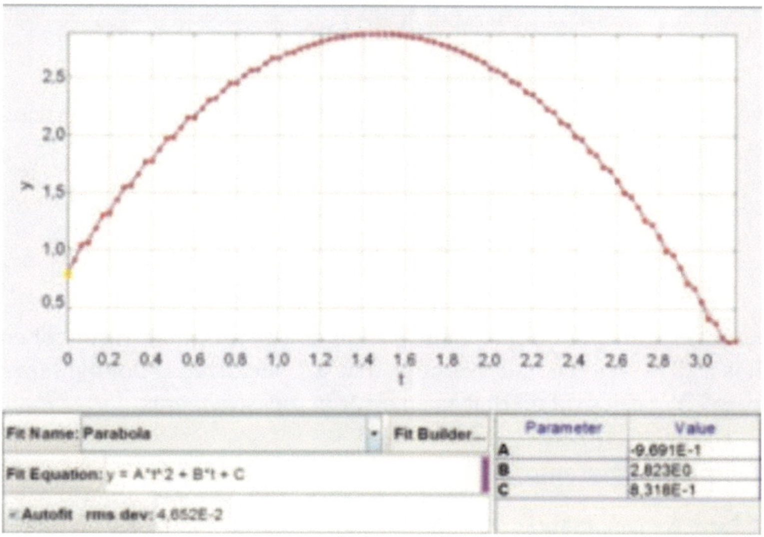

Figure 12. From Equation (7), we can see that acceleration (A) in vertical direction is *a*/2, which gives us a result acceleration equal to 1.9 U/ s^2. From the measurement, we can also read the vertical component of velocity (B), which is 2.8 U/s, and height (C), which is 0.8 U.

From the result, we wanted to determine what was the size of our basic unit. We measured acceleration in vertical direction as 1.9 U/ s^2. We placed our experiment on Earth so acceleration should be equal to gravitational acceleration, which is 9.8 m/ s^2 [24,25]. From that, we can calculate what was the size of our basic unit, and we get the result that our slingshot was 5.1 m high because the size of the slingshot was set as our basic unit. When we get our basic unit, we can calculate our velocity in vertical and horizontal directions so that we simply multiply our measured values with 5.1 m, and as result, we get that v_{0y} is 14.2 m/s and v_{0x} is 16.7 m/s. From this point, we can calculate initial velocity as follows:

$$v_0 = \sqrt{{v_{0x}}^2 + {v_{0y}}^2}, \tag{8}$$

and we get that v_0 is 21.9 m/s. From these measurements, we can also calculate our starting height $h_{starting}$, which is 4.2 m. When we obtain the starting height, we can also calculate the maximum height as follows:

$$h = \frac{v_{0y}^2}{2g} + h_{starting}. \tag{9}$$

We get that the maximum height h is 14.5 m. It is also interesting to know from which angel did we shoot the bird:

$$\theta = \tan^{-1}\left(\frac{v_{0y}}{v_{0x}}\right) \tag{10}$$

As a result, we get $\theta = 40.4°$. When we all needed information, we can also calculate the range d of the bird's flight using the following equation:

$$d = \frac{v_0}{g}\sqrt{v_0^2 + 2gh_{starting}}, \tag{11}$$

where we get range corresponding to value 52.8 m. We get a similar result when the range is 10.5 U, which is 53.0 m. We see that the range that we calculated is not the same as the range that we measured. We can explain that as an error in measurements.

8.4. Use of example in classroom

We have seen how we can analyze physics with the red angry bird, which does not have any special abilities. This type of analysis and understanding would be more appropriate for pupils in secondary school, in which pupils could use this particular experiment to determine the actual size of birds and the actual size of the slingshot, like we have shown in our example. We can also use experiment for teamwork, where we could divide pupils in two groups. the first group would have to explain the physics of vertical motion, and the second group would have to explain the physics of horizontal motion. At the end of the experiment, both explanations can be merged, and the physics of projectile motion can be explained. Our example can be also used in primary school, where we would have to lower the difficulty of tasks for pupils. We could teach them how to use the programs LoiLo and Tracker for simple analysis not only in *Angry Birds* but also in any other experiment footage. With this experiment, they can get familiar with graphs and errors in measurement. We also know that there is much more physics that can be explained with the use of *Angry Birds* for physics lessons. For additional work, students could explore the initial acceleration and midair acceleration of the yellow angry bird when we use his special ability. It would be also interesting to check the physics background of the blue angry bird, where students could check what is happening with momentum when he splits into three same-sized birds and if the mass of all three birds is the same. We already mentioned materials that show up in the game. For additional project work, students could analyze how different angry birds affect the same material.

9. Research

We showed an example of an experiment that could be used in the class. However, the question is if teachers would even use *Angry Birds* as a didactical tool. That is why we started research where we wanted to see teachers' responses on the proposal of teaching with *Angry Birds*. Our

http://dx.doi.org/10.5772/60604

targeted group of teachers was mostly middle-aged teachers (age 36 years and older). We know that the use of ICT is in average a bigger problem in older teachers rather that new young teachers. That is why the middle-aged group is much more interesting. On the question if they know the computer game *Angry Birds*, 35% of the teachers answered yes (Figure 13), which is actually impressive according to age-group that was questioned.

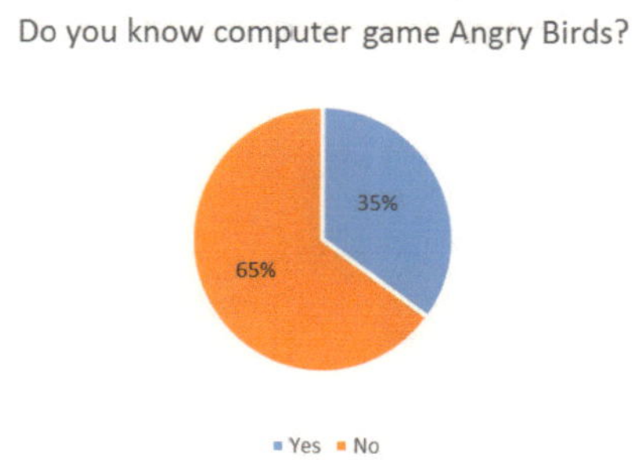

Figure 13. Chart where we can see how many teachers know the computer game *Angry Birds*.

With this, we have determined our group of teachers who actually know the game. Later on, we wanted to know how well they know the game. Hence, we set some common questions about the effects of the birds in the game and which of the physical content they see in the game is also included in physics curriculum. As a result, we learned that teachers who played *Angry Birds* know the game pretty well; 83% knew the effects of the birds in the game. The more interesting part comes when they had to determine the physical contents they found in the game, and the result was amazing. We found that physics teachers have noticed 9 different physics themes (Figure 14) in the computer game *Angry Birds*, which shows us that game really is suitable for physics class.

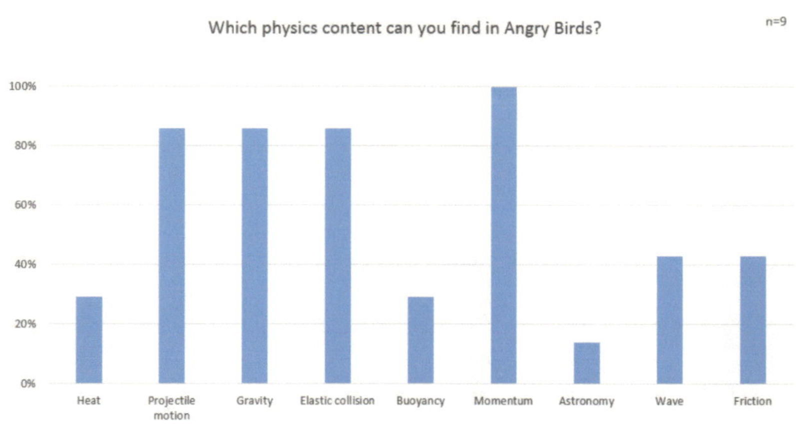

Figure 14. In the chart, we can see what teachers have found in the game *Angry Birds*: heat, projectile motion, gravity, elastic collision, buoyancy, momentum, astronomy, wave, and friction. The vertical axis shows the percentage of teachers who found certain physics content in the game. The horizontal axis shows the different physics contents.

We figured out that teachers can definitely see that game contains content for teaching physics. We also wanted to gain insight what teachers think about the suitability of the game in teaching physics in elementary and high school. Thus, we asked them how appropriate do they find the computer game *Angry Birds* for teaching physics in elementary school. None of teachers evaluated the computer game *Angry Birds* as inappropriate, and more than half of them find it appropriate for teaching physics (Figure 15).

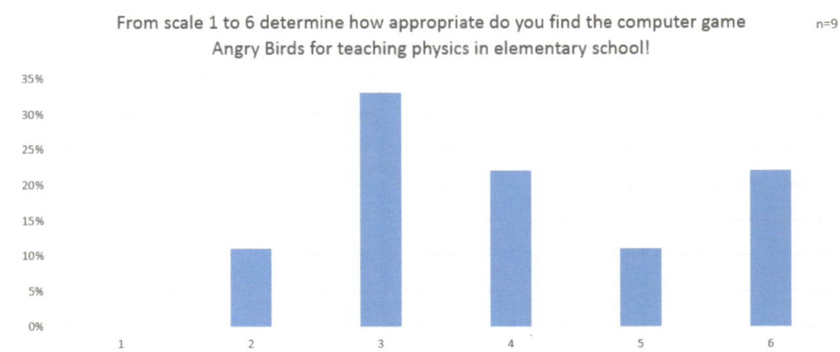

Figure 15. On the vertical axis, there is percentage of teachers who evaluated suitability for elementary school from 1 to 6, where 1 indicates completely inappropriate and 6 indicates perfectly suitable for teaching physics in elementary school, which could be found on the horizontal axis. We see that more than half of teachers found the computer game *Angry Birds* for teaching in elementary school as appropriate; 22% of them found it also perfectly suitable for teaching physics in elementary school.

We also asked them how they would evaluate the suitability of the computer game *Angry Birds* for lessons in physics in high school (Figure 16). We got results that more than half of teachers find it appropriate for teaching physics in high school.

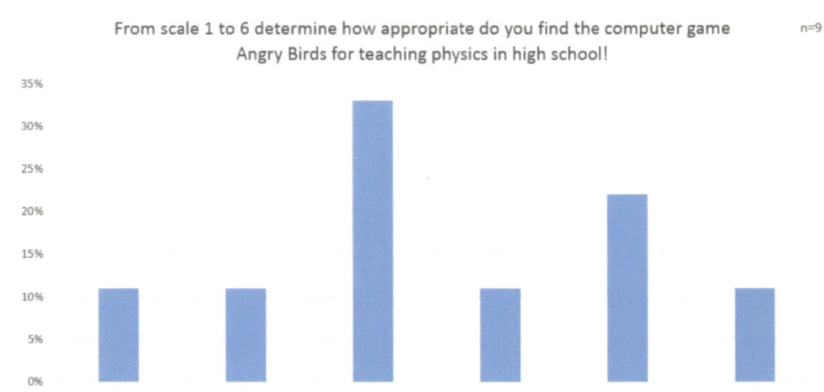

Figure 16. On the y axis, there is a percentage of teachers who evaluated suitability for high school from 1 to 6, where 1 indicates completely inappropriate and 6 indicates perfectly suitable for teaching physics in elementary school, which could be found on the x axis; 11% of them found it also perfectly suitable for teaching physics in high school.

http://dx.doi.org/10.5772/60604

In our survey, we also asked if the computer game *Angry Birds* is appropriate as a motivational tool in lessons in elementary and high school. As a result, 78% of the teachers find the computer game *Angry Birds* as a great motivational tool for both elementary and high school. The most impressive result was when we asked them if they would use the game for teaching physics. All of the teachers that know the computer game *Angry Birds* would use it for teaching physics.

9.1. Methodology

For our research, we used free online survey tool 1ka.si [26]. The tool offers many options to design an electronic survey. We took into account all basic rules of making survey where we limited the number of questions per page on 5 and separated the different topics of question in separate pages so the survey itself was not too harsh for respondents. In the survey, we also made a break point where we eliminated teachers who do not know the computer game *Angry Birds*. If they answered "no" on a question where we asked them if they know the computer game *Angry Birds*, the survey was finished; if they answered "yes," they could continue with the survey. We sent our survey through e-mail. The results that we introduced were analyzed in Excel table, where we merged our results in charts appropriate for the type of data that we got. In the research, we included 41 physics teachers who finished their study between the year 2005 and 2015 at our faculty and students of educational physics study. We got the response of 26 persons, 9 of them ware familiar with the game *Angry Birds*.

10. Conclusion

In this article, we determined that the use of ICT in learning is a skill that every teacher should acquire during his education. If we look in the present and, even more important, if we look in the future, ICT will be a main tool for learning. We also learn what the difference is between EG and fun CG. We found out that some computer games like *Angry Birds* could be more appropriate material for teaching because if its motivational fun factor. In educational game, designers mostly forget about it because their main point is focused on teaching, and game mechanics are obstructed by learning processes, in which most children forget that learning new things can also be fun. We become familiar with two new programs LoiLo Game Recorder and Tracker, which can be used for analysis. We also show an example of how we could use *Angry Birds* for teaching projectile motion where we explain the physics of *Angry Birds*. At the end, we also check the applicability of *Angry Birds* and how it can be used for further courses. We also conducted one research where we found out that most of the teachers think that Angry Birds is appropriate for teaching physics in high school and elementary school.

Author details

Robert Repnik[1*], Dominik Robič[1] and Igor Pesek[1,2]

*Address all correspondence to: robert.repnik@um.si

1 Faculty of Natural Sciences and mathematics, University of Maribor, Maribor, Slovenia

2 Institute E-um, Ptuj, Slovenia

References

[1] Wenning C.J. Why the resistance to inquiry-oriented science teaching. Journal of Physics Teacher Education Online 2010; 5(3): 1–2. http://www2.phy.ilstu.edu/~wenning/jpteo/issues/jpteo5%283%29win10.pdf (accessed 8 December 2014).

[2] Carnoy M. ICT in education: possibilities and challenges. In: Inaugural Lecture of the OUC 2004-2005, UOC, Barcelona; 2004

[3] Levy F., Murnane R. J. The New Division of Labor: How Computers Are Creating the Next Job Market. Princeton University Press; 2004.

[4] NCREL & Metiri Group. enGauge 21st Century Skills: Literacy in the Digital Age; 2003.

[5] McClarty K.L., Orr A., Frey P., Dolan R., Vassileva V., McVay A. A Literature Review of Gaming in Education. Research report. Pearson; 2012.

[6] Salen K., Zimmerman E. Rules of Play: Game Design Fundamentals. Cambridge MIT Press, 2003.

[7] Wolf M. J. The Medium of the Video Game. Texas: University of Texas Press; 2002.

[8] Granic I., Lobel A., Engels C.M.E. The benefits of playing video games. American Psychologist 2014; (69): 66–78.

[9] Razak, A.A., Connolly M.T., Hainey T. Teachers' views on the approach of digital games-based learning within the curriculum for excellence. International Journal of Game-Based Learning 2012; 33: 33–51.

[10] Gruden B., Kreuh N., Možina Podbršcek I., Flogie A., Razbornik I., Trstenjak B. Path to E-Competency & E-Education Project: The Future of Education. Florence; 2013.

[11] Shan Fu J. ICT in education: a critical literature review and its implications. International Journal of Education and Development using Information and Communication Technology 2013; 9(1): 112–125.

[12] Nordine J. Motivating calculus-based kinematics instruction with *Super Mario Bros.* Physics Teacher 2011; 49: 380.

[13] Jurcevic J.S. Learning Projectile Motion with Computer Game "Schorched 3D." Physics Teacher 2008; 46: 48.

[14] Rovio Entertianment Ltd. *Angry Birds*. http://www.rovio.com/en/our-work/games/view/1/angry-birds (accessed 8 December 2014).

[15] Wikia Inc Angry Birds *Wiki*. http://angrybirds.wikia.com/wiki/Birds (accessed 21 March 2015).

[16] Pardhan H. Engagement enhance interest in physics. Alberta Science Education Journal 2003; 36(2): 25–30.

[17] Azuma T., Nagao K. An inquiry into the reproduction of physics-phobic children by physics-phobic teachers. Bulletin of Faculty of Education, Ibaraki University 2007; 56: 91–102.

[18] Pierson S. ASA Community, 20 December 2013 [Online]. http://community.amstat.org/blogs/steve-pierson/2013/12/20/statistical-science-degree-comparisons-updated-through-2012

[19] CERN. The Curricula of Various Countries. CERN and High School Teachers Programme, 18 July 2002 [Online]. http://teachers.web.cern.ch/teachers/materials/syllabus.htm#Belgium (accessed 21 March 2015).

[20] Haliday D., Resnick R., Walker J. Fundamentals of Physics 8th edition. Cleveland: John Wiley& Sons; 2007.

[21] S. Iyer. Angry Birds Space update splashes underwater with new Pig Dipper episode. NDTV Convergence Limited, 2013 [Online]. http://gadgets.ndtv.com/apps/news/angry-birds-space-update-splashes-underwater-with-new-pig-dipper-episode-316283 (accessed 21 March 2015).

[22] LoiLo. LoiLo Game Recorder. http://loilo.tv/us/ (accessed 8 December 2014).

[23] Douglas B. Tracker: Video analysis and modeling tool. http://www.cabrillo.edu/~dbrown/tracker/ (accessed 8 December 2014).

[24] Rodrigues M., Simeäo Carvalho P. Teaching physics with *Angry Birds*: exploring the kinematics and dynamic of the game. Physics Education 2013; 48: 431. http://iopscience.iop.org/0031-9120/48/4/431/article (accessed 8 December 2014).

[25] Condé Nast Digital. WIRED. Allain R. The physics of Angry Birds. http://www.wired.com/2010/10/physics-of-angry-birds/ (accessed 8 December 2014).

[26] Faculty of Social Sciences "1ka," University of Ljubljana; Faculty of Social Sciences, 2002–2009 [Online]. https://www.1ka.si/ (accessed 21 March 2015).

Chapter 10

Challenges of Business Simulation Games — A New Approach of Teaching Business

Andrej Jerman Blažič and Franc Novak

Additional information is available at the end of the chapter

http://dx.doi.org/10.5772/61242

Abstract

Serious games are part of the new emerging world of education environment that is based on sophisticated technology with elements of entertainment. They have been seen as good supplements for supporting the learning processes due to their capability to increase visualisations and challenge the student creativity. They have the potential to significantly improve training and education activities and initiatives. As a part of serious computer games, business simulation games support training and learning focused on the management of economic processes. They have been proven to be useful in empowering and mediating learning business content. This chapter addresses the simulation business games used in the educational process by analysing selected popular games regarding their properties that are considered as important in the learning process. The first part presents a short introduction in the field of business games and the approach used in selection of the studied games. The next part provides a review of related articles and brief overview of the state of the art that has guided the selection of business simulation games to be analysed and assessed. The game parameters used in the assessment have been defined and described. The analysis and the assessment report are followed with brief concluding remarks.

Keywords: Serious Games, Business Simulation Games, E-Learning, Problem-Based Learning, Education

1. Introduction

Digital games have the potential to change the landscape of education as we know it. From the early isolated reports on conferences and books reflecting about possible application of digital games for learning, more and more practitioners and researchers embraced the idea, including the e-learning community [1]. However, today serious games are accepted terms for games with an educational intent despite the lack of supporting evidences about their effectiveness in the learning process. Their popularity in the past decade has increased significantly and continues to increase [2]. It is widely accepted by the educators that the games used in education should be engaging, although not necessarily funny, while the learning can be implicit or explicit. Despite the fact that many games to be used in education are now readily available, commercial off-the-shelf, no uniform game pedagogy was developed and it could be said that does not exist. It is safe to be assumed also that in the literature a deep research is missing, which links the games to various properties with the type of learning [3]. Earlier games tended to be based on the behaviorist model but there were other games that tried to incorporate experiential, situated and socio-cultural pedagogical models [4]. Among the researchers in the field, it was widely accepted that the learning outcome, when the games are incorporated in the educational process, is dependent upon the appropriate pedagogy and the underlying game mechanics [5].

Serious games are also used as part of the treatment of some mental disorders such as attention deficit in children, as a way of training for keeping long period attention [6]. Several authors also point out that games can be used to improve self-monitoring, problem recognition and solving, decision making, better short-term and long-term memory, increase social skills such as collaboration, negotiation and shared decision-making as pointed out in ELSPA [7] and by Mitchell & Savill-Smith [8].

As a part of serious computer games, the games known as business simulation games support training and learning focused on the management of economic processes. Business simulation games bring effective methods of learning and experience through business challenges that students usually need to meet before setting foot in the real world [9]. In a business simulation game, the participants can select different decisions without any fear for a real loss to the organization in case participants make mistakes. Participants can select actions and can have experience regarding the consequences of those actions.

The selection of business simulation games for assessment purpose has been made with an intention to demonstrate what kind of business knowledge and skills can be acquired through the gaming. The discussion that follows the assessment points to the limitations of the selected game set. Overall, with game parameters presented and assessment discussed, this chapter attempts to bring educators closer to the real expectations they can have, regarding the achievement of the learning objectives, when an adequate combination of business simulation games and training is applied in a particular education process.

2. Overview of the current state

2.1. Brief introduction in the area of business simulation games

Wikipedia explains that business simulation games are not a new phenomenon. Computer-supported business simulation has an origin in the military war games and came into existence during the late 1950s [10]. By the beginning of the 1960s, 89 different business games have been developed by industrial firms, business associations, educational institutes, or governmental units [11]. They have been used as a learning tool for teaching management [12, 13]. They are regularly in use at the universities with business and management programs, and in particular at the world's major business schools. As an example, the University of Washington has been using business simulation games in classes since 1957 [14]. As an educational tool, business simulation games have grown considerably in past 50 years and have moved from being a supplemental exercise in business courses to a central mode of business instruction [15].

Up to the present time, numerous business games appeared to be of different types or genre. To establish the adequate comparison between all of them and to make the proper survey, it is almost impossible due to the expanding list of business games, as new games are growing day to day. According to the studied literature and Internet reviews, this chapter attempts to present the survey of several games found to be typical for the business environment as they cover the most important educational content that can be gamified.

2.2. Study framework

Business simulation games can be usually presented as a training technique in which participants consider sequence of problems required to be solved by them or to take decisions. The main component of most of the games is the simulation of the ecosystem. They model the realities of the business world by simulating basic – and in some cases advanced – business theories and practices in controlled game environments. Because they simulate the real-world system, they can often be used as a teaching method for executive education as well [16]. The benefits of business simulations are in the possibilities of the students to experience and test themselves in situations before encountering them in real life, give them the chance to experiment and test hypotheses. Within the business simulations offered within a serious game, subjects seem much more "real" to the students or learners than when taught passively from pdfs, PowerPoint, or from blackboards. Extensively, business game simulations in professional world are used most frequently. The game applied is usually based on a request for sequential decision-making exercise structured around a hypothetical model of the operations of an organization. The participants can select different decisions without any fear for a real loss to the organization in case mistakes are made. Participants get experience through the consequences of those actions that can be positive or negative for the game purpose or goal. The learners/students are using their newly acquired skills and knowledge by applying them to a competitive challenge provided within the game.

Business simulations are also in experiments related to learning and cognition. These experiments and the studies that followed have revealed that people often have an attitude for mastering systems without the necessity to comprehend the underlying principles [17]. As a consequence, business education is nowadays criticized for being mainly theoretically driven and without a component that triggers critical thinking, creativity and innovation [18, 19, 20]. These properties, which are considered as major challenges in university-level education nowadays, were found to be missing in many graduated students. As the process of the globalization and liberalization of the business world has changed the types and qualities of the human capital required by the corporate sector, the business graduates are expected to have not only theoretical understanding of business but also communication and thinking skills [21], in addition to the ability to apply the multi-disciplinary knowledge acquired during their study. The current popularity of business simulation games in education follows from these findings. The interest in using simulation games is also driven by the effectiveness in presenting knowledge and theory. Instructional simulation researchers believe that a game-based method is effective because of the full-mind involvement in the learning process [22]. The activities in simulation games used in the area of business teaching usually involve observation and reflection, the creation of concepts, the integration of observations into theories and the application of theories into decisions and problem-solving. Students learn through the sequential process of cause and effect, and learning by doing. The underlying sequential processes are intended to motivate the students to explore, to experiment and to learn independently [23].

2.3. Terminology used

According to the variety of literature in this area, several mixed response about the definition of the business simulation games and its terminology is possible to be found.

Wikipedia (2014) [24] gives the following description of business simulations games: *They are games that generally focus on the management of economic processes, usually presented in the form of a business process. They allow students to practice business by use of relevant economic terminology and concepts. In most cases, the term business (simulation) game and management (simulation) game can be used interchangeably and there is no well-established difference between these two terms.* Wikipedia also mentions the approach of Greenlaw et al. (1962) [25] in game definition as a sequential decision-making exercise structured around a model of a business operation, in which participants assume their role of managing the simulated operation offered in the game. Keys and Wolfe (1993) [26] have defined a management game as a simplified simulated experimental environment that contains enough illusion of reality enabling real-world-like responses by those participating in the exercise.

Other authors define business simulation games as games that are designed for a primary purpose other than pure entertainment [27]. Serious games are considered by Squire [28] as an important response from the education technologist to the "digital natives", which is a generation of students who are raised on digital gadgets and interactive games. For them, the expectation to have interactive experiences in the education media seems very natural.

There are also other views that contribute to the conclusion that there is no pure agreement regarding the definition what exactly can be defined as business simulation games. However, in this chapter for the purposes of the study carried out the following definition is used: Business simulation games are considered as a type of serious games that focus on simulating management or business processes, using the economic terminology and real-life business environment simulation.

2.4. Use of the business games (The "Why and How")

Business simulation games are used in several educational areas; however, their purpose is to provide effective training. Schurr and Thole et al [29, 30] state that usage of business simulation games is mainly focused on acquiring skills as they permit students to experience and test themselves in situations before they encounter them in the real life; in addition, they permit students to experiment with business hypotheses and test them. Faria et al [15] state in their study based on review of the 304 business simulation educations and learning articles that the capabilities/properties of the business simulation games are related to provision of:

- Getting experience,
- Learning strategy
- Getting decision-making experience,
- Getting better learning outcomes,
- Getting teamwork experience.

Each of these properties can be found in more than 20% of the business education and learning articles published in Simulation & Gaming Journal [15].

However, other authors, e.g. Whicker et al. [31], argue that business simulation games are used merely to enhance students' decision-making skills, especially under conditions defined by limited time and information. They vary in their focus from how to undertake a corporate takeover and how to expand a company's share of the market. Typically, the player feeds information into a computer program and receives back a series of optional or additional data that are conditional upon the player's initial choices.

Business simulation games can be also potentially used to manage skills mediation. Riedel [32] pointed out two types of skills that can be mediated or promoted by usage of games for business and industry: soft skills (team building, communication, inter-personal skills, negotiation skills, creativity, collaboration skills, learning skills) and hard skills (product/ service knowledge, sales, discipline-based training, customer service, project management, decision-making skills, innovation, risk management, health and safety). Here it should be mentioned that: "the increased usage of the business simulation games [15] has been influenced by the usage of the emerging technology of Internet and the computer technology power".

The Internet as a vehicle combined with inexpensive hosting and memory storage services has triggered the proliferation of the distributed computing to happen as the national and even international reach for business simulation game providers became very easy. This perspective of business simulation games development enables the grouping of as: web-based and desktop-based group of business simulation games. The business simulation games also may come in different shapes and sizes. Some business simulation games are small and require no download from the Internet and can be played on-line. These types of games are run by modern browsers which have latest java script enabled or fresh updated flash player. Some of them can be played on user's computer once they have been loaded. In this group, it could be found that good examples of small business simulation games do not require a download process and are often described as web-based games. Then there are other business simulation games that require to be downloaded in order to play them. These come in two types: the stand-alone games that users are playing by themselves once they have downloaded the game and installed on their computer (often described as desktop-based), and the multi-player business simulations that players play online with others once they have downloaded the game. These business simulation games are the most intricate, well designed and engaging. To manage and to play this kind of business simulation games, the following must be done. The game has to be downloaded (with the purchased license, if the game is commercial type) to the user's computer and afterwards an installation must be done. Once the user has the game installed on his/her computer, the playing is enabled. While user's computer is connected to the game's serves online, the multi-player environment is created by other users and amazingly, there can be over 100,000 users or more playing one of these popular business simulation games at a given time, each of whom is running the game they downloaded on their computer with a connection to the central game servers [33].

In some cases when players want to play a massive multi-player business simulation game that requires to be downloaded and installed, they are usually asked to set up a profile at the game's website first, before they download the game. When the game connects to the game's site for the first time after it was installed, the software recognises the user's computer and the game is ready to be played. However, not all business simulation games are available for download; they can also be available only in a form of CD-ROME or DVD format accompanied with an installation guide and game tutorial.

The proliferation of accessible business simulation games has enabled the educators to be capable to set up and conduct business simulation exercises easily and on almost on no cost. Student access to the Internet is pervasive, which makes the administration of the business simulation games to be easy. In addition to the technical advantages offered by the Internet-based simulation games, students are in the same time accustomed to communicate and to play on the Internet. They interact within the social networks such as Facebook, LinkedIn. They play MMOG (Massive multi-player real-time online games). Among them, the well-known World of Warcraft (www.worldofwarcraft.com) is very popular. Faira has found that the students expect and prefer computerised simulations games to be administered in this fashion [15].

3. Selection of the game parameters

In recent years, much debate has taken place about the classification framework for business-simulation games designed for teaching and training purposes [34]. In fact, many teachers or tutors who are using business games as an educational tool for teaching business knowledge or skills often need to make a pre-view or assessment of the game in order to determinate whether the game will accomplish or fulfil their learning objects/goals. Since most of the educational games require constant interaction, teachers need to select the game carefully, as an appropriate training tool with properties that meet their curriculum targets.

Since the first adoption of business games, their classifications have been constantly changing due to the changeable forms and origins of business games, as well as with technology development. One of the first classifications in terms of the design characteristics was introduced by Elion [35] and Greenlaw [36] (total enterprise or functional, interacting or non-interacting, computer or non-computer) and according to their accepted use, e.g., either

- as part of a general management training program;
- or teaching new techniques or procedures for selling;
- or for conducting research (e.g. on the behaviour of systems, on the decision-making processes of individuals);
- or for studying the interaction of individuals within a team.

Many of these early, hand-scored business games did not make the transition to the era of the desktop computer. Instead, new, computer-based, business-simulation games appeared at the start of the new digital era [37]. Important work in this area was conducted by Keys and Wolfe [26] in their attempt to classify computerised, business management simulations. They produced an overview of business games based on the Greenlaw taxonomy [36]. However, an important finding in this work was the multi-dimensional character of business games and the possibility to classify them in a number of ways. Later, many authors were trying to classify business simulation games according to their content environment and their educational goals. For example, Wolfe [38] established his classification of business simulation games using three main fields of application:

- Top-management games
- Functional games
- Concept simulation games

This chapter uses the classification of business simulation games as described by Jerman [39], based on Keys' [26] and Biggs's [40] classification of business simulation games. The classification properties are presented in two major groups. The first group – **the technical classification** – presents the properties derived from the technical data that describe the business simulation game and the second group – **the usability classification** – presents the variety of dimensions that describes the types of the usability characteristics important in the training and education process. All properties are described in the following sections and have been used in the Table 1 [39].

Technical Properties

The technical properties are defined by the following technical dimensions:

- **Web-based/desktop:** Whether the game can be played via modern browser or with installation package.
- **Distribution:** Whether the game is free for use, played by license, on cd-rom, or run by downloaded application/client.
- **Year of publishing**: The year that game was started to be available for public use.
- **Users:** How many registered users the game has (up to 2010)?

- **Label:** The name of development team.
- **Single/multi-user:** Whether the game can be played by one or many players.
- **Dimension:** Whether the game is present in 2D/3D environment.

Usability Properties

- **The time period simulated:** For example, day/week/quarter/year.
- **Industry-specific or generic:** In industry-specific game, the authors attempt to replicate closely the actual industry. In generic games, only general business relationships are replicated.
- **Degree of complexity:** Game decision input variable complexity, or the computer model complexity.
- **Functional or total enterprise:** Designed to focus specifically on problems of decision-making as seen in one functional area or designed to give participants experience in making decisions at a top executive level and in which decisions from one functional area interact with those made in other areas of a firm
- **Competitive or non-competitive:** Whether the decisions or participants influence the other participants or not.
- **Feedback system:** Whether the results are shown by gained scores, experience points, upgrade level or summary reports.
- **Deterministic or stochastic:** The stochastic alternative is probabilistic, including chance of elements.
- **Briefing systems:** The level and usability of briefing screen.
- **Learning objectives:** Types of learning skills that can be obtained, e.g., business strategy/strategic management, finance.
- **Background knowledge:** Whether a basic/advanced or none business knowledge is recommended in order to play a game.
- **Interactivity type:** In an interactive game, participants respond to the questions at the computer, receive an immediate response and then submit additional decisions. In a non-interactive game, decisions are submitted to the game administrator.

3.1. Selection of business simulation games for the assessment

The list of business simulation games that can be found on Internet is countless. Wikipedia [24] provides a list of several hundred business games ordered in alphabetical and chronological order. The problem of this list is the fact that they are considered to be more entertainment-oriented than edutainment and as a consequence, their use as a learning tool is questionable. The classification as the group of educational business simulation games requires much more. The game has to be realistic, engaging, motivating, popular and user-friendly and with clear educational objective [39].

The selection of business simulation games analysed in this contribution was based on a review of business-game-related articles that address educational problems and issues related to particular business simulation games. The selection was influenced by the results of two projects: the COSIGA project and GALA project (http://www.elios.dibe.unige.it/gala). Two other authors [32] have listed another selection of 39 serious games that address educational topics such as finance, management, product management, industry management, leadership, etc. The revision of the mentioned lists enabled the selection of games that can be considered as representatives by their popularity and by the topic addressed (considered as important in the area of management education as well as in politics). Once the selection was completed, our research team started to play them and started to improve the results of assessments. The following games have been selected.

3.1.1. eRepublik

eRepublik (www.erepublik.com) is considered as a massively multi-player online strategic game that combines social networking elements (Facebook, LinkedIn, etc.). It was developed by Republik Labs. Launched in October 2008, the game is currently translated into 18 languages. The game itself is a free-to-play web-based game, which means it can be played absolutely for free via the Internet (the registration is required), and it runs in most modern Internet browsers. It was developed and programmed using PHP program language and Symphony framework. eRepublik has spawned a number of similar games due to commercial success.

The game is set up in a mirror world called the New World. The players take the role of citizens where they can participate in daily activities. As the citizens of the New World, they can choose which country they wish to join. Each country is named after an actual country in the real world, and is generally located similarly according to the real world. The player who has German nationality will probably join to Germany, and Italian to Italy, etc. After joining to their desired country, players can act as employees, where they can own a business, run a factory, start a political activity, form a political party, write newspaper articles, run for the president, become members of Congress or country presidents, where they can help formulate national economic and social policies as well as initiating wars with their neighbors (as a virtual version of real-life countries) and/or tread the path of a private citizen working, fighting and voting for their state. In the beginning of the game, each player has to seek for an employment at a company within the country he has joined that will provide him with monthly salary and daily needs. While becoming an employee, he/she is offered the opportunity to be trained as a soldier for his/her country. Training and working at a company are done on a daily basis. The game has an official eRepublik wiki (wiki.erepublik.com) and official blog (blog.erepublik.com) where players can obtain all the information that may help them to get deeply involved into the game of eRepublik.

To begin a game, each player can get the mentor (or watch video tutorial), who guides him/her through introduction of eRepublik and provides an explanation of the basics of the game. The game consists of four modules: My Land, Politics Module, War Module and News Module. In My Land, a player has a patch of land where they can construct various buildings (farms, factories, storages, etc.) that can be constructed with a local currency or gold. The effectiveness of economy buildings depends on the natural resources which nation (country) has. In Politics module, a player can join a party, when they reach a certain level. If his/her political party or party campaign become successful, he/she can take the higher role such as a congress member or a president of the nation he/she belongs to. On the fifth of every month, eRepublik holds presidential elections, on the fifteenth the congressional elections. All activities that are connected to the warfare systems are situated in the War Module. When the president or the congress of the country proposes a Natural enemy law, a war on other countries can be declared. Players are able to train as a soldier and be ranked up in the military by fighting battles or go to war when he/she signs up to army of his/her country. Wars are taking potentially essential role by increasing the economic or political power of the country. A nation that has experienced and battle hardened citizens can become a global power and grow global economy business.

The role-play of the world of eRepublik consists of combining the capabilities of the above modules to reach goals and become leader in one or more domains. Using newspapers in the News Module, they can share their political ideas and changing and shaping the directions of political system and beliefs. The congress of a country sets taxes to enforce economic policies. To wage successful wars, the economy of a country has to sustain it and citizens have to be motivated.

Regarding the graphics, the game has no advanced or attractive graphical interface. It is created with merely few visual elements and is primarily text-based in nature, yet overall the game is nicely illustrated. The game also has a sleek interface, so it is very easy to find what you are looking for.

The eRepublik is aiming to do the best to reflect the nature of 21st century business/political world and 21st century life in general. The player will not learn the all expected business "know-how" abilities and processes as the time allowed for playing is limited (the game can be played from 10 minutes (14 minutes equals one day in eRepublik world) up to 15 minutes per day). The nature of the business in the game is politically oriented.

The workflow functionality of the game is a basic simple click-to-do, but it provides a great source of income for a player. Regular "working" increases players' experience level, and the higher level you are, the more things you can do. The game requires a "long-term" regular playing where players embrace the full role of managers and politicians. The main problem that can be noticed is lack of specific situated business or business-project tasks that could be potentially involved.

On the other hand, the game of eRepublik provides some interesting psychology aspects. One nation can be in favor with the real life being either political or economic situation in the New World. Just for example, in the real world, Slovenia and Croatia are negotiating for years about Adriatic open-sea border agreement, which is causing potential political and economic tension between them. The potential players that were solving this problem can simply declare the war and take over the other country through military invasion or economical destruction of the weaker country.

Overall, eRepublik is a strong multi-player simulator from the current world, based on a website and textual elements with a search enabling easy navigation, well reflecting the real world where citizens of different countries interact.

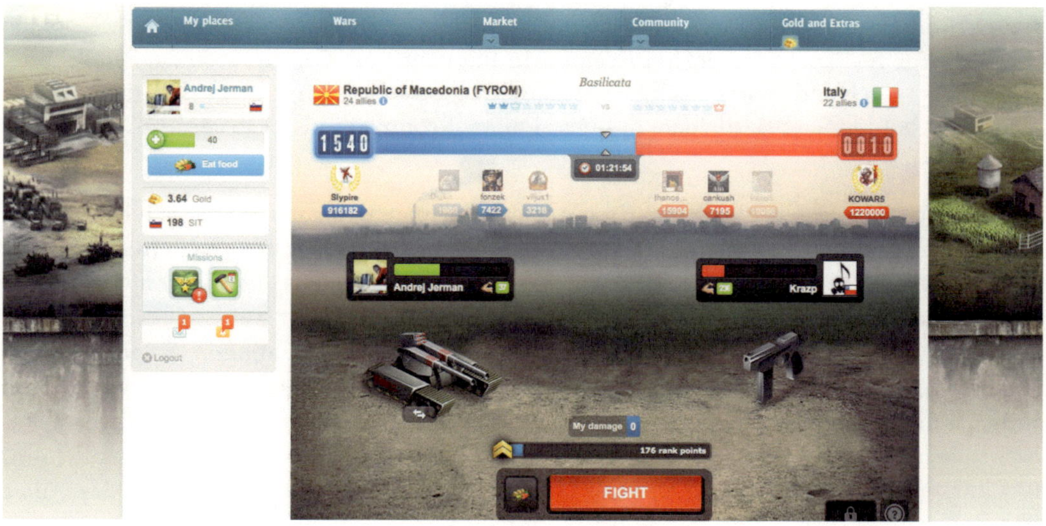

Figure 1. eRepublik (A screenshot of eRepublik game, showing the current war between the Republic of Macedonia and Italy)

3.1.2. *Virtonomics*

Virtonomics is another business-strategy-oriented online (web browser) game, played as a MMOG game where basics of management are tested. It is an Internet game with massive players, which reflects wild range of interests. It has been developed by Russian developers, and it was launched by Virtonomics team in May 2009. For 3 years of its existence, the project managed to join more than 400.000 users in Russia, Ukraine Germany, Belorussia, Kazakhstan, Baltic States and other regions (Wikipedia, 2013). It is designed for fans of the economic and strategic games, and to study the basics of management. The game itself requires an understanding of laws of real-life economy, business and finance, yet players do not need a deeper understanding of economics or any special background education for taking part in this game. The game is helpful in meeting interesting people with common interests and making useful connections (Jerman Blazic & Arh, 2013). The game can be presented as a unique business community where participants can find new business partners and potential employers. Economic experts can find Virtonomics as an inexhaustible source of useful observations and a place where they can try different business strategies. Virtonomics is versatile. It combines logical and business gaming, real economy simulation and economics strategy. This is a game where player's knowledge and efforts are the source of real income. There are a few fields of economy represented in the game, which has more than 100 different products. New countries and manufacturing sectors are being introduced as well as products and productions. The main purpose and aim is managing a company, where a player has to compete with artificial intelligence agents as well as with other players participating in the game realms from all over the world. Currently, there are 700,000 registered users (http://en.wikipedia.org/wiki/Virtonomics), (Virtonomics is translated to English, Spanish, German, Russian, Chinese and French and more). It is integrated with popular social networks (Facebook, LinkedIn, Twitter.). From all over the world, players can cooperate, compete, form a partnership and have price wars for the products which they sell, etc. It is a unique system for business training. All the possible industries of real economy are represented in the game: agriculture, mining, retail trade, scientific research and others. Each player is free to choose his own strategy: whether to build a complex holding and participate in several market competitions or to carve an individual and original way.

When starting a game, a player can choose and participate in the game realms where he/she will run his/her successful business. Currently, the game has five realms – Vera (Russia), Olga (Russia), Mary (English, France), Lien (English, Canada) and Anna (English, France, Canada, Russia). Each realm has its current characteristic: number of current companies involved the turnover value, technology level and the countries that are participating in the game realm. Dynamic movement is tested, when slowing down with the business, the chances of bankruptcy is increasing. Quick decisions are player's key to success. For those who like everything exclusive and equal game opportunities, there is a separate game world (the Anna Realm) functioning according to the principles of a subscription model (free of charge for 10 days, after that subscription starts from 8.25$ per month). All achievements depend on the player's capability of planning, thinking and implementing. The fight for survival begins in the very first moment when the player registers his/her own company and creates the working office. For beginners, the Virtonomics offers to a player a gift: a company left from "your uncle", with all the needs to start the capital in a full-progress business world. It does not matter which strategy the player will choose (adapting the old business or start a new one), the main goal is to establish and make a profitable and successful business. The opportunity is given to a player to become a tycoon, in order to develop his/her own company, competing with thousands of real components, winning the new markets, providing financial and political power of its corporations. To do this, a player has to engage in trade, manufacturing, research, exploration of natural resources, agriculture, trade in the currency market, manage personnel, finance, marketing, logistics and other business processes. By controlling the corporation, a player must hire and train stuff, establish sales and deliver, monitor the activities of competitors, improve the quality of his/her products, enter into business alliances and more. The game runs on virtual money. Every player receives a sum at the very first registration. This fund is used for the construction of business units, the payment of expenses and investments. Money that is being earned can be used for development of the company. The game can constantly grow. New countries can be created; new industries, new products added and new type of productions can be implementing.

The Virtonomics as any other MMOG game takes place in its own game world as a mirror of the real world. Game world is built from cities, woods, fields and farms. Several cities with similar profit tax are creating a region. Several regions with similar custom duties create a biggest economic unit – a country. All the rules from a real-world business are present, such as the correlation of export and import duties expresses development priorities for each country. The game is turn-based, which means the game can be played without staying online for full time. Visiting website once per day for 30 min makes enough time to completely review the player's business status and challenge of the new tasks. The game is a sort of business simulator, where a regular player can offer to the "serious" players to obtain different specific skills in management, marketing, economic cooperation, business optimisation, finance control, etc.

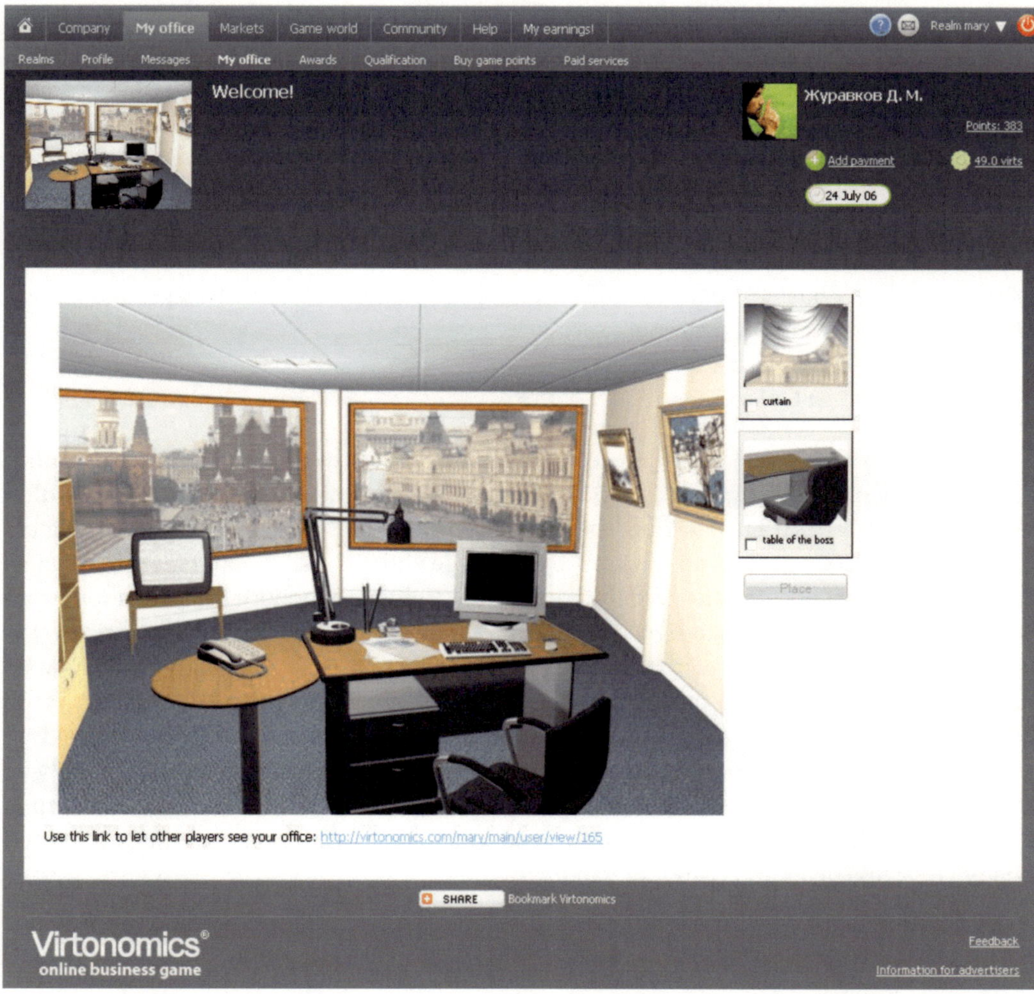

Figure 2. Virtonomics (Screenshot from the online game Virtonomics – player's equipped office).

Graphically, game is very poor. Virtonomics is a strictly text-based game with minor graphic elements. Visually, it looks like a wide complex forum community. The lack of realm maps and city maps is well noticed. The menu bar consists of seven sections: Company, My Office, Markets, Game world, Community, Help and My earnings. Each section has a sub-menu bar.

The most activities deal with the first three sections. In the "My office" section, a player can read messages, change the profile, restart a business, monitor the realm, study the reports, manage the paid service, etc. In the "Market" section, a player deals with markets like: Enterprise market, State enterprise market, Franchise market or participate in Enterprise auctions, award auctions, gift shops and deposits.

Virtonomics is not just a web-based online game, it can also be considered as a training system. It might be very useful for the students of business schools and economic colleges, as well as for already graduated managers who want to know more about the economic principles in practice and try themselves in various business situations. There is a market research that needs to be done (study and review reports to begin with), managing the retail and suppliers of products and on the other side, training of staff and pricing the players' purchased goods with reference to existing market's sales (both local suppliers and competitors), qualities and brands of the goods. All this characteristics can refer to the overall review that would describe as the "not-so-user-friendly" web-based business game. Many business schools and universities recommend Virtonimics as a unique business training simulator for modeling various business strategies and tactics, solving business cases, as well as a unique business community where users can find new business partners and potential employers. Economic background knowledge is well recommended, yet is not necessarily required.

3.1.3. Business Tycoon OnLine

Business tycoon online (bto.dovogame.com) is an innovative, well-known, massively multiplayer online game that originated in Asia. The game supports thousands of players simultaneously. The game has been developed and launched in 2010 by Dovogame. Playing a Business Tycoon Online (BTO) game is absolutely free of charge with no instillation required. It can be played on almost any computer with Internet connectivity and modern browser supporting Adobe Flash Player 10.0. It is designed as a business simulator where players must rise to the top of the social ladder as industrial tycoons. The players take the role of entrepreneurs who make their way by living in the Liberty City. In the tough business world, a player starts his/her own business and breaks through constant challenges to eventually end with building up a universal corporation or a powerful business empire. BTO comprehends a variety of business items that are being simulated through the game: realistic financial accounting, business interaction, trading and commerce processing, designing empire buildings, and even "shady" business deals and corporate sabotages.

In the very beginning of creating the company in the world of the Liberty city, players can open more than 100 different kinds of stores where their success or failure is in their hands. In addition to opening the stores and running them successfully, the players need to recruit employees and arrange their training. Every day, different kind of business meeting will be required to attend. The performance in the business simulation game will affect the Directors' impressions that players will make. In order to become well-connected socialites of Liberty city and expand the player's network, players are obligated to widen their social circles and interact with other entrepreneurs around them. When faced with fierce market competition, the player is making preparation for any and all challenges that will come on his/her way.

http://dx.doi.org/10.5772/61242

The game itself is played in the strategy-oriented nature where the business decisions and leadership are tested in the direction of the progress of the game. By recruiting smart secretaries brings you benefits where they can help you to improve working efficiency. Each secretary is presented as an attractive female drawn character model, showing what kind of impressions are they giving, and background info about their private life (hobbies, interests). On the other hand, with good leadership skills a player can increase his/her own company's revenue. The objective is creating your very own company in one of four industries (Entertainment industry, Sales industry, Catering industry, Service industry), from a single shop to a major large company with hundreds of employees. In Entertainment industry, a player deals with managing stores like Jazz clubs, arcades, Billiard Halls, while Casinos and Horse Racing courses await entertainment tycoons. The management of Sales industry can be difficult but it is bringing a big payoff. Player's engagement is dealing with open markets, bookshops, gift shops and eventually shopping malls. In Catering industry, the player meets the world of hotel and resorts business. Service industry involves a management of service-related stores such as barbershops, massage paroles and tattoo shops. Depending on which industry a player will choose, he/she will be limited to a handful of stores he/she can open and to each store special benefits are tied to it. For example, if a player chooses Sales industry, he/she will enjoy a 5% production and raw material supply rate increase from the player's factory.

By gaining more experience and success, the player receives level points and rewards. Being a successful businessman in Liberty City will not bring the participant to play an easy task, it will certainly involve him in managing store fronts, factories, and training employees, building relationships with the media and with the local government. Media system takes also an important role to evolve the player's business strategy. Through media (newspapers, TV, radio, Internet), a player can publish comments to promote their companies or to attack the competitors.

BTO is structured to be a real business-oriented web-based game with involving a building aspect that makes it also a construction and management simulations. As in most of those games, players start with an "easy-to-use" tutorial system, which guides them to the general features and game-play mechanics the players will need to become familiar with. In the meantime, investors are also playing a big role during the game where they provide you a series of missions to walk you through step-by-step. Each mission accomplished is not just one step closer to establishing a business empire, but also a position where a player gets some good treats, such as money and gold, which plays a major part in the game.

Overall, the game does not require economic or business background knowledge, but is very well welcomed. It is easy to play where lots of "real-life" plot twists and interesting spins on traditional business simulators are presented.

Graphically, the game seems to do a good work in comparison to other web-based strategy games or simulations. Yet, the menu system has a little to many features which can make players confused at the very beginning, and the "web-design" gives the impression of "online poker portal". In order to really enjoy the game, some studying, spending money and learning "how to be patient" and "forgiving" will be required. But as a feedback, BTO gives to the player a variety of directions how to obtain some good strategy skills and management-decision processes that can be mirrored to the "real-life" world.

Figure 3. Business Tycoon OnLine (Screenshot of BTO users interface)

3.1.4. INNOV8 2.0

The INNOV8 is a serious game which was developed by IBM as part of their Academic Initiative programme. It is based as a role-playing game that simulates business process management in a 3D environment. The IBM SOA (self-oriented architecture) team originally created the game to help educate potential SOA clients. The initial version was only open to the academic community and has been in use at over a 1,000 universities and colleges (as far and wide as Beijing and Manchester) since its launch in 2007 [39]. The 2.0 version was released on May 2009 and has two extra scenarios – smarter supply chain and smarter traffic – in addition to the original customer service track. The original scenario of the game deals with a call centre where the players are using the call centre environment to develop more efficient ways to respond to customers. In each of these three scenarios, a player's goal is to model a new business process in order to come up with solutions that improve the efficiency. Online version of the game is also available and is open to the public.

The game employs a first-person role-playing approach where the player assumes the role of a consultant within a company that is experiencing challenges. The player is given a goal which he/she must achieve in order to successfully complete the game. The goal is to re-engineer a call centre process for the company in order to make it more efficient and effective. In order to achieve this goal, the player has to complete certain tasks which evolve as the game progresses. The game starts on the very first moment when a player takes the role of a female virtual character that has been hired by After Incorporate Company. A players' mission is to invest a critical process from the inside of organisation that deals with the customer service. The goal is clear: improve customer service and maximise profits while running a call centre. A player uses drag-and-drop graphics to advance through the game. Since main parts of the game are taking place in 3D environment, the game gives the very impressions of the "first-person-shooter"-like game play.

While different tasks are completed, the game tries to "force" the players to make decisions as they seek more efficient ways to manage a call centre and respond to customers. When the business meeting takes place, a player has to play with different variables of business modeling and see how player's changes vary the outcome, preparing them for the day they need to make real decisions.

This game focuses on the experience that is gathered by the individuals who are starting to learn about business project management and processing of the information and decisions. There are three levels to Innov8 2.0: process discovery and process modeling, collaboration-driven simulation and iterative process improvement, and real-time business management. INNOV8 2.0 gives players also the option to collaborate to map out business processes, identify process bottlenecks and explore what-if scenarios. Some parts of the game, which even has virtual characters in a shape of heroes and villains, use "Second Life-like" graphics.

Figure 4. IBM innov8 (a screenshot of 3D environment of Innov8 game)

Graphically, the game is very rich. In the beginning of every scenario, there is a short movie scene provided, where the objective goal is explained. It has virtual avatars (characters) that have audio voice, when a player has a meeting discussion. The interface consists of no menu bar tools. The GUI (Graphic User Interface) is manly concentrated on point-to-click and drag-and-drop issues, where a player sets the parameters to simulate the right solution for business process management problem that is being issued. The overall visualisation of a game gives the expression that the game origins from the commercial-designed game market.

Overall, INNOV8 is an interactive, 3D business simulator designed to teach the fundamentals of BPM. BPM enabled by SOA delivers continuously to provide lifecycle improvement, drives innovation in the business process and business model. Capabilities from both the software and the expertise follow a logical lifecycle approach for modeling, optimising, designing, deploying and managing business processes.

3.1.5. Wall Street Survivor

Wall Street Survivor (www.wallstreetsurvivor.com) is web-based financial (stock market) game with real market data, real stock symbols and real market tracking, all tracked and accounted for on an impressive simulated trading platform. It simulates real-time bid/ask trade fills, streaming profit and loss pages. The "virtual stock market" site offers a fantasy stock-trading platform, real-time quotes for the most realistic paper-trading experience, as well as educational articles and forums. In addition, to play the advanced version the subscription with payment is needed. Wall Street Survivor is considered as a "biggest simulated trading game on the internet with thousands of people learning the ropes of trading every day". It was launched on September 2011, where it has currently come up to 350,000 registered users and 3.5 million page views per month (www.finovate.com). Players can interact in the platform to share trading tips and make new connections as they learn how to trade and gain confidence in their decisions.

In order to play a game, the profile account needs to be created and registered. Once a user is registered at Wall Street Survivor, he/she receives an account with $100,000.00 in simulated money to trade with. The account also includes a margin, meaning that a player can use up to 2 times the amount of money in the account for trading, in other words $200,000.00. As a safeguard to help a user to learn, Wall Street Survivor do not allow more than 25% of users balance to be traded in any one position at a time. Players (investors and traders) can also win prizes if they land on the top gainers category. The game also has a resource section on their website which is full of articles explaining the most important trading topics, including stocks, options, futures and other important trading ideas. Wall Street Survivor also gives out $100,000 in prizes every year to its players, which is a very nice thing for them to do. It is easy to navigate around the website, which makes Wall Street Survivor different from other stock market simulation.

Getting help at Wall Street Survivor is easy as click and send. The FAQ page is well supplied with helpful data while a user is logged in to this simulated stock market game. One of the most important lessons that one can learn in Wall Street Survivor is that he/she cannot play unless he/she meets the understanding of dynamics of the stock market. Wall Street Survivor articles, which are regularly uploaded on official page, do not guarantee you to higher gains, but it rather guides you to important skills such as choosing the best deals, comprehensive usage of best strategies, and finding hints which are hot or preferred stocks to be bought (www.wallstreetsurvivor.com).

However, in placing a trade at Wall Street Survivor, the quotes shown for a particular stock are delayed 15–20 minutes. This delay matters so much in real trading; but for the sake of learning day-trading strategies, this delay might be justified in order to make the most out of Wall Street Survivor by using different strategies or position sizing methods. This enables as well as to learn how to close out positions. At the end of each day, Wall Street Survivor would make users to realise that practice can move him/her further in the ladder of success. Perhaps being conscious that no money, and therefore no emotions, is involved, this certainly allows users to practice the game without any bad consequences (www.wallstreetsurvivor.com).Graphically, the game is strictly text-based with a view of different types of charts with various technical indicators. Wall Street Survivor is not for every user. For users that have no desire to learn about the stock market or get involved in to the real stock market world, it is highly not recommended, yet for people who want to "hone" their trading skills and simulate real trading before doing real business with real money, Wall Street Survivor is a good place to start.

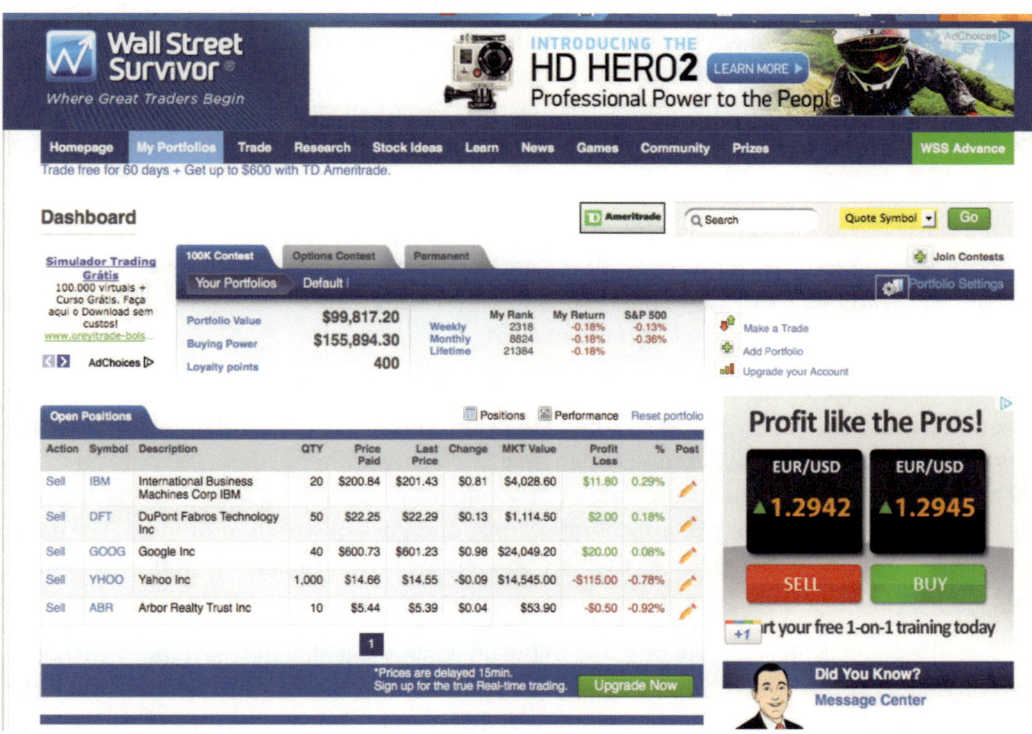

Figure 5. Wall Street Survivor (Screenshot of online Wall Street Survivor virtual stock)

3.1.6. Big Oil: Build an Oil Empire

Big Oil: Build an Oil Empire is a business strategy game where users take a role of oil baron who is set in times of the oil industry pioneers, in order to build his own oil empire by taking control of the entire oil business process, from surveying, drilling and extracting to refining, selling and market investments. The game was released in July 2006 and developed by Try Synergy. The game can be played in a single-player mode or multi-player mode online or via a local network with up to six players [39].

Big Oil lets users to build an oil empire by drilling for oil, shipping it to refineries around the world, and eventually processing it into products that can be sold to the public. To play a game, user/player can choose from more than 15 scenarios based on historical events such as the Oil Crisis, Lenin's death, Apartheid, World Wars or the Great Depression [39]. Each scenario has unique rules and conditions for success. However, they can all be played about the same, which is to say, they all play poorly. A player can also choose a free play campaign, where he/she starts from scratch and builds oil wells and refineries, researches new technology to improve transportation and creates new products and develops cities that provide more workers. There are two difficulty modes to choose from: easy mode and advanced mode. When choosing the easy mode, the player is receiving a constant help from a virtual assistant that guides the player through so-called "getting familiar" process with the users interface and makes recommendations to user's decisions in order to automatically undertake certain menial tasks, like sending a virtual team to test a potential oil field, with user's permission. Big Oil is a commercial-strategy-game alike. With all the functionality that is provided, Big Oil gives more or less the expression of Dune 2000 (http://www.gamespot.com/dune-2000/) or series of war craft games (http://eu.battle.net/wow/en/) where the competition of your opponents is running all the time. The player's progress is showed by the money budget he/she receives in order to how his/her oil business is growing.

Big Oil starts out at the top of its difficulty curve, forcing potential players to spend a couple of hours learning the "ins" and "outs" of the game's extremely confusing user interface. This sort of complexity tends towards the "status quo" for simulations, but even for simulations like the one in Big Oil, it is hard to get the hang of.

Like any open-ended game, there are a large multitude of choices to be made that allow for a different game play experience each time. However, the high initial difficulty curve of the game, as well as the underwhelming experience of playing it after getting a handle on it, Big Oil game will probably spend more time in the desk drawer gathering dust than in CD drive. Big Oil starts with a generally unappealing premise and goes downhill from there. The game is difficult regarding the controls as they are somehow hectic and boring. At the same time, they are packaged in an uninspiring shell of semi-poor graphics.

Overall, the game itself is merely oriented to the oil business, which means if users are not so passionate about the world of oil business, they can easily be confronted with the hectic learning curve and subsequent extreme dullness that Big Oil offers; however, on the contrary for "oil-tycoon-wannabes", there is true possibility that they might find the game to be endlessly fascinating.

Figure 6. Big Oil: Build Oil Empire (Screenshot of GUI of Big Oil: Build Oil Empire).

3.1.7. Virtual Leader

Important area in the management education is the building of leadership. The training in that context is possible with the Virtual Leader game. The game is dedicated to acquiring leadership skills. Being a good leader is considered as a capacity to have suitable power in influencing the employers for making an effective and productive atmosphere that will enable successful accomplishment of the task and the project at the end. This can be achieved by many components in a form of communication and increasing awareness of verbal and non-verbal communication cues. Virtual leader as a simulator provides a user step-by-step practices, by preset communication dialogs over the course of several sessions or one long session with virtual co-workers. It uses a meeting environment to allow the users to interact with other characters. There is also a well-written guide that describes the theories behind the content.

Virtual Leader is a standalone game, which means when the game is installed to a computer it can be played. Once the game starts, users need to register and create his/her account and begin to play. In the beginning, the player can take short introductions about Leadership fundamentals and framework showing how communication affects the principles of leaderships. As well as the player can choose two other options which are either to begin the learning of the principles through tutorial practices or to be engaged into the simulator through variety of leaderships scenarios. Player takes the role of the character named Corey that Nordic enterprise hired to work as a sector leader at the customer service call center. It is all about getting work done. Virtual Leader uses meeting scenarios where Corey is getting to interact to virtual characters to get the right combination of ideas completed. At each meeting sessions, the goal is to introduce ideas, support them and make them happen after finishing the meeting. By achieving the goal, a user must create the right amount of tension and using the right amount of gained power to make the virtual character accept and support the leader's ideas. All this components of maintaining the power are constantly monitored in a shape of 3-color graph that can be seen as a practice mode. When the meeting is finished, learner is given a summary of how he/she used the key tenets of leadership skills to manage the expectations of the meeting. A set of graphs and numbers are presented where players can analyse how to improve the strategy of increasing or decreasing the elements of a good leadership.

Virtual Leader does not try to simulate a real-life conversation. The learning objective mainly focuses to make the learning experience to develop intuitive skills so that people can understand the people's intent in a real-life situation without hesitation.

Figure 7. Virtual Leader (a screenshot of business meeting at Virtual Leader Simulation)

3.1.8. Shark World – A Project Management Game

This game is considered as an excellent addition to the basic project management training. The main focus is in experimentation and gaining experience about key aspects of efficient project management in a highly entertaining and motivating setting. The game is played online, enabling a creation of convincing virtual environment, close to the reality in which a particular project is developed in real time. The game proceeds in an interactive way that urges the students to react when things go wrong or more preferably before they happen. The game can be played both through online and mobile channels which make the game accessible any time and in any location. Projects are developed in (accelerated) real-time (24/7) so players have to keep up with the fast pace and to act or intervene almost immediately. The game is propelled by an underlying suspense story that blurs the line between the reality and the fiction. The game offers life-like content as a test case for inspiring the trained future project managers. The screenshot of Sharkworld's GUI is presented in Figure 8.

Shark World combines simulation elements with a story and characters, to create an engaging project management experience. With the help of picture and video material, players are taken on a trip to China. Once they arrive in China, players start to manage their project. They can use conversation, chat and email, in order to take care of the interests of the boss, client and team. They also make project schedules and project budgets. The choices that players make during the game decide whether the project becomes a success or turns into a disaster (www.ranj.com).

The game play is based on the usage of various media such as emails from game characters, newspaper and TV news in order to give extra depth to the experience. When players are not behind the computer, they get text and voice messages from game characters on their mobile phones.

Once the user is registered (create our profile and enter the mobile number), the game is ready to be played. The game begins with an automated mobile call, where the virtual female assistant lets the player know that she is waiting to pick up the player on the Shanghai airport. After the game started, the introduction video begins, where the female assistant meets the player at the meeting spot (Shanghai airport) and explains the background story and the aim of the project to be processed. She describes the challenges the player should expect during the play. On a location near the city of Sha Cheng, a large-scale shark aquarium is being re-built and is combined with a swimming paradise named "Sharkworld". The Virtual Dutch (international) installation company with the name "Spector Install" has acquired the project. The company is experienced for building swimming pools, congress halls, hospitals and dolphin aquariums, but has never worked with sharks before. Their corporate website provides a nice overview of several installation and construction projects in both utility and industrial fields, with diversity of cases, but without any shark aquarium.

The game continues with the news that the appointed project manager on site has mysteriously disappeared and the player is a person that applies for his job, gets the job and is sent to China immediately. The player lands in the middle of an ongoing project and must bring the project to a good end. What the player does not know at the start of the game is that not everything in the game is what it seems to be. Some things, e.g. obstacles, will turn out to be setups as they are designed to test the player's project management abilities (www.sharkworldgame.com). During the game, a player is expected to achieve and display essential soft skills, by making conversations with people who are involved in the project. When a player has a dialog with the game characters, the "mood icon" of the characters appears on the upper right corner of GUI (graphical user interface presented on Figure 4). When the game character is satisfied with the player's answer, the "mood icon" shows a "happy face"; and on the contrary, when the game character does not like the answer or the undertaken step, the "mood icon" changes into an "angry face". During the game, a player must maintain the three very important type of atmosphere:

- Team satisfaction
- Boss satisfaction
- Client satisfaction

Figure 8. Shark World (a screenshot of Graphic User's Interface).

The levels of these attributes are shown on the status bar, with a little pointer that shows where on the scale of satisfactory presented skills the player is. For example, if the pointer is colored green, the satisfaction is high and the red color indicates low satisfaction. In order to bring the project to a successful end, all three satisfaction types have to get the highest satisfaction levels, meaning that the pointer has to be in the area of a green color on a the scale bar. The performance of solving problems is also followed during the game. Whenever in a game a challenge comes up, the player must perform a task in order to solve the problem presented as a challenge. The player provides solution to the problem with calculation of the data information gathered during the game for an assessment of risk management. Depending on a player's decisions, the result of the challenges is shown in the project overviews. After the accomplishment of the task, the game displays the achieved performances in problem-solving being categorized as extremely poor or professionally successful.

4. Assessment and evaluation

The brief presentation of the selected games makes possible the assessment of the game properties to be presented in the form of table in the section that follows.

4.1. Value of the assessment parameters

Below we present the value of assessment parameters presented in Section 4 for each of the selected games.

	eRepublik	Virtonimics	Shark World	IBM innov8	Virtual Leader	Big Oil	Wall Street	The Beer Game	Business Tycoon Online
Web-based/ Desktop	Web-based	Web-based	Web-based	Desktop	Desktop	Desktop	Web-based	Web-based	Web-based
Distribution	Republik Labs	Virtonomics team		IBM	SimuLearn	Try Sinergy	Wall Street Survivor	MTI Sloan	Dovogame
No. of users	**400.000	**550.000	n/a	n/a	n/a	n/a	350.000	n/a	**600.000
Year of publishing	2008	2009	2008	2009	2003	2006	n/a	n/a	2010
Dimension	2D	2D	2D	3D	2D	3D	2D	2D	2D
Platform	Any	Any	Any	PC-Windows	PC-windows	PC-Windows	Any	Any	Any
Free of use	Yes	Yes	Purchase required	Registration approved	Purchase required	Purchase required	Yes	Yes	Yes
Time period	Min. 1 month	Min. 1.5 month	Min. 1 month	2–4 hours	6–9 hours	8–10 hours	Min. 1 month	1–1.5 hours	Min. 1 month
Industry or	Generic	Generic	Industrial	Industrial	Industrial	Industrial	Generic	Industrial	Industrial

	eRepublik	Virtonimics	Shark World	IBM innov8	Virtual Leader	Big Oil	Wall Street	The Beer Game	Business Tycoon Online
generic									
Degree of complexity	Low	Medium	Medium	Low	Medium	Low	Low	Low	Medium
Functional or enterprise	Enterprise	Total enterprise	Total enterprise	Enterprise	Enterprise	Functional	Functional	Functional	Total enterprise
Competitive or non-competitive	Competitive	Competitive	Non-competitive	Non-competitive	Non-competitive	Competitive	Competitive	Competitive	Competitive
Feedback system	Experience points	Virtual Money income	Customer influence	Points received	Statistic charts	Points received	Virtual money	Statistic charts	Points received
Deterministic or stochastic	Deterministic	Deterministic	Deterministic	Deterministic	Deterministic	Deterministic	Stochastic	Deterministic	Stochastic
Briefing systems	Tutorial video of personal mentor	Poorly supports with mail from virtual administrator	Supported with mails from virtual administrator	The virtual Note support	Text Instructions and audio/video tutorial	Virtual assistant provided	Text tutorial	Text tutorial	Text tutorial
Learning objectives	Strategy skills, politics-management skills	Strategy skills, politics-management skills	Project management skills, hard skills, soft skills	Business Process management skills	Leadership skills	Business strategy skills	Financial skills, stockbroker skills	Coordination, logistic skills	Strategy business – decision-making skills
Background knowledge	Not required	Required	Required	Required	Not required	Not required	Required	Not required	Not required
Interactivity type	Yes	Yes	Yes	No	No	No	No	No	No

Table 1. (Assessment parameters and results) Immersive business simulation games: an innovative pedagogical approach to e-learning

5. Discussion

The assessment of selected business simulation games has provided some summarised results. The parameters that assess the properties for achievement of the educational goals are considered as most important. In that context, it is important for the game scenario to meet the educators' and the learners' expectations. Games that answer to this requirement usually have highly developed segments or levels of reality. In addition, the game has to lead the player through several situations that require decision-making. The game should help the learner with proper guidance and explanation in case the decision was not selected as it was expected. This type of game enables faster transfer of experiences, getting skills more easily and good outcomes when the achievement of learning objectives is analysed. By inspection of Table 1, it can be concluded that Shark World game appears to represent the real-case situation most effectively. The game provides excellent underlying storyline (which turn is also entertaining), the fictional characters are played by the real actors and the video material is a very nice attempt that makes the players to feel like being part of a real business project in a real-life environment. The game eRepublik provides scenarios in a fictional war situation where users are gaining their economical power; however, this is most likely hard to happen in the real world.

The way of presenting the game content, the game scenarios and the users' satisfaction are also important aspects how the game is structured. Another good example among the selected games is certainly the IBM's INNOV8. This game is based on high rich graphics, cut scenes, scenarios and attractive walkthrough. It gives a good opportunity to explore how to learn the basic about the management of business process and how to collaborate with participants of the business processes, how to identify process bottlenecks and how to explore what-if scenarios when a decision is expected to be taken by the player. The game provides clear and easy-to-learn player's interface which enables an easy control of the game. On the contrary, Virtual Leader, give an impression of poor level regarding the properties required in the player training and learning. The gameplay focuses on a selection of the right set of dialogs with virtual characters. Functionally, there is nothing much to do within the presented scenario. With no sufficiently presented scenario, players are more likely to be confronted with a hectic learning curve and subsequent extreme dullness. However, it should be noticed that the game gives an excellent case for imitation of human behavior and for practicing tenets of three-to-one leadership with simulations of business meeting sessions which can be mirrored into the real-life situations.

The technical properties studied in the games, e.g. GUI (graphical user interface), the screen briefings, the tutorial supports also differ from game to game. IBM's INNOV8 and Shark World are good examples as they contain clear and easy-to-learn player's interface, while Big Oil game (Build an Oil Empire) requires from the player to spend a lot of time for learning the usage of of the game GUI.

On the other hand, the MMOG business games (Virtonomics, eRepublik, Business On-Line Tycoon, eRepublik) have shown to be bad examples regarding the user's guidance. Players need to learn the whole functionality of the games "menu-bar" and game GUIs tool bars, without any comprehensive tutorial support in the background. These games are time-consuming and are a temptation for the players' motivation and satisfaction. We may consider them as helpful in some cases as they demonstrate some aspects of business strategy, decision-making processes, business management and organisation activities.

6. Concluding remarks

The research on modern students' education methods and techniques has proven that education based on practical usage of knowledge and training in a target activity environment is the most effective way of learning and educating [41]. Business simulation games are developed to implement different real scenarios and virtual worlds enabling the player motivation to be upgraded and the learning goals achieved. They specially try to make a good attempt in capturing and combining the virtual reality technologies and engaging components of video games for simulation of the real eco-systems. The current study is a contribution to the assessment of the business simulation games to be perceived as an interesting and desired form of gaining experience to be used in later professional practice [42].

However, business simulation games can be allocated to different game types or categories, based on the variety of "learning" content and their technical capabilities. In that context is extracting the in-built learning activities which were proved to be the most important in the game assessment within the educational and training environment. The presented study is a contribution to this area of research. The selected business simulation games from the current stage of "world of business games" and their study are not attempts to cover the whole knowledge area that can be met in business education [39], but complement the current research in this field which is considered to cover some of the most important methods of acquiring technical and problem-related knowledge. When a combination of business simulation games is adequately set up within particular educational process, this becomes a practical teaching-related arrangement that successfully combines the natural predisposition of the players with planned and directed knowledge acquirement. With most of the other teaching methods, this is rarely the case.

This contribution has pointed out to the fact that different games provide different skills and practice and that is one of the reason why the selection of most appropriate game should be based on criteria and property evaluation. By deciding/selecting which "field" of business education needs to be "trained", suitable set of games can be found as the market of business games is sufficiently large and rich. However, the market changes with time to time and business simulation games are offered with variety of expectations, limitations (games can be out of date, they can be commercial, they work just on certain platforms) and (dis)advantages that should be carefully considered.

With all positive effects found in the training with business simulation games, it is necessary to point out that digital learning games, on the other hand, can also have some negative aspects. Games and gaming behaviors can in many ways be fundamentally incompatible with the institutional education environment. As Caillois [43] outlines, this can be formulated by consideration of the six formal qualities of games regarding the incompatibleness with the institutional environment:

- Freedom
- Separation (from events outside of the game world and the structure of the game)
- Uncertainty of outcome
- Non-productiveness

- Government by rules
- Make-believe (not real)

Freedom of action means that the games are time-consuming and diffuse, tending to frustrate attempts to focus efforts on a single, measurable curricular element. Separation of the gaming world from the outside world may make it difficult to connect gaming outcomes to established learning standards, and the uncertainty of outcome can make it difficult to measure formal learning in any case.

Game designers in that case need to re-assess the business games in order for the business models to be re-built for more realistic simulation of the market situations. Moreover, a properly designed game should allow one to generate results that would show its participants the increase in the knowledge gained during the game in the normal course of game usage (during the game).

We may conclude as well as that the business simulation games make great attempts to seize technologies for presenting the virtual reality and the entertaining components from digital games world. By capturing the massive size of resources and technology from the video games industry, business games can bring learners in to new environment where business (management) processes can play a major role in everyday life.

These are the processes that are identified as critical to different type of organizations (energy sector, banking, health care, supply chain, logistic infrastructures, traffic systems, customer service, telecom service, politics, etc.), This chapter does not bring solutions for "how to select" a business simulation game for particular educational case. It does not provide also advices to which level business games should be used in the game-based learning environments, but it provides ideas about the appropriateness of several indicative games and how to assess some aspects of their educational capabilities in achieving learning goals. This chapter contributes also to the widening of the educator's horizons and opens a window towards the "massive world" of continuously rising the world of business simulation games. The chapter has shown as well that the "great teachers-designers" need to step forward together with people with visions in the area of e-learning for better harnessing of the wide range of business simulation game world.

Another concluding remark goes to the request of simulation games to be used as didactic tools within the new learning methods, that is, they must be extremely precise in the simulation of the business market realities. Game developers should monitor continuously everyday business ecosystem, so they can adequately present the predicted market situations that make the virtual world as close as possible to the real world.

Author details

Andrej Jerman Blažič* and Franc Novak

*Address all correspondence to: andrejcek@e5.ijs.si

Laboratory for Open Systems, Jožef Stefan Institute, Ljubljana, Slovenia

References

[1] Pivec M. Editorial: play and learn: potentials of game-based Learning. British Journal of Educational Technology 2007;38(3):387–93. DOI: 10.1111/j.1467-8535.2007.00722.x.

[2] Arnseth HC, McFarlane A. Simulation/gaming as a discipline. J Simulation Gaming 2010;41(6):898–920.

[3] Wilson KA, Bedwell WL, Lazzara EH, Salas E, Burke CS, Estock JL, Orvis KL, Conkey C. Relationships between game attributes and learning outcomes. J Simulation Gaming 2009;40(2):217–66.

[4] Amory A, Seagram R. Educational game models, conceptualisation and evaluation. South African Journal of Higher Education 2004;17(2):206–17.

[5] Suittie N, Louchart S, Lim T, Macvean A, Westera W, Brown D, Djaouti D. Introducing the "Serious Games Mechanics" A Theoretical Framework to Analyse Relationships Between "Game" and"Pedagogical Aspects" of Serious Games. In: Proceedings, VS-GAMES 2012, Procedia Computer Science. 29-31 October, Genoa, Italy 2012;15:314–315.

[6] Navarro JI, Marchena E, Alcalde C, Ruiz G, Llorens I, Aguilar M. Improving attention behaviour in primary and secondary school children with a computer assisted instruction procedure. International Journal of Psychology 2003;38(6):359–65.

[7] ELSPA Unlimited learning – computer and video games in the learning landscape. 2006, http://www.org.id.tue.nl/IFIP-TC14/documents/ELSPA-report-2006.pdf [Accessed:2015-03-12]

[8] Mitchell A, Savill-Smith C. The use of computer and video games for learning: a review of the literature. Learning and Skill Development Agency, 2004. (www.LSDA.org.uk) [Accessed:2015-04-10]

[9] Jerman BA, Ribeiro C, Fernandes J, Pereira J, Arh T. Analysing the required properties of business simulation games to be used in e-learning and education. Intelligent Informaton Management 2010;4(6):348–56. DOI: 10.4236/iim.2012.46039.

[10] Wells RA. Management games and simulations in management development: an introduction. Journal of Management Development 1990;9(2):4–6, DOI: 10.1108/02621719010002108.

[11] Greenlaw PS, Herron LW, Rawdon RH. Business Simulation in Industrial and University Education. Englewood Cliffs, New Jersey: Prentice Hall, 1962.

[12] Jackson JR. Learning from experience in business games. California Management Revision 1959;1(2):92–107.

[13] Andlinger G.R. Business games – play one! Harvard Business Review 1958;28:115–25.

[14] Saunders D. Games and Simulations to Enhance Quality Learning. Routledge: Falmer, 1996, ISBN 0749418664.

[15] Faira AJ, Hutchinson D, Wellington WJ, Gold S. Developments in busines gaming – a review of the past 40 years. Simulation & Gaming. 2009;40(4):464–487.

[16] Farkas GM. Social software in libraries: building collaboration, communication, and community online. Information Today, Inc. 2007, p. 216. ISBN 157387275X.

[17] Hogarth RM. Educating Intuition. University of Chicago Press. 2001, p. 184. ISBN 0226348601.

[18] Ben-Zvi T, Carton TC. Applying bloom`s recised taxonomy in business games. Develop Bus Simulation Exp Learning. 2008;35:265–72.

[19] Hughes T, O'Regan N, Wornham D. The credibility issue: closing the academic/practitioner gap. Strategic Change Journal. 2008;17(7):215–33.

[20] Snyder LG, Snyder MJ. Teaching critical thinking and problem solving skills. Delta Pi Epsilon J 2008;2(1):90–9, North Carolina State University, Business Communication – Business Education – Teaching and Learning.

[21] [21 Suittie N, Louchart S, Lim T, Macvean A, Westera W, Brown D, Djaouti D. Introducing the "Serious Games Mechanics" A Theoretical Framework to Analyse Relationships Between "Game" and"Pedagogical Aspects" of Serious Games. In: Proceedings, VS-GAMES 2012, Procedia Computer Science. 29-31 October, Genoa, Italy 2012;15:314–315.

[22] Feinstein AH, Mann S, Corsun DL. Charting the experiential territory: clarifying definitions and uses of computer simulation, games, and role play. J Manage Develop 2002;21(10):732–44, retreived from http://dx.doi.org/10.1108/02621710210448011.

[23] Abdullah N L, Hanafiah MH, Hashim NA. Developing creative teaching module: Business simulation in teaching strategic management. International Education Studies. 2013;6(6):95–107.

[24] Wikipeida (2014) http://en.wikipedia.org/wiki/Business_simulation_game [Accessed: 2014-12-18]

[25] Greenlaw PS, Herron LW, Rawdon RH. Business Simulation in Industrial and University Education. Englewood Cliffs, New Jersey: Prentice Hall, 1962.

[26] Keys B, Wolfe J. The role of management games and simulations in education and research. J Manage 1990;16(2):307–36. http://library.marketplace6.com/papers/pdfs/Keys-Wolfe-1990.pdf

[27] Michael D, Chen S. Serious Games: Games that Educate, Train, and Inform. Boston, MA: Thomson Course Technology, 2006.

[28] Squire K, Giovanetto L, DeVane B, Durga S. From users to designers building a self-organizing game-based learning environment. Technol Trend 2005;49:32–42.

[29] Schurr S.(1994) Dynamite in the Classroom: A How-to Handbook for Teachers. National Middle School Association. 1994, p. 73. ISBN 1560900415.

[30] Thole, Heinz-Jürgen; Claus Möbus, Olaf Schröder (1997). "Domain Knowledge Structure, Knowledge Representation and Hypotheses Testing". Artificial Intelligence in Education: Knowledge and Media

[31] Whicker ML, Lee S. Computer Simulation Applications, An Introduction. Sage Publications, London, 1991.

[32] Riedel JCKH, Hauge JB. State of the art of serious games for business and industry. 17th International Conference on Concurrent Enterprising, 20–22 June. Germany. 2011; p.1–8.

[33] Herman A, Coombe R, Lewis K. Your second life? Goodwill and the performativity of intellectual property in online digital gaming. 20 Cultural Studies 2005; 20(3):184–210.

[34] Djaouti D, Alvarez J, Jessel JP. Can game 2.0 help design serious games? A comparative study, in Proceedings of the 5th ACM SIGGRAPH Symposium on video games, 2010; 11–18. Doi:10.1145/1836135.1836137.

[35] Elion S. Management games. J Operation Res Soc 1963;14(2):137–49.

[36] Greenlaw PS, Herron LW, Rawdon RH. Business Simulation in Industrial and University Education. Englewood Cliffs, New Jersey: Prentice Hall, 1962.

[37] Fritzsche DJ, Burns AC. The role of ABSEL in the development of marketing simulations in collegiate education. Simulation & Gaming 2001;32(1):85–96.

[38] Wolfe J. A History of business teaching games in English-Speaking and post-socialist countries: the original and diffusion of a management education and development technology. Simulation &Gaming 1993;24:446–63.

[39] Jerman BA, Arh T. Immersive business simulation games: an innovative pedagogical approach to e-learning and education. In: Proceedings of 30th ascilite Conference, Carter H, Gosper M, Hedberg J. (eds.) Electric Dreams. 1-4 december 2013 Sydney, 2013, p. 427–437.

[40] Biggs WD. Introduction to computerized business management simulations. In: Gentry J. (ed.) Guide to Business Gaming and Experiential Learning. East Brunswick, NJ: Nichols/GP, 1990,pp.23–35.

[41] Hodkinson, H. & Hodkinson, P. (2005). Improving schoolteachers' workplace learning. Research Papers in Education, 2, p. 151-182.

[42] Wawer M, Milosz M, Muryjas P, Rzemieniak M. Business simulation games in forming students' entrepreneurship. Int J Euro-Mediterranean Studies. 2010;3(1):49–73.

[43] Caillois, R. Man, Play and Games. (N. Trans Meyer Barash, Ed.) Meyer Barash. New York. The Free Press of Glencoe (Vol. Reprint, p. 224). University of Illinois Press.

Chapter 11

Using Phonically Based E-books to Develop Reading Fluency

Charles Potter

Additional information is available at the end of the chapter

http://dx.doi.org/10.5772/61607

Abstract

The purpose of this chapter is to describe the 'Tales of Jud the Rat' reading fluency programme and its logic, and to present preliminary results from its use as a form of e-learning. The first section of the chapter provides an overview of the development of the 'The Tales Jud the Rat' series. Literature relevant to the neurolinguistic basis of the materials is then reviewed. Results from initial case study and the first cohort of children who have worked on this programme with their parents are presented in the third section, while the final section of the chapter provides an evaluation of the current status of the programme and indicates its potential uses.

At this stage in the development of the programme, there is plenty of material available, and the ebooks and supporting methodology are currently being used by the parents, therapists and teachers of over seventy children with reading difficulty across our country. Some of the children live over a thousand kilometres from my rooms. Others are in schools or clinics. The results have been promising both with primary school children as well as with adolescents in high school. Parents, therapists, teachers and children have also provided positive evaluations of the effects improved reading fluency has had on reading ability more generally, as well as on school work.

Keywords: Reading difficulties, dyslexia, reading fluency, rate of work, structured phonics, analytical phonics, seven vowel system, large print, ebooks, visual tracking, 3 × 3 oral impress method, distance education

1. Introduction

'Learning to read requires mastering the system by which print encodes the language.' [1]

I am an educational psychologist who specialises in work with children with learning and reading difficulties. As part of this work, I have been developing a reading fluency programme based on a series of ebooks.

The text of the ebooks has been written based on neurolinguistic theory[1], and the ebooks are designed to be used with a form of oral impress procedure based on paired reading. This is simple to implement. It differs from the type of paired reading procedures documented in the literature, as it involves additional repetition to develop phonic associations and automaticity in reading.

The ebooks are set in large print with wide spaces between words to provide maximal visual cues and also to prevent crowding, which has emerged in recent literature as a factor affecting reading in dyslexic children. The oral impress procedure also builds in visual tracking to maintain visual attention. Repetition on both the phonological and the visual level is thus provided both in the text of the ebooks as well as in the procedures used to work with the children. Visual attention is maintained through the use of a pointer working from the top of the line, and not from the bottom, for the reason that the top of the line provides greater visual cues than the bottom of the line.

As the materials are in electronic form, they provide a form of e-learning which can be used in contact, as well as at distance. The ebooks are designed to be used by parents and can also be used by therapists, teachers and schools to develop fluent reading. Assessment and evaluation are built into the programme's structure, linked to an awards system for children using the materials.

This chapter is written in three parts. The first part of the chapter presents a literature review. The second part describes the development of the characters and setting of a set of reading materials called 'The Doctor Skunk Stories', which were developed for a child who lived some 6,000 miles away from my rooms. This part of the chapter is based on a longitudinal case study. The third part of the chapter then describes the subsequent development of the materials into an assessment-based reading programme and presents results of the first cohort of children who have worked on this programme with their parents.

At this stage in the development of the programme, there is plenty of material available, and the ebooks and supporting methodology are currently being used by the parents, therapists and teachers of over seventy children with reading difficulty across our country. Some of the children live over a thousand kilometres from my rooms. Others are in schools or clinics. The results have been promising with younger children as well as adolescents. Parents, therapists, teachers and children have also provided positive evaluations of the benefits improved reading fluency has had on reading ability more generally, as well as on school work.

---

1 The approach to automaticity in reading adopted in this chapter is based on the work of the Russian neuropsychologist A.R. Luria, and the term "neurolinguistic" follows Luria's work on the physiological basis of language-based functions (Luria, A.R. (1976). Basic Problems of Neurolinguistics. The Hague: Mouton B.V.) as well as the approach suggested by Arbib and Caplan of the Center for Systems Neuroscience at the University of Massachusetts, Amherst (Arbib, M.A. and Caplan, D . (1979). Neurolinguistics must be computational. Behavioral and Brain Sciences, 2, 3, pages 449- 460) in which neurolinguistics draws insights from modern neuroanatomy, neurochemistry and neurophysiology.

2. Literature on automaticity in reading

2.1. Orientation

The literature on reading is complex on a theoretical level, and it is impossible in a short literature review to do justice to this. I have thus written the first section of the literature review which deals with automaticity in reading from a functional and applied perspective, and would refer readers interested in psycholinguistic theories of reading to a good source, such as Adams [2] or Perfetti [3, 4, 5].

The definitions of the terms I am going to provide at the beginning of this chapter are functional ones for the reason that the first stage in development of 'The Tales of Jud the Rat' materials was based on applied work conducted over a number of years with one child. As these initial materials were used by a parent and a peer tutor implementer working in Europe, 6,000 miles away from my rooms in Johannesburg, the initial literature I am going to review is based on research on reading fluency programmes implemented through parent and peer-tutored paired reading. This is followed by review of the neurolinguistic literature which has provided the theoretical basis for the development of the 'The Tales of Jud the Rat' materials in their current form.

2.2. Definition of terms

Reading decoding involves a child or adult's ability to read words both individually and in sequence. This involves the ability to use sound–letter associations to sound out individual words by analysing their parts and then to link these parts together to form words. The process of analysis and synthesis of individual words then needs to be done sequentially, with sufficient fluency to comprehend both the individual words and strings of words being read.

Fluent reading involves the ability to decode individual words and join the parts together quickly and accurately, so that the words can be understood both individually and in sequence. Cognitive processes of perception, language, sequencing and working memory are involved in fluent reading, and for this reason, assessment of reading also involves side-by-side assessment of perceptual, language, working memory and sequential abilities.

Reading can be defined as a complex cognitive process of making meaning from text, which depends on adequately developed perception, language, working memory and sequential abilities. As reading comprehension is affected by reading fluency, reading fluency can be defined as:

'The ability to read phrases and sentences smoothly and quickly, while understanding them as expressions of complete ideas.' [6]

Smooth, quick reading is based on the notion of automaticity [7], which underpins the abilities to read with speed and accuracy as well as expression. Automaticity is developed in reading when there has been sufficient practice to enable a complex functional act to become fluent enough to form the basis for higher mental processing. As Logsdon [8] suggests:

'Reading fluency refers to the ability to read with adequate accuracy, speed, expression, and automaticity. Reading fluency is very important to one's overall ability to understand, or comprehend, what is read.'

2.3. Automaticity in reading

On a theoretical level, automaticity in reading is based on the suggestions made by Luria [9] concerning the development of automaticity in the hierarchical processing of information by the working brain. LaBerge and Samuels [10] were the first researchers to focus on automaticity as a function of how reading fluency develops. They proposed a model of information processing in reading, in which visual information is transformed through a series of processing stages involving visual, phonological and episodic memory systems until it is finally comprehended in the semantic system.

LaBerge and Samuels further proposed that the processing occurring at each processing stage was learned while the degree of learning could be assessed with respect to two criteria: *accuracy* and *automaticity*. At the accuracy level of performance, attention was assumed to be necessary for processing; at the automatic level, it was not.

Again following Luria [11], who had suggested the value of repeated modelling and practice in developing automaticity in writing, Samuels suggested that automaticity in reading could be trained through procedures involving repeated reading, As Samuels commented,

'It is important to point out that repeated reading is not a method for teaching all reading skills. Rather, it is intended as a supplement in a developmental reading program. While the method is particularly suitable for students with special learning problems, it is useful for normal children as well.' [12]

Support for LaBerge and Samuels' work was provided independently by Carol Chomsky [13] at Harvard University. Chomsky concluded that the repeated reading procedure she had used with students had been facilitating for both slow and halting readers, 'increasing fluency rapidly and with apparent ease'. Other researchers such as Carbo [14], Morgan and Lyon [15] and Ashby-Davis [16] provided additional support through studies using different repeated reading methods to model and develop automaticity through repetition.

The goal of each of these different studies was the development of reading fluency, which Allington [17] pointed out was a characteristic of poor readers, but was seldom treated. The notion of fluency has then recurred in subsequent literature. Adams [18], for example, has suggested that the most salient characteristic of skillful reading is the speed with which text is reproduced into spoken language.

Fluency is thus associated with oral reading. Fuchs et al. [19] have defined oral reading fluency as the oral translation of text with speed and accuracy. On the basis of review of theoretical arguments and several studies substantiating this phenomenon, Fuchs et al. concluded that oral reading fluency is an indicator of overall reading competence.

The U.S. Congress [20] has defined the essential components of reading instruction as involving explicit and systematic instruction in:

a. phonemic awareness;

b. phonics;

c. vocabulary development;

d. reading fluency, including oral reading skills; and

e. reading comprehension strategies.

(SEC. 1208. DEFINITIONS).

There would thus be justification for incorporating the assessment of reading fluency as one aspect of psychometric measurement of reading, with implications for both research and practice based on assessment of reading ability (e.g. [21]).

2.4. Developing reading fluency through paired reading methods

The literature suggests that reading fluency can be developed by paired reading methods, which have been described differently by different researchers. Carol Chomsky [22] called the technique 'repeated reading'. Carbo [23] used tape-recorded books with struggling readers to good effect and called her method 'talking books'. Morgan and Lyon [24] called their technique 'paired reading', while Ashby-Davis [25] called her method 'assisted reading'. Other terms used by researchers include 'neurological impress' [26, 27, 28] and 'reading by immersion' [29].

The use of these different terms would suggest that paired reading is an umbrella term, in which there are a number of variations in method. For this reason, I have used the term '3 × 3 oral impress method' to describe the procedure for paired oral reading I have developed, as the method I use differs from the strategies for developing reading fluency used in the studies reviewed in the rest of this section.

The earliest study indicating the value of paired reading in a classroom setting was conducted by Heckelman [30, 31], who reported that 24 students involved in using what he called 'the neurological impress method' made exceptional gains in reading ability. The mean gain in reading comprehension was 1.9 grade levels after using the method daily for 15 min (a total of seven and a quarter hours) over a 6-week period. Heckelman hypothesised that this method was 'one of the most direct and fundamental systems of reading' involving a 'combination of reflexive neurological systems'.

Hollingsworth [32] also reported positive results from the use of an impress method in teaching reading and defined impress or neurological impress techniques as the use of unison reading methods in which teacher and student read aloud simultaneously. No attention would be called to the pictures accompanying the story, nor would the teacher attempt to teach sounds of words or word recognition skills.

Morgan and Lyon [33] involved parents in the process of providing tuition for children with reading difficulties and called the technique 'paired reading'. In Morgan and Lyon's study, the paired reading tuition procedure was described as a simple and flexible remedial technique for general application, incorporating simultaneous reading and verbally reinforced individual reading, and utilising textual material suited to the child's interests and chronological age rather than his reading age.

In Morgan and Lyon's study, the parents of four reading-retarded children were trained in how to provide paired reading tuition at home for a quarter of an hour daily. Over 12 to 13 weeks of tuition, the group's reading ages improved markedly. Marked advances in reading comprehension were also noted.

The researcher who has done most to promote and popularise paired reading methods, however, has been Topping [34–37], who has been Professor of Educational Psychology and Director of the Centre for Paired Learning at the University of Dundee. Topping's Centre has focused in particular on the development and evaluation of the effectiveness of methods for non-professionals (such as parents or peer tutors) in providing support in the acquisition of basic skills in reading, spelling, writing, science, maths and information technology. As part of this work, Topping has published widely on paired reading as well as peer tutoring and other forms of cooperative learning.

Topping [38] focused on the value of paired reading in the context of a large-scale dissemination project, and reported on the instructional procedures and outcomes from ten different peer tutoring projects. Pre-and post-test data were reported for all these ten evaluative studies. Four of the studies also provided baseline data and two studies provided comparison group data. Two studies then provided follow-up data for the short and long term respectively.

The evidence reviewed under these different conditions suggested that peer tutored paired reading accelerated children's reading progress in all these settings. All children were reported to have made progress, with peer tutors gaining more than tutees. On the basis of these positive results, Topping [39] also suggested that peer tutoring and paired reading were two potentially powerful techniques which could be combined, and that structured pair work between children of different ability had great potential for effective cooperative learning. Good organisation by the teacher was the key.

2.5. Parent involvement in paired reading

Based on the work of a number of paired reading programmes, Topping [40] suggested that paired reading methods provided an ideal way for teachers to involve parents in the process of developing reading competence. He also wrote a handbook [41] indicating ways in which parents could use paired work with their children to develop basic skills in reading, spelling and writing.

In addition, Topping reported the results of a number of studies indicating the effects of paired reading on reading ability based on reading age gains relative to increase in chronological age [42–44]. Based on analysis of results of 18 studies which focused on the effects of paired reading, Topping concluded that variables such as the duration of the intervention period and the acceleration of learning did not affect the results. In addition, based on analysis of the results of projects which included follow-up data and as there were no reports to the contrary in any of the other studies, Topping concluded that gains in reading ability appeared to be sustained.

Other researchers have also indicated the value of parental involvement in children's reading. Morgan and Lyon [45] described paired reading tuition procedure as a simple and flexible remedial technique which incorporated simultaneous reading and verbally reinforced individual reading. Parents could be trained to use the method. Hewison and Tizard [46] reported that the factor which emerged as most strongly related to reading achievement was whether or not the mother regularly heard the child read. IQ differences did not account for the superior reading performance of the coached children. Maternal language behaviour also had little effect on the association between coaching and reading performance. The important variable was the amount of parental coaching received by the children, which had a highly significant positive association with reading test scores.

In addition, there has been evidence of the value of paired reading programmes involving parents cross-culturally. Vanwagenen, Williams and Mclaughlin [47] reported positive effects of assisted reading on reading rate, accuracy and comprehension on three 12-year-old Spanish-speaking children learning English, while in South Africa, Overett and Donald [48] trained 29 parents from low socio-economic backgrounds to use a paired reading technique. Overett and Donald then compared their results with those of a control group composed of 32 parents. The results indicated a statistically significant increase for the experimental group, with statistically significant improvements in reading accuracy and comprehension, as well as reading attitude and involvement. A broader ecosystemic analysis was also conducted, which suggested that positive relationships between children and significant others in the family were nurtured and other children in the family were benefiting. Interactions between family and school, and school and the local community library were also enhanced.

Positive results have also been reported in other cultural contexts. In Hong Kong, Lam et al. [49] involved parents in paired reading with pre-schoolers, working with 195 preschoolers (mean age = 4.7 years) and their parents. The sample was drawn from families with a wide range of family income, and the preschoolers were then randomly assigned to experimental and control groups.

Training was provided to the parents in the experimental group, who received 12 sessions of school-based training on paired reading over a period of 7 weeks. These parents were then asked to do paired reading with their children at least four times a week in each of these 7 weeks.

At the end of the 7-week intervention, Lam et al. reported that the children in the experimental group had better performance in word recognition and reading fluency than their counterparts in the control group. The children who had been exposed to paired reading were also reported as more competent and motivated in reading by their parents.

In addition, parental changes in relationships and self-efficacy were found to mediate the impact of the intervention on some of the child's outcomes. Lam et al. reported that the parents in the experimental group had higher self-efficacy in helping their children to be better readers and learners, and that these parents also had better relationships with their children. However, family income did not moderate the effectiveness of the programme, with families with high and low income deriving similar benefits from the programme.

2.6. Are parents and peer tutors effective in assisting their children to learn to read?

Overall, the literature reviewed in this section would suggest that both practice and modelling of the reading process by a competent reader are important in paired reading. Repetition is also a crucial factor, especially in working with children with reading or reading fluency difficulties. Parents as well as peer tutors can be used to provide support to struggling readers for the reason that it is the contact, support and modelling of the reading process which are important factors as opposed to variations in implementation of paired reading procedure. Organisation and clear direction are also important factors in implementing a successful paired reading programme.

In their review of the literature on paired reading, Cadieux and Boudreault [50] concluded that paired reading is an effective means of improving reading performance and that nothing indicates that reading gains made through paired reading are not sustained over time. Those studies which have examined processes demonstrate variable levels of compliance with the paired reading technique. However, this factor does not appear to be closely linked with reading gains.

There is also a wider literature supporting parental involvement in assisting their children to read. Hannon, Jackson and Weinberger [51] reported considerable similarities between the parents' and teachers' strategies in terms of the relative frequencies with which they made different kinds of responses while hearing their children read. The most frequent responses for each group were providing words or giving directions about reading, with a greater proportion of parents' responses being made after reading mistakes or miscues, while teachers were likely to make responses both after reading mistakes or miscues, as well as at other times.

Hannon, Jackson and Weinberger reported that both parents and teachers used phonic techniques in responding to reading mistakes or miscues. For parents, this usually meant 'sounding out' words, while for teachers this meant a wider range of responses. Both parents and teachers focused on children's understanding, but for the parents this was generally in response to reading mistakes or miscues, while for teachers this was generally to establish that what the children had read had been comprehended. Hannon, Jackson and Weinberger reported differences in the pattern of positive feedback, praise and criticism between parents and teachers but suggested that these could be due to differences in the social context of reading in the parent and school settings.

Overall, Hannon, Jackson and Weinberger concluded that no justification exists for considering that parents are incompetent in working with their children in developing reading ability. They also concluded that there was scope for reviewing the roles of both parents and teachers in developing reading competence in early childhood education, and this could be facilitated by further research.

Ellis [52] utilised a pre-test/post-test experimental design to investigate the effects of a 12-week parent and child reading intervention on the reading ability and self-perceptions of reading ability in second- and third-grade students. Twenty parents, randomly assigned to the experimental group, participated in the weekly programme sessions. The sessions emphasised

http://dx.doi.org/10.5772/61607

simple techniques that parents could use at home to help their child in reading, such as relaxed reading, paired reading and praise and encouragement.

Ellis reported significantly greater improvements in reading as measured by the number of errors made on graded passages for the experimental group. No significantly greater improvements were made by the experimental group in terms of the number of errors made on graded word lists or graded comprehension questions, or in self-perceptions of reading ability. Overall, the findings supported the notion of parental involvement in reading to improve reading ability.

2.7. Type and difficulty level of materials used in paired reading

The literature is not as clear on the type of reading materials to use in paired reading programmes, and also reflects different opinions on difficulty level of materials in paired reading. Carol Chomsky [53] reported that struggling readers decoded slowly and with difficulty and that, despite their hard-won decoding skills, they were also passive to reading. Chomsky recommended that what was needed was material which would engage attention and also make large amounts of textual material available.

Other researchers have used taped books in paired reading (e.g. [54]), or instructional level materials (e.g. [55]). Based on Wasik's review of volunteer tutoring programmes in reading [56], Cadieux and Boudreault gave a standard material package of instructional level material to all participants in their study of paired reading, which was based on available materials reflecting the type and progression of instruction in reading and word attack skills received in school. The package included flash cards containing phonograms (letters, consonant–vowel syllables and consonant–vowel–consonant syllables) which were used for letter reading and syllable recognition activities, as well as first-grade books containing illustrations which were used to practice reading using text. The children received two or three books at each tutoring session, chosen to suit the level of the reading abilities of the child and parent.

In contrast, Deegan [57] has suggested that the student and teacher should select a text that is near frustration level reading and around 200 words in length. Deegan has also suggested that textual characteristics influence the effectiveness of paired reading and that rhythmic and repetitive texts can increase student participation.

Given difference of opinion relating to difficulty level, Morgan, Wilcox and Eldredge's [58] study is of particular interest. These researchers investigated the effect of difficulty levels on second-grade delayed readers using dyad reading, with the aim of establishing how far above a poor reader's instructional level dyad reading should be conducted. The aim was to establish which level of difficulty was associated with the greatest improvement in reading level, word recognition, comprehension and rate. In their study, 51 poor readers were randomly assigned to three experimental groups: (a) dyad reading using materials at their instructional reading level, (b) dyad reading using materials which were two grades above their reading level and (c) dyad reading using materials which were four grades above their reading level. The research was conducted over 95 sessions, with all groups involved in paired reading for 15 min daily during their classroom reading time.

At the end of the school year, Morgan, Wilcox and Eldredge compared reading gain scores of the three groups. They also compared the post-test scores for word recognition, comprehension and reading rate for each group. No significant differences were found between classrooms. The results indicated that all three groups had made gains in reading skills regardless of the difficulty level of the materials used. The second and third groups which read material significantly above their reading level made greater gains than those reading at their instructional level.

Morgan, Wilcox and Eldredge reported that those students who were assisted in reading material two years above their level made the greatest gains. From informal observations, it appeared that poor readers in the third group (i.e. poor readers reading difficult material) seemed to be less motivated to read books four years above their reading level. Morgan, Wilcox and Eldredge commented that these books had significantly less pictures and more words and the children did not seem ready to make the transition from picture books to chapter books. At this level of difficulty, some students appeared to be turned off and paid less attention.

Overall, while all the children improved with dyad reading regardless of the difficulty levels of materials, the results suggested that the difficulty level of materials used for dyad reading may make a difference in student progress. The researchers did not indicate the exact point at which frustration defeated the purpose of paired reading, but suggested that additional research was needed to establish this. Nevertheless, Morgan, Wilcox and Eldredge concluded that children did not have to be taught with instruction-level materials. Poor readers appeared to improve significantly more when they read with a partner at higher levels that exposed them to more unknown words and complex language structures. The results also indicated that to progress more rapidly, students need to be exposed to more difficult material.

Stahl and Heubach [59] reported the results of a 2-year project in which they re-organised the basal reading instruction provided in 14 classes so as to stress fluent reading and automatic word recognition. The reorganised reading programme consisted of three parts: a basal reading lesson which included repeated reading and partner reading, a choice reading period during the day and a home reading programme. The reorganised reading programme was then implemented over a period of 2 years.

Stahl and Heubach reported that the children in all 14 classes made significantly greater than expected growth in reading achievement. All but two children who entered second grade were reading at grade level or higher by the end of the year, while growth in fluency and accuracy appeared to be consistent, reflecting over the whole year. Students' and teachers' attitudes towards the programme were also positive.

In evaluating the contribution of the different components in their programme, Stahl and Heubach reported that self-selected reading partners appeared to work best. Children chose partners primarily out of friendship, and tended to choose books that were at or slightly below their instructional level. However, children in the study also benefited from more difficult materials, provided that scaffolding and support were provided.

http://dx.doi.org/10.5772/61607

2.8. Implications

The literature on paired reading reviewed in this section reflects some differences in preferred methodology, as well as some difference between recommendations concerning the type of materials felt to be most appropriate for use in the process. Overall, however, there would appear to be consensus concerning the value of paired reading, with all of the studies indicating the potential of including parents as well as peer tutors as partners in the process of teaching children to read fluently.

In many of the studies reviewed in this section, paired reading showed positive results on reading fluency over a relatively short period of time. In addition to effects at the reading fluency level, transfer effects of paired reading into reading comprehension were also noted. This would suggest benefits from paired reading methods not only at the level of automaticity (i.e. on speed and accuracy of reading) but also on the higher-level cognitive processes involved in comprehension.

There are also areas of lack of clarity in the literature. Difficulty level of materials would be an important variable to consider in developing paired reading programmes. Certain authorities suggest the value of fun reading materials, others the value of instructional level reading materials and others the value of reading material chosen to be at or near frustration level. There is thus a lack of consensus in this area.

What is clear from the literature, however, is that quality of scaffolding and support in paired reading is important, especially where difficult materials are chosen for use in paired reading programmes. How reading errors are corrected would appear to be less important, as the literature suggests that a wide variety of strategies have been used for doing so, particularly by teachers. It would, however, be important that the procedures used in paired reading are clear enough to be consistently used by parents, tutors and teachers, and that recommended procedures for correcting the errors made by children are also defined.

Overall, it would also be important to stress that while paired reading methods have potential value for developing reading fluency, other methods have also produced positive results. A study by Homan, Klesius and Hite [60], for example, compared repeated reading strategies with non-repetitive strategies on students' fluency and comprehension. In their study, they focused on the transfer effects of the previously mentioned procedures on both comprehension and fluency with sixth-grade students. Homan, Klesius and Hite's results indicated equivalent benefits for repetitive and non-repetitive methods, with significant comprehension improvement over a 7-week period.

Similarly, working in a developing country context, Shah-Wundenberg, Wyse and Chaplain [61] investigated parental support for children's reading of English in an inner-city school in India. The children in the study had oral proficiency in the regional language but were beginning to acquire conventional forms of literacy in English. A quasi-experimental design involving a sample of 241 children was used to evaluate the effectiveness of two approaches to parents supporting reading: paired reading and hearing reading. Interviews and observations with a smaller sub-sample of parents and children were also used to explore the implications of the data more deeply.

In Shah-Wundenberg, Wyse and Chaplain's study, paired reading and hearing reading were found to be equally effective in developing children's beginning English reading skills, reading accuracy and comprehension, relative to controls. The data also indicated that parents had engaged in a variety of mediation behaviours to enhance their children's English reading development. In addition, parents reported that participating in their children's reading in both conditions had been both enriching and empowering, suggesting that parental involvement can benefit children's English reading development.

The development of the reading fluency programme described in the rest of this chapter should thus be viewed as one of a number of potential approaches to enhancing the development of reading ability. Its potential advantages to parents, therapists, teachers and schools lie in the fact that it is based on a theory of structured phonics which has been developed with children who have had reading and spelling difficulties, that the material is delivered via the internet and email, and that the programme can be used at distance. 'The Tales of Jud the Rat' thus provides a form of e-learning which has the potential to enable paired reading methods to be used in a variety of contexts to develop fluent reading. There would also be potential for combining this programme with other instructional approaches [62].

3. Literature relevant to the Phonological Side of 'The Tales of Jud the Rat' reading fluency programme

3.1. Phonological and language correlates of reading ability

A wide variety of different studies have indicated an association between phonological and language development and reading ability. Based on meta-analysis of 61 samples of data, Scarborough [63, 64] reported that the highest average correlations and effect sizes were between measures requiring the processing of print (e.g. letter-sound knowledge) and reading ability, followed by measures of oral language proficiency (e.g. phonological awareness). There were a number of average predictive correlations above 0.50 and still more above 0.40, but of the oral language predictors, only phonological awareness was found to have a causal relationship with learning to read [65, 66].

Overall, the evidence from predictive research within the phonologically based paradigm was both convergent and compelling [67, 68, 69]. In addition, a number of neurolinguistic studies (e.g. [70, 71, 72]) indicated that dyslexic readers process written stimuli atypically, suggesting abnormal functioning of the left hemisphere reading system.

These neurolinguistic studies were of particular interest in suggesting particular areas of the brain associated with reading difficulties. Schulte-Körne and her colleagues [73] used mismatch negativity (MMN) to investigate the relationship between dyslexia and central auditory processing in 19 children with spelling disability and 15 controls at grades 5 and 6 level. While there were no group differences for tone stimuli, a significantly attenuated MMN was found in the dyslexic group for the speech stimuli, suggesting that dyslexics have a specific speech

http://dx.doi.org/10.5772/61607

processing deficit at the sensory level which could be used to identify children at risk at an early age.

Shaywitz et al. [74] reported that learning to read requires phonological awareness, which can be defined as an awareness that spoken words can be decomposed into the phonologic constituents that the alphabetic characters represent. Phonological awareness is characteristically lacking in dyslexic readers, for the reason that dyslexic readers have difficulty in mapping alphabetic characters onto the phonologic constituents of the spoken word.

Shaywitz and her colleagues used functional magnetic resonance imaging (MRI) to compare brain activation patterns in dyslexic and non-impaired subjects as they performed tasks that made progressively greater demands on phonologic analysis. Brain activation patterns were found to differ significantly between the groups with dyslexic readers showing relative underactivation in posterior regions (Wernicke's area, the angular gyrus and striate cortex) and relative overactivation in an anterior region (inferior frontal gyrus). Shaywitz et al. thus concluded that the impairment in dyslexia is phonologic in nature and that brain activation patterns may provide a neural signature for this impairment.

Similar conclusions were reached by Brunswick et al. [75], who reported that dyslexic readers process written stimuli atypically, based on abnormal functioning of the left hemisphere reading system, and that the deficits are localised in the neural system underlying lexical retrieval. Klingberg et al. [76] used MRI analysis to examine the structure of white matter in dyslexic and normal adult readers and found differences between normal readers and individuals with poor reading ability. These differences occurred bilaterally in the temporo-parietal white matter underlying perisylvian cortical areas. An overlapping region in the left temporo-parietal white matter also yielded significant correlation between white matter microstructure and reading ability across all 17 subjects. This correlation was apparent both in the poor reading group and in the control group, indicating a structural neural correlate of reading skill in both normal and poor readers and also indicating that white matter underlying left temporo-parietal cortex plays a critical role in reading ability.

Burton [77] reported that there were functional sub-regions within the inferior frontal gyrus that correspond to specific components of phonological processing (e.g. orthographic to phonological conversion in reading, and segmentation in speech). Temple et al. [78] suggested that difficulties in reading are associated with both phonological and orthographic processing deficits, and that dyslexia may be characterised in childhood by disruptions in the neural bases of both phonological and orthographic processes important for reading.

In addition, the neurolinguistic literature indicated that a number of areas of the cortex were involved in fluent reading, as well as in processing different types of reading material. Bentin et al. [79] conducted research based on the analysis of event-related potentials (ERPs) elicited by visually presented lists of words. Based on this evidence, Bentin et al. concluded that different levels of processing are involved for visual, phonological/phonetic, phonological/lexical and semantic material in both hemispheres of the brain, and that a cascade-type process involving different but interconnected neural modules may be involved in the processing of print material, each responsible for a different level of processing of word-related information.

Similar conclusions were reached by Brown et al. [80] on the basis of examination of the MR images of 16 men with dyslexia and 14 control subjects, and comparison of these using a voxel-based analysis. Brown et al. reported evidence of decreases in gray matter in dyslexic subjects, not only in the left temporal lobe and bilaterally in the temporo–parieto–occipital juncture but also in the frontal lobe, caudate, thalamus and cerebellum. Brown et al. thus concluded that widely distributed morphologic differences affecting several brain regions may contribute to the deficits associated with dyslexia.

The above research thus suggested associations between impaired neurological processing and reading disability in dyslexic children. Equally important, however, were the indications from the neurolinguistic literature that reading difficulties were not immutable and that improvements in reading ability also had physiological correlates. Specifically, the development of reading ability would be accompanied by improvement in connectivity between the variety of cortical and sub-cortical centres involved in the reading process. These studies are reviewed in the following section.

3.2. The development of reading ability has correlates on a neurological level

A number of studies suggest that there are associations between the development of reading ability and improvement in neurological processing of print material. Patterns of central processing might initially not be well developed in dyslexic children, but would be responsive to instruction.

Simos et al. [81] studied magnetic source imaging scans during a pseudoword reading task with a sample of eight children aged from 7- to 17-years-old, both before and after 80 hours of intensive remedial instruction. All children were initially diagnosed with dyslexia, having severe difficulties in both word recognition and phonological processing. After remedial training, the dyslexia-specific brain activation profiles became normal, suggesting that change in central processing of print had occurred following intensive remedial training.

Shaywitz et al. [82] reported that provision of a phonologically mediated reading intervention over a period of a year improved both reading fluency and the development of the fast-paced occipito-temporal systems serving skilled reading. After the year-long intervention, children taught with the experimental intervention had made significant gains in reading fluency and demonstrated increased activation in left hemisphere regions, including the inferior frontal gyrus and the middle temporal gyrus, These improvements appeared to be stable; as 1 year after the experimental intervention had ended, these children were activating bilateral inferior frontal gyri and left superior temporal and occipito-temporal regions. This indicated the phonologic reading intervention had facilitated the development of those fast-paced neural systems that underlie skilled reading.

Similar conclusions concerning change in neurological processing in children were reached by Maurer et al. [83], who investigated the development of coarse neural tuning for print by studying children longitudinally before and after learning to read, and compared these patterns to those exhibited by adults who were skilled readers. Maurer et al. reported that coarse neural tuning for print peaked when children learned to read. Coarse N1 tuning, which

http://dx.doi.org/10.5772/61607

had been absent in non-reading kindergarten children, emerged less than 2 years later after the children had mastered basic reading skills in second grade. The coarse N1 tuning had become larger for words than symbol strings in every child. Coarse N1 tuning was also stronger for faster readers. On this evidence, Maurer et al. concluded that fast brain processes specialise rapidly for print when children learn to read, and play an important functional role in the fluency of early reading.

3.3. Neural connectivity is associated with fluent reading

Shankweiler et al. [84] also concluded that cortical integration of speech and print in sentence processing varies with reader skill. These researchers used functional magnetic resonance imaging (fMRI) to investigate the association between literacy skills in young adults and the distribution of cerebral activity during comprehension of sentences in spoken and printed form. The results from different analyses all pointed to the conclusion that neural integration of sentence processing across speech and print varies positively with the reader's skill. Further, Shankweiler et al. identified the inferior frontal region as the principal site of speech–print integration and a major focus of reading comprehension differences.

Additional studies used advances in fMRI to identify a relationship between white matter structure (as an indicator of myelination) and reading ability (e.g. [85, 86]). This area of the neurolinguistic literature was based on the premise that myelination was not only an index of the maturity of the insulation of individual fibres in the brain but was also an index of efficiency in neurological transmission [87, 88].

Hasan et al. [89] used diffusion tensor imaging to study the structure and distribution of white matter within the corpus callosum areas connecting the two hemispheres of the brain in children with dyslexia and those of typically developing readers of comparable age and gender. Hasan et al. reported that the posterior corpus callosum area was enlarged in children with dyslexia relative to the same area as measured in typically developing children. In addition, there were microstructural differences (e.g. the mean diffusivity of the posterior middle sector of the corpus callosum), which correlated significantly with measures of word reading and reading comprehension. Reading group differences between dyslexic and typically developing children were also found when using fractional anisotropy, mean diffusivity and radial diffusivity to measure the microstructural characteristics of the posterior corpus callosum.

Vandermosten et al. [90] also used diffusion tensor imaging tractography to examine the integrity of the three-dimensional white matter tracts connecting the left temporo-parietal region and the left inferior frontal gyrus, for which atypical functional activation and lower fractional anisotropy values have been reported in dyslexic readers. Their study revealed structural anomalies in the left arcuate fasciculus in adults with dyslexia. In addition, Vandermosten et al. were able to demonstrate a correlational double dissociation, which suggested that the dual route reading model has neuroanatomical correlates. In the sample studied, the left arcuate fasciculus seemed to sustain the dorsal phonological route underlying grapheme–phoneme decoding in reading, while the left inferior fronto-occipital fasciculus seemed to sustain the ventral orthographic route underlying reading by direct word access.

3.4. Repetition of phoneme-grapheme relationships is likely to build neural connectivity

Later in this chapter, there is reference to the longitudinal work I conducted in the 1990s with a dyslexic child called Q. There were indications from the neurologist's reports that Q's dyslexia was linked to a disorder of neural network connections, as well as a function associated with possible cortical immaturity (Dr Graeme Maxwell, personal communication). The research evidence reviewed in the previous sections was not available at this time, and it was only at the end of the 1990s that neurolingustic evidence began to emerge that many dyslexic children process reading material at a central level in ways different to normally developing readers [91, 92, 93].

Subsequent evidence suggested that the neural connections formed through the reading process involved a number of cortical areas [94], while also indicating a developmental trajectory by which exposure to written language engages areas originally shaped by speech on the path toward successful literacy acquisition [95, 96]. Equally important was the evidence from studies reviewed in the previous section (e.g. [97, 98, 99]), which suggested that connectivity in the brain could be enhanced through involvement in the process of learning to read, and that phonologically and phonemically based instruction could be particularly helpful in this process.

What my own clinical observations and the literature implied was that in Q's development as well as in the development of other dyslexic children, neural connections would not initially be strongly developed. Changes in connectivity as well as in white matter structure would also be likely to accompany phonologically based reading acquisition.

On a programmatic level, this implied that repeated reading of phonically based material would be likely to develop connections between the variety of cortical areas involved in fluent reading. Conversely, where repeated reading of phonically based material leads to observable changes in reading fluency, this would probably also point to increased functionality in the neural connections which underpin central processing of printed material.

In short, there was a two-way association involved. This suggested that in children with reading difficulties, increased time on task in reading tasks involving repetition of phoneme–grapheme relationships would be likely to build greater reading ability, as well as greater neural connectivity. This has informed the development of the 'Jud the Rat' reading materials described later in this chapter.

3.5. Limitations in correlational research

While the research reviewed in this section implies two-way associations between phonological- and language-based factors, reading ability, instruction in reading and brain connectivity, it is important to note that there are a number of limitations in correlational research.

As Scarborough [100] has suggested, two-way associations in the literature on reading may not be linear ones, for the reason that the development of reading is a multi-faceted process. In addition, Scarborough has suggested that there are many inconsistencies within the evidence on the relationship between phonological and language factors and reading disabilities, which may indicate that there is a second causal chain (e.g. a persisting underlying condition which may account for all the two-way associations observed).

Studies by Galaburda [101], Poldrack [102] and Stein [103] have also suggested the high likelihood that some other mechanism (e.g. of magnocellular, auto-immune system or genetic origin) may account for the anatomical differences between the brain structures of dyslexics and normal readers. Underlying attentional or working memory factors (what Ahissar et al. [104, 105], have called an

anchoring-deficit) may also account for the evidence that only 5–10% of children who are fluent readers in the early grades at school stumble later, while between 65% and 75% of children designated as reading disabled early continue to read poorly throughout their school careers (and beyond), despite evidence that these readers have learned to read [106]. Anchoring deficit factors could also account for periods of 'illusory recovery', in which symptoms of reading disability appear to be remediated, but then reappear at later stages in schooling, suggesting that language skills may develop in a non-linear fashion [107].

In short, while the evidence of the associations between phonological and language factors and reading disability would appear to be compelling, other underlying factors besides a core phonological deficit may contribute to reading disability [108, 109, 110]. A number of other theories (e.g. those relating to how print material is processed visually) are thus reviewed in the following section. These theories have provided the rationale behind the use of large print in the 'Jud the Rat' materials, as well as the use of visual attentional cueing in the process of implementing the materials.

4. Literature relevant to the visual and visual-attentional sides of 'The Tales of Jud the Rat' reading fluency programme

4.1. Rapid visual and auditory processing as predictors of reading difficulty

A number of studies have indicated that developmental dyslexics do poorly in tests requiring rapid visual and auditory processing. Witton et al. [111] reported that neuronal mechanisms that were specialised for detecting stimulus timing and change were dysfunctional in many dyslexic individuals. The dissociation observed in the performance of dyslexic individuals on different auditory tasks also suggested a sub-modality division in the auditory system similar to that already described in the visual system.

Both Farmer and Klein [112] and Stein and Walsh [113] reported that dyslexia was associated with difficulties with moving visual stimuli. Hari and Renvall [114] also reported that dyslexic subjects often suffered from impaired processing of rapid stimulus sequences and suggest that sluggish attentional shifting can account for the impaired processing of rapid stimulus sequences in dyslexia. Amitay et al. [115] concluded that disabled readers suffered from both visual and auditory impairments, showing impaired performance in both visual and auditory tasks requiring fine frequency discriminations.

Talcott et al. [116] reported that both visual motion sensitivity and auditory sensitivity to frequency differences were robust predictors of children's literacy skills and their orthographic and phonological skills. Cohen-Mimran and Sapir [117] reported auditory temporal processing deficits in children with reading disabilities, and that children with reading difficulties had difficulty in discriminating between pure tones with short, but not long, interstimulus intervals, whereas controls performed well with both short and long interstimulus intervals.

Rapid auditory processing deficits have also been found to be consistent predictors of later reading achievement [118]. Lervåg and Hulme [119] reported that rapid automatised naming (RAN) measured with non-alphabetic stimuli before reading instruction had begun was a predictor of later growth in reading fluency, and continued to exert an influence on the development of reading fluency over the next 2 years after reading instruction had begun. Equally important were indications that there was no evidence of reciprocal influence of reading fluency on the growth of RAN skill. This would suggest that RAN is a function which taps the integrity of the left-hemisphere object-recognition and naming circuits which form critical components of the child's developing visual word-recognition system.

4.2. The influence of instruction on rapid processing ability

The literature, however, also indicates that rapid processing dysfunctions are responsive to training. Temple et al. [120] reported disruption of the neural response to rapid acoustic stimuli in dyslexia, with normal readers showing left prefrontal activity in response to rapidly changing, relative to slowly changing, non-linguistic acoustic stimuli. Dyslexic readers, in contrast, showed no differential left frontal response. Temple et al. also reported that dyslexic readers who participated in a remediation program showed increased activity in left prefrontal cortex after training.

Temple et al.'s results would suggest that the left prefrontal regions are normally sensitive to rapid relative to slow acoustic stimulation, but are insensitive in the case of dyslexic readers. Equally important are the indications that the left prefrontal cortex would appear to be plastic enough in adulthood to develop such differential sensitivity after intensive training.

Gaab et al. [121] reported that children with dyslexia had a fundamental deficit in processing rapid acoustic stimuli, but that this was responsive to training. While typical-reading children showed activation for rapid compared to slow transitions in left prefrontal cortex, children with developmental dyslexia did not show differential response in these regions to rapid and slow transitions in acoustic stimuli. After 8 weeks of remediation which provided training in rapid auditory processing, phonological processing and language skills, Gaab et al. reported that the children with developmental dyslexia showed significant improvements in both language and reading skills. They also showed activation for rapid relative to slow transitions in the left prefrontal cortex after training. Gaab et al. thus concluded that neural correlates of rapid auditory processing were disrupted in children with developmental dyslexia, but could be ameliorated with training.

These findings suggested that many children with reading difficulties have difficulties with rapid visual processing, difficulties with rapid auditory processing, as well as impairments of perceptual processing of rapidly changing acoustic stimuli. These findings also suggest that reading disabilities are often accompanied by impaired perceptual skills as well as specific perceptual deficits and perceptual difficulties which have neurological correlates. As with other areas of functioning, the relationship between behaviour and underlying neural connectivity would appear to be a two -way association, in which improved perceptual processing leads to improved neural connectivity, and vice versa.

4.3. The magnocellular theory of dyslexia

Overall, the research reviewed in the previous section would suggest that many children with dyslexia or poor reading ability have difficulties in processing rapidly changing signals, both auditorally as well as visually [122]. Visual processing difficulties, as well as auditory processing difficulties, have neurological correlates, suggesting the possibility of a general underlying attentional or processing difficulty affecting the development of reading ability.

The magnocellular theory of dyslexia [123, 124] suggests that underlying difficulties in auditory and visual processing can be traced to difficulties in the magnocellular component of the visual system. As Stein and Walsh comment:

'Developmental dyslexics often complain that small letters appear to blur and move around when they are trying to read. Anatomical, electrophysiological, psychophysical and brain-imaging studies have all contributed to elucidating the functional organization of these and other visual confusions. They emerge not from damage to a single visual relay but from abnormalities of the magnocellular component of the visual system, which is specialized for processing fast temporal information. The m-stream culminates in the posterior parietal cortex, which plays an important role in guiding visual attention. The evidence is consistent with an increasingly sophisticated account of dyslexia that does not single out either phonological, or visual or motor deficits. Rather, temporal processing in all three systems seems to be impaired. Dyslexics may be unable to process fast incoming sensory information adequately in any domain.' [125]

Stein and Walsh's conclusions have been supported by a number of studies. Salmelin et al. [126] used magnetoencephalography to identify impaired word processing in the occipito-temporal areas of dyslexics, while Livingstone et al. [127] reported that dyslexic subjects exhibited diminished visually evoked potentials to rapid, low contrast stimuli, but normal responses to slow or high contrast stimuli. Livingstone et al. suggested that the abnormalities in the dyslexic subjects' responses to evoked potentials were associated with a defect in the magnocellular pathway at the level of visual area 1 or earlier.

Livingstone et al. also compared the lateral geniculate nuclei from five dyslexic brains to five control brains, reporting abnormalities in the magnocellular, but not the parvocellular, layers in the dyslexic brains studied. As previous studies using auditory and somatosensory tests had shown that dyslexics perform poorly on tasks requiring rapid discriminations, Livingstone et al. hypothesised that many cortical systems can be divided into a fast and a slow subdivision; and further that that dyslexia is associated with difficulties in rapid processing within these fast subdivisions.

Similarly, Vidyasagar and Pammer [128] reported that impaired visual search in dyslexia relates to the role of the magnocellular pathway in attention, leading Vidyasagar [129] to suggest that attentional gating in primary visual cortex provides a physiological basis for dyslexia. Sireteanu et al. [130] also investigated the performance of children with developmental dyslexia on a number of visual tasks requiring selective visual attention and found that dyslexic children did not show the overestimation of the left visual field (pseudoneglect) characteristic of normal adult vision. Dyslexic children also showed shorter reaction times and a dramatically increased number of errors on these tasks, suggesting that children with developmental dyslexia have selective deficits in visual attention.

Misra et al. [131], for example, have identified a number of neurological correlates of rapid processing deficits, reporting that the majority of children and adults with reading disabilities also exhibit pronounced difficulties on naming-speed measures such as tests of rapid automatised naming, which required speeded naming of serially presented stimuli. In their study, functional magnetic resonance imaging was used to evaluate the neural substrates that were associated with performance on rapid naming tasks. Activation was found in neural areas associated with eye movement control and attention as well as in a network of cortical structures implicated in reading tasks, including the inferior frontal cortex, temporo-parietal areas and the ventral visual stream. Whereas the inferior frontal areas of the network were similarly activated for both letters and objects, activation in the posterior areas varied by task. These results suggested that rapid naming tasks recruited a network of neural structures which were also involved in more complex reading tasks, and suggested that rapid naming of letters pinpointed key components of this reading network.

4.4. Prevalence of magnocellular deficits: Evidence from multiple case studies

Vidyasagar and Pammer [132] have proposed that dyslexia is a deficit in visuo-spatial attention, not in phonological processing. However, the evidence from multiple case studies of disabled readers suggests that dyslexics may suffer from visual and auditory impairments but only a few suffer from a specific magnocellular deficit.

Amitay et al. [133], for example, reported that only six out of the thirty reading disabled subjects in their study had impaired magnocellular function, and that the performance of the other twenty four reading disabled subjects on magnocellular tasks did not differ from that of controls. Amitay et al. also reported that many of the reading disabled children showed impaired performance in both visual and auditory non-magnocellular tasks which required fine frequency discriminations. Overall, Amitay et al. concluded that some reading disabled subjects have generally impaired perceptual skills, while many reading disabled subjects have more specific perceptual deficits. The 'magnocellular' level of description, however, did not capture the nature of the perceptual difficulties in any of the reading disabled individuals in the sample, as the six subjects with impaired magnocellular function were also consistently impaired on a broad range of other perceptual tasks.

Similarly, Ramus et al. [134] analysed sixteen dyslexic subjects and reported that all sixteen dyslexics suffered from a phonological deficit. Ten of the subjects could be characterised as suffering from an auditory deficit, four from a motor deficit and two from a visual magnocellular deficit. The results thus indicated that a phonological deficit can appear in the absence of any other sensory or motor disorder. A phonological deficit is also sufficient to cause a literacy impairment, as demonstrated by five of the dyslexics. Auditory disorders, when present, aggravated a phonological deficit, contributing to the literacy impairment.

These data thus indicated that auditory deficits could not be characterised simply as rapid auditory processing problems, as would be predicted by the magnocellular theory. Nor were they restricted to speech. Contrary to the cerebellar theory, Ramus et al. also found little support for the notion that motor impairments had a cerebellar origin or reflected an automaticity deficit. Overall, Ramus et al. concluded that the phonological theory of dyslexia could account for all sixteen of the subjects in their sample. There were also additional sensory and motor disorders in certain individuals.

Ziegler et al. [135] reported that children with dyslexia had significant deficits for letter and digit strings, but not for symbol strings. Visual-attentional theories of dyslexia could not explain these findings, as visual attentional theories postulated identical deficits for letters, digits and symbols in dyslexics. Ziegler et al. also reported that dyslexics showed normal W-shaped serial position functions for letter and digit strings. This finding suggested that their deficit could not be attributed to an abnormally small attentional window. In addition, the data indicated that the size of the deficit was identical for letters and digits, suggesting that poor letter perception in dyslexic children was not just a consequence of lack of reading.

What could account for Ziegler et al.'s data was that the process of mapping symbols onto phonological codes was impaired, as this was the case for both letters and digits. In contrast, symbols that did not map onto phonological codes were not impaired. This dissociation suggested that impaired symbol-sound mapping rather than impaired visual-attentional processing was the key to understanding dyslexia.

4.5. Both visual and visual attentional factors need to be taken into account in teaching reading

Despite convergent evidence that dyslexia is a language disability which has its foundations in difficulties in phonological and phonemic processing, both Schulte-Körne and Bruder's [136] review and Stein's more recent [137] review of current literature suggest that rapid processing, attentional and magnocellular factors are important influences on reading ability which should not be overlooked. Research from both Australia [138] and from Italy [139] also indicate that it is important to take account of visual attentional factors in remediating language-based learning difficulties.

In addition, visual features stemming from layout of reading material have been found to influence reading as well as comprehension outcomes [140]. Spinelli et al. [141] have suggested that dyslexic readers are affected by crowding of multiple characters and large numbers of words onto printed pages. Visual features of text such as print size [142], visual span [143], spacing of letters [144], spacing between letters [145, 146], as well as font size and spacing between words relative to print size and visual acuity limits [147] are also important to consider when publishing materials for poor readers.

The above research has implications for the development of reading materials for dyslexic children. As I had found in working with Q, research post 2000 indicated that dyslexic children would be likely to respond best to reading material which took account of factors such as length of words [148, 149], amount of text in paragraphs [150] and amount of text on pages [151].

How I have taken account of phonological and phonemic factors, as well as crowding, visual and visual-attentional factors, in writing the 'Tales of Jud the Rat' series as well as in developing the procedures used in the implementation of the materials is covered in the rest of this chapter.

5. The first stage of development of the 'Tales of Jud the Rat' programme: Extended case study

5.1. The need for graded reading materials of gradually increasing difficulty

Janet Lerner [152, 153, 154] has suggested that the methods used for children with learning difficulties can be used with all children. The reason for this is that all children respond to good teaching. Shaywitz et al. [155] also emphasise continuities across normal and dyslexic readers, interpreting dyslexia as occurring at the lower end of a normal distribution of reading abilities. While a diagnosis of dyslexia often has a high degree of stability over time, there are also a large number of children who are diagnosed as dyslexic in early grades who no longer meet dyslexic criteria in later grades at school. Thus the distinction between developmental dyslexics and other poor readers may be of limited usefulness.

Similarly, Elliott and Grigorenko [156] argue that the evidence suggests that both dyslexics and other poor readers benefit from structured phonological treatment. This implies that if a method is workable for a child who has severe reading difficulties, it is also likely to work for a child who has less severe learning difficulties, or for a child who has no difficulties at all.

This has been the principle guiding the development of the materials used in the reading fluency programme. These have been developed in two stages, working with children involved my practice in Johannesburg.

The first stage in the development of the reading fluency programme was based on the need for graded reading materials of gradually increasing difficulty for a child who was severely dyslexic (Child Q). These needed to be implemented at a distance of 6,000 miles from my rooms.

5.2. Implementation side-by-side with a method for teaching structured phonics which was both visual and verbal

Child Q worked with me over a number of years. She and her parents were South African but lived in Europe. The referral came internationally, and I was then consulted by the child's mother, who indicated that her child (called Q for the purpose of case study) had severe learning problems. These were intractable.

Q had been assessed as having developmental learning problems in Britain from age 5. This had been followed by a number of language and remedial interventions, which had been

http://dx.doi.org/10.5772/61607

effective in developing skills, but not effective in increasing reading ability. When Q first came to see me at the age of 8, she did not know all her letters. It was also evident that she had both language and reading difficulties. Despite major phonological and expressive language difficulties, Q was of high intelligence, and had well-developed visual imagery and visualisation abilities.

As available instruction was not working effectively, Q's mother spent 2 h in Q's school daily, working individually with her child on a programme sent to her first by fax, and then by email. The initial programme I provided focused on phonically based instruction using synthetic phonics material. In addition, as the five vowel system previously used with Q had not been effective and as Q's strengths lay in visualisation, I utilised a system for teaching structured phonics to develop both word attack and spelling ability. This was both visual and verbal, based on a seven vowel system and colour coding.

Initially, developmental reading materials were provided by the teachers at Q's primary school, while the material provided by myself was designed to support the word analysis, spelling and sequential writing sides of Q's instructional programme. I also sent Q's mother material to teach number concept and arithmetic, with which Q had major difficulties.

Over the first year Q's progress was steady, but as her programme entered its second year, it became clear that there was insufficient graded reading material available in the school to support the gradual increase in the level of reading instruction which Q needed. Additional reading schemes were bought by the school; but as the second year progressed, we simply ran out of reading books which were available at the school and at her level. There was no alternative other than to develop reading material specifically designed to support the gradual increase in the level of phonic skills Q needed, as well as the amount of reinforcement of phonic skills required in her reading programme.

5.3. The Doctor Skunk stories

As Q was a South African child living abroad, the first two reading books I wrote were stories written about South African wild animals. However, I struck an immediate problem on a phonic level. South African wild animals have names like 'giraffe', 'elephant', 'eland', 'gemsbok', 'lion', 'leopard' and 'cheetah'. How would I be able to reconcile these indigenous names with Q's phonological and phonic needs?

To determine Q's phonic needs, I was using both standardised tests as well as a self-developed clinical test called the phonic inventories [157, 158, 159, 160], which classroom-based research [161, 162, 163, 164, 165, 166, 167, 168, 169] had identified as both valid and reliable, as well as predictive of learning difficulties at both junior and high school levels [170, 171, 172, 173]. Used clinically, the information yielded by the instrument was diagnostic and indicated that Q needed phonic materials targetting word endings such as 'ss', 'ff', 'll', 'ck', 'ng', 'tch' and 'dge', as well as vowel digraphs such as 'ai', 'ee', 'ea', 'oa', 'ay' and 'ou'.

In the first two reading books I wrote, it was impossible to reconcile the names of South African animals with these phonic needs. The word 'lion', for example, was spelled in a completely opposite way to the diphthong 'oi', which was one of the vowel digraphs which Q had not yet established. 'Cheetah' included the 'ee' vowel digraph, and also included a schwa sound made by an 'a' followed by a silent 'h' at the end of the word. 'Buck' had a short vowel and a 'ck' ending. Tiger also met long vowel phonic criteria, but unfortunately tigers are not found on the South African veld.

I thus abandoned the aim of indigenising Q's reading material. As Q lived near a park, I focused instead on creating a more universal reading world of a small village set next to a park. In the village lived a number of phonically regular short vowel animals such as 'rat', 'cat', 'dog' and 'skunk'. The books were set in large print to increase the visual cues from the letters and words, and the paragraphs were kept short to enable Q to focus on the words she was reading by avoiding clutter. As the stories progressed, the short vowel animals interacted with long vowel animals such as 'mole', 'bird' and 'owl' and more complex polysyllabic but phonically regular animals such as 'rabbit', 'weasel', 'hamster', 'hedgehog' and 'badger'.

The main characters in the stories became the phonically regular short vowel 'Jud the Rat' and 'Jill the Dog', who first interacted with other short vowel characters such as 'Tom the Cat' and 'Doctor Skunk', and later with long vowel characters such as 'Max the Mole' and 'Mrs Weasel', and then with polysyllabic characters such as 'Len Hamster', 'Mr and Mrs Rabbit' and 'Bill the Hedgehog'. As the stories progressed, the characters met others who lived at a distance from the village such as 'Mrs Horse', 'Captain Ferret' and 'Colonel Tortoise'.

At basic levels in the stories there was a 'shop' and each character had a 'house' in the village. There was also a 'farm' close by where there were 'cows' which provided 'milk' and 'hens' which provided 'eggs', while further away from the village and at higher levels in the stories there were more phonically complex 'mountains', 'a valley', 'a country club' and even 'Benjamin Horse's Stud Farm'.

At basic levels in the stories, the animals entertained themselves by having 'fun' and at intermediate levels by having 'tea and cake' and 'a picnic', while at higher levels the animals met with 'brothers' and 'sisters' and 'in-laws' and 'cousins'. One of the 'uncles' drove a 'shiny red motorbike with a bright green sidecar', while other animals rode 'from up the valley' on the 'bus from town' driven by 'Sid the Badger'.

At higher levels in the stories there was 'a party' in 'Farmer Jim's barn' with music provided by 'Harry Hopper and the Doodlebugs', who accompanied 'Cheryl Crow' and 'The Mice Girls'. Harry Hopper's band played polysyllabic 'guitars' and 'saxophones' and 'trumpets' through 'amplifiers'. More traditional music was also provided at the party on phonically counter-intuitive 'violins' by 'The Veteran Insects String Band', until Doctor Skunk came along and performed as the phonically intuitive 'Screaming Lord Skunk' and then wrecked the proceedings.

It will be gathered from the above that the Doctor Skunk stories were based on structured phonic principles which gradually increased in level, and were designed to teach as well as to entertain. For in the absence of other appropriately graded reading materials, it was important to keep Q interested, with material which appealed to her well-developed visual imagery and her delightful sense of humour, while at the same time addressing the basic progression in phonic complexity which Q needed to learn to read fluently.

http://dx.doi.org/10.5772/61607

5.4. What were the effects of this type of reading instruction?

In her longitudinal case study of the effects of instruction on Q's phonic, reading and spelling development, Sfetsios (2002) [174] described the development of the reading materials used in Q's programme as follows:

'Simultaneously with the introduction of rule-based instruction through the spelling, dictation and written side of the programme, an attempt was made to sequence the skills introduced in the reading side of the programme, in order for the written and reading sides of the programme to reinforce one another.

It was evident that Q needed a gradual progression when reading, and found changes in language register confusing (Professor Potter, personal communication, 2002). What had been established through the written side of the programme was that constant reinforcement was necessary before Q was able to use a particular phonic rule in reading, or orthographic rule as this applied in writing and spelling. Difficulties were pronounced where this involved a combination of vowels or chunking of letters. The Phonic Inventories (see Appendix A) indicated that she had particular difficulty with the consonant clusters commonly used in word endings, and the decision was made to target these and focus on the rules involving combinations of consonants used at the ends of words after short vowels. This was the focus before any attempt was made to target the long vowel sounds represented in vowel digraphs and diphthongs.

The reading materials available in Q's school essentially moved too quickly to provide the basis for learning and overlearning necessary to reinforce the alphabetic rules introduced in the written side of the programme, and the type of consistent use of a gradually expanding core vocabulary necessary for Q to progress (Professor Potter, personal communication, 2002). The indication on the reading side was thus for a reading programme which reinforced the skills introduced in the written side of the programme, and which did not increase in complexity too quickly. Here we found that conventional reading schemes were not sufficient, either singly or in combination as a part of a broader reading scheme. The font size used in the books was also problematic, in that Q responded better to larger as opposed to smaller font sizes.

Against this background, the decision was taken to develop one story and a core set of characters and extend them in the beginning, creating a context and world of meaning with which Q could become familiar, and then extending these parameters to new and wider contexts. The story would need to work from the familiar, and introduce a graded and gradually extending vocabulary. Q was very interested in animals. She also lived in an area adjacent to parkland in Holland. These two aspects were therefore selected as contextual features of the story created. The Doctor Skunk stories (see Appendix R, pp.1xxxiv–1xxxvii) revolved around a group of animals who lived in a parkland, each animal representing human qualities to which Q could relate and enjoy. The story had a strong comical angle and ensured that Q maintained interest in the antics of the growing number of characters over the 6-year remedial period.

In practice, the Doctor Skunk stories provided the vehicle both for the development of reading as well as a springboard for the development of Q's imagery and imagination, and for her own descriptive and creative writing (see Appendix R, pp. xciii–xcv). It should be borne in mind that owing to her developmental difficulties, Q had lost out on many situations involving social interaction through play and involvement with other children as a contributing and functional partner in learning activities at school. The key to Q's learning to read was the fact that she was able to discover humour and enjoyment in the reading act, and to maintain her interest in reading while experiencing success in working with text, both in reading and writing (Professor Potter, personal communication, 2002).

Four years later at the time Q went to high school, she was still interested in the characters in the Doctor Skunk stories and their antics, and had covered 23 books involving several thousands of pages of text in large print. The gradually increasing difficulty of the orthography used in the text had taken her from the level of short vowels and three letter words to the ability to decode the work she was required to handle at school (see Appendix R, p.1xxxvii). By the time it was possible to reduce the font size on the printed page after 4 years of this type of work, she had also developed the skills required to read more widely, and for enjoyment.' [175]

The gains in reading, spelling and dictation made by Q over a four and a half year period are presented in Table 1 below

	July 1997 M's age: 10 years 2 months	**February 1998** M's age: 10 years 9 months	**June 1998** M's age: 11years 1 month	**June 2000** M's age: 12 years 11 months	**April 2001** M's age: 13 years 11 months	**August 2001** M's age: 14 years 3 months	**December 2001** M's age: 14 years 7 months
	Age	**Age**	**Age**	**Age**	**Age**	**Age**	**Age**
Oral Reading							
Rate	7.9	7.7	7.9	8.9	7.10	8.2	8.0
Comprehension	7.11	8.7	9.5	9.8	9.1	9.11	9.11
Silent Reading							
Rate	7.0	7.5	7.4	8.0	7.3	7.9	8.0
Comprehension	8.6	9.7	9.12	10.3	9.2	10.2	9.5
Listening	9.2	9.2	9.2	10.2	9.2	10.2	9.2
Flash Words	7.10	8.0	8.2	9.6	9.2	9.7	9.11
Word Analysis	8.0	8.3	8.2	9.11	9.5	9.11	9.11
Spelling (Durrell)	7.3	8.0	8.0	9.6	8.2	8.8	8.2
Handwriting	7.4	8.3	8.3	8.9	9.2	9.0	8.5
Spelling							
Schonell Form A	7.2	7.6	8.4	8.7	8.5	9.4	8.6
Schonell Graded Dictation							
Test A	-	-	7.6	8.1	-	-	-

Test B			*No score	8.0	8.0	9.6	8.0
Test C	-	-	-	7.6	8.5	10.0	7.0
Test D	-	-	-	-	-	-	6.1
Daniels and Diack							
Graded Reading Test	7.2	-	-	-	-	-	-
Standard Spelling Test	7.3	-	-	-	-	-	-
Visual Memory	7.9	7.0	8.5	8.8	8.8	8.8	8.8
Hearing Sounds in Words	8.6	7.11	9.0	-	-	-	-
Auditory Phonic Spelling	-	-	8.8	10.8	10.2	10.2	7.3

*There is no score as it was found that Q was not ready for this level of dictation

Table 1. Q's Progress as Measured by Durrell Analysis of Reading Difficulty Age Scores

From Table 1, it will be clear that Q made gains, despite weaknesses in the phonological, phonemic and language areas, and difficulties with rate of reading. Her strengths lay in visual imagery and visualisation, which were utilised in her reading programme, as well as in the methods used to teach her spelling and sequentialisation. However, despite a programme which focused on phonological and phonemic development combined with tailor-made reading, writing and spelling programmes, Q did not develop to be a fluent reader. Both rate of reading and rate of work continued to be particular problems. She was nevertheless able to cope mainstream schooling up to the end of junior high school, requiring scaffolding and support to do so. She then completed her final years of schooling in a remedial school.

Summarising Q's progress, Sfetsios commented,

'Gains made with Q in reading, spelling and dictation have been hard won. Success has been a result of much dedication and support of her mother and father, remedial therapists and tutors, however, above all, it is a credit to Q's motivation and persistence. Her continuing willingness to undertake a programme that has been built step-by-step and skill-by-skill has resulted in her moving from only being able to recognise 16 letters of the alphabet to successfully attending a mainstream British High School.' [176]

6. The second stage of development of 'The Tales of Jud the Rat' reading fluency programme

6.1. A set of graded phonic ebook materials for paired reading

It is very infrequently that I encounter children in my practice who have as intractable reading and spelling difficulties as those of Q. Early in 2013, however, I encountered another child (A) who was not making progress in reading, despite therapy directed at phonological and phonemic development, combined with a programme of reading, writing and spelling support. It was evident that there were major difficulties in A's reading fluency, despite progress in the development of phonological and phonic skills, as well as word analysis and sentence reading abilities.

As with Q, the report from A's neurologist (Dr Graeme Maxwell, personal communication) [177] indicated that there were attentional difficulties combined with attentional lapses, stemming from cortical immaturity and a slow myelinisation process. On a functional level, it was evident that A was not making progress in reading despite the fact that his school was sending out a variety of graded reading books which were then read orally at home and in his remedial support sessions in the afternoons.

At this stage (mid 2013), I took the decision to relook at the Doctor Skunk stories, and to develop additional material in a format in which they could be used to support A's need to become a more fluent reader. This required writing more graded material based on phonic associations which were introduced and then repeated. This set of ebooks ('The Tales of Jud the Rat') would then be sent to A's parents by email and implemented via a form of paired reading aimed at using repeated reading to develop automaticity and reading fluency.

I first tried out the material with A in my sessions with him. Once it was evident after 6 months of instruction that this type of programme was producing effects, the material was then made available for wider use; at the beginning of 2014, I suggested to the parents of seven other children in the practice who were not fluent readers that they should also use the programme. In this way, an initial cohort of children started working with the reading fluency materials.

This consisted of three children (A, B and C) of junior primary school level, three (D, E and F) were at upper primary school level and two children (G and H) who were at junior high school level. Each of these children had been diagnosed as being of average to upper intelligence with scatter in the IQ profile, and as having learning and reading difficulties. Each of these children was also being seen by the same neurologist, who had diagnosed attentional deficits and cortical immaturity linked to slow rate of myelination.

The ebook-based reading fluency programme followed by this initial cohort of children is described in the next section. This will be followed by discussion of the neurolinguistic research which has provided the theoretical basis of the programme materials and the oral impress method and visual tracking methods used in programme implementation. The assessment and evaluation process will then be described, followed by presentation of results. Implications will then be discussed at the end of the chapter.

6.2. An ebook series of gradually increasing level of difficulty

It was only near the end of the first stage in the development of the 'Doctor Skunk' stories that the books I had written began to be delivered as attachments to emails. During the second stage of development of the programme, email delivery was used with all children. One reason for this was that a large amount of additional graded material had been written over the second half of 2013, based on recent (post 2000) neurolinguistic literature. In addition as, there were now eight children of different ages and reading levels in the 2014 cohort, ebook delivery of

http://dx.doi.org/10.5772/61607

the second series materials ('The Tales of Jud the Rat') became an integral feature of the reading fluency programme.

An additional reason for ebook delivery is that many children's parents travel considerable distance to the rooms in Johannesburg where I run my practice. One family travels 500 kilometers weekly. A number of other parents in the practice live over a hundred kilometers away from my rooms, travelling long distances to see me. The reason that they do so is that there is a high level of demand for instruction as well as materials for children with reading difficulties, particularly from areas outside Johannesburg. This is probably a feature linked with deteriorating schools in the public sector in South Africa, as well as a dearth of appropriate scaffolding and support in the schools close to where many parents live.

All parents in my practice, however, have email, and for this reason, 'The Tales of Jud the Rat' reading fluency programme has been developed in a form in which it can be delivered by email and then downloaded and used by parents at home. As the reading fluency materials have been designed to complement the sessional work I do, parents are provided with tutorial support by email, as well as questions and answers by cellphone. As new books in the series are also sent out by me, I am able to monitor the rate at which the children are covering the material, and through this establish the amount of paired reading done using the programme at home.

My own sessions thus work side-by-side with the implementation of the reading fluency programme by parents. In this way, I can focus in my sessions on developing basic skills in phonological and phonic development, as well as the sequentialisation and working memory skills which underpin writing, spelling and learning at school. I am also able to do work to develop the abilities to use these basic skills in reading comprehension and school-related work.

The aim has been to provide a large body reading fluency materials which are appropriately graded, which are readily available and inexpensive, and which can be used daily at home. As the materials have been written to meet the needs of parents of children in my practice who have rate of work problems linked to reading fluency difficulties, through the materials parents have thus become partners in the learning process.

6.3. Use of phonic strategies in writing the materials

My experience in working with Q had informed the decision that the 'Doctor Skunk' stories should be written on phonemically based principles. Developments in the neurolinguistic literature post 2000 then ensured that this principle should be carried forward into "The Tales of Jud the Rat" series. Specifically, I ensured that all words used in the ebooks would be able to be decoded using phonically based strategies. In addition, words used would then be repeated.

This would be done so that 'The Tales of Jud the Rat' materials would be suitable to be used by teachers and therapists working in a phonologically based paradigm. They would also be suitable for use by parents to develop automaticity in sound–letter associations through repeated reading. In addition, being phonically based, the materials could also be used for the purposes of teaching phonic analysis and spelling rules.

In short, my experience in working with Q suggested that repetition of phonic associations was necessary in developing fluent reading, and that there were side-by-side improvements in connectivity on a neural level (Dr Graeme Maxwell, Q's neurologist, personal communication) [178]. As this reciprocal link was also indicated in the neurolinguistic literature post 2000, there was clear support for the use of phonic strategies in writing 'The Tales of Jud the Rat' materials.

6.4. Use of repetition of phonic associations to build decoding ability

As with the 'Doctor Skunk' stories used with Q, the 'Tales of Jud the Rat' materials were designed to enable repetitions which were phonically based, and exposure to phonic rules which proceeded up in level very gradually. As there was a need for plenty of repetition, there was also a need for plenty of material.

The 'Doctor Skunk' stories had been implemented side-by-side with instruction in phonics, using a combination of the synthetic phonic principles embodied in the Orton/Gillingham [179] approach and the analytical phonics principles suggested by Sister Mary Caroline [180]. As the field had now moved on, 'The Tales of Jud the Rat' materials were designed to provide the degree of repetition necessary to reinforce remedial teaching done within both the Orton/Gillingham paradigm as well as teaching done within more modern phonologically based paradigms (e.g. [181]).

Underpinning both sets of materials was an assumption that repetition of phonic associations would lead to probable benefits at a neurological level. The 'Doctor Skunk' stories were based on the Wernicke-Geschwind hypothesis [182], the assumption being that a combination of amount of time on task and amount of repetition would enable associations to form within the occipito-temporal areas of the left hemisphere of the brain.

Given the more precise indications concerning neural connectivity which had emerged from neurolinguistic research post 2000, 'The Tales of Jud the Rat' materials assumed that neural connectivity would be improved by repetitive exposure to phonically graded material set in large print, specifically between the left occipital and parietal lobes in which large print would be processed, the temporal/occipital lobes in which sound–letter associations would be processed and also those areas of the left temporal and frontal lobes in which higher levels of language processing take place. Writing and spelling based on these associations would then be encoded in medial areas of the left side of the brain in both right-handed people as well as in the majority of left-handed people.

In short, stronger associations at a central level would be likely to lead to positive results, as a number of studies reviewed in this chapter had indicated that this would be likely to be the case.

6.5. Use of material set in large print: Visual features of the ebooks

The literature post 2000 also indicated that there are visual features in text which may influence the way in which dyslexic children learn to read [183, 184]. 'The Tales of Jud the Rat' materials were thus also designed to take into account visual attentional as well as visual features of text.

A feature of ebooks and electronic print is that they can be set in different fonts and print sizes. The ebooks in 'The Tales of Jud the Rat' series were set in large print and made use of short sentences and paragraphs as well as large amounts of white space on the page. This was done so that the material could avoid crowding, as this was to likely to affect dyslexics on a visual level (e.g. [185, 186]).

Print size was one important variable. O'Brien, Mansfield and Legg [187] had reported constant reading rates across large print sizes in dyslexics, but that a sharp decline in reading rates occurs once print is presented below a critical print size, indicating that dyslexic readers would require larger critical print sizes to attain maximum reading speeds. O'Brien, Mansfield and Legg's results indicated that reading rate-by-print size curves followed the same two-limbed shape for dyslexic and non-dyslexic readers. The reading curves of dyslexic children, however, showed higher critical print sizes and shallower reading rate-by-print size slopes below the critical print size. Non-dyslexic reading curves also showed a decrease of critical print size with age. Statistical analysis indicated that a developmental lag model of dyslexic reading had not accounted for the results, since the regression of critical print size on maximum reading rate differed between the two groups.

Research reported by Brennan, Worrall and McKenna [188] indicated that a number of other aspects of the design and formatting of materials used in written communication (e.g. use of simplified vocabulary and syntax, large print and increased white space) can influence comprehension. Brennan, Worrall and McKenna worked with aphasic adults, and reported that adding pictures, particularly Clip Art pictures, may not significantly improve the reading comprehension of people with aphasia, but that simplified vocabulary and syntax, large print and increased white space were significant features to consider when using all written communication with people with aphasia.

Martelli et al. [189] suggested the value of using white space when presenting materials for dyslexic children learning to read, for the reason that crowding may influence reading speed. Levi [190] also pointed out that crowding was an important influence on visual discrimination and object recognition which has a relationship with dyslexia. Based on review of the literature, Levi suggested that there were two stages involved in the development of object recognition which can be localised to the cortex. The first stage involves the detection of simple features, while the second stage is required for the integration or interpretation of the features of an object. In addition, there is evidence that top–down effects (i.e. effects of interpretation and comprehension) mediate the bottom–up effects of crowding, while the role of attention in this process remains unclear.

Overall, Levi suggested that there is a strong effect of learning in shrinking the spatial extent of crowding, indicating that instruction ameliorates the influence of crowding on reading ability. Legge and Bigelow's review [191] also indicated that both size and shape of printed symbols determine the legibility of text, and for this reason, the PDFs of the ebooks in 'The

Tales of Jud the Rat' series were set in large print, using Arial, which is a simple uncluttered font.

6.6. Use of visual tracking to maintain visual attention in the implementation process

Stein's review [192] indicates that visual attentional factors are likely to influence reading ability. In addition, Sireteanu et al. [193] have suggested that children with developmental dyslexia show selective visual deficits in attention, with dyslexic children showing shorter reaction times as well as dramatically increased numbers of errors.

For this reason, the procedures used for implementing 'The Tales of Jud the Rat' materials have been designed to provide a combination of phonically based material and large print, as well as visual tracking. The assumption is that this combination would assist developing phonological and visual associations while also maintaining visual attention, and that this combination, in turn, would be helpful in building connectivity on a magnocellular level.

Visual tracking is thus built into the implementation process of 'The Tales of Jud the Rat' materials, with a pointer being used from the top of the line focus attention on words read, as well as attention on those visual features in words which provide maximum cues in the decoding process. Visual and visual attentional decoding processes are then combined with phonic repetition throughout the core series of ebooks. The reason for this is that research evidence suggests that rapid automatised naming (RAN) is a correlate of early reading skills and that RAN continues to exert an influence on the development of reading fluency over the next 2 years after reading instruction has started [194].

Given needs for longitudinal intervention where reading problems are major or intractable (such as in Q's case), the series of 'The Tales of Jud the Rat' ebooks has been designed to provide enough graded reading material for the programme to be used for at least 2 years and for up to 4 years with any child, should this be necessary. This means that the combination of use of large print, visual tracking and phonic repetition can be continued for an extended period, until an age appropriate level of reading fluency has been developed.

How this is done is described in the following sections.

7. Provision of material of gradually increasing complexity: The core and extension readers

7.1. The core large-print reading series

Carol Chomsky [195] has suggested that struggling readers decode slowly and with difficulty and that, despite their hard-won decoding skills, they are also passive to reading. Chomsky also suggests that what is needed is material which will engage attention, and also make large amounts of textual material available.

The core series of large print readers is designed to provide a large amount of material which can be used to develop reading fluency. There are currently 19 ebooks which are graded in terms of level. The titles of the ebooks in the core reading fluency programme can be found on

http://dx.doi.org/10.5772/61607

my website at http://www.charlespotter.org, while the programme as a whole is designed as follows:

Core Series: Title of book	Extension	Award
1. JUD THE RAT AND TOM THE CAT		
2. TOM THE CAT TRIES TO TRICK JUD THE RAT, BUT GETS VERY WET AND COLD		
3. TOM THE CAT TRIES TO BE CLEVER, BUT LANDS UP SICK IN BED	Supplementary Series One: The Stories of Sid the Badger – Basic Level Readers	Supplementary Series One: The Stories of Sid the Badger – Basic Level Readers
4. JILL THE DOG		
5. TOM THE CAT MAKES A MISTAKE, BUT LANDS UP BEING SUCCESSFUL		
6. HOW JUD THE RAT REALISES HE HAS BEEN TRICKED, AND TRIES TO SAVE FACE	Supplementary Series Two: The Stories of Bill the Hedgehog – Intermediate Level Readers	Certificate: Reading Fluency Level Two + Book Prize
7. JUD THE RAT'S HOUSE		
8. THE SMELLY END OF THE STREET		
9. TOM THE CAT CATCHES JUD THE RAT, BUT JUD STILL GETS AWAY	Supplementary Series Three: The Chronicles Doctor Skunk: Part One – Higher Level Readers	Certificate: Reading Fluency Level Three + Book Prize
10. JILL THE DOG'S SHOP		
11. TOM THE CAT'S SECRET		
12. JILL THE DOG SOLVES PART OF THE PUZZLE		
13. SID THE BADGER FINDS THE ANSWER		
14. TOM THE CAT'S TRAP	Supplementary Series Four: The Chronicles of Doctor Skunk Part Two – Higher Level Readers	Certificate: Reading Fluency Level Four + Book Prize
15. JUD THE RAT AND MAX THE MOLE		
16. DOCTOR SKUNK'S VISIT		
17. HOW DOCTOR SKUNK GOT BACK TO THE STREET AND THEN WENT HOME		
18. JUD THE RAT SPOILS TOM THE CAT'S BIKE RIDE		
19. TOM THE CAT GETS HIS OWN BACK	Supplementary Series Five: Stories of the Valley and Legends of the Deep Woods -- Extension Readers	Certificate: Reading Fluency Level Five + Book Prize

Table 2. Dr Charles Potter's reading fluency programme: design

Each of the elements in the programme is ebook-based, supported by email tutorials. The ebooks are also designed to be delivered by email. This provides the flexibility for the core programme of large print readers to be implemented both as a support programme for parents working with me on a sessional basis, or at distance.

7.2. Reducing font size and extending vocabulary: The extension readers

The evidence from the literature is convergent in indicating that reading difficulties are language based [196], though a combination of auditory and visual as well as attentional factors may also influence reading abilities [197], There is also evidence that increased reading fluency influences reading comprehension [198] and that conversely, top–down effects involved in language and reading comprehension mediate the influence of auditory, visual and attentional and fluency factors on reading ability [199].

For this reason, it will be evident from Table 2 above that reading fluency is conceptualised as a variable having stages. These stages can be determined both from reading behaviour as well as performance on reading tests measuring reading accuracy and reading rate.

As certain children may require substantial work before an age-appropriate level of reading fluency is developed, there are five supplementary series in the programme. Each of these supplementary series consists of between five and seven ebooks. At lower levels in the programme, there are extension stories based on rhythm and rhyme, as well as stories based on sequenced storytelling. At higher levels, there are extension stories drawn from the original 'Doctor Skunk' series written for Q, as well as extension stories designed to link with tales of imagination and legends. There are also procedures for use of the materials for building skills in analytical phonics, spelling and sequential spelling, as well as an awards programme for children completing a certain number of books and reaching particular levels of reading fluency. Despite having a large number of ebooks available, the aim is that the materials in the programme should be used only as long as is necessary to develop an age appropriate level of reading fluency. What this means is that decisions concerning the need for continued use of large print and repetition are evidence-driven and taken both quantitatively as well as qualitatively. In addition, as the evidence from the paired reading literature is not convergent concerning optimal levels of difficulty of reading material, the books in the core series are written based on predominantly short words which can be decoded using phonic rules. Books in the extension material also include more complex vocabulary.

Specifically, once there is evidence that reading fluency is developing from one stage to the next and evidence that age-appropriate top-down effects are operating (i.e. improvements in reading fluency as well as comprehension are taking place), children working through the 'The Tales of Jud the Rat' series are directed to supplementary and extension materials. In these ebooks both print size and repetition of words are reduced, At the same time, the amount of repetition in the paired reading procedures used for implementation of the reading fluency programme is also reduced.

http://dx.doi.org/10.5772/61607

7.3. Reading fluency as one element in a broader intervention

It will be apparent from the above that the 'Tales of Jud the Rat' programme can be used for purposes of clinical teaching as well as in other situations in which observation is used to determine needs for intervention. The assumption is that one size may not fit all, and that as Scarborough [200] suggests, the variables involved in reading acquisition may not be linear. In addition, multiple case studies suggest variation in the aetiology of adult dyslexics [201] as well as children [202].

What this means is that not all children need the same thing, and that not all dyslexic children are likely to respond to the same treatment. The reading fluency programme is thus conceptualised as one element in a broader intervention. Its value lies in its potential for providing sufficient time on task for automaticity in reading to be developed. At the same time, the results obtained also reflect the skill of the teacher or therapist in using the tools and the programmes available to him or her, and 'The Tales of Jud the Rat' series is only one of a number of possible tools and programmes.

What this also means is that for optimum results, paired reading using 'The Tales of Jud the Rat' programme should be combined with other programmes involving phonic teaching [203] as well as exposure to other texts in which vocabulary is broader and difficulty levels are higher [204]. As reading and spelling are linked processes, how this is done (i.e. how the programme is structured and how other additional instructional programmes are organised and implemented) is essentially based on assessment, evaluation and clinical judgement as interpretive processes, as described in the following sections.

7.4. Assessment and evaluation as informing clinical judgement

The ebooks in the reading fluency programme are not a panacea. They can best be described as an exercise programme designed to provide a structured and sequenced means for developing reading fluency as one element in a broader instructional programme. If the reading fluency programme is implemented by parents for 20 min a number of times a week, its potential value lies in enabling time on task in reading to be substantially increased, using graded materials which have been developed on a conceptual basis linked to recent developments in neurolinguistic research.

As it is important to establish the need for as well as the effects of the 'Tales of Jud the Rat' programme as well as the need for other interventions targeting the development of phonic analysis, reading comprehension, spelling and sequential writing ability, there are systems for assessment and evaluation linked to the materials. These are based on a process of action research [205], in which assessment is used to establish needs for intervention, followed by a process of planning and implementation in which evaluation is integral.

Placement in the programme is initially made on the basis of reading level. Based on the process of evaluation, awards are also made both for effort as well as improvement. These awards are linked to extension activities, in the form of ebooks which are at a higher level, as well as end books for broader reading.

Children are placed in the programme based on a system of assessment and evaluation involving quantitative indicators from four core reading, spelling and sequential spelling tests. Reading fluency and reading comprehension are also assessed via other reading tests, and supported by additional testing of phonemic knowledge and reading comprehension abilities. During implementation, these data are then linked to qualitative indicators of reading fluency based on parental reports. This is done by informal interviews as well as questionnaires.

The evaluation is thus multi-method [206, 207], based on both quantitative and qualitative evidence linked to other available data on school and classroom performance as well as reading habits. Once placement has been made at a particular level in the reading materials, the first ebook is sent out by email. This is supported by a written tutorial, and if possible a trial session in how to support the paired reading procedure with visual tracking, and how to pace repeated reading.

Once parents have tried out the materials, a formative evaluation questionnaire is completed. Only at this stage is the child brought into the programme. As the sequence of the core reading series is published on the author's website, the child's progress through the core reading materials can be tracked both by parents and their teachers or therapists. Summative evaluation is then completed after a number of books have been worked through, as the basis for achieving awards, as well as entry into the intermediate- and higher-level series.

This decision is based on clinical judgement and can be made at any level in the programme, but generally occurs once the child has reached reading fluency level three. Parents are involved in this process, as well as in the system of awards and the summative evaluation process conducted at the end of each calendar year, which involves post-testing.

8. Results

Though 'The Tales of Jud the Rat' reading programme has been developed on a clear theoretical rationale, in the final analysis any reading programme is merely a tool which is as good as the user. I have learned a great deal from working with parents as well as other therapists and teachers as part of the formative and summative evaluation process. This has shaped not only the sequence of the programme but also the awards system and the use of supporting and extension reading materials which now form an integral part of the structure of the programme.

Overall, the results have been very promising. Based on use of the materials for a period of 6 months as part of a broader-based remedial intervention, the results of the first cohort of children are presented in Table 3 below.

It will be evident from the above that all children in the initial cohort placed on the programme have made good progress, as indicated by gains in reading age after 6 months programme usage. Evaluative comments made by both parents and children have also been very positive. These can be summarised in Table 4 as follows.

Perhaps, the most important qualitative indicator, however, is that all parents who were using the materials at the end of 2014 have asked to continue using them this year (2015). Equally important is the evidence that many of the children using the programme have reported improvements in rate of work at school. Based on these positive indicators, an increasing number of children are currently working with the materials, some working with their parents as part of their weekly contact with me, and some working with their parents or with teachers or other therapists at distance from my rooms.

Children in Reading Fluency Programme	Grade Level at School	Schonell One Word Reading Test	Holborn Sentence Reading Test	Schonell Single Word Spelling Test	Schonell Dictation Tests
Child A *Pretest*	*start Grade 2*	*6 years 9 months*	*6 years 9 months*	*6 years 6 months*	-
Child A Post-test	end Grade 2	7 years 7 months	8 years 3 months	7 years 5 months	< 6 years 0 months
Child *B Pretest*	*start Grade 3*	*7 years 7 months*	*8 years 6 months*	*7 years 8 months*	*6 years 0 months*
Child B Post-test	end Grade 3	8 years 8 months	9 years 2 months	8 years 7 months	9 years 0 months
Child C *Pretest*	*start Grade 3*	*7 years 0 months*	*7 years 7 months*	*7 years 5 months*	*< 6 years 0 months*
Child C Post-test	end Grade 3	8 years 11 months	8 years 6 months	9 years 0 months	7 years 6 months
Child D *Pretest*	*start Grade 5*	*7 years 7 months*	*8 years 6 months*	*7 years 4 months*	*7 years 5 months*
Child D Post-test	end Grade 5	9 years 0 months	9 years 2 months	9 years 1 month	8 years 6 months
Child E *Pretest*	*start Grade 5*	*7 years 7 months*	*8 years 0 months*	*8 years 1 month*	*< 6 years 0 months*
Child E Post-test	end Grade 5	9 years 2 months	8 years 11 months	8 years 7 months	8 years 8 months
Child F *Pretest*	*start Grade 7*	*8 years 2 months*	*8 years 6 months*	*6 years 8 months*	*6 years 9 months*
Child F Post-test	end Grade 7	10 years 7 months	9 years 10 months	8 years 8 months	7 years 9 months
Child G *Pretest*	*start Grade 8*	*8 years 11 months*	*9 years 2 months*	*8 years 6 months*	*8 years 9 months*
Child G Post-test	end Grade 8	11 years 3 months	9 years 10 months	9 years 6 months	8 years 9 months
Child H *Pretest*	*start Grade 8*	*10 years 6 months*	*9 years 2 months*	*9 years 11 months*	*10 years 7 months*
Child H Post-test	end Grade 8	"/> 12 years 6 months	13 years 5 months	10 years 11 months	12 years 0 months

Table 3. Progress of 2014 Cohort as Measured by Reading, Spelling and Dictation Age Scores

Children in Reading Fluency Programme	Improvement in Reading Accuracy	Improvement in Reading Rate	Improvement in Reading Hesitancy and Confidence	Improvement in Ability to Read New Material	Improvement in Reading Comprehension
Child A	*	*	*	*	*
Child B	*	*	*	*	*
Child C	*	*	*	*	*
Child D	*	*	*	*	*
Child E	*	*	*	*	*
Child F	*	*	*	*	*
Child G	*	*	*	*	*
Child H	*	*	*	*	*

Table 4. Summary of Qualitative Evaluations by Parents: 2014 Cohort

Overall, the experience has been a very positive one. While the results we have are preliminary, the evidence so far would also suggest that parents can use the programme with their children and that schools, teachers and therapists can also use the materials to support the work they are doing. The evidence also suggests that those children who proceed through the programme at the rate of one ebook a month make substantial progress.

9. Summary and evaluation

This chapter has presented eight major assets of 'The Tales of Jud the Rat' series.

a. The material has been developed based on clinical teaching as well as neurolinguistic theory.

b. The material is graded, based on structured phonic principles.

c. The material is set in large print to increase visual cues as well as reduce crowding.

d. There is plenty of material available, and there is enough for the core reading materials to be used for as long as is necessary to develop reading fluency, even with readers who require a 2-year intervention (or more) as their reading problems are severe or intractible,

e. The material is available in electronic ebook form. This implies that all material can be sent out by email and used at a distance. All core tests and evaluation procedures can also be applied at a distance.

f. There are established procedures for implementation, which include visual tracking.

g. Once downloaded, 'The Tales of Jud the Rat' material is implemented using repeated paired reading to develop automaticity in reading.

h. The implementation and evaluation procedures are simple, and can be used by parents and peer tutors, as well as by teachers and therapists.

While the research evidence reviewed in this chapter would suggest that automaticity forms the foundation for both increases in reading rate and accuracy as well being associated with improvement in reading comprehension, there are a number of disadvantages of the programme.

- The material targets reading fluency and does not overtly target reading comprehension.
- While the literature suggests that the development of automaticity is an essential skill and the evidence from parent use of 'The Tales of Jud the Rat' material suggests that the children who have used the programme have improved in a number of different aspects associated with fluent reading, the results we have so far are not definitive.
- The 'Tales of Jud the Rat' programme has so far only been used under clinical settings, and my own clinical experience suggests that the results of any one programme will only be as good as the other aspects of instruction which accompany it. Put another way, any educational programme is merely a tool. It will produce best effects where the programme implementer is skilled, and in situations where the programme is used in conjunction with other instructional programmes which also target improvement.

Despite these potential weaknesses, we have had good results with 'The Tales of Jud the Rat' series, and there are probably a number of reasons why this is so. The first reason is that the material is phonically based and proceeds up in level very gradually. There is plenty of repetition. The programme is also compatible with other instructional programmes. If one believes in Gillingham and Stillman's approach, for example (and many therapists still do), what this means is that 'The Tales of Jud the Rat' material can be used to reinforce remedial teaching done within the Orton/Gillingham paradigm [208], teaching done using an analytical phonics approach (e.g.[209]), as well as teaching done within more modern phonologically based paradigms (e.g. [210]).

Given the potential for increase in time on task in reading using material which involves frequent repetition of phonic associations, there are also probable benefits at a neurological level. In addition, visual tracking is built into programme implementation and this is also likely to lead to probable benefits at a neurological level. In short, increased time on task would be likely to develop automaticity in reading, implying stronger associations at a central level. As the literature suggests that the directionality in these associations is two-way, automaticity at a central level would be likely to lead to positive results in reading more generally, and the studies reviewed in this chapter indicate that this is indeed likely to be the case.

Based on the literature, there are also a number of other probable reasons for positive results. One is that 'The Tales of Jud the Rat' materials are repetitive, and take into account visual attention as well as visual features of text [211, 212]. The ebooks are set in large print and make use of short sentences and paragraphs as well as large amounts of white space on the page. What this means is that the material is likely to avoid crowding, which has been emerging in the literature as a feature affecting dyslexics on a visual level (e.g. [213, 214]). In addition, there are theoretical reasons why a combination of phonically based material and large print would be helpful on a magnocellular level, especially in a situation in which both repetition of phonic associations and visual tracking are built into programme implementation.

However, it is important to state that there is no empirical evidence that this is actually so, and these theoretical bases of a programme remain possibilities until there is empirical evidence available to support assertions like these, or prove otherwise. Though the results presented in this chapter are positive, they are small-scale and preliminary. In addition, there are many weaknesses in data from pre-test, post-test and pre-experimental designs, especially when these designs are used clinically. Specifically, difficulties in weak research designs are likely to be compounded where therapy or instruction is undertaken with the aim of improving test scores and where a variety of teaching strategies are used to do so.

As they are based on clinical evidence and case study, the results presented in this chapter are positive but difficult to disaggregate, and larger-scale comparative research would be necessary to do so. Nevertheless, the clinical evidence presented is recurrent and indicates that there is likely to be benefit from using the materials even in the absence of both longitudinal and/or comparative studies. The value of both partner reading and peer tutored reading as well as parental involvement in assisting children with their reading is already clear from the literature (e.g. [215, 216, 217, 218, 219]). This is essentially what 'The Tales of Jud the Rat' programme provides, and the evaluative issue may thus not be whether this particular method is better than any other, but whether it is able to provide an appropriately structured and low-cost way for parents or peer tutors to achieve improvements in reading fluency.

The results we have obtained would support the indications in the literature of the value of increasing the amount that children read, as well as providing exposure to accessible texts. As Fisher and Berliner [220] have suggested, the amount that students read in classrooms is critically related to their reading achievement. In addition, Hiebert and Fisher [221] have suggested that children of lower primary school age performing in the bottom quartile require the following experiences with text:

Accessible Text

Provision of text which is accessible through being decodable, which includes both high-imagery and high-frequency words, which limits the number of unique words per text, and which repeats key words.

Increased Text

Provision of increased opportunities for reading involving exposure to text during classroom instruction, with the aims of increasing both word recognition and fluent reading skills.

Repeated Text

Provision of opportunities for repeated reading of text, with the aims of increasing exposure to new words and developing reading fluency.

The evidence from my practice would suggest the value of providing greatly increased time on task in reading accessible, graded texts using a methodology combining repetition with visual tracking. Both parents and children in my practice report steady improvement in reading fluency, and evaluate the 'Tales of Jud the Rat' reading fluency materials positively Positive qualitative evaluations have been accompanied by the changes in test scores presented in Tables 3 and 4 in this chapter.

The evidence from my practice would also support Hiebert and Martin's [222] comment that repetition has been the forgotten variable in reading instruction. Both parents and therapists have commented positively on the phonic structure of the programme as well as the use of repetition within the texts as well as in the methodology used in implementing the programme. It is also of interest that, despite the large amount of repetition which is a feature of the programme, the stories have been rated as entertaining by both children and their parents.

There have also been wider benefits. One parent reports that her child receives the books. His older sister then reads them. The family's domestic help then reads them, and her children then also use them to learn to read. The ebooks are also currently being used as the basis for reading fluency programmes being implemented with ten higher- and twenty lower-income families in Mpumalanga province. I await the results of these pilot programmes with interest.

In summary, I have found in my own work that 'The Tales of Jud the Rat' material provides a way of enabling parents to provide graded daily reinforcement of reading, by using ebooks which target reading fluency and automaticity in decoding at home. The majority of the children I work with have reading difficulties, and in this context 'The Tales of Jud the Rat' programme has been very helpful.

In implementing the programme, clear guidelines are given to parents in how to engage productively in improving the reading fluency of their children, and this enables me to ensure that time on task in reading is increased at home. The involvement of parents then leaves me with more time to focus in therapy on programmes which improve other aspects of reading and writing ability. These include programmes for developing synthetic and analytical phonic skills and word attack, as well as tasks involving oral and written language skills designed to build oral and written language comprehension skills. I am also able to spend more time in assessment and counselling of children and parents, as well as in working on programmes for developing skills in silent reading, as well as word analysis, single word spelling and sequential writing and spelling.

What can be claimed is that a great deal of material in 'The Tales of Jud the Rat' programme is already available but I am still developing parts of it, and also revising aspects of the material where formative evaluation has shown that this is necessary. It can also be claimed that the programme has provided clear benefits based on observable differences as well as changes in test scores. Based on positive evaluations, the materials are being added to, but are already in a form in which they can be used by others.

The number of families using the programme has increased rapidly, and the material may also have wider relevance for use in the classroom. Low-cost material of this type is often difficult to obtain especially in developing world contexts, or where parents, teachers and therapists live at distance from major towns or from educational bookshops. Positive results with the 'Tales of Jud the Rat' series so far suggest that the material provides a low-cost path to reading improvement which can be used in direct contact or at distance by parents, peer tutors, teachers, therapists and schools.

Author details

Charles Potter*

Address all correspondence to: pottercs@gmail.com

Private Practice, Johannesburg, South Africa

References

[1] Rieben L, Perfetti CA (Eds.) Learning to Read: Basic Research and Its Implications. New York: Routledge, 2013, p. vii.

[2] Adams MJ. Beginning to Read: Thinking and Learning About Print. Cambridge, MA: MIT Press, 1990.

[3] Perfetti CA. Psycholinguistics and reading ability. In: Gernsbacher MA. (Ed.) Handbook of Psycholinguistics. San Diego, CA: Academic Press, 1994, pp. 849–894.

[4] Perfetti CA. The universal grammar of reading. Sci Stud Reading 2003;7(1):pp.3–24.

[5] Perfetti CA. Representations and awareness in the acquisition of reading competence. In: Rieben L, Perfetti CA. (Eds.) Learning to Read: Basic Research and Its Implications. New York: Routledge, 2013, pp. 33–44.

[6] Logsdon A. What is reading fluency? http://learningdisabilities.about.com/od/glossar1/g/rdgfluency.htm, 2012a.

[7] Luria AR. The Working Brain: An Introduction to Neuropsychology. Harmondsworth, UK: Penguin Education, 1973.

[8] Logsdon A. What is reading fluency? Learn about reading fluency. http://learningdisabilities.about.com/od/readingstrategies/a/What-Is-Reading-Fluency.htm, 2012b.

[9] Luria AR. The Working Brain: An Introduction to Neuropsychology. Harmondsworth, UK: Penguin Education, 1973.

[10] Laberge D, Samuels JS. Toward a theory of automatic information processing in reading. Cogn Psychol 1974;6(2):293–323.

[11] Luria AR. The Working Brain: An Introduction to Neuropsychology. Harmondsworth, UK: Penguin Education, 1973.

[12] Samuels SJ. The method of repeated readings. The Reading Teacher 1979;32(4):403–8.

[13] Chomsky C. After decoding: what? Language Arts 1976;53(3):288-–96.

[14] Carbo M. Teaching reading with talking books. The Reading Teacher 1978;32(3):267–73.

[15] Morgan R, Lyon E. Paired reading — a preliminary report on a technique for parental tuition of reading retarded children. J Child Psychol Psychiatr 1979;20(2):151–60.

[16] Ashby-Davis C. A review of three techniques for use with remedial readers. The Reading Teacher 1981;34(5):534–8.

[17] Allington RL. Fluency: the neglected reading goal. The Reading Teacher 1983;36(6): 556–61.

[18] Adams MJ. Beginning to read: Thinking and learning about print. Cambridge, MA: MIT Press, 1990.

[19] Fuchs LS, Fuchs D, Hosp MK, Jenkins JR. Oral reading fluency as an indicator of reading competence: a theoretical, empirical, and historical analysis. Sci Stud Reading 2001;5(3):239–56.

[20] U.S. Congress. No Child Left Behind Act: Reauthorization of the Elementary and Secondary Education Act (PL 107–110). www.ed.gov/offices/oese/esea/. 2001.

[21] Norton ES, Wolf M. Rapid automatized naming (RAN) and reading fluency: implications for understanding and treatment of reading disabilities. Annu Rev Psychol 2012;63:427–52.

[22] Chomsky C. After decoding: what? Language Arts 1976;53(3):288–96.

[23] Carbo M. Teaching reading with talking books. The Reading Teacher 1978;32(3):267–73.

[24] Morgan R, Lyon E. Paired reading — a preliminary report on a technique for parental tuition of reading retarded children. J Child Psychol Psychiatr 1979;20(2):151–60.

[25] Ashby-Davis C. A review of three techniques for use with remedial readers. The Reading Teacher 1981;34(5):534–8.

[26] Heckelman RG. A neurological impress method of reading instruction. RG Heckelman – 1962 – Merced County Schools Office, Merced CA.

[27] Heckelman RG. A neurological-impress method of remedial-reading instruction. Acad Therap 1969;4(4):277–82.

[28] Heckelman RG. N.I.M. revisited. Acad Therap 1986;21(4):411–20.

[29] Hoskisson K, Krohm B. Reading by immersion: assisted reading. Elementary English 1974;51(6):832–6.

[30] Heckelman RG. A neurological impress method of reading instruction. RG Heckelman – 1962 – Merced County Schools Office, Merced CA.

[31] Heckelman RG. A neurological-impress method of remedial-reading instruction. Academic Therapy 1969;4(4):277–82.

[32] Hollingsworth PM. An experiment with the impress method of teaching reading. The Reading Teacher 1970;24(2):112–4.

[33] Morgan R, Lyon E. Paired reading — a preliminary report on a technique for parental tuition of reading retarded children. J Child Psychol Psychiatr 1979;20(2):151–60.

[34] Topping K. Paired reading: a powerful technique for parent use. The Reading Teacher 1987a;40(7):608–14.

[35] Topping K. Peer tutored paired reading: outcome data from ten projects. Edu Psychol: Int J Exp Edu Psychol 1987b;7(2):133–45.

[36] Topping K. Peer tutoring and paired reading: combining two powerful techniques. The Reading Teacher 1989;42:488–94.

[37] Topping K. Paired, Reading, Spelling and Writing: The Handbook for Teachers and Parents. London: Cassell, 1995.

[38] Topping K. Paired reading: a powerful technique for parent use. The Reading Teacher 1987;40(7):608–14.

[39] Topping K. Peer tutoring and paired reading: combining two powerful techniques. The Reading Teacher 1989;42:488–94.

[40] Topping K. Peer tutored paired reading: outcome data from ten projects. Edu Psychol: Int J Exp Edu Psychol 1987b;7(2):133–45.

[41] Topping K. Paired, Reading, Spelling and Writing: The Handbook for Teachers and Parents. London: Cassell, 1995.

[42] Topping K. Paired, Reading, Spelling and Writing: The Handbook for Teachers and Parents. London: Cassell, 1995.

[43] Topping KJ, Lindsay GA. Paired reading: a review of the literature. Res Papers Edu 1992;7(3):199–246.

[44] Topping K, Wolfendale S. (Eds.) Parental involvement in children's reading. New York: Nichols, 1985.

[45] Morgan R, Lyon E. Paired reading — a preliminary report on a technique for parental tuition of reading retarded children. J Child Psychol Psychiatr 1979;20(2):151–60.

[46] Hewison J, Tizard J. Parental involvement and reading attainment. Edu Psychol 1980;50(3):209–15.

[47] Vanwagenen MA, Williams RL, Mclaughlin TF. Use of assisted reading to improve reading rate, word accuracy, and comprehension with ESL Spanish-speaking students. Perceptual Motor Skills 1994;79(1):227–30.

[48] Overett J, Donald D. Paired reading: effects of a parent involvement programme in a disadvantaged community in South Africa. Br J Edu Psychol 1998;68(3):347–56.

[49] Lam S, Chow-Yeung K, Wong BPH, Kiu Lau K, In Tse S. Involving parents in paired reading with preschoolers: Results from a randomized controlled trial. Contemp Edu Psychol 2013;38(2):126–35.

[50] Cadieux A, Boudreault P. The effects of a parent-child paired reading program on reading abilities, phonological awareness and self-concept of at-risk pupils (1). The Free Library. 2005 Project Innovation (Alabama) 24 Feb 2015. http://www.thefreelibrary.com/The±effects±of±a±parent-child±paired±reading±program±on±reading...-a0142874180

[51] Hannon P, Jackson A, Weinberger J. Parents' and teachers' strategies in hearing young children read. Res Papers Edu1986;1(1):6–25.

[52] Ellis MG. Parent-child reading programs: Involving parents in the reading intervention process. ERIC Number: ED397377, 1996.

[53] Chomsky C. After decoding: what? Language Arts 1976;53(3):288–96.

[54] Carbo M. Teaching reading with talking books. The Reading Teacher 1978;32(3):267–73.

[55] Cadieux A, Boudreault P. The effects of a parent-child paired reading program on reading abilities, phonological awareness and self-concept of at-risk pupils (1). The Free Library. 2005 Project Innovation (Alabama) 24 Feb 2015. http://www.thefreelibrary.com/The±effects±of±a±parent-child±paired±reading±program±on±reading...-a0142874180

[56] Wasik BA. Volunteer tutoring programs in reading: a review. Reading Res Quart 1998;33:266–92.

[57] Deegan J. Impress method. Downloaded from websites.pdesas.org/jamesdeegan/2013/9/12/520805/file.aspx, 2007.

[58] Morgan A, Wilcox BR, Eldredge JL. Effect of difficulty levels on second-grade delayed readers using dyad reading. J Edu Res 2000;94(2):113–9.

[59] Stahl SA, Heubach KM. Fluency-oriented reading instruction. J Literacy Res 2005;37(1):25–60.

[60] Homan SP, Klesius JP, Hite C. Effects of repeated readings and nonrepetitive strategies on students' fluency and comprehension. J Edu Res 1993;87(2):94–9.

[61] Shah-Wundenberg M, Wyse D, Chaplain R. Parents helping their children learn to read: the effectiveness of paired reading and hearing reading in a developing country context. J Early Childhood Literacy 2013;13(4):471500.

[62] MacDonald P. Paired reading: a structured approach to raising attainment in literacy. Support Learning 2010;25(1):15–23.

[63] Scarborough HS. Early identification of children at risk for reading disabilities: Phonological awareness and some other promising predictors. Specific Reading Disability: A View of the Spectrum 1998a;75–119.

[64] Scarborough HS. Predicting the future achievement of second graders with reading disabilities: contributions of phonemic awareness, verbal memory, rapid naming, and IQ. Anna Dyslexia 1998b;48(1):115–36.

[65] Scarborough HS. Developmental relationships between language and reading: reconciling a beautiful hypothesis with some ugly facts. In: Catts HW, Kamhi AG. (Eds.) The Connections between Language and Reading Disabilities. New Jersey: Lawrence Erlbaum, 2005, pp. 3–22.

[66] Scarborough HS. Connecting early language and literacy to later reading (dis)abilities: evidence, theory and practice. In: Fletcher-Campbell F, Soler J, Reid G. (Eds.) Approaching Difficulties in Literacy Development: Assessment, Pedagogy and Programmes. New York: Sage, 2009; pp. 23–38.

[67] Potter CS, Grasko D, Pereira C. Using spelling error patterns to identify children with learning difficulties. SAALED International Conference "Reading for All". Nelspruit, September, 2006.

[68] Potter CS, Fridjhon P, Grasko D, Pereira C, Ravenscroft G. Spelling error profiles: an index for evaluating the learning needs and progress of children in the classroom. Pretoria, ASEASA International Conference, July, 2008.

[69] Potter CS, Fridjhon P, Grasko D, Pereira C, Ravenscroft G. Identifying patterns of phonic errors in children with learning disabilities. Salt Lake City, UT: 46th International Conference of the Learning Disabilities Association of America, February, 2009.

[70] Shaywitz SE, Shaywitz BA, Pugh KR, Fulbright RK, Constable RT, Mencl WE, Gore JC. Functional disruption in the organization of the brain for reading in dyslexia. Proc Nat Acad Sci 1998;95(5):2636–41.

[71] Schulte-Körne G, Deimel W, Bartling J, Remschmidt H. Auditory processing and dyslexia: evidence for a specific speech processing deficit. Neuroreport 1998;9(2):337–40.

[72] Brunswick N, McCrory E, Price CJ, Frith CD, Frith U. Explicit and implicit processing of words and pseudowords by adult developmental dyslexics: a search for Wernicke's Wortschatz? Brain 1999;122(10):1901–17.

[73] Schulte-Körne G, Deimel W, Bartling J, Remschmidt H. Auditory processing and dyslexia: evidence for a specific speech processing deficit. Neuroreport 1998;9(2):337–40.

[74] Shaywitz SE, Shaywitz BA, Pugh KR, Fulbright RK, Constable RT, Mencl WE, Gore JC. Functional disruption in the organization of the brain for reading in dyslexia. Proc Nat Acad Sci 1998;95(5):2636–41.

[75] Brunswick N, McCrory E, Price CJ, Frith CD, Frith U. Explicit and implicit processing of words and pseudowords by adult developmental dyslexics: a search for Wernicke's Wortschatz? Brain 1999;122(10):1901–17.

[76] Klingberg T, Hedehus M, Temple E, Salz T, Gabrieli JDE, Moseley ME, Poldrack RA. Microstructure of temporo-parietal white matter as a basis for reading ability: Evidence from diffusion tensor magnetic resonance imaging. Neuron 2000;25(2):493–500.

[77] Burton MW. The role of inferior frontal cortex in phonological processing. Cognitive Sci 2001;25(5):695–709.

[78] Temple E, Poldrack RA, Salidis J, Deutsch GK, Tallal P, Merzenich MM, Gabrieli JDE. Disrupted neural responses to phonological and orthographic processing in dyslexic children: an fMRI study. Neuroreport 2001;12(2):299–307.

[79] Bentin S, Mouchetant-Rostaing Y, Giard M, Echallier J, Pernier J. ERP manifestations of processing printed words at different psycholinguistic levels: time course and scalp distribution. J Cognitive Neurosci 1999;11(3):235–60.

[80] Brown WE, Eliez S, Menon V, Rumsey JM, White CD, Reiss AL. Preliminary evidence of widespread morphological variations of the brain in dyslexia. Neurology 2001;56(6):781–3.

[81] Simos PG, Fletcher JM, Bergman E, Breier JJ, Foorman BR, Castillo EM, Davis RN, Fitzgerald M, Papanicolaou AC. Dyslexia-specific brain activation profile becomes normal following successful remedial training. Neurology 2002;58(8):1203–13.

[82] Shaywitz BA, Shaywitz SE, Blachman BA, Pugh KR, Fulbright RK, Skudlarski P, Mencl WE, Constable RT, Holahan JM, Marchione KE, Fletcher JM, Lyon GR, Gore JC. Development of left occipitotemporal systems for skilled reading in children after a phonologically-based intervention. Biol Psychiatr 2004;55(9):926–33.

[83] Maurer U, Brem S, Kranz F, Bucher K, Benz R, Halder P, Steinhausen H, Brandeis D. Coarse neural tuning for print peaks when children learn to read. Neuroimage 2006;33(2):749–58.

[84] Shankweiler D, Mencl WE, Braze D, Tabor W, Pugh KR, Fulbright RK. Reading differences and brain: cortical integration of speech and print in sentence processing varies with reader skill. Develop Neuropsychol 2008;33(6):745–75.

[85] Poldrack RA. A structural basis for developmental dyslexia: evidence from diffusion tensor imaging. In: Wolf M.Ed.) Dyslexia, Fluency, and the Brain. Baltimore, MD: York Press, 2001; pp. 3–17.

[86] Shaywitz BA, Shaywitz SE, Blachman BA, Pugh KR, Fulbright RK, Skudlarski P, Mencl WE, Constable RT, Holahan JM, Marchione KE, Fletcher JM, Lyon GR, Gore JC. Development of left occipitotemporal systems for skilled reading in children after a phonologically-based intervention. Biol Psychiatr 2004;55(9):926–33.

[87] Poldrack RA. A structural basis for developmental dyslexia: evidence from diffusion tensor imaging. In: Wolf M. (Ed.) Dyslexia, Fluency, and the Brain. Baltimore, MD: York Press, 2001, pp. 3–17.

[88] Fields D. Myelination: an overlooked mechanism of synaptic plasticity? Neuroscientist 2005;11(6):528–31.

[89] Hasan KM, Molfese DL, Walimuni IS, Stuebing KK, Papanicolaou AC, Narayana PA, Fletcher JM. Diffusion tensor quantification and cognitive correlates of the macrostructure and microstructure of the corpus callosum in typically developing and dyslexic children. NMR in Biomedicine 2012;25(11):1263–70.

[90] Vandermosten M, Poelmans H, Sunaert S, Ghesquière P, Wouters J. White matter lateralization and interhemispheric coherence to auditory modulations in normal reading and dyslexic adults. Neuropsychologia 2013;51(11):2087–99.

[91] Shaywitz SE, Shaywitz BA, Pugh KR, Fulbright RK, Constable RT, Mencl WE, Gore JC. Functional disruption in the organization of the brain for reading in dyslexia. Proc Nat Acad Sci 1998;95(5):2636–41.

[92] Brunswick N, McCrory E, Price CJ, Frith CD, Frith U. Explicit and implicit processing of words and pseudowords by adult developmental dyslexics: a search for Wernicke's Wortschatz? Brain 1999;122(10):1901–17.

[93] Temple E, Poldrack RA, Salidis J, Deutsch GK, Tallal P, Merzenich MM, Gabrieli JDE. Disrupted neural responses to phonological and orthographic processing in dyslexic children: an fMRI study. Neuroreport 2001;12(2):299—307.

[94] Frost SJ, Landi N, Mencl WE, Sandak R, Fulbright RK, Tejada ET, Jacobsen L, Grigorenko EL, Constable RT, Pugh KR. Phonological awareness predicts activation patterns for print and speech. Anna Dyslexia 2009;59(1):78–97.

[95] Vellutino FR, Fletcher JM, Snowling MJ, Scanlon DM. Specific reading disability (dyslexia): what have we learned in the past four decades? J Child Psychol Psychiatr 2004;45(1):2–40.

[96] Shaywitz BA, Shaywitz SE, Blachman BA, Pugh KR, Fulbright RK, Skudlarski P, Mencl WE, Constable RT, Holahan JM, Marchione KE, Fletcher JM, Lyon GR, Gore JC. Development of left occipitotemporal systems for skilled reading in children after a phonologically-based intervention. Biol Psychiatr 2004;55(9):926–33.

[97] Simos PG, Fletcher JM, Bergman E, Breier JJ, Foorman BR, Castillo EM, Davis RN, Fitzgerald M, Papanicolaou AC. Dyslexia-specific brain activation profile becomes normal following successful remedial training. Neurology 2002;58(8):1203–13.

http://dx.doi.org/10.5772/61607

[98] Shaywitz BA, Shaywitz SE, Blachman BA, Pugh KR, Fulbright RK, Skudlarski P, Mencl WE, Constable RT, Holahan JM, Marchione KE, Fletcher JM, Lyon GR, Gore JC. Development of left occipitotemporal systems for skilled reading in children after a phonologically-based intervention. Biol Psychiatr 2004;55(9):926–33.

[99] Maurer U, Brem S, Kranz F, Bucher K, Benz R, Halder P, Steinhausen H, Brandeis D. Coarse neural tuning for print peaks when children learn to read. NeuroImage 2006;33(2):749–58.

[100] Scarborough HS. Developmental relationships between language and reading: Reconciling a beautiful hypothesis with some ugly facts. In: Catts HW, Kamhi AG. (Eds.) The Connections between Language and Reading Disabilities. New Jersey: Lawrence Erlbaum, 2005, pp. 3–22.

[101] Galaburda AM. Ordinary and extraordinary brain development: Anatomical variation in developmental dyslexia. Anna Dyslexia 1989;39(1):65–80.

[102] Poldrack RA. A structural basis for developmental dyslexia: evidence from diffusion tensor imaging. In: Wolf M. (Ed.) Dyslexia, Fluency, and the Brain. Baltimore, MD: York Press, 2001, pp. 3–17.

[103] Stein J. Dyslexia: the role of vision and visual attention. Curr Develop Disord Rep 2014;1(4):267–80.

[104] Ahissar M, Lubin Y, Katz HP, Banai K. Dyslexia and the failure to form a perceptual anchor. Nat Neurosci 2006;9(12):1558–64.

[105] Ahissar M. Dyslexia and the anchoring-deficit hypothesis. Trend Cogn Sci 2007;11(11):458–65.

[106] Scarborough HS. Connecting early language and literacy to later reading (dis)abilities: evidence, theory and practice. In: Fletcher-Campbell F, Soler J, Reid G. (Eds.) Approaching Difficulties in Literacy Development: Assessment, Pedagogy and Programmes. New York: Sage, 2009, pp. 23–38.

[107] Scarborough HS, Dobrich W. Development of children with early language delay. J Speech Language Hearing Res 1990;33(1):70–83.

[108] Galaburda AM. Ordinary and extraordinary brain development: anatomical variation in developmental dyslexia. Anna Dyslexia 1989;39(1):65–80.

[109] Poldrack RA. A structural basis for developmental dyslexia: evidence from diffusion tensor imaging. In: Wolf M. (Ed.) Dyslexia, Fluency, and the Brain. Baltimore, MD: York Press, 2001, pp. 3–17.

[110] Stein J. Dyslexia: the role of vision and visual attention. Curr Develop Disord Rep 2014;1(4):267–80.

[111] Witton C, Talcott JB, Hansen PC, Richardson AJ, Griffiths TD, Rees A, Stein JF, Green GGR. Sensitivity to dynamic auditory and visual stimuli predicts nonword reading ability in both dyslexic and normal readers. Curr Biol 1998;8(14):791–7.

[112] Farmer ME, Klein RM. The evidence for a temporal processing deficit linked to dyslexia: a review. Psychonom Bull Rev 1995;2(4):460–93.

[113] Stein J, Walsh V. To see but not to read; the magnocellular theory of dyslexia. Trend Neurosci 1997;20(4):147–52.

[114] Hari R, Renvall H. Impaired processing of rapid stimulus sequences in dyslexia. Trend Cogn Sci 2001;5(12):525–32.

[115] Amitay S, Ben-Yehudah G, Banai K, Ahissar M. Disabled readers suffer from visual and auditory impairments but not from a specific magnocellular deficit. Brain 2002;125(10):2272–85.

[116] Talcott JB, Witton C, Hebb GS, Stoodley CJ, Westwood EA, France SJ, Hansen PC, Stein JF. On the relationship between dynamic visual and auditory processing and literacy skills: Results from a large primary-school study. Dyslexia, 2002;8(4):204–25.

[117] Cohen-Mimran R, Sapir S. Auditory temporal processing deficits in children with reading disabilities. Dyslexia 2007;13(3):175–92.

[118] Ziegler JC, Pech-Georgel C, Dufau S, Grainger J. Rapid processing of letters, digits and symbols: what purely visual-attentional deficit in developmental dyslexia? Develop Sci 2010;13(4):F8–14.

[119] Lervåg A, Hulme C. Rapid automatized naming (RAN) taps a mechanism that places constraints on the development of early reading fluency. Psychol Sci 2009;20(8):1040–8.

[120] Temple E, Poldrack RA, Salidis J, Deutsch GK, Tallal P, Merzenich MM, Gabrieli JDE. Disrupted neural responses to phonological and orthographic processing in dyslexic children: an fMRI study. Neuroreport 2001;12(2):299–307.

[121] Gaab N, Gabrieli JDE, Deutsch GK, Tallal P, Temple E. Neural correlates of rapid auditory processing are disrupted in children with developmental dyslexia and ameliorated with training: an fMRI study. Restor Neurol Neurosci 2007;25(3–4):295–310.

[122] Stein J. Dyslexia: the role of vision and visual attention. Curr Develop Disord Rep 2014;1(4):267–80.

[123] Lovegrove B. Dyslexia and a transient/magnocellular pathway deficit: the current situation and future directions. Austral J Psychol 1996;48(3):167–71.

[124] Stein J, Walsh V. To see but not to read; the magnocellular theory of dyslexia. Trend Neurosci 1997;20(4):147–52.

[125] Stein J, Walsh V. To see but not to read; the magnocellular theory of dyslexia. Trend Neurosci 1997;20(4):147.

[126] Salmelin R, Kiesilä P, Uutela K, Service E, Salonen O. Impaired visual word processing in dyslexia revealed with magnetoencephalography. Annal Neurol 40(2):157–62.

[127] Livingstone MS, Rosen GD, Drislane FW, Galaburda AM. Physiological and anatomical evidence for a magnocellular defect in developmental dyslexia. Proc Nat Acad Sci 1991;88(18):7943–7.

[128] Vidyasagar TR, Pammer K. Dyslexia: a deficit in visuo-spatial attention, not in phonological processing. Trend Cogn Sci 2010;14(2):57–63.

[129] Vidyasagar TR. Attentional gating in primary visual cortex: a physiological basis for dyslexia. Perception 2005;34(8):903–11.

[130] Sireteanu R, Goebel C, Goertz R, Wandert T. Do children with developmental dyslexia show a selective visual attention deficit? Strabismus 2006;14(2):85–93.

[131] Misra M, Katzir T, Wolf M, Poldrack RA. Neural systems for rapid automatized naming in skilled readers: unraveling the RAN-reading relationship. Sci Stud Reading 2004;8(3):241–56.

[132] Vidyasagar TR, Pammer K. Dyslexia: a deficit in visuo-spatial attention, not in phonological processing. Trend Cogn Sci 2010;14(2):57–63.

[133] Amitay S, Ben-Yehudah G, Banai K, Ahissar M. Disabled readers suffer from visual and auditory impairments but not from a specific magnocellular deficit. Brain 2002;125(10):2272-85.

[134] Ramus F, Rosen S, Dakin SC, Day BL, Castellote JM, White S, Frith U. Theories of developmental dyslexia: insights from a multiple case study of dyslexic adults. Brain 2003;126(4):841–65.

[135] Ziegler JC, Pech-Georgel C, Dufau S, Grainger J. Rapid processing of letters, digits and symbols: what purely visual-attentional deficit in developmental dyslexia? Develop Sci 2010;13(4):F8–14.

[136] Schulte-Körne G, Deimel W, Bartling J, Remschmidt H. Auditory processing and dyslexia: evidence for a specific speech processing deficit. Neuroreport 1998;9(2):337–40.

[137] Stein J. Dyslexia: the role of vision and visual attention. Curr Develop Disord Rep 2014;1(4):267–80.

[138] Brennan A, Worrall L, McKenna K. The relationship between specific features of aphasia-friendly written material and comprehension of written material for people with aphasia: an exploratory study. Aphasiology 2005;19(8):693–711.

[139] Martelli M, Di Filippo G, Spinelli D, Zoccolotti P. Crowding, reading, and developmental dyslexia. J Vision 2009;9(4):article 14.

[140] Legge GE, Bigelow CA. Does print size matter for reading? A review of findings from vision science and typography. J Vision 2011;11(5):article 8.

[141] Spinelli D, De Luca M, Judica A, Zoccolotti P. Crowding effects on word identification in developmental dyslexia. Cortex 2002;38(2):179–200.

[142] O'Brien BA, Mansfield JS, Legge GE. The effect of print size on reading speed in dyslexia. J Res Reading 2005;28(3):332–49.

[143] Yu D, Cheung S, Legge GE, Chung STL. Effect of letter spacing on visual span and reading speed. J Vision 2007;7(2):article 2.

[144] Chung STL. The effect of letter spacing on reading speed in central and peripheral vision. Investig Ophthalmol Visual Sci 2002;43(4):1270–6.

[145] Yu D, Cheung S, Legge GE, Chung STL. Effect of letter spacing on visual span and reading speed. J Vision 2007;7(2):article 2.

[146] De Luca M, Burani C, Paizi D, Spinelli D, Zoccolo Z. Letter and letter-string processing in developmental dyslexia. Cortex 2010;46(10):1272–83.

[147] Arditi A, Knoblauch K, Grunwald I. Reading with fixed and variable character pitch. J Optics Soc Am 1990;7(10):2011–15.

[148] Di Filippo G, Brizzolara D, Chilosi A, De Luca M, Judica A, Pecini C, Spinelli D, Zoccolotti P. Naming speed and visual search deficits in readers with disabilities: evidence from an orthographically regular language (Italian). Develop Neuropsychol 2006;30(3):885–904.

[149] De Luca M, Burani C, Paizi D, Spinelli D, Zoccolo Z. Letter and letter-string processing in developmental dyslexia. Cortex 2010;46(10):1272–83.

[150] Martelli M, Di Filippo G, Spinelli D, Zoccolotti P. Crowding, reading, and developmental dyslexia. J Vision 2009;9(4):article 14.

[151] Spinelli D, De Luca M, Judica A, Zoccolotti P. Crowding effects on word identification in developmental dyslexia. Cortex 2002;38(2):179–200.

[152] Lerner JW. Children with learning disabilities: theories, diagnosis, teaching strategies. Boston: Houghton Mifflin, 1976.

[153] Lerner JW. Educational interventions in learning disabilities. J Am Acad Child Adolesc Psychiat 1989;28(3):326–31.

[154] Lerner JW. Attention deficit disorders: assessment and teaching. Pacific Grove CA: Brooks/Cole, 1995.

[155] Shaywitz SE, Escobar MD, Shaywitz BA, Fletcher JM, Makuch R. Distribution and temporal stability of dyslexia in an epidemiological sample of 414 children followed longitudinally. New Eng J Med 1992;326:145–50.

[156] Elliott JG, Grigorenko EL. The dyslexia debate (No. 14). Cambridge MA: Cambridge University Press, 2014.

[157] Potter CS. Using informal phonic inventories to identify spelling error patterns in children with learning difficulties. Johannesburg: University of the Witwatersrand, International Conference on Learning Disabilities, Division of Continuing Medical Education, July, 1979.

[158] Potter CS. The Phonic Inventories: an ipsative instrument for analysing the error patterns of children. Johannesburg: University of the Witwatersrand, Department of Psychology, 1996.

[159] Potter CS. The Phonic Inventories: Test Administration Manual Version One (South African Edition). Johannesburg: University of the Witwatersrand, Department of Psychology, 2009a.

[160] Potter CS. Information for test users of the Phonic Inventories Version One (South African Edition). Johannesburg: University of the Witwatersrand, Department of Psychology, 2009b.

[161] Rebolo C. Phonic inventories: a comparison of the development of spelling patterns and errors of normal and dyslexic children in grades one to seven. Honours research dissertation. Johannesburg: University of the Witwatersrand, Department of Psychology, 2002.

[162] Els K. The use of mental imagery in improving the English spelling, reading and writing abilities of Grade IV learners with learning disabilities. Honours research dissertation. Johannesburg: University of Witwatersrand, Department of Psychology, 2003.

[163] Els K. The Use of Mental Imagery in Improving the Simultaneous and Successive Processing Abilities of Grade V Learners with Learning Disorders of Reading and Written Expression. Unpublished Masters thesis. Johannesburg: University of Witwatersrand, 2005.

[164] Grasko D. The Phonic Inventories. Unpublished Masters thesis. University of the Witwatersrand, Johannesburg, 2005.

[165] Pereira C. An analysis of the short and long-term validity of the Phonic Inventories. Unpublished Masters thesis. Johannesburg: University of the Witwatersrand, 2008.

[166] Potter CS, Grasko D, Pereira C. Using spelling error patterns to identify children with learning difficulties. SAALED International Conference "Reading for All". Nelspruit, September, 2006.

[167] Potter CS, Fridjhon P, Grasko D, Pereira C, Ravenscroft G. Spelling error profiles: An index for evaluating the learning needs and progress of children in the classroom. Pretoria, ASEASA International Conference, July, 2008.

[168] Potter CS, Fridjhon P, Grasko D, Pereira C, Ravenscroft G. Content, construct, predictive, pragmatic and viable validity: Evaluating a test's conceptual properties and utilisation potential. Johannesburg: University of the Witwatersrand, Programme Evaluation Group, Virtual Conference on Methodology in Programme Evaluation, 2010, http://wpeg.wits.ac.za

[169] Potter CS, Fridjhon P, Grasko D, Pereira C, Ravenscroft G. The Phonic Inventories: A Technical Manual. Johannesburg: University of the Witwatersrand, Department of Psychology.

[170] Callander A. Using Phonic Inventories to identify children with learning disorders or barriers to learning. B.Ed Honours research report. Johannesburg: University of the Witwatersrand, Department of Psychology, 2007.

[171] Mazansky K. Using Phonic Inventories to identify children with learning disorders/ barriers to learning with specified spelling difficulties in a mainstream Grade 6 classroom in South Africa. B.Ed Honours research report. Johannesburg: University of the Witwatersrand, Department of Psychology.

[172] Ravenscroft G, Potter CS, Fridjhon P. Using Information and Communication Technology (ICT) to identify error patterns amongst children and guide their remedial intervention. Barcelona, Proceedings International Conference ICERI 2009, pdf 1294, November, 2009.

[173] Kruger M. A comparison of reading and spelling test scores and frequency of phonic errors in a remedial and a mainstream high school. Honours research dissertation. Johannesburg: University of Witwatersrand, Department of Psychology, 2011.

[174] Sfetsios N. The Use of Mental Imagery in the Treatment of a Child with Severe Learning Difficulties. Honours research dissertation. Johannesburg: University of Witwatersrand, Department of Psychology.

[175] Sfetsios N. The Use of Mental Imagery in the Treatment of a Child with Severe Learning Difficulties. Honours research dissertation. Johannesburg: University of Witwatersrand, Department of Psychology, 2002, pp. 82–3.

[176] Sfetsios N. The Use of Mental Imagery in the Treatment of a Child with Severe Learning Difficulties. Honours research dissertation. Johannesburg: University of Witwatersrand, Department of Psychology, 2002, pp. 83–4.

[177] Dr Graeme Maxwell, neurosurgeon, Sandton Clinic, Johannesburg, telephone conversations 1995, 1996, 1997 on child Q, 2013 and 2014 on child A; diagnosis checked by reading draft of this chapter 2015.

[178] Dr Graeme Maxwell, neurosurgeon, Sandton Clinic, Johannesburg, telephone conversations 1995, 1996, 1997, 2013 and 2014; conclusions checked by reading draft of this chapter 2015.

[179] Gillingham A, Stillman BW. The Gillingham manual: remedial training for students with specific disability in reading, spelling, and penmanship. Toronto and Cambridge MA: Educators Publishing Service, 1997.

[180] Caroline, Sister M. Breaking the Sound Barrier. New York: Macmillan, 1956.

[181] Lindamood PC, and Ages PDLA. LiPS: The Lindamood phoneme sequencing® program for reading, spelling, and speech. Globe 1998;864:288–3536.

[182] Geschwind N, Levitsky W. Human brain: left-right asymmetries in temporal speech region. Science 1968;161:186–7.

[183] Schulte-Körne G, Bruder J. Clinical neurophysiology of visual and auditory processing in dyslexia: a review. Clin Neurophysiol 2010;121(11):1794–809.

[184] Stein J. Dyslexia: the role of vision and visual attention. Curr Develop Disord Rep 2014;1(4):267–80.

[185] Spinelli D, De Luca M, Judica A, Zoccolotti P. Crowding effects on word identification in developmental dyslexia. Cortex 2002;38(2):179–200.

[186] Martelli M, Di Filippo G, Spinelli D, Zoccolotti P. Crowding, reading, and developmental dyslexia. J Vision 2009;9(4):article 14.

[187] O'Brien BA, Mansfield JS, Legge GE. The effect of print size on reading speed in dyslexia. J Res Reading 2005;28(3):332–49.

[188] Brennan A, Worrall L, McKenna K. The relationship between specific features of aphasia-friendly written material and comprehension of written material for people with aphasia: an exploratory study. Aphasiology 2005;19(8):693–711.

[189] Martelli M, Di Filippo G, Spinelli D, Zoccolotti P. Crowding, reading, and developmental dyslexia. J Vision 2009;9(4):article 14.

[190] Levi DM. Crowding—An essential bottleneck for object recognition: a mini-review. Vision Res 2008;48(5):635–54.

[191] Legge GE, Bigelow CA. Does print size matter for reading? A review of findings from vision science and typography. J Vision 2011;11(5):article 8.

[192] Stein J. Dyslexia: the role of vision and visual attention. Curr Develop Disord Rep 2014;1(4):267–80.

[193] Sireteanu R, Goebel C, Goertz R, Wandert T. Do children with developmental dyslexia show a selective visual attention deficit? Strabismus 2006;14(2):85–93.

[194] Lervåg A, Hulme C. Rapid automatized naming (RAN) taps a mechanism that places constraints on the development of early reading fluency. Psychol Sci 2009;20(8):1040–8.

[195] Chomsky C. After decoding: what? Language Arts 1976;53(3):288–96.

[196] Shaywitz BA, Shaywitz SE, Blachman BA, Pugh KR, Fulbright RK, Skudlarski P, Mencl WE, Constable RT, Holahan JM, Marchione KE, Fletcher JM, Lyon GR, Gore JC. Development of left occipitotemporal systems for skilled reading in children after a phonologically-based intervention. Biol Psychiatr 2004;55(9):926–33.

[197] Legge GE, Bigelow CA. Does print size matter for reading? A review of findings from vision science and typography. J Vision 2011;11(5):article 8.

[198] Fuchs LS, Fuchs D, Hosp MK, Jenkins JR. Oral reading fluency as an indicator of reading competence: A theoretical, empirical, and historical analysis. Sci Stud Reading 2001;5(3):239–56.

[199] Stein J. Dyslexia: the role of vision and visual attention. Curr Develop Disord Rep 2014;1(4):267–80.

[200] Scarborough HS. Connecting early language and literacy to later reading (dis)abilities: evidence, theory and practice. In: Fletcher-Campbell F, Soler J, Reid G. (Eds.) Approaching Difficulties in Literacy Development: Assessment, Pedagogy and Programmes. New York: Sage, 2009, pp. 23–38.

[201] Ramus F, Rosen S, Dakin SC, Day BL, Castellote JM, White S, Frith U. Theories of developmental dyslexia: Insights from a multiple case study of dyslexic adults. Brain 2003;126(4):841–65.

[202] Ziegler JC, Pech-Georgel C, Dufau S, Grainger J. Rapid processing of letters, digits and symbols: what purely visual-attentional deficit in developmental dyslexia? Develop Sci 2010;13(4):F8–14.

[203] MacDonald P. Paired reading: a structured approach to raising attainment in literacy. Support for Learning 2010;25(1):15–23.

[204] Morgan A, Wilcox BR, Eldredge JL. Effect of difficulty levels on second-grade delayed readers using dyad reading. J Edu Res 2000;94(2):113–9.

[205] Potter CS. Vision, intention, policy and action: dimensions in curriculum evaluation. J Edu Eval 1999;8:1–29.

[206] Potter CS. Programme evaluation. In: Terreblanche M, Durrheim K. (Eds.) Research Methodology in the Social Sciences in Southern Africa, 2nd edition, Cape Town: University of Cape Town Press, 2006, pp. 209–26.

[207] Potter CS. Multimethod research. In: Wagner C, Kawulich B, Garner M. (Eds.) Doing Social Research: A Global Context. Maidenhead, Berkshire: McGrawHill, 2012, pp. 161–74.

[208] Gillingham A, Stillman BW. The Gillingham manual: Remedial training for students with specific disability in reading, spelling, and penmanship. Toronto and Cambridge MA: Educators Publishing Service, 1997.

[209] Caroline, Sister M. Breaking the Sound Barrier. New York: Macmillan, 1956.

[210] Lindamood PC, Ages PDLA. LiPS: The Lindamood phoneme sequencing® program for reading, spelling, and speech. Globe 1998;864:288–3536.

[211] Schulte-Körne G, Bruder J. Clinical neurophysiology of visual and auditory processing in dyslexia: a review. Clin Neurophysiol 2010;121(11):1794–809.

[212] Stein J. Dyslexia: the role of vision and visual attention. Curr Develop Disord Rep 2014;1(4):267–80.

[213] Spinelli D, De Luca M, Judica A, Zoccolotti P. Crowding effects on word identification in developmental dyslexia. Cortex 2002;38(2):179–200.

[214] Martelli M, Di Filippo G, Spinelli D, Zoccolotti P. Crowding, reading, and developmental dyslexia. J Vision 2009;9(4):article 14.

[215] Hewison J, Tizard J. Parental involvement and reading attainment. Edu Psychol 1980;50(3):209–15.

[216] Stahl SA, Heubach KM. Fluency-oriented reading instruction. J Literacy Res 2005;37(1):25–60.

[217] Topping KJ. Peer tutored paired reading: outcome data from ten projects. Edu Psychol: Int J Exp Edu Psychol 1987b;7(2):133–45.

[218] Topping KJ. Tutoring. Genf, Switzerland: International Academy of Education, 2000.

[219] Topping KJ. Trends in peer learning. Edu Psychol 2005;25(6):631–45.

[220] Fisher CW, Berliner DC. (Eds.) Perspectives on instructional time. New York: Longman, 1985.

[221] Hiebert EH, Fisher CW. Fluency from the first: what works with first graders. In: Rasinksi T, Blachowicz CLZ, Lems K. (Eds.) Fluency Instruction: Research-based Best Practices. New York: Guilford Press, 2006, pp. 279–95.

[222] Hiebert EH, Martin LA. Repetition of words: the forgotten variable in texts for beginning and struggling readers. Finding the right texts: what works for beginning and struggling readers, 2007, 47–69.

Section 2

Organizational Strategy and Management

Quality of Undergraduate Distance Courses in Brazil — The Points of View of Human Resource Managers from Industrial Organizations

Ana Alice Vilas Boas and Gustavo Henrique Nogueira de Andrade

Additional information is available at the end of the chapter

http://dx.doi.org/10.5772/60657

Abstract

The main objective of this study was to assess the perception of human resource managers of industrial organizations in relation to the quality of undergraduate distance courses in the state of Minas Gerais. We asked human resource managers to analyze some attributes of graduated employees. We also requested them to compare some features between in-classroom education and distance education. According to the results, both undergraduate courses lack practical application of knowledge learned, since many of the graduates come to the market too naïve. This situation is more easily bypassed by graduates from distance courses, because they normally belong to an older age group. Regarding training of new cadres, many organizations highlighted the democratic role of distance education for continuous development of work force. It is because distance education is the main enabler of formal education for people with families and those without the availability of time to attend formal courses. These managers pointed out that responsibility is one of the most important characteristic of the employees graduated at distance courses. They are also better to associate theory and practice and to deal with modern technology. Moreover, the possibility of developing other complementary experiences to the course seems to be an interesting opportunity.

Keywords: E-Learning Assessment, Human Resources Management, Distance Education, Market

1. Introduction

In recent years, given a new federal government policy, there is a significant movement to increase enrollment in undergraduate programs of public and private universities in Brazil, with remarkable expansion of places for distance education. According to the Anuário Brasileiro Estatístico de Educação Aberta e a Distância, more than 2.5 million of Brazilians studied in distance education courses in Brazil in 2007, as in reference [1].

For this reason, Palloff and Pratt state that it is still necessary to increase the efforts to improve the quality of the services offered at distance education [2]. For these authors, it is indispensable that course coordinators, teachers and professors, course designers, and other professionals involved with distance courses search more and conduct more efforts regarding students treatment. In this matter, social psychology can contribute assisting in determining students' expectations and desires in order to assess the needs of apprenticeship. Additionally, other sciences, such as Management and Economy, may help to access market expectations regarding the performance and quality of employees who attended distance courses.

Bastos highlights that professional qualification can be understood as an important justification to the success of organizations and even to countries to keep competitive in the scenario of uncertainty and turbulences. Besides, the re-structuration of the production process demands new forms of action and reaction in the market, thus requiring new skills and competences to stay competitive worldwide [3].

As a result, many studies and researches about distance education are gaining strength around the world. In Brazil, we may give attention to authors who are investigating the institutions practicing distance education through methods that evaluate their competences. Among them, we may point out in [4-17]. Outside the country, we may give attention to other authors such as in references [18-26].

When thinking about quality and assessment, we must think about appropriate methodologies to the new market reality. Thus, according to Carlini and Ramos, in reference [6], the concept of evaluation should be understood by the following aspects: diagnostic, formation and somatization, as a practice that search to understand, ameliorate, qualify and quantify the processes of apprenticeship, giving them particular meanings and orientation to decision-making process in both in-classroom and distance education. In this matter, authors in references [11, 27, 13, 28] state that it is necessary to have a rigorous process of evaluation and improvement of the adopted techniques and methodologies just to provide credibility and recognition to distance education in Brazil.

In this context, this chapter will focus on the following questions: Do undergraduate distance courses produce a process of qualified and effective learning that contributes to the practices of people development in the market? If so, how do human resource managers from industrial organizations in the state of Minas Gerais evaluate the performance of their employees graduated at in-classroom and distance courses? In other words, what are the perceptions of human resource managers regarding the quality of the distance undergraduate courses offered in the market? Thus, the main objective of this study is to assess the perception of human resource managers from industrial organizations in relation to the quality of undergraduate courses offered in Minas Gerais.

It is assumed that graduated students from distance management courses contribute to the organizations because these courses empower individuals to work at marketplace without increasing management costs of people's management.

In order to verify this perception related to formation of undergraduate students, this research deals with themes relating to the aspects perceived by the organizations that demonstrate the effectiveness of the learning process of distance courses. We also identified the most relevant attributes that undergraduate students should have to be well accepted in the market, and the differences between graduated students from in-classroom courses and distance courses. The advantages and disadvantages resulting from the integration process of a newly formed employees, as well as the main contributions that have been raised from these graduate employees were identified and evaluated according to the points of view of human resource managers of industrial Organizations. It was also requested to human resource managers a comparison between in-class and distance courses that made possible the identification of common and divergent features of the two learning methods.

Keeping in mind the issues discussed above, this chapter will elucidate the quality assessment of distance education courses made by managers of industrial organizations in Brazil. The chapter will be divided into five sections: a brief introduction and justification of the theme dealt in the chapter; some considerations about the theoretical bases for discussing the fieldwork research; methodological procedures adopted to carry on the fieldwork; presentation of the results and discussions compared with the literature review; and final considerations or conclusion.

2. Literature review

This chapter deals with a literature review about distance education, contextualization of distance education in Brazil, quality in distance education, human resources management and employee's qualification, and the new roles of human resources regarding distance education in order to discuss the findings about quality of undergraduate courses in Brazil from the perspective of human resource managers from industrial organizations.

2.1. Distance education

Contemporary society has undergone many changes, which in turn has generated substantial impact on the educational process. Souza mentions that the technological, informational and scientific revolutions have had a lasting impact on the history of humanity. This unique and remarkable period can be understood through two primary factors: a scientific scenario extremely developed with a technological breakthrough that covered all fields of knowledge and the dissemination of knowledge that quickly affects people from different social classes [29].

Given the above, where the changes are quickly and intensely present in society, formal education is becoming more important. This is because education improves the employee's income, develops better institutions and organizations and brings economic and social development to the region or country [30].

Within this context, together with the beat and intense workdays, there is the rapid appearance of distance education in different countries. Nunes believes that the choice of distance education modality emerged as a means of providing educational institutions with instruments to meet the new demands for education and agile, quick and qualitatively superior training [31]. On the other hand, Moore and Kearsley present distance education as a planned learning that normally occurs in a different place of education, and because of this, it requires special techniques of course design, special education techniques, special methods of communication through electronic and other technologies, as well as specific organizational and administrative arrangements [32].

Additionally, Preti states that distance education is, therefore, an actual form of non-traditional teaching that is typical nowadays. It offers different ways of teaching and learning, using new methods, techniques and resources available for companies too, since most of its students have some particular characteristics [33]. These students are usually adults in the job market, live in distant places from educational centers, failed approval in regular courses, are very heterogeneous and with little time to study in classroom teaching.

In this scenario, these students seek this learning technique because they found it easier to plan their programs of study and evaluate the progress they made, and because they prefer to study alone than to study in regular classes.

Discussions on distance education (EAD) have multiplied in recent years. According to Suga, one of the reasons is that this system extends educational opportunities to a large segment of the population [30]. A great part of the population benefited from EAD system is made up of people who cannot attend classroom courses for various reasons such as long distances.

It is important to understand that distance education should be like a system that enables quality of knowledge and access to education, besides contributing to the democratization of knowledge. In other countries, this method has won its performance space and recognition for its quality and methodological innovation in addition to being regarded as the education of the future, in the societies mediated by information processes and technology [33].

When thinking about quality, we should consider evaluation methodologies consistent with this new reality. According to Carlini and Ramos, the concept of evaluation is understood through the following aspects: diagnosis, training and somatization, and practice that seeks to understand, improve, qualify and quantify the processes of teaching and learning thus giving them unique meanings and helping in taking new decisions, whether in in-classroom education or in virtual education [6].

In the technological age, where changes are so accelerated, knowledge management becomes critical to maintaining a competitive advantage in the market. Authors in references [10, 11, 34, 13, 35] state that companies have felt the need to develop their own educational systems geared to meet market needs, as well as to improve their relations with employees, customers, suppliers and the community in general. Due to this phenomenon, organizations have invested in the formation of the profile of future professionals, providing them with continuous learning opportunities and the development of attitudes, skills and abilities beyond the concern with theoretical knowledge.

Some time ago, companies began to realize that their greatest competitive advantage was at the level of training, knowledge and commitment of the entire team, including customers and suppliers. That said, it is observed that the effective validity of university undergraduates and graduate students is becoming increasingly reduced; that is, if the employee does not stay permanently updated, he will be outdated in a short time, even with a "suitable" title.

Thus, Vilas Boas believes that traditional training programs no longer meet the training needs and updated knowledge is required by market dynamics [10]. As a result, organizations face a competitive environment and seek in the lifelong learning process a way to build a competitive business intelligence that can proactively respond to the demands of the globalized world.

In this context, this study seeks to make a theoretical and practical analysis of distance education as an innovative element in the educational model, highlighting this mode as a resource of people's training and improvement in the business environment.

It is indisputable that in Brazil distance education is booming and has established itself, especially at university level. Some of the main reasons for this rapid growth are the repressed demand of not attended students, mainly for economic reasons, flexibility of time to attend in-classroom courses and geographical access to learning places. Another relevant aspect is that education for work is considered by many people as the best way to promote greater social equity and reduce the differences in constant competition for a place in the labor market [36].

Therefore, it is essential to improve the process of evaluation of distance education systems in Brazil and elsewhere. In addition to its wide dissemination in the country and its social and economic impact, EAD is a relatively new methodology that must be remodeled to suit the different needs of students and the market. It is also necessary to have a rigorous process of evaluation and improvement of techniques and methodologies adopted in distance education courses, just to provide credibility and recognition to this modality of education in the country as in references [27, 28, 15, 16, 17].

2.2. Contextualizing distance education in Brazil

The history of distance education in Brazil, and in the world, is not new. Brazil has nearly a century of experience. Over the years, it was not only successes and recognitions that have marked its existence. Probably, the first experiences in distance education in Brazil have been unregistered, since the first known data belong to the twentieth century.

It appears that since the 1970s there have been attempts to systematize the experience in distance education in Brazil, which effectively are not solidified because of government intervention, at the time of the military regime. With the transition to democracy in the 1980s, distance education had been overlooked and forgotten, because there were political differences about the projects and programs developed by the government. However, the 1990s saw a growing need for continuous and permanent education, as well as a debate on technological advances, which obviously made distance education emerge as a real opportunity to expand the education for the entire population, especially those who were outside of the traditional educational system [37].

For these reasons, it is relevant to highlight that between the 1970s and 1980s, private foundations and non-governmental organizations have initiated the provision of distance supplementary courses, at tele-education model, with satellite classes, supplemented by printed materials. This practice marked the arrival of the second generation of distance education in the country. It is also noteworthy that only in the 1990s the majority of Brazilian higher education institutions mobilized for distance education using new communication and information technologies. A study carried out by Chang and Smith showed that when information on the organization and operation of courses and programs in distance education are more transparent, and the students are more conscious about their rights, duties and skills, the experience of distance education will be more profitable for Brazilian students. Apart from that, they observed that the greater the credibility of the institutions, the better would be the experiences in distance education [38].

The enrichment of distance education came only with the Law number 9394/96 – Law of Guidelines and Bases of National Education, which included EAD in the education system and recognized it as a legitimate educational modality of the education system in Brazil. Even then, many misconceptions regarding this type of education still remain, hindering its enrichment and recognition as a specific field of information and as a specific and unique methodology of education [37].

According to a survey conducted by the Brazilian Statistical Yearbook of Open Education and Distance Learning (ABRAEAD), in its edition of 2008, more than 2.5 million Brazilians studied in courses with distance methodologies, in 2007, in the country. The data do not only include students in institutions of courses accredited by the education system but also large projects of regional or national importance, such as Bradesco Foundation, Roberto Marinho Foundation and the Group S (SESI, SENAI, SENAC, SEBRAE, etc) [1].

Several studies and researches on distance education have become increasingly important on the world stage. In Brazil, we can highlight some authors who are investigating the institutions that practice this type of education by methods that assess their skills, including [31, 4-10, 15-17, 39].

The development of distance education in Brazil, as well as in the world, is due to the technological growth of the media. It had moments of success as well as failures and resistance that remains nowadays in some countries. Some people maintain very large bias within distance education. Thus, researchers who believe that distance education is suitable to attend special needs fight to highlight its place in the education system. In this context, studies about the quality of distance education courses are gaining value in this sector.

2.3. Quality in distance education

Distance education has been consolidated as an important alternative to capacitate students in Brazil. It is worth noting that according to Abraead, there are 2,504,483 students officially enrolled in distance education, comprising all forms of distance education offered in the country. Specifically, among graduate students, there are 813,550 students registered in undergraduate courses [1].

Comparing the number of places in higher education in Brazil from 2003 to 2010, we can see clearly the role of distance education in the volume of places offered. It presents a strong growth over the years, even though it is notable that there is still a very long way to go and many spaces to be filled, as shown in Table 1. The number of students enrolled in distance education has grown from 49,911 students in 2003 to 930,179 students in 2010.

Year	In-classroom Students	Growth %	Students EAD	Growth %	Total
2003	3,887,022	11.7	49,911	22.6	3,936,933
2004	4,163,733	7.1	59,611	19.4	4,223,244
2005	4,453,156	7.0	114,642	92.3	4,567,798
2006	4,676,646	5.0	207,206	90.7	4,883,852
2007	4,880,381	4.4	369,766	78.5	5,250,147
2008	5,080,056	4.1	727,961	96.9	5,808,017
2009	5,115,896	0.7	838,125	15.1	5,954,021
2010	5,449,120	6.45	930,179	10.9	6,379,299

Source: In reference [40]

Table 1. Growth of in-classroom education × growth of distance education

According to data from Abraead, the average age of distance education students compared to students in in-classroom courses is seven years higher, and their age group corresponds to the range of 30–40-years-old. These kinds of students require special attention in order to get their attention to learn in this special mode [1].

Thus, it is essential to define a pedagogical approach to attend to those students and to assure quality of a distance course. There are many special features to be observed, as pointed out by Vilas Boas, Hamtini, Ferreira and Furtado. This pedagogical approach is a kind of guideline that determines since the planning of the course and its operation until the grasp of the objectives, represented by the presentation of content, the role played by its participants, the forms of interaction between them and the assessment of learning. The focus should be on the quality of material and in the fulfillment of the complexity of current educational setting [17].

Regarding distance education courses, they have shown over the years a functionalist approach, with presentation of content in modules, use of tutorials and objective assessments. In fact, an attempt to replicate the classroom model. However, in education as a whole, new concepts have been adopted as alternative models to explain the acquisition of knowledge, among them cognitive and interactionist theories – constructivism and social cognition, for example. They are looking for learning as a process of knowledge construction departing from critical reflections involving the active participation of the student, who must learn by interacting with the environment and with other components of the communities to which they belong.

Thus, studies and researches are being implemented by EAD proposals to adapt to the new reality. Nowadays, it is easy to have technological resources that facilitate communication and interaction. This technology brings new experiences from the perspective of distance and time, improving presentation of courses, the role of educators and learners, and the use of new forms of communication to compensate for the absence of physical contact. In addition to this, participation and evaluation can be reformulated to meet the dialectic of teaching and learning at a distance. The proposal for active learning is only possible in environments that generate interaction, collaboration, knowledge production and the possibility of customization or personalization of education. These aspects are directly related to constructivist, reflective, collaborative and interactivist theories that enable autonomous learning processes.

The concept of distance education is related to different situations, its features have more to do with historical, political and social circumstances than with the very type of education itself. These conditions, according to Pimentel, mean that there is a dizzying development of Information and Communication Technologies (ICT), mediated with satellites transmissions, Internet and multimedia material. So many variables contributed also to diversify the definitions of what is meant by EAD [12].

Cooperative work facilitates group learning and allows the creation of a deeper knowledge. According to Palloff and Pratt, the development of cooperation requires an environment and an appropriate way to study with the following features: (a) enable student groups to formulate a common goal for your learning process; (b) encourage students to make use of problems, special interests and personal experiences as a resource for motivation; and (c) take the dialogue as a fundamental tool of investigation, as in reference [2].

Collaborative learning development process begins with a plan that would lead to the formulation of a community that glimpses a common goal for learning. One of the steps to increase collaboration in educational processes would be proposing activities that enable students to associate everyday life to the problems presented in the course. Offering students the opportunity to explore and relate their personal experiences in working groups can become an important feature to stimulate participation and discussion related to the subjects they are studying. In this collaborative approach, the course pedagogical program directs the activities submitted to the groups, valuing the collective construction, individual knowledge and the application of this in contexts brought by students to contribute to the solution of the problem.

All these efforts towards the distance education allowed an evolution in educational applications, providing countless possibilities, with the convergence of different media technologies, hypertext, online video conferences and wireless technology, leading to many different pedagogical solutions. The resulting software ranges from solutions developed by specific university trainings to corporate integrated solutions packages, which are ready for the development of courses, and tools that can be coupled to other software and environments that provide support to various stages of the educational process. In fact, the biggest concern is not the technological product itself, but the pedagogical proposal of the institution that should be focused on the student and his learning procedure.

Distance education mediated by the internet, that is, an education with its own characteristics, possibilities and risks, has a number of challenges to be overcome in the pursuit of quality education. Initially, we emphasize the need for infrastructure, comprising software, hardware and telecommunication technology. These can be provided by the school itself or through its poles, or even provided by the student himself. However, there is in addition the need for easy handling, as pointed by Palloff and Pratt in [2]. In addition to this, there are the pedagogical level of challenges. Klering, Guadagnin and Biancamano point out some challenges to be overcome for successful distance education, as in [42]:

a. Need for attractiveness of content: due to greater autonomy of students in distance education, it is necessary that the content and materials should be of more interest to them to achieve a suitable performance;

b. Spirit of community: "to intensify the interaction between people with common interests, the virtual community tends [...] to lead to dissemination and knowledge generation and strengthen cooperation in the search for satisfaction of needs and objectives" [42, p.5]. This is the collective knowledge creation, only possible to the extent that there is involvement of students among each other. This integration between students should be encouraged by teachers and tutors and by the proper distance education system;

c. Development of an own cultural code: This code is necessary for the proper consolidation of the community spirit and a sense of belonging to an exclusive group;

d. Evaluation as a learning tool: the assessment should consider the rhythm of the students, allowing them to reach proposed goals. Thus, there is a need to assess to what extent the challenges that EAD brings have been overcome nowadays.

In this context, it is important to consider the roles of human resources team in providing adequate infrastructure and training to guarantee quality in distance education projects. These projects can be addressed to schools or universities, or companies.

2.4. Human resources management and employee's qualification

Binotto and Nakayama, in reference [43], explains that until the 1960s, human resources management in companies received simply the name of "personnel department" and "industrial relations", assuming a limited role of bookkeeping and records. With the evolution of administrative theories, the advent of the Theory of Human Relations, and with also the improvement of the theories of organizational behavior, human resources management started to move towards activities such as selection, definition of positions and salaries, training, benefits and social work.

Nowadays, human resources management tends to align itself more with the organizational strategy and to focus simultaneously on the internal customer (employee) and external costumer (market), as in [34, 13, 35, 44, 45]. In this context, most researchers and managers prefer to call it as people management. For this reason, a transition of the human resources management from a "department" to a "business unit" is observed. The results must be observed far beyond cost reduction and optimization of employee management activities. In other words, human resources management or people management starts to produce both operational results as well as knowledge within the organization. Consequently, the companies are able to convert these results into financial resources.

People management in organizational environment has become the object of study and practical performance, more and more intense. This statement stems from the typical phenomenon of this time such as globalization, outsourcing and new business models. Besides, managers are witnessing a time where technology development and the increasing industrial automation has caused significant changes to organizations, therefore demanding a constant qualification of its workforce [46].

Professional qualification delivers results for individuals, and consequently it will lead to gains for the organization. This qualification can occur both as in-the-job training or out-of-the-job training. According to Esi, educational activities are characterized as operating strategy in the pursuit of quality and productivity in organizational environment [47]. As a result, it enhances versatility, enrichment of tasks and increases employees' responsibility.

Human learning in organizations is divided into two major groups: the natural learning, which is configured by trial and error and the induced learning, which is obtained through carefully planned and structured situations [48].

An important aspect is that qualification involves at least three social actors: government, workers and businesses. So far, government qualification provides a way to ensure the productivity and competitiveness of the country itself, for workers qualification brings a strengthening of their autonomy and self-worth, and for companies that practice is associated with productivity and their own survival [10-11].

2.5. The new roles of human resources and distance education

Currently, human resources management tends to remodel, aiming to respond to the new challenges posed by the globalized world. There is also the tendency of aligning themselves more with the organizational strategy and to focus simultaneously on the internal (employee) and external costumers (market).

Then occurs a transition of human resources management from the "department" to the "business unit". The results must be observed far beyond cost reduction and optimization of employee management activities. In other words, HR starts to produce both operating results as well as knowledge across the organization, and consequently these results that become financial resources.

Ulrich, in reference [49], advocates that in a company, the current HR task is to achieve organizational excellence. Thus, HR has to assume a new role, focusing on results and not the traditional activities of HR, such as hiring and remuneration. According to the same author, "this sector should not be defined by what it does, but for what it is – results that enrich the company's value for customers, investors and employees" [49, pp.35–36].

http://dx.doi.org/10.5772/60657

Consequently, all of these changes in HR have influenced Training and Development processes (T&D) in businesses. Odenwald and Matheny, in reference [50], explain that the future of the business world trends is reflected even in the terminology, which is now adopted with respect to the development of human resources, such as control for autonomy, supervisor for mentor, competition for collaboration, matrix by network, provider for helpmate and driving by facilitation.

In this context of change, different factors led organizations and individuals to opt for distance education courses in order to keep update and attend market's requirements. On one hand, the inability of the student to have access to classroom teaching due to downtime or costs required to attend traditional classrooms or even the imposition of being constantly updated to meet the labor market requirements. On the other, companies that cannot dispense their employees for daytime training and companies in need of reducing training costs and qualification for many reasons. In response to these needs, not only the educational institutions have been offering this type of education as an alternative to personnel training, as well as the organizations themselves, seeking to qualify employees without interruption at work [35].

Thus, Carnoy emphasizes the importance of educational institutions as sources of knowledge transmission, and because they can also re-insert individuals in new companies built with high information technology [51].

3. Methodology

Companies of the industrial sector of Minas Gerais that have control over the academic training of their professionals were defined as the object of study. This choice is due to the importance this segment has on the state's economy and consequently, the role this state has on the country. According to the objectives of this study, we choose to perform a research divided into two distinct phases. Firstly, we performed semi-structured interviews with 12 human resource managers of small, medium and large industries. These interviews were carried on from August to September 2011. This number was established when it was observed the interruption of the marginal contribution of the interviews. That is, the interviews from this point did not contribute with more relevant information.

The first part of this work is qualitative; therefore, semi-structured interviews were conducted to establish a better interaction with the theme and research problem in order to gather more information that complement the quantitative method. The qualitative method, in turn, has characteristics of an exploratory study that are designed to increase knowledge about a particular problem. According to Triviños, this type of research, apparently simple, explores the reality seeking greater knowledge that allows planning a descriptive research in the sequence to deepen the knowledge about the subject under study [52].

For Triviños, in reference [52, p.146], semi-structured interview is characterized by basic questions that are supported by theories and hypotheses that are related to the subject of research. The questions bear fruit to new hypotheses arising from the responses of informants. The main focus would be placed by the researcher–interviewer.

The second part of the study relied on quantitative method characterized by a "survey". Thus, this descriptive research seeks to know more about the reality under study, their characteristics and their problems. Survey helps to accurately describe the facts and given reality of a phenomena [52].

The population for this research consists of 18.591 industries characterized according to the methodology of the Brazilian Institute of Geography and Statistics – IBGE, as small, medium and large industries, in the state of Minas Gerais. Survey respondents were made of human resource managers of these industrial organizations with more than 10 employees. They were asked to inform if these companies employ undergraduate students. From this universe, we got a sum total of 377 questionnaires answered through Google Docs. Data were collected from October 2011 to January 2012. The answers of the quantitative research were submitted to descriptive analysis.

4. Results and discussion

4.1. Profile of human resource managers and their organizations

Subsequently, in the semi-structured interviews we interviewed 377 human resource managers of industries in order to expand the analysis performed in the group of twelve interviews to a larger number of respondents, thus allowing statistical inferences to the population. Consequently, the interviews allowed us to raise the profile of managers of industrial organizations from the state of Minas Gerais.

To assess the profile of the current human resource managers of industrial organizations is crucial to characterize the scenario of people management policies, so it is important to have a panel about the age of the current human resource managers as shown in Table 2. We may observe that 52% of the managers have undergraduation degree or post-graduation degree. It is worth to mention that 6.6% of them did not finish high school or intermediate level of education yet.

	Frequency	%	% Total
Incomplete high school	25	6.6	6.6
Complete high school	74	19.6	26.3
Incomplete college	82	21.8	48.0
Undergraduate	98	26.0	74.0
Postgraduate	98	26.0	100.0

Source: Research data

Table 2. Managers' educational level

Table 3 shows the time managers are on their positions. We may observe that 54.4% of the respondents have less than 5 years in function. Another relevant fact is that there is a very

http://dx.doi.org/10.5772/60657

significant number of managers (32.6%) between 11 and 20 years in function, this shows stability in the company and job.

	Frequency	%	% Total
Up to 3 years	18	4.8	4.8
3 to 5 years	187	49.6	54.4
6 to 10 years	49	13.0	67.4
11 to 20 years	123	32.6	100.0
More than 21 years	0	0.0	100.0

Source: Research data

Table 3. Managers' time working in that industry

The respondents are up to 40-years-old in 67.4% of the cases, but the largest group of respondents are between 31 and 40-years-old, as shown in Table 4. Only 6.6% of the managers are older than 51 years.

Age	Frequency	%	% Total
Up to 20-years-old	0	0.0	0.0
21 to 30-years-old	107	28.4	28.4
31 to 40-years-old	147	39.0	67.4
41 to 50-years-old	98	26.0	93.4
More than 51-years-old	25	6.6	100

Source: Research data

Table 4. Age of the human resource managers

It is important to notice that in the age group from 31 to 40, we found more managers (18%) still taking their undergradution, as shown in Table 5. However, among the managers from 21 to 30-years-old, we found out that 14.3% of them already have their undergraduation degree. We can infer that some of these managers are studying at distance courses and we may say that nowadays many professionals are having more access to formal education than people used to have in the past. It can be also supported by data in the same table showing that among managers over 51-years-old, only 2.2% of them are undergraduates or are still studying.

From the point of view of the size of the organizations, according to IBGE definition, we observe that 47.7% of the organizations are small industries, as they have 11–50 employees (Table 6). Following the same definition, we have 39.3% of medium-sized industries, of 51–250 employees and 13% of large industries, over 251 employees.

Age	Incomplete High school	High school	%	Undergraduate	Post Graduate
Up to 20-years-old	0.0%	0.0%	0.0	0.0%	0.0%
21 to 30-years-old	0.0%	0.0%	2.7	14.3%	11.4%
31 to 40-years-old	0.0%	4.2%	18.0	6.6%	10.1%
41 to 50-years-old	4.2%	14.9%	0.8	3.2%	2.9%
More than 51-years-old	2.4%	0.5%	0.3	1.9%	1.6%
Source: Research data					

Table 5. Age of the HR managers × educational level

	Frequency	%	% Total
Between 11 and 30 employees	25	6.6	6.6
Between 31 and 50 employees	155	41.1	47.7
Between 51 and 99 employees	123	32.7	80.4
Between 100 and 250 employees	25	6.6	87.0
More than 251 employees	49	13.0	100.0
Source: Research data			

Table 6. Size of the organizations

Within the division of the activities of the responding organizations, there is a predominance of industries related to food production, beverages and tobacco (30%), as shown in Table 7. The textile sector is the second sector represented by 24.9% of the companies surveyed. In sequence comes automotive industries and transport of materials, the mining industries, metallurgic and fuel industries.

	Frequency	%	% Total
Mining	23	6.1	6.1
Food, beverage and tobacco	113	30.0	36.1
Textile	94	24.9	61.0
Fuels	19	5.0	66.0
Metallurgy	34	9.0	75.0
Automotive and transport	41	10.9	85.9
Other Industries	53	14.1	100.0
Source: Research data			

Table 7. Economic sector of the industries from Minas Gerais

Regarding the regions of the state of Minas Gerais, it is observed that the central region of the state of Minas Gerais have the biggest number of industries in this sample (Table 8). In the sequence comes west region with 21.8% of the industries. Central region has also the highest scores of formal education with 11.9% of managers still carrying on their undergraduate courses and 11.1% already graduated. However, we can see that west region has the highest score of managers with post-graduation degree.

Age	Frequency	%	Inc. High School	High School	Incomplete College	Undergraduate	Post-Graduate
South region	49	13.0	0.3%	3.7%	1.3%	4.5%	3.2%
East region	49	13.0	1.3%	3.2%	3.2%	3.7%	1.6%
North region	49	13.0	4.0%	5.0%	2.1%	1.3%	0.5%
Central region	148	39.2	0.8%	5.8%	11.9%	11.1%	9.5%
West region	82	21.8	0.3%	1.9%	3.2%	5.3%	11.1%

Source: Research data

Table 8. Region of the organizational industries × managers' educational level

The human resource managers interviewed indicate that higher education institutions located in the region where the industries operate meet partially the company's needs for 39% of respondents, as shown in Table 9. Another 34.7% stated that regional educational institutions do not meet their professional needs. Only 26.3% of the respondents said regional institutions meet well their professional needs. This shows that regional universities should look better for their courses in order to meet industries' requirements. It is probably related to the quality and kind of courses offered.

	Frequency	%	% Total
Partially yes	147	39.0	39.0
Yes	99	26.3	65.3
No	131	34.7	100.0

Source: Research data

Table 9. Superior educational institutions from Minas Gerais meet industrial needs

4.2. Mapping the graduates' skill and characteristics

According to the respondents, one of the skills observed in undergraduate employees is integration in the market. Table 10 shows that 44.8% of the managers stated that the level of integration of the graduate employees is suitable. However, 22.3% mentioned that their forms of integration in the company is very good. According to Vilas Boas, the qualification provides conditions to ensure productivity and competitiveness of workers, and therefore for their organizations, since qualification strength their own autonomy and self-worth, as in reference [10]. For companies, this practice is associated with their productivity and own survival.

	Frequency	%	% Total
Too bad	0	0.0	0.0
Bad	25	6.6	6.6
Indifferent	99	26.3	32.9
Good	169	44.8	77.7
Very good	84	22.3	100.0

Source: Research data

Table 10. Graduates' integration on the job

When questioned about the productivity of undergraduates, it appears that there is a prevalence of 64.5% of positive points of view; however, 13.3% of managers pointed out that productivity of undergraduates is not good, as shown in Table 11. This information about the productivity is supported by the information collected in semi-structured interviews where some respondents have mentioned the issues of low productivity of the new professionals.

	Frequency	%	% Total
Too bad	0	0.0	0
Bad	50	13.3	13.3
Indifferent	84	22.3	35.5
Good	193	51.2	86.7
Very good	50	13.3	100.0

Source: Research data

Table 11. Graduates' productivity

Productivity refers to the greater or lesser use of resources in the production process where raw materials are combined to provide an output, that is, how much one company can produce with limited resources. According to Megginson, Mosley and Pietri Jr. "Productivity is the amount of goods or services produced by an employee in a given period of time, taking quality into account." [53, p.534] Thus, an increase in productivity leads to a better use of employees, machinery, energy, fuels, raw materials, among others.

Given the above, it can be seen in Table 12 that motivation has the same characteristics as the understanding of the tasks where there is a high prevalence of positive assessment (65.8%) in this sample. Only 5.3% of the respondents pointed out that the level of motivation of the new employees is bad.

	Frequency	%	% Total
Too bad	0	0.0	0.0
Bad	20	5.3	5.3
Indifferent	109	28.9	34.2
Good	174	46.2	80.4
Very good	74	19.6	100.0

Source: Research data

Table 12. Graduates' motivation

According to Table 13, the skills of understanding tasks was appointed as indifferent by almost half of the interviewed managers (48.8%). It meets the speeches of the managers interviewed in the first phase of this research. Work activity synthesizes and integrates different factors structuring work process [54]. Thus, in real work situation, the activities give visibility to the determinants that affect their interaction with the environment and motivate people.

	Frequency	%	% Total
Too bad	0	0.0	0.0
Bad	25	6.6	6.6
Indifferent	184	48.8	55.4
Good	118	31.3	86.7
Very good	50	13.3	100.0

Source: Research data

Table 13. Graduates' task comprehension

4.3. Comparison between classroom and EAD graduates

In order to compare the perception of human resource managers regarding quality features of students' in-classroom courses and distance courses, we asked them to choose the options in a specific scale about quality features of undergraduate students as shown on tables 14, 15, 16, 17, 18 and 19. More information on these results can be seen in reference [39]. It can also be related to information in previous literature about distance education and e-Learning as in [3, 8, 10, 11, 17, 21, 22, 25, 30, 34, 48, 50, 55]. When it comes to the ability to deal with information technology, 75.3% of respondents pointed out predominance of the distance courses in relation to classroom courses, as shown in Table 14. This result is justified by the intense interaction with the technological tools used in distance courses.

	Frequency	%	% Total
Slightly favorable to classroom courses	0	0.0	0.0
Favorable to classroom courses	23	6.1	6.1
Indifferent	70	18.6	24.7
Slightly favorable to distance courses	215	57.0	81.7
Favorable to distance courses	69	18.3	100.0
Source: Research data			

Table 14. Comparison between ability to deal with information technology

Managers were asked to compare the quality of job performed by graduates from in-class courses and distance courses. Table 15 shows that 36.1% of the managers stated that graduates from in-class courses perform better their job. On the other hand, 34.7% of them said graduates from distance education courses perform better their job. The difference between the two groups is very short and not significant statistically. In addition, almost one third of the respondents are indifferent to this issue.

	Frequency	%	% Total
Slightly favorable to classroom courses	81	21.5	21.5
Favorable to classroom courses	55	14.6	36.1
Indifferent	110	29.2	65.3
Slightly favorable to distance courses	69	18.3	83.6
Favorable to distance courses	62	16.4	100.0
Source: Research data			

Table 15. Comparison regarding the quality of the job performed by graduates

Association between theory and practice by graduates is extremely important for industrial organizations. Regarding this attribute, the respondents stated they are favorable (46.4%) to graduates from distance education courses, as shown in Table 16. Thus, this is a useful indicator of the quality for distance education courses. Consequently, when industries invest in adoption of new equipment and mechanisms that require application of theory in practice, they may relay well on graduates of distance education programs. On the other hand, 41.2% are favorable to in-classroom courses for the association between theory and practice.

http://dx.doi.org/10.5772/60657

	Frequency	%	% Total
Slightly favorable to classroom courses	73	19.4	19.4
Favorable to classroom courses	82	21.8	41.1
Indifferent	47	12.5	53.6
Slightly favorable to distance courses	117	31.0	84.6
Favorable to distance courses	58	15.4	100.0

Source: Research data

Table 16. Comparison between association of theory and practice

Table 17 presents the comparison regarding the actuality of learned content. According to this table, both in-class courses and distance courses are both updated in terms of the content they offer to their students. However, there is 24.4% of managers who did not know well to inform, it is because they marked indifferent to this question.

	Frequency	%	% Total
Slightly favorable to classroom courses	61	16.2	16.2
Favorable to classroom courses	83	22.0	38.2
Indifferent	92	24.4	62.6
Slightly favorable to distance courses	95	25.2	87.8
Favorable to distance courses	46	12.2	100.0

Source: Research data

Table 17. Comparison regarding update of learned content

Regarding responsibility of the graduates of distance education courses and in-class courses, 67.4% of managers are favorable to distance courses (Table 18). This result indicates that by requiring a straight discipline to the conclusion of the courses, distance education provides further development of the issues related to individual responsibility. It is relevant to mention that discipline and responsibility to follow the activities and study to achieve suitable results are essential to this kind of course, but it also brings this quality feature regarding the degree of responsibility of the graduates from this kind of education.

	Frequency	%	% Total
Slightly favorable to classroom courses	33	8.8	8.8
Favorable to classroom courses	33	8.8	17.5
Indifferent	57	15.1	32.6
Slightly favorable to distance courses	172	45.6	78.2
Favorable to distance courses	82	21.8	100.0

Source: Research data

Table 18. Comparison in terms of graduates' responsiblity

When comparing the models of in-class and distance courses for the development of skills related to leadership, we observed that the regular courses present a large advantage over distance courses. In this case, managers informed that the development of leadership in-class courses is better in 54.9% of the cases (Table 19). On the other hand, 31.6% of the managers stated that graduates from distance courses are more skillful on leadership. In this case, closest physical contact may enhance the development of leadership.

	Frequency	%	% Total
Slightly favorable to classroom courses	73	19.4	19.4
Favorable to classroom courses	134	35.5	54.9
Indifferent	51	13.5	65.4
Slightly favorable to distance courses	49	13.0	88.4
Favorable to distance courses	70	18.6	100.0

Source: Research data

Table 19. Comparison between in-classroom and distance courses regarding leadership

Contributions from superior education institutions (IESs) can still be materialized by the transfer of trained personnel to companies and research institutes through agreements of technical cooperation and use of laboratories and library collections [56]. Therefore, this set of relationships replaces IESs in the center of the competitive dynamics of industry while playing a key role in sustaining the flow of innovations. For this reason, we asked industrial managers their opinions about the services offered by regional IESs to meet industrial needs in the region of the respondents, as in the main study, in reference [39].

According to the results shown in Table 20, the majority of the respondents stated they attend their needs partly (41.6%). Only 23.6% of the managers said IESs from Minas Gerais attend their employees' needs. This is an important general overview about the quality of courses and kind of courses offered in the region. A total of 34.7% of the respondents pointed out that superior education institutions do not attend their needs. It means educational institutions should get closer to industrial managers to know their needs and make strategies to invest in new courses or new models of teaching.

Region	No	Partly yes	Yes	Total
South	2.1%	7.7%	3.2%	13.0%
East	2.9%	5.0%	5.0%	13.0%
North	9.0%	3.2%	0.8%	13.0%
Central	11.9%	20.2%	7.2%	39.3%
West	8.8%	5.6%	7.4%	21.8%
Total	34.7%	41.6%	23.6%	100.0%

Source: Research data

Table 20. IESs from Minas Gerais meet industrial needs

http://dx.doi.org/10.5772/60657

5. Final considerations

This study aims to assess the perception of human resource managers regarding the quality of distance undergraduate courses. In search of a broader understanding of this phenomenon, we sought to characterize the managers from Minas Gerais industries and the industries of this state to map the most relevant attributes and the main differences between graduates attending in-classroom courses and distance courses. To achieve these purposes, we used a semi-structured interview with 12 managers and a survey with 377 managers from industries based in the state of Minas Gerais. The interviews allowed the researchers to construct the questionnaire and offered some relevant information to the whole research.

We observed that the development of a teaching and learning model does not necessarily exclude the other model, thus it is concluded that the challenge of human resource managers is to get the most of their graduates regarding the positive aspects of each modality. On the other hand, universities may use this information to improve the quality of their courses and even amplify their profile of courses, in both modalities of undergraduate courses.

According to the results, in-class and distance course lack practical application of learned knowledge, since many of the graduated students arrive, in the market, with few work experiences. However, this situation is more easily bypassed by graduated students from distance courses, because most of them belong to a older age group and many of them are already in the market when they attend undergraduate distance courses. This is an important feature regarding the quality of formal education.

In addition to this, we noticed that industrial managers pointed out responsibility as one of the most important characteristics of graduates from distance courses. According to these managers, graduates from distance courses are also better to associate theory and practice and to deal with modern technology. Although, they pointed out that graduates from in-classroom courses are better in terms of leadership. This conclusion proves that distance courses have to find a form of improving leadership skills on their students because leadership is an important issue regarding human resource managers and their organizations.

To sum up, we would like to suggest that new researches on this subject includes samples from other states. It is also important to consider analyzing the perception of managers from other economic sectors. The collection of more qualitative data is also relevant to have deeper perception about the good and bad sides of these two educational modalities. This research agenda can be seen as an attempt to deepen the knowledge about the use of distance education as an instrument of human resource managers. It is because industries can be directly beneficiated with qualification that their employees carry on through formal in-classroom and distance education.

We also suggest that new studies compare the performance of the same group of employees before and after attending undergraduate courses, since this study did not analyze quality education features in this perspective. Otherwise, it can be done in the first semester that some specific employees start in-classroom or distance undergraduate courses and in the first semester they graduate.

Author details

Ana Alice Vilas Boas* and Gustavo Henrique Nogueira de Andrade

*Address all correspondence to: ana.alice2006@yahoo.com

The Federal University of Lavras, Brazil

References

[1] ABRAEAD – Anuário Brasileiro Estatístico de Educação Aberta e a Distância. São Paulo: Instituto Monitor, 2008.

[2] Palloff RM, Pratt K. O aluno virtual: um guia para trabalhar com estudantes on-line. Porto Alegre: ArtMed, 2005.

[3] Bastos AVB. Trabalho e qualificação: questões conceituais e desafios postos pelo cenário de reestruturação produtiva. In: Borges-Andrade JE, Abbad G, Mourão L. (Orgs.) Treinamento, desenvolvimento e educação em organizações e trabalho: fundamentos para a gestão de pessoas (pp.23–40). Porto Alegre: Artmed. 2006.

[4] Bielschowsky CE. Educação superior a distância: uma estratégia para avaliação institucional. In: Desafios da educação a distância na formação de professores. Brasília: Secretaria de Educação a Distância, 2006. 237 p

[5] Moran JM. Avaliação do Ensino Superior a Distância no Brasil. São Paulo, ECA/USP 2007. Disponível em <http://www.eca.usp.br/prof/moran/avaliacao.htm>. Acesso em 20 de ago. de 2009.

[6] Carlini AL, Ramos MP. A avaliação do curso. In: Litto FM, Formiga MMM. (Orgs). Educação a distância: o estado da arte. São Paulo: Pearson Education do Brasil, 2009.

[7] Queiroz VC. Avaliando a EAD. EAD, Unicamp. Revista Digital. March 2003.

[8] Neves CMC. Referenciais de qualidade para cursos à distância. Ministério da Educação, Secretaria de Educação a Distância. 2003.

[9] Rodrigues R. Modelo de avaliação para cursos no ensino a distância: estrutura, aplicação e avaliação. Florianópolis. Dissertação (Mestrado em Engenharia de Produção) – Universidade Federal de Santa Catarina. 1998.

[10] Vilas Boas AA. EaD e Gestão do Conhecimento: A Experiência no Ambiente Empresarial. In: 12º CIED – Congresso Internacional de Educação a Distância, Florianópolis – SC. 12º CIED – Congresso Internacional de Educação a Distância, 2006.

[11] Vilas Boas AA, Martins LRV, Oliveira G de J Meeting Expectations in Higher Degree Programmes through Education at Distance: a new paradigm for rural sector. *ECHAE CZU, Prague, Tchech Republic. 2006.*

[12] Pimentel NM. Educação a distância. Florianópolis: SEAD/UFSC, 2006. 142p.

[13] Oliveira G de J, Trinta Z, Vilas Boas AA EAD x UAB: um processo de formação continuada dos profissionais da educação. In: Anais do 4th International Conference on Information System and Technology Management, Sao Paulo: USP, 2007.

[14] Vilas Boas AA, Oliveira G de J. Distance Education and the Brazilian Open University. In: 4th International Conference on Social and Organizational Informatics and Cybernetics, 2008, Orlando - Florida. Proceedings of the 2nd International Multiconference on Society, Cybernetics and Informatics, 2008.

[15] Vilas Boas A A, Silva SA, Oliveira G de J O Processo de Construção do Portal de Ensino do Exército Brasileiro. In: Anais do 6th International Conference on Information Systems and Technology Management, São Paulo: USP, 2009.

[16] Vilas Boas AA, Andrade GHN De, Hamtini TJ, Sousa SA de. Tutors and University Teachers' Perception about Quality Assurance in Distance Education: the case of the Undergraduate Management Course in Minas Gerais – Brazil. In: IEEE EDUCON 2011 – Learning Environments and ecosystems in Engineering Education, 2011, Amman – Jordan. Proceedings of the IEEE EDUCON 2011. IEEE Education Society: Amman, 2011;1:1–7.

[17] Vilas Boas AA, Hamtini TJ, Ferreira PA, Furtado RPM. Quality assurance in distance education in Brazil. In: Muyinda PB. (Org.) Distance Education. 1ed. Croatia: InTech, 2012; 1:157–80.

[18] O'Malley J, McCraw H. Students' perceptions of distance learning, online learning, and the traditional classroom. Online J Distance Learning Administration, 2010;2(4). Retrieved on October 11.

[19] Phipps R, Merisotis J. Quality on the line: Benchmarks for success in Internet-based distance education. Blackboard and National Education Association. 2000.

[20] Peters L. Through the looking glass: student perceptions of online learning. The Technology Source 5(5): 2001.

[21] Young K. The effective deployment of e-learning. Industrial and Commercial Training 2001;33(1):5–11.

[22] Rosenberg M. E-learning: estratégia para a transmissão do conhecimento na era digital. São Paulo: Makron Books, 2002.

[23] Jurczyyk J, Benson SNK, Savery JR. Measuring student perceptions in web-based courses: a standards-based approach. Online J Distance Learning Admin 2004; 7(4) 37-45.

[24] Johnston J, Killion J, Oomen J. Student satisfaction in the virtual classroom. Internet J All Health Sci Pract 3(2), 17–29, 2005. v.3.

[25] Belcheir MJ, Cucek M. Faculty perceptions of teaching distance education courses. Research Report. Boise State University Institutional Assessment Report. 2002.

[26] Willis B. Distance Education at a Glance. Series of Guides prepared by Engineering Outreach at the University of Idaho, 1996.

[27] Vilas Boas A A, Oliveira G de J, Martins N S An evaluation methodology for distance education in a regional consortium experience. Proceedings of the 1st International Conference on Technology Supported Learning & Training - Online Educa Moscow. September/October, 2007.

[28] Vilas Boas AA, Oliveira, G de J The Evolution of the Evaluation Methodology in a Regional Consortium Experience in Rio de Janeiro – Brazil. Proceedings of the 3rd International Conference on ICT for Development, Education and Training. Ghana, May 2008.

[29] Souza RP. Educação na sociedade do conhecimento. In: Fronteiras do pensamento: retratos de um mundo complexo. Org. Fernando Schüler, Gunter Axt, Juremir Machado da Silva. São Leopoldo: Ed. UNISINOS, 2008.

[30] Suga N. Educação à distância para melhoria da renda e do bem-estar social. In: O Brasil e o conflito social moderno: crescimento econômico x distribuição de renda/ Cira Souza e outros. Brasília, DF Instituto Tancredo Neves, 2001.

[31] Nunes IB. Noções de educação à distância. Revista Educação à Distância n. 5, Abr./ 1994 Brasília, Instituto Nacional de Educação a Distância, pp. 7-25

[32] Moore M, Kearsley G. Distance education: a systems view. Belmont: Wadsworth, 1996.

[33] Preti O. Educação a distância: uma prática educativa mediadora e mediatizada. Cuiabá: UFMT, 1996.

[34] Trinta Z, Oliveira G de J, Vilas Boas AA. Universidade Corporativa: uma vantagem estratégica. In: III Simpósio de Excelência em Gestão e Tecnologia, 2006, Resende. Anais do III Simpósio de Excelência em Gestão e Tecnologia, 2006.

[35] Costa Duarte, AF, Vilas Boas, AA, Capobianco, L. Preparing future EAD managers through a distance education training course. CIANTEC, Aveiro, Portugal, 2009.

[36] DIEESE - DEPARTAMENTO INTERSINDICAL DE ESTATISTICAS E ESTUDOS SÓCIO-ECONÔMICOS. A situação do mercado de trabalho em regiões metropolitanas. 2009. Disponível em: http://www.dieese.org.br Acesso 12/11/2010.

[37] Maia C, Mattar J. ABC da EaD.1 ed. São Paulo: Pearson Prentice, 2007.

[38] Chang SHH and Smith RA. "Effectiveness of personal interaction in a learner-centered paradigm distance education class based on student satisfaction." Journal of Research on Technology in Education 40.4 (2008): 407-426.

[39] Andrade GHN de. Qualidade dos Cursos de Graduação a Distância: a opinião dos gestores de recursos humanos. Dissertação, mestrado PPGA – UFLA, 2012.

[40] Vianney J. A EAD como inclusão social: O perfil socioeconômico dos alunos (2011). Disponível em <http://www.ricesu.com.br/colabora/n17/artigos/n_17/id02c.htm>. Retrieved on October 2012.

[41] Palloff RM, Pratt K. Building Learning Communities in Cyberspace. San Francisco: Jossey-Bass 1999.

[42] Klering, L. R., Guadagnin, L. A., da Rocha Biancamano, M., Kihs, M. A., & Pilla, B. S. (2004). Educação a distância para gestores locais: potencialidades e desafios. *RENOTE, 1*(2).

[43] Binotto E and Nakayama, MK. "Educação a distância no agronegócio sob a ótica das teorias da aprendizagem organizacional." *Distance education in agribusiness under the optics of the theories of organizational learning). Brazilian Congress of Rural Management–ABAR, Goiânia. (in Portuguese).* 2001.

[44] Vilas Boas AA, Andrade, ROB de. Gestão Estratégica de Pessoas, Rio de Janeiro/ Elsevier/Campus 2009.

[45] Vilas Boas AA, Oliveira, G de J, Capobianco L, Hamtini TJ Open University of Brazil: a pioneer experience in training professionals in the education sector. *ECHAE CZU, Prague, Tchech Republic. 2010.*

[46] Mourão L. Oportunidades de Qualificação Profissional no Brasil: Reflexões a partir de um Panorama Quantitativo RAC, Curitiba, v. 13, n. 1, art. 8, p. 136-153, Jan./Mar. 2009

[47] ESI MC. "The education of future and the integrating dimension of the new learning technologies." *Conference proceedings of "eLearning and Software for Education" (eLSE).* No. 01. 2011, 574-581.

[48] Abbad G, Borges-Andrade JE. Aprendizagem humana em organizações de Trabalho. In: Zanelli JC, Borges-Andrade JE, Bastos AVB (Orgs.) Psicologia, Organizações e Trabalho no Brasil (pp.237–275). Porto Alegre: Artmed.2004.

[49] Ulrich D. Recursos humanos estratégicos: novas perspectivas para os profissionais de RH. Futura, 2000.

[50] Odenwald SB and Matheny MG. Impacto global tendências mundiais em treinamento e desenvolvimento. Futura, 1996.

[51] Carnoy, M. O impacto da mundialização sobre as estratégias da reforma de educação. Mundialização e reforma da educação: o que os planejadores devem saber. Brasília: UNESCO/Brasil, 2003. p. 55-86.

[52] Triviños ANS. Introdução à pesquisa em ciências sociais: a pesquisa qualitativa em educação. São Paulo: Atlas, 1987.

[53] Megginson LC, Mosley DC and Pietri Jr PH. Administração: Conceitos e Aplicações. 4ª edição. Trad. Maria Isabel Hopp. Ed. Harbra. SP, 1998.

[54] Béguin, Pascal. "Design as a mutual learning process between users and designers." Interacting with computers 15.5 (2003): 709-730.

[55] Wentling T. e-Learning: a review of literature. Urbana-Champaign: University of Illinois, 2000.

[56] Monck JS, Letteri CA, Languis M, Dunn R. Learning Style Profile - Learning strategies of adult ESL learners in the US: a collaborative study. University of Alabama, Tuscaloosa, AL (1989) Unpublished manuscript.

Chapter 13

Increasing Access to Higher Education Through E-Learning

Susan L. Renes

Additional information is available at the end of the chapter

http://dx.doi.org/10.5772/60906

Abstract

Students with disabilities, rural students, students with parental responsibilities, and military students are populations who now have increased access to higher education due to E-Learning. Access limited by the location of the student, life circumstances that cannot be changed, or responsibilities that cannot be ignored, no longer act as barriers to higher education. This chapter examines how E-Learning benefits each of these populations and examines possibilities for international collaborations. The online environment has caused educators at all levels to re-examine how education might be delivered and who might benefit from this increased access.

Keywords: E-Learning, Access, Higher Education, Technology

1. Introduction

This chapter focuses on increased access to higher education that has resulted from E-Learning and reviews the literature addressing (a) students with disabilities, (b) rural students, (c) students with parental responsibilities, and (c) students currently serving in the military. A discussion of potential international collaborations that can occur thanks to the online environment is also included.

The National Center for Education Statistics [1] defined distance education as:

a formal educational process in which the instructor and the student are not in the same location. Thus, instruction might be synchronous or asynchronous, and it may involve communication through the use of video, audio, or computer technologies, or by correspondence (which may include both written correspondence and the use of technology such as CD-

ROM)...Hybrid/ blended online courses were defined as a combination of online and in-class instruction with reduced in-class seat time for students. (para. 1)

E-Learning in higher education has reached many unique populations. Students who have accessed higher education through E-Learning include (a) students with disabilities [2-7], (b) rural students who find it difficult to relocate [8-13], (c) parents with children [6, 14, 15], (d) military personnel [16-18], (e) students working full time [6, 19], and (f) urban students who find it easier to time-shift rather than space-shift [20, 21]. Renes and Strange [22] pointed out, "The National Center for Education Statistics reported in the 2006-07 academic year, 66 percent of the 4,160 2-year and 4-year Title IV degree-granting postsecondary institutions in the nation offered college-level distance education courses" (p. 204).

Students who have done well in E-Learning formats include:

(a) adult learners [23], (b) students who are self-directed learners [24], (c) students in rural areas [8, 25], (d) students who value interdependence [26], (e) students who must remain employed and require flexibility [25], and (f) students needed by their communities [8, 27]. [22, p. 204]

2. Students with disabilities

E-Learning has increased access to higher education for students with disabilities and allows many of these students to pursue their education in a place more suited to their needs than the college classroom. Some of the earliest work in distance education designed to meet the needs of these students occurred after World War II and the Korean War [28]. Texts were made available on tape; lectures were recorded; and students were taught using tutors, tape recorders, and the telephone. Herbert Rusalem was a pioneer who advocated for students with disabilities.

As Madeus [28] pointed out, in 1962 Rusalem wrote:

Physically handicapped college students requiring one or more special educational services are no longer a rarity on the American campus. Having the same goals as other students, they are enrolling in increasing numbers, encouraged by better public and private school preparation, improved rehabilitation services, the availability of scholarship funds, and a changing attitude toward disabled persons in our society. Since these sources of encouragement will probably become more influential in the future, in seems likely that the problems of educating the physically handicapped student will be receiving increasing attention. (p. 161)

Rusalem's [29] belief was that students with disabilities could achieve the high standards expected in higher education when certain modifications were made available.

In addition to students with visual or hearing impairments, students with disabilities who might benefit from E-Learning include students with cognitive or neurological disabilities (such as attention deficit disorder, autism, post traumatic stress disorder, traumatic brain injury, or memory impairments); physical disabilities (such as arthritis, repetitive stress injuries, quadriplegia, or paraplegia); and more temporary disabilities resulting from recent injuries or surgery [30].

There is currently momentum to evaluate and enforce the federal accessibility standards for online courses and this enforcement is significant, as it will allow students with or without disabilities to choose the learning delivery system that is most beneficial, given their particular circumstances [22, 30]. Three federal laws currently direct E-Learning programs with regard to accessibility standards: the Americans with Disabilities Act (ADA) and Section 504 and 508 of the Rehabilitation Act of 1973 [5, 28, 30-32]. Equal access to education is required by the ADA, and Section 504 provides for equal access to education but also stipulates that any educational institution receiving federal funding must ensure that web based programs, including E-Learning opportunities, are accessible to students with disabilities. Section 508 requires that types of technology are defined and include provisions that establish a minimum level of accessibility. The types of technology referred to in Section 508 include web-based and software applications, telecommunication products, and multimedia products [32].

E-Learning instructors often make their courses inaccessible without realizing it, as few instructors are trained to be aware of barriers for students with disabilities or barriers to accessibility in E-Learning courses [32]. However, it is the instructors' responsibility to make sure all students have access to course materials [33]. Courses designed to meet the needs of students with disabilities might also assist other students [34-36]. R. Mace in 1997 coined the term Universal Design for Learning (UDL) to describe a course design that improves the accessibility of course to students with different learning styles, different backgrounds, different abilities, and disabilities [32, 35, 37]. Far from being a "one size fits all," when done well, UDL offers various assignments and alternative learning tools to assist students. Roberts and colleagues [30] say students often do not want to disclose their disability for a variety of reasons and frontloading courses following UDL principles is especially helpful for these students. Tandy and Meachum [32] suggest that universal design helps "normalize" the experience of being disabled as UDL practices meet a variety of needs for students. For example, when an E-Learning instructor includes an audio and written description of the tools available to enhance watching a YouTube video, no student is singled out and all students might benefit from the enhancements in some way.

When designers follow UDL guidelines, physical environments, communication options, and the products developed are accessed by people with various characteristics including but not limited to:

age, race, ethnicity, gender, native language, and levels of ability to hear, see, move, and speak. When the range of characteristics of potential students is considered, distance learning course designers create learning environments where all students and instructors can fully participate, just as architects design buildings that can be used by those who walk independently, walk with crutches, push baby strollers, and use wheelchairs. [37, p. 236]

Some of the more common tools include (a) captions for lived synchronized media, (b) insuring colored images are available in text format, (c) providing spoken versions of the text, and (d) lectures that can be repeatedly paused and restarted.

The technology required for E-Learning might take time for students with disabilities to learn [35]. However, the career commitment held by many persons with disabilities is often a key factor in their completion of a higher education program delivered in a distance format [38]. The number of students with disabilities desiring higher education is on the rise and addressing their needs could increase the number of students participating in E-learning courses [30, 33]. "An accessible course makes it possible for students or instructors with disabilities to interact with others in the class regardless of impaired mobility, speech, or vision" [32, p. 314].

3. Rural students

Information communication technology now available to a large number of rural students has increased the higher education opportunities for these students, but E-Learning for rural students is still challenged by significant barriers. The success of the rural student appears dependent on adequate preparation of (a) the faculty, (b) the rural student, and (c) the college or university supporting E-Learning. Lack of preparation by any one of these three potentially reduces the effectiveness of E-Learning. Owens and colleagues [9] interviewed 49 non-indigenous graduate and undergraduate students located in remote areas in Australia who completed distance education courses between 2003 and 2007. Three significant barriers were identified: (a) feelings of isolation, (b) the knowledge and attitude of the teaching staff, and (c) the ability to use the required technology. The quality of interaction between the student and the institution and the amount of communication was seen as the key to success. Communicating frequently with individuals who appeared caring and supportive deterred feelings of isolation, but the perception of not being treated as well as the students on campus undermined the distance learning experience. These conclusions are similar to what other studies have found [e.g., 39].

Training for faculty for e-learning online instruction in higher education varies significantly across institutions [2, 12, 40-43]. Faculty willing to accept the challenge, who are not overwhelmed by the expertise needed to both develop and then deliver a course in this manner, are often small in number [44]. Understanding rural students so instructors can teach in a culturally responsive way and improve the students' learning experiences requires another level of expertise [9, 45, 46]. Instructors serving rural students need to acknowledge the reasons their rural students do not want to leave their communities to attend school. Are they needed in their home communities and families to serve a vital role, are the travel costs prohibitive, are they hoping to avoid some of the discrimination and racism that exists on college campuses? Remaining sensitive to the needs of their rural students is vital for faculty serving rural students through E-Learning. Serving rural students from Indigenous communities will be more effective if the unique learning styles of the Indigenous people are understood and incorporated and if cultural and linguistic traditions including Indigenous knowledge are invited in to the E-Learning classroom [46].

Getting started in E-Learning can be challenging for rural or remote students due to possible insecurities about learning, potential disruptions to family life, and the financial cost of education [9, 11]. However, a strong desire on the part of rural students to pursue higher education has also been reported [13, 22, 44, 47], along with an understanding of the self-disciplined and self-regulated style required by E-Learning and an appreciation of the access to qualified or specialized instructors. The partial anonymity offered in E-Learning can actually make participation easier for rural students [25, 48].

The sense of isolation often felt by students engaged in E-Learning, including rural students, is well documented [22, 36]. Rural students, many who are first generation college students or members of other underrepresented groups in higher education, appreciate consistent and respectful communication with instructors and other members on the main college campus [47]. Prompt feedback from the instructor on how they performed on assignments is reported to reduce anxiety and the sense of isolation for rural students. Students are not generally looking for social interaction in the E-learning classroom but they do want to interact with their peers, their instructors, and the course content.

Institutional factors necessary to successfully launch and maintain e-learning programs are documented elsewhere [22, 25, 40, 49, 50], but a factor pertinent to successfully serving rural students is an understanding of the digital divide [11, 13, 41, 44, 51, 52]. The digital divide is a term used to describe economic and social inequality that exists for certain populations with regard to their access to, use of, or understanding of information and communication technologies [53]. In other words, who does or does not have fast, reliable Internet service and who is or is not able to use it. Higher education institutions hoping to serve rural students must appreciate the limitations of technology in both student access and student understanding of the technology. Many rural students do not have access to personal computers, requiring students to rely on the computers available in local schools or community centers, if available, and many rural students do not have access to computer training skills or access to a fast broadband connection [9, 13, 51]. Colleges and universities committed to (a) increasing student access to technology, (b) increasing student understanding of technology, and (c) improving the types of Internet access available are likely to see an increase in student enrollment and improve the chances for rural students to succeed in higher education.

4. Students with parental responsibilities

Students who are balancing student life, family life, and possibly job commitments often find E-Learning courses fit more easily in to their schedules. Like the students who live in urban environments, having the ability to time-shift rather than space-shift makes higher education more manageable [20, 21]. Specifically, women who have families and jobs, [14, 58], students parenting young children [6], and students who are pregnant [54] were found to benefit from E-Learning. Parents can see the task of getting to and from campus (with possibly a side trip to child care) as overwhelming when other responsibilities are looming. Another factor that makes E-Learning appealing for students with parental responsibilities is their experience of feeling "out of place" on a college campus, which can jeopardize their academic success [55]. The E-Learning environment often puts students who are parenting in touch with other students who are juggling the same responsibilities of wanting time to study, wanting to spend time with their children, and needing to earn a living [56].

The scheduled time for many face-to-face classes often conflicts with family responsibilities. However, parents who pursue higher education are often doing so for their children as much as for themselves, as they see themselves as role models for their children [56, 57]. Integrating their children in to the educational process by showing them the E-Learning platform, talking about assignments, and discussing successes as well as setbacks was reported to help with the flexibility parents need when completing college courses through E-Learning.

Students who are supporting families are part of the category of adult learners, defined as students age 25 and older who have multiple responsibilities, experiences that contribute directly to their learning, and goals based on well defined needs [58]. According to the National Center for Education Statistics (NCES), between 2008 and 2019, the number of students between the ages of 25 and 34 is projected to increase by 28 percent and for students 35 years of age and older, the projected increase is 22 percent. This compares to the 12 percent projected increase for "traditional" college students aged 18 to 24.

Following a critical review of the characteristics of adult students and adult learning theories, Cercone [23] determined that high quality E-Learning for adult students includes (a) collaboration and social interaction with peers, (b) the opportunity to connect new information with past experiences, (c) immediate application of the new knowledge, and (d) the opportunity for self-reflection and self-regulation of learning. Integrating these elements allows for what Majeski and Stover [10] describe as deep learning, a learning that is collaborative in nature, includes self-reflection, integrates new knowledge, and is directed toward an application. Deep learning moves learning from memorizing facts to integrating new knowledge with that which is already known, enriched by the fact that it occurs in a social environment.

5. Military populations

More than any group of soldiers in the past, current servicemen and servicewomen have the financial and technological resources to pursue higher education while still active in the military [17]. Even when remotely deployed, the E-Learning environment has made higher education accessible, making almost irrelevant the geographical requirements that used to exist for higher education. The current unparalleled availability of E-Learning along with an understanding of the benefits of higher education among prospective soldiers makes distance learning an effective tool for military recruitment. Prospective soldiers are aware of the benefits of higher education that will be available to them in their post military lives [17, 18]. Most men and women who are enlisted recruits do not have a college degree because, in general, they enlist before attending college [18]. However, approximately 90% of the recruits have a high school diploma or have obtained a GED, making recruits eligible to apply to colleges and universities.

While the structure of the E-Learning might fit well for military populations, the success of the military student will depend, in part, on the instructor's understanding of military culture [16,

59, 60]. Soldiers who are also students often work very hard and can set high standards in the E-Learning environment as they have been trained in the importance of duty and discipline. Students who are in the military often show great respect to the instructor, and are often willing to follow instructions and meet deadlines, as these have been reinforced in their daily lives as members of the military.

Higher education may support military students moving up the ranks and because their focus is "mission based," they often benefit from structure and well-defined goals with activities that lead directly to those goals [60]. The well-structured format along with clear and active communication between students and their instructors is essential when teaching distance students who might be unexpectedly taken away from the online environment or might be working in threatening and stressful environments. Letting students know ahead of time how TDY (Temporary Duty Yonder), PCS (Permanent of Station) or unexpected military assignments will be handled will be greatly appreciated by military students, as is constructive, consistent feedback from the instructor to let them know how they are performing in the class. Colleges and universities offering classes in an E-Learning environment to military students should understand that military students often do not complete their degrees until after their military service is done due to the threat, stress, and the unpredictability they might be dealing with [17].

6. International collaborations

International collaboration among students and instructors occurs easily in online formats [25]. With online international collaboration, learning is expanded beyond the local context. Including various cultural groups in the online format invites new ideas and views in to the learning community, potentially enriching the lives of the students and teachers involved [61-63]. The increased diversity that international collaborations offer in the E-Learning environment increases awareness of global and cultural issues and allows experts from other countries to participate and share their expertise. Online international collaborations that develop can be structured in a variety of ways and often develop from ordinary people taking on what Ife [64] describes as "globalization from below," an approach by interested local parties not driven by governments or institutions, that often result in international exchange that is more participatory in nature.

Students, teachers, schools, as well as institutions, and governments can benefit from international collaborations [61]. Leppisaari and Lee [65] investigated an international collaboration between students in Finland and Korea focused on environmental education. Leppisaari and Lee found that students in the study were enthusiastic about the subject matter; the students shared information and documented real world solutions to environmental problems using mobile phones and digital cameras. This sharing of information allowed students in both countries to view environmental problems from a new perspective, allowing them to better understand their own communities. Along with the subject matter, the students were also excited to learn about the culture and customs of another school. As the result of the pilot study, Leppisaari and Lee stated that the collaboration showed the possibilities of "cyber space pedagogy" (p. 244).

Colleges and universities hoping to increase diversity in both the face-to-face and E-learning classroom have entered in to agreements with developing countries that have a need for postsecondary education, resulting in networks of international education [61, 62]. These networks can result in aid for developing nations and academic publications and other academic acknowledgements for the faculty. Successful frameworks are now available and describe how to develop successful collaborations.

With the new opportunities now available for international collaboration come new caveats. When a classroom has an international community, the instruction coming from one culture might not follow the norms of the other students' cultures [66, 67] and questions asked from a western viewpoint might not be relevant to students living elsewhere [68]. Differences in communication styles and differences in teaching styles, both heavily influenced by the culture of the teacher and the student, make pedagogical sensitivity essential [69]. Part of this sensitivity includes an understanding of electronic colonialism [70], which means imposing western values on students from non-western cultures in E-Learning environments. Leppisaari and Lee [65] point out that while international learning communities develop around common interests, the pedagogy often has not caught up with the technology. Organization, continuous technical support, time allotted for development of the structure of the collaboration, and time allotted to develop trust between the collaborators are all key to successful collaborations [62, 63, 68].

The development of successful online collaborations requires that each group of collaborators understand their goals, hopes, fears, the time commitment involved in setting up and actually collaborating, and their beliefs about what will occur in the collaboration [71]. International collaboration can be a dynamic experience when there is sufficient planning and understanding among all the parties involved [68]. When teaching critical thinking skills and creative problem solving, it is essential that students examine situations from a variety of perspectives, and international collaborations in E-learning offer this environment. Mitroff and Linestone [72] stated, "because of long and arduous years involved in mastering a particular discipline, the academic/professional mind easily becomes the prisoner of a particular way of viewing the world" (p.34).

7. Conclusion

Information communication technology has increased the number of ways students and instructors interact with each other, the location of students who do the interacting, and the types of learning and student communities that can develop. The UDL principles that assist students with disabilities were found to improve the learning environment for all students. When working with rural students, understanding the digital divide and addressing these barriers will further increase their access to higher education. Understanding higher education as it relates to recruitment and rank in the military and understanding the military culture will allow better experiences for military personnel who choose to pursue higher education through E-Learning. Suspending the demand for a four-year completion rate now seen in higher education will ease the pressure on all of these populations, probably more for students with parental responsibilities than any other student group. Finally, while acknowledging the "cyber space pedagogy" [65, p. 244] that could develop as the result of international colonialism, the possibility of electronic colonialism described by Boshier and colleagues [70] must also be acknowledged and prevented.

Can E-Learning also be a platform that does not support oppression and allows education to be de-colonized, offering opportunities for all those who for various reasons have been denied the opportunity? In examining the new opportunities now available to students with disabilities, rural student, students with parental responsibilities, military populations, and the opportunities for international collaborations because of the E-learning environment, it is obvious that access to higher education can be increased due to E-Learning. The challenge now available for E-Learning is how to make this new learning environment less oppressive, more inclusive, and more collaborative than learning environments in the past. Successfully addressing this challenge will not only benefit the E-Learning but improve the face-to-face classroom environment as well.

Author details

Susan L. Renes

Address all correspondence to: slrenes@alaska.edu

School of Education, University of Alaska Fairbanks, Alaska

References

[1] National Center for Education Statistics. (2008). Distance education at degree-granting postsecondary institutions: 2006-07. Retrieved from http://nces.ed.gov/pubsearch/pubsinfo.asp?pubid=2009044

[2] Austin, G. A. (2010). Administrative challenges and rewards of online learning in a rural community college: Reflections of a distance learning administrator. *New Directions for Community Colleges, 150,* 27–36. doi: 10.1002/cc.402

[3] Crow, K. L. (2008). Four types of disabilities: Their impact on online learning. *TechTrends: Linking Research and Practice to Improve Learning, 52*(1), 51–55.

[4] McNab, L. (2005). Interview: Speaking personally with Chris Dede. *American Journal of Distance Education, 19*(2), 119–123.

[5] Musick, K. (2001). Distance education: Promoting access and equity for adult learners with disabilities. *Rehabilitation Education, 15*(1), 63–77.

[6] Nightengale, B. (2014). Teaching honors online at a public college. *Journal of the National Collegiate Honors Council, 15*(1), 61–62.

[7] Spaniol, M., Klamma, R., Springer, L., & Jarke, M. (2006). Aphasic communities of learning on the web. *International Journal of Distance Education Technologies, 4*(1), 31–45.

[8] Chaney, E., Chaney, J., Eddy, J., & Stellefson, M. (2008). Making the case for distance education in the health education and health promotion profession. *International Electronic Journal of Health Education, 11*(1), 5–18.

[9] Kawalilak, C., Wells, N., Connell, L., & Beamer, K. (2012). E-Learning access, opportunities, and challenges for aboriginal adult learners located in rural communities. *College Quarterly, 15*(2), 1–18.

[10] Majeski, R., & Stover, M. (2007). Theoretically based pedagogical strategies leading to deep earning in asynchronous online gerontology courses. *Educational Gerontology, 33*(3), 171–185. doi: 10.1080/03601270600850826

[11] Owens, J., Hardcastel, L., & Richardson, B. (2009). Learning from a distance: The experience of remote students. *Journal of Distance Education, 23*(3), 57–74.

[12] Ozdemir, Z. D., & Abrevaya, J. (2007). Adoption of technology-mediated distance education: A longitudinal analysis. *Information & Management, 44*(5), 467–479. doi: 10.1016/j.im.2007.04.006

[13] Philpott, D., Sharpe, D., & Neville, R. (2009). The effectiveness of web-delivered learning with aboriginal students: Findings from a study in coastal Labrador. *Canadian Journal of Learning and Technology/La Revue Canadienne de L'apprentissage et de La Technologie, 35*(3). Retrieved from http://www.cjlt.ca/index.php/cjlt/article/view/545

[14] Carnevale, D. (2002). Distance education attracts older women who have families and jobs, study finds. *The Chronicle of Higher Education, 49*(11), A33.

[15] Ke, F., & Xie, K. (2009). Toward deep learning for adult students in online courses. *Internet and Higher Education, 12*(1), 136–145. doi: 10.1016/j.iheduc.2009.08.001

[16] Garner, G., & Keynard, C. (2000). Serving the underserved--distance learning: An alternative for the military. *Community College Journal, 70*(5), 44–51.

[17] McMurry, A. J. (2007). College students, the GI bill, and the proliferation of online learning and contemporary challenges. *Internet & Higher Education, 10*(2), 143–150.

[18] Vardalis, J. J., & Waters, S. N. (2011). Factors influencing military police officers in their decision in selecting higher educational institutions. *Journal of Criminal Justice Education, 22*(4), 479–492. doi: 10.1080/10511253.2010.534487

[19] Talbert, J. J. (2009). Distance education: One solution to the nursing shortage? *Clinical Journal of Oncology and Nursing, 13*(3), 269–270.

[20] Whitaker, R. (2007). Teaching online in the Bronx: Local distance education. *On the Horizon, 15*(3), 145–156. doi: 10.1108/10748120710825031

[21] Zhao, J. J., Alexander, M. W., Perreault, H., Waldman, L., & Truell, A. D. (2009). Faculty and student use of technologies, user productivity, and user preference in distance education. *Journal of Education for Business, 84*(4), 206–212.

[22] Renes, S., & Strange, T. (2011). Using technology to enhance higher education. *Innovative Higher Education, 36*(3), 203–213. doi: 10.1007/s10755-010-9167-3

[23] Cercone, K. (2008). Characteristics of online learners with implications for online learning design. *Association for the Advancement of Computing in Education Journal, 16*(2), 137–159.

[24] Salinas, M. (2008). From Dewey to Gates: A model to integrate psychoeducational principles in the selection and use of instructional technology. *Computers & Education, 50*(3), 652–660. doi: 10.1016/j.compedu.2006.08.002

[25] Appana, S. (2008). A review of benefits and limitations of online learning in the context of the student, the instructor, and the tenured faculty. *International Journal on E-Learning, 7*(1), 5–22.

[26] Smith, K. A., Sheppard, S. D., Johnson, D. W., & Johnson, R. T. (2005). Pedagogies of engagement: Classroom-based practices. *Journal of Engineering Education, 94*(1), 87–101.

[27] Southernwood, J. (2008). Distance learning: The future of continuing professional development. *Community Practitioner: The Journal of the Community Practitioners' and Health Visitors' Association, 81*(10), 21–23.

[28] Madaus, J. (2011). The history of disability services in higher education. *New Directions for Higher Education, 154*, 5–15. doi: 10.1002/he.429

[29] Rusalem, H. (1962). The physically handicapped student and the college faculty. *College and University, 37*(2), 161–67.

[30] Roberts, J. B., Crittenden, L. A., Crittenden, J. C. (2011). Students with disabilities and online learning: A cross-institutional study of perceived satisfaction with accessibility compliance and services. *The Internet and Higher Education, 14*(4), 242–250. doi: 10.1016/j.iheduc.2011.05.004

[31] Madaus, J., Kowitt, J., & Lalor, A. (2012). The Higher Education Opportunity Act: Impact on students with disabilities. *Rehabilitation Research, Policy, and Education, 26*(1), 33–41.

[32] Tandy, C., & Meachum, M. (2009). Removing the barriers for students with disabilities: Accessible online and web enhanced courses. *Journal of Teaching in Social Work, 29*, 313–328. doi: 10.1080/08841230903022118

[33] Hollins, N., & Foley, A. (2013). The experiences of students with learning disabilities in a higher education virtual campus. *Educational Technology Research & Development, 61*(4), 607–624. doi: 10.1007/s11423-013-9302-9

[34] Edmunds, C. D. (2004). Providing access to students with disabilities in online distance education: Legal and technical concerns for higher education. *American Journal of Distance Education, 18*(1), 51–62. doi: 10.1207/s15389286ajde1801_5

[35] Seale, J. (2010). Editorial: Disability, technology, and e-learning: Challenging conceptions. *ALT-J Association for Learning Technology Journal, 14*(1), 1–8. doi: 10.1080/09687760500480025

[36] Simminolli, A., & Hinson, J. M. (2008). College students' with learning disabilities personal reactions to online learning. *Journal of College Reading & Learning, 38*(2), 49–62.

[37] Burgstahler, S., Corrigan, B., & McCarter, J. (2004). Making distance learning courses accessible to students and instructors with disabilities: A case study. *The Internet and Higher Education, 7*(3), 233–246. doi: 10.1016/j.iheduc.2004.06.004

[38] Kim-Rupnow, W. S., Dowrick, P. W., & Burke, L. S. (2001). Implications for improving access and outcomes for individuals with disabilities in postsecondary distance education. *American Journal of Distance Education, 15*(1), 25–40.

[39] Ravoi, A., & Barnum, K. (2003). Online course effectiveness: An analysis of student interactions and perceptions of learning. *Journal of Distance Education, 18*(1), 57–73.

[40] Keramidas, C. G., Ludlow, B. L., Collins, B. C., & Baird, C. M. (2007). Saving your sanity when teaching in an online environment: Lessons learned. *Rural Special Education Quarterly, 26*(1), 28–39.

[41] Leist, J., & Travis, J. (2010). Planning for online courses at rural community colleges. *New Directions for Community Colleges, 150*, 17–25.

[42] Menchaca, M. P., & Bekele, T. A. (2008). Learner and instructor identified success factors in distance education. *Distance Education, 29*(3), 231–252. doi: 10.1080/01587910802395771

[43] Nicolle, P. S., & Lou, Y. (2008). Technology adoption into teaching and learning by mainstream university faculty: A mixed methodology study revealing the "how, when, why, and why not". *Journal of Educational Research, 39*(3), 235–265. doi: 10.2190/EC.39.3.c

[44] Cjeda, B. D. (2007). Connecting to the larger world: Distance education in rural community colleges. *New Directions for Community Colleges, 137*, 87–98. doi: 10.1002/cc.273

[45] Carter, L., & Graham, R. D. (2012). The evolution of online education at a small Northern Ontario University: Theory and practice. *Journal of Distance Education, 26*(2), 1–7.

[46] Renes, S. (2014). Amplifying indigenous voices. *Hybrid Pedagogy*. Retrieved from http://www.hybridpedagogy.com/journal/amplifying-indigenous-voices/

[47] Priebe, L. C., Ross, T. L., & Low, K. W. (2008). Exploring the role of distance education in fostering equitable university access for first generation students: A phenomenological survey. *International Review of Research in Open and Distance Learning, 9*(1), 1–12.

[48] Sullivan, P. (2002). "It's easier to be yourself when you are invisible": Female college students discuss their online classroom experiences. *Innovative Higher Education, 27*(2), 129–144.

[49] Dykman, C. A., & Davis, C. K. (2008). Part one: The shift toward online education. *Journal of Information Systems, 19*(1), 11–16.

[50] Mapuva, J. (2009). Confronting challenges to e-learning in higher education institutions. *International Journal of Education & Development using Information & Communication Technology, 5*(3), 1–14.

[51] Craduck, L. (2012). The future of Australian e-Learning: It's all about access. *E-Journal of Business Education & Scholarship of Teaching, 6*(2), 1–11.

[52] Raturi, S., Hogan, R., & Thaman, K. H. (2012). Learners' access to tools and experience with technology at the University of the South Pacific: *Readiness for E-learning. Australasian Journal of Educational Technology, 27*(3), 411–427.

[53] U.S. Department of Commerce, National Telecommunications and Information Administration (NTIA). (1995). Falling through the net: A survey of the have nots in rural and urban America. Retrieved from http://www.ntia.doc.gov/ntiahome/fallingthru.html

[54] Hordzi, W. H. K. (2004). The challenges faced by University Of Education, Winneba distance education student-mothers during examinations. *IFE PsychologIA, 16*(2), 243–254. doi: 10.4314/ifep.v16i2.23814

[55] Perna, L. W. (2010). Understanding the working college student. *Academe, 9*(4), 30–32.

[56] Reay, D., Ball, S., & David, M. (2002). 'It's taking me a long time but I'll get there in the end': Mature students on access courses and higher education choice. *British Educational Research Journal, 28*(1), 5–19. doi: 10.1080/01411920120109711

[57] Vaccaro, A., & Lovell, C. (2010). Inspiration from home: Understanding family as key to adult women's self-investment. *Adult Education Quarterly, 60*(2), 161–176.

[58] Kimmel, S., Gaylor, K., Grubbs, R., & Hayes, B. (2012). Good times to hard times: An examination of adult learners' enrollment from 2004-2010. *Journal of Behavioral & Applied Management, 14*(1), 18–38.

[59] Artino, A. (2008). Motivational beliefs and perceptions of instructional quality: Predicting satisfaction with online training. *Journal of Computer Assisted Learning, 24*(3), 260–270. doi: 10.1111/j.1365-2729.2007.00258.x

[60] Smucny, D., & Stover, M. (2013). Enhancing teaching and learning for active-duty military students. *American Sociological Association Footnotes, 41*(3), 1–8.

[61] Hastie, M., Chun Hung, I., & Chen, N. S. (2010). A blended synchronous learning model for educational international collaboration. *Innovations in Education & Teaching International, 47*(1), 9–24. doi: 10.1080/14703290903525812

[62] Holland, D. (2010). Notes from the field: Lessons learned in building a framework for an international collaboration. *New Directions for Higher Education, 150,* 31–41. doi: 10.1002/he.388

[63] Rautenbach, J. V., & Black-Hughes, C. (2012). Bridging the hemispheres through the use of technology: International collaboration in social work training. *Journal of Social Work Education, 48*(4), 797–815. doi: 10.5175/JSWE.2012.201100114

[64] Ife, J. (1995, November). *Globalization from below: Social services and the new world order.* Paper presented at the Asia-Pacific Regional Social Services Conference, Christchurch, New Zealand.

[65] Leppisarsi, I., & Lee, O. (2012). Modelling digital natives' international collaboration: Finnish-Korean experiences of environmental education. *Journal of Educational Technology & Society, 15*(2), 244–256.

[66] Keengwe, J., Onchwari, G., & Onchwari, J. (2009). Teaching and student learning: Toward a learner-centered teaching model. *AACE Journal, 17*(1), 11–22.

[67] Moore, M. G. (2006). Editorial: Questions of culture. *American Journal of Distance Education, 20*(1), 1–5. doi: 10.1207/s15389286ajde2001_1

[68] Vosit-Stellar, J., Morse, A. B., & Mitrea, N. (2011). Evolution of an international collaboration: A unique experience across borders. *Clinical Journal of Oncology Nursing, 15*(5), 564–566.

[69] EBS (2008). *The East and the West.* Seoul, Korea: Educational Broadcasting System. Retrieved from https://www.youtube.com/watch?v=RnyaD1ZjS-s

[70] Boshier, R., Wilson, M., & Qayyum, A. (1998). Lifelong education and the world wide web: American hegemony or diverse utopia? *International Journal of Lifelong Learning, 18*(4), 275–285. doi: 10.1080/026013799293694

[71] Samuel, M. A., & Mariaye, H. (2014) De-colonising international collaboration: The University of KwaZulu-Natal-Mauritius Institute of Education Cohort PhD programme, *Compare: A Journal of Comparative and International Education, 44*(4), 501–521. doi: 10.1080/03057925.2013.795100

[72] Mitroff, I., & Linestone, H. (1993). The unbounded mind: Breaking the chains of traditional business thinking. New York, NY: Oxford University Press.

Chapter 14

Differences in Perceived Benefit, Use, and Learner Satisfaction between Open Source LMS and Proprietary LMS

Ahmad Rafi, Khairulanuar Samsudin and
Hafizul Fahri Hanafi

Additional information is available at the end of the chapter

http://dx.doi.org/10.5772/60670

Abstract

Currently, many institutions are using expensive proprietary learning management systems (LMSs). Open source LMSs have been introduced to offer affordable solutions; however, these solutions have not been fully embraced. The researchers undertook a study to examine the differences between these two types of LMSs. This study used a survey to collect data pertaining to perceived benefit, LMS use, and learner satisfaction. The survey sample comprised 608 information technology (IT) major undergraduates from two Malaysian universities. Two groups were set up based on the LMSs used, where the first group (n = 290) and the second group (n = 318) used the proprietary and open source solutions, respectively. Students were asked to fill out a questionnaire to elicit their opinions concerning constructs *perceived benefit*, *use*, and *learner satisfaction*, and data were analyzed using SPSS (ver. 19). Independent sample t-tests were performed, indicating that there were significant differences in the three constructs, which favored the open source solution. Correlational analysis showed that each construct correlated significantly with each other, suggesting that each contributes to the overall effectiveness of the system. These findings reinforce the imperative of deploying open source learning solutions that are not only affordable but also effective to support students' needs for effective online learning.

Keywords: Learner satisfaction, open source LMS, perceived benefit, proprietary LMS, use

1. Introduction

Today's educational realm is witnessing an ongoing tremendous transformation in the teaching and learning process as the result of the continual advancement of technology. For decades, learners were immersed in learning settings that were dictated by physical learning tools (which was naturally cumbersome), confined learning spaces, and the presence of the teacher. Then, this learning landscape changed to a better setting, with the introduction of the then technology – the monochrome television (TV). The teacher, on certain occasions, showed students the scheduled broadcast over the educational channel containing pre-recorded teaching topics relevant to the current learning objectives. In the same period, many public universities that offered distance-learning courses began to conduct such learning classes by broadcasting live lectures to students in their designated classes, which were geographically spread across the country. Even though this type of learning environment was not exactly perfect, many students managed to learn quite effectively with minimum cost. Later, this learning setting morphed into a revolutionized teaching and learning environment in response to the advancement of the personal computing platform together with the introduction of the Internet, especially the World Wide Web. Hence, the birth of electronic learning (e-learning) was inevitable, bringing in tremendous benefit to the educational, social, and economical spheres. From the educational perspective, students' independent learning becomes more intense with more online materials and contents being delivered over the Internet and Intranet. This intensification of independent learning has shifted the role of instructors – from being the teacher to the facilitator, especially in collaborative learning classes.

Given the enormous economic and educational potential of e-learning, many solutions have been introduced since the late 1990s. These solutions assume many different terms or names, such as course management system (CMS), learning content management system (LCMS), virtual learning environment (VLE), virtual learning system (VLS), learning portal, or e-learning platform, which reflects the many flavors of their functionalities. Among these, LMS is the dominant term commonly used in the educational sphere that focuses on learners rather than learning contents. The literature is quite replete with many definitions of LMS. For example, an LMS is "[a] comprehensive, integrated software [application] that the development, delivery, assessment, and administration of courses in traditional face-to-face, blended, or online learning environments" [1]. In a similar tone, Ref. [2] defined an LMS as "... as a software application for the administration, documentation, tracking, reporting and delivery of e-learning education courses or training programs."

Many learning management system (LMS) companies have entered the market to provide online learning solutions to many institutes of higher learning (IHLs). Invariably, these proprietary LMSs were, and still are, prohibitively expensive to other branches of educational sphere, such as public schools, colleges, and training institutions. The licenses of the LMSs are notoriously exorbitant, ranging from tens of thousands to hundreds of thousands (depending on the scale of users). In fact, the costing of LMS covers not only the cost of acquisition, but installation, customization, and maintenance costs as well. To highlight the impact of the preceding factors, the finding of a survey by eLearning Guild survey [3] involving 909 of its members serves as a guideline for any prospective organizations that decide to implement these learning solutions. Depending on the scale and needs of an organization, the cost of acquisition, installation, and customization can range from as low as $10,000 to more than $1 million. On top of this cost, the maintenance of such a system will incur additional cost, ranging from $10,000 to more than $250,000 annually. Clearly, the overall cost of running these learning management systems is quite staggering, especially for small organizations. Despite these cost constraints, many institutions still prefer to use proprietary LMSs because of several factors, such as ease of upgrades, security, downtime, and support, which are relatively better handled by proprietary systems [4].

In view of the high initial cost of implementation, many non-profit organizations, such as the open source software (OSS) community (which consists of dedicated individuals or teams) have begun developing their own version of LMS, with considerable degree of success. According to a white paper by Ref. [5], "[o]pen-source solutions are software for which the source code is provided under a license that permits users to access, change, and improve it." Likewise, Ref. [6] defined open source software solutions as "... computer solutions or applications that are developed, tested, updated, and distributed among the community members." The development of open source LMSs entails the utilization of open source platforms, such as PHP/MySQL, Java, Python, Ruby on Rails, or on open source content management systems (CMS), such as Joomla and Drupal [7]. In addition, open source LMSs, such as Moodle, Sakai, and Wordpress, are built on content management systems, such as Joomla and Drupal. Initially, open source systems were built for education, but now they have been adopted by both educational organizations and some companies as well [7].

From the initial outlay perspective, "several OSS systems can help mitigate the ever-increasing licensing fee of commercial providers" [8]. In fact, in certain functionalities, they may have surpassed certain performances of the proprietary LMSs. For example, better customization, intuitive navigation, "simple chat tool" [9] and "highly interactive" [10] are some of the features of the OSS systems that users found to be appealing. "Ample evidence can be gleaned from the relevant literature that supports the use of affordable OSS systems to help improve student leaning" [9,11,12]. Then again, the superiority of one system over the others may no longer hold true when the latter may have made further improvements, far exceeding the former. Nonetheless, there are bound to be intrinsic differences between OSS and licensed LMSs, which cover a range of features, functionalities, and characteristics. These differences in functionalities or features could make – depending on the background of a range of stakeholders, such as the end user (e.g., students and lecturers) and the system administrator – certain LMS systems more preferable compared to others. For example, the end user would naturally prefer an LMS system that is easy to use, while the system administrator would desire an LMS system that is easy to maintain. Irrespective of the types of LMSs, these learning solutions should be able to perform the following core functions for educational purposes as follows [2]:

- Centralize and automate administrative functions
- Use self-service and self-guided services

- Assemble and deliver learning content rapidly
- Consolidate training initiatives on a scalable web-based platform
- Support portability and standards
- Personalize content and enable knowledge reuse

Figure 1 shows a snapshot of the learning materials interface of an LMS system indicating available lecture and presentation notes to registered students of a particular course, serving as the third core function (i.e., Assemble and deliver learning content rapidly) of any LMS systems as mentioned above.

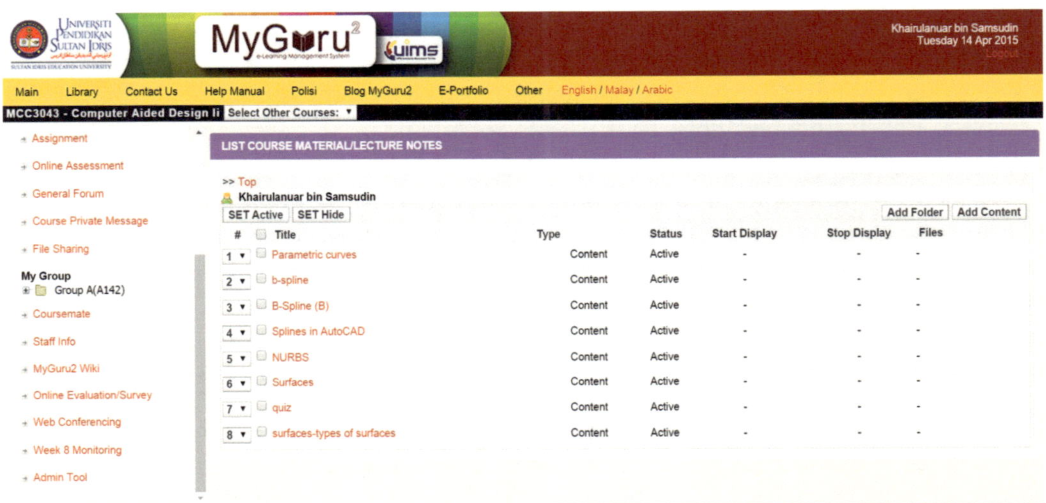

Figure 1. A snapshot of a learning materials interface

Implementing LMSs for learning purposes that involves audiences consisting of students, teachers, and administrators would entail the following features [13]:

- Registration and Enrollment options to teachers and students.
- Adding/Deleting Courses by the University/Educational Bodies.
- Setting the different User Roles and user account.
- Setting the course calendar.
- Uploading and Retrieving Assignment and Resources
- Forum module

Figure 2 shows a snapshot of the group forum interface of an LMS system that can setup to facilitate discussion among a group of students involved in a project or an assignment. Through this online forum, students will be able to discuss their ongoing work without the usual constraints faced by face-to-face discussion, namely, time and place. At any time, at any place every member of the group can compose and post comments to collaborate on that work.

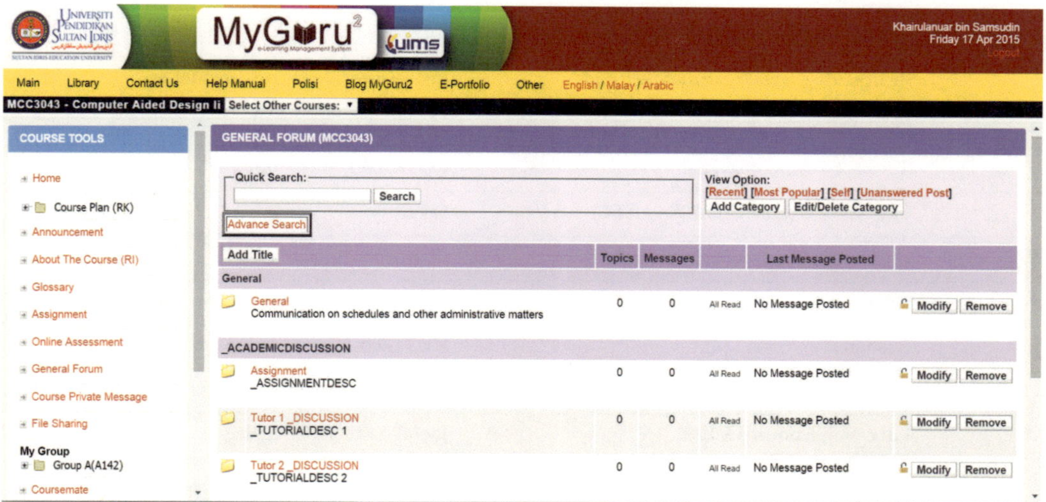

Figure 2. A snapshot of a group forum interface

In general, there are two main categories of learning management system, namely Education LMS and Corporate LMS [7]. The former primarily focuses on learners and learning facilities, launching and monitoring of online learning, and keeping record of learning activities. On the other hand, even though the latter shares similar functionalities as the former, corporate LMS is also equipped with e-Commerce capability, regulatory compliance, competency, performance, human capital, and talent management [7]. For Education LMS, there are two categories: a) commercial (proprietary) Education LMS, and b) open source Education LMS. In fact, there is another category involving systems (which is small in number) that were developed by the universities themselves. Examples of the university-built systems include Brigham Young University, Maryland University, University of Phoenix, Western Governors University, and the Oberta University in Catalonia, among others. Currently, there are about 214 commercial Education LMSs available. In contrast, for open source Education LMSs, the number is about 60, and this number is expected to grow enormously as they become more technically mature over the years, enabling improved installation and customization. Table 1 shows some examples of both types of Education LMSs commonly used by universities worldwide.

Leading commercial Education LMS include Blackboard Learn (Blackboard Inc.), Desire2Learn (D2L) Brightspace, Edmodo (Edmodo LLC), Instructure Canvas (Instructure Inc.), Pearson LearningStudio, and Schoology (Schoology, Inc.). For open source Education LMS, popular systems include ATutor (University of Toronto), eFront (Epignosis Ltd.), ILIAS 4 e-Learning, Instructure Canvas (Instructure Inc.), Moodle (open source), OpenOLAT, Sakai, and Chamilo. Clearly, commercial Education LMSs still dominate the educational landscape

No.	Commercial Education LMS	Open source Education LMSs
1	Blackboard Learn (Blackboard Inc.)*	ATutor (University of Toronto)*
2	Desire2Learn (D2L) Brightspace *	eFront (Epignosis Ltd.)*
3	Edmodo (Edmodo LLC) *	ILIAS 4 e-Learning*
4	Instructure Canvas (Instructure Inc.) *	Instructure Canvas (Instructure Inc.)*
5	Pearson LearningStudio	Moodle (open source)*
6	Schoology (Schoology, Inc.) *	OpenOLAT*
7	CourseWebs (Case Consulting, LLC)	Sakai*
8	Collaborise Classroom (DemocraSoft)	Chamilo*
9	AdrennaLearn (Adrenna Inc.)	CourseWork (Stanford University)
10	Academic Systems LMS	LMS Global BusinessLMS
11	Destiny One (Destiny Solutions Inc.)	Google Classroom
12	Education Elements HLMS	JoomlaLMS (JoomlaLMS)
13	eScholar (eScholar LLC)	Open LMS
14	FrogLearn (FrogEducation Ltd.)	EctoLearning (Ecto, LLC)
15	Helix LMS (Helix Education)	Sensei (Woothemes)
16	InYourClass (InYourClass.com)	Uzity (Foradian Technologies)
17	JoomlaLMS (Joomla LMS)	Metacoon Metastudy
18	Krawler LMS (Krawler Networks)	OpenSWAD
19	McGraw-Hill Connect	Whiteboard Courseware System
20	Top Scholar (Top Scholar)	WeBWorK

* Leading, popular LMS

Table 1. Some examples of commercial and open source Education LMSs used by universities

compared to open source Education LMSs. This is not surprising given the former's earlier adoption by many major corporations for the training of their personnel. However, open source Education LMSs are tailing closely behind their commercial counterparts for reasons as explained earlier. With greater effort by the open source movement, this type of learning systems is poised to make greater inroad in online learning environments in the near future.

In general, IHLs can adopt two categories of LMSs – either licensed (proprietary) systems or non-licensed (OSS) systems. WebCT, Blackboard, MyGuru, eCollege, and LearningSpace are some of the examples of the former category; on the other hand, Moodle, ILIAS, ATutor, and Claroline represent some of the latter systems. Undisputedly, deciding on which one of the two will rely on many aspects, such as user acceptance, technical support, maintenance, training, servicing, and cost of ownership, which will have an overall significant impact on the use of the system.

http://dx.doi.org/10.5772/60670

For any technology implementations, the ultimate aim is to ensure that the intended users (e.g., students, executives, trainees, or personnel) will be able to improve their knowledge and skills after using such systems. More importantly, users must be made to realize that the systems are indispensable to the efforts to make them more competent. From the managerial perspective, it becomes the imperative of the instructors, teachers, or administrators to select and implement the right system in their organization lest the implementation will run into problems, which could be costly and damaging. To achieve a successful implementation of any LMS system will entail conditions that help users to appreciate the full potential of the solution. In other words, they should perceive the system to be highly beneficial to their training or leaning. Of course, there are interrelated factors that come into play in shaping the perceived usefulness or perceived benefit of such systems.

To explain the factors and their relations, several researchers have formulated a few models such as *Technology Acceptance Model (TAM)* [14], *Unified Theory of Acceptance and Use of Technology (UTAUT)* [15], *DeLone and McLean model (DL&ML)* [16], and *Educational Technology Model (ETM)* [17]. Invariably, some of the newer models were formulated based on older models, thus some having the same underlying constructs, such as system quality, service quality, course quality, learner satisfaction, LMS use, and *perceived benefit* [18]. In this paper, the constructs that were examined were learner satisfaction, LMS use, and perceived benefit given that the remaining constructs mainly deal with the technical aspects of the systems. According to Ref. [19], user (learner) satisfaction, which measures learner's attitude toward the system, is " the extent to which users believe the information system available to them meets their information requirements." Thus, if the user perceives the system to be poor, the system is rendered inferior. In contrast, higher learner satisfaction of the system will lead to higher "intention to use," which in turn improves usage [16].

Based on these interrelations, satisfied learners will perceive the system to be beneficial to their learning and will most likely use the system more persistently. "The construct LMS use measures the extent to which learners use the LMS, which in effect serves as a barometer that shows the success (or failure) of such a system implementation" [16]. With frequent use of the system, learners will be more likely to improve their knowledge and skills – the positive impact of which will resonate throughout the organization. Accordingly, measuring the net benefit of the system entails the evaluation of the system along with the purpose of the system. "One of the practical ways to measure the perceived net benefit is through eliciting learners' perception on the benefit of the system" [18]. In unison, all these factors will have a serious impact of the selection and use of such a LMS. Furthermore, the use of such a system will also be influenced by several mediating, notably demographic factors, which need to be considered when implementing online learning for students.

As with other computer-based solutions, both proprietary and non-proprietary systems are readily available. Given the availability of both types of the systems, undertaking a comparative study of these two systems will not only be interesting but purposeful, as the lessons to be learned will help universities' administrators to make an informed decision on the final choice of a particular system type to be used in their organizations. Such a choice will have an overwhelming impact on the learning and teaching process in the long term. Thus, three research questions that focus on perceived benefit, LMS use, and learner satisfaction were formulated to guide the study as follows:

a. Is there a significant difference in perceived benefit between the open source LMS and the proprietary LMS as reported by the participants?

b. Is there a significant difference in perceived LMS use between the open source LMS and the proprietary LMS as reported by the participants?

c. Is there a significant difference in perceived learner satisfaction between the open source LMS and the proprietary LMS as reported by the participants?

Based on the three research questions, three corresponding research hypotheses were also formulated as follows:

a. Perceived benefit of the open source LMS will differ significantly from the perceived benefit of the proprietary LMS.

b. LMS use of the open source LMS will differ significantly from the LMS use of the proprietary LMS.

c. Learner satisfaction of the open source LMS will differ significantly from the learner satisfaction of the proprietary LMS.

2. Research method

In this study, the researchers used a quantitative research method based on a survey to collect the required data from a group of students. Using this approach helped the researchers to test the preceding research hypotheses by employing relevant participants, research instruments, and procedure. The details of the research method are as follows.

2.1. Participants

The sample of the survey comprised a group of 608 undergraduates, who were majoring in information technology at two institutions of higher learning in Malaysia. In terms of gender composition, this sample consisted of 401 female undergraduates and 207 male undergraduates. Their mean age was 21.5 years, and, on average, they had been using the LMSs for more than 2 years. Their participation in this survey was based on voluntary basis.

2.2. Research instruments

The research instrument used in this study was mostly based on the questionnaire used by Ref. [18] to collect data pertaining to the constructs LMS use, learner satisfaction, and perceived benefit. There were 11 items in the questionnaire, which were split into three categories. The first category comprised four items to measure LMS use, the second category comprised three items to measure learner satisfaction, and the third category consisted of four items to measure perceived benefit. The participants were asked to state their opinions with regard to the three constructs along 5-Likert-type scales, ranging from "1" (*strongly disagree*) to "5" (*strongly agree*). Cronbach's alpha coefficients for construct reliability measurement of LMS use, learner satisfaction, and perceived benefit were 0.89, 0.88, and 0.91, respectively. These coefficients suggest that the internal consistency of the items are good, exceeding the acceptable value of 0.7 [20]. Table 2 summarizes the 11 items, constructs, and internal consistencies as reported in Ref. [18].

Item	Construct	Statement	Cronbach's alpha coefficients
1	LMS use	I use LMS to help me to interact with my instructor.	0.79
2		I use LMS to access learning resources electronically	0.80
3		I use LMS to communicate and share knowledge with my colleagues.	0.81
4		I use LMS to accomplish and submit my assignments.	0.77
5	Learner Satisfaction	I am pleased with the LMS.	0.69
6		I am very satisfied with the course content I access from LMS.	0.80
7		Overall, my interaction with LMS is very satisfying.	0.79
8	Perceived Benefit	Using LMS has helped me to accomplish my learning tasks more quickly.	0.76
9		Using LMS has made my learning activities become much easier than before.	0.82
10		My learning performance has enhanced since I started using LMS.	0.82
11		I find the system useful in my studies.	0.81

Table 2. Items, constructs, and internal consistencies

2.3. Procedure

Two groups of participants were formed based on their locations of study. The first group comprised 290 undergraduates (204 females, 86 males) of a private university, who used a proprietary (licensed) LMS. The second group comprised 318 undergraduates (197 females, 121 males) of a public university, who used use a non-proprietary (open source) LMS. The participation of the undergraduates was secured through personal contact of the researchers to allow them to send an online survey questionnaire to the students. This questionnaire also contained a brief introduction of the purpose of the survey and an assurance that their answers would remain confidential. Collected questionnaires were analyzed using Statistical Software for Social Science (Ver. 19.) The statistical procedures to address the research questions were a series of independent t-tests and Pearson correlation. The former procedure was used to examine any significant differences in the perceived constructs. The latter procedure was employed to examine the relations among the constructs. "Pearson correlation is commonly used in social science studies to examine the size and direction of the linear relationship between two continuous variables" [21].

3. Findings

Participants' responses to the questionnaire items were processed to produce the required descriptive statistics, namely, the mean scores, maximum scores, minimum scores, and standard deviations. The overall mean scores (standard deviations) of LMS use, learner satisfaction, and perceived benefit were 3.95 (.68), 3.97 (.69), and 3.78 (.65), respectively, as shown in Table 3.

	Construct (Measure)					
Type of LMS	**LMS use**		**Learner Satisfaction**		**Perceived Benefit**	
	Mean	*SD*	Mean	*SD*	Mean	*SD*
Open source ($n = 318$)	4.02	0.62	4.04	0.64	3.85	0.52
Proprietary ($n = 290$)	3.86	0.73	3.87	0.72	3.72	0.76
Overall ($N = 608$)	3.95	0.68	3.97	0.69	3.78	0.65

Table 3. Mean scores and standard deviations of the three constructs

An independent-samples t-test indicated that LMS use's mean scores were significantly higher for the group that used open source system ($M = 4.02$, $SD = 0.62$) than for the group that used the proprietary systems ($M = 3.86$, $SD = 0.73$), $t(606) = 2.91$, $p < 0.05$. The same test also indicated that learner satisfaction's mean scores was significantly higher for the group that used open source system ($M = 4.04$, $SD = 0.64$) than for the group that used the proprietary systems ($M = 3.87$, $SD = 0.72$), $t(606) = 2.77$, $p < 0.05$. Similarly, the perceived benefit's mean score was significantly higher for the group that used open source system ($M = 3.85$, $SD = 0.52$) than for the group that used the proprietary systems ($M = 3.72$, $SD = 0.76$), $t(606) = 2.32$, $p < 0.05$.

Bivariate correlations between pairs of constructs were also computed using the Pearson correlation procedure. Perceived benefit and LMS use were significantly correlated, $r(606) = 0.11$, $p < 0.05$. Likewise, perceived benefit and learner satisfaction were also significantly correlated, $r(606) = 0.12$, $p < 0.05$. For constructs LMS use and learner satisfaction, their correlation was found to be strong and highly significant, $r(606) = 0.95$, $p < 0.001$. Table 4 summarizes the correlations among perceived benefit, LMS use, and learner satisfaction.

Construct (Measure)	1	2	3
1. Perceived benefit	—		
2. LMS use	0.112*	—	
3. Learner satisfaction	0.120*	0.95**	—

*p <.05, p < 0.001

Table 4. Pearson correlations among perceived benefit, LMS use, and learner satisfaction

4. Discussion and conclusion

One of the major findings of the independent-samples t-test indicates that the participants who used the open source LMS rated the perceived benefit of their LMS significantly higher than their counterpart who used the proprietary LMS. In other words, the difference in perceived benefit between the two types of LMSs as reported by the participants was significant. Thus, this finding supports the first research hypothesis of the study. Similarly, the LMS use of the open source LMS was observed to differ significantly from the LMS use of the proprietary LMS, which lends support for the second research hypothesis of the study. Likewise, another finding of the independent-samples t-test indicates that the participants who used the open source LMS tended to rate Learner satisfaction significantly higher than those who used the proprietary LMS. There was a significant difference between the two groups in this measure, thus supporting the third research hypothesis of the study.

Given the support of all research hypotheses, there is growing evidence to suggest that learning management solutions developed by the open source community might have matured to a level that is on par with licensed solutions – or, as demonstrated in this case, the former might have surpassed the latter in terms of perceived benefit, LMS use, and learner satisfaction. Clearly, when these measures are perceived to be important by users, it can be inferred that the implementation of such a leaning management system is successful to a certain extent. Undisputedly, "there are numerous technical and socio-psychological factors" [22,23,24] "involving all the stakeholders that can determine the success (or failure) of LMSs" [25]. In this study, the perceived benefit (perceived usefulness), learner satisfaction, and LMS use of the open source LMS were highly rated. In addition, based on the correlational analysis, all the three factors were also significantly correlated with each other. More notably, the significant positive association between learner satisfaction and perceived benefit is consistent with earlier findings. This finding reinforces the contention that users will accept an LMS to be beneficial when they "are satisfied with the performance of such a system" [26]. This significant positive relation will in turn make users utilize the system more often and readily to support their learning process. Continued use of such systems will not only benefit students and instructors but administrators as well. In view of this revelation, it is important for both teaching staff and academic administrative personnel to institute several initiatives to highlight the benefits of LMS to their students. Through such initiatives, students will be able to recognize and appreciate the immense potential of an LMS. With the right frame of mind, students, especially the freshmen, will be primed to adapt to new, novel learning environment.

Interestingly, in this study, perceived benefit, LMS use, and learner satisfaction of an open source LMS were rated higher than the proprietary LMS. This finding suggests that solutions developed by the open source organizations or individuals have a promising future in providing online learning opportunities to a wide spectrum of users. Though the proprietary LMS entered the educational landscape much earlier than the open source LMS and dominated the online learning environment, the ongoing and relentless efforts by the open source community have made the latter system a formidable solution on par with the former system. Given its relatively inexpensive outlay, many institutions, especially cash-strapped schools, can now afford to implement open source, non-proprietary learning solutions. As demonstrated in this study, the open source LMS was rated high by students who used it to support their learning, especially outside the classroom. The high ratings of the perceived benefit, LMS use, and learner satisfaction strongly suggest that "features and functionalities of open source LMSs to support online independent learning have improved over the years to provide the essential teaching and learning needs" [27].

Despite the many advantages of open source LMSs, some factors may hinder successful implementation of such systems. Even though the acquisition of open source LMSs are almost without cost, a highly trained personnel (e.g., a system analyst) is required to manage the systems, which encompasses a wide range of technicalities. Without proper system management, the solution put in place will ultimately become inefficient and ineffective. Like any other database systems, LMSs require constant monitoring, updating, and maintenance over time as the number of users is growing. In addition, there is concern that some of the open source LMSs do not provide the level of security that is needed by certain educational institutions. Hence, important information could be comprised, which is detrimental to the organizations' reputation. Of course, there are other factors as well that can make an open source implementation challenging, but these two factors represent the major concern that can make such adoption either a success or a failure. Given these issues, adopting an open source solution entails appropriate planning that holistically focuses on all aspects pertaining to technical, training, and cost considerations.

In this study, even though the open source Education LMS was highly rated higher than the proprietary Education LMS in terms of the three constructs, the researchers strongly believe that the success of any LMS system – irrespective of being either proprietary or open source – will rely on technical, managerial, institutional, and attitudinal aspects. For example, at the institutional level, universities should not view LMS as a mere technological tool, but more importantly, this system should be implemented with careful, comprehensive planning. To plan such an implementation would entail a rigorous review of existing infrastructure, current teaching and learning practices, and policies. Failure to factor in these aspects in the planning process could make the system underutilized. The researchers opine that for any universities to embark on an LMS project, a dedicated team drawn from various and relevant background should be set up to plan all the necessary details to help guide the selection, installation, testing, and full deployment of a proper LMS system. Ideally, these team members should work in a unit, which may be called (as an example) an e-learning unit under the ambit of the academic affairs department.

This team should be given sufficient empowerment to study, formulate, and deploy strategies for effective LMS deployment. This team should examine existing infrastructure to help determine the capabilities of available hardware to support the proposed learning management system. Having the knowledge of the performance of this hardware would help IT personnel to carry out appropriate upgrading or retrofitting work to run the proposed learning management system. It is worthy to note that implementing learning management system is not only about the software per se, but the hardware to run the system is equally important. In other words, the importance of the symbiotic relation between software and hardware to operate such a learning management should not be downplayed. Thus, a thorough review of existing equipment and IT tools is not only important but also mandatory. Likewise, a review of existing teaching and learning practice of a university should be performed with utmost importance. After all, the main aim of deploying LMS is to improve the existing process of teaching and learning, thus this review would help identify weak spots or areas that require redress. Problems associated with teaching and learning in many universities worldwide have increased without respite given the ever-increasing number of students enrolling in diverse academic programs. Face-to-face lectures have become a serious problem to many educational institutions as infrastructure is stretched to its limits, putting great constraint on it capability. Naturally, lectures have to be complemented by other means, notably online learning to cater vast student populations. Nowadays, many universities have adopted blended learning as a solution to handle the teaching needs and learning needs of lecturers and students, respectively.

In addition, the introduction of learning management systems in institutes of higher learning would entail a sound, appropriate policy to make their implementations a success. Ultimately, these systems would be deemed worthwhile and beneficial if all the stakeholders (students, lecturers, and administrators) could fully utilize these solutions. For example, a part of the policy may contain provisions to necessitate (or to enforce) all lecturers to use the LMS in the following teaching activities: a) uploading lecture notes on LMS, b) making online announcements, c) setting up online discussion groups, d) conducting online quizzes and tests, e) providing online feedback of students performance, and f) posting online information and news. With all these teaching activities performed on the learning management system, students would be more prone to partake in online learning activities to complement their face-to-face learning. Hence, the use of the system would be more intense, leading students to perceive the system to be highly beneficial. Sustaining this level of teaching and learning activities would in the end make the adoption of the LMS a success.

Overall, the findings of this study provide some assurances that open source education learning management systems are on par with their proprietary counterparts for the constructs learner satisfaction, LMS use, and perceived benefit. In fact, the latter system has been demonstrated to be rated higher than the former system for the three constructs. However, this finding is informative in terms of the continually increasing capability of open source education learning management systems, but not conclusive to stake claim that these open source systems are better than proprietary systems. Many factors are involved in making the adoption of learning management systems a success; thus, the interpretation of this finding should be embraced with caution as this study was based on students' opinions. Other stakeholders' opinions and feedback are needed to ascertain the performance of any learning management systems with some degree of certainty.

In summary, open source education learning management systems are beginning to be seriously viewed as an effective, efficient learning solution from the student perspective. Now, more learning opportunities will be made available to a greater pool of learners across the nation to help them pursue their academic programs in an environment that suits today's educational landscape – more precisely, digital landscape in which more and more contents and materials are in electronic form. Therefore, it is incumbent on the management of universities, training centers, and institutions that are currently using expensive learning solutions to seek affordable solutions, which are equally effective, to further enhance their students' online learning experiences. More importantly, schools, especially the public ones, which do not have such systems in place, should try to learn from others that have successfully implemented the open source education learning management systems so that their pupils can experience online learning at the early age.

Author details

Ahmad Rafi[1*], Khairulanuar Samsudin[2] and Hafizul Fahri Hanafi[2]

*Address all correspondence to: rafi@mmu.edu.my

1 Faculty of Creative Multimedia, Multimedia University, Cyberjaya, Selangor, Malaysia

2 Computing Department, Faculty of Art, Computing and Creative Industry, Sultan Idris University of Education, Tanjung Malim, Perak, Malaysia

References

[1] Wright, C.R., Lopes, V., Montgomerie, C., Reju, S.A., & Schmoller, S. Selecting a learning management system: Advice from an academic perspective. EDUCAUSE review, April 21, 2014. Available from: http://www.educause.edu/ero/article/selecting-learning-management-system-advice-academic-perspective [2015-03-17].

[2] Ellis, R.K. Field Guide to Learning Management Systems. Alexandria: ASTD Learning Circuits, 2009.

[3] Shank, P. Learning management systems, the eLearning guild. 2010. Available from: http://www.elearningguild.com/research/archives/index [2015-03-17].

[4] Kano-Bower, E. Open source vs. commercial learning platforms: Total cost of ownership and total cost of effective use. 2010. Available from: http://www.itslearning.net/Websites/itstest/Images/Documents/TCO.pdf [2015-03-17].

[5] Monarch Media, Inc. Open-source learning management systems: Sakai and Moodle. Monarch Media, Inc., Business White Paper. 2010.

[6] Feller, J., & Fitzerald, B. A framework analysis of the open source software development paradigm University College Cork Ireland. 2000. Available from: http://www.josephfeller.com/publications/ICIS2000.pdf [2000-02-10].

[7] McIntosh. D. Vendors of learning management and e-learning products. Available from: http://www.trimeritus.com/vendors.pdf [2015-04-10].

[8] Wheeler, B. The open source parade. EDUCAUSE Review. 2004; 39 (5): 68–69.

[9] Hotrum, M., Ludwig, B., & Baggaley, J. Open source software: Fully-featured vs. "the devil you know." International Review of Research in Open and Distance Learning. 2005; 6 (1). Available from: http://cde.athabascau.ca/softeval/reports/R430410.pdf [2015-03-17].

[10] Beatty, B., & Ulasewicz, C. Online teaching and learning transition: Faculty perspectives on moving from Blackboard to Moodle learning management system. TechTrend. 2007; 50 (4): 36–45.

[11] Awang, N., & Darus, M.Y. Evaluation of an open source learning management system: Claroline. Procedia – Social and Behavioral Sciences. 2012; 67: 416–426.

[12] Cavus, N., Uzunboylu, H., & Ibrahim, D. Assessing the success of students using a learning management system and together with a collaborative tool in web based teaching of programming languages. Journal of Education Computer Research. 2007; 36 (3): 301–321.

[13] Ankita, S., & Vatta, S. Role of learning management systems in education. International Journal of Advanced Research in Computer Science and Software Engineering. 2013; 3 (6): 997–1002.

[14] Davis, F.D., Bagozzi, R.P., & Warshaw, P.R. User acceptance of computer technology: A comparison of two theoretical models. Management Science. 1989; 35 (8): 982–1003.

[15] Venkatesh, V., Morris, M.G., Davis, G.B., & Davis, F.D. User acceptance of information technology: Toward a unified view. MIS Quarterly. 2003; 27 (3): 425–478.

[16] DeLone, W.H., & McLean, E.R. The DeLone and McLean model of information systems success: A ten-year update. Journal of Management Information Systems. 2003; 9: 9–30.

[17] Almarashdeh, I.A., Sahari, N., Zin, N.A.M., & Alsmadi, M. The success of learning management system among distance learners in Malaysian universities. Journal of Theoretical and Applied Information Technology. 2010; 12 (2): 80–91.

[18] Mtebe, J.S., & Raisamo, R. A model for assessing learning management system success in higher education in Sub-Saharan countries. The Electronic Journal of Information Systems in Developing Countries. 2014; 61 (7): 1–17.

[19] Ives, B., Olson, M., & Baroudi, J.J. The measurement of user information satisfaction. Communications of the ACM. 1983; 26: 785–793.

[20] DeVon, H.A., Block, M.E., Moyle-Wright, P., Ernst, D.M., Hayden, S.J., Lazzara, D.J. et al. A psychometric toolbox for testing validity and reliability. Journal of Nursing Scholarship. 2007; 39 (2): 155–164.

[21] Goodwin L.D., & Leech, N.L. Understanding correlation: Factors that affect the size of *r*. The Journal of Experimental Education. 2006; 74 (3): 251–266.

[22] Abrahams, D. Technology adoption in higher education: A framework for identifying and prioritising issues and barriers to adoption of instructional technology. Journal of Applied Research in Higher Education. 2010; 2 (2): 34–49.

[23] Al-Busaidi, K., & Al-Shihi, H. Key factors to instructors' satisfaction of learning management systems in blended learning. Journal of Computing in Higher Education. 2012; 24: 18–39.

[24] Liaw, S., Huang, H., & Chen, G. Surveying instructor and learner attitudes toward e-learning. Computers & Education. 2008; 49: 1066–1080.

[25] Naveh, G., Tubin, D., & Pliskin, N. Student LMS use and satisfaction in academic institutions: The organisational perspective. Internet and Higher Education. 2010; 13: 127–133.

[26] Sun, P., Tsai, R., Finger, G., Chen, Y., & Yeh, D. What drives a successful e-learning? An empirical investigation of the critical factors influencing learner satisfaction. Computers & Education. 2008; 50: 1183–1202.

[27] Fariha, Z. & Zuriyati, A. Comparing Moodle and eFront software for learning management system. Australian Journal of Basic and Applied Sciences. Special Issue 2014; 8 (4): 158–162.

Chapter 15

Model for Blended Supervision of Post-Graduate Students

Mildred Atieno Ayere

Additional information is available at the end of the chapter

http://dx.doi.org/10.5772/60656

Abstract

Supervision of eLearning students at Maseno University poses a great challenge to the normal institutional order because most senior lecturers qualified for postgraduate supervision are technologically illiterate, semi-literate, or challenged [10]. The recommended lecturer to student ratio for postgraduate supervision in Maseno University is 1:5 and 1:3 for master's and PhD students, respectively, but the actual ratio is 1:12 [23]. The challenge of high student numbers in three different campuses, low numbers of qualified supervisors; and fully online students is a big problem. ELearning is not new to the developed world but a fairly new concept in Africa [2, 6, 7]. Through eLearning, Maseno is fulfilling the global demand for universal lifelong learning [26]. Introducing blended supervision was a strategy seeking to harness the opportunities in the online platform by reducing distance between students while increasing the rate and quality of feedback [8, 21, 31]; leveraging the affordances of virtual learning to create an interactive environment for learners and faculty [11, 18, 15]. Objectives of this project were to develop policy and procedures for online supervision, Identify postgraduate supervision milestones, and Build a collaborative research environment. The study used the critical case study design [28] and was hinged on constructivist theory [15]. The population consisted of 513 students, 42 lecturers from the 5 schools with postgraduate courses at eCampus, and 8 university administrators. Purposive sampling led to 149 students, 11 lecturers, and 3 administrators from one school that fully embraced the model. Data were collected using online discussions, observations, and interviews. Data were analyzed using time series analysis to identify milestones in the supervision process while predicting best interaction models for online supervision. Regression logic model further helped predict expected completion rates based on existing supervisor to student ratios. The study identified key supervision milestones as assistance in drafting an acceptable concept paper and proposal, quality interaction and feedback from supervisor, provision of adequate tools to support research processes, identification with a collaborative research team, and exposure to research seminars and presentations. From the milestones, the study school identified a group of qualified supervisors and offered them training on use of the online platform and resources in supervision. This study concluded that a pilot model for blended postgraduate supervision is in its formative stages, the collaborative postgraduate research course area is being piloted in six schools, online supervision has enabled most schools to share supervisors with other research institutions at no extra cost, predicted completion rate for postgraduate research is one year on the blended model, and research outputs from post-graduate students have increased by 50% on average. It is recommended that results from this study need to be replicated in other schools before it can fully inform university wide policy, making it a continuing work in progress.

Keywords: eLearning, online supervision, eCampus, postgraduate research, blended supervision

1. Introduction

1.1. The eCampus of Maseno

The eLearning Centre of Maseno University was established in the year 2007 to spearhead the development of institutional policies and strategies for promoting innovative use of Information and Communications Technologies (ICTs) to benefit learning, teaching, and research activities at the university [10]. In January 2012, it evolved into an eCampus and continued to support academic staff empowerment in modern communication and collaborative learning techniques, to enable them to contribute significantly to quality learning experiences among learners at the university, regardless of their physical location.

The eCampus of Maseno University, therefore, is one of the greatest innovations by Maseno University to facilitate online delivery of high-quality certificate, diploma, and degree programs to learners in various parts of the country, the East African region, and beyond. Maseno University has indeed successfully pioneered the use of modern technology to not only to realize equitable access to higher education through eLearning, but also to improve the quality of educational experience for its face to face learners [18]. The eCampus, which was previously known as the eLearning Centre, has been defined as such in the Maseno University Statutes 2012.

It admitted its first online learners in September, 2011. These were 160 students (102 undergraduates and 58 postgraduates) spread across five university programs housed in three different schools. This number has since increased to 892 students admitted in 15 different programs across six schools within the university. Out of these, there are 366 undergraduate and 526 postgraduate students, a pointer to the popularity of the programs by postgraduate learners. Actually, the number of postgraduate students in the online platform is half the total number of postgraduate students in the whole university, making them very significant to the university research fraternity.

1.2. Background to the problem

Postgraduate supervision of eLearning (fully online) students at Maseno University poses a very great challenge to the normal institutional order because there is no policy or guidelines catering for online supervision. At the same time, most senior lecturers who take part in postgraduate supervision are technologically illiterate, semi-literate, or challenged [10]. The lecturers were already having problems with high numbers of postgraduate students being supervised, which increases significantly when eLearning students are added. It means therefore that there is need to use blended supervision as opposed to the old mode (Face to face). This requires a new policy and procedures for supervision to cater for this unique need, capacity building for lecturers, and a medium to facilitate the new mode [4, 9, 7, 16]. This change is the content of this chapter.

The recommended lecturer to student ratio for postgraduate supervision in Maseno University is 1: 5 and 1:3 for master's and PhD students, respectively [23]. The average ratio of lecturer to postgraduate student supervision is 1:25 for most schools [24]. This challenge of high student numbers, high workload, and low numbers of qualified supervisors needs an immediate solution given this novel mode of learning introduced by eLearning [13]. eLearning has created a chance for a large yet busy group of working learners to go back to class from the comforts of their "homes" and "offices" [7]. By adopting this mode of learning, Maseno University is fulfilling a global demand for lifelong learning [27]. Despite the successful delivery of fully online instruction, the university is yet to formulate policy to institutionalize blended supervision [29]. Therefore, this project is an intervention to help the university come up with policy and procedures that would mainstream blended supervision in its institutional structures.

The eCampus has so far attracted international students from Iraq, Uganda, Tanzania, Somalia, Rwanda, Nigeria, and Belgium: a fact that has brought an international feel to the university. The greatest challenge with admitting international students is the examinations, which is done face to face [25]. This has denied many learners a chance to enroll because of costs associated with the travel for face to face examinations. For postgraduate supervision, the challenge is much greater given that an eLearning postgraduate student would have to travel back and forth for supervision, which adds to not only the cost but also the time constraints [7, 9, 16]. There is therefore an urgent need to develop an intervening strategy (blended supervision) to deal with supervision of purely online students, high number of postgraduate students, and lack of an online interaction interface for the postgraduate students [30]. The need is further compounded by the fact the university has three face to face campuses (approximately 150km apart), manned by the same pool of lecturers who teach and supervise postgraduate students. An interactive online supervision platform, when created, would create a pool of researchers (postgraduate students and supervisors), who could be resident in any of the campuses. This idea capitalizes on the affordances of a virtual learning environment through the eCampus LMS to build a collaborative learning environment for postgraduate research students to interact with faculty and peers to share, support, encourage, and learn from each other [1, 3, 7, 9]. The LMS has the advantage of not only closing physical space and bringing everyone closer through the new ICTs but also keeping a record of activities [5].

2. Research section

This section explains how the project was undertaken as a research venture. The aim was to find a solution with a research backing, hence the scientific approach to the project. It was to be done in phases, and this section reports the research undertaken in phase one 1 of the project.

2.1. Statement of the problem

The problem that needed urgent attention at the eCampus of Maseno University was the fact that it had embarked on an innovative mode of learning which attracted a high number of postgraduate students (526 in 3 years). The ideal would have been to have these fully online students supported by supervisors through the same platform (LMS). At the same time there was no institutional structure (policy, structured platform, capacity building for supervisors) for the kind of support needed. Compounding the problem was the need to manage high numbers of postgraduate students ready for supervision against a limited human resource. Online supervision was seen as way of mitigating against the problem because it would provide a platform for team supervision and peer education in the course of the research process.

In summary, this project hopes to harness the opportunities in the online platform through a tried and tested LMS to institutionalize blended supervision as a way of managing the postgraduate research process. This would enable the university to reduce the distance between a postgraduate student and supervisor thus increasing the rate and quality of feedback, leveraging the affordances of virtual learning to create an interactive environment for learners and faculty, and in the process, developing institutionally accepted procedures for online supervision out of which a policy on online supervision could be developed.

2.2. Purpose and objectives of the project

The purpose of this study was to develop a model for blended postgraduate supervision for fully online students at the eCampus of Maseno University. In particular, it was set to:

i. Identify ways of managing postgraduate supervision milestones in the online platform

ii. Develop policy and procedures for blended supervision of postgraduate students

iii. Build a collaborative learning environment for postgraduate students and their supervisors

2.3. Research questions

The research questions that would need to be answered in the course of this research include the following:

i. How should supervision milestones be managed in the online platform at Maseno University?

ii. What policy and procedures should guide the online postgraduate supervision at Maseno University?

iii. How can the university build a collaborative learning environment for postgraduate research students and their supervisors?

http://dx.doi.org/10.5772/60656

2.4. Significance of the project

The results from this project may influence the mode and quality of postgraduate supervision at Maseno University and possibly other public universities in Kenya. It may introduce capacity building for supervisors as an in-built component in the online supervision course area, which would have an impact in the quality of research outputs. Supervisors and students would also benefit greatly from a reduced workload brought about by mutual sharing and interactivity on the online platform. It also has a global contribution to the supervision process in introducing mentorship of new supervisors by experienced supervisors. The envisaged interaction model and outcome is represented in the figure that follows.

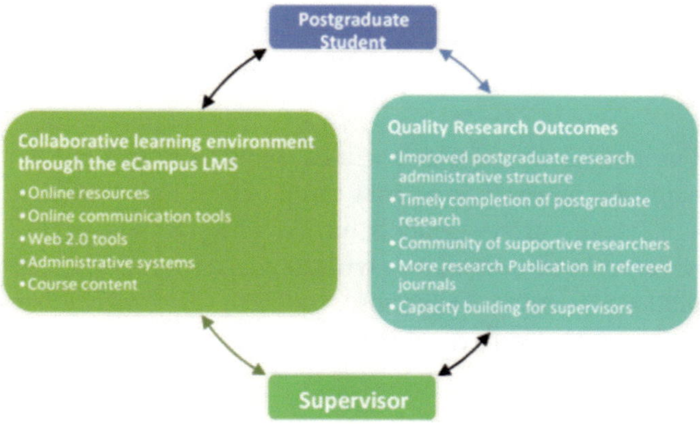

Figure 1. Post Graduate Students' Interactions

2.5. Research methodology

The project used the critical case study design to show-case the Maseno University eCampus operations. The case study design was chosen *"Because of its strength as an applied field where processes, problems, and programs can be examined to bring about understanding that in turn can affect and perhaps even improve practice. Case study has proven particularly useful for studying educational innovations, evaluating programs, and informing policy"* [17].

The population consisted of 526 students, 42 lecturers from the 5 schools with postgraduate courses at eCampus, and 8 university administrators. Purposive sampling was used to select 165 students, 11 lecturers, and 3 administrators from one school that fully embraced the blended supervision model in its formative state. Data were collected using online discussions, observations, and interviews. The collected data were analyzed using time series analysis to identify milestones in the supervision process while predicting best interaction models for online supervision. Regression logit model further helped predict expected completion rates based on existing supervisor to student ratios.

A team of four supervisors who formed the project secretariat designed a supervision course area and piloted it by working with one supervisor from each school who supervised at least two students purposively selected. A team of administrators representing school of graduate studies, the eCampus, school coordinators, and technical team leaders were to brainstorm and harmonize policy and procedures for online supervision of postgraduate research at Maseno University. The project secretariat were to use the final protocol developed to train supervisors towards building a collaborative learning environment for postgraduate research students and their supervisors at Maseno University.

During piloting, data were collected and used to make adjustments in the protocols. Policy documents were then discussed, reviewed, and consultations will be made to determine the extent to which they support implementation of the protocol and areas that need to be harmonized. A validation workshop was held with relevant stakeholders before preparing a final report containing the revised supervision protocol and the necessary policy revision for implementation.

2.6. Project plan

The following activities (see figure below) will be undertaken in a bid to operationalize the project with the help of a research secretariat composed of four researchers. Each associate researcher will be in charge of two schools having postgraduate studies at the eCampus. Besides overseeing the school activities, they will also assist with specialized areas like creating the collaborative platform, training of supervisors, and engaging with university management. The actual project plan will be carried out in the steps set out in the figure that follows:

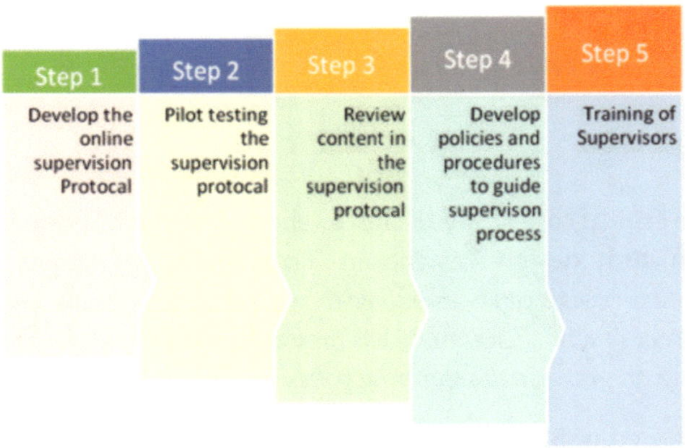

Figure 2. projected Project Plan

2.7. Expected outcomes

It is expected that at the completion of this project, Maseno University would have developed a policy for blended post graduate supervision; at least 50% (Based on the number of schools offering courses online) of the lecturers undertaking post graduate supervision would have been trained to undertake online supervision of postgraduate students. A reviewed supervision policy for online supervision of postgraduate students will be available for use by all postgraduate students at the university, thus improving completion rates because of the community of researchers available to the student researchers. At the same time, the eCampus will have grown the capacity to mentor other universities. This may involve training and knowledge transfer. Lastly, the project will nurture postgraduate students to publish more in refereed journals.

3. Results and conclusion

This section reports the results from the project so far and makes conclusions that were possible at the end of phase 1 of this project. The reported results are mainly from the one school that had already embraced the online supervision model as it was in its formative stage and was using the course area created by the project team.

3.1. Results

It should be noted that the project being reported is a work in progress and will take time to complete. The results reported here refer to what has been achieved so far. The project objectives had been set as follows:

i. Identifying ways of managing postgraduate supervision milestones in the online platform

ii. Developing a policy and procedures for online supervision of postgraduate research

iii. Building a collaborative learning environment for postgraduate research students and their supervisors

The results being reported in this book therefore are what has been achieved so far as the project continues on.

3.1.1. Managing the supervision milestones

The analysis of data collected was done through a time series analysis on trends of supervision milestones [12], which gave provided the results presented using the graph that follows in terms of postgraduate supervision in research. To arrive at the four key issues analyzed for trends, online interviews were done to help arrive at possible areas of need for the students.

The trends were analyzed from data collected from students in four successive semesters (Categories 1 to 4) through a five-scale rated discussion and questionnaire. The responses were rated with respect to assistance given to students in drafting concept paper and proposal (series 1), provision of tools to support the research process (series 2), identifying with a research team (series 3), and exposure to seminars and presentations (series 4).

It is apparent from the trends that the main supervision milestones given in order of preference were as follows: exposure to research seminars and presentations (4.325), giving students' assistance in drafting an acceptable concept paper and proposal (3.95), provision of adequate

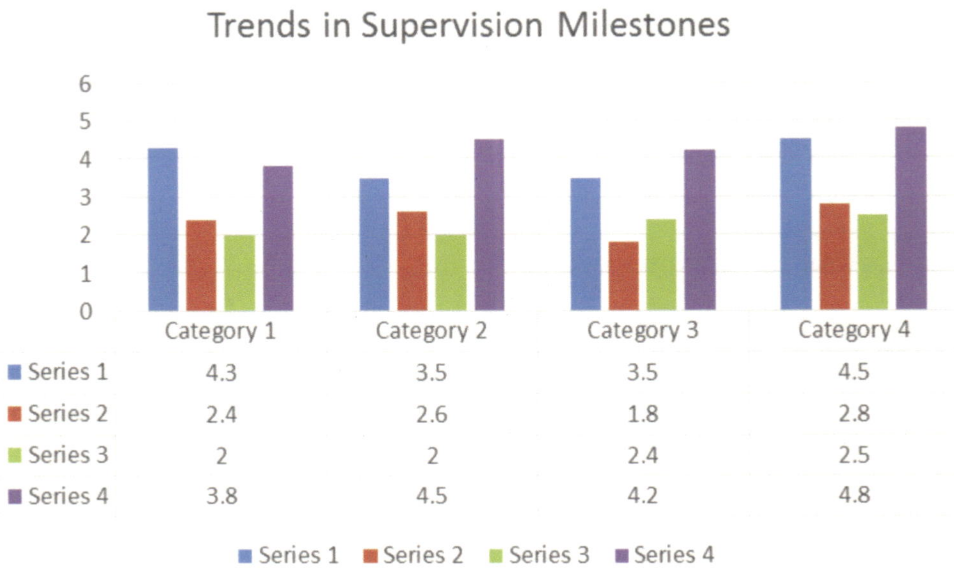

	Category 1	Category 2	Category 3	Category 4
Series 1	4.3	3.5	3.5	4.5
Series 2	2.4	2.6	1.8	2.8
Series 3	2	2	2.4	2.5
Series 4	3.8	4.5	4.2	4.8

tools to support the research process (2.4), and identifying with a collaborative research team (2.225).

The milestones are further discussed below in order of preference from the research outcomes:

i. Giving students assistance in drafting an acceptable concept paper and proposal. This is mainly because the research area has interactive and self-directing instructions together with resources that allow learners to discuss and learn from each other.

ii. Provision of adequate tools to support the research process. This is because the main tool used in the postgraduate research area is an LMS used at the eCampus, which is supported by Moodle. Therefore, all the interactive tools in-built in the Moodle and web2 tools supported by Moodle are available for online supervision. Moodle has innumerable communication, learning, and interactive tools.

iii. Identifying with a collaborative research team. From the questionnaire, it was reported by all the students surveyed that most postgraduate students are isolated and lonely. Looking closely at the issues raised by the students, it is apparent that all these issues would be adequately dealt with by having a chance to interact with peers and supervisors.

iv. Exposure to research seminars and presentations. All schools involved in this project resorted to holding seminars and presentations during the face to face meeting held once a term by the eCampus. This practice brought about learning in the process of presentations. Students ask questions which are tackled jointly by all faculty members present.

3.1.2. *Building a collaborative learning environment*

The table below gives a list of issues raised by postgraduate students after their course work

Issues facing postgraduate students after course work	Percentage number of students affected
Problems on access to adequate resources	80
Uncertainty as a learner a progresses in different stages of research work	85
Inadequate role models	70
Delayed feedback on work submitted	90
Procrastination on tasks	80

Looking closely at the issues raised by the students, it is apparent that all the issues would be adequately dealt with by having a chance to interact with peers and supervisors.

This researcher used a novel method for converting educational log data collected by observing learner interactions in the course into features suitable for building predictive models of student success as reported by [26]. They further acknowledge that unlike cognitive modeling or content analysis approaches, these models are built from interactions between learners and resources, an approach that requires no input from instructional or domain experts and can be applied across courses or learning environments. It is from the results of these analyses that a model of interaction was suggested for the eCampus. The model is presented in the diagram that follows.

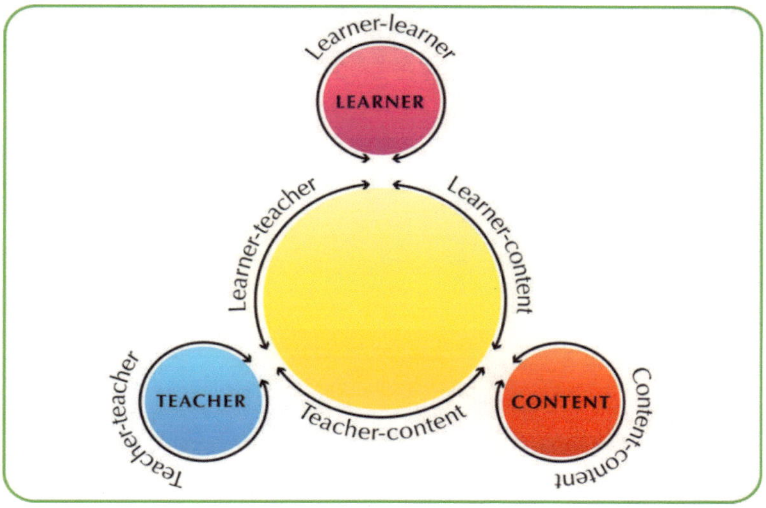

Figure 3. Post Graduate Students' Interactions

Quality interaction and feedback from supervisor and peers was one of the emerging practices realized from building a collaborative learning environment. This came about because the course area is open to all postgraduate students and other supervisors; therefore, a supervisor is compelled to ensure the feedback they give is holistic and humane. The interactions identified in the postgraduate research area so far may be symbolized by the diagram that follows.

It is clear from the diagram that the depicted interaction is not only between the student and the supervisor but also between the student and the content as well as among the peers. It results in a win–win situation for all involved as supervisors get to improve their skills by interacting not only with learners but also with content availed in the research area. Students on the other hand get assistance from other supervisors interacting in this common area.

3.1.3. Emerging research outcomes

The qualitative data reviewed from the lecturers taking part in this project resulted in significant outcomes that cannot fully be ignored. These had to do with schools thinking of novel ways of mitigating against the high learner to supervisor ratio. It emerged that the project school had only four qualified lecturers against 85 students needing supervision after completing course work. They took advantage of the existing interactive course area to outsource for supervisors external to the department and the university who needed the experience and could spare time to assist with the supervision tasks.

Furthermore, the logit model was used to predict the learner completion rates and expected research outputs from the postgraduate students. For these predictions to be possible, the outcome (response) variable is binary, i.e., complete or drop out (1 or 0). The predictor variables of interest are as follows: frequency of contact with supervisors, interaction with peers, online tools support provided, and identification with a research team. Categories in the curve refer to semesters when the data are collected. The predictor logistic line is presented below:

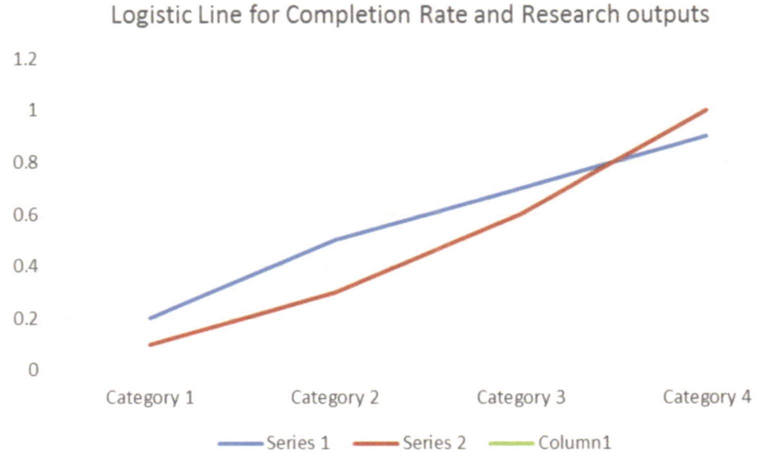

The results indicated that a learner is likely to complete research in four semesters, which is just over a year if all the predictor variables are present (series 2). At the same time, the research outputs are likely to increase by slightly more than 50% (series 1). These outputs range from publications to presentations at conferences and seminars to innovative outputs.

3.2. Conclusion

In conclusion, it was noteworthy that the project enabled the university to arrive at the following in its phase 1 of implementation:

- The university through the eCampus was able to conceptualize a blended postgraduate supervision model to be used and was tried out by at least one school with its postgraduate students even though the interaction model is still in its early formative stages.
- The eCampus, through the schools having postgraduate students, managed to set up a collaborative postgraduate research course area, which is still being piloted in six schools.
- Most schools with a high number of students at the eCampus are co-opting supervisors from other research institutions at no extra cost to the university.
- It is predicted that with this model in use, the completion rate for postgraduate research will be just one year using the blended model.
- Research outputs from postgraduate students are expected to increase by 50% on average with more students having the ability to publish in refereed journal and making presentations in conferences and departmental seminars.

With all these initiatives taking place through the eCampus, the final outcome from this project is expected to be a policy document being formulated based on research outcomes to guide blended research processes on blended supervision.

Author details

Mildred Atieno Ayere*

Address all correspondence to: ayeremildred@yahoo.com

eCampus, Maseno University, Kenya

References

[1] Abdel Hafez A. M. M.. Postgraduate Students' Knowledge and Attitudes towards good Supervisory Practice at Exeter. 1st ed. United Kingdom: Exeter University; 2007.

[2] Brew A., Peseta T.. Changing postgraduate supervision practice: A program to encourage learning through reflection. Innovations in Education and Teaching International. 2007;41(1):5-52.

[3] Carlson-Dakes C.. Creating a Collaborative Learning Environment: A Guide Book. Centre for Integration of Research, Teaching and Learning [Internet]. 2005. Available from: http://www.cirtl.net.

[4] Chiappetta-Swanson C., Watt S.. Good Practice in the Supervision and Mentoring of Postgraduate Students. 1st ed. McMaster University: Centre for Leadership and Learning; 2011.

[5] Conrad L.. Five ways of enhancing the postgraduate community: Student perceptions of effective supervision and support. In: HERDSA; 2003; Brisbane. Griffith University:

[6] Cullen D., Pearson M., Saha L. I., Spear R. H.. Establishing Effective PhD Supervision. Canberra: AGPS; 1994.

[7] De Beer M., Mason R. B.. Using blended approach to facilitate postgraduate supervision. Innovation in Education and Teaching International. 2009;46(2):213-226.

[8] Delany D.. A Review of the Literature on Effective PhD Supervision.. 1st ed. Trinity College: Centre for Academic Practice and Student Learning; 2012.

[9] Donnely R., Fitzmaurice M.. Creating Spaces for Voices: The portfolio as a Framework to support Inquiry into Third Level Learning and Teaching [Internet]. 2004. Available from: Education-Line Database http//www.leeds.ac.uk/educo/documents/00003437.html

[10] eCampus. The eCampus of Maseno: 1 year on. Maseno University. Forthcoming.

[11] Edward B.. Postgraduate Supervision: Is having a PhD enough?. In: Australian Association for Research in Education Conference; 2002; Brisbane. Australia:

[12] Given M. L.. The Sage Encyclopedia of Qualitative Methods [Internet]. 2008. Available from: http://dx.doi.org/10.4135/9781412963909

[13] Grant B. Walking on a rackety bridge: mapping supervision [Internet]. 1999. Available from: Higher Education Research Development Society of Australia. http://www.herdsa.org.au/branches/vic/Cornerstones/pdf/grant.pdf

[14] James R., Baldwin G.. Eleven Practices of Effective Postgraduate Supervisors. 1st ed. University of Melbourne, Victoria: Centre for Higher Education and the school of Higher Education; 1999.

[15] Jonassen D. H., Rohrer-Murphy L.. Activity theory as a framework for designing constructivist learning environment. Educational technology: Research and Development. 1999;46(1):215-239.

[16] Malfroy J. Doctoral supervision, workplace research and changing pedagogic practices.. Higher Education Research and Development. 2005;24(1):165-178. DOI: 10.1080/07294360500062961

[17] Merriam S.. Qualitative Case study Research in Qualitative Research: A Guide to Design and Implementation. 1st ed. John Wiley & Sons INC; 2009.

[18] Ministry of Education. National Information and Communication Strategy for Education and Training. 1st ed. Nairobi: Government Printers; 2006.

[19] Pearson M., Brew A.. Research training and supervision development. Studies in Higher Education. 2002;27(2):135-150.

[20] Powles M. How's the Thesis Going? Former Students and their Supervisors' Views on Completion Times and Dropout. 1st ed. University of Melbourne: Centre for the Study of Higher Education; 1989.

[21] Seagram B. C., Gould J., Pyke S. W.. An investigation of gender and other variables on time to completion of doctoral degrees. Research in Higher Education. 1998;39(3): 319-335.

[22] Schaffner C.. Formalising Supervision: A step toward better quality. [Internet]. 2004. Available from: Report from the Lisbon Congress round table on supervision, Aston University, Birmingham http://www.est-translationstudies.org/

[23] School of Graduate Studies. Rules and Regulations for Postgraduate Studies. 1st ed. Maseno University: SGS; 2013.

[24] School of Graduate Studies. School of Graduate Studies Report. Maseno University. 2014;4(1)

[25] Swedish Coordinating Centre. International Students Mirror Catalonia, Finland, Ireland and Sweden [Internet]. 2006. Available from: Stockholm: Swedish National Agency for Higher Education http://www.hsv.se/reports/2006/internationalpostgraduatestudentsmirrorcataloniafinlandirelandandsweden

[26] Thompson C., Brooks C., Teasley S.. A Time Series Analysis Method for Building Predictive Models of Learners using Log Data. 1st ed. New York: ACM; 2015.

[27] United Nations. Global experts call for lifelong learningas a cornerstone of development. In: Dakar Conference on Education; 2013; Dakar. UN joint Press Release;

[28] Yin R. K.. Case Study Research: Designs and Methods [Internet]. 2009. Available from: Thousand Oaks: Sage Publications INC http://amazon.com/case-study-research-methods-applied

[29] Wiskers G., Robinson G., Shacham M.. Postgraduate research success: Communities of practice involving cohorts, guardian supervisors and online communities. Innovations in education and Teaching. 2009;44(3)

[30] White T., Coetzee E.. Postgraduate supervision: email as an alternative. Africa Education Review. 2014;11(4)

[31] Wolf R. Judging Educational Research Based on Experiments and Surveys [Internet]. 2005. Available from: Paris: UNESCO http://www.unesco.org/iiep

[32] Zhao F.. Postgraduate supervision: A process of knowledge management [Internet]. 2001. Available from: E-journal:UltiBASE, 2001-providersedge.com [Accessed: 4th October 2014]

Chapter 16

Leadership in Implementing Technology-Enhanced Learning in Educational Institutions

John Wall

Additional information is available at the end of the chapter

http://dx.doi.org/10.5772/61108

Abstract

Conventional designs of educational programs are usually based on implicit instructional design approaches that look equally at all learners. However, research indicates that learning is a complex activity involving a number of different aspects. Using technology to deliver and support learning adds another layer of complexity. In a rapidly changing environment a template to map the implementation of blended learning is proposed to contribute to the ongoing debate in higher education in implementing blended learning approaches. In a challenging economic environment, some of the key strategic leadership challenges that institutions must address are articulated. Much of the research into deploying e-learning initiatives suggests that it is a complex undertaking and that educational institutions are at various stages in the development and deployment of technology-facilitated initiatives. A number of key leadership challenges are outlined that academic leaders must address in delivering the curriculum using technology. A proposed framework for deploying blended learning coupled with a template for educational managers to embrace in their strategic deployment of technology in delivering the curriculum is presented.

Keywords: E-learning, blended learning, leadership

1. Introduction

While higher education has traditionally been slow in implementing change, external changes are challenging higher education's resistance to change [1]. More educational providers are being encouraged to move towards more online and blended courses to meet existing students' needs and reach new students [2]. As stated by Folkers [1] coupled with these external changes, higher-level institutes face the continued growth of Internet use, decline in governmental support for education, and the emergence of a new student population. As highlighted by

Hirshon [3] the nature of education is changing in terms of (i) what higher-level institutes do and (ii) the financial resources available to perform their role. There are three themes that are influencing strategic planning in higher education: (i) population demographics, (ii) the increased importance and changing characteristics of non-traditional students on college campuses, and (iii) the economics of higher education [4]. As acknowledged Bradwell [5], the forces now confronting education in many respects represent a "perfect storm" of institutions expected to offer a more varied provision to a growing number of students in an era where funding is reducing. These are key strategic challenges that institutions must address in order to sustain the delivery of learning opportunities in the medium to long term. One of the leadership challenges that educational institutions face is maximizing the effectiveness of technology to underpin the support and delivery of the curriculum.

One of the most significant levers of changes in higher education will be technology. More programs are incorporating Web sites, more staff and students are using e-mail for in-depth communication and more high-level institutions are facilitating their students in transacting administrative requirements via the Internet [6]. Technology has begun to change the relationship between knowledge boundaries, creating new types of communications and underpinning work in novel ways [7].

2. Successful approaches to integrating Information and Communications Technology (ICT)

E-learning is not only an application of technology to teaching but it is also a new business model for higher education [8]. As highlighted by Chan and Welebir [9] e-learning not only creates new opportunities but also introduces new obstacles for the traditional higher-level institution. The Internet is facilitating new competition from both profit and non-profit competition to enter the higher education market free of traditional institutions' on-going requirements to invest in capital assets and personnel that reduce the capacity to affect and manage change to deliver e-learning programs [10].

It is insightful to review examples of successful educational institutions that have embraced many components of technology in the delivery of e-learning. Table 1, taken from [11], illustrates an effective strategy by comparing two educational institutions that have successfully engaged technology in the delivery of learning within a typical large US university. The key message that this highlights is the flexibility that exists within both the Open University and University of Phoenix models that may not exist in traditional US third-level institutions.

The greatest advantage which non-traditional providers of education have in their deployment of learning to remote participants is their financial and administrative model of operation [11]. The profit for educational institutions is that they do not educate those whom they find too expensive to educate on account of the demands of discipline which require investments in faculty and facilities to educate to a higher standard [7]. In 2003, while many virtual learning providers were experiencing challenging times, the University of Phoenix enrolments were

Characteristic	University of Phoenix	Open University	Composite of typical large US university
Total enrolment / Distance Learning (DL) enrolment	230,000 / 115,000	220,000 / 170,000 (many classes offer varying DL options)	10,000 / 1,000
Number of full-scale DL degree programs	20 undergraduate; 37 masters; 6 Phd	Over 200 degree options / combinations	Typically, none or one
Full-time cadre for DL (professors and staff)	1,500 (for DL and traditional)	1,120 (for DL and traditional)	50
Part-time DL instructors	9,600	8,000	5–50
Cost per credit hour	$570	$70–$200	$200–$500 public $500–$1,200 private
Student support infrastructure	Excellent (135 centers)	Excellent (352 regional / study centers)	Fair (most local campus facilities)
Sophistication of courseware	Excellent	Excellent	Fair (varies by course and instructor)
Teaching model	Part-time instructor / many materials provided	Part-time tutors / comprehensive materials provided	Full-time instructor / individualized training material
Typical per course salary	Adjunct $1,500–$2,000	Adjunct $1,500–$2,000	Full-time $10,000; adjunct $2,000
Program offerings	Undergraduate through PhD plus certificates	Undergraduate through PhD plus certificates	Undergraduate and graduate primarily plus certificates
Placement success of DL graduates	Good	Good	Good
Typical class size for DL graduate courses	12 (classes are 5 or 6 weeks in duration)	20	30+

Source: Ruth [11] (page 24, 2006).

Table 1. Comparison of e-learning program characteristics

rising at a compound yearly rate of approximately 20% and had enrolments of over 100,000 [12]. By 2005 this number was over 200,000 [13]. Wilson [14] states that the University of Phoenix is now the second largest higher education institution in the US with over 450,000 students. It is also insightful to note that neither the University of Phoenix nor the Open University use the online model exclusively but offer a range of options along the blended learning continuum [11]. Wilson [14] states that the University of Phoenix has 200 campuses in 39 states including Canada, Mexico, the Netherlands, and Puerto Rico.

It has been argued that electronic education should not attempt to replace traditional education but to support both staff and students through the provision of services that facilitate teaching, learning, and education-related administrative tasks [15]. The drivers of greater flexibility required by participants, third-party competition, and further rivalry among educational institutions mean that technology will play an ever-increasing role in the delivery of learning.

3. Challenge for educational management

Technology has to be taken seriously as a strategic asset and should be harnessed as a solution and a tool for the way educational institutions will support learning and research into the future [5]. Since 2002, the Sloan Consortium has surveyed chief academic offices with respect to the strategic importance of online learning to their institutions. Since the 2005 survey, the percentage of institutions agreeing with this statement has reached a plateau of approximately 60% [16].

A potentially useful framework, identified by the Higher Education Funding Council for England [17], suggests that there are benefits of using technology at three levels in educational institutions:

i. Efficiency – existing processes can be carried out in a more cost-effective, time-effective, sustainable, or scalable manner

ii. Enhancement – improving existing processes and the outcomes

iii. Transformation – radical, positive change in existing processes or introducing new processes.

The design, development, and implementation of e-learning in the delivery of learning can represent a significant investment without any guarantee of success. Therefore, it is vital that a strategic approach is embraced in deploying any initiative using technology. Embracing a strategic approach can result in the successful deployment of a blended program meeting the needs of participants and other external stakeholders.

A study by the Association of Public and Land-Grant Universities (2009) [18] identified a number of key leadership and policy issues for institutions leaders to consider. These include the following:

i. Leaders need to understand the characteristics of the online teaching populations in their institutions and use communication strategies that engage all faculty members

ii. Leaders should maintain consistent communication with all administrators and faculty regarding the role and purpose of online learning programs as they relate to the academic mission and academic quality. Faculty, administrators, and managers must work together to improve the quality and perceived quality of online learning outcomes

iii. In a climate where financial resources are declining, educational leaders need to regularly re-examine institutional policies regarding faculty incentives

iv. By better understanding what motivated faculty to teach online, leaders of educational institutions have the potential to expand faculty engagement in online instruction.

McPherson and Nunes [19] suggest that the role of academic leadership is to balance the dramatic effect that the political and social changes have had on teaching and learning within higher education institutions and guide institutions through the development of sound strategic change. Their research suggests that if "top-down" strategies are devised to implement e-learning strategies, it is the duty of academic leaders to ensure that appropriate levels of staffing and support are put in place. The critical success factors to facilitate this are captured in Table 2.

Provideinspirationalleadership	Examplesofissuesforconsideration
Realize agreed strategy · Involve staff in change processes · Focus on changing role of educational professionals	Have issues of ownership and Internet protocol been clarified? Have issues of culture/class/gender been resolved? Opens up options for students but may be threatening to tutors – could a slow and gradual transition be put in place? Is it possible to encourage a culture of open and evolving commitment?
Understand motivation for engagement · Offer recognition for staff commitment · Appreciate motivation of learners	Have motivational factors of the educational staff been determined? Is there a way to acknowledge dedication of teaching staff? Is motivation of virtual learning environment providers and developers the same as delivery staff? Are there incentives for the application of an e-learning framework? Has it been determined whether students are sufficiently independent and motivated to able to undertake computer-based learning? Can students see the benefits? Where e-learning is deemed desirable, are targets and customers well-defined? What are motivational factors for learners, i.e., rewards for learners?
Understand what is deemed acceptable and usable	Can academic staff be convinced that e-learning will work, i.e., do they have a wish to use and develop new tools? How are teaching staff going to use it? Do students' users want it and will they use it?
Ensure sufficient resourcing · Create (or at least measure) the demand for e-learning as a method of learning · Guarantee sufficient funding	Can teaching staff be persuaded of the need for convergency and flexibility to enhance students learning experiences? Can a move away from expectation of two lecturers, one lab, one tutorial, etc., per week be encouraged? Have issues of affordability and viability been determined? Has time resourcing, e.g., more time to teach online, been taken into account?

Source: McPherson and Nunes [19].

Table 2. Criticalsuccessfactorontologyfore-learningdelivery: Leadershipissues

The challenge for educational institutions is to get the best from the available resources and ensure that the program meets the objectives of participants in the context of the resources available. Even when the financial resources are available to invest in e-learning content, it does not ensure the success of the program. In the absence of resources to develop sophisticated e-learning content, the instructor must be empowered to embrace blended learning and acknowledge that his or her role must change. This presents significant strategic challenges for leaders in educational institutions.

4. Blended learning

The term blended learning has been widely adopted to depict combinations of face-to-face and technology-based learning [20]. Blended learning is a balanced learning design with this balance achieved by the combination of classroom instruction with self-paced instruction that is delivered over the Internet [21]. No two blended learning designs are identical, which introduces the great complexity of blended learning [22].

Blended learning, therefore, potentially offers the advantages of both traditional instruction and online learning. There is a need for a more formal approach to the development of policies and operations required in supporting blended learning approaches [23]. As stated by Pailing [24], blended learning may bring about major changes in the way educational material is designed, developed, and delivered to people who want to access learning but have other constraints that affect the process of learning. Blended learning, therefore, potentially offers the advantages of both traditional instruction and online learning.

5. Implementing technology-facilitated learning

Garrison and Kanuka [23] suggest that for academic administrators and leaders, the successful adoption of a blended learning approach requires the following:

1. Creation of clear institutional direction and policy
2. Frame the potential, increase awareness, and commit
3. Establishment of a single point of support, quality assurance, and project management
4. Creation of an innovation fund to provide the financial support and incentives to faculty and departments to initiate blended learning course transformation
5. Strategic selection of prototype projects that prove to be exceptionally successful exemplars of effective learning
6. Development of formal instructional design support available through a blended format
7. Systematic evaluation of satisfaction and success of the teaching learning, technology, and administration of new course
8. Create a task group to address issues, challenges, and opportunities as well as communicate and recommend new directions for the higher education community.

Delivering distance learning can involve a host of teaching and learning practices that can offer convenience for students but may be far more labor intensive for staff in higher-level institutes. For staff it includes (i) creating courses, (ii) maintaining chat rooms, (iii) responding to students queries by email around the clock, (iv) the new expectations of students on these programs including "anytime, anyplace learning," "round-the-clock availability of instructors," and "24/7 advising" [24, 25]. Newton [26] in an analysis of funded research by the Learning and Technology Support Network – Information and Computing Studies Group identified the following barriers to using technology in teaching and learning within the academic community in the UK: (i) increased time commitment, (ii) lack of incentives or rewards, (iii) lack of strategic planning and vision, (iv) lack of support, (v) lack of training in use of the technology, (vi) lack of support for pedagogical aspects of developments, and (vii) philosophical, epistemological, and social objections.

At an institutional level, the Higher Education Authority report [27] titled "Open and Flexible Learning – HEA Position Paper" suggested that matters such as innovative and imaginative timetabling, off-campus and workplace provision, etc., need to be addressed in encouraging staff involvement and facilitating greater engagement from learners. Research by the Joint Information Systems Committee [28] highlighted through a series of case studies that the tangible benefits of integrating technology in program delivery can be categorized as (i) cost savings / resource efficiency, (ii) recruitment and retention, (iii) skills and employment, (iv) student achievement, (v) inclusion, (vi) widening participation and social equality, and (vii) other benefits. Some suggestions as to how this can be capitalized upon within higher education institutions are proposed in Table 3.

Benefit	Explanation	Possible strategy to deploy in institutions
Cost savings / resource efficiency	Probably the most readily quantifiable cost savings were identified in the area of e-assessment where automated marking of exams for large cohorts of students now takes seconds rather than hours. Other savings resulted from the ability to cope with larger numbers of students, perhaps geographically spread, and the use of e-portfolio solutions for Personal Development Planning (PDP).	Investigate use of online assessment on modules and programs. Integrate e-Portfolio solutions (i.e., Mahara) as part of centrally project including industrial placement integration.
Recruitment and retention	The possibility of offering online courses has opened up new markets abroad. Technology has enabled institutions to support additional student numbers and improved personalization and mentoring has helped students who might otherwise feel isolated. E-Assessment has led to greater student satisfaction with their program of study.	Use of technology to delivery blended programs - leverage the expertise gained further within the Institute. Integrate technology further as part of assessment. Further offering of programs on an international basis.

Benefit	Explanation	Possible strategy to deploy in institutions
Skills and employment	Many of the initiatives studied were aimed at equipping graduates to be "fit for purpose." The broad skills agenda features across the full spectrum of examples but employability and employer engagement were specific features of many developments.	Build capacity through delivery of core foundation modules across all programs using technology to support learning. Identify key modules that will enhance employability of students and support using technology. Capture best practice on work placement models ensuring consistency across an institution.
Student achievement	There is clear evidence that e-learning offers increased opportunities for formative assessment leading to real benefits in terms of student retention and achievement. There was evidence of improvements in pass rates and overall marks and a high degree of student engagement with the process.	Build capacity to integrate technology to build in formative assessment, improving retention rates.
Inclusion	E-learning offers opportunities to support learners with a range of learning difficulties in ways which would simply not have been possible in the past. Many case studies explored how this was achieved, and again, e-assessment and flexibility were significant factors.	Learning resources to support students with learning difficulties such as dyslexia can be developed. The archiving of audio files can assist participants who may have visual impairments.
Widening participation and social equality	Case studies demonstrated that the use of e-learning has undoubtedly widened participation in UK higher education, be this participation by overseas students who would not previously have been able to attend courses in the UK, by professionals who need to fit study into a busy working life, or by the groups of "non-traditional" learners who form the target of government widening participation strategies.	Support resources such as language learning facilities for non-English speakers might be developed. Through strategic partnerships, use technology to deliver programs remotely, the capacity exists to build this further into postgraduate programs in particular. Reach a new student cohort who value flexibility.
Other benefits	Other benefits which may appear less immediately tangible, but nonetheless significant, include the external (international) recognition of the quality of UK higher education, the professional development of staff, improved pedagogic approaches, and beneficial effects on the development of research communities.	Capturing of best practices through the use of technology and using exemplars to further integrate technology into curriculum delivery.

Source: JISC [28]– Column 3 is proposed strategies to build capacity in an Educational Institution in Ireland.

Table 3. Potential tangible benefits of e-learning within higher education

It is incumbent on management in higher education to make a strategic decision on the role of technology in the delivery of learning. If the strategic decision is to embrace technology in the delivery of learning, then budgets need to be dedicated to resourcing appropriately the technological infrastructure, support and training mechanisms, and appropriate rewards and recognition systems for staff involved in the programs.

6. Evolution of E-learning content

Bruce [29], when discussing the evolution of technology, states that there are three scaling laws that apply: (i) Moore's Law – processor capabilities double every eighteen months, (ii) Saltzer's observation – solid-state and rotating memory double every twelve or so months, and (iii) Metcalfe's Law – the price of commodity bandwidth decreases by 50% every nine months. With the continued evolution of the Internet, providers of training and learning continue to integrate new technologies to improve the learning experience for the learner. Web 2.0 technologies have increased the availability and accessibility of content for both learners and instructors. Web 2.0 has enabled both instructors and learners to produce content, blurring the line between the instructor and the learner.

The range of initiatives and options available in the use of technology in the delivery of learning has promoted the option for educational institutions to collaborate in the development of content. Repositories of digital materials are now available in many disciplines to access e-learning material [30]. Some of the more established initiatives in this field in the sharing of experiences and creation of communities of practice in the delivery of learning content are Multimedia Educational Resource for Learning and Online Teaching (MERLOT) in the US, JISC in the UK, and National Digital Learning Repository (NDLR) in Ireland. This trend towards repositories is an attempt to share knowledge and reduce the cost of learning content development. It also offers the advantage of shared experiences and collaboration allowing for shared risk and rewards in content development. There is evidence that developers of content are creating learning material referred to as reusable learning objects and are sharing them by placing them in learning object repositories [31]. However, Cormier and Siemens [32] suggest that the significant number of high-profile open courseware initiatives from elite universities suggest that content of itself is not a sufficient value point on which to build the future of higher education.

7. Looking to the future

A report titled "Enhancing Learning and Teaching through the Use of Technology – A Revised Approach to HEFCE's Strategy for e-Learning" [17] has developed a framework to assist institutions in maximizing the strategic benefits of technology outlined in Table 4. Underpinning this report is recognition of the diverse institutional missions and strategic priorities meaning that it would be counter-productive to prescribe institutional activities. The intention of this HEFCE report is to highlight those strategic areas where institutions may see a benefit from investing in technology and to help institutions map those benefits to specific institutional goals, strategic plans, or internal documents.

The framework is designed to help classify priorities for development. The implementation scaffolding is designed to be flexible, and HEFCE anticipate that institutions will adjust this framework to suit their specific requirements. In order to plan effectively for enhancement, institutions will need to convert these into specific goals, development pathways, and measures of success.

Activity area	Strategic priorities	Harnessing technology for strategic gain – examples of development goals
1. Pedagogy, curriculum design, and development	Enhancing excellence and innovation in teaching and learning Enhancing flexibility and choice for learners Enhancing student achievement Improving employability and skills Attracting and retaining learners Supporting research-based or enquiry-based learning Engaging employers (or other stakeholders) in curriculum design and delivery Improving efficiency of curriculum design and delivery processes	Tutors have access to a wide range of tools to support teaching, and a wide range of high-quality resources to engage students. Innovative uses of technology for learning are supported by the curriculum design process. Technology is used to enhance the responsiveness and flexibility of curriculum offerings. Technology is used to help identify learners with specific aptitudes or needs. Information and information systems are used effectively to support curriculum planning. Web 2.0 technologies are harnessed to support communities of learning and research. E-assessment technologies are used to support innovative practices such as just-in-time assessment and peer review. Students are developing their digital and learning literacies throughout their studies. Technologies for teaching and research are joined up in ways that support scholarship across the institution.
2.Learning resources and environments	Enhancing flexibility and choice for learners Enhancing student achievement Improving employability and skills Widening participation and improving access Effective management of learning resources Designing and maintaining effective environments for learning	Students can access information, support, expertise and guidance, and communicate with each other, wherever they are studying. Students can access personalized services within institutional environments, and use personal tools to suit their individual needs. Tools for scholarly communication are widely used, for example for feedback, collaborative research, and peer review. Tutors are collaborating in subject communities to produce high-quality, reusable learning resources.

Activity area	**Strategic priorities**	**Harnessing technology for strategic gain – examples of development goals**
		Tutors have access to relevant learning resources, and support for adapting, integrating, and enhancing them. There is continuity across learning, teaching, research, and administrative environments to support joined-up processes.
3. Lifelong learning processes and practices	Improving employability and skills Enhancing flexibility and choice for learners Widening participation and improving access to learning opportunities Supporting diverse learners' needs Retaining learners and meeting learners' expectations Co-operating with other institutions, colleges, and campuses	Students can record, access, reflect on, and present their achievements in ways appropriate to a variety of situations. Assistive and personal technologies are used effectively to support students with diverse needs and aptitudes. Local and regional communities are involved with the institution via electronically supported networks, for example, through lifelong learning networks. Students can access information online to make informed choices about their programs of study including choices about how and where to access learning. Technology is used to help students connect formal study with other aspects of life and work. Joined-up information systems support students in transition or while studying at more than one location or institution.
4. Strategic management, human resources, and capacity development	Enhancing excellence in teaching Enhancing excellence in research Workforce development Business/community links Improving efficiency and effectiveness of institutional processes	All staff have opportunities to develop and practise skills for enhancing learning through the use of technology. Staff skills for technology-enhanced learning are recognized in their roles and responsibilities and in reward structures. Technology is being used to join up and make more efficient the administrative and information management processes of the institution. Content resources are managed in an integrated way, allowing institutional assets to be exploited effectively for learning, teaching, and research. Institutional strategies (for example, for learning, teaching, and assessment; widening participation; learning spaces; information management; and human resources) include consideration of potential enhancements through technology. Staff and student time are used effectively through appropriate technical interventions.
5. Quality	Institutional quality processes can support objectives and enhance benefits in all the other areas	Institutional quality processes are agile enough to respond quickly to learners' and employer's needs.

Activity area	Strategic priorities	Harnessing technology for strategic gain – examples of development goals
		Streamlined quality processes allow institutions to feel confident in the quality of their provision at a reduced administrative burden. Enhancements through use of technology are taken into account in quality assurance arrangements.
6. Research and evaluation	Enhancing excellence in learning and teaching Enhancing excellence in research Enhancing understanding of learning and teaching processes Enhancing institutional processes (especially quality assurance and review)	Staff have access to research, evidence, and scholarship to inform curriculum development and research-based teaching. Staff engage actively with the scholarship of teaching and are involved in innovation in using technology for learning and teaching. Institutions have effective mechanisms for evaluating learners' experiences of learning, including learning with technology. Learners, and staff involved in teaching, participate actively in strategic decisions about technology in the learning environment.
7. Infrastructure and technical standards	Enhancing flexibility for learners Supporting diverse learners' needs Enhancing efficiency of institutional processes Enhancing the technical infrastructure Enhancing the information environment Ensuring effective ICT investments and effective use of existing ICT resources Sustainability ("green" computing)	Technology is being used to join up and make more efficient the core administrative and information management processes of the institution. Due to more coherence and collaboration, technical issues have been addressed to give better value for money. Institutions are making good technology investments and finding the right balance of commercially developed, open source, and bespoke solutions. Institutions are providing technical support at an appropriate level to staff and students as users. Institutions are taking an informed approach to adoption and implementation of standards to support system interoperability and coherence. Institutions are making effective use of the network services and resources invested in by the sector as a whole.

Source: HEFCE [17].

Table 4. Enhancing learning and teaching through the use of technology: A suggested framework for institutions

8. Proposed strategy for educational institutions

As Taylor [33] states, the Internet can be a wonderful tool for instructors. Creating a new course or transforming a traditional instructor-led program to an online format involves much more than converting notes to HTML pages. Howell et al. [34] suggest seven strategies to be adopted and applied in facilitating the delivery of distance learning using technology. These are as follows:

- Enable higher-level institutes and departments to accept more responsibility for distance education activities
- Provide faculty with more information about distance education programs and activities
- Encourage faculty to incorporate technology into their traditional classrooms
- Provide strong incentives for faculty to participate in distance education
- Improve training and instructional support for distance education faculty
- Build a stronger education faculty community
- Encourage more distance scholarship and research.

Source: Howell et al. [34].

9. Proposed strategic deployment model

If one considers the delivery of blended learning to include (i) e-learning content, (ii) virtual learning environment (VLE), (iii) instructor-delivered content, instructor support for students, (iv) student engagement, (v) student support, (vi) assessment and evaluation, and (vii) accreditation similar to a supply chain, the key strategic decisions that need to be made are with respect to what can be potentially outsourced, where collaboration may be possible, and what elements should remain in the domain of educational institutions.

One possible model of the redefined supply chain could be as outlined in Figure 1.

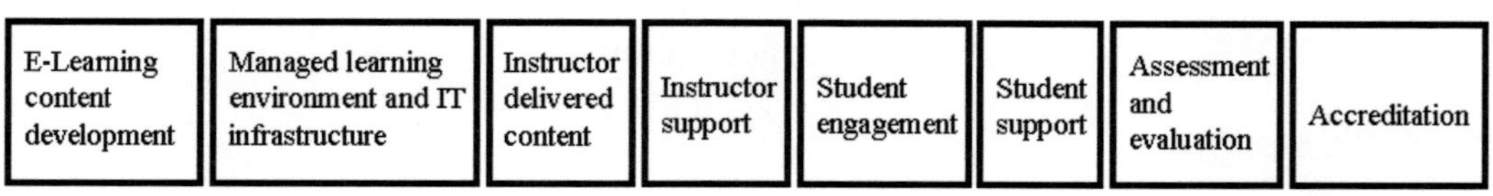

Figure 1. Supply Chain Model of Education

As technology has become ubiquitous, having the capacity to manage the IT infrastructure to support learning is an element in the delivery of learning that educational institutions should continue to develop a competency in house. Outsourcing content delivery and creation or collaborative approaches to develop content may result in potential saving for institutions. Educational institutions are best placed to support students, engage in the assessment of learning and accreditation of participants learning. This module is illustrated in Figure 2.

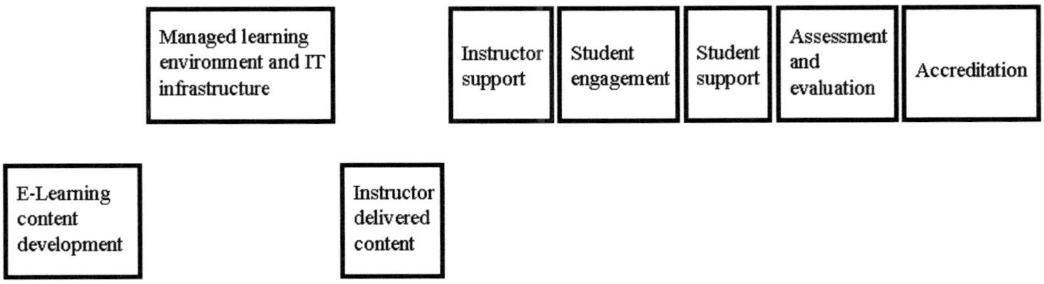

Figure 2. Proposed supply chain model for e-learning deployment

Socialization is a key reason for participants engaging with traditional models of education. It may be useful to construct a framework that will assist in deploying lifelong learning using technology. This framework, outlined in Figure 3, is constructed around four key parameters:

1. Participants
2. The delivery of the instruction
3. Online learning
4. Traditional instruction.

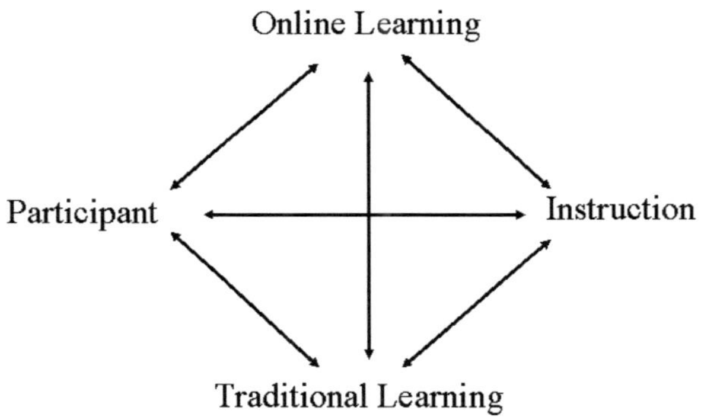

Source: Wall [35].

Figure 3. Framework of parameters in blended learning

There should be a balance between online learning and traditional learning and between the participant and the relationship formed with the instructor as part of any module to be delivered. A change in any one of these parameters has consequences for any other elements of the framework. The emphasis on instruction method, the balance between online and traditional instructions, and the degree of directed and independent learning will change, based on the individual's learning preferences, the material to be learned, the skills, ability, and instructional methodology of the instructor and the prior experience of the individual.

Blended learning offers institutions the opportunity to engage in using technology in conjunction with traditional delivery to offer learning. The issue then becomes how to configure this blend? There are often clear differences between the various subject disciplines in terms of technological and pedagogical innovation and what appears well embedded in one subject area may be quite innovative in another. Institutions are challenged to identify appropriate strategies for the various subject discipline areas.

On the basis of detailed research carried out in Waterford Institute of Technology in Ireland, where the deployment of a blended learning initiative was evaluated from both participants' and instructors' perspectives, a proposed framework for deploying lifelong learning is outlined in Table 5, identifying milestones, looking at key aspects of each milestone, suggesting possible activities to be undertaken to address the key aspects identified, and identifying the possible benefits as a result.

Milestone	**Aspect**	**Key considerations**	**Potential benefits**
1	Appreciate the learning process	Appreciate that everyone learns differently, so use multiple instructional methodologies. Recognize that a "one-size-fits-all" approach will not work. Individuals have different prior learning experiences. Use Learning Style Profiling Tool(s).	Instructors are aware that various instructional methodologies in both the classroom and online environment can enhance the learning experience. Can plan for instructional methods to capture peer learning.
2	Learning Management System (LMS)	Investigate current LMS system in organization. Invest in LMS, either purchase or use open sources system.	An established protected environment with a series of resources, administrative functions, and tools that can act as the platform for more sophisticated development and integration of resources over time.
3	Agreed standards in the delivery of material	Posting notes on LMS. All communication through LMS. Assignments posted through LMS. Use a voice over Internet Protocol (IP) communication platform.	Consistency from the participants' perspective. Different possible communications platforms that address learners' needs, increasing flexibility, overcoming any sense of isolation and ensure that participants are continuously engaged.
4	Agreed breakdown of classroom and online elements	Once module has been designed and learning outcomes agreed, agree on elements that will be delivered in a traditional setting and the elements that may be delivered online.	Overcomes the sense of isolation that participants may experience.
5	Assessment	Agreed breakdown of assessment methodologies.	More engaged with work / improved work performance.

Milestone	Aspect	Key considerations	Potential benefits
		Attempt to integrate assessment with work.	Can encourage work-based learning.
6	Agreed dates for traditional delivery and program of work at the commencement of the program	Appoint a leader to coordinate the scheduling of assignments, dates for delivery of traditional instruction, and online instruction and collaboration.	Participants can plan both work and private life, as they are informed in advance, for the times when formal traditional instruction takes place.
7	ICT infrastructure of participants	Survey participant's ICT ability and infrastructure at both work and home. Consider including purchase of laptop or distribution of a CD with requisite course material and software loaded.	Understanding of IT ability and infrastructure of the participants may help in tailoring some elements of the instructional methodologies to better meet participants' needs and circumstances.
8	Provide adequate induction	Develop guides Using of LMS Voice over IP communication Relevant software packages Library infrastructure / remote access facilities	Less administrative and communication challenges once program is up and running.
9	Use of multiple methods of communication with participants	Email (both work and student email) LMS Mobile devices Voice over IP communication	Emails to work act as a reminder to participants. Voice over IP allows for collaboration and collaborative learning to take place. Use of video and audio presentations where appropriate can facilitate collaborative learning. Discussion boards or blogs can be an effective learning resource.
10	Plan in social events	Informal get-together for meal or drinks events at commencement and throughout the program.	Breaks down barriers. Participants may find it easier to contribute particularly in the online environment as barriers have been broken down. Allows for further networking opportunities.
11	Creation of online resources	Can be costly and staff delivering the program may not have the expertise to develop sophisticated online resources.	Can enhance the learning experience when instructionally effective resources are developed.

Milestone	Aspect	Key considerations	Potential benefits
		Strategic decision to set aside funding on a continuing basis to facilitate online resource development and training.	Research integration of existing available resources.
12	Look at new / novel methods to focus on active learning	Use of problem-based learning; integrate existing developed resources such as games / simulations as part of modules / assessment.	Encourages collaborative and peer learning. Allows for informal learning to take place.
13	Recognition of the effort of staff delivering modules	Provide adequate training. Allow staff sufficient time to develop resources. Provide adequate reward scheme. Staff required to be more flexible in dealing with participants.	Staff more motivated. New skills sets developed. Broadens the institution's reach into industry.

Source: Wall and Ahmed [36].

Table 5. Proposed framework for deploying blended lifelong learning

This framework builds on the literature review and analysis of the formal blended learning program in Waterford Institute of Technology (WIT). It is fundamental at the outset to appreciate the learning process. By acknowledging that learning is complex, instructors and educational institutions should be open to new ideas / increased flexibility. The use of a learning style profiling tool such as Kolb Learning Style Inventory can assist in making instructors aware that there are many learner types and plan for a variety of instructional strategies, ensuring the benefits of understanding the variety of learner types. Establishing the appropriate infrastructure and standards of delivery will ensure a minimum standard of consistency. This still recognizes that instructors may be at different levels of confidence and experience in the use of technology in the delivery of learning. It will also encourage instructors who gain confidence to become more sophisticated and advanced in their use of technology over time.

By agreeing the breakdown of classroom and online elements prior to the commencement of the program, instructors know what is expected and participants can plan how to integrate formal continuing professional development (CPD) into their work and personal life. It helps plan dates and times for traditional delivery in advance. By focusing explicitly on assessment at the outset, instructors can plan a coherent assessment strategy and an evenly distributed workload can be achieved. Recognizing the ICT infrastructure of the participants' highlights at the outset of any potential problems, allowing for these challenges to overcome/mitigate early during the program. This will help in providing an appropriate level of induction, ensuring a smooth delivery and administration of the program. The use of multiple methods of communication allows the integration of both asynchronous and synchronous communications and also acknowledges the variety of possible learning styles as mentioned earlier. The usefulness of social events should not be underestimated. As regards breaking down barriers, it can help build community morale on the program.

Identifying the creation of online resources as a discrete milestone challenges institutions to take a strategic approach to deploying blended learning. Searching for new/novel methods to encourage active learning helps build on the experiential learning of the group and encourages a continuous search for new instructional approaches. Finally, recognizing the key role of staff will ensure the initial and ongoing level of success or otherwise of the blended approach.

10. Conclusion

Current methods of working in educational institutions will be difficult to sustain in an environment where (i) the funding to institutions is reducing, (ii) demand for services is increasing, (iii) the demographics of students are changing, (iv) students are becoming more technologically literate and demanding, (v) the requirements to broaden access are growing, and (vi) there is an increasing need to provide flexible lifelong and work-based learning opportunities while maintaining the reputation for excellence in teaching, innovation, and research.

As funding mechanisms continue to change and rapid advances in ICT continue to transform the way education is delivered, developing a framework to deploy learning to address the diverse learning needs of future learners presents many challenges to higher education. The adoption of ICT to support and facilitate the development of educational programs can be at various stages of the technological adoption cycle in higher education. In many cases, it remains unknown and as such carries significant risk in terms of costs if not deployed successfully. Higher education institutions are under pressure to find new strategies and delivery models to enhance student learning. There is no unique formula to apply for the successful development and delivery of blended learning. Deploying blended learning is a complex and demanding undertaking from pedagogical and technological perspectives, which places new roles and responsibilities on both the participant and the instructor. Recognizing the rapidly changing landscape of education challenges, leaders in higher education institutions need to respond in a proactive manner. The frameworks proposed in this paper are put forward as a "roadmap" that may assist institutions plan the "route" to further integrating technology in both curriculum development and delivery.

Author details

John Wall*

Address all correspondence to: jwall@wit.ie

Waterford Institute of Technology, Waterford, Ireland

References

[1] Folkers D.A. 2005. Competing in the marketspace: Incorporating online education into higher education – An organisational perspective. *Information Resources Management Journal*, vol. 18, no. 1, pp. 61–77.

[2] Schrum L., Burbank M. and Capps R. 2007. Preparing future teachers for diverse schools in an online learning community: Perceptions and practice. *Internet and Higher Education*, vol. 10, pp. 204–211.

[3] Hirson A. 2005. A Diamond in the Rough Divining the Future of E-Content. Educause Review, 2005, pp. 34 – 44.

[4] Falk C.F. and Blaylock B.K. 2010. Strategically planning campuses for the "newer students" in higher education. *Academy of Educational Leadership Journal*, vol. 14, no. 3, pp. 15–38.

[5] Bradwell P. 2009. The Edgeless University: Why higher education must embrace technology. Accessed February 15, 2010, http://www.demos.co.uk/files/Edgeless_University_-_web.pdf.

[6] Johnstone S. 2002. Signs of the times change in coming for e-learning. *Educause Review*, pp. 15–24.

[7] Mellow G. and Woolis D. 2010. Teetering between eras: higher education in a global, knowledge networked world, *On the Horizon*, vol. 18 no. 4 pp. 308-319.

[8] Steinberg D.C. 2004. The Business model of e-learning in UK higher education: Optimization, through outsourcing. *Industry and Higher Education*, vol. 18, no. 3, pp. 187–198.

[9] Chan P.S. and Welebir B. 2003. Strategies for e-education. *Industrial and Commercial Training*, vol. 35, no. 5, pp. 196–202.

[10] Graves W.H. 2001. Virtual operations challenges for traditional higher education. *Educause Review*, vol. 36, no. 2, pp. 46–56.

[11] Ruth S.B. 2006. E-learning – A financial and strategic perspective. *Educause Review*, no. 1, pp. 22–30.

[12] McCredie J. 2003. Does it matter to higher education? *Educause Review*, vol. 38, no. 6, pp. 15–22.

[13] Buchen I.H. 2005. The future of higher education and professional training. *Foresight*, vol. 7, no. 4, pp. 13–21.

[14] Wilson R. 2010. For-profit colleges change higher education's landscape, *The Chronicle of Higher Education*. Accessed 15th July 2015 http://chronicle.com/article/For-Profit-Colleges-Change-/64012/

[15] Lehner F., Nosekabel H. and Lehmann H. 2003. Wireless e-learning and communication environment: WELCOME at the University of Regensburg. *E-Services Journal*, vol. 2, no. 3, pp. 23–42.

[16] Allen E. and Seaman J. 2010. Class differences: Online education in the United States, 2010. The Sloan Consortium. Accessed March 5, 2010, http://www.sloanconsortium.org

[17] HEFCE. 2009. Enhancing learning and teaching through the use of technology - A revised approach to HEFCE's strategy for e-learning. Accessed February 15, 2010, www.hefce.ac.uk/Pubs/hefce/2009/09_12/

[18] Association of Public and Land-Grant Universities. 2009. Online Learning as a Strategic Resource, Volume I: A Resource for Campus Leaders. Accessed February 15, 2010, www.aplu.org/NetCommunity/Document.Doc?id=1879

[19] McPherson M.A. and Nunes J.M. 2008. Critical issues for e-learning delivery: What may seem obvious is not always put into practice. *Journal of Computer Assisted Learning*, vol. 24, no. 5, pp. 433–445.

[20] Stubbs M., Martin I. and Endlar L. 2006. The structuration of blended learning: Putting holistic design principles into practice. *British Journal of Educational Technology*, vol. 37, no. 2, pp. 163–175.

[21] Voci E. and Young K. 2001. Blended learning in a leadership development programme. *Industrial and Commercial Training*, vol. 33, no. 5, pp. 157–160.

[22] Garrison D.R. and Kanuka H. 2004. Blended learning: Uncovering its transformative potential in higher education. *Internet and Higher Education*, vol. 7, no. 2, pp. 95–105.

[23] Pailing M. 2002. E-learning: Is it really the best thing since sliced bread? *Industrial and Commercial Training*, vol. 34, no. 4, pp. 151–155.

[24] Alexander S. 2001. E-Learning developments and experiences. *Education + Training*, vol. 43, no. 4/5, pp. 240–248.

[25] Levine A. and Sun J.C. 2002. Barriers to distance education, American Council on Education Center for Policy Analysis. Accessed January 17, 2005, http://acenet.edu/bookstore

[26] Newton R. 2003. Staff attitudes to the development and delivery of e-learning, *New Library World*, vol. 104, no. 1193, pp. 412–425.

[27] Higher Education Authority. 2009. *Open and Flexible Learning – HEA Position Paper.*

[28] JISC. 2008. Tangible benefits of e-learning, does investment yield interest? Accessed February 15, 2010, www.jisc.ac.uk/media/documents/publications/bptangiblebenefitsv1.pdf

[29] Bruce J.D. 2003. Beyond bandwidth. *Educause Review*, pp. 23–31.

[30] Ruiz J.G., Teasdale T.A., Hajjar I., Shaughnessy M. and Mintzer M.J. 2007. The consortium of e-learning in geriatrics instruction. *Journal of American Geriatrics Society*, vol. 55, no. 3, pp. 458–463.

[31] Bond S., Ingram C. and Ryan S. 2008. Reuse, repurposing and learning design – Lessons from the DART project. *Computers & Education*, vol. 50, no. 2, pp. 601–612.

[32] Cormier D. and Siemens G. 2010. Through the open door: Open courses as research, learning and engagement. *Educause Review*, vol. 45, no. 4, pp. 30–39.

[33] Taylor R.W. 2002. Pros and cons of online learning – a faculty perspective. *Journal of European Industrial Training*, vol. 26, no. 1, pp. 24–37.

[34] Howell S.L., Saba F., Lindsay N.K. and Williams P.B. 2004. Seven strategies for enabling faculty success in distance education. *Internet and Higher Education*, vol. 7, pp. 33–49.

[35] Wall J. 2009. The Development of Technology Facilitated Learning for Continuing Professional Development of Construction Managers. PhD Thesis, University of Salford, Salford, UK.

[36] Wall J. and Ahmed V. 2008. Lessons learned from a case study in deploying blended learning continuing professional development. *Engineering* Construction and Architectural Management, vol. 15, no. 2, pp. 185–202.

Chapter 17

Considerations on Barriers to Effective E-learning toward Accessible Virtual Campuses

Salvador Otón, Héctor R. Amado-Salvatierra, José Ramón Hilera, Eva García and Antonio García

Additional information is available at the end of the chapter

http://dx.doi.org/10.5772/60605

Abstract

Nowadays, the implementation of virtual campuses is a reality, both in academic settings and in the workplace. However, there are several challenges associated with the implementation of effective learning outcomes via e-learning. In this chapter in particular, the use of e-learning to reach students with disabilities and the barriers that they may have will be presented. In this sense, e-learning solutions adopted by several institutions are encouraged to validate and promote accessibility in a virtual campus. A large myriad of research related to accessibility in distance education systems is available in literature, and the most relevant studies and standards are presented in this chapter as a starting point for education institutions looking at improving the accessibility in their own virtual campuses. This work is intended to be relevant both to teachers and lecturers who use e-learning for their courses, and to those involved in the design, setup, and maintenance of e-learning systems, whether from a pedagogical or technical perspective to take into account the accessibility for students with disabilities. This work will explore on the accessibility of the basic stone of the e-learning process, the learning objects. An analysis of the IMS AfA v3.0 specification will be presented as a starting point to develop an accessible and adaptable online course, based on the student's preferences, within an accessible virtual campus.

Keywords: accessibility, learning objects, adaptability, disability, e-inclusion

1. Introduction

A virtual campus is an environment based on a web technology that provides facilities for the development, management, and publication of content that contributes to the process of teaching and learning. The process of teaching and learning enhanced by technology is commonly known as e-learning. The virtual campus is the fundamental element on which a virtual education project is based. If it is an accessible virtual campus, it must be ensured that all functionality can be used by any user, including users with disabilities.

There are several challenges associated with the implementation of effective learning outcomes via e-learning within a virtual campus. In this chapter in particular, the considerations on the use of e-learning to reach students with disabilities and the barriers [1–5] that they may have will be analyzed, providing the basic knowledge to prepare an accessible virtual campus.

This chapter is structured as follows: A state of the art on accessibility related to virtual campuses, highlighting studies related to the application of accessibility standards to improve the e-learning systems is presented in the first section. The first section explores on the main accessibility requirements for an e-learning campus. Then a review on the basic knowledge that the stakeholders involved in e-learning education should have in order to preserve and promote accessibility is presented. In particular, the authors propose an evaluation guideline on accessibility for virtual campus administrators. Finally, the considerations on the accessibility requirements of learning objects (LOs) are presented using the IMS Access for all v3.0 specification, the main objective of which is to simplify the definition of the accessibility metadata for learning objects and the preferences and needs of the users of these objects tracing them to students' related disabilities.

2. State of the art on accessibility related to virtual campuses

A virtual campus is an environment based on a web technology that provides facilities for the development, management, and publication of content that contribute to the process of teaching and learning. In this work, a virtual campus will be also referred as e-learning system and learning management system (LMS). In terms on legislation related to students with disabilities in e-learning, Edmonds [6] explored the different laws available and highlights the legal and technical concerns for education institutions. International legislation in terms of technological evolution related to e-learning is reflected on the Convention on the Rights of Persons with Disabilities (CRPD) in Article 9 (points 2.g an 2.h) [7]. The CRPD highlights the importance of promoting access to information and communications technology (ICT) for people with disabilities (PWD) and specially producing accessible content in early stages at minimum costs. Related to education, the (CRPD) in Article 24 recognizes the right to education. Countries that signed the CRPD must make sure that students with disabilities are able to get access not only to general education but also to tertiary education, vocational training, adult education, and lifelong learning without discrimination and on an equal basis with others.

In terms of accessibility, the International Organization for Standardization (ISO) defines accessibility as "the usability of a product, service, environment or facility by people with the widest range of capabilities" [8]. The World Wide Web Consortium (W3C), the organization in charge of developing web standards, created the Web Accessibility Initiative (WAI) with the aim of studying the problems of accessibility and propose solutions. One of its most known results is the Web Content Accessibility Guidelines (WCAG) 2.0 that establishes four principles that give the foundation of web accessibility: web content must be perceivable, understandable, operable, and robust [8].

In terms on learning objects accessibility, it is important to take into consideration the standard ISO/IEC 24751 [9–11] to describe the process of using an accessible online educational system, which takes into account the needs and preferences of the student and contains accessibility metadata of the learning objects. This chapter will explore also on the metadata for the learning objects using the IMS Access for All v3.0 specification [12], the main objective of which is to simplify the definition of the accessibility metadata for learning objects and the preferences and needs of the users of these objects.

2.1. General requirements for accessibility of learning management systems (LMS)

Learning management systems (LMS) are mainly based on web technologies through a client–server model, with an interface prepared to work base on HTML markup and presented in a web browser. For this type of systems, accessibility requirements should be followed, especially guidelines provided by the Web Accessibility Initiative (WAI) [13] part of the World Wide Web Consortium (W3C). These guidelines are summarized as follows:

- Authoring Tool Accessibility Guidelines (ATAG) [14]—guidelines intended to software used to create web sites and content
- User Agent Accessibility Guidelines (UAAG) [15]—addresses web browsers and media players, and especially related to assistive technologies interaction
- Web Content Accessibility Guidelines (WCAG) [8]—guidelines intended to improve information on a web site, including text, images, videos, etc.
- Accessible Rich Internet Applications (WAI-ARIA) [16]—defines a way to make dynamic web content and web applications based on new interactive technologies as Ajax, HTML5 more accessible

2.2. Accessibility requirements for content and user interfaces

Learning management systems (LMS) work with web technology, so their user interfaces can be evaluated based on the basic principles for creating accessible web content as presented in WCAG 2.0. The universality of these guidelines is evidenced by the fact that it was approved in 2012 as an international standard: ISO/IEC DIS 40500 [8]. WCAG 2.0 identifies twelve guidelines and numerous compliance criteria ("*success criteria*"). WCAG 2.0 is based around four main principles, which provide the necessary basis for anyone to access and use a system. The four principles are described as follows:

- Perceivable: This principle is related to how information and user interface components must be presentable to users in ways they can perceive without limitations. This means that users must be able to perceive the content and information available in a web, the information presented in any part of the web must be visible to all of their senses.

- Operable: This principle is based on the fact that user interface components and navigation through a web must be operable. This is important so that users must be able to operate the interface, avoiding to ask the user some interaction that she cannot perform.
- Understandable: This means that users must be able to understand the information as well as the operation of the user interface without more details provided.
- Robust: Content presented in a web must be really robust, in a way that it can be interpreted easily by a wide variety of user agents, especially software and hardware prepared as assistive technologies. This means in other works that users must be able to access the content independently as technologies advance and evolve.

Under each of the four principles, there is a list of guidelines that address the principle. There are a total of 12 guidelines. One of the key objectives of the guidelines is to ensure that content is directly accessible to as many people as possible. There are success criteria related to each guideline, which describe specifically what must be achieved in order to conform to the WCAG 2.0 standard [8]. Each success criterion is written as a statement that will be either true or false when specific web content is tested against it. Table 1 presents the 12-guideline part of the standard.

Principles	**Guidelines**
Perceivable	1.1 Provide text alternatives for any non-text content so that it can be changed into other forms people need, such as large print, Braille, speech or simpler language.
	1.2 Provide alternatives for time-based media.
	1.3 Create content that can be presented in different ways (for example, simpler layout) without losing information or structure.
	1.4 Make it easier for users to see and hear content, including separating foreground from background.
Operable	2.1 Make all functionality available from a keyboard.
	2.2 Provide users enough time to read and use content.
	2.3 Do not design content in a way that is known to cause seizures.
	2.4 Provide ways to help users navigate, find content, and determine where they are.
Understandable	3.1 Make text content readable and understandable.
	3.2 Make web pages appear and operate in predictable ways.
	3.3 Help users avoid and correct mistakes.
Robust	4.1 Maximize compatibility with current and future user agents, including assistive technologies.

Table 1. Accessibility guidelines for web content WCAG 2.0

The group of principles, guidelines, and success criteria based on WCAG 2.0 [8] are applicable to any web pages and digital content. In the case of e-learning systems (e.g., LMS), these systems are a group of web pages and educational digital content so WCAG 2.0 can be applied to each element. As a summary, the following six basic accessibility principles should be included in every e-learning system [17]:

1. Allow users to customize their portal based on their preferences.
2. Provide equivalents to every time-based media and visual elements.
3. Use different ways to present information in an interface.
4. Provide information appropriate compatible with assistive technologies.
5. Allow access to all functionalities via keyboard.
6. Provide background information and status and location information to the user at all times.

From WCAG 2.0 [8] guidelines and different accessibility related laws, in terms of basic functionality, e-learning systems (learning content management systems) should have the following basic characteristics:

1. Structure
   a. Absence of markup code errors in pages (HTML, CSS)
   b. Setting of accessibility preferences as default configuration, available for user personalization
   c. Accessibility check for content creators (HTML editors) and images selectors (e.g., alternative texts for each image)
   d. Summary of last activity within the system
2. Keyboard navigation
   a. Definition of a logical order to display tab indicators, provide a visual place mark to identify where the user is in a particular moment
   b. Provide links to jump to main content
   c. Functionality to simplify configuration to minimize secondary content pages and menus
   d. Functionality to select options using a simple combination of keys
   e. Provide complete access to all functionality via keyword, including HTML editors, controls in multimedia viewers, and Web 2.0 functionalities (e.g., Drag and drop")
   f. Enable keyboard shortcuts (hotkeys) and provide a definition page with all combinations
   g. Provide a complete sitemap structure for navigation in all systems
   h. If a key is pressed by mistake, provide the ability to undo and return to previous state
3. Magnification of screen size and functionality to change colors contrast
   a. Provide a standard design of the interface through all systems in order to find similar functionality on all tools

b. Provide integration for assistive technologies

c. Provide a selector to change style sheets for user personalization

d. Avoid the communication of system information based on colors (e.g., buttons with a specific color and meaning)

e. Provide the ability to change user preferences to change font size and style

f. Maximize compatibility with assistive technologies

g. Compliance-oriented design to improve interoperability with assistive technologies

h. Consistent and unique design of headings, links, buttons and images description

i. Provide descriptive forms including support for errors correction. Identification of the location of the users when filling a form

j. Minimal use of frames, appropriate use of title in frames, provide adoption of ARIA standard attributes and navigational marks ("role landmarks"), structural tags, and alerts

4. Multimedia (audio) functionalities

2.3. Accessibility requirements for content authoring tools

Authoring tools are software and services included in e-learning systems (LMS), used for teachers and students to produce web content as educational material. Authoring tools related to LMS include desktop applications, multimedia authoring tools, and mainly HTML editors (e.g., what-you-see-is-what-you-get WYSIWIG editors). These tools should follow the Authoring Tool Accessibility Guidelines (ATAG) 2.0 [14].

The Authoring Tool Accessibility Guidelines (ATAG) explain to developers how to make and adapt the authoring tools to be accessible so that people with disabilities can access and create educational content. The guidelines explain how to help authors (teachers and students) to create more accessible web content (learning material) with inline validators, forms with hints and reminders.

Accessibility, from the perspective of authoring tools, is related to content creators and then for final users (especially people with disabilities). Thus, ATAG [14] is divided into two parts, each reflecting a key aspect of accessibility with respect to authoring tools. Part A "Make the authoring tool user interface accessible" relates to the accessibility of authoring tool user interfaces to authors with disabilities. Part B "Support the production of accessible content" relates to support by authoring tools for the creation, by any author (teachers and students, not just those with disabilities), of web content that is more accessible to end users with disabilities.

Besides general authoring tools, which are referred by ATAG, it is important to keep in mind that in the field of e-Learning, educational resources are usually packaged in containers for interoperability and reusability. Following ATAG [14] recommendations, tools used to prepare educational containers should take into account the accessibility requirements.

The format most commonly used is Sharable Content Object Reference Model (SCORM). This is a set of standards and specifications for creating structured teaching objects [18]. With SCORM, it is possible to create content that can be imported into different learning management systems providing SCORM compatibility. Based on the original definition of SCORM (ADL) [18], it is important to mention the six motivations of the standards: accessibility, adaptability, affordability, durability, interoperability, and reusability. In this chapter, Section 4 will elaborate on two aspects: accessibility and adaptability for the learning objects, building blocks for this standard.

2.4. Accessibility requirements for multimedia tools

The users of an e-learning campus use different tools as media players, web browsers, and assistive technologies to be part of the educational process. These tools are known as user agents. The User Agent Accessibility Guidelines (UAAG) [15] explain how to make user agents accessible to people with disabilities, particularly to increase accessibility to web content, a basic building block for educational material in a virtual campus. As described in the working draft of UAAG Guidelines, in addition to helping developers of browsers and media players, UAAG 2.0 benefits developers of assistive technologies because it explains what types of information and control an assistive technology may expect from a user agent that follows UAAG 2.0. Assistive technologies not addressed directly by UAAG 2.0 [15] (e.g., Braille rendering) are still essential to ensuring web access for some users with disabilities.

UAAG is organized in guidelines, principles, and success criteria elements. There are five principles: "perceivable, operable, understandable, programmatic access, and specification and conventions." Following the principles, there are 27 guidelines [15].

2.5. Accessibility requirements of dynamic content and rich user interfaces

Nowadays, web applications, in our work the case of virtual campuses based on learning management systems, are increasingly using more advanced and complex user interface controls such as tree controls for site navigation, drag-and-drop functionality, or technologies developed with Ajax or DHTML. To prevent accessibility issues, the Web Accessibility Initiative (WAI) [13] proposed a recommendation called "Accessible Rich Internet Applications," usually known as WAI-ARIA [16]. This suite of recommendations defines a way to make web content and web applications more accessible to people with disabilities. It especially helps with dynamic content and advanced user interface controls developed with Ajax, HTML, JavaScript, and related technologies.

More specifically, WAI-ARIA provides a framework for adding attributes to identify features for user interaction, giving hints on how they relate to each other, and their current state. The WAI-ARIA framework [16] identifies innovative navigation techniques to mark regions and common web structures as menus, primary content, secondary content, banner information, and other types of web structures. As a working example for developers, with WAI-ARIA, it is possible to identify regions of pages and enable keyboard users to easily move among regions rather than having to press the tab key many times.

WAI-ARIA also includes technologies to map controls, Ajax live regions, and events to accessibility application programming interfaces (APIs), including custom controls used for rich Internet applications. WAI-ARIA [16] techniques apply to widgets such as buttons, drop-down lists, calendar functions, tree controls (for example, expandable menus), and others usually available in virtual campuses so it is important that LMS administrators.

3. Knowledge required for users related to an accessible virtual campus

Once a virtual campus reaches an acceptable level of accessibility, this accessibility must be constantly maintained. The content and learning material published by the teachers and administrators will be periodically updated, and it is important to teach stakeholders on how to create and adapt learning content to be accessible following most used guidelines. Among the actions to be carried out periodically to maintain accessibility in a virtual campus are the following:

- Training for teachers and students in techniques for creating accessible digital contents
- Training for teachers in Universal Learning Design techniques
- Providing in the virtual campus the functionality of online accessibility checkers when final users work with basic actions such as uploading images and alternative text, providing context information for links, validating information in content editors, etc.

3.1. Techniques for creating accessible documents

It is important to take into consideration that when digital content is created by teachers or students in any type of format (textual, graphic, audio, or multimedia), it is necessary to keep in mind that final users of such content may be people with physical, sensory, or cognitive limitations, who could find barriers to access the information. In fact, at some point in our lives, we all probably will have limitations that can affect our access to digital content. Among the difficulties that teachers are facing when preparing learning content in digital format is the diversity of authoring tools available to create the content. In [19], a collection of the basic considerations to create accessible digital content are presented and for diversity, the Accessible Digital Office Document (ADOD) initiative [20] prepared different recommendations based on the content creator used.

The Accessible Digital Office Documents (ADOD) Project [20] is an initiative created to provide guidelines on the accessibility of office documents, office document formats, and office applications independent of the tool used to create the content. ADOD provides both an "ADOD Assessment Framework" and a suite of practical guidance documents that are intended to help stakeholders in the educational process to make decisions about office applications. Currently, ADOD is based primarily on the WCAG and ATAG recommendations presented in Section 2.

The recommendations provided for office tools are also applicable to PDF documents. Among the recommendations to create accessible PDF documents with learning content, based on WCAG 2.0 guidelines [21], are the following:

1. Check that all nontext elements should include alternative text.
2. Check for background color and foreground contrast.
3. Specify the text language in all documents to help assistive technologies.
4. Check if hyperlinks are correctly formatted and functional.
5. Provide labeling of elements and correct use of styles.
6. Provide alternative texts and contextual information for hyperlinks.
7. Provide information for abbreviations and acronyms.
8. Check for language changes in the text if more than one language is used.
9. Identify decorative elements in headers and footers.
10. Add markers (bookmarks) that allow the user to jump to a specific part of the document.
11. Verify that the default reading order, according to the structure of tags, makes sense and is consistent.
12. Check for the proper security settings, avoiding sharing a document with password.
13. If the PDF contains an image from a scanned document, an OCR process has to be prepared to provide the text as background alternative for assistive technologies.
14. In case the PDF contains a form, the fields properties should have a detailed description to help the user to fill in the requested information.

Besides the ADOD project and the recent book [19], other initiatives and guidelines for creating electronic documents accessible are found in [22–24].

As an alternative, authors can export a document in DAISY format, which is a good way to ensure that a document is accessible. DAISY is a multimedia format that maintains and promotes a system of Access to standard printed documents for blind, low vision or other problems. The format was developed by the DAISY consortium in 1996 and is currently based on the definition of ANSI/NISO Z39.86-2005 standard [25].

The text content can be exported in DAISY format with plug-ins for Word processors as Microsoft Office Word and LibreOffice Writer. This format can be tested with a DAISY complaint software, for example, the AMIS software (http:/www.daisy.org/amis). Exporting content to DAISY [25] format allows authors to check the accessibility of a document to a person with vision problems because the software prepares and audio book based on the content.

Administrators for a virtual campus based on learning management systems (LMS) should not assume that the users (e.g., teacher, instructor, tutor, student, etc.) have all the knowledge concerning WCAG guidelines or principles of Universal Learning Design. It is important to incorporate and provide descriptive aid in the different interfaces and provide validators to allow users to know whether the content is accessible based on the minimal requirements established by the educational institution.

Examples of basic functionality to be included to help final users creating contents are as follows:

- Basic code validator (HTML) included in WYSIWYG content editors usually used in application for discussion forums, wikis, information box, etc. (e.g., AChecker plug-in (www.achecker.ca) for ATutor LMS)
- Validator for images and alternative text aids for users editing content
- Validator for accessibility in equation writer editors

3.2. Automatic analysis using validation tools

The evaluation of the accessibility of a virtual campus and its contents is performed in two main phases.

1. Automatic analysis with validation tools
2. Manual analysis/heuristic evaluation by experts and end users

The first phase is proposed to use an online automatic validator based on the WCAG guidelines. Some of the identified tools available online are as follows:

- Examinator (based on WCAG 2.0 guidelines) (www.examinator.ws)
- AChecker (based on WCAG 2.0, HTML y CSS) (www.achecker.ca)
- TAW (based on WCAG 2.0) (www.tawdis.net)
- CynthiaSays (based on WCAG 2.0) (www.cynthia-says.com)
- Tingtun (based on WCAG 2.0) (accessibility.tingtun.no)
- HERA (based on WCAG 1.0) (www.sidar.com/hera)
- WebAim (Web Accessibility Evaluation Tool) (http://wave.webaim.org)
- HTML validator (http://validator.w3.org/)
- CSS validator (http://jigsaw.w3.org/css-validator/)

The assessment of accessibility should identify a simple of pages related to the main actions from users within the virtual campus. The main actions to be evaluated are as follows:

1. Start using the virtual campus.
    a. Visit the homepage of the educational institution.
    b. Visit the accessibility information for the educational institution.
    c. Pages that the user needs to visit to reach the virtual campus login pages.

http://dx.doi.org/10.5772/60605

   d. Registration, enrollment, and log into the virtual campus.
   e. Change the personal settings and preferences for the user.
   f. Follow the steps to visit a course page.

2. Use basic functionality for students.
   a. Find and review content within a course, including multimedia content.
   b. Contribute to course content assigned to the student (wiki tool or upload a file form).
   c. Find, check, and submit and assessment.
   d. Find a questionnaire, read the instructions, answer all questions, and send the completed questionnaire (quiz).
   e. Find and check the gradebook.
   f. Read news and announcements published by the teacher.
   g. Find, publish, and interact in a course blog.
   h. Find the discussion forums application and be part of a conversation.

3. Use basic functionality for teachers.
   a. Create and publish content in a course page.
   b. Create content on the course with conditional availability (hide and enable content).
   c. Create a task assignment.
   d. Create a questionnaire with different types of questions.
   e. Reorganize and sort items in the course menu.
   f. Copy items from one section of the course to another section.
   g. Login and manage the student gradebook.
   h. Evaluate and comment a student assignment.

The pages included in the virtual campus (dynamic content and login required pages) usually cannot be verified easily by automatic analysis tools. To perform this analysis, it is possible to use installed tools as plug-ins (e.g., WAVE tool) or download the pages to be evaluated as static content.

The second phase of the evaluation is the heuristic evaluation by experts and end users. Automatic validation tools offer a partial view on the accessibility, but it is important to have a group of accessibility experts and final users with disabilities to test the main functions and have a contrasted opinion and recommendations to improve the accessibility of the virtual campus.

4. Requirements to create accessible learning objects

Learning objects (LOs) are the minimum unit in which educational content is organized so that it can be easily published for a better understanding. One of the most popular definitions of LO is that offered by Wiley "as any digital resource that can be reused to support learning" [26].

The main goal of an LO is their reuse in more than one training activity. To do this, it is necessary that the LO can be found in a simple manner. To achieve this, we need to describe the LO's characteristics, including their metadata, which are a set of fields that provide information about the LO such as, for example, its title, its description, the language in which it is written, or its scope. There are some specifications and standards commonly used to define the LO metadata for their correct description. The most popular are Dublin Core [27] and LOM [28].

LOs, besides regular metadata, must have associated accessibility metadata that describe their accessibility characteristics and that make them accessible to all people. These metadata are the fields used for searching accessible LOs.

Repositories are used to store LOs and to facilitate their search and therefore their reuse. Search operations are performed based on their metadata, hence the importance of clearly and correctly describing the resources, which provides more precise searches. One of the most known repositories is Merlot [29], which have an interesting advanced search function.

When users need to perform a training activity, they use these repositories to find the learning objects that better adapt to that training, thus drawing up a new course from the learning objects found in the repository or repositories to they can access.

Metadata should be inserted in an XML (extensible markup language) file [30], composed of each of the fields (each field corresponds to a metadata) described following one of the standards published for this purpose, such as, for example, learning object metadata (LOM) [28]. This work is provided by metadata editors such as, for example, LomPad, known for being one of the most used [31].

As shown in Figure 1, the LomPad editor allows completing the LOM metadata fields. Once all data have been inserted, an XML file containing all information is generated.

The process for sharing content and distributing it among different information systems is to pack it in a compressed file composed of the content and metadata that describe it. In this scope, there are two specifications widely used, such as Sharable Content Object Reference Model (SCORM) [18] and IMS Common Cartridge [32]. Just as there are editors to help content authors to describe the metadata, there are also editors that help to pack this content along with metadata. One of the most known editors is Reload Editor [33].

Reload not only allows packing content based on SCORM specification but also allows to describe resources with metadata (analogously to LomPad) and to organize the sequencing of these resources.

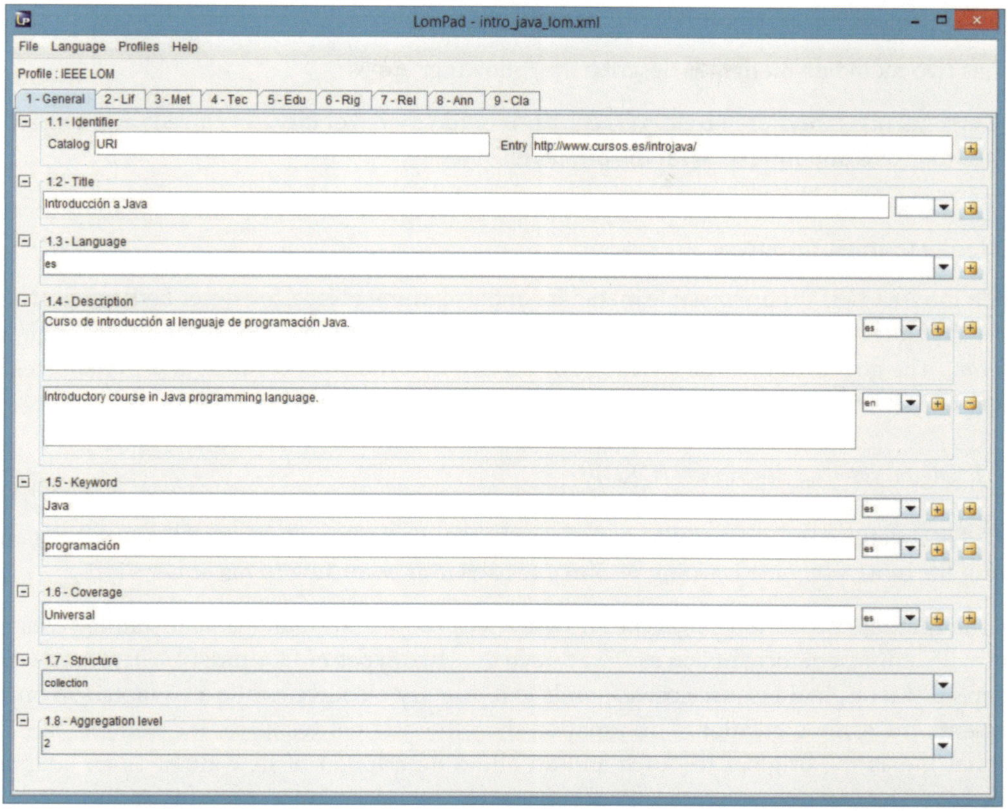

Figure 1. LomPad editor.

4.1. IMS Access for All (AfA) V3.0

IMS AfA v3.0 specification [12] is a way to add accessible metadata to a learning object. Using this, we can describe what is the best sensory form to access the learning object. The specification is created with the aim of simplifying the ISO/IEC 24751 standard [9–11] due to the difficulties encountered when putting it into practice. Both standard and specification in version 3.0 cover the entire process from reading the user needs to the search mechanism needed to find the LO that meets those needs or preferences. The main objectives of IMS AfA v3.0 specification are as follows [12]:

- Being simple and easy to understand
- Facilitating its modification to suit the needs of the organizations requiring some parts of the model
- Facilitating integration with other metadata and specifications
- Allowing integration with devices' properties standards for accessibility
- Allowing integration with user agents, accessibility APIs, and productivity-oriented accessibility standards

- Allowing inclusion in accessibility frameworks and tools

It has two metadata models to describe the following:

- Personal needs and preferences (PNP): description model of the users' needs and preferences to access and interact with the digital resources

- Digital resource description (DRD): description model of the accessibility metadata for the digital training resources

With the AfA DRD, the accessible metadata of the learning objects are described and with the AfA PNP the students can provide their personal needs (or those due to disability environments). The goal is to find the learning objects that best match user needs and preferences in an automated way, solving the metadata similarities between PNP and DRD.

4.1.1. Digital resource description (DRD)

AfA DRD defines the accessibility metadata of a resource that will be used for searching and using the most adequate learning resource to each user according to his or her PNPs.

The adaptation of a learning object occurs when we produce one with the same training content but with a different form of access. To achieve this, two types of LOs must exist: original and adapted. An original resource corresponds to a primary resource, while an adapted resource presents the same educational information than the original resource, for example, a PDF format file as the original resource and an audio description of its content as an adapted resource. The first one presents textual access, while the adaptation presents auditory access to the same educational content.

Original resources may have any number of adaptations, which may be total or partial, i.e., or they are adaptations of the whole educational content or they are just a part of this.

Figure 2 shows the accessibility properties or metadata of a resource and how they relate to each other, as IMS AfA v3.0 specification presents them. As seen in the figure, in order to simplify as much as possible the data model, the metadata have been organized in two clearly distinguished levels:

1. Those belonging to a basic core (Core Profile), containing the most important metadata, necessary for a proper description of the resource

2. Those belonging to the full specification, which extent and complement the basic core information

4.1.2. Personal needs and preferences (PNP)

The specification shows a common information model to define and describe the student's or user's PNPs with a different sensory perception mode or who is in a disability context. The user's PNPs may be environmental (for example, "in the dark"), may be related to the communications technology or the available and specific information services (for example,

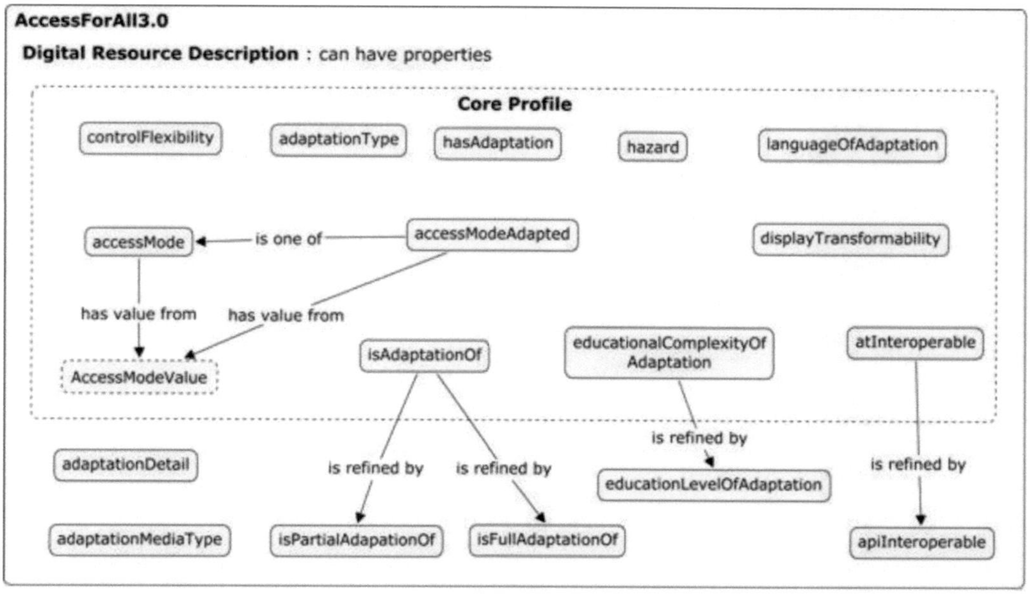

Figure 2. Digital resource description (DRD) properties.

"when a Braille device is available"), or may relate to social situations (for example, "when my nurse is present") or other scenarios.

The recommended method to generate the student's PNPs is the presentation of a form with various options (like aforementioned or preferred sensory mode). The PNPs will be generated from students' responses to these questions.

The declaration of PNPs is associated to one person. In turn, one person can generate several sets of PNPs for being used in the environment he or she is at each moment (for example, in the dark or in a noisy area). Like any software application, user's PNPs should be easily modified by editing the user profile and by allowing its extension, replacement, or removal.

Figure 3 shows the user's accessibility properties and how they relate to each other. In the same manner as specification AfA DRD, there are properties belonging to the basic profile (Core Profile) and those belonging to the full specification.

4.2. Application scenario

In this section, a scenario of use of IMS AfA v3.0 specification [12] is described in addition to other e-learning specifications and standards previously explained, describing all stages for getting an accessible learning object.

First, a content author plans to carry out a learning resource that contains a video tutorial (original resource) of an educational course. An alternative content (adapted resource) is created to provide access to this resource to the students with disabilities (especially those with

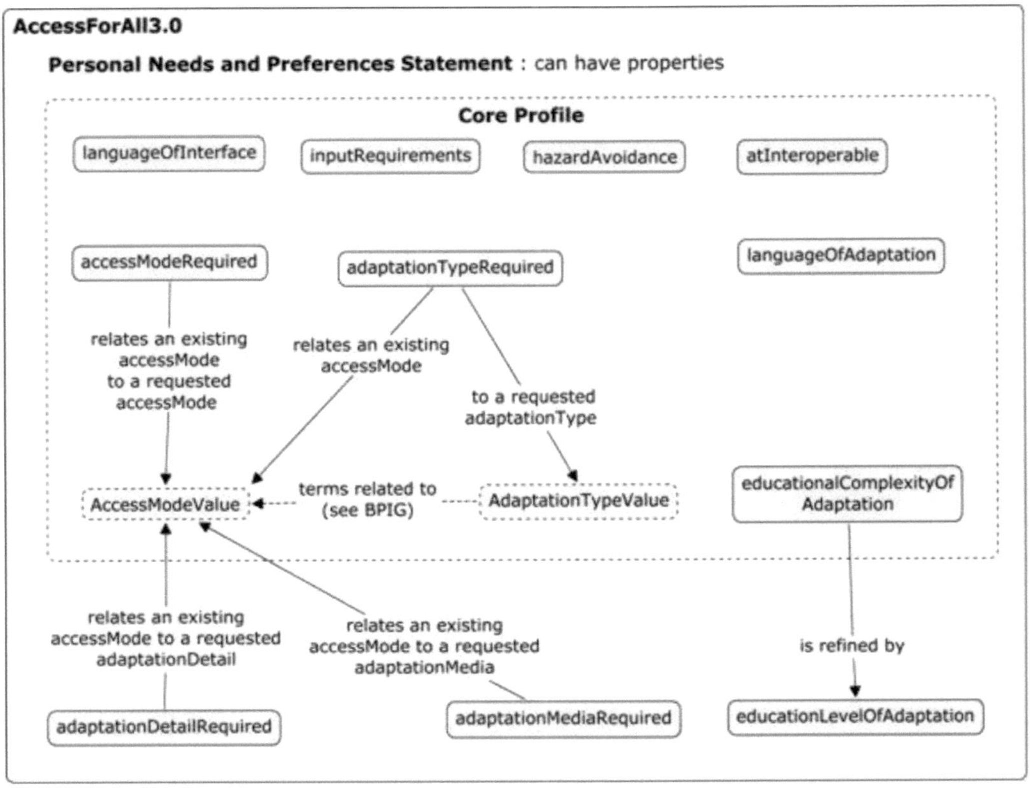

Figure 3. Personal needs and preferences (PNP) properties.

visual problems). This resource consists of an audio description (audio file that describes the images containing meaningful information).

The content author uses LomPad [31] or Reload [33] to describe the LOM metadata of the video tutorial, thus describing the educational material so that it can be located and reused in different training activities.

Then it is necessary to include the accessibility metadata of the original resource; thus, the type of sensorial perception is described, which is needed to understand the training content. As this is a video, both the visual and the auditory senses are needed. For inserting the accessibility metadata by following IMS AfA specification, the author can use LomPad-AfA tool [34], as shown in Figure 4, whose ultimate goal is to generate the XML file, as shown in Figure 5. LomPad-AFA allows the content authors and the learning platform users to insert accessibility metadata of LOs (DRDs) and students' PNPs, respectively, generating both XML format files. This tool allows to complete the properties of DRDs and PNPs graphically and to generate the corresponding XML file following the IMS AfA v3.0 specification.

In the XML file generated, which is shown in Figure 5, it is described that the original resource has two access modes: visual and auditory. It has one adaptation: OR_1_A1, and it can be controlled using the keyboard and mouse.

The following step will be creating the description for the adapted resource, which contains the audio description. Using LomPad-AfA, the accessibility metadata are filled and the XML file is generated (Figure 6).

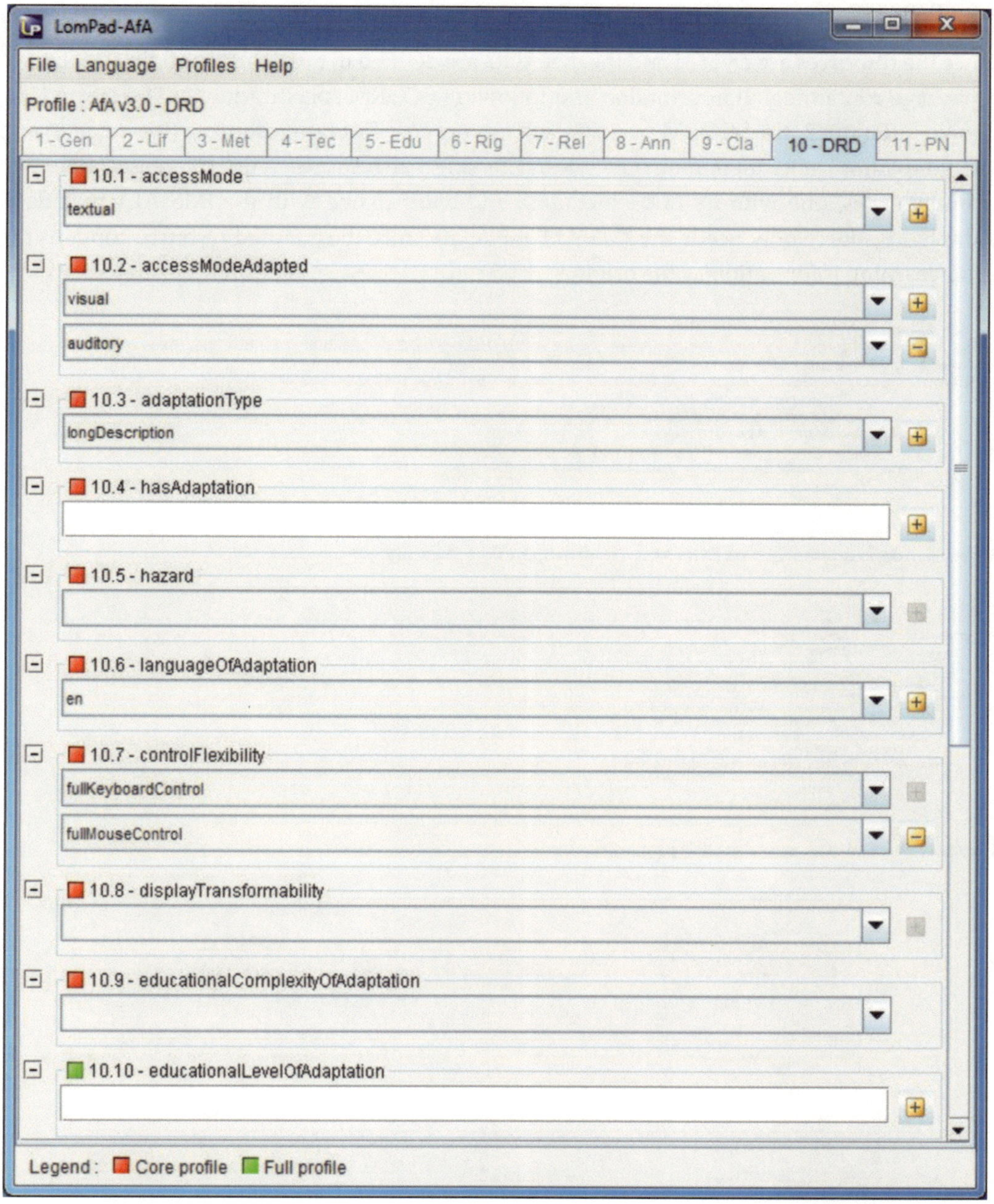

Figure 4. Original resource's DRD XML (afadrdv3p0_OR_1.xml).

In the XML file generated, which is shown in Figure 6, it is described that the adapted resource has an auditory access mode, and it adapts a visual one. More details about the type of adaptation are given through property "adaptation type," and it is specified that it is an audio description. It has full control by keyboard and mouse. It is an adaptation of the original resource OR_1, and it is a partial adaptation. Finally, it states that the audio is recorded using a human voice.

Once the resources are created and the metadata are defined in their corresponding XML files, a package containing all information and following SCORM specification will be created. As shown in Figure 7, the SCORM package will be composed of two resources (the original and the adaptation) and their metadata files. The original resource will have associated two metadata files, one with its LOM metadata and another one with the IMS AfA metadata. Adapted resource only needs the IMS AfA metadata since the adapted resource contains the same learning information as the original.


```xml
<?xml version="1.0" encoding="UTF-8"?>
- <accessForAllResource xsi:schemaLocation="http://www.imsglobal.org/xsd/accessibility/afadrdv3p0/imsafav3p0drd_v1p0
imsafav3p0drd_v1p0.xsd" xmlns:xsi="http://www.w3.org/2001/XMLSchema-instance"
xmlns="http://www.imsglobal.org/xsd/accessibility/afadrdv3p0/imsafav3p0drd_v1p0">
    <accessMode>afaterms-visual</accessMode>
    <accessMode>afaterms-auditory</accessMode>
    <hasAdaptation>OR_1_A1</hasAdaptation>
    <controlFlexibility>afaterms-fullKeyboardControl</controlFlexibility>
    <controlFlexibility>afaterms-fullMouseControl</controlFlexibility>
</accessForAllResource>
```


Figure 5. Adapted resource's A1 DRD XML (afadrdv3p0_OR_1_A1.xml).


```xml
<?xml version="1.0" encoding="UTF-8"?>
- <accessForAllResource xsi:schemaLocation="http://www.imsglobal.org/xsd/accessibility/afadrdv3p0/imsafav3p0drd_v1p0 imsafav3p0drd_v1p0.xsd"
xmlns:xsi="http://www.w3.org/2001/XMLSchema-instance" xmlns="http://www.imsglobal.org/xsd/accessibility/afadrdv3p0/imsafav3p0drd_v1p0">
    <accessMode>afaterms-auditory</accessMode>
    <accessModeAdapted>afaterms-visual</accessModeAdapted>
    <adaptationType>afaterms-audioDescription</adaptationType>
    <languageOfAdaptation>en</languageOfAdaptation>
    <controlFlexibility>afaterms-fullKeyboardControl</controlFlexibility>
    <controlFlexibility>afaterms-fullMouseControl</controlFlexibility>
    <isAdaptationOf>OR_1</isAdaptationOf>
    <isPartialAdaptationOf>OR_1</isPartialAdaptationOf>
    <adaptationDetail>afaterms-recorded</adaptationDetail>
</accessForAllResource>
```


Figure 6. LomPad-AfA resource DRD properties.

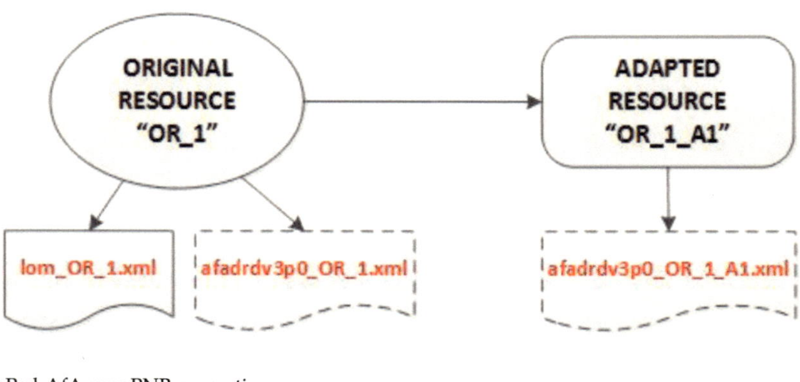

Figure 7. LomPad-AfA user PNP properties.

Furthermore, LomPad-AfA tool allows generating XML files containing the users' PNPs. For example, if a blind person or a person with visual problem wants to describe his or her preferences, he or she has to fill the metadata, as shown in Figure 8, and generate the XML file, as shown in Figure 9.

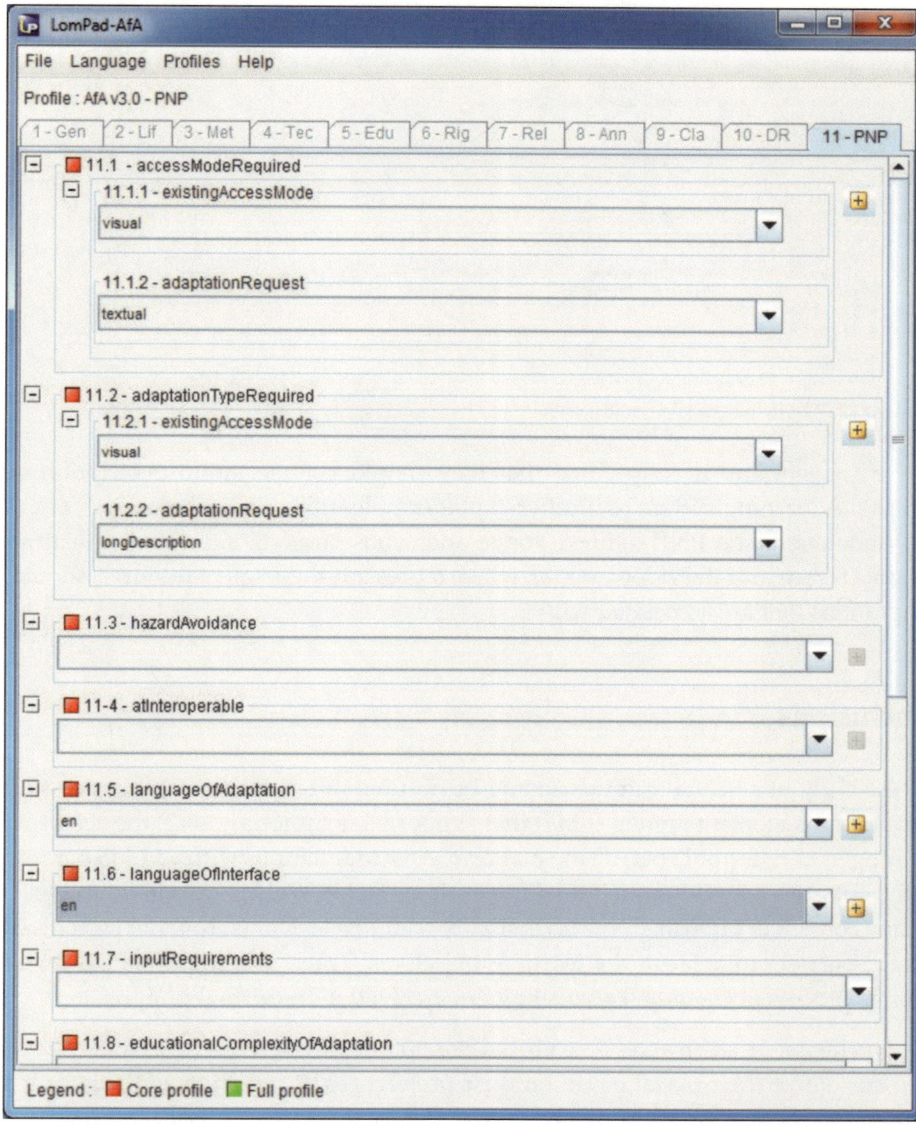

Figure 8. SCORM content.

In the XML file generated, as shown in Figure 9, it is described that, for visual content, the user prefers adapted resources that have an auditory or textual access mode. By means of property "adaptation type required," more details about the type of desired adaptation for visual

```
<?xml version="1.0" encoding="UTF-8"?>
- <accessForAllUser xsi:schemaLocation="http://www.imsglobal.org/xsd/accessibility/afapnpv3p0/imsafa3p0pnp_v1p0
  imsafa3p0pnp_v1p0.xsd" xmlns:xsi="http://www.w3.org/2001/XMLSchema-instance"
  xmlns="http://www.imsglobal.org/xsd/accessibility/afapnpv3p0/imsafa3p0pnp_v1p0">
  - <accessModeRequired>
      <existingAccessMode>afaterms-visual</existingAccessMode>
      <adaptationRequest>afaterms-textual</adaptationRequest>
    </accessModeRequired>
  - <accessModeRequired>
      <existingAccessMode>afaterms-visual</existingAccessMode>
      <adaptationRequest>afaterms-auditory</adaptationRequest>
    </accessModeRequired>
  - <adaptationTypeRequired>
      <existingAccessMode>afaterms-visual</existingAccessMode>
      <adaptationRequest>afaterms-audioDescription</adaptationRequest>
    </adaptationTypeRequired>
  - <adaptationTypeRequired>
      <existingAccessMode>afaterms-visual</existingAccessMode>
      <adaptationRequest>afaterms-longDescription</adaptationRequest>
    </adaptationTypeRequired>
    <languageOfAdaptation>en</languageOfAdaptation>
    <languageOfInterface>en</languageOfInterface>
  - <adaptationDetailRequired>
      <existingAccessMode>afaterms-visual</existingAccessMode>
      <adaptationRequest>afaterms-enhanced</adaptationRequest>
    </adaptationDetailRequired>
  </accessForAllUser>
```


Figure 9. User PNP XML (afapnpv3p0_USR1.xml).

content are given, and it is specified that they should contain audio description or long description. A learning system (educational platform, learning object repository, etc.) that is able to understand the PNP defined above and whose user is interested in learning the educational resource of the video tutorial, which represents the original resource, should show the adaptations that are associated with it.

5. Conclusions

The accessibility of a virtual campus should be ensured at two levels: (1) the accessibility of the learning management system (LMS) that supports the campus and (2) the accessibility of the learning materials published on the platform. A virtual campus with an LMS platform that meets the criteria under different guidelines as described in WCAG 2.0 will be accessible, but when new content is published, the accessibility could be lost, and students with disabilities could face barriers to achieve the learning objectives. Thus, it is important to maintain a continuous process of training for stakeholders involved in the virtual campus.

The main principles that an accessible virtual campus should provide are as follows: (1) allow users to customize their portal based on their preferences, (2) provide equivalents to every time-based media and visual elements, (3) use different ways to present information in an interface, (4) provide information appropriate compatible with assistive technologies, (5) allow access to all functionalities via keyboard, and (6) provide background information and status and location information to the user at all times.

Training for users of virtual campus, publishing learning content is an ongoing process that should primarily include the following components: (1) training teachers and students in

http://dx.doi.org/10.5772/60605

techniques for creating accessible documents, (2) training teachers on universal learning design techniques, and (3) training LMS administrators to maintain the accessibility and configure the LMS to provide validators of accessibility in content editors, to ease the process of learning objects publication.

IMS AfA v3.0 specification presents to the content authors and developers the technical way to follow for achieving an accessible online teaching. According to ISO/IEC 24751-2-3 standard and IMS AfA v3.0 specification, the basic steps in developing an accessible online course are as follows: creating accessible learning objects (LOs), both original and adapted, by means of inserting the accessibility metadata; reading the users' personal needs and preferences (PNP); and searching and presentation of LOs meeting those PNPs.

For an LO that can be used in an educational platform, it is necessary to pack all files shaping the LO with the files containing its metadata, including the accessibility ones, and following the standards established. There is a great lack of technical applications and human resources to provide assistance in developing accessible resources.

Acknowledgements

This work is funded by the University of Alcalá (Spain) and Galileo University (Guatemala) (grant ESVIAL project). Authors also want to acknowledge support from the Master in Software Engineering for the Web and the TIFyC research group.

Author details

Salvador Otón[1*], Héctor R. Amado-Salvatierra[2], José Ramón Hilera[1], Eva García[1] and Antonio García[1]

*Address all correspondence to: salvador.oton@uah.es

1 Universidad de Alcalá, Spain

2 Universidad Galileo, Guatemala

References

[1] Power C., Petrie H., Sakharov V., Swallow D.. Virtual learning environments: another barrier to blended and e-learning.. In: Miesenberger K., Klaus J. Zagler W., Karshmer A.I., editors. ICCHP2010; Springer; 2010.

[2] World Wide Web Consortium. How People with Disabilities Use the Web [Internet]. [Updated: 2014]. Available from: http://www.w3.org/WAI/intro/people-use-web/ [Accessed: 01-03-2015]

[3] Amado-Salvatierra H. R., Hernández R., García-Cabot A., García-López E., Batanero C., Otón S.. Towards a methodology for curriculum development within an accessible virtual campus. In: Computers Helping People with Special Needs; 2014; Springer; 2014. pp. 338–341.

[4] Armstrong H.L.. Advanced IT education for the vision impaired via e-learning. Journal of Information Technology Education. 2009;8(1):243–256.

[5] Burgstahler S., Corrigan B., McCarter J.. Making distance learning courses accessible to students and instructors with disabilities: a case study. Internet and Higher Education. 2004;7(3):233–246.

[6] Edmonds C.D.. Providing access to students with disabilities in online distance education: legal and technical concerns for higher education.. American Journal of Distance Education. 2004;18(1):51–62.

[7] United Nations. Convention on the Rights of Persons with Disabilities [Internet]. 2008. Available from: http://www.un.org/disabilities/default.asp?id=150 [Accessed: 01-03-2015]

[8] ISO. ISO/IEC 40500:2012. W3C Web Content Accessibility Guidelines 2.0 [Internet]. 2012. Available from: http://www.iso.org/iso/iso_catalogue/catalogue_tc/catalogue_detail.htm?csnumber=58625 [Accessed: 01-03-2015]

[9] International Standard Organization. ISO/IEC 24751-1:2008, Information Technology —Individualized Adaptability and Accessibility in E-learning, Education and Training. Part 1: Framework and Reference Model. [Internet]. [Updated: 2008]. Available from: http://www.iso.org/iso/catalogue_detail?csnumber=41521 [Accessed: 01-03-2015]

[10] International Standard Organization. ISO/IEC 24751-2:2008, Information Technology —Individualized Adaptability and Accessibility in E-learning, Education and Training. Part 2: "Access for All" Personal Needs and Preferences for Digital. [Internet]. [Updated: 2008]. Available from: http://www.iso.org/iso/catalogue_detail?csnumber=41521 [Accessed: 01-03-2015]

[11] International Standard Organization. ISO/IEC 24751-3:2008, Information Technology —Individualized Adaptability and Accessibility in E-learning, Education and Training. Part 3: "Access for All" Digital Resource Description. [Internet]. [Updated: 2008]. Available from: http://www.iso.org/iso/catalogue_detail?csnumber=41521 [Accessed: 01-03-2015]

[12] IMS Global Learning Consortium, Inc.. IMS Access For All Version 3.0 [Internet]. Available from: http://imsglobal.org/accessibility [Accessed: 01-03-2015]

[13] World Wide Web Consortium. WAI Guidelines and Techniques [Internet]. [Updated: 2014]. Available from: http://www.w3.org/WAI/guid-tech.html [Accessed: 01-03-2015]

[14] World Wide Web Consortium. Authoring Tool Accessibility Guidelines (ATAG) 2.0 [Internet]. [Updated: 2014]. Available from: http://www.w3.org/TR/ATAG20/ [Accessed: 01-03-2015]

[15] World Wide Web Consortium. User Agent Accessibility Guidelines (UUAG) 2.0. Working Draft [Internet]. [Updated: 2014]. Available from: http://www.w3.org/TR/UAAG20/ [Accessed: 01-03-2015]

[16] World Wide Web Consortium. Accessible Rich Internet Applications (WAI-ARIA) 1.0 [Internet]. [Updated: 2014]. Available from: http://www.w3.org/TR/wai-aria/ [Accessed: 01-03-2015]

[17] Moodle Community. Especificación de accesibilidad Moodle [Internet]. [Updated: 2012]. Available from: http://docs.moodle.org/dev/Moodle_Accessibility_Specification [Accessed: 01-03-2015]

[18] Advanced Distributed Learning (ADL). Sharable Content Object Reference Model (SCORM). http://www.adlnet.org/scorm/

[19] Hilera J.R., Campo E., García-López E., García-Cabot A.. Guide for Creating Accessible Digital Content: Documents, Presentations, Videos, Audios, and Web Pages. Alcalá de Henares, España: Universidad de Alcalá; 2015. DOI: 978-84-15834-82-3

[20] Inclusive Design Research Centre. Accessible Digital Office Document (ADOD) Project [Internet]. [Updated: 2010]. Available from: http://adod.idrc.ocad.ca/ [Accessed: 10-02-2015]

[21] World Wide Web Consortium. Técnicas PDF accesibilidad WCAG 2.0 [Internet]. [Updated: 2014]. Available from: http://www.w3.org/WAI/GL/WCAG20-TECHS/ [Accessed: 01-03-2015]

[22] Australian Agency for International Development.. Guidelines for preparing accessible content [Internet]. [Updated: 2013]. Available from: http://www.ausaid.gov.au/business/Pages/web-content-accessibility-guidelines.aspx [Accessed: 01-02-2015]

[23] Moreno L.. Recursos para elaborar documentación accesible.. Universidad Carlos III, España; 2013.

[24] Sama V., Sevillano E.. Guía de accesibilidad de documentos electrónicos. España: Universidad Nacional de Educación a Distancia, España.; 2012.

[25] DAISY. DAISY Consortium—Creating the Best Way to Read and Publish [Internet]. [Updated: 2014]. Available from: http://www.daisy.org/ [Accessed: 01-02-2015]

[26] Wiley D. Connecting Learning Objects to Instructional Design Theory: A Definition, a Metaphor, and a Taxonomy, in The Instructional Use of Learning Objects.. Reusability:2001.

[27] Dublin Core Metadata Initiative. Dublin Core [Internet]. Available from: http://dublincore.org/ [Accessed: 01-03-2015]

[28] Institute of Electrical and Electronics Engineers. IEEE Learning Object Metadata (LOM) [Internet]. [Updated: 2002]. Available from: http://www.ieeeltsc.org/ [Accessed: 01-03-2015]

[29] MERLOT cooperative. MERLOT (Multimedia Educational Resource for Learning and Online Teaching) [Internet]. Available from: http://www.merlot.org/ [Accessed: 01-03-2015]

[30] World Wide Web Consortium. Extensible Markup Language (XML). [Internet]. [Updated: 2008]. Available from: http://www.w3.org/XML/ [Accessed: 01-10-2015]

[31] Licef. LomPad, learning object metadata editor. [Internet]. [Updated: 2004]. Available from: http://helios.licef.ca:8080/LomPad/en/index.htm [Accessed: 01-05-2014]

[32] IMS Global Learning Consortium, Inc.. IMS Common Cartridge [Internet]. Available from: http://www.imsglobal.org/commoncartridge.html [Accessed: 01-03-2015]

[33] Liber O., Olivier B., Beauvoir P.. Reusable eLearning Object Authoring & Delivery [Internet]. [Updated: 2013]. Available from: http://www.reload.ac.uk/ [Accessed: 01-02-2015]

[34] Otón S., García A., García E., Barchino R., Amado-Salvatierra H.. Transforming LOMPad to Support IMS Access for All v3.0. In: Advanced Learning Technologies (ICALT), 2014 IEEE 14th International Conference on; 2014; IEEE; 2014. pp. 599–600.

Chapter 18

Barriers to e-Learning in SMEs — Are they Still There?

Andrée Roy

Additional information is available at the end of the chapter

http://dx.doi.org/10.5772/61131

Abstract

Facing pressure from an increasingly competitive business environment, small and medium-sized enterprises (SMEs) are called upon to implement e-Learning strategies to support their organizational training and developmental efforts. The purpose of this study is to identify the barriers and constraints SMEs experience when they want to use e-Learning and to determine, through a multiple case study, if the barriers to e-Learning actually experienced by SMEs in Atlantic Canada are the same as those that larger organizations are experiencing, and if they remain the same after all these years. Another purpose of this study is to present different approaches, such as the need to develop an e-Learning culture in Atlantic Canada and Canada in general, to create greater awareness and promotion of e-Learning, to determine an overall learning strategy to upgrade the technological skills of the employees and the SMEs, that can assist SMEs in surmounting the barriers they face when they want to use e-Learning.

Keywords: Barriers, constraints, e-Learning, SMEs, training,

1. Introduction

Small and medium-sized enterprises (SMEs) are considered a source of economic growth and are seen as a key sector for creating employment in many countries around the world. Consequently, training and learning are considered critical to SMEs' growth in many countries. To this end, references [1, 2] consider that in knowledge-based economies, a firm's investment in training and updating its employees' skills is a key element of its growth. However, SMEs do not provide sufficient training mainly because they cannot spare time for employees to attend external training programs and because internal training is too expensive. Therefore, SMEs should logically turn to e-Learning to provide training as the benefits associated with it are supposed to solve these problems. But the logic is not working. SMEs have not rushed to embrace e-Learning in order to train their employees. Why? What are the barriers and constraints they face?

In Canada, particularly Atlantic Canada, SMEs have played an important role in the economic development in various ways and their contribution towards a healthy economy has been recognized. They are defined as businesses having fewer than 500 employees and they represent the majority of businesses [3]. They are the fastest growing segment of the economy, and are considered the foundation of economic development [3–5]. Due to their great flexibility and adaptability, they represent the economy sector that creates the most employment [3, 6] and they remain critical to the economic prosperity of the region as in other parts of the world [see, for example, 7–9]. Yet, despite their great contribution to the region's economy, there are very few studies on them and even less on the training barriers they face, and this despite the fact that the most successful economies are those with the best trained individuals [1, 2, 10].

Capability development of small and medium firms remains critical to economic prosperity in Atlantic Canada as well as in other parts of the world [for example, see 3, 5, 7–9,11–13]. It is therefore important to know the barriers faced by SMEs regarding training, more specifically e-Learning, in order to be in a position to help them ensure their growth and their sustainability.

The purpose of this study is descriptive and prescriptive. After having identified the barriers and constraints SMEs experienced when they wanted to use e-Learning using a survey of the literature on the issue, the first objective is to determine through multiple case studies if the barriers to e-Learning actually experienced by SMEs in Atlantic Canada are still the same after all these years. If so, the second objective is to introduce possible solutions to assist SMEs in surmounting these barriers.

Thus, the remainder of this chapter is arranged as follows. Section 2 presents the method used for the study. Section 3 presents a literature census on the various barriers and constraints to the use of e-Learning by businesses. Section 4 determines through multiple case studies the barriers and constraints to e-Learning actually encountered by SMEs in Atlantic Canada and proposes different approaches to overcome those barriers. The conclusion and discussion will be included in section 5. The references are in section 6.

2. Method

Given the present state of knowledge on training in SMEs and on e-Learning, the method used for this study includes a census of the literature on training and e-Learning combined with a qualitative and exploratory research approach, i.e. multiple case studies. The literature census covers more specifically the barriers and constraints businesses faced when they wanted to use e-Learning. The case study method is well adapted in situations where theoretical propositions are few and field experience is still limited [14]. Multiple-site case studies allow one to understand the particular context and evolution of each firm in regard to e-Learning. Sixteen SMEs located in the Atlantic Region of Canada were studied in 2006, four in each of the provinces of New Brunswick, Nova Scotia, Prince Edward Island and Newfoundland. In 2012, 6 years later, four other SMEs located in New Brunswick and Prince Edward Island have been studied to verify if the businesses were still encountering the same problems in regard to e-Learning. These 20 businesses were selected because they were sufficiently successful (at least 10 years in business) and representative in terms of industry and size, for theoretical generalization purposes. These manufacturing SMEs stem from various sectors such as: construction, textile, oil and gas, pulp and paper and processed food sector. Following North American research [4, 15], a small enterprise (SE) is defined as having 20 to 99 employees, whereas a medium-sized enterprise (ME) has 100 to 499.

Data were collected through semi-structured tape-recorded interviews ranging approximately 2 hours each with the owner-manager or CEO and with the firm's HR manager or manager responsible for training. E-Learning users were also interviewed. The interviews consisted of a series of standardized open-ended questions related to e-Learning. The standardized open-ended interview, as explained by reference [16], is a structured approach in which participants are always asked identical questions designed to generate an open-ended response. This approach was utilized to solicit a variety of viewpoints based on individual experiences, but also to control researcher biases. All narrative interviews were transcribed, coded and analysed using open line-by-line coding to identify themes following reference [17] prescriptions with the assistance of the Atlas.ti application. For confidentiality reasons, fictitious names of individuals and firms participating in the study were used. For example, the first business interviewed is represented by the letter A, and a name starting with the letter A (Arthur, Andy) is given to the representatives of this business. The second business interviewed is represented by the letter B, and a name starting with a B (Bert, Bob) is used and so on. As presented in the research results section, these firms range in size from 60 to 490 employees and operate in industries whose technological intensity varies from low to high. All export except for one firm (M). The SMEs interviewed in 2006 were regrouped in four e-Learning profiles of increasing intensity based on the extent of their awareness and use of e-Learning (none, weak, average, strong). The four businesses interviewed in 2012 are grouped together, but not based on their e-Learning profiles of awareness and used of e-Learning. Three of these businesses were using e-Learning, and one was not.

3. Literature census

Some researchers such as references [18, 19] have identified the barriers to the traditional training taken up by SMEs. Some of the problems identified are lack of training time, delivery of tailored training programs, cost versus financial resources available for training, lack of knowledge on training opportunities available, returns on training offered and the fear of poaching by other businesses or losing the employees to another business. The lack of employees' desire for training and learning combined to a lack of awareness by SMEs of the necessity of having more skilled employees for business success have also been identified.

Barriers to e-Learning as a method of training for learners, both for businesses and educational institutions, have also been identified by various studies. For example, reference [20] mentions that the main barriers to the use of e-Learning in Canada are learners and technical infrastructure. Among other barriers mentioned by reference [20], we find the lack of knowledge towards e-Learning, the accessibility, the lack of commitment from senior management, the lack of quality courses, the development costs and the priorities of investment. According to reference [21], the bandwidth, the access to the Internet, the reluctance of the employees to use the technologies, the lack of investment on the part of companies in technology and the lack of university-level courses and non-academic courses relevant to the needs of businesses are also some barriers to e-Learning. In addition to the lack of relevant courses, the reluctance of employees towards training, the lack of expertise or technical capacity of the employees, reference [22] also mentions the lack of realism of businesses towards what e-Learning can and cannot do. Businesses' lack of realism towards what e-Learning can and cannot do is also mentioned by reference [23]. The barriers to e-Learning seem to be perceived differently by working adults and full-time students, with working adults viewing technology access and time for studying their principal constraints [5].

A more recent report, the State of e-Learning in Canada, done by reference [24] also mentions the learners and the technology as some of the main barriers. Other barriers mentioned in the 2009 report are the lack of support for the learners, the lack of knowledge towards e-Learning by the organization and, the financial problems, in which the e-Learning project are underfunded and, therefore, could not produce the anticipated gains. Other challenges and constraints mentioned in the 2009 State of e-Learning report are the reluctance to use chat rooms and discussion groups by the learners, the fact that many Canadians discontinue use of the Internet and the difficulty to harness the potential of the Internet to enhance learning opportunities. A similar study conducted in seven European countries by reference [25] also mentions that technology and attitudes of managers and employees seem to form the main drawbacks to e-Learning initiatives in SMEs. For reference [26], learners and the necessity for them to be self-motivated and self-disciplined are also a barrier to e-Learning. They also noted the lack of desire to assign a specific amount of time to learn during the work day and the lack of a good human resources development policy towards learning as some barriers to e-Learning.

Other researches done on Canadian SMEs also mentioned that the barriers encountered by SMEs in the use of e-Learning are the lack of access to the necessary technology, the lack of training and support both for SMEs and for the employees and the lack of knowledge on the e-courses and the content relevant to the needs of SMEs including false expectations of SMEs as to what e-Learning can and cannot do. The purchase costs of tailored courses and internal development costs are also barriers for SMEs. Finally, the level of interaction in the e-courses and the learners are also problematic according to references [27, 28].

According to reference [29], organizations reported more barriers to adopting e-Learning in 2011 than in 2010 but the top barriers remain the same: the lack of skills among employees, the lack of knowledge of technology, the lack of skills by training staff to implement e-Learning, the reluctance by line managers and unreliable ICT. The barriers facing companies when they want to use e-Learning are summarized in Table 1.

Barriers	Explanation of barriers
Accessibility	Difficulty for the learner and trainer to acquire or have access to the necessary technology (hardware, software, bandwidth) [5, 20–25, 27–44].
Training and support not available	Teachers and learners do not always understand how to use the technology required for the course (computers, software, Internet, TV, etc.) [5, 21, 27–30, 36, 38, 40–42, 44–47]. Support service not available or inadequate for teachers and learners [24, 26–29, 36, 40, 41, 44, 46, 47]. Lack of support from senior administration [5, 20, 21, 24–29, 36, 40, 41, 44]. Lack of involvement of different stakeholders and lack of strategic plan [25, 26, 36, 44, 48, 49].
Course and course content	Determine the purpose of the course: learning through technology or learning technology [26, 50]. Determine the course content and the order of the presentation of content [27, 28, 32, 44, 51–53]. Align the course's objectives with the course content and assessments [27, 28, 32, 34, 44, 46, 52]. Choose the method of training (an active method, which allows the learner to construct their learning, and have access to a teacher if necessary, is a better method than an affirmative one) [27, 28, 40, 45, 47, 52]. Determine the duration and cost [26–28, 34, 38, 46, 54]. Lack of university-level courses and non-academic relevant to businesses [20, 21, 27, 28, 41]. Lack of knowledge on e-Learning and e-courses and what e-Learning can and cannot do [22–24, 27, 28].
Interaction	Lack of human interaction (face to face) [27, 28, 31, 33, 35, 49, 55].
Learners	The profile of the learner may not always match the desired profile (including lack of skills of the learners) [21–25, 27–29, 37, 43, 52]. The following characteristics are desirable in order to ensure the success of the training: self-motivated [5, 20, 26–28, 31, 32, 45, 46, 51, 55, 56], able to work alone [27, 28, 45, 56], self-disciplined [5, 20, 26–28, 32, 44, 51, 55, 56], 'focused' [20, 27, 28, 32, 44, 51, 55].
Environment	The political, social and economic forces which may influence the choice of courses offered, the quality of courses and the place [23, 32, 41, 49].
Costs	Costs (infrastructure, development and/or purchase of course) required to support e-Learning [23, 27, 28, 31, 32, 38, 40, 44, 57–59].

Table 1. Barriers to the use of e-Learning

4. Research results

The majority of SMEs who participated in the 2006 case were well aware of e-Learning, but it remained to be defined for some. A detailed study of these SMEs stated knowledge about e-Learning and their use of it enables us to qualify their level of use. This analysis also allows us to categorizing SMEs into four distinct profiles of e-Learning users. There are SMEs that use e-Learning a great deal (strong use), those that use it quite a bit (average use), those that don't use it much (weak use) and those that don't use it at all (non-existent use) as indicated in Table 2.

The four SMEs who participated in the 2012 case study were all aware of e-Learning even the one who was not using it (profile V in Table 2). One of the SMEs in profile V was using e-Learning a great deal (strong use – SME name Q), one SME was using it quite a bit (average use – SME name R), one didn't use it much (weak use – SME name S) and the last SME didn't use it at all (non-existent use – SME name T).

Year			**2006**		**2012**
	Profile I *Strong* (C, D, K, L)	Profile II *Average* (B, E, M, O)	Profile III *Weak* (A, F, I, J)	Profile IV *Non-existent* (G, H, N, P)	Profile V *Mixed* (Q, R, S, T)
Size					
Number of employees	300 to 485	60 to 280	150 to 350	75 to 400	150 to 490
E-Learning					
Utilization	Strong	Average	Weak	Non-existent	Mix

A 'strong' use means that the business regularly uses e-Learning to train its employees. An 'average' use means that the business has developed at least two courses in e-Learning format and that the production employees must take these courses. A 'weak' use means that only a few employees use it in the business and a 'non-existent' use means that the business does not use e-Learning to train its employees and that they do not use it to develop their knowledge. A 'mixed' use means that there is an SME for each of the above criteria.

Table 2. Profiles of e-Learning's utilization by SMEs.

SMEs encounter some barriers when they want to use e-Learning as a means of training. Even SMEs who rarely or never use e-Learning are aware that certain barriers may be encountered with e-Learning.

4.1. Perceived barriers of e-Learning by SMEs

The barrier which was most often mentioned in the 2006 case study (for more details on the 2006 case study, see references [27, 28, 60]), in fact which was mentioned by all SMEs interviewed, was the one connected with the bandwidth, which is part of the accessibility. The capacity to download e-Learning courses was not available because the required bandwidth was not always available in the workplace or in regions where employees reside. This problem was illustrated by the comments of Gérôme, who said at the time: « *The bandwidth is insufficient. It takes an eternity to download an e-mail, forget videos and other sophisticated things. It would be difficult to administer training of this style with the system such as it operates at present. By the time a course would be online, the employees would have left home* » (G:181–186).The bandwidth problem was never mentioned in the 2012 study. This may be due to the fact that several initiatives have been undertaken during the last years, both by the provincial government and the federal government, to improve access to the Internet across Canada and especially in remote areas.

In the 2006 study, some SMEs pointed out that they didn't have a training room equipped with the necessary equipment for this type of training, and some employees didn't have a computer at home. This barrier was not mentioned in the 2012 case study. However, one SME brings up the point that they only have computers in the 'office'.

Another barrier mentioned by the majority of SMEs, in both 2006 and 2012 cases, is the level of knowledge of employees towards computers. There are several employees whose level of knowledge is not sufficient, and some even have no interest in computers. The comments of Jules illustrate the problem; he says: « *There are some employees who are fascinated by computers and there are others who don't want to touch them... Is that the medium that is most suitable for these people to learn* » (J:652–654). Stan's comments give us another example of this persisting barrier; he says: « *Many of our employees have not finished their high school... they are not interested in computers... well, not learning on a computers* » (S:427–430). The lack of motivation and discipline to take a course online, and the lack of knowledge and capacity to support e-Learners by the organization were also mentioned in both studies. Theresa gives us an example of the lack of capacity to support e-Learners; she says: « *We don't have computers technicians here, we only have computers in the office...* » (T:223–224).

The lack of knowledge about the courses available is another barrier highlighted in both studies. It is not known what courses are offered, where they can be found, what their level of interaction is, what the possibilities of mentoring are, what the possibilities for evaluation are and what level of security is necessary in order to avoid problems and to ensure that it is the right person participating in the course. Hector gives us an example of the lack of knowledge about what is available; he says: « *There's no directory, or if there is one, I am not aware of it* » (H: 145–146). Quynh give us another example; she says: « *There was no college or university-level courses relevant to our business... we develop a partnership with a private college to fulfill our needs* » (Q:328–331).

The lack of human interaction in some courses was mentioned in the 2006 study and is still mentioned as a barrier in the 2012 study. Ron gives us an example of how the lack of interaction is a barrier that made it difficult to stay focused on the subject covered by the e-course. He says: « *You know, sometimes with some of these webinars, it gets so boring... The guy is speaking and speaking... I leave my computers on and I work on others things... I still hear what they are saying* » (R: 221–223). Denise gives us another example where interaction in e-Learning courses is important and the lack of it could be a barrier; she says: « *I prefer interaction in e-Learning. I prefer when there are discussions, and it is more my learning style to have conversations and discussions. I learn better when I can discuss and exchange ideas* » (D:803–805: 816–817: 869–870).

Another barrier stated by the SMEs in both studies is the profile of the learners and the SMEs. It appears that the profile of the learner and the profile of the SME do not always match the desired profile for e-Learning. Jules gives us an example of how the profiles of the SME and the employees could be barriers; he says: « *The 'learning by doing' method is frequently used to learn certain jobs. It is our preferred manner of training and we've used it since the beginning of the company in 1964... Some employees have chosen e-Learning, but it is usually on an exception basis, to develop their work knowledge and it was suggested by the employee and not the employer... They have to be self-disciplined and motivated to finish the course on-line and get their diploma* » (J:447–449: 989–919: 954–955). Quynh gives us another example how the profile of the employee could be a barrier; she says: « *The employees have to be dedicated, they have to be motivated and self-disciplined... it is not easy to find the time when you are working full time* » (Q:656–658). Denise gives us another example of barrier to e-Learning if the employee is not self-disciplined and self-motivated; she says: « *Since I have a three year-old daughter and that my work schedule is rather full, I can complete the work (course) at 3:00 AM...* » (D:82–83).

Finally, the cost of e-Learning was and is still an important barrier for SMEs. Denise, from the 2006 study, gives us an example; she says: « *The costs for a course like an MBA (on-line) are very high* » (D:687–693). Edna, also from the 2006 study, gives us another example of how the cost is a barrier; she says: « *The cost and time of development in-house are high* » (E:419–423). Lastly Quynh, from the 2012 study, is telling us how cost of e-Learning is affecting their business and is a barrier. She says: « *It costs us a lot of money to have courses developed and tailored for us... We could easily have done something else with that money* » (Q:917–918: 921–923).

The barriers cited by SMEs in the use of e-Learning, during the 2006 study and 2012 study, are illustrated in Table 3. These barriers, as shown in Table 4, can be grouped into broad categories, namely: lack of access to computers or the Internet (accessibility), the lack of training and support both for SMEs and for the employees (training and support), lack of knowledge on the courses and content relevant to the needs of SMEs including false expectations of SMEs as to what e-Learning can and cannot do (course and content), the level of interaction (interaction), the cost of purchases or development (costs) and the learner himself (learners). The barrier of the environment was not mentioned during the study conducted in 2006 nor during the study conducted in 2012. It is important to reiterate that the barrier associated to the bandwidth doesn't seem to be there anymore. The barriers faced by SMEs are similar to those found in the review of the literature.

According to reference [31], many SMEs may be more willing to engage in the use of the Internet and e-Learning if they can overcome the barriers that are preventing them from moving forward in this digital economy. Therefore, in order for e-Learning to be a doable and viable solution for all SMEs, we must eliminate or at least mitigate some of these barriers. Activities to promote e-Learning, at all levels of the firms, also have to be undertaken by different stakeholders. The various approaches presented below are a step in that direction.

- « *The necessary bandwidth is not available in all regions.* » Gérôme (G:264–267)
- « *The necessary bandwidth is not available everywhere.* » Ivan (I:886–896)
- « *Some employees do not have access to the Internet at home.* » Jules (J:1055–1064)
- « *We don't have* the *facilities for such courses. [...] They were conditioned to receive training in a certain way, with a teacher. It will be difficult to change this.* » Arthur (A:509–513: 613–617)
- « *Not all of our employees have a computer at home. We will have to organize a class with computers and give* the *employees some free time in order to get trained. There are costs associated with that.* » Jules (J:1086–1107)
- « *The employees don't have* computers access here. » Theresa (T:336)
- « *Employees do not have all the necessary knowledge.* » Ivan (I:822–830)
- « *As mentioned earlier, many of our employees don't have their 12th grade.* » Stan (S:477–477)
- « *First we would have to know what is available [...] The information is missing. There is no directory of what is available or, if there is one, I don't know* about it. » Hector (H:140–147)
- « *It is difficult to find courses relevant to what you need and it takes time.* » Bert (B:719–726)
- « *We had too many employees who were not studying but surfing on the Internet ... We had to restrict access to the Internet.* » Bert (B:531–543)
- « *There are people who need to be in class* in order *to learn. It depends on the type of learner you are. If you are able to learn alone and you do not need interaction, it is OK.* » Monique (M:637–647)
- « *It's scary when you do not know what it is.* » Gilbert (G:264–267)
- « *Some of our employees have done some courses over the Internet.* [...] *They are motivated ... they needed the courses for their job.* » Ron (G:826–829)
- « *The cost and time for development at the internal are high.* » Edna (E:419–423)
- « *The costs for a course like an MBA(on-line) are very high.* » Denise (D:687–693)
- « *It is expensive to develop courses in-house and it takes a lot of time. We need a champion to lead the case. [...] It took us a while to find the right platform.* » Bert (B:576:581–584:1044)
- « *It will be too expensive ... too expensive for what we need.* » Theresa (T:773–775)

Table 3. Illustrations of the barriers encountered by SMEs in the use of e-Learning

Barriers	SME (2006)																SME (2012)			
	Profile I Strong				Profile II Average				Profile III Weak				Profile IV Non-existent				Profile V Mixed			
No. of employees	300 to 485				60 to 280				150 to 350				75 to 400				150 to 490			
	C	D	K	L	B	E	M	O	A	F	I	J	G	H	N	P	Q	R	S	T
Accessibility		x			x						x	x	x			x				
Training and support					x			x	x	x	x		x				x	x	x	x
Course and content					x		x				x		x	x	x	x	x	x	x	x
Interaction		x	x								x			x		x	x	x		
Learners	x			x	x		x			x		x					x	x	x	
Environment																				
Costs	x	x		x	x	x		x		x		x					x	x	x	x

Table 4. Barriers to the use of e-Learning according to SMEs

4.2. Approaches to overcome barriers to the use of e-Learning by SMEs

As mentioned earlier, the investment of a company in the training and update of the employees' skills is a key element of growth in the knowledge-based economies [1, 2]. Consequently, SMEs need to exploit e-Learning to address their training needs in order to ensure their growth and their sustainability [1, 2, 28, 61–63]. However, if we want businesses to use e-Learning, barriers need to be removed or at least reduced [24, 27, 28, 57, 59]. In addition, a culture more favourable to e-Learning must be developed [21, 24, 27, 28, 62, 64]. The culture change must also be transmitted and adopted by all stakeholders, i.e. by SMEs, governments and the various players in economic development and society in general [23, 24, 27, 28, 65]. Therefore, the approaches to incite SMEs to use e-Learning must include both actions to develop a culture more conducive to e-Learning and actions to remove or reduce barriers in using e-Learning [27, 28].

The development of a culture of learning and e-Learning passes, among other things, by valuing learning and having a better understanding of the e-Learning [2, 27, 28, 64, 66]. The comment issued by Denise illustrates indeed the need to develop a culture of learning and enhance learning. She says: « *We must develop a learning culture in society in general because without education or training, businesses cannot survive* » (D:985–999). For its part, the comment issued by Jules illustrates the need to learn more about e-Learning. He says: « *It is important that SMEs see practical examples of e-Learning, things that are already used by another company if you want them to invest or move in that direction. The best way to educate a group is to present the success of customers or other SMEs and to recommend them to verify this with them. [...] It is also necessary to develop success stories* » (J:1546–1551: 1557–1565: 1582). Developing a culture of learning and e-Learning is also about building and sustaining an environment that inspires and supports employees to pursue learning [67]. The comment issued by Quynh illustrates the need for a business to create an environment that motivates and supports employees to pursue learning; she says: « *In our field, it is very important for us that our employees keep their skills up-to-date. This is why we develop a partnership with a private college in order to develop e-Learning courses to fulfill our needs. [...] We also reimburse some university courses taken by our employee* » (Q:991–993:997–998).

Champions of learning and e-Learning are another way to develop a culture of learning and e-Learning [27, 28, 67]. Champions, at every level of the organization, can help towards the promotion and awareness of e-Learning. This promotion and awareness can be done by internal champions of e-Learning [27, 28, 67–70] as well as by external champions [1, 27, 28, 71, 72]. However, champions must have credibility and knowledge of e-Learning [27, 28]. The comment issued by Bert clearly illustrates the need for internal champions of e-Learning. He says: « *Developing courses in-house is expensive and it takes a lot of time. We need a champion to lead the case* » (B:576: 581–584). Ron's comment illustrates how internal champions can have an impact on the choice of taking or not an e-Learning course. He says: « *Word of mouth is important. Some of our employees have taken some e-Leaning courses because someone else has taken the course and given a good review. Some of our employees lead the show in regards of e-Learning* » (R:946–949). For its part, Edna illustrates the need for external champions of e-Learning. She says: « *I think it should be up to someone like an economic development agency to tell SMEs about what is available* » (E:613–615). Monique's comment also illustrates the need for external champions. She says:

« *The information spreads quickly around here. If a person is satisfied with e-Learning, it won't take long for everyone to know. You can use agencies or groups to circulate the information. [...] I think we should encourage suppliers to give seminars to show what they have as courses. They could provide examples of people or businesses that use their courses. [...] They could show the different possibilities of e-Learning for various industries* » (M:423–427: 848–851: 861–866).

As previously mentioned, in addition to actions in developing a culture more conducive to e-Learning, actions should be undertaken to remove or reduce barriers in using e-Learning if we want to encourage SMEs to use e-Learning. To this end, various actions including the improvement of the accessibility to e-Learning, the upgrading of SMEs' and employees' skills in technology and e-Learning and the offering of technical support must be undertaken.

Accessibility has been one of the major barriers to e-Learning in the 2006 study. The lack of bandwidth in some regions was reducing the ability of companies and employees to download training courses in e-Learning format. Ivan's comment goes in this direction. He says: « *The Internet is the Internet. There are places where it is not fast [...] We need more bandwidth* » (I:886–898). Gérôme also mentions the need for more bandwidth; he says: « *The speed of the line (bandwidth) has to be greater, we should have a better network* » (G:268–270). For its part, Jules says: « *Some employees may not have access to the Internet at home* » (J:1055–1064).

Initiatives have been undertaken in the last years to overcome the accessibility barrier and in the 2012 case study, none of the SMEs mentioned this barrier, which tends to support references [26, 29] findings. According to reference [26], technological improvement and the design of high-capacity networks for sharing data have allowed for solving most of the limitations of the traditional learning methodology both by facilitating access to information and by adapting programs to individual needs. According to reference [29], the increase in bandwidth is now achieved.

One of the factors which also discourage businesses to use e-Learning is the lack of support available [27, 28]. The lack of support was a barrier to the use of e-Learning in the 2006 study and is still a barrier. Thus, in order to ensure that SMEs and learners do not drop out or refuse to use e-Learning, they must be given the necessary support to use e-Learning [2, 23, 24, 27, 28, 57, 59, 64, 73, 74]. To this effect Ivan said: « *It will take some support. There are some people who do not know how to download and install the necessary software* » (I:886–901). He adds: « *Universities or another organization should make resources available by e-mail or telephone to provide a consulting service for SMEs. They could also leave a phone number that people could call, say between 4:00 pm and 6:00 pm, if they have questions. The questions would be answered by students. This would be part of their training, and this would be an improvement for the business community. This would be a way to get people interested* » (I:1086–1098). For its part, Denise says: « *It is necessary to speak the language of SMEs and employees* » (D:1020). Theresa gives us another example of the need of some support in order to use e-Learning; she says: « *We will need some external support. As I have said earlier, we don't have computers on the floor and we don't have computers technicians here* » (T:442–443).

In firms where the availability of resources is limited, e-Learning based on cloud computing could be an interesting alternative since it creates virtualized resources (hardware and software) that can be made available to users [75–81]. Users connect their devices (computers, tablets, smart phones, etc.) to the server where applications have been installed and use them to train themselves [75, 79, 80]. There is no burden of maintenance. Software and hardware updates are done by the providers [81]. Users can also receive external computing support from the cloud supplier [77, 78]; which is an important aspect for smaller firms [77]. Nevertheless, top management commitment and support is still a requirement for cloud e-Learning [77].

The lack of knowledge towards e-Learning and the technology is among the factors that discourage SMEs and employees from using e-Learning [2, 24, 25, 27–29, 74]. The comment of Hector is an example; he says: « *First, it is necessary that SMEs are equipped with people who can prepare the material for e-Learning. The IT equipment and the applications have to work. [...] People who do the promotion have to know what they are talking about. It will take trained people to promote e-Learning to other businesses* » (H:386–398: 410–412). Thus, in order to ensure that learners do not drop out or refuse to use e-Learning, we must ensure that employees have the equipment, the software, the skills and the necessary knowledge needed to use e-Learning [24, 31, 64, 69, 74]. Reference [58] suggests offering training seminars in IT skills to people working in SMEs in order to help small firms integrate information and communication technologies in their business activities and improve their competitiveness. Ivan gives us an example of the necessity to train employees; he says: « *Employees do not have all the necessary knowledge. We might have to train them before they can use computers and e-Learning* » (I:822–830). It is also necessary to provide basic courses to those who do not know how to use computers. Jules's comment goes in this direction; he says: « *Some of our employees do not have the knowledge and skills necessary [...]* » (J:654–658). Stan's comment also expresses the need for better-trained employees. He says: « *Some of our employees don't have what's needed... we will have to offer them some training* » (S:611–612). For her parts, Theresa expresses her firm's incapacity to support e-Learning; she says: « *We don't have computers technicians here...* » (T:223).

Cloud-based e-Learning could be an alternative to the lack of knowledge on technology since the SMEs and the employees don't have to be knowledgeable on the necessary technologies because the technology itself is being offered by the provider [77–80]. Moreover, since the e-Learning applications run on provider's infrastructure, the need to keep high-end computers and highly qualified technicians is eliminated with cloud-based e-Learning [81].

The lack of information about what is available on the Internet is one of the barriers identified in the use of e-Learning [27] by both authors and SMEs themselves despite references [73, 82] showing a large number of courses available on the Internet. To overcome this barrier, some researchers [for example, see 82–84] suggested using tools to explore the availability of e-Learning, and thus better understand what is available on the Internet. For their part, references [27, 28, 69] suggest creating and distributing tools to help companies use e-Learning. Reference [58] also suggests the development of information counters in order to provide information and empirical evidence to SMEs. The comment of Gérôme illustrates well the need of a toolbox; he says: « *The most interesting way would be to bring me a catalogue and to tell me what is available as training [...]* » (Gérôme G:595–597). Edna also expresses the need for a toolbox for SMEs or access to different resources. She says: « *I think if the economic development agencies have libraries of courses pertinent to SMEs to train their employees, SMEs would see e-Learning as a very effective way to provide training. I think that it is necessary to develop inventories of existing courses or to give access to portals such as 'Soft Skill' where there is a library that contains hundreds of useful courses to SMEs to train their employees* » (Edna E:615–625: 627–643). Ron's comment also expresses the need for help finding what is available in terms of e-Learning. He says: « *If someone could tell us what is available as training [...]. Which courses are good ones [...]. It would be very helpful* » (R:974: 977: 980).

Costs are also a barrier to e-Learning. In-house development or external tailored development of e-Learning courses and/or buying general e-courses can cost a lot of money [27, 28, 31, 32, 38, 40, 44, 58, 59, 64]. Ron is giving us an example how in-house development can cost a lot of money to a small business; he says: « *It takes a lot of time to develop courses in-house and it is expensive* » (R:815–816). The comment of Quynh is an example of how buying external courses could be expensive; she says: « An on-line MBA costs a lot of money, especially one with a good university such as... » (Q:717–719). To overcome this barrier, reference [2] suggests ensuring that the costs of education and training be shared. Reference [2] also suggests that governments can design financial incentives and tax policies that encourage individuals and employers to invest in education and training. For reference [64], some changes in the supports available to e-Learning funding are required for Canada to 'leapfrog' to a stronger adoption of e-Learning. Facilitating SMEs' access to funding will also help improve SME's access to training interventions, according to reference [58].

Since cloud e-Learning's task is to ensure that users, such as SMEs, can simply use the computing resources (infrastructure, software, platform) and e-Learning resources (courses) on demand and pay money according to their usage [75–77, 79, 81], cloud computing is a cost alternative for providing training in SMEs [75, 78–80]. By lowering operation costs through cloud computing, a firm can redirect the saved money towards the development of in-house content or purchase content developed by other organizations [80].

5. Conclusion and discussion

In recent years, e-Learning has grown into a widely accepted learning model by larger organizations and to some extent by SMEs. The technological advances along with a reduction of their costs allow SMEs to reconsider the e-Learning model in order to train their employees.

In Atlantic Canada, a growing number of SMEs are aware of e-Learning, and use it to train their employees. During this study, three quarters of the SMEs participating used e-Learning to various degrees to train their employees. Nevertheless, they encounter numerous barriers when they want to use e-Learning.

The barriers that need to be addressed and are preventing SMEs in using e-Learning are the same as those which larger organizations are facing. The lack of training and support for both SMEs and employees is a major barrier. There is no support service regarding technology and e-Learning in some firms and the technical infrastructure is inadequate in others. The learners' lack of skills is another problem. There is a large number of employees whose level of knowledge is inadequate for e-Learning and who don't have any interest in computers, even less in e-Learning. The lack of knowledge on e-courses and content relevant to the needs of SMEs including false expectations of SMEs as to what e-Learning can and cannot do is another barrier. The level of interaction of e-courses is also a challenge for SMEs. E-courses where there is some level of interaction are judged more interesting and appropriate for effective learning. The cost of purchases of e-courses or the cost of in-house development is an important barrier. Finally, the culture towards learning and e-Learning is also an obstacle. The accessibility which was a barrier in the 2006 study doesn't seem to be a barrier anymore for SMEs, nor for the employees/learners at home.

Therefore, in order for e-Learning to be a viable and feasible solution for all SMEs and for the full potential of e-Learning to be achieved by SMEs, conditions favourable to e-Learning must be created and maintained. Efforts are required to eliminate or at least alleviate some of the barriers SMEs run into while using e-Learning. Activities to promote e-Learning have to be undertaken at all levels of the firms as well as different stakeholders if we want SMEs to fully engage in the use e-Learning. The various actions presented below to alleviate and to eliminate some of these barriers are a start in that direction.

Indeed, a number of actions could facilitate the adoption of e-Learning by SMEs and address the barriers they face in its adoption. The first set of actions should focus on the need to develop an e-Learning culture within the SMEs: an e-Learning culture where managers and employees are truthfully committed and motivated to lifelong learning using e-Learning because they believe it is essential to their individual development and their firm's growth. This requires greater awareness and promotion of learning and e-Learning's value through the dissemination of knowledge among SMEs as to the nature, possibilities and advantages of e-Learning for workplace training. It also requires a better awareness and promotion of the supply and appropriateness of e-Learning services and products available.

A second set of actions should focus on eliminating or at least alleviating the barriers to the efficient and effective use of e-Learning by SMEs. Inadequate infrastructure, technological problems and lack of support services are major barriers to e-Leaning and can eliminate the motivation to learn through e-Learning. Inadequate or lack of necessary skills of the employees to learn through e-Learning is also a barrier faced by SMEs. This implies that employees must possess the computer knowledge and skills required to use e-Learning effectively, and that they should be provided with computers and e-Learning software at work that are user-friendly and appropriate to the task at hand if we want to eliminate these barriers. This also implies better management and technical support of employees in regard to e-Learning, support which was found lacking in a number of SMEs. Cloud-based e-Learning could be a solution since it can alleviate some of these barriers. Finding relevant courses to the need of SMEs is also a barrier. This implies a need for a better dissemination of information on existing e-courses and other possibilities. Finally, the cost of in-house development of e-courses and of purchases of external tailored e-courses is another major barrier to the use of e-Leaning. Cloud-based e-Learning could be a solution here and at the same time lower the burden of cost.

http://dx.doi.org/10.5772/61131

Considering the limitations of our research, it should be noted that our sample includes 16 SMEs in the first case studies and 4 SMEs in the last case studies. This constrains the possible generalization of results; thus further research is needed in order to confirm our conclusion. Nevertheless, this research sheds light on the barriers faced by SMEs when they want to use e-Learning to fulfil their training needs and introduces some ideas on how to address these barriers.

For e-Learning's full potential to be achieved, favourable conditions to learning must be created and maintained in Atlantic Canada and Canada in general. Stakeholders such as governments, economic development agencies, SMEs, employees, learning institutions and society in general have an important role to play in developing a culture more conducive to learning and e-Learning. Stakeholders also have a role to play in facilitating access to e-Learning in order to ensure the growth and sustainability of SMEs.

Author details

Andrée Roy*

Address all correspondence to: andree.roy@umoncton.ca

Université de Moncton, Moncton, Canada

References

[1] OECD. (2004) *OECD Employment Outlook.* Paris: OECD Publishing.

[2] OECD. (2012) *Better Skills, Better Jobs, Better Lives: A Strategic Approach to Skills Policies.* Paris: OECD Publishing.

[3] APECA. (2005) *État de la petite entreprise et de l'entrepreneurship dans la région de l'Atlantique 2005.* Moncton: Direction générale des politiqueset des programmes.

[4] Mittelstaedt, J.D., Harben, G.N. and Ward, W.A. (2003) 'How small is too small? Firm size as a barrier to exporting from the United States', *Journal of Small Business Management,* Vol 41, No. 1, pp 68–84.

[5] Roffe, I. (2007) 'Competitive strategy and influences on e-learning in entrepreneur-led SMEs', *Journal of European Industrial Training,* Vol 31, No. 6, pp 416–434.

[6] Brady, A. (1995) 'Small is as small does', *Journal of Business Strategy,* Vol 16, No. 2, pp 44–52.

[7] Varum, C.A. and Rocha, V.C. (2013) 'Employment and SMEs during crises', *Small Bus Econ,* Vol 40, pp 9–25.

[8] Yoshida, Y. (2012) SMEs' important role in creating jobs in the post-crisis. In *Skills Development Pathways in ASIA* (pp 133–135). Paris: OECD Publishing.

[9] Kongolo, M. (2010) 'Job creation versus job shedding and the role of SMEs in economic development', *African Journal of Business Management*, Vol 4, No. 11, pp 2288–2295.

[10] Smith, A. and Hayton, G. (1999) 'What drives enterprise training? Evidence from Australia', *The International Journal of Human Resource Management*, Vol 10, No. 2, pp 251–272.

[11] Bowale, K.E. and Ilesanmi, A.O. (2014) 'Determinants of factors influencing capacity of small and medium enterprises (SMEs) in employment creation in Lagos State, Nigeria', *International Journal of Financial Research*, Vol 5, No. 2, pp 133–141.

[12] Jayawarna, D., MacPherson, A. and Wilson, A. (2007) 'Training commitment and performance in manufacturing SMEs; Incidence, intensity and approaches', *Journal of Small Business and Enterprise Development*, Vol 14, No. 2, pp 698–720.

[13] Matlay, H. (1999) 'Vocational education and training in Britain: A small business perspective', *Education & Training*, Vol 41, No. 1, pp 6–13.

[14] Yin, R.K. (1994) *Case Study Research: Design and Methods*, 2nd Edition. Thousand Oaks, CA: Sage Publications.

[15] Wolff, J.A. and Pett, T.L. (2000) 'Internationalization of small firms: An examination of export competitive patterns, firm size, and export performance', *Journal of Small Business Management*, Vol 38, No. 2, pp 34–47.

[16] Gall, M.D., Gall, J.P. and Borg, W.R. (2003) *Educational Research: An Introduction*, 7th Edition. Boston, MA: A & B Publications.

[17] Miles, M.B. and Huberman, A.M. (1994) *Qualitative Data Analysis: An Expanded Sourcebook*, 2nd Edition. Thousand Oaks, CA: Sage Publications.

[18] Joyce, P., McNulty, T. and Woods, A. (1995) 'Workforce training: Are small firms different?', *Journal of European Industrial Training*, Vol 19, No. 5, pp 19–25.

[19] Westhead, P. and Storey, D. (1996) 'Management training and small firm performance: Why is the link so weak?', *International Small Business Journal*, Vol 14, No. 4, pp 13–24.

[20] Bolan, S. (2001) 'Canada behind in e-learning', *Computing Canada*, Vol 27, No. 9, p 4.

[21] Schweizer, H. (2004) 'E-learning in business', *Journal of Management Education*, Vol 28, No. 6, pp 674–692.

[22] Economist Intelligence Unit. (2004) *Europe Company: Making the Most of e-Learning*. New York, NY: EIU ViewsWire.

[23] Medarova, V., VladimírBures, V. and Otcenaskova, T. (2012) 'A review of obstacles to successful e-Learning deployment in SMEs', *Journal of Innovation Management in Small & Medium Enterprises*, Vol 2012, No. 2012, pp 1–9.

[24] Canadian Council on Learning. (2009) *State of e-Learning in Canada 2009*. Ottawa: Canadian Council on Learning available at: www.ccl-cca.ca

[25] Admiraal, W. and Lockhorst, D. (2009) 'E-Learning in small and medium-sized enterprises across Europe: Attitudes towards technology', *Learning and Training. International Small Business Journal*, Vol 27, No. 6, pp 743–767.

[26] Calvo, N. and Rungo, P. (2010) 'Analysis of emerging barriers for e-Learning models: An empirical study', *European Research Studies*, Vol 13, No. 4, pp 33–43.

[27] Roy, A. (2010) 'SMEs: How to make a successful transition from conventional training towards e-Learning', *International Journal of Advanced Corporate Learning*, Vol 3, No. 2, pp 21–27.

[28] Roy, A. (2013) E-Learning: Tool to ensure growth and sustainability of SMEs. In *Collectif, Case Studies in e-Learning Research: For Researchers, Teachers and Students* (pp 122–140). Reading, UK: Academic Conferences and Publishing International Limited.

[29] Little, B. (2012) 'The rise and rise of do-it-yourself e-learning', *Training & Management Development Methods*, Vol 26, No. 3, pp 613–618.

[30] Banes, D. (2005) 'Accessible e-learning', *E.learning Age*, November 25, p 28.

[31] Collins, C., Buhalis, D. and Peters, M. (2003) 'Enhancing SMTEs' business performance through the Internet and e-learning platforms', *Education + Training*, Vol 45, No. 8/9, pp 483–494.

[32] Dunn, R.L. (2003) 'Getting into e-learning for workplace training', *Plant Engineering*, Vol 56, No. 9, pp 63–71.

[33] Melymuka, K. (2002) 'Executive education on a shoestring', *Computerworld*, Vol 36, No. 11, pp 24–25.

[34] Noble, D. F. (2002) *Digital Diploma Mills: The Automation of Higher Education*. Toronto: Between the Lines.

[35] Nonprofit World. (2002) 'Reach out and train someone: The many faces of distance learning', *Nonprofit World*, Vol 20, No. 2, pp 24–29.

[36] Rayfield, R. and Imel, L. (2002) 'Making interactive video distance learning work', *Principal Leadership*, Vol 2, No. 4, pp 56–61.

[37] Retová, J. and Pólya, A. (2012) 'The accessibility of e-learning systems for disabled', *Studia Commercialia Bratislavensia*, Vol 5, No. 17, pp 124–130.

[38] Sambrook, S. (2003) 'E-learning in small organizations', *Education & Training*, Vol 45, No. 8/9, pp 506–516.

[39] Sanderson, P.E. (2002) 'E-learning strategies for delivering knowledge in the digital age', *Internet and Higher Education*, Vol 5, No. 2, pp 185–188.

[40] Sharma, K., Pandit, P. and Pandit, P. (2011) 'Critical success factors in crafting strategic architecture for e-learning at HP University', *International Journal of Educational Management*, Vol 25, No. 5, pp 423–452.

[41] Swensson, L., Ellstrom, P.-E. and Aberg, C. (2004) 'Integrating formal and informal learning at work', *Journal of Workplace Learning*, Vol 16, No. 7/8, pp 479–491.

[42] Tiene, D. (2002) 'Digital multimedia & distance education: Can they effectively be combined?', *T.H.E. Journal*, Vol 29, No. 9, pp 18–25.

[43] Thomas, D. (2007) 'Accessibility and e-learning', *E.learning Age*, June 2007, pp 12–14.

[44] Uhomoibhi, J.O. (2006) 'Implementing e-learning in Northern Ireland: Prospects and challenges', *Campus-Wide Information Systems*, Vol 23, No. 1, pp 4–14.

[45] Moore, K.B. (2002) 'Professional development through distance learning', *Scholastic Early Childhood Today*, Vol 16, No. 6, pp 6–7.

[46] Perez, S. and Foshay, R. (2002) 'Adding up the distance: Can developmental studies work in a distance learning environment?', *T.H.E. Journal*, Vol 29, No. 8, pp 19–24.

[47] Serwatka, J.A. (2002). 'Improving student performance in distance learning courses', *T.H.E. Journal*, Vol 29, No. 9, pp 46–51.

[48] Servage, L. (2005) 'Strategizing for workplace e-Learning: Some critical considerations', *Journal of Workplace Learning*, Vol 17, No. 5/6, pp 304–317.

[49] Spaulding, S. (2002) 'Distance education, broadcast media, virtual reality, and cyberspace: Is the future passing us by?', *Comparative Education Review*, Vol 3, No. 46, pp 119–130.

[50] Fulton, L. (1998) 'Learning in a digital age: Insights into the issues', *T.H.E. Journal*, Vol 25, No. 7, pp 7–10.

[51] Cutshall, S. (2002) 'Going the distance: When online learning works', *Techniques*, Vol 77, No. 5, pp 22–23.

[52] O'Dell, T. (2009) *Generational Difference in Satisfaction with e-Learning in a Corporate-Learning Environment* [thesis]. ProQuest Dissertation and Theses.

[53] Phillips, V. (1998) 'Virtual classrooms, real education', *Nation's Business*, Vol 86, No. 5, pp 41–45.

[54] Stevenson, N. (2000) *Distance Learning Online for Dummies*. New York, NY: Hungry Minds Inc.

[55] Jha, S.K., Shahabadkar, P.K. and Singhal, S.K. (2012) 'Developing architecture of an e-learning system – A case study', *Journal of Information and Operations Management*, Vol 3, No. 1, pp 129–132.

[56] Brandao, C. (2002) 'Teaching online: Harnessing technology's power at Florida Virtual school', *T.H.E. Journal*, Vol 29, No. 10, pp 37–42.

[57] Industrie Canada (2001) *L'évolution de l'apprentissage en ligne dans les collèges et les universités*. [online], http://www.rescol.ca/mlg/sites/acol-ccael

[58] Panagiotakopoulos, A. (2011) 'Barriers to employee training and learning in small and medium-sized enterprises (SMEs)', *Development and Learning in Organizations*, Vol 25, No. 3, pp 15–18.

[59] Web-Based Education Commission. (2000) *The Power of the Internet for Learning: Moving from Promise to Practice*. Washington, DC: Government Printing Office.

[60] Roy, A. (2009) 'The training process of SMEs: What motivates SMEs to use e-Learning', *International Journal of Advanced Corporate Learning*, Vol 2, No. 3, pp 66–73.

[61] Berris, J. (2006) 'A job like mine', *E.learning Age*, October 26, p 26.

[62] Edwards, M.G. (2009) 'An integrative metatheory for organisational learning and sustainability in turbulent times', *The Learning Organization*, Vol 16, No. 3, pp 189–207.

[63] Filipczak, B. (1994) 'The training manager in the '90s',*Training*, Vol 31, No. 6, pp 31–35.

[64] Contact North. (2012) *Online Learning in Canada: At a Tipping Point – A Cross-Country Check-Up 2012*. Ontario: Ontario's Distance Education & Training Network available at: http://contactnorth.ca/sites/default/files/pdf/trends-and-directions/onlinelearningincanadareport_june_2012_-_final_0.pdf

[65] Middleton, C. (2003) 'The rate of learning must be greater than the rate of change', *Industrial and Commercial Training*, Vol 35, No. 6/7, pp 306–308.

[66] Taran, C. (2006) 'Enabling SMEs to deliver synchronous online training – Practical guidelines', *Campus-Wide Information Systems*, Vol 23, No. 3, pp 182–195.

[67] BC Public Service Agency (2012) *Developing the Best: A Corporate Learning Strategy for the BC Public Service*. [online], http://www2.gov.bc.ca/local/myhr/documents/learning_education/corporate_learning_strategy.pdf

[68] Clawson, T. (2004) 'Teach the boss', *Human Resources*, Vol 12, pp 38–40.

[69] Tanquist, S. (2001) 'Marathon e-learning', *T + D*, Vol 55, No. 8, pp 22–24.

[70] Terry, L. (2000) 'Get Smart Online', *Upside*, Vol 12, No. 5, pp 162–164.

[71] Manufacturiers et exportateurs du Québec. (2003) *La formation par les TIC ou e-learning: le pourquoi et le comment: guide d'aide à la décision en contexte manufacturier*. Montréal: Manufacturiersetexportateurs du Québec.

[72] TechnoCompétences. (2002) *E-learning: guide pratique de l'apprentissage virtuel en entreprise*. Montréal: TechnoCompétences.

[73] Roffe, I. (2004) 'E-learning for SMEs: Competition and dimensions of perceived value', *Journal of European Industrial Training*, Vol 28, No. 5, pp 440–455.

[74] Zielinski, D. (2000) 'Can you keep learners online?', *Training*, Vol 37, No. 3, pp 64–75.

[75] Masud, A.H. and Huang, X. (2012) 'An e-Learning system architecture based on cloud computing', *World Academy of Science, Engineering and Technology*, Vol 6, No. 2, pp 736–740.

[76] Marston, S., Li, Z., Bandyopadhyay, S., Zhang, J. and Ghalsasi, A. (2011) 'Cloud computing – The business perspective', *Decision Support Systems*, Vol 51, No. 1, pp 176–189.

[77] Alshamaila, Y., Papagiannidis, S. and Li, F. (2013) 'Cloud computing adoption by SMEs in the north east of England: A multi-perspective framework', *Journal of Enterprise Information Management*, Vol 26, No. 3, pp 250–275.

[78] Dong, B., Zheng, Q., Yang, J., Li, H. and Qiao, M. (2009) An e-Learning ecosystem based on cloud computing infrastructure. In: *Ninth IEEE International Conference on Advanced Learning Technologies (ICALT '09)*, 15–17 July 2009, Riga (pp 125–127). Latvia: IEEE.

[79] Bora, U.J. and Ahmed, M. (2013) 'E-Learning using cloud computing International', *Journal of Science and Modern Engineering*, Vol 1, No. 2, pp 9–13.

[80] Karim, F. and Goodwin, R. (2013) 'Using cloud computing in e-learning systems', *International Journal of Advanced Research in Computer Science & Technology*, Vol 1, No. 1, pp 65–69.

[81] Mitakos, T., Almaliotis, I., Diakakis, I. and Demerouth, A. (2014) 'An insight on e-learning and cloud computing systems', *Informatica Economica*, Vol 18, No. 4, pp 14–25.

[82] Harris, P. (2005) 'Small businesses bask in training's spotlight', *T + D*, Vol 59, No. 2, pp 46–52.

[83] Charp, S. (2002) 'Assisting educators on the use of technology', *T.H.E. Journal*, Vol 29, No. 11, pp 10–11.

[84] Pantaziz, C. (2002) 'Maximizing e-learning to train the 21st century workforce', Public Personnel Management, Vol 31, No. 1, pp 21–26.

Section 3

Developments in E-learning Technology

Chapter 19

E-Learning Platforms for Professional Training Providers

Nicoleta Nicolau Gudanescu

Additional information is available at the end of the chapter

http://dx.doi.org/10.5772/60851

Abstract

The aim of this chapter is to identify alternative financial resources and practical ways for people (employed, unemployed, young bachelors, managers from public and private economic environment) to participate in lifelong learning programmes, in order to have a quality human capital in our country. The financial opportunity is the European Structural Funds, and the practical opportunity is the building and using of e-learning platforms which solve more problems: the money, the time and the professional progress using IT applications. The concerns are related to the participants' satisfaction and the interest manifested by the organization owners and managers for this kind on training.

Also the chapter presents a short history of the e-learning system and the steps of entering on the educational market anad become one of the main learning tools today.

At the end of the chapter is presented such a platform created entirely by a private training provider, the system being created with European financing.

In the process of creating and using an e-learning platform the organization must take into account mainly the satisfaction of the clients (employees, young bachelors, unemployed people who need to reconvert professionally) which are saving time and money in the educational process.

Keywords: E-learning, Training, Lifelong learning, Project, Management

1. Introduction

Professional training is an important component of Romanian education for adult system, a part of 'lifelong learning' process. The actual concerns regarding lifelong learning in Romania are concentrated on the elaboration of a national strategy, coherent and integrated, through all the interested parts and factors to act for the development of the domain.

The main obstacles in the efforts of adopting a right strategy and applying the Lisbon and Europe 2020 Strategy directives are:

- Underdeveloped culture of permanent education in Romanian organizations
- Absence of a policy for adult professional education
- Differences between regions regarding lifelong learning
- Missing correspondences between education policies and financial resources allocated
- Insufficient implication in education policies for human development of the responsible actors

The responsible ministry and authorities established a set of objectives to overcome the problems of adult education system which are:

- Increase the rate of participation in lifelong learning programmes of the young people and adults
- Increase the level of using nonformal education in organizations
- Develop education programmes for rural population
- Increase the access to education for vulnerable categories of population
- Develop IT and foreign language programmes in many organizations
- Develop and implement on-line training systems
- Identification of financial resources in state institutions and private organizations dedicated to training programmes and human resource development
- Using the structural funds for the development of the lifelong learning programmes

Due to the financial and economic global crisis, the resources dedicated to training and human resource development are very reduced or missing integrally. The solutions for this are on-line courses at low costs because of the reduced expenses vs. face-to-face courses which involve logistic costs.

The most appropriate way to finance lifelong learning in Romania in present conditions when the crisis is ameliorated but not overpassed totally are the European Structural and Cohesion Funds for Economic Competitiveness and Human Resource Development. The two national programmes together can be used for financing lifelong learning for adults.

2. What is e-learning and Learning Management System (LMS): A short history

E-learning is learning to utilize electronic and informational technologies to access educational curriculum outside of a traditional classroom. In most cases, it refers to a course, programme or degree delivered completely on-line.

A learning management system (LMS) is an electronic educational technology (so-called e-learning) through which are developed courses and training programmes.

The system (LMS) has incorporated Internet facilities, forums for on-line collaboration and virtual library with courses and materials for training at any level.

The benefits of using this kind of learning systems are dedicated to the ones who learn but also the teachers that have more time to interact on-line with the students and to prepare more interesting materials.

2.1. Short history

Distance learning appeared for the first time in the eighteenth century in the same time with postal services. Using postal services, Prof. Isaac Pitman, from the UK, in 1840 begins distance courses with his students, sending them materials and tests.

In the USA, the first distance courses were introduced in 1874 at Illinois Wesleyan University, where the distance learning was accepted as a form of education.

At the beginning of the twentieth century, Prof. Sidney Pressey, from Ohio University, developed a mechanical device used to test the students; the device was like a typewriting machine with buttons for answers and a window for questions.

After the test the system will show a page with the answers and the evaluation result.

In 1920 appeared the first elements of distance learning by TV or radio.

In 1960, the University of Illinois launched the PLATO [1] 1 programme (Programmed Logic for Automated Teaching Operations) for advanced computer-assisted instruction. At the beginning of the 1970s, the instruction was extended on 1,000 terminals. The system functioned for 4 years with improvements.

After the World Wide Web apparition in 1989 and HTML language (Hypertext Markup Language), the learning digital technologies were introduced by many universities, colleges and high schools at the global level.

In the 1990s, the LMS were used worldwide. The software were improved, and many schools and universities started to develop their own LMS and present their solutions on the market [2].

Students and teachers could use functionalities like:

- Extract and exchange learning materials

- Examinations and on-line tests
- Communicate with colleagues and teachers
- Track the progress and do tests and evaluations

The environment and the busy people facilitate the use of e-learning technologies at a large level in present days. This kind of learning extended from universities and high schools to adult education by participating in professional improvement of skills on-line.

In Romania, the process was slower than in the USA or UK.

The first e-learning system in Romania was created and implemented in 1989 at the Polytechnic University of Timisoara and was named 'Distance Learning Centre'. This is still functional today also with specific improvements and helps students to learn without being present every day or helps students without financial possibilities to learn and work at the same time.

The second e-learning system appeared in 2001 and was developed by the Education Ministry for high school exams and national yearly evolutions.

The e-learning systems are the future of learning due to the adaptability meant to meet the needs of the participant as individual, of the small and big groups without big costs and time spent [3].

3. Learning methods [4]

Learning in modern society is not linked with classroom. This situation allows development of new teaching and learning methods, dedicated to individual learning for big groups of people that are geographically located at distance. In the latest years appeared different methods of implementation for:

Problem-Based Learning (PBL) – by this method, the instructed ones are taught how to learn; there is cooperation in the group in order to solve real problems. These problems are simulated and are used to create the wish for knowledge, thinking and using resources at the participants in a specific domain.

Case Study – an active method by which there are analysed concrete problems together with the solutions known or unknown. In the learning process, the formable group receives a proposal of concrete situation to solve. There are required optimal solutions for solving the problem. Finally, every member proposes a solution; all are analysed and the best one in the given situation is found.

Collaborative Learning – the learning method by which different persons with different preparation levels act together in order to solve common problems. Learning responsibilities are distributed for each group member which is participating at the course and the most prepared member become responsible for the youngest colleagues learning process.

The method allows development of critical thinking and communication capacities. The groups include different categories of persons, from different institutions and from different geographic areas. The method is named collaborative instruction, for the organizational and communicative components.

Team-Based Learning – it is an instruction strategy elaborated for the creation and development of the instructed teams which can solve high performance problems. The teams are formed for the entire period of learning and the activity is permanently evaluated. For the evaluation are used also the time resources of the course. The importance of own evaluation in the group and the permanent control of the team progress is critical.

For all these learning methods exist many categories of software instruments classified by the Centre for Learning & Performance Technologies from Great Britain like:

- Programmes for Web navigation – this allows to access Web pages, search systems, visualize the information on the network and interact with other instructing programmes (Firefox, Google Chrome).
- E-mail – electronic post applications. These permit the creation and utilization of the electronic post accounts, receiving, reading and sending the messages as well as attached files (Google, Yahoo).
- Integrated instruments for social networks – allow the communication with network members, the creation of own profile and the establishment of connections with network members, virtual activities on the network (Twitter, Facebook).
- Personal panels – applications for public posting of personal information (iGoogle).
- The collection and posting of news (RSS feed) – informational programmes for the news websites, in one or more activity domains specified by the posting in a specific location (work surface, gadget window) (Google Reader, Bloglines).
- Synchronic communication instruments – allow instant transmission and reception of the messages: texts, video and sound (Skype).
- Instruments for blogs and microblog creation – allow using the maximum automatic instruments for the creation of a blog. Also exists space for the posted information (WordPress, Blogger, Twitter).
- Instruments for Web page creation – allow using the maximum automatic instruments for the creation of a website. Also, exists space for the posted information (Google sites, Dreamweaver).
- Instruments for on-line working on documents – these are applications that allow the access of documents (text documents, calculation tables, presentations, databases) are kept and can be visualized and edited in common with other users (Google Docs, Zoho).
- Instruments for presentation creation – allow to create, edit and visualize the multimedia presentation with external resource introduction (PowerPoint, Impress).
- Instruments for storing and publishing the presentations – allow the publishing of the created presentations on the network; these are accessible from any place and can be the subject of on-line discussions (SlideShare, Prezi).

- Applications for Web conferences – allow the synchronic communication for many persons using the Internet resources. The communication can be realized by video, sound and text (Dimdim, Adobe Connect, Skype).
- Web images and storage organization – the applications for creating and editing the images (local) and posting it in on-line albums (Snagit, Adobe Photoshop/Picasa, Flickr/network posting).
- Applications for video and sound transmitting – systems for sound and video image with network storage. Allow the access, synchronic or not (YouTube, Flip, Livestream/video, Audacity, iTunes/Sunset).
- Instruments for time management – allow the optimal organization of the activities (schedules, meetings) for a period of time (Google calendar, Evernote).
- Instruments for the mind mapping – applications for creating a structured thinking and solving problems. Also these are strategic applications for decision-making (FreeMind, Bubbl.us).
- Instruments for course authoring (educational resources) – applications for the educational resource organizing. Allow the creation of structure for the course and for the testing systems and simulating processes and educational games (Articulate, Lectora, Adobe Captivate, Camtasia).
- The library, dictionary, maps and on-line encyclopaedias – specialized resources for studies that allow getting information for the interested ones, as exact definitions or images (Google maps, Google Books, Wiki, DEX online).
- Storage and organizing course systems – complex applications that organize the e-learning system in educational institutions (Moodle, Blackboard).
- Social platforms for learning – integrated instruments for open learning, team learning and collaborative learning for students or employees (Elgg).

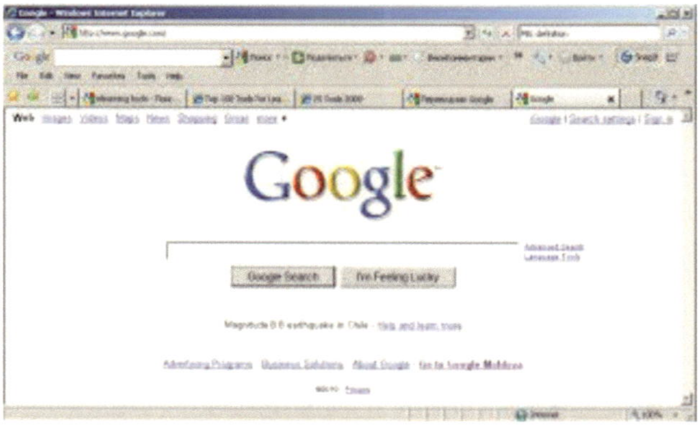

Figure 1. Google Image

Studying the above instruments for e-learning, we can observe a domination coming from Google (the image of opening page of Google application is presented in Fig 1). These applications are the often used and accessed and in the future will be extended in the educational area. From this point of view, they are preferred because they are free or at low cost. Every time someone wants information, Google platform is the preferred one.

4. Google image

Considering the above description the conclusion is that, we have presented the essence of the e-learning systems and the most important instruments that help implement such systems.

5. Why e-learning is the most effective method of training employees and unemployed people

Today's organizations' experience says that there is insufficient training and a lack of knowledge sharing that prevent teams from achieving their greatest potential:

- Almost 80 % of low-performing organizations and 62 % of high-performing organizations are not investing enough money and time in human resource development.
- Dysfunctional teams in different organizations affect the productivity.
- More than 25 % of employees leave their present job if they see no opportunity for training and professional development.

Traditional training methods do not cut it anymore because of the fact that up to 85 % of trainings fail to deliver a positive return on investment.

5.1. Results obtained by using e-learning

- E-learning can be used for own-employee training; they can consult the platform whenever they feel that an information is missing.
- Using on-line training, more than 60 % of employees are motivated to remain in the organization.
- It is already known that the learning curve increases by 60 % in using e-learning than participating in face-to-face training sessions.
- It is studied that e-learning covers courses and application materials five times more than in face-to-face learning.
- Participants in e-learning programmes have 9 % higher knowledge than the ones in face-to-face courses.

5.2. Costs saved by e-learning

- Fifty percent of costs from traditional learning are saved by using e-learning.
- E-learning decreases instructional time by up to 60 %.
- E-learning consumes 90 % less energy than traditional courses.
- The productivity of an employee increases by 30 % using on-line courses.

5.3. E-learning helps organizations grow

Companies with a strong learning culture are 46 % more likely to be the leader in their industry:

- Forty-seven percent of organizations use mobile devices for learning.
- By 2016, 80 % of learners will be on mobile.
- Increasing with 37 %, the employees' productivity.
- Increasing with 34 %, the response of the employees at the customer needs and requests.
- Increasing with 26 %, the ability of workers to create quality products.
- Increasing of employee engagement with 18 %.
- Increasing with 72 %, the competitive advantage by using e-learning as training tool for employees.

6. Good practice example: E-learning platform for training

A good practice example is a project implemented by a Romanian organization named RADINC – a consultancy and training provider which activates on the specific market from 2009. The activity of the organization is focused on training provided in European-financed projects or in private contracts for young bachelors, employees of different organizations with low level of preparation and unemployed people. The training is provided also for own employees that have to be well prepared and competitive to be able to train other people.

The vision of the management related to development and evolution regards:

- Personalized training plans for own employees and for any other clients
- Effects on employees and on their current activity by using new competencies
- Development of the programmes that help in optimizing the activity of the companies (clients)
- Establishing the professional path for each employee

In order to achieve all the objectives established, the organization applied for European funds to build an e-learning platform that will be used to develop training programmes for those who are employed and unemployed in various domains.

Following this chapter, we will present the project and the e-learning facilities for training and e-commerce module – build for the payment of the courses by the on-line participants.

The project is financed from Competitivity Program – ITC dedicated to public and private sector, operation,, Sustaining e-economy'' increase the competitiveness of economic operators'' and consists from building and implementation an e-learning platform for on-line training. The training services are supplied to employees, unemployed, young bachelors, future employees etc. E-learning is a training system consisting of methods and instruments using the Internet, by which educational activities in the time they can do it are ensured, without time constraints and obligations to participate in training sessions.

Specific objectives:

- To increase the competitiveness of SMEs by assimilating new knowledge for the employees themselves
- To realize the infrastructure necessary for e-learning system implementation (IT&C and peripheral equipment, licenses, software)
- To train the personnel that is going to ensure the maintenance of the new e-learning system
- To translate the interface in the English language

Project components and activities:

- Consultancy services for business plan elaboration that include market analysis, selecting the organization who will realize the plan, contracting services and receiving documentation
- Publicity on the project including information of public opinion interested in project implementation and building a website and maintaining it
- Acquisition of IT equipment, licenses and services for e-learning software and infrastructure equipment
- Project audit
- Project management and implementation

The project manager is the GM of the organization, which is also the legal responsible in the relation with the financing authority and the person that checks the expenses and operational activities of the project. The project team includes also persons for financial responsibility and technical responsibility.

The methodology for implementation involves following and achieving the budget, timeline records of the project and performance criteria.

The actual IT infrastructure formed from one classroom which has 28 computers used for face-to-face courses, 8 computers for support employees and management, 1 server, 2 printers and 1 projector was changed for the necessities of implementing the project, buying new equipments necessary for the good functioning of the platform.

The e-learning platform created by project is dedicated to all categories of people who want to learn and allows transmitting the knowledge by electronic instruments. The learning can be asynchronic (self-learning) and synchronic (with on-line teacher and other participants) as can be seen in Fig. 2.

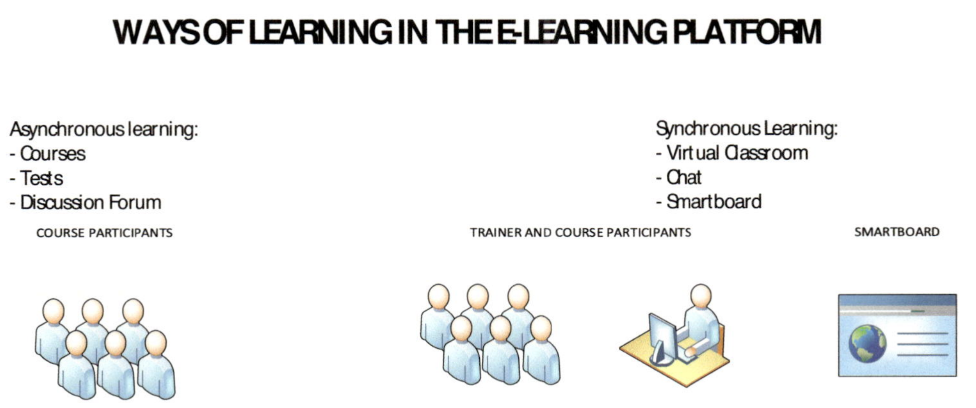

Figure 2. Ways of learning using E-learning platforms

The system created has two components:

1. Software component that includes:

- Operating systems for servers (hypervisor)
- Database system
- Software platforms for streaming – cluster configured
- The application and Web servers for the on-line solution
- Content for the platform(courses, teaching and learning materials, tests)
- The logical architecture of the e-learning platform is presented in Fig. 3.

What can the user (participant of the course) do on the platform?

- Access all the functionalities for users (log in, change password).
- Each user can be registered to many courses and can set a personal calendar for the courses where is registered.
- Each user has a 'TO DO' section for himself to establish personal tasks.
- Users have access to forum and e-mail notifications.

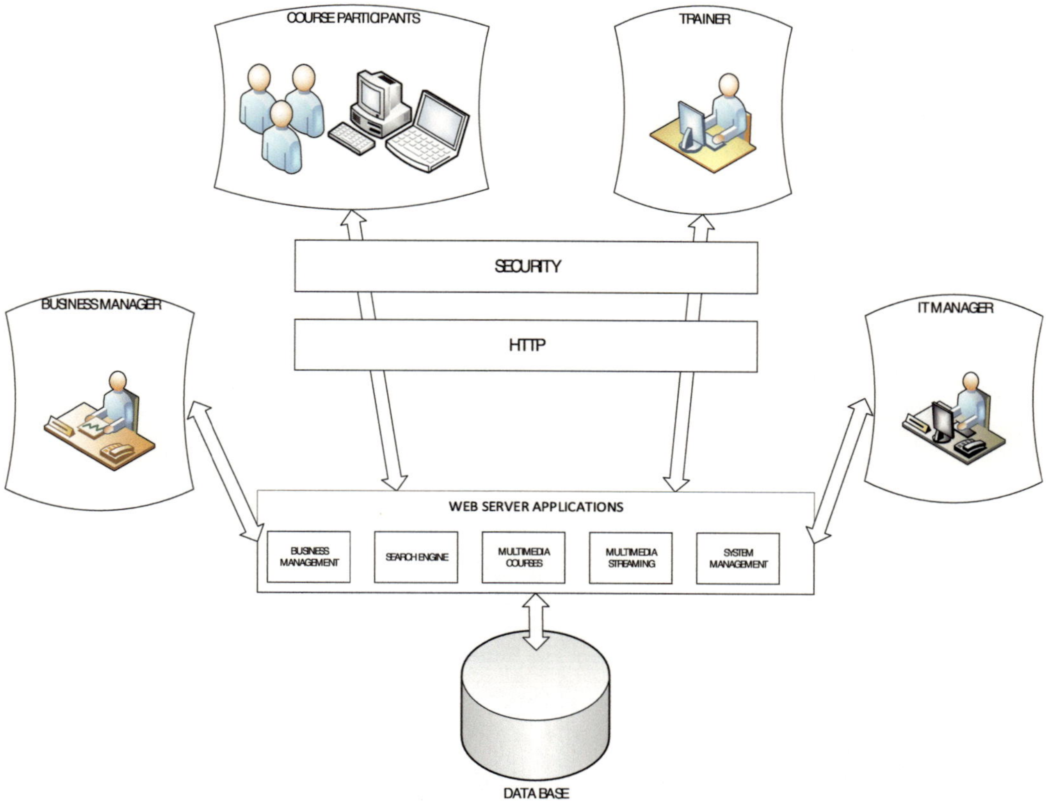

Figure 3. E-learning System's Components

- Users can send/post documents and materials on the platform for trainers and colleagues.
- Users can see the history of the course followed.
- All the users can pay the course on-line using the e-commerce facility of the platform.
- The interface allows the teaching and learning in many languages.
- The evaluation is based on sets of questions for each course (with multiple answers, true/false or writing responses).
- The finalized test is sent automatically to the trainer for the final evaluation.
- The content for a specific course is used only by the registered participants.
- Users can participate in interactive learning sessions with colleagues and trainers.

2. Hardware component includes:

  - Blade servers – 3 ride servers with different functionalities
  - Internet gateway

- Routers, switch and other accessories
- Software for servers
- SAN – storage area network
- Monitors
- Interactive blackboard
- Printers
- Video projector

The technical configuration is presented in Fig. 4.

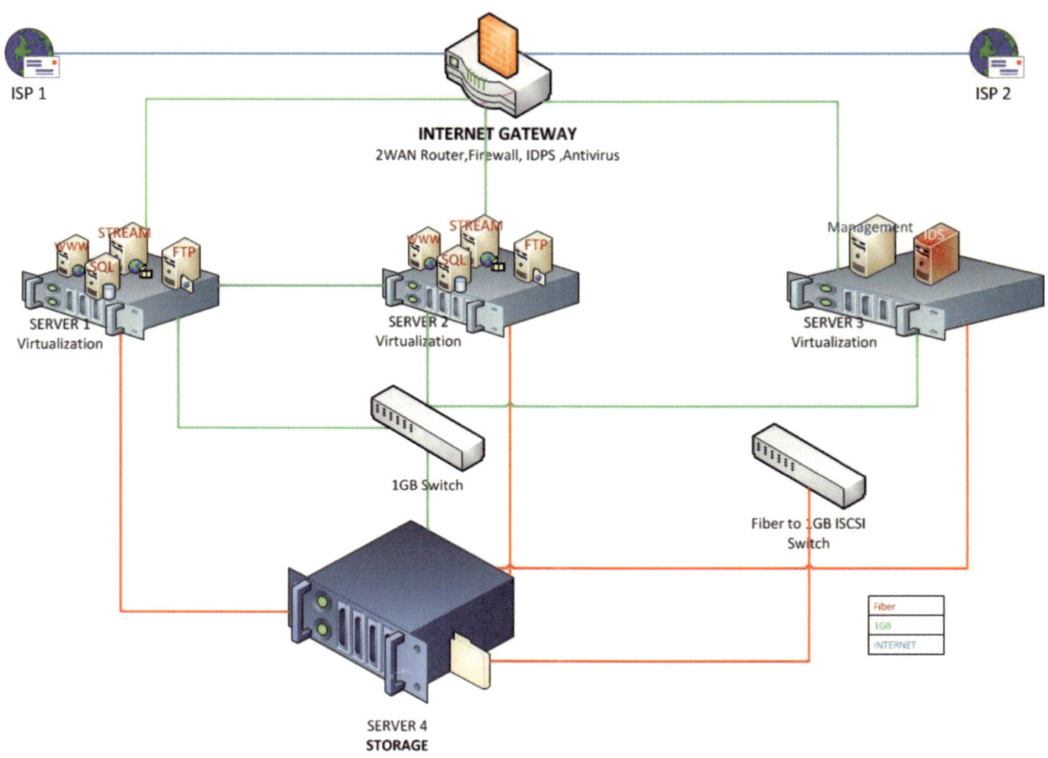

Figure 4. Technical configuration of the e-learning system

At present, the project is implemented and functional; on the platform are studying over 1,000 people.

Some images with the e-learning platform are presented in Figs. 5, 6, 7, 8 and 9.

http://dx.doi.org/10.5772/60851

Figure 5. Authentication window – e-learning platform

Figure 6. Login user (course participant)

Figure 7. Home page – e-learning platform

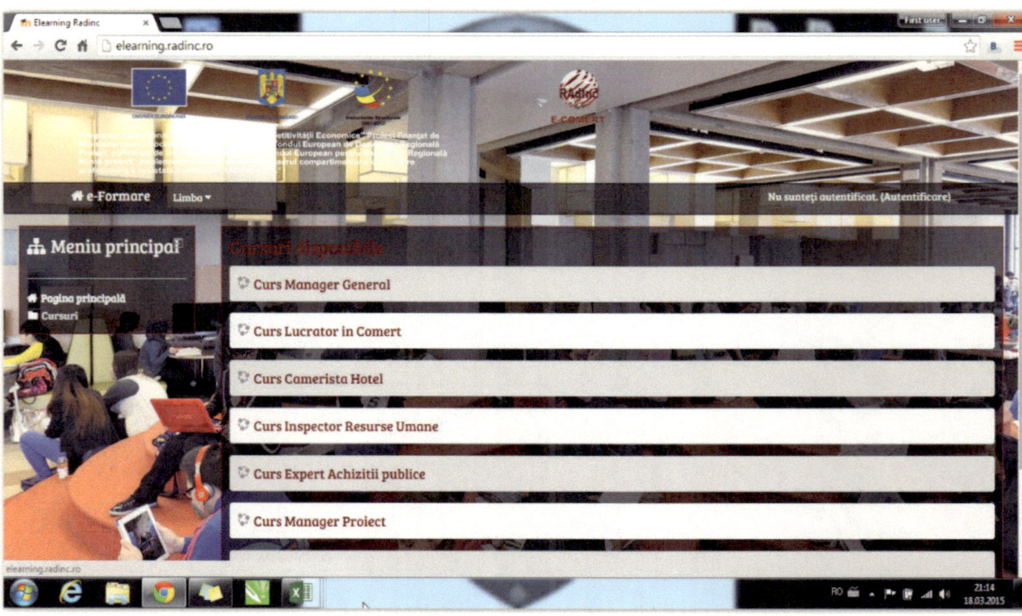

Figure 8. Courses offered

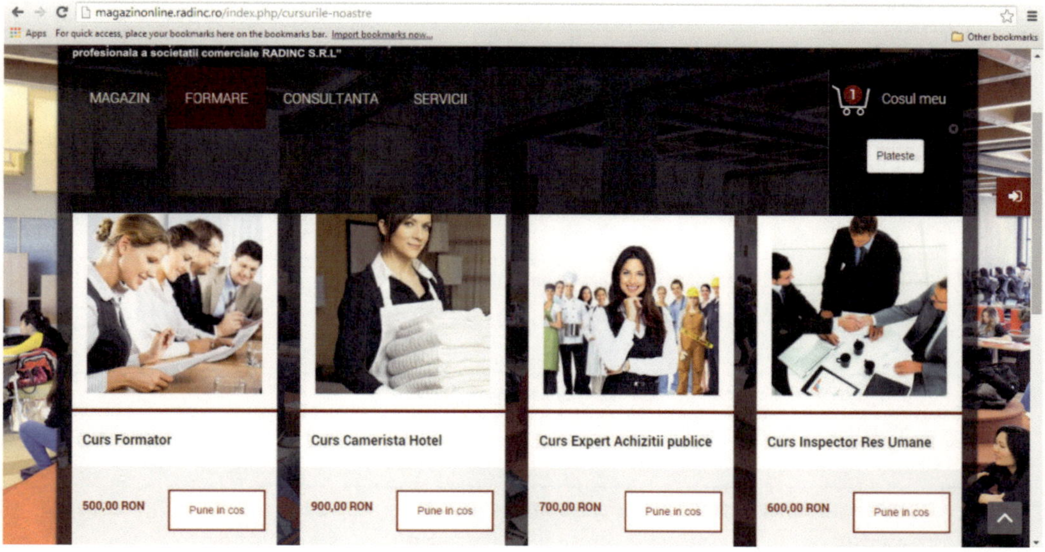

Figure 9. Training page with different course presentations

7. Analysis of the results of a survey realized on clients of the e-learning platform

7.1. Effective Learning/Teaching in E-learning Systems

CRT.NO.	Question	Answers
1.	Have you used by now an e-learning platform to study?	Yes No I tried but it is difficult
2.	Is this the proper modality to learn for you (taking into consideration the demographic data of the participants)?	Yes No I will use it in the future
3.	Is this technology easy to use for you? Is the interface friendly?	Yes No Can be improved
4.	Does the platform facilitate the process of learning?	Yes No It helps the process of combined learning (e-learning and face to face)

CRT.NO.	Question	Answers
5.	Is the interactivity at a right level (reading, visualizing and listening and communicating with the teachers/trainers)?	Yes No Can be improved
6.	Is the speed of the technology at the right level?	Yes No Can be improved
7.	What is the level of satisfaction in participating in the courses on this e-learning platform?	High Moderate Low
8.	Did the participation of this kind of courses saved you from costs (money)?	Yes No Partially
9.	Will you participate in the future in this kind of courses?	Yes No I am thinking twice
10.	Did you find the tests and evaluation methods facile and effective?	Yes No Can be improved
11.	What did you like the most in these courses?	The quality of the material posted The interactivity The tests and evaluation methods

Table 1. Survey tests on the platform

8. Analysis

The test has been completed by 30 people, participants at different courses.

The answers were:

Question 1 – 20 persons responded Yes and 10 people responded No.

Question 2 – 23 persons responded Yes and 7 people responded I will use it in the future.

Question 3 – 30 persons responded Yes.

Question 4 – 27 persons responded Yes and 3 people responded It helps the process of combined learning (e-learning and face to face).

Question 5 – 30 persons responded Yes.

Question 6 – 30 persons responded Yes.

Question 7 – 30 persons responded High.

Question 8 – 30 persons responded Yes.

Question 9 – 30 persons responded Yes.

Question 10 – 30 persons responded Yes.

Question 11– 11 persons responded (a), 8 persons responded (b) and 11 persons responded (c).

The respondents are very happy with the friendly interface, with the facility of learning at distance from home, with the interactivity of the platform at the technical level, the lower costs than a face-to-face course, the testing modalities and all the participants intend to participate to this kind of courses in the future. Paying on-line is another facility appreciated by the participants; they can pay each module separately on the e-commerce facility.

The main interest in using this platform is the fact that after following the course, the participants have more opportunities like if he/she has practice and is not qualified in a specific field, after participating in the course on the platform, he/she can go to a competencies evaluation centre of national authority for professional training and obtain a diploma or he/she can do the practical part of the course in an organization, pass a practical test and participate together with the theoretical part learned on the platform at a graduation exam.

The advantages are available also for the organization that created the platform by reducing the costs with the trainers which are working from the office without being necessary the displacement at every location where the groups of participants are gathered. Also, the trainer can prepare more materials useful to the participants and can respond in time to their questions on the forum section of the platform. The cost for the accountant which has to prepare invoices for every participant is reduced or is eliminated because the payment is on-line and the participant prints the invoice himself. The time and the money are valuable resources and have to be preserved, from the organizations' and from the participants' point of view.

The on-line learning is preferred also by other organizations that request by contract to use the platform and train their own employees internally or with a diploma of professional training.

9. Short conclusions

Why is e-learning important as training method today (considered the method of the century)? Because it saves time and money for the people who participates in training, for trainers and also for the employers.

The e-learning [5] appeared as consequence of evolution in the technologic field and from the necessity of communication in real time for the people.

The interest manifested by the participants and future participants was tested using questionnaires applied directly on the platform and among the persons selected to participate in different projects at the training sessions.

Also my own experience as teacher and trainer for more than 18 years was the main determinant to write this work (chapter). As project manager of various projects with the main objective to implement e-learning platforms in universities or in any other types of organization, I could observe the hostility of the people at the beginning and the satisfaction after using such platforms. So we can affirm that the e-learning is the future regarding the educational systems.

Author details

Nicoleta Nicolau Gudanescu

Address all correspondence to: n.gudanescu@gmail.com

Hyperion University, Bucharest, Romania

References

[1] Plato ist2 terminal, Available from: http://en.wikipedia.org/wiki/ File:Plato_ist2_terminal.jpg, [Accessed: 2014-12-03]

[2] Ellis, Ryann K., Field Guide to Learning Management Systems, ASTD Learning Circuits, 2002

[3] Gibbons, A. S., Nelson, J. M., & Richards, R., The Nature and Origin of Instructional Objects. In D. A. Wiley (Ed.), 2002

[4] Team based learning, Available from: http://teambasedlearning.apsc.ubc.ca/v/clip11/clip11.htm, [Accessed: 2014-12-10]

[5] E-learning fundamentals. History of e-learning, Available from: http://www.leerbeleving.nl/wbts/1/history_of_elearning.html, [Accessed: 2014-12-10]

http://dx.doi.org/10.5772/60851

Chapter 20

Improving E-Learning in SMEs through Cloud Computing and Scenarios

Ileana Hamburg

Additional information is available at the end of the chapter

http://dx.doi.org/10.5772/61009

Abstract

Small and medium sized enterprises (SMEs) assure economic growth in Europe. Generally, many SMEs are struggling to survive in an ongoing global recession and are often reluctant to release or pay for staff training. E-Learning has tried to address issues of time and cost in SMEs, by allowing employees to access learning resources remotely, but its use in SMEs is not efficient. Cloud Computing offers many opportunities and could help companies to improve their business and use technology more efficiently also for E-Learning. In addition to Cloud Computing, Scenario-based E-Learning introduces the learners to real-life situations close to their business allowing them to gather skills or information for future use, and also improves Learners' engagement and motivation to understand core concepts like the Cloud.

In this chapter, learning methods particularly E-Learning in European SMEs is described in part 1. The advantage of using Cloud Computing in E-Learning including models of cloud architectures for E-Learning are presented in part 2 and Scenario-based E-Learning in part 3. In part 4, examples and conclusions are given.

Keywords: SME, E-Learning, Cloud Computing, Scenarios, ICT

1. Introduction

Small and medium sized enterprises (SMEs) assure economic growth in Europe. In the European Union 28 (EU28), in 2013 some 21.6 million SMEs employed 88.8 million people and generated 3.666 trillion in values added [1]. The financial crisis and the economic recession have hit SMEs hard in the EU28 and the economic conditions remain difficult. Many of these companies are micro enterprises, have few resources, and difficulties in facing technological, economic, and financial changes.

Generally, many SMEs are struggling to survive in an ongoing global recession and are often reluctant to release or pay for staff training. Research has highlighted the role of training and skills development on business success. However, in difficult times training budgets are often the first to be reduced or removed. This is often because owner/managers of SMEs do not have enough knowledge about the long-term value of training in sustaining competitive advantage and about suitable, efficient, and chip learning solutions.

E-Learning has tried to address issues of time and cost in SMEs, by allowing employees to access learning resources remotely. The learning material is easy to keep updated; the trainers can integrate multimedia content which facilitates understanding and motivate the participants, but this form of learning is not used efficiently in SMEs. Some disadvantages of E-Learning could be its weakness on scalability at the infrastructure level; inefficient utilization of resources during the night and holidays; cost related to computer maintenance, installation, and technical support for individual software packages.

Cloud Computing offers many opportunities and can help companies improve their business and use technology more efficiently also for E-Learning.

Marston et al. [2] define Cloud Computing as "an information technology service model where computing services (both hardware and software) are delivered on-demand to customers over a network in a self-service fashion, independent of device and location."

Agility, elastic scalability, low costs are some benefits of using Cloud Computing; data can be moved smoothly without boundaries. Cloud platforms are an alternative to traditional computer centers. Cloud can be viewed as being Education Software as a Service. The learning resources could be accessed anywhere and anytime, costs for software installation and maintenance are reduced, SMEs can pay by subscription based on usage of learning resources, etc.

In addition to Cloud Computing, Scenario-based E-Learning introduces learners to real-life situations close to their business allowing them to gather skills or information for future use. There are many reasons why scenarios help to improve learners' engagement and motivation and to understand core concepts like the Cloud.

In this chapter, learning methods and the use of blended learning and particularly E-Learning in European SMEs are described in part 1. The advantages of using Cloud Computing in E-Learning including models of cloud architectures for E-Learning are presented in part 2 and Scenario-based E-Learning in part 3. In part 4, examples and conclusions are given.

2. SMEs in Europe

Different countries and sectors define SMEs differently and there are many classifications for different fields [3] with regard to employment, sales, or investment [4]. So there is no common definition for SME at present. The European Commission has developed criteria for SME [3] including employee numbers, turnover, and balance sheet statistics [5], which make an equal consideration possible.

2013 could be considered a turning point for European SMEs [1]. After years of an uncertain economic situation, 2013 is the first year with combined increase in employment and value-addition in European SMEs.

Figure 1 shows the degree of recovery of SMEs from 2008 to 2013.

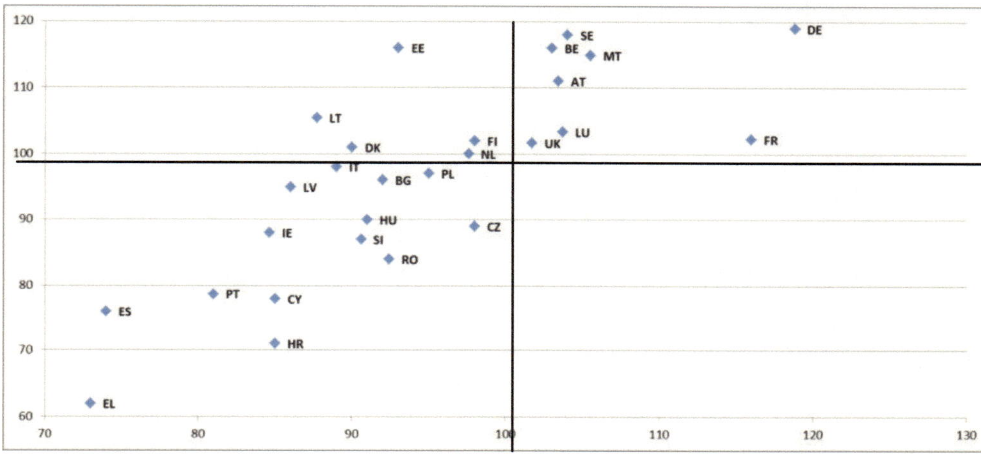

Figure 1. SME degree of recovery from 2008 to 2013, value-addition and employment [1]

It is known that the current business SME environments are characterized by increasing competition and the day-to-day pressure of running an efficient enterprise. Low demand for the goods and services, which SMEs produce, explains why the SMEs' performance did not reach previous values in some member states.

The most important SME sectors are the wholesale and retail sectors and the largest ones are manufacturing, construction, accommodation, and food. In 2013, positive growth was reported in business services, retail and wholesale trade; the construction industry has suffered severely.

Many SMEs are not in export-oriented sectors, particularly the micro and small enterprises. Generally, many SMEs are struggling to survive in an ongoing global recession and are often reluctant to release or pay for staff training which can improve staff competences and contribute to improve this situation.

In all companies, also in SMEs, computing became more pervasive within the organization; the complexity of managing the whole infrastructure of heterogeneous information architectures and distributed data and software increases the costs for computing in organizations. For small and medium businesses with limited capital and cash flow, it is difficult to afford investments for Information and Communication Technologies (ICT) infrastructure. So Cloud

Computing promises to deliver all the functionality of existing information technology services, reducing the upfront costs of computing that hinder many organizations in deploying new innovative IT services [6].

3. Learning in SMEs

The economic pressure requires continuous improving of company efficiency, of staff knowledge, of training and learning to survive or stay competitive. Due to limited resources, often financial ones, the managers reduce learning activities and the introducing of new technologies in their companies. E-Learning is rarely used in SMEs, although it is suitable to quickly and up-to-date the requirements typical for SMEs [7], [8].

Some managers, who do not know the advantages of E-Learning, would like to preserve instructor, classroom-based learning as the learning culture of the company. Managers and staff should be aware of integrating training/learning in the company business contributing to their growth. Figure 2 shows some important variables reported in the literature contributing to a better understanding of the role of training and education for SMEs in order to compete nowadays.

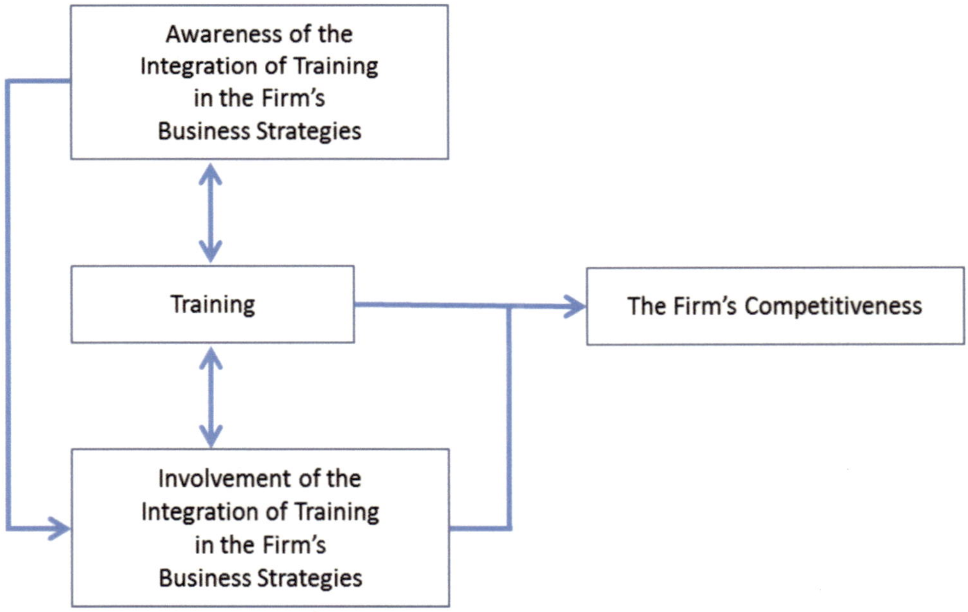

Figure 2. Variables for training [9]

With regard to learning, the most popular form of learning in SMEs among staff is the informal one, which accounts for over 75% of the learning taking place in organizations today. Informal learning is the unofficial, unscheduled, impromptu way people learn to do their jobs. Most learning does not occur during formal training programs. It happens through processes that are not structured or supported by an employer or an organized formal course. Most companies, however, focus on and recognize only formal learning programs, losing valuable opportunities and outcomes.

Blended learning can combine the positive aspects of different learning approaches, classroom-based learning and E-Learning, formal and informal ones [7]. By mixing learning styles and different dimensions of learning suitable for SMEs at the course level, the use of blended learning opportunities as a suitable way to learn in SMEs could be improved so that this increases or keeps up competitiveness/survival of the companies.

The term blended learning is used in the literature for an integrated combination of traditional offline methods of learning with on-line methods (i.e., web-based ones) [10]. Within blended learning, classroom-based learning is combined with computer-mediated instructions [11], but also various event-based activities (face-to-face classrooms, live E-Learning, self-paced learning) are combined.

Results of projects show that SMEs are restricted in the efficient use of different forms of learning and technology for learning and in adequate management learning approaches [12].

An informal and predominant training method, workplace training for daily tasks, is known to have "low learning cost" [13]. The integration with formal strategic training is often not planned. Also the blending of face-to-face training with self-paced E-Learning is not efficiently used [14].

Some important aspects of blended learning for SMEs could be Self-Paced Learning, Mix of Methods and Media, Quality, Time Flexibility, Learner-Centred, Motivation, Flexibility, Accessibility, and Workplace-Related Learning.

The trainees have the possibility to choose when they study; distance and schedules becoming irrelevant. The students are not required to take into account each other's time restrictions; they can also choose content necessary to their tasks. In some projects like SIMPEL [7], coordinated by the author, the use of E-learning in SMEs has been particularly analysed. The conclusions were that properly developed training based on E-Learning not only contributes to improving competences of SME staff, but also to create a growing repository of knowledge. This knowledge can be continuously provided to employees at a determined time and in a way that can be individualized, to be more efficient. E-Learning has a great potential for the expansion of educational opportunities but it is also necessary to note that "social presence is a strong enabler of satisfaction also in a computer conference" [14].

Results of the EU ARIEL project (Analysing and Reporting on the Implementation of Electronic Learning in Europe www.ariel-eu.net), [15], financed within the E-Learning initiative and coordinated by the author, show that SMEs have problems in introducing and using E-Learning. Problems that appear relate to organizational technology and human resource development.

Some models of the E-Learning are cited by Psycharis [16], [17].

In the publication of Rosenberg [18], four factors are identified: Culture, Champions, Communications, and Change. Twenty questions to classify the factors in categories were developed by him.

The main factors identified by Chapnick [19] are: the psychological readiness, the sociological readiness, the environmental readiness, the readiness of the human resources, and the economic readiness.

According to Broadbent [20], the successful implementation of E-Learning in an organization requires the right people, the right place, and the right resources.

From the author's point of view, learning refers less on the basis of technical implementation, but more on the need of organisation development and organisational integration. Some important issues when applying the models to SMEs are as follows:

- A decision should be made whether this is the best choice of training delivery or not.
- Special pedagogical requirements and face-to-face contact have to be considered.
- Organizational readiness is a difficult problem for SMEs.
- All staff should answer the questions of these models.
- The models should include the fields needed to be ready before starting E-Learning.

The author worked in the European project ReadiSME [21] where the evaluation of E-Learning readiness was researched and a list of questions for the evaluation of E-Learning readiness supporting knowledge improvement was developed.A reference catalogue taking into consideration the categories Organization/Management, Technology/Services, Staff/Human Resources (Figure 3) was developed and used within ReadiSME and in other projects.

After the collection of data by using this catalogue, the results were evaluated by an E-Learning consultant of the company and completed/detailed in direct discussions with the staff and management of the company.

The next step was to determine knowledge needs and gaps and to develop corresponding approaches. Further steps are shown in Figure 4.

The design of the appropriate content for E-Learning-based training guided by the SME's knowledge requirements should be taken into consideration. It helps to improve products and services offered to clients, and knowledge concerning new markets, customers, and suppliers that needs to be transferred to the staff.

The design of blended learning material has a great importance and several authors have developed frameworks to guide this process.

Managers of SMEs need to be aware of the importance of mixing E-Learning with other forms of learning like mobile learning, webinars, access to on-demand learning resources, and social learning supported by social media for up-to-date skills and information [8].

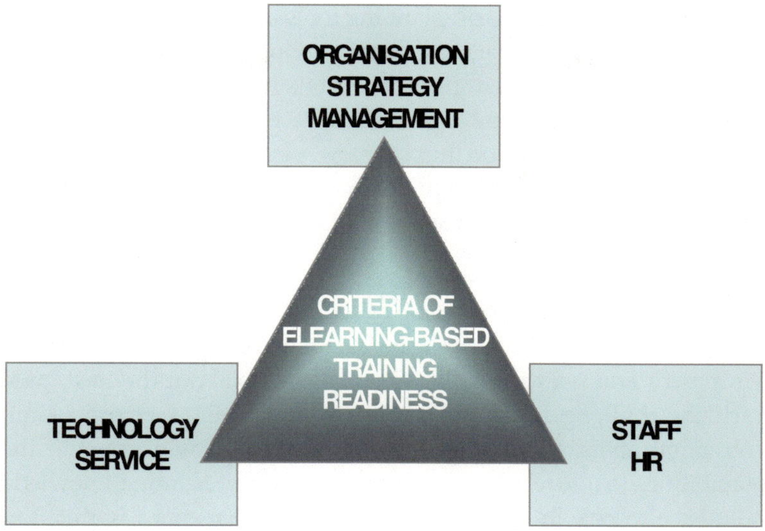

Figure 3. Categories [21]

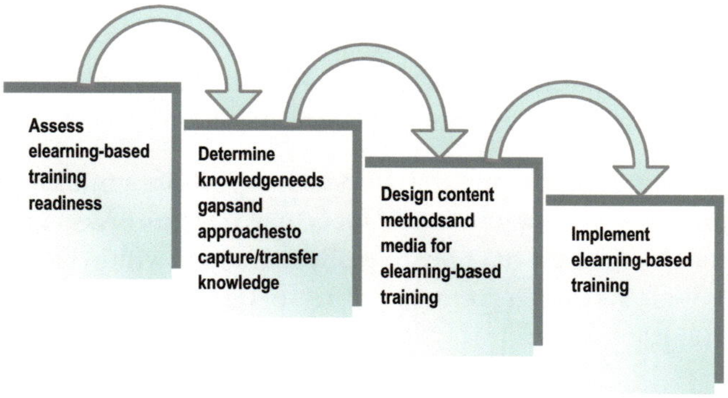

Figure 4. Value chain [21]

4. Scenarios

Scenarios are particularly useful to explore a range of possible futures and driving forces what could lead to these futures. Scenario methodology has a major advantage over some methods – it can be participatory [22]. If used within learning in companies, it could engage learners and provide them with resources to improve their knowledge.

System thinking used in conjunction with scenario planning leads to plausible scenario story lines because the causal relationship between factors can be demonstrated. Scenarios are used by decision makers to explore ways to avoid risks and to improve opportunities. A common language and tools should be developed, so people from a variety of disciplines and backgrounds can work together effectively.

There are a number of different scenario planning tools available; they each provide a means of looking at reality [23] and encourage a company to look at the current situation, different events that can occur, how they can impact on the business, and how the business can plan effectively to take advantage or combat the negative effects of these events. They can be categorized depending on the direction the company wishes to take. In addition, it "simplifies the avalanche of data into a limited number of possible states" [22].This is particularly appropriate in today's knowledge environment where the amount of data is growing exponentially each day.

Chermak and Swanson [24] examined the use of scenario planning as a learning tool in which knowledge is developed. "Scenario planning is designed to support exploration of a constantly changing environment and uses multiple narrative stories about the past, present, and the future to stretch the thinking inside the organization." Thus, scenario planning involves gathering information about events that have occurred and will occur in the future and understand possibilities to address these. Thus, it involves generating knowledge and skills. Scenario planning is also heavily influenced by the social elements advocated by the organizational history and culture elements of Vygotsky's constructivist learning theory as "Scenario planning is also dependent upon the situation in which it is employed as a tool for learning and planning" [24].

Scenario planning combined with learning can help SMEs to identify the future state of their organization if they use new technologies like Cloud Computing technologies, accounting for all the limitations and issues that they need to consider [8].

Scenario-based E-Learning [25] can put the learners into real-life situations that allow them to gather skills or information that they will need for actual or future tasks. Information regarding the work context enables learners not only to easily manage it within their working tasks, but also to commit it to their long-term memory for future use. Some characteristics for scenario-based learning are [25]:

- Realistic, in order to fully engage learners providing students or employees with the required information.
- Learner-centric, drawing upon learners' core strengths and allowing them to use skill sets that they are developing, while at the same time improving upon their weak points.
- Involving learning strategies which use skills or knowledge that learners have already gathered and which can be applied to the current tasks.
- Due to their interactive character, the learners achieve real-world experience rather than theoretical information.

Scenario-based E-Learning:

- Improves the learners' engagement and understanding of core concepts.
- Motivates the learner.
- Allows the learner to directly see the E-Learning rewards.

- Challenges the learner without overwhelming their mental capacity.

Some important issues for Scenario-based techniques in E-Learning could be

- Design the E-Learning course with a thorough understanding of your learners' needs.
- Include as much interactivity as possible.
- Ensure that the context of the scenario is realistic and manageable.

Scenario-based E-Learning help trainers to create E-Learning/blended learning courses that are fully engaging for staff and provide them with the resources to solve current work tasks, to enhance their performance and their overall knowledge base for future work. These scenarios can enable them to use already established skills and draw upon real-life experience to achieve E-Learning experience in different environments.

5. Cloud Computing to Support Learning in SMEs

The NIST (National Institute of Standards and Technology) definition of Cloud Computing is as follows: "Cloud computing is a model for enabling convenient, on-demand network access to a shared pool of configurable computing resources (e.g., networks, servers, storage, applications, and services) that can be rapidly provisioned and released with minimal management effort or service provider interaction" [26].

Useful characteristics of Cloud Computing [6] [26] for SMEs are:

- On-demand self-service. The user can benefit from capabilities such as server time and network storage, without requiring human interaction with each service provider.
- Broad network access. Capabilities are available over the network and accessed through standard mechanisms.
- Resource pooling. The resources are pooled to serve multiple users who generally have no control or knowledge over the exact location. Examples of resources include storage, processing, memory, network bandwidth, and virtual machines.
- Rapid elasticity. Capabilities can be rapidly and elastically provisioned.
- Measured Service. Resource usage can be monitored, controlled, and reported providing transparency for both the provider and user of the utilized service.

Figure 5 shows the most deployed models of Cloud Computing. They define the type of access to the cloud, i.e., how the cloud is located?

Cloud can have any of the four types of access: Public, Private, Hybrid, and Community.

Private Cloud:

- Is Cloud infrastructure operated solely for a single organization.
- Is managed internally or by a third-party and hosted internally or externally.

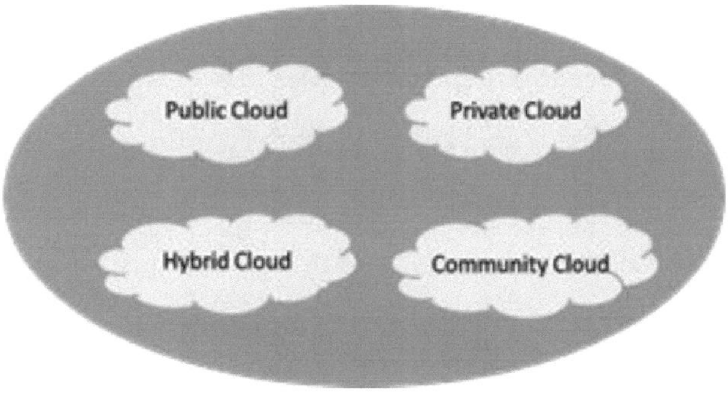

Figure 5. Models of Cloud

- Has attracted criticism because users "still have to buy, build, and manage them."

Public Cloud:

- It has services that are rendered over a network that is open for public use.
- It is technically little different from private cloud in architecture, but security considerations may be substantially different.
- It does not require users to manage the Cloud service.
- The hybrid Cloud is a composition of a public and private Cloud.
- Sensitive applications are handled in an internal private Cloud, while others are practiced in a public Cloud.
- A primary advantage is that an organization only pays for extra compute resources when they are needed.

A community Cloud is a multitenant infrastructure that is shared among several organizations from a specific group with common computing concerns. Service Models are the reference models on which the Cloud Computing is based. These can be categorized into three basic service models as listed below [26]:

- Cloud Software as a service (SaaS). Cloud Service Providers (CSP) applications running on a Cloud infrastructure are accessible from various client devices through a thin client interface such as a web browser.
- Cloud Platform as a service (PaaS). The user develops on the Cloud infrastructure or acquires applications created using programming languages and tools supported by the provider.
- Cloud Infrastructure as a service (IaaS). The CSP provide the user with storage, networks, and other fundamental computing resources where the consumer is able to deploy and run arbitrary software, which can include operating systems and applications.

Figure 6 shows the hierarchy of the three basic service models.

http://dx.doi.org/10.5772/61009

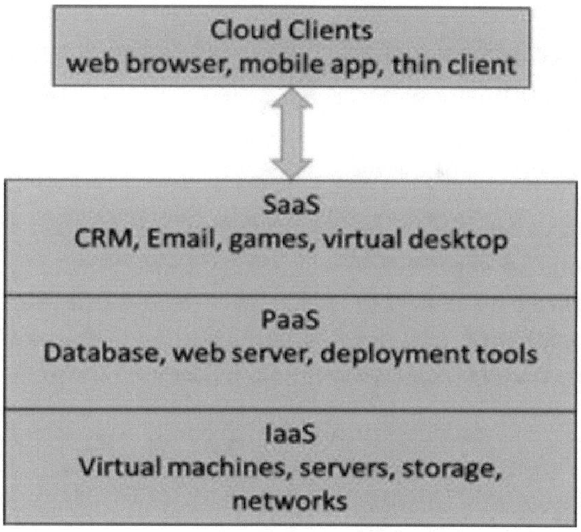

Figure 6. Service models

By using Cloud services SMEs can avail of opportunities that allow them to compete in an innovative ICT environment, and give a level playing field required to succeed in business [6].

In the discussion with German SMEs, the following advantages of Cloud Computing emerged:

- Up-to-date low-cost software solutions
- Unlimited data storage
- Access to data from anywhere and anytime means portability and flexibility; giving more time and effort to be placed on business strategies and solutions
- High levels of security protocol that ensures business and data protection
- Improved business performance
- Simplified data management

As with any technology, there are also a number of limitations or issues with Cloud Computing. One of the main issues is the reliability and security of data and the accessibility of this on a 24/7 basis, particularly when the Cloud service provider has an outage. Many companies will have problems about the lack of control over their ICT systems and the impact of a CSP on these [3].

These issues may inhibit an SME's decision to migrate to a Cloud Computing environment. In addition, there are other factors which may influence the decision:

- The lack of understanding of the infrastructure, cost, and appropriateness to the needs and scenarios of different companies from different business environments.
- The ICT skill levels of users, managers, and entrepreneurs.
- The readiness of SMEs to adopt Cloud Computing from a business perspective.

- Less time.

Some of these issues can be addressed by educating employees on the concept of Cloud Computing and developing business-based ICT skills in SMEs. This will allow them to make informed decisions about the appropriateness of Cloud Computing to their business strategy and what aspects can benefit them the most.

Besides advantages within business, Cloud Computing can be used for improving learning. Some aspects which could be improved by using Cloud Computing to implement E-Learning are scalability of E-Learning systems at the infrastructure level, development and assigning of resources only for determined tasks, need to configure and add new resources making the costs and resource management less expensive [27], [28].

Two main characteristics of Cloud Computing which could be an alternative to traditional ICT centres and could improve the E-Learning approaches in SMEs are the use of resources "on demand" and the transparent scalability so that the computational resources are assigned when they are necessary without the necessity of infrastructure understanding by the users.

Cloud Computing supports the efficient utilization of E-Learning resources following a dynamic rule of use. Costs related to computer infrastructure maintenance disappear.

Masud and Huang identified [29] some consequences and implications when the E-Learning services are deployed using Cloud Computing environments:

- Accessed via Web.
- Subscribers do not pay for installation, software maintenance, deployment, and server administration.
- Pay by subscription based on usage.
- Very high of security should be given by CSP because subscriber data are held on an SaaS server.

Ouf et al. [30] highlighted potential values of Cloud Computing, such as the following:

- When client computer crashes, there are almost no data lost because everything is stored in the Cloud.
- Students can work from different places, can find their files and edit them through the Cloud and browser-based applications accessed through various devices.
- Virtualization which makes possible the rapid replacement of a Cloud-located server.
- Centralized data storage.
- Easier monitoring of data access.

Figure 7 shows the architecture of a

Cloud Computing platform for E-Learning, which is usually common to most E-Learning approaches on the Cloud. Source [31]

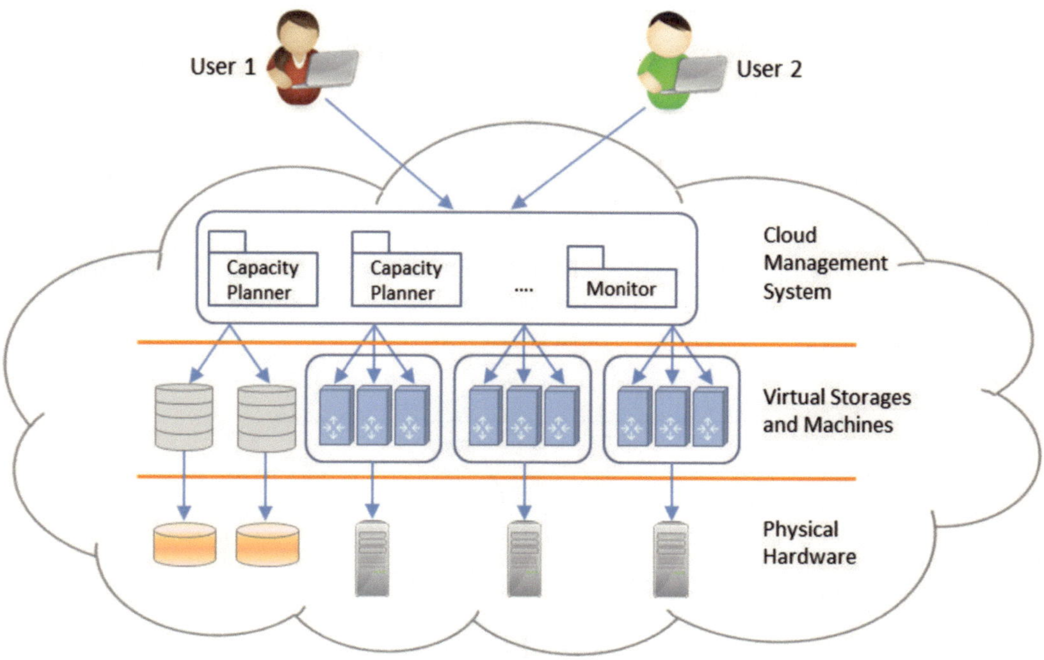

Figure 7. The architecture of a Cloud computer platform for E-Learning [31]

E-Learning could be used also to develop ICT skills in Cloud Computing for SMEs.

Few studies have been conducted into the emerging ICT skills required for Cloud Computing. Much research has focused on the technological aspects of Cloud Computing rather than the skills and preparation that companies require to allow them to avail of the strategic benefits this technology offers. Laugesen et al. [32] conducted an in-depth study of such skills with 72 companies, experts, public sector representatives, and representative institutions on e-skills requirements for Cloud Computing [32]. They found that the focus from primarily technical skills has moved to business skills, primarily those that are concerned with enabling and managing ICT as well as strategy development and managing change. Skills in the security of information were viewed as one of the most important. They also investigated the courses available to satisfy these skills needs and found that they were very technical, slow moving, and only covered partial elements. In addition, there were few courses that were "vendor neutral." Thus, it is important that contextualized business-related ICT skills are developed simultaneously with technology that informs companies of the range of technologies available out there and how they can assist with competitive advantage.

6. Examples

The European observatory project ARIEL [15] had partners from research institutes, universities, and E-Learning development firms of five European countries, and analysed fields of application and factors leading to concepts about the future development of E-Learning in Europe through four alternative scenarios (Figure 8).

Within ARIEL, basic scenarios were developed with the help of a scenario matrix containing descriptors, which are important to answer ARIEL problems.

In Germany, the factors "vocational training system" and "business" are considered as the most important factors.

The results and scenarios developed in ARIEL have been used within the new EU-supported valorisation project SIMPEL, to provide sustainable models of E-Learning, in cooperation with SMEs and consultants, supporting the business of SMEs.

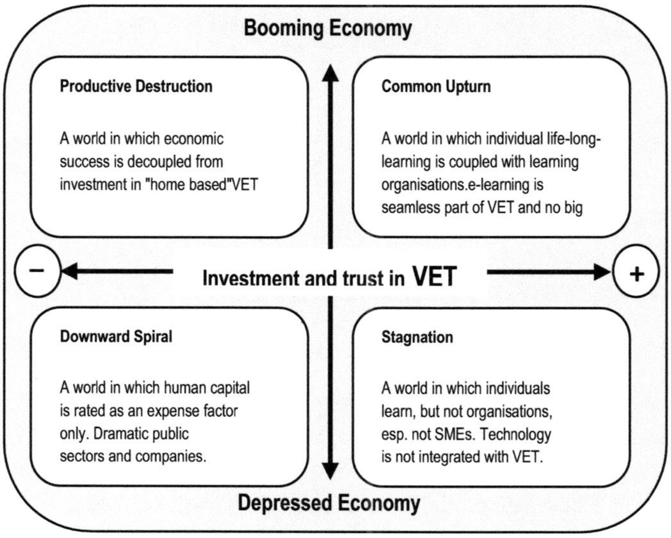

Figure 8. Ariel Scenarios [15]

Comparative analysis of the results of projects undertaken by the SIMPEL partners and results of national seminars within this project, show aspects that have to be considered when implementing E-Learning and using informal learning as a part of the strategy of the company in order to be competitive.

Partners from universities and SMEs in Germany, Ireland, Portugal, Romania, and Hungary worked within the EU Leonardo project Lifelong Learning – LLL Readiness in SMEs (Read-iSME – www.readisme.com [8]).

The project was based on the results of ARIEL and SIMPEL and was focused on methods to establish degrees of learning readiness based on E-Learning in SMEs and on impacting knowledge management. A step-by-step approach was used to implement learning concepts according to different levels of readiness, whilst simultaneously working toward higher levels of readiness [7], [15].

Within ReadiSME, 20 German SMEs have been interviewed and 2 case studies have been carried out in order to evaluate learning readiness of German SMEs and methods used taking into consideration categories like Organization, Technology, and Human Resources (Figure 3). Results of interviews not only from Germany but also from project partner countries are summarized below.

The majority of companies responded that E-Learning and blended learning are not sufficiently applied and they are still not up taking them as competitive tools. In previous studies done in projects like Ariel and SIMPEL, regarding barriers to training issues in SMEs, some similar issues, like in the ReadiSME, have been found.

A framework was developed within ReadiSME which uses the readiness results and suggests measures to improve learning readiness and steps to develop learning strategies. It uses a combination of the trans-theoretical model, which is a model for behaviour change and recommendations from the ARIEL and SIMPEL projects.

The framework developed within ReadiSME is based on a top-down and bottom-up approach taking into consideration both organizations and individuals. Last but not least, the frame proposed some steps which companies can use to implement sustainable learning strategies.

The European project Net Knowing 2.0 (www.netknowing.com/) aimed at improving E-Learning, knowledge management, and use of new technologies in SMEs.

Within Net Knowing 2.0, an E-Learning self-learning basic course was developed. It focused on benefits of informal learning for SMEs and how to learn using Web 2.0, social networks and net collaborating practices. A second course dealt with E-Learning focused on the implementation of Web 2.0-based informal learning, networking strategies, and mentoring in SMEs and other organizations.

Figure 9 presents a screenshot from the advanced course of the learning suite within Net Knowing 2.0. Within the project Net Knowing 2.0, scenarios have been used in companies providing a common vocabulary and an effective basis for communicating conditions and options.

The German SMEs affirm that scenarios can help them by:

- Identifying connections between old and new economies.
- Motivating stakeholders to make changes for transformation and to articulate the future of a city, region, etc.
- Initiating innovation for new products and services replacing traditional ones.
- Creating an organization's vision and purpose.

A scenario which was developed after the analysis of a German company situation and was used in the project for learning is the following:

A medium-sized retailer – active in Germany with about 20 locations – would like to position itself with a new strategy, because it was difficult to compete successfully in the highly

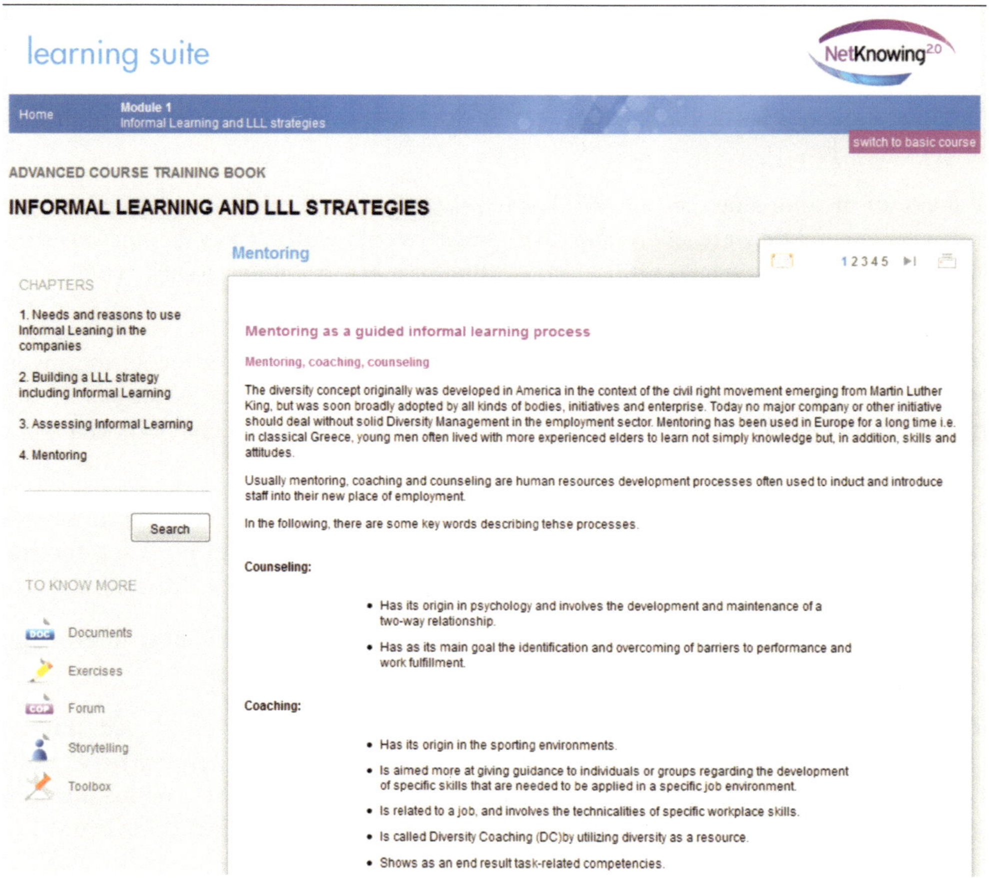

Figure 9. Advanced E-Learning course

competitive market. The new strategy for the next year should include a realistic assessment of the company goals. Using the technique of scenario, the thinking in options was encouraged and some future versions were discussed with the staff in a one-day workshop. The final decision is presented in the scenario below.

The conclusion was that the company has, on the one hand, a strong business unit with a diverse range of products. On the other hand, the company's focus cannot be identified. The company offers products in many areas, but it is not really excellent or clearly perceptible in any one of these areas. In future, new media should be used to advertise the products and increase the focus on the customers. More knowledge of competitors' products is necessary. The staff should participate in qualification courses and informal learning should be recognized as a learning method in the company. These changes have been discussed during another workshop by using scenario-based learning.

To present the scenarios at the workshop, the workshop leaders held presentations supported by animations and web-based material about possible strategies. So the company staff was informed and motivated about the actual situation and future solutions. This method of Scenario-based learning can also take place internally in a company.

E-Learning scenarios could be built by using Microsoft PowerPoint or Articulate Presenter (www.articulate.com) for example. The Articulate Presenter is working with core features including branching, hyperlinking, slide masters and customizing player templates to create multiple learning paths.

In order to research the needs and problems of the German SMEs in adopting Cloud technology, some interviews were conducted by the authors with managers from SMEs. After the analysis of the interviews it became clear that Scenario-based E-Learning for the introduction of Cloud Computing in SMEs following the results of the interviews were necessary [33].

Another project, in which the authors use E-Learning scenarios, is SmartPA (www.smart-pa.eu). Within the project SmartPA, mentors will be trained for accountants and staff from public administrations and SMEs to use Cloud services [12].

The EU Erasmus+ project, supporting problem-based learning in SMEs through ICT-facilitated mentoring – Archimedes – will develop a framework for organizational problem-based learning and support the use of this form of learning, which should be widely adopted in SMEs, as well as informal/social learning. It will be realized through formal and informal mentoring processes. The project will use E-Learning content encouraging the use of Cloud Computing and ICT-based social networking [14].

7. Conclusions

To conclude from literature research and projects, it is evident that small and medium sized companies remain vital to the European economy but many of them fail in the first five years; so it is important to ensure the survival of these companies and encourage them to grow. In today's business world, SMEs are competing with a larger number of companies, many of these are multinationals; they have a greater number of staff and a wider pool of skills. So it is important for SMEs to acquire the relevant strategic skills as quickly as possible to remain ahead of the competition. To do this while trying to sustain an organization can be difficult as a lot of SME managers' time is spent on ensuring the company's survival. By allowing SMEs to leverage off external expertise through the use of E-Learning through the latest technologies such as Cloud Computing, new skills can be accessed in time.

New media can allow managers to access real-time information in a chunked manner as needed. Cloud Computing can allow them to access the material anytime, anywhere. But the advantages as well as risks of Cloud Computing to support business and learning in SMEs are not thoroughly explored.

The results of focus discussion groups with SME staff and education experts organized in the projects presented briefly in this paper, and workshops and work sessions organized at different conferences sustain our hypothesis that besides adequate education and training, by using E-Learning, blended learning, and other forms, Scenario-based E-learning can motivate SME staff to learn and prepare for future work.

Acknowledgements

This paper describes work of the European projects ARIEL, SIMPEL, ReadiSME, Net Knowing 2.0, and SmartPA, within the Lifelong Learning Program and the ongoing Erasmus+ project Archimedes.

Author details

Ileana Hamburg*

Address all correspondence to: hamburg@iat.eu

Institut Arbeit und Technik - IAT, Gelsenkirchen, Germany

References

[1] European Commission: Annual Report on European SMEs 2013/2014: A Partial and Fragile Recovery, pp.10.

[2] Marston, S., Li, Z., Bandyopadhyay, S., Zhang, J., Ghalsasi, A.: "Cloud computing – The business perspective." *Decision Supp Sys*, 51, 2011. pp. 176-189.

[3] Hamburg, I., Marian, M.: "Supporting knowledge transfer and mentoring in companies by e-learning and cloud computing." ICWL 2012 International Workshops, KMEL, SciLearn, and CCSTED, Sinaia, Romania, September 2-4, 2012; revised selected papers. Heidelberg: Springer: pp. 231-240.

[4] Ayyagari, M., Beck, T., Demirguc-Kunt, A.: "Small and medium enterprises across the globe." *Small Bus Econ*, 29, 2007. pp. 415-434.

[5] Tiwari, R., Buse, S.: "Barriers to Innovation in SMEs: Can the Internationalization of R&D Mitigate Their Effects." http://iri.jrc.ec.europa.eu/documents/10180/12569/Barriers% 20to% 20innovation% 20in% 20SMEs% 20-% 20Can% 20the% 20internationalization% 20of% 20R% 26D% 20mitigate% 20their% 20effects?version=1.0&t=1369908833719,2007. pp. 3-9.

[6] Layo, I.: "Cloud computing advantages for SMEs." http://cloudtimes.org/2013/09/18/cloud-computing-advantages-for-smes/, 18th Sept 2013, accessed on the 18th June 2014.